International Environmental Law and Policy Series

The Peaceful Management of Transboundary Resources

Series General Editor

Stanley P. Johnson

Advisory Editor

Günther Handl

Other titles in the series

The Environmental Policy of the European Communities, S. P. Johnson and G. Corcelle
(ISBN 1-85333-225-9)
Transferring Hazardous Technologies and Substances, G. Handl and R. E. Lutz
(ISBN 0-86010-704-3)
Understanding US and European Environmental Law: A Practitioner's Guide, T. T. Smith and
P. Kromarek
(ISBN 1-85333-305-0)
*Air Pollution Control in the European Community: Implementation of the EC Directives in the
Twelve Member States*, G. Bennett (ed.)
(ISBN 1-85333-567-3)
International Responsibility for Environmental Harm, F. Francioni and T. Scovazzi (eds.)
(ISBN 1-85333-579-7)
International Law and Global Climate Change, R. Churchill and D. Freestooc (eds.)
(ISBN 1-85333-629-7)
Environmental Protection and International Law, W. Lang, H. Neuhold and K. Zemanek (eds.)
(ISBN 1-85333-611-4)
International Legal Problems of the Environmental Protection of the Baltic Sea, M. Fitzmaurice
(ISBN 0-7923-1402-6)
The Antarctic Environment and International Law, J. Verhoeven, P. Sands, M. Bruce (eds.)
(ISBN 1-85333-630-0)
Basic Documents of International Environmental Law, H. Hohmann (ed.)
(ISBN 1-85333-628-9)
*The Earth Summit: The United Nations Conference on Environment and Development
(UNCED)*, S. P. Johnson
(ISBN 1-85333-784-6)
Environmental Pollution Control: An Introduction to Principles and Practice of Administration,
J. McLoughlin, E. G. Bellinger
(ISBN 1-85333-577-0)
*Amazonia and Siberia: Legal Aspects of the Preservation of the Environment and Development
in the Last Open Spaces*, M. Bothe, T. Kurzidem, C. Schmidt (eds.)
(ISBN 1-85333-903-2)
Civil Liability for Transfrontier Pollution, G. Betlem
(ISBN 1-85333-951-2)
Pollution Insurance: International Survey of Coverages and Exclusions, W. Pfennigstorf (ed.)
(ISBN 1-85333-941-5)
The Environment After Rio: International Law and Economics, L. Campiglio, L. Pineschi,
D. Siniscalco and T. Treves (eds.)
(ISBN 1-85333-949-0)
European Environment Law, J. R. Salter
(ISBN 1-85966-050-9, looseleaf)
*Negotiating International Regimes: Lessons Learned from the UN Conference on Environment
and Development*, S. Gunnar, B. Spector, W. Zartman
(ISBN 1-85966-077-0)
Precautionary Legal Duties and Principles of Modern International Environmental Law,
H. Hohmann
(ISBN 1-85333-911-3)
(Please order by ISBN or title)

International Environmental Law and Policy Series

The Peaceful Management of Transboundary Resources

Editors

Gerald H Blake, William J Hildesley, Martin A Pratt
Rebecca J Ridley, Clive H Schofield

Graham & Trotman / Martinus Nijhoff
Members of the Kluwer Academic Publishers Group
LONDON/DORDRECHT/BOSTON

Graham & Trotman Limited
Sterling House
66 Wilton Road
London SWIV 1DE
UK

Kluwer Academic Publishers Group
101 Philip Drive
Assinippi Park
Norwell, MA 02061
USA

© Graham & Trotman 1995
First published 1995

British Library Cataloguing in Publication data is available

Library of Congress Cataloging in Publication data is available

ISBN: 1-85966-173-4
Series ISBN: 1-85333-275-5

Printed and bound in Great Britain by Athenaeum Press Ltd, Gateshead, Tyne & Wear.

Table of Contents

Water

Environment and Conservation

Fisheries

Notes on Contributors

Ewan W. Anderson, Department of Geography, University of Durham, UK.

Mohammed Asafuddowlah, Planning Commission, Government of the People's Republic of Bangladesh; formerly Secretary to the Ministry of Irrigation, Flood Control and Water Development.

James E. Bailey, Visiting Professor of Law, Northwestern School of Law at Lewis and Clark College, Portland, Oregon, USA.

Gideon Biger, Department of Geography, Tel Aviv University, Tel Aviv, Israel.

Gerald H. Blake, Director, International Boundaries Research Unit, University of Durham, UK.

Rodman R. Bundy, Partner, Frere Cholmeley Bischoff, Paris, France.

Dante A. Caponera, Chairman, Executive Council of the International Water Law Association, Rome, Italy; former chief of the Legislation Branch of the Food and Agriculture Organization of the United Nations.

Jeremy P. Carver, Partner and head of the Public International Law Group, Clifford Chance, London, UK; Chairman of British Invisibles' CIS Advisory Panel.

Héctor Ceballos-Lascuráin, Co-ordinator, IUCN Ecotourism Programme, Tepepan, Tlalpan, Mexico.

Prachoom Chomchai, Mekong Development Research Network, Institute of Asian Studies, Chulalongkorn University, Bangkok, Thailand.

Kevin Crean, School of Geography and Earth Resources, University of Hull, UK.

Douglas Day, Professor of Geography, Saint Mary's University, Halifax, Nova Scotia, Canada.

William V. Dunlap, Associate Professor of Law, Quinnipiac College School of Law, Bridgeport, Connecticut, USA.

Greg Englefield, Public International Law Group, Clifford Chance, London; formerly Research Director, International Boundaries Research Unit, University of Durham.

Monica Gangas Geisse, Associate Professor, Institute of Geography, Pontifical Catholic University of Chile, Santiago, Chile; Research Associate, Institute of Political Science, Chile (State) University; board member, Geopolitical Institute of Chile.

David Goldberg, Clifford Chance, Washington DC, USA; formerly Deputy General Counsel, Legal Department, World Bank, and consultant to the Water Resources Committee of the International Law Association.

Ieuan Ll. Griffiths, School of African and Asian Studies, University of Sussex, Brighton, UK.

A.R. Harborne, Coral Cay Conservation, London, UK.

Moritaka Hayashi, Principal Officer, Division for Ocean Affairs and the Law of the Sea, Office of Legal Affairs, United Nations, New York, USA.

Glen Hearns, Research Associate, Centre for Asian Legal Studies, Faculty of Law, The University of British Columbia, Canada.

Glen Herbert, Dalhousie University, Halifax, Nova Scotia, Canada.

Ellen Hey, Faculty of Law, Erasmus University, Rotterdam, The Netherlands.

Mladen Klemencic, Miroslav Krleza Lexicographical Institute, Zagreb, Croatia.

Nurit Kliot, Professor of Geography, University of Haifa, Israel.

Miroslav B. Liska, Slovakian Government, Bratislava, Slovakia.

Laurel A. Meuhlhausen, Northwestern School of Law at Lewis and Clark College, Portland, Oregon, USA; formerly Business Development Manager, North American Collection and Location by Satellites, Landover, Maryland, USA.

P.J. Mumby, Coral Cay Conservation, London, UK.

Stephen P. Mumme, Department of Political Science, Colorado State University, Fort Collins, USA; President of the Association of Borderlands Scholars of the USA.

Gordon R. Munro, Department of Economics, University of British Columbia, Vancouver, Canada; Co-ordinator, Pacific Economic Cooperation Council Task Force on Fisheries Development and Cooperation.

Suparna Nag, Senior Research Fellow, Division of Political Geography, School of International Studies, Jawaharal Nehru University, New Delhi, India.

David Ong, The Law School, University of Hull, UK.

Alex G. Oude Elferink, Research Associate, Netherlands Institute for the Law of the Sea (NILOS), Utrecht University, The Netherlands.

P.S. Raines, Coral Cay Conservation, London, UK.

J.M. Ridley, Coral Cay Conservation, London, UK.

Charles Robson, Partner, Lovell White Durrant, London, UK.

Hernan Santis Arenas, Professor, Institute of Geography, Pontifical Catholic University of Chile, Santiago, Chile; Professor, Institute of Political Science, Chile (State) University; Manager, Geopolitical Institute of Chile.

R.C. Sharma, Professor of Political Geography at the School of International Studies, Jawaharal Nehru University, New Delhi, India.

William G. Stormont, Research Associate, Centre for Asian Legal Studies, Asia-Pacific Ocean Cooperation Program, University of British Colombia, Vancouver.

Richard E. Swarbrick, Department of Geological Sciences, University of Durham, UK; associate of the International Boundaries Research Unit.

David Symes, School of Geography and Earth Resources, University of Hull, UK.

Ian Townsend-Gault, Director, Centre for Asian Legal Studies, and Co-Director, Asia-Pacific Ocean Cooperation Program, University of British Colombia, Vancouver; Director, Pacific Office, Oceans Institute of Canada.

Peter Tyedmers, Research Associate, Centre for Asian Legal Studies, Faculty of Law, The University of British Columbia, Canada.

Joeli Veitayaki, Co-ordinator, Ocean Resources Management Programme, University of the South Pacific, Suva, Fiji.

Melissa Waterman, Senior Planner, Gulf of Maine Program, Augusta, Maine, USA.

Introduction:
Boundless Resources?

Gerald Blake

'The peaceful management of transboundary resources' was the theme chosen for the third conference of the International Boundaries Research Unit at Durham University in April 1994. The subject appears to have generated even more interest than IBRU's earlier conferences in Durham in 1989 and 1991, both of which were regarded as successful gatherings of boundary specialists from around the world. The reasons for the popularity of the resource theme are not hard to discern. In a world where rapidly growing populations and rising expectations create an ever increasing demand for food, raw materials, and recreational space, there are powerful incentives to seek out and exploit resources in areas which are both geographically and politically marginal. As commodities become scarcer, so states grow more anxious about their ability to procure and control resources. Against this background, the number of international boundaries has also increased markedly in recent years. Most of these boundaries have been delimited without taking into account the location of natural resources. The number of land boundaries has gone up from about 280 in the late 1980s to 308 in 1994. There are also approximately 320 potential maritime boundaries world-wide, about one-third of which have been formally agreed. Each year up to half a dozen more maritime boundaries are agreed, raising questions about access to living and non-living resources in the partitioned ocean.

The concept of borderland resources can be interpreted broadly. The most obvious resources on land are oil, gas, minerals, groundwater and surface water. At sea, hydrocarbon resources and fisheries are predominant, both of which are high value commodities. Borderland resources may also be taken to include high quality landscapes, important ecological regions such as forests or coral reefs, wildlife, timber, and historic or cultural sites representing tourist potential. There is thus clearly a great array of transboundary resources, each of which presents different legal, technical, and managerial challenges. The simplest to manage are those such as coal and timber which are conveniently fixed in space. The most difficult are those resources such as water, oil and migratory fish stocks which move across international boundaries. Unfortunately these types of resource are the most prevalent. Without exception, all transboundary resources are most conveniently and efficiently managed and exploited in the context of collaborative arrangements of some kind between neighbours. This is well understood. In recent years there has been a great deal of discussion about how collaboration can best be achieved, and there is a considerable volume of literature on the legal framework and practical arrangements necessary for transboundary resource management and fisheries. 'The Transboundary Resources Report', published by the International Transboundary Resources Center at the University of New Mexico gives a good idea of the range of topics in the literature.

The earliest collaborative agreements over marine hydrocarbon resources were reached in the 1950s and 1960s. Some of the most celebrated river basin regimes were established long before that; several more river agreements followed in the 1960s and 1970s. The earliest national park to be established jointly on an international boundary was at Waterton Lakes (Canada–USA) in 1932. In other words, the concept of transboundary collaboration over resources is neither new, nor is it without substantial theoretical and practical underpinning. There is already abundant evidence to show that the peaceful management of transboundary resources is achievable, and that collaboration can be made to work. In view of this, it is both surprising and disappointing that in relation to the size of the task, relatively little progress has been made, in spite of some glittering success stories. Even in cases where agreement has been reached there is often a big gap between theory and practice. For example, the results of several of the international river basin agreements in Africa have been very disappointing (Blake, 1994).

Table 1 attempts a summary of chapters in this volume which deal for the most part with specific case studies. While the table is at best a caricature of the contents of some detailed and complex conference papers, the right-hand column nevertheless gives a crude indicator of the extent of formal transboundary resource collaboration. The list is very far from comprehensive, nor does it imply that the authors listed wrote exclusively on the case studies mentioned. Most include important discussions and commentary. There thus appears to be a lot of consultation going on and many potential collaborative schemes are being suggested, but the number of cases where there is solid agreement and fruitful action remains quite limited. River basins illustrate the point very well. World-wide, 240 river basins are shared between two or more states, and five are shared between seven or more states. There are today well over 2,000 bilateral agreements on river basins covering topics including navigation, research, fishing, flood control, water allocation, etc, but there are still very few integrated river basin projects. Several chapters in this volume offer ample evidence of the difficulties to be overcome in the implementation of proper river basin management schemes including those by Nurit Kliot, R.C. Sharma, Mohammed Asafuddowlah, and Monica Gangas Geisse and Hernan Santis Arenas. The political and practical problems being encountered where no such agreement exists are also discussed. In several regions, such as the Middle East and the Indian sub-continent the absence of agreement carries potentially very serious political consequences. As with all transboundary resources, there may be many reasons why agreement

Table 1 Case Studies in This Volume

Author	States/Region	Resource	Status
Anderson	Jordan and neighbouring states	Water	No agreements
Asafuddowla	Bangladesh, India	Ganges River	Short-term agreements
Biger	Israel, Jordan	Dead Sea minerals	Informal discussions
Carver, Englefield	Central Asia, Transcaucasia	Hydrocarbons	Discussion
Ceballos-Lascurain	Belize, Guatemala, Mexico Honduras	Cultural/environmental	Planning discussions
Chomchai	Cambodia, Laos, Thailand Vietnam	Lower Mekong River	Mekong Committee set up in 1957
Day, Herbert	Canada, USA of Maine	Fisheries in the Gulf	Transboundary violations
Elferink	Sea of Okhotsk	Fisheries in high seas	No agreement
Gangas Geisse Santis Arenas	Bolivia, Chile	Lauca River	No agreement
Harborne, Mumby, Raines, Ridley	Belize, Mexico	Marine environment	Proposed informally
Hearns, Tyedmers	China, Taiwan, Philippines	Marine, environment/fisheries	Proposed informally
Klemencic	Bosnia, Croatia	Zrmanja, Cetina, Trebisnica rivers	Local agreements only
Kliot	Israel, Jordan, Lebanon Syria	Jordan-Yarmouk rivers	No agreement
Liska	Hungary, Slovakia	Danube water and energy	Agreement in 1977
Mumme	Mexico–USA	Borderland water management	Agreement in 1944
Munro	Pacific Island Nations Region/ASEAN	Western Pacific tuna fisheries	Informal diplomacy WPFCC established in 1988
Ong	Malaysia–Thailand Australia–Indonesia Malaysia–Vietnam	Hydrocarbons	Agreements in 1979 1989 and 1991
Robson	UK–Norway, Australia–Indonesia	Hydrocarbons	Agreements in 1976 and 1991
Santis Arenas, Gangas Geisse	Chile–Ecuador, Peru Chile–Peru	Fisheries, transit of goods	Special Maritime Zone 1954 Lima Convention 1993 (unratified)
Sharma, Nag	Bangladesh–India India–Nepal	Ganges River basin	Short-term agreements
		River basins	No agreement
Veitayaki	South Pacific states	Fisheries	Several active agreements
Waterman	Canada / USA	Gulf of Maine	Agreed in 1989

cannot be reached, including legal questions and technical complexities, but most often the chief obstacle is political. If relations between states are poor, collaborative ventures are unlikely to have any chance of success.

The Durham conference was convened as a forum for the exchange of information, ideas and practical experiences of transboundary resource management. By publishing most of the papers given at that conference we hope to make a contribution to transboundary collaboration. Most would agree that the best boundaries are those which permit the maximum degree of peaceful interaction between the peoples on either side, and that the negative effects of international boundaries should be eliminated as far as possible. On the other hand it is almost inconceivable that there will ever be a borderless world; international boundaries will continue to exist although their locations and functions will change through time. They are likely to continue to delimit state sovereignties, while states will be forced increasingly into collaborative schemes with their neighbours. Paradoxically, international boundary lines will be delimited with more and more precision using global positioning system (GPS) techniques (Adler, in press, 1994). At the same time many boundaries will become highly permeable. One of the ways in which boundaries are changing from being 'hard' to 'soft' is in relation to resource management. This is a welcome trend – but the difficulties standing in the way of more rapid progress must not be underestimated. It is significant that many of the following pages are devoted to the discussion of unsettled legal questions associated with international resource management, since these present some of the trickiest problems. There is, however, some cause for optimism, because painstaking efforts to devise model agreements are having some success after many years of work. For example, the British Institute of International and Comparative Law undertook the daunting task of drawing up a model agreement for joint development zones for offshore oil and gas. A revised 20-page model agreement was finally published in 1990 after many months of work by a team of distinguished lawyers (Fox, 1990). To date the model does not appear to have been used, but only two joint zones (Malaysia–Thailand and Malaysia–Vietnam) have been established since it was published. There are still only 15 joint zones world-wide, whereas approximately 145 formal maritime zones have been agreed. Maritime joint zones nevertheless seem likely to proliferate in future. The legal issues are complex (as discussed for example by Rodman Bundy, Charles Robson, and Ian Townsend-Gault and William Stormont), and there are difficult technical problems such as the apportionment of oil and gas reserves, as so clearly demonstrated by Richard Swarbrick. Nevertheless joint hydrocarbon zones are nothing like as challenging as those associated with river basin management. International river law has taxed the brains of some of the finest lawyers since the middle of the last century, and it remains a bewildering and sometimes rather confused scene. Dante Caponera's paper provides a masterly briefing for beginners, while Ellen Hey and David Goldberg ably demonstrate the complexities of the subject. Since 1970 the UN's International Law Commission has been examining the laws associated with the non-navigational uses of international watercourses with a view to their development and codification. While much has been achieved, the law of international watercourses remains unsettled, and a deterrent to collaborative ventures between states.

Much the same can be said about groundwater resources, which are so often forgotten in spite of the fact that, according to David Goldberg, they contribute 97% of freshwater outside the polar ice-caps. It took a group of experts seven years to come up with a draft treaty in respect of groundwater in the Mexico–United States borderlands. The treaty (which takes its name from Bellagio in Italy, where discussions began) might be adopted as a model for groundwater management. The aim of the treaty is to achieve joint optimum use of shared groundwater while avoiding disputes between the parties (Hayton and Utton, 1985).

Fisheries experts have similarly sought to hammer out acceptable international agreements for the management of straddling fish stocks and highly migratory fish stocks. UN conferences convened for this purpose in 1993 and 1994 are discussed by Moritaka Hayashi. The problems are associated both with fish stocks shared by coastal states and the high seas beyond their exclusive economic zones, and between neighbouring coastal states. James Bailey's suggestions that the effective enforcement of fishing agreements could be greatly assisted by the use of satellite monitoring, provides a most valuable supplement to the legal discussion.

Perhaps least known of all the initiatives to provide a framework for transboundary resource management are those of the International Union for the Conservation of Nature (IUCN) and the United Nations Environment Programme (UNEP) which have promoted the idea of transboundary national parks in borderland regions. Boundary parks are seen as desirable for the conservation of important ecological areas, and also as a starter for confidence building between neighbours. The potential is clearly considerable as Ieuan Griffiths shows for Africa. There are, for example, 70 national parks adjacent to international boundaries world-wide, many of which might conveniently have counterparts on the other side. Here again, the number of transfrontier national parks operating jointly even at a basic level is disappointingly small in relation to the potential (Thorsell, 1990). In 1992 UNEP gave special consideration to the role of transfrontier reserves in promoting peace and security with special reference to Indo-China (Westing, 1993). The UNEP report includes a draft agreement for a transfrontier reserve in Indo-China which might usefully provide the basis for a model to be applied elsewhere.

This is no volume for the starry-eyed idealist. While it underlines the pressing need for states to collaborate to develop shared resources in their borderlands, it also points to many obstacles along the way. We should, however, be encouraged by the evidence of this volume that there are specialists in many fields all over the world who are willing and able to grapple with the problems. Much is being achieved by the exchange of views between disciplines and between states. The joint endeavours of boundary scholars and practitioners seem likely to be rewarded by a growing number of international agreements over resource management in the closing years of the century.

References

Adler, A. (1995) 'Positioning and mapping international land boundaries', *Boundary and Territory Briefing, 2.1* Durham: International Boundaries Research Unit.

Blake, G.H. (1994) 'International transboundary collaborative ventures' in W.A. Galluser (ed.) *Political Boundaries and Co-existence,* Berne: Peter Lang: 359–71.

Fox, H. (ed.) (1990) *Joint Development of Offshore Oil and Gas.* Vol 2 London: British Institute of International and Comparative Law: 3–33.

Hayton, R.D. and Utton, A.E. *Transboundary Groundwaters: The Bellagio Draft Treaty,* New Mexico: International Transboundary Resources Center.

Thorsell, J. (ed.) (1990) *Parks on the Borderline: Experience in Transfrontier Conservation,* Gland, Switzerland: IUCN.

Acknowledgements

This volume is the outcome of a conference held at St Aidan's College Durham from 14–7 April 1994. The richness and diversity of the papers presented owes much to the helpful suggestions and advice of our chief collaborators, the International Geographical Union Commission on the World Political Map, the World Conservation Monitoring Centre, Cambridge, (Dr James Payne), the Netherlands Institute for the Law of the Sea, Utrecht (Dr Alex Oude Elferink), and the International Transboundary Resources Centre, University of New Mexico (Professor Albert Utton). We are also extremely grateful to international lawyers Messrs Lovell White Durrant of London who provided generous sponsorship to enable us to bring distinguished scholars and experts to Durham who would not otherwise have been able to attend. These included Professor Chen Degong (China Institute for Marine Development Strategy, Beijing) and Dr Prachoom Chomchai (Mekong Development Research Network, Bangkok). British Petroleum also contributed towards conference costs and we are most grateful to them.

So many people helped the staff of the International Boundaries Research Unit (IBRU) to organise the conference that it is impossible to thank every one of them. We were especially grateful to our conference organiser Karen Harris who was indefatigable in her efforts long before and during the conference. She was admirably supported by Julia Morgan, Anna Oxbury, and Rebecca Ridley of IBRU and by a team of volunteers including Alice Burt, Simone Gunzenhauser, Andrew Harris, Debbie Hillyer, Lisa Leombrone, Dan Park and Roly Sinker. Dr Jim Crowe of Newcastle University, Department of Archaeology, led a memorable trip to that ancient international divide, Hadrian's Wall.

These conference proceedings have been jointly edited by IBRU staff but the lion's share of the credit must go to Rebecca Ridley, whose energetic editorial skills produced a fine manuscript in a short time out of a complicated collection of papers. The Cartographic Unit at the Department of Geography in Durham University drew many of the maps, under the capable direction of Arthur Corner.

Finally, the International Boundaries Research Unit would like to thank all those from more than 30 countries who participated in our conference and made it such an enjoyable and fruitful occasion. We hope this volume will be a fitting tribute to their enthusiastic involvement, and to the hard work of those who prepared and delivered papers and acted as session chairpersons. A few of the papers given at the conference are published elsewhere, and do not appear in this volume.

Gerald Blake
Durham   November 1994

Hydrocarbons and Minerals

1

Transboundary Petroleum Reservoirs: Legal Issues and Solutions

Charles Robson

Introduction

This paper discusses international boundaries in the context of petroleum resources. Historically, natural resources in the region of international boundaries have had a significant impact on the relations between neighbouring states. It is the value of the resource, real or perceived, which motivates states to exert their sovereignty. Petroleum, as a principle source of energy and a major feedstock for the chemicals industry, is of considerable commercial and strategic value in an increasingly energy-intensive and high-technology world. With the industrialisation of developing countries its strategic value can only increase.

Effective and efficient exploitation of a single petroleum reservoir which straddles an international boundary requires co-operation between the states concerned and their respective licensees or contractors.

The presence of petroleum in an area in which an international boundary is yet to be determined can have a profound effect on the delimitation of the boundary. It can accelerate or delay agreed delimitation. It can influence the position of the boundary. It can cause states to abandon attempts at delimitation (temporarily at least) and pursue a strategy of joint development.

Although nobody should completely discount the possibility of states resorting to acts of aggression in order to resolve disputes with their neighbours over natural resources, it is clear that the international community espouses peaceful co-operation in the settlement of such disputes more universally and more explicitly than ever before:

It is necessary to ensure effective co-operation between countries through the establishment of adequate international standards for the conservation and harmonious exploitation of natural resources common to two or more states in the context of the normal relations existing between them (UNGA 3129).

In the exploitation of natural resources shared by two or more countries, each state must co-operate on the basis of a system of information and prior consultation in order to achieve optimum use of such resources without causing damage to the legitimate interest of others (UNGA 3281).

In addition to verbal statements of principle, individual state practice has, in some cases, put these principles into practice. For example, the UK–Norway Frigg Reservoir Agreement and the Australia–Indonesia Timor Gap Treaty, both of which are considered in this paper.

The legal issues raised by transboundary petroleum resources are examined in two parts here. The first part deals with issues raised where delimitation of the international boundary is undertaken at a time when the transboundary resource has not been identified specifically (although a general potential may have been identified). The second part deals with the issues raised where a specific potential petroleum resource has been identified in an area between or adjacent to two or more boundaries but where international boundaries have not been delimited.

The factors recognised in international law as being relevant to the delimitation of the continental shelf between states (whether opposite or adjacent) are principally geographical and anthropological. Geomorphology has been held to be a relevant factor in some cases.[1] Decisions of the International Court of Justice are not entirely consistent as to whether the presence of natural resources, including petroleum, is to be recognised as a relevant factor.[2] Whether or not the presence of natural resources is a factor to be given weight as a matter of law, it is certainly a factor which will influence states in their dealings with one another concerning a common boundary.

This paper does not seek to address the merits of the various potentially relevant factors to be taken into account in delimiting continental shelf boundaries. It assumes in the first part that the relevant states are able to agree a delimitation and it examines the issues which arise concerning the exploitation and development of subsequently identified petroleum resources which cross the agreed boundary or boundaries. In the second part it assumes that the relevant states are able to agree to exploit the petroleum resources jointly, pending a final delimitation of the boundary and it examines the issues which arise concerning a joint development strategy.

Before looking in detail at the issues raised in each of these situations, the paper reviews the nature of states' legal rights to petroleum in the continental shelf and the physical properties of petroleum which give rise to the issues discussed.

EXCLUSIVE RIGHT OF EXPLOITATION

Subject to the legitimate claims of its neighbours, every coastal state has the exclusive right to exploit the natural resources of the sea-bed and subsoil of the submarine area that extends from its land territory to a distance of 200 nautical miles or to the edge of the continental margin, whichever is the greater (UNCLOS Article 76).[3] It has jurisdiction to regulate all activities undertaken in such area for the exploration for and exploitation of such natural resources. This jurisdiction is generally exercised either through a system of regulations applied to licences awarded for designated areas or blocks, or through a system of contracts between the state (normally acting through a state-owned enterprise) and contractors for areas designated in such contracts.

The matters which states agree with their neighbours regarding the exploitation and development of transboundary resources will be implemented by each state through its licensing or contracting system to ensure that activities are carried out (or not carried out) by their respective licensees or contractors in accordance with the agreement between states.

PHYSICAL PROPERTIES WHICH GIVE RISE TO PROBLEMS

Petroleum is fluid. Whether liquid or gas, it cannot resist shear stress. It is stable in the horizontal plane only if all points in that plane are subject to uniform stress. If the stresses at one point in the plane are different from the stresses at another point, the petroleum will move until the stress differential is equalised. This is the phenomenon which gives rise to the expression 'water always finds its level'.

Where a single petroleum reservoir extends across a continental shelf boundary (which will almost always be a non-physical dividing line), each state has the exclusive right to exploit the natural resources (including the petroleum in that reservoir) which are within the sea-bed and subsoil of its continental shelf. Such exploitation can, because of the fluid nature of petroleum, interfere with the neighbouring state's equivalent rights to the petroleum in the reservoir by causing it to flow from one side of the boundary to the other.

This physical property of petroleum clearly operates in the same way for all non-physical boundaries whether they are between states or between individual landowners, licensees or contractors within a single state.

UNITED STATES EXPERIENCE

In the early days of the oil industry in the United States, the fluid nature of petroleum threatened to stifle the development of this important industry.

By and large, each US landowner had legal title to the petroleum in any reservoir which lay under his land and the exclusive right to exploit that resource. That is broadly the position which applies under customary international law to petroleum reservoirs between states. Because of the fluid nature of the resource, where a reservoir extended underneath both the US landowner's and his neighbour's land, exploitation by one would almost certainly interfere with the other's equivalent right to exploit. Therefore, by exploiting his resource each landowner was exposed to an action in damages for wrongful interference with his neighbour's resource.

LEGAL ISSUES

This dilemma gave rise to a rule of law known as the rule of capture. The rule stated that petroleum produced from a shared deposit was the property of the party who produced it. The principle of the rule was probably based on the concept of possession. By analogy with the ancient common law rules relating to wild animals and birds, the principle was that until reduced to possession no-one had title to petroleum.

The effect of the rule of capture, however, was to make petroleum production a race. Wells were drilled along boundaries by adjacent landowners and petroleum was produced on both sides of the boundary as fast as possible. This hasty development was disorderly, inefficient and wasteful. The percentage of petroleum in place which is ultimately recoverable from a petroleum reservoir can be affected greatly by the placing of wells and the rates of production from them.

It was not long before most of the petroleum producing states in the United States had implemented legislation providing for compulsory co-operation in the exploitation of common petroleum reservoirs. One method of co-operation, unitisation, has now become the most common basis for co-operative exploitation of petroleum reservoirs world-wide, both nationally and internationally.

UNITISATION

Unitisation is an arrangement between all parties with an interest in a petroleum reservoir under which terms for its development as a unit are agreed before development operations begin. It is a contractual arrangement under which the parties' respective interests are pooled and which determines their respective rights and obligations, including the apportionment of petroleum produced from the reservoir.

A unitisation agreement will normally contain many of the provisions found in a joint operating agreement, a very common arrangement between oil companies which regulates the activities of the consortia into which they commonly organise themselves for reasons of risk-management. Whereas joint operating agreements normally relate to activities undertaken jointly pursuant to a single licence or contract, unitisation agreements relate to activities to be undertaken jointly by two or more consortia, each operating by virtue of a different licence or contract. In addition to the provisions found in a joint operating agreement, a unitisation agreement will deal with the apportionment of the reservoir or 'unit' between the licence blocks or contractual areas and, in the case of an international unitisation, the apportionment of the unit between the respective continental shelves of the states concerned.

The scope of a unitisation agreement typically includes:

1   The extent of the unit and corresponding surface area, in order to define the area which is the subject of the unitisation agreement
2   The proportion of the unit for which each interested party or consortium has independent rights of exploitation ('tract participation' and 'unit interest')
3   Redetermination of tract participation and unit interests
4   The establishment of a management committee to supervise operations including voting passmark and voting interests
5   The scope of the rights and obligations of the unit operator
6   Unit expenditure – work programmes and budgets
7   Allocation and disposal of petroleum
8   Payment of taxes
9   Accounting

The process of unitisation necessarily involves co-operation between all parties with an interest in the reservoir concerned. In international unitisations this includes the states as well as their respective licensees or contractors. In some cases it can be necessary for the states to bring a degree of pressure to bear on the licensees or contractors in order to encourage that co-operation, and licensing or contracting systems commonly include mechanisms for doing so.

Delimitation of the International Boundary Before Specific Potential Petroleum Resources Have Been Identified

In many ways the legal issues raised in this part of the paper are easier to deal with than those raised in the second part. They are very similar to those which arise in relation to a petroleum reservoir which crosses a property boundary between individual landowners or a boundary between individual blocks within a single licensing regime.

COMPULSORY UNITISATION

A party with an interest in a transboundary resource has no inherent *right* to insist on unitisation. Hopefully, common sense and the parties' common interest in the efficient and effective exploitation of the resource will operate as an effective incentive to co-operate and agree a unitised development. Experience shows that this is not always the case, however, and it is common for the licensing or contracting systems of states to provide that the government may require adjoining concessionaires or licensees to agree a unitisation plan or accept a unitisation plan imposed by the government.[4] Even this does not confer a right for concessionaires or licensees to require unitisation. It confers a power on the government which is designed to ensure that any development is undertaken efficiently and effectively.

Not all states have such legislation. If there is no such legislation, licensees cannot be compelled to unitise the resource, no matter how desirable that may be from the point of view of efficient and effective development.

Lastly, although there is some debate on the issue,[5] there is probably no obligation under international law for states to co-operate in the development of a transboundary resource. Notwithstanding United Nations General Assembly Resolution 3281, a working group of the British Institute of International and Comparative Law concluded:

> In light of the conflict of views it would seem that international law only entails an obligation to consult and negotiate where states have broadly agreed on the delimitation of their maritime boundaries. There would seem to be no body of state practice upon which to underpin such a general obligation in the case where no boundary has been drawn in the disputed area (BIICL, 1989: 35).

International law probably does no more than to oblige states to refrain from unilateral development where a risk of irreparable prejudice to rights or of physical damage to the sea-bed or subsoil is involved.

In summary, as a matter of municipal law, the obligation to unitise must be imposed on licensees or contractors in the licence or contract. As a matter of international law, there is no duty on states to co-operate with their neighbours regarding the development of transboundary resources, unless the states involved have agreed otherwise.

AGREEING OTHERWISE

In light of this, it is very common for states to include in treaties delimiting international boundaries 'mineral deposit clauses' which oblige each state to seek to reach agreement as to the manner in which any transboundary structure or field is to be exploited and the manner in which the proceeds of exploitation are to be apportioned.

The first such clause was included in a treaty between the United Kingdom and Norway in 1965. The same basic form has been used in many other delimitation treaties since then.

> If any single geological petroleum structure or petroleum field or any geological structure or field of any other mineral deposit, including sand or gravel, extends across the dividing line and the part of such structure or field which is situated on one side of the dividing line is exploitable, in whole or in part, from the other side of the dividing line, the Contracting Parties shall, in consultation with the licensees, if any, seek to reach agreement as to the manner in which the structure or field shall be most effectively exploited and the manner in which the proceeds derived therefrom should be apportioned (UK–Norway, 1965: Article 4).

The obligation to co-operate is triggered if any part of the structure or field situated on one side of the dividing line is exploitable, in whole or in part, from the other side of the dividing line.

Other treaties have included obligations to co-operate which are triggered simply by the existence of a transboundary resource. For example, the 1971 treaty between Denmark and the Federal Republic of Germany (Germany–Denmark, 1971). Others have included obligations which are triggered only if any part of the structure or field situated on one side of the dividing line can be exploited by directional drilling from the other side of the dividing line. For example, the 1969 Iran–Qatar treaty. Although the circumstances which trigger the obligation to endeavour to reach agreement may differ, the principle is the same. Each of the states undertakes to co-operate in the development of any transboundary resource in order to protect its own interests in the resource, to facilitate the exploitation of the resource and to preserve good relations with its neighbours.

FRIGG RESERVOIR AGREEMENT

The Frigg Field lies in the northern North Sea about 60°N, 2°E, straddling the continental shelf boundary delimited by the United Kingdom and Norway in 1965 (UK–Norway, 1965: Cmnd. 2757). It was discovered in May 1972 and is estimated to have had recoverable reserves originally present of 185 billion m³ of natural gas, 39.18%

of which is agreed to have been within the United Kingdom sector (DTI, 1993).

Pursuant to the 1965 treaty, representatives of the United Kingdom and Norway met to agree the manner in which the Frigg Field could be exploited most effectively and the manner in which the proceeds deriving therefrom should be apportioned. The resulting Frigg Reservoir Agreement was signed in London on 10 May 1976.

The agreement has stood the test of time, operating effectively to regulate the exploitation of the Frigg Reservoir for over 18 years. The Frigg reservoir is now in decline and discussions are underway to revise the agreement to make it appropriate for the importation into the United Kingdom of other Norwegian gas via the pipelines originally constructed for the transmission of gas from the Frigg Field.

The main provisions of the agreement can be summarised as follows:

1   The reservoir is to be exploited as a single unit by a unit operator in accordance with a development plan approved by both states
2   The states must both agree the type and location of installations to be used in the exploitation of the reservoir
3   Each state is obliged to require its licensees to enter into agreements between themselves and the licensees of the other state to regulate the exploitation of the reservoir in accordance with the agreement between the states, such licensee agreements being expressly subordinate to the agreement between the states
4   Each state is obliged to agree a determination of the limits of the reservoir, the estimated total reserves of the reservoir and an apportionment of those reserves between them
5   Each state is obliged, in default of agreement, to submit disputes to an arbitral tribunal
6   Each state is obliged, subject to safety considerations, to permit the drilling of wells comprised in the development plan produced by the licensees and permit the free movement of persons and materials between installations
7   Provision is made for the redetermination of the limits of the reservoir and the total amount of the reserves every four years and at any other time when further reservoirs are discovered and which are proven to contain gas which is capable of flowing into the Frigg Reservoir at the start of production, at the request of either state
8   Each state is obliged to require any person not a party to the agreements referred to at 3 above, but who holds a production licence in respect of an area into which the reservoir is proved to extend, to enter into such agreements
9   Each state is obliged to ensure that at the time production from the Frigg Reservoir ceases the share of production received by the

licensees of each state corresponds to the apportionment agreed between the states

10 Each state is obliged to consult the other on safety matters but subject to it having the final right to determine the safety measures which govern the installations under its jurisdiction

11 The basis upon which the licensees are to be taxed by either state in relation to Frigg Field operations is provided for and each state agrees not to tax on any other basis

12 Each state is obliged to ensure that its licensees do not transfer their interest or grant similar rights to third parties without the consent of the licensing state and before granting any such consent each state is obliged to consult the other state

13 The agreement establishes a commission consisting of six persons, three appointed by each state, for the purpose of facilitating the implementation of the agreement

14 The agreement includes an express acknowledgement that:
   (a) nothing in it affects the jurisdiction of each state under international law; and
   (b) nothing in it prejudices or restricts the application of the laws of either state or the exercise of jurisdiction by their courts, in conformity with international law.

The obligation to require licensees to enter into agreements regulating the exploitation of the reservoir is the principal operative provision. This serves as the working link between the two states' separate exploitation regimes. The details of these arrangements are left, subject to approval by the states, to the licensees.

The character of the agreement as a working link between two separate exploitation regimes is reinforced by the acknowledgements regarding the states' jurisdictions.

SUMMARY

The principle objects of the agreement are to:

1 Agree mechanisms for apportioning the reserves of the reservoir between the states' respective continental shelves;
2 Co-ordinate the exploitation activities of the states' respective licensees; and
3 Ensure that mechanisms are in place for the resolution of disputes which may arise in the course of exploitation.

It does not establish the basis upon which the reserves are to be apportioned: the basis for apportionment was established by the agreed delimitation of the continental shelf areas. Nor does it establish the detailed legal framework for the exploitation: that is comprised in the terms of the licences granted by each state to its licensees.

It obliges each state, through its own licensing system, to require its licensees to develop and adhere to a single development plan which is approved by both states. By doing so, it serves as a working link between the states' respective licensing systems to enable the development of a shared resource.

Structures or Fields in Areas Where the International Boundary Has Not Been Delimited

The identification of a promising geological structure or stratum in a continental shelf area between two or more states which has not been delimited can make delimitation of the boundary more difficult.

If the states are unwilling or unable to agree a delimitation through negotiation, development of the resource will be hampered at least, and possibly prevented, to the economic detriment of all concerned. If the political will is present on all sides, development may be enabled by the creation of a zone over which the states concerned exercise joint control. Arrangements of this type do not overcome the problem of delimitation directly: they do not address that problem. However, by enabling the development of the resource on a co-operative basis, they may remove an element of competition from the process of delimitation and thereby facilitate a resolution.

This approach is also consistent with the spirit of the United Nations Convention on the Law of the Sea, 1982, which provides that:

> pending agreement [on delimitation] the states concerned in a spirit of understanding and co-operation, shall make every effort to enter into provisional arrangements of a practical nature and, during this transitional period, not to jeopardise or hamper the reaching of a final agreement. Such arrangements shall be without prejudice to the final delimitation (UNCLOS Article 83(3)).

This approach has been adopted in a number of instances of state practice. Over the course of time, if state practice is sufficiently consistent regarding the circumstances in which this approach is used and in the scope and nature of the provisional arrangements, the zone of joint development may even develop into a new norm of customary international law. That development might, in turn, act as an added incentive for states to overcome their differences regarding a definitive, agreed, continental shelf delimitation.

The 1969 offshore boundary agreement between Qatar and Abu Dhabi provides for equal sharing of production from the al-Bunduq Field, over which the state parties exercise joint sovereignty.

In 1979, Thailand and Malaysia established a joint development zone the exploitation of which is controlled by a joint commission (Thailand–Malaysia, 1979).

In 1989, Australia and Indonesia entered into a treaty (Timor Gap Treaty) which created a zone of co-operation in the area known as the Timor Gap, which is between the island of Timor and the north coast of Australia.

TIMOR GAP TREATY

The Timor Gap is the name given to a zone of co-operation of approximately 16,129 square nautical miles between Indonesia's East Timor province and the north coast of Australia in the vicinity of Joseph Bonaparte Gulf.

Australia and Indonesia settled the majority of their continental shelf boundary in 1972. At that time East Timor was a colony of Portugal and Portugal refused to negotiate the delimitation of the continental shelf between East Timor and Australia. In 1975 East Timor became part of Indonesia. After some initial, fruitless, negotiations regarding the delimitation of the continental shelf, the parties began to concentrate on the creation of a joint zone of co-operation. On 11 December 1989 the Timor Gap Treaty was signed and it entered into force on ratification by the Australian government on 9 February 1991.

The zone is divided into three areas. The northern area is 1,576 square nautical miles and is designated Area C. In this area Indonesia controls the granting of rights to explore for and exploit natural resources but it has agreed to pay to Australia 10% of any taxation revenue it derives by virtue of such operations. The southern area is 5,178 square nautical miles and is designated Area B. Australia controls the granting of exploration and exploitation rights in this area but must account to Indonesia for 10% of any taxation revenue it derives from such activities. The central area is 9,375 square nautical miles and is designated Area A. A Ministerial Council and a Joint Authority, on both of which each state is equally represented, control the granting of exploration and exploitation rights.

Annexed to the Treaty are a petroleum mining code for Area A, a model production sharing contract between the Joint Authority and contractors and a taxation code for the avoidance of double taxation.

The preamble to the Treaty records that the Treaty is founded on the principle of Article 83 of the 1982 UN Convention on the Law of the Sea.[6] The Timor Gap Treaty was entered into on the basis that it would not affect the final delimitation of the continental shelf boundary. It contains an express reaffirmation by Indonesia and Australia of their commitment to agreeing such a delimitation.

CIRCUMSTANCES GIVING RISE TO THE CREATION OF THE JOINT ZONE

At the time the Treaty was being negotiated Indonesia claimed its continental shelf margin on the basis of distance. Australia's claim was based principally on the geomorphology of the sea-bed. The area of overlapping claims was considerable. In fact the northern boundary of the zone eventually established is an approximation of the Australian claim line and is based on the axis of the principal geomorphological feature of the area, the Timor Trough. The southern boundary of the zone is based on the Indonesian claim of a shelf 200 nautical miles wide.

In 1988 Australia's proven oil reserves were approximately 1,345 million barrels. The Gippsland Field provided 76% of those reserves. Output from the Gippsland Field was declining. Since offshore oil provides approximately 87% of Australian oil production, the Australian authorities were concerned to discover whether the zone contains any commercial oil fields. A commercial oil field has been discovered at Jabiru, about 100 nautical miles west of the zone and the very large Kelp anticline in the northern sector of Area A is thought to be an attractive prospect.

Indonesia, in contrast to Australia, does not appear to have had such pressing economic reasons for exploring the zone. Its proven oil reserves stood at about 9,000 million barrels and only 34 of 60 potential oilfields had been explored. The Kelp structure is comparatively large, however, and this may have been an influential factor. It may be that the incentive for Indonesia to enter into the Treaty was principally political. The references in the Treaty to 'the Indonesian Province of East Timor' amount to an acknowledgement by Australia of Indonesia's sovereignty over East Timor. That acknowledgement may be regarded by Indonesia as particularly valuable in light of Portugal's continuing claims of sovereignty. It is worth noting that Area B is about three times larger than Area C.

The Timor Gap Treaty is interesting for a number of reasons. It is probably the most comprehensive treaty of its kind. The states have established a regime for the joint exploitation of natural resources which is exhaustive in its detail with the intention of removing, to the greatest extent possible, the scope for fundamental disagreement in future as to how exploitation activities in the zone should be regulated. It provides a model for the creation of the joint administrative bodies which are required to regulate activities within such zones of co-operation. Also, the creation of a zone divided into three areas is a strategy which may have broader application elsewhere.

THE THREE AREAS

The Treaty divides the zone into three Areas.

In relation to the exploration for and the exploitation of petroleum resources in Area A, the rights and responsibilities of the two states are to be exercised by the Ministerial Council and the Joint Authority in accordance with the treaty. The object of the Ministerial Council and the Joint Authority is to achieve optimum commercial utilisation of petroleum resources within Area A and equal sharing between the two states of the benefits of their exploitation. Petroleum operations in this Area must be carried out through production sharing contracts. The Joint Authority must enter into such production sharing contracts with limited liability corporations specifically established for the sole purpose of performing such contracts. That provision applies equally to the successors and assignees of such corporations.

The requirement that special purpose vehicles be used as the contracting parties is interesting. There is no requirement that these corporations must be incorporated in a particular jurisdiction. The concept of limited liability protects the shareholders (or other promoters) of these corporations from direct action by parties who deal with the special purpose vehicle (including the states concerned). The requirement that the special purpose vehicle do nothing other than carry out operations pursuant to the production sharing contract provides the states with some comfort that the valuable asset which is the corporation's rights under the production sharing contract will not be subject to claims by third parties.

In relation to the exploration for and the exploitation of petroleum resources in each of the other Areas, the controlling state must notify the other of the grant, renewal, surrender, expiry and cancellation of rights granted by the controlling state and pay to the other state 10% of the tax revenue from such operations. In the event that either of the states changes the basis upon which the relevant tax is calculated or the tax regime applicable in the area which it controls, both states are obliged to review the stipulated percentages or formulation set out in the Treaty and agree on new percentages or formulations so as to ensure that the relative shares of revenue paid by each of the states remains the same.

THE MINISTERIAL COUNCIL

The Ministerial Council is made up of ministers designated from time to time by the two states, provided that at any one time there must be an equal number of ministers appointed by each state. The council meets annually, or as often as may be required, alternately in Australia and Indonesia. Decisions of the council are made by consensus, in other words unanimously.

The Ministerial Council has overall responsibility for all matters relating to the exploration for and the exploitation of petroleum in Area A and such other functions as the states entrust to it. It is responsible, for example, for giving directions to the Joint Authority as necessary, amending the petroleum mining code and model production sharing contract to facilitate operations, approving production sharing contracts which the Joint Authority proposes to enter into and approving their termination.

THE JOINT AUTHORITY

The Joint Authority is stated in the Treaty to have juridical personality and such legal capacities under the laws of both states as are necessary for the exercise of its powers and the performance of its functions. To lawyers, at least, it is an interesting entity. It has separate legal personality but is not exclusively the creature of either national legal system. Its legal capacities under the laws of both states are determined not by the national laws of those states but as a matter of fact, the test being: is the legal capacity in question necessary for the exercise of the Joint Authority's powers and the exercise of its functions under the Treaty?

The Joint Authority is made up of executive directors appointed by the Ministerial Council comprising equal numbers of persons nominated by each of the states, three directorates (technical, financial and legal) which are responsible to the executive directors and a corporate services directorate for the provision of administrative support to the other three directorates.

The Joint Authority is responsible for the management of activities relating to the exploration for and the exploitation of petroleum resources in Area A in accordance with the Treaty and, in particular, the petroleum mining code and the production sharing contracts. It is responsible, for example, for dividing Area A into contract areas, co-ordinating the solicitation and revue of applications and making recommendations to the Ministerial Council for production sharing contracts, entering into such contracts and undertaking the day to day administration and control of activities within Area A.

The Joint Authority is financed from fees collected under the petroleum mining code. In the event that the Joint Authority cannot meet an obligation under an arbitral award arising from a dispute under a production sharing contract, the states have agreed to contribute all necessary funds in equal shares to enable it to do so.

CO-OPERATION ON CERTAIN MATTERS

The Treaty makes specific provision for co-operation in relation to certain matters, including surveillance, security measures, search and rescue, air traffic etc. In particular, there is an obligation to share information derived from hydrographic and seismic surveys carried out in Area A and to co-ordinate the carrying out of marine scientific research into non-living resources of the continental shelf in Area A.

UNITISATION

The Treaty contains a mineral deposit clause. If any single accumulation of petroleum extends across any of the boundary lines of Area A and the part of the accumulation that is situated on one side of the line is exploitable, in whole or in part, from the other side of the line the states must seek to reach agreement on the manner in which the accumulation can be most effectively exploited and on the equitable sharing of the benefits deriving from such exploitation. Similarly, if the effective exploitation of a petroleum accumulation inside Area A requires the construction of facilities outside Area A, each state must provide every assistance to the contractors and the Joint Authority to enable the construction and operation of those facilities. The construction and operation of those facilities will, however, be subject to the laws and regulations of the relevant state.

LAW APPLICABLE TO PRODUCTION SHARING CONTRACTS

The Treaty provides that the law applicable to any production sharing contract is to be stipulated in that contract. It does not require that the applicable law be that of either state.

TAXATION

The Treaty makes three basic provisions regarding taxation. First, for the purposes of taxation related directly or indirectly to the exploration for or the exploitation of petroleum resources in Area A or acts, matters circumstances and things touching or concerning such exploration and exploitation, each state agrees to treat Area A as (and agrees that Area A is deemed to be) part of that state. Secondly, in the application of taxation law in Area A or to interest and royalties paid by a contractor, each state grants relief from double taxation. Finally, each state agrees not to impose a tax not covered by the provisions of the Taxation Code in respect of or applicable to the exploration for and the exploitation of petroleum resources in Area A unless the other state consents to the imposition of that tax.

ANCILLARY MATTERS

The Treaty also makes provision for the application of customs, migration and quarantine laws and for the employment, health and safety of workers. As regards criminal jurisdiction, the Treaty broadly provides that a national or permanent resident of one of the states is subject to the laws of that state. Nationals and permanent residents of third states are subject to the criminal laws of both states provided that such a person cannot be subject to criminal proceedings under the laws of one state if he has already been tried (and punished if guilty) under the laws of the other state. The states are obliged to consult with each other to determine which criminal law is to be applied in each particular case.

DISPUTE RESOLUTION

Any dispute arising between the states concerning the interpretation or application of the Treaty is to be resolved by consultation and negotiation.

Each production-sharing contract entered into by the Joint Authority must contain provisions to the effect that disputes are to be referred to a specified form of binding commercial arbitration. Each state is obliged to facilitate the enforcement in their respective courts of arbitral awards made pursuant to such arbitration.

TERM

The Treaty is to remain in force for 40 years from the date of its entry into force.[7] Unless the states agree otherwise, the Treaty is to continue in force thereafter for successive terms of 20 years unless by the end of each term (including the initial term) the two states have concluded an agreement on a permanent continental shelf delimitation.

SUMMARY

The scope of the Timor Gap Treaty is considerably wider than that of the Frigg Reservoir Agreement. It does more than link together the states' individual licensing systems: it creates, in Area A, a new licensing system which is independent from the states' individual systems. The guiding principle in that Area is an equal sharing of the benefits of exploitation.

Conclusions

The Frigg Reservoir Agreement provides a useful model for a workable international agreement for the exploitation of a shared petroleum resource (ie, a resource which has been apportioned). Similar frameworks are being used in a wide variety of situations around the world. The conclusion of such agreements is greatly facilitated if a mineral deposit clause has been included in the relevant delimitation treaty.

The creation of a joint zone for the exploitation of a common petroleum resource (ie, a resource which has not been apportioned) entails the establishment of institutions and administrations which are not under the direct control of any one state: in the case of the Timor Gap Treaty they are the Ministerial Council, the Joint Authority and the four directorates. Entities like this are necessarily bureaucratic and expensive. Whether the Timor Gap institutions are workable at all remains to be seen. Businessmen in international oil companies may say that the time and expense invested in their creation and operation will be justified only if the zone proves to contain very significant quantities of petroleum. Students of public international law, on the other hand, may take the view that, irrespective of the success or otherwise of the drilling, the Timor Gap Treaty has developed the theoretical concept of joint exploitation considerably. If the structure established by the Treaty proves to be workable in practice, it may also have advanced the case for treaties of this sort to be used elsewhere in the development of petroleum resources.

Both types of agreement have a role to play in promoting the peaceful management of transboundary petroleum resources.

Notes

1   For comment on the limitations of geomorphology as a relevant factor see ICJ (1985: 13).
2   For example, The North Sea Continental Shelf Cases (Federal Republic of Germany v. Denmark, Federal Republic of Germany v. The Netherlands) (ICJ, 1969: 3) cites the presence of natural resources as a relevant factor, whereas The Case Concerning the Continental Shelf (Tunisia/Libyan Arab Jamahiriya) (ICJ, 1981) merely states that the presence of oil wells in an area to be delimited may, depending on the facts, be an element to be taken into account.
3   The 1982 United Nations Convention on the Law of the Sea is widely regarded as embodying relevant customary international law and it will enter into force (and become binding on the parties to it) on 16 November 1994.

4   For example, model clause 28 of the UK's Petroleum (Production) (Seaward Areas) Regulations 1988.
5   See, for example, Onorato (1985: 541).
6   See note 2 above.
7   ie, until 9 February 2031.

Bibliography

BIICL (1989) *Joint Development of Offshore Oil and Gas: A Model Agreement for States for Joint Development with Explanatory Commentary,* London: BIICL.
DTI (1993) 'Development of the oil and gas resources of the United Kingdom, a report to Parliament by the Minister for Energy', April, London: Department of Trade and Industry.
Onorato, W. (1985) 'A case study on joint development: the Saudi Arabia/Kuwait partitioned neutral zone', *Energy* 10: 539.

LEGAL REFERENCES

(Iran–Qatar) (1969) Agreement Concerning the Boundary Line Dividing the Continental Shelf between Iran and Qatar, 20 September, *Limits in the Seas* 25.
(Germany–Denmark) (1971) Agreement between the Federal Republic of Germany and the Kingdom of Denmark Concerning the Delimitation of the Continental Shelf under the North Sea, 28 January, *UNMBA*: 65.
(Qatar–Abu Dhabi) (1970) Agreement on Settlement of Maritime Boundary Lines and Sovereign Rights over Islands between Qatar and Abu Dhabi, 20 March, *Limits in the Seas* 18.
(Thailand–Malaysia) (1979) Memorandum Of Understanding between the Kingdom of Thailand and Malaysia on the Delimitation of the Continental Shelf Boundary between the Two Countries in the Gulf of Thailand, 24 October, *Maritime Boundary Agreements (1970-84)* 217 (1987).
(UK–Norway) (1965) Agreement between the Government of the United Kingdom of Great Britain and Northern Ireland and the Government of the Kingdom of Norway relating to the Delimitation of the Continental Shelf between the Two Countries, 10 March *UNTS* 551: 214.
Frigg Reservoir Agreement (1976) Agreement between the Government of the United Kingdom of Great Britain and Northern Ireland and the Government of the Kingdom of Norway relating to the exploitation of the Frigg Field reservoir and the

transmission of gas therefrom to the United Kingdom, 10 May, ISBN 0 10 164910 X.

ICJ (1969) 'The North Sea continental shelf cases (Federal Republic of Germany v. Denmark, Federal Republic of Germany v. The Netherlands)', *ICJ Reports:* 3.

—— (1981) 'The case concerning the continental shelf (Tunisia/Libyan Arab Jamahiriya)', *ICJ Reports:* 43.

—— (1985) 'Case concerning the continental shelf (Libyan Arab Jamahiriya/Malta)', *ICJ Reports*: 13.

Timor Gap Treaty (1989) Treaty between Australia and the Republic of Indonesia on the Zone of Cooperation in an Area between the Indonesian Province of East Timor and Northern Australia, 11 December, J.I. Charney and L.M. Alexander (eds) (1993) *International Maritime Boundaries,* Dordrecht: Martinus Nijhoff: 1245–328.

UNGA (1973) *United Nations General Assembly Resolution* 3129 (XXVIII) 13 December.

—— (1974) *United Nations General Assembly Resolution* 3281 (XXIX) 12 December.

Transmission on the Accession to the Reserves Preservation Scheme, 37 J.

—Transmission of the Accession to the United Kingdom, 30 March 1976, ISBN 0 11 164910 X.

ICJ (1969), The North Sea continental shelf cases (Federal Republic of Germany v. Denmark, Federal Republic of Germany — The Netherlands), ICJ Reports 3.

—(1951), The case concerning the continental shelf (Tunisia/Libyan Arab Jamahiriya), ICJ Reports 18 February 1982, ICJ Reports.

—(1985), The case concerning the continental shelf (Libyan Arab Jamahiriya/Malta), ICJ Reports 13.

Tobar Gil, Teddy (1989), Treaty between Austria and the Kingdom of ... et al. Limited of the Zone of Co-operation in an Area between the Indonesian Province of East Timor and Northern Australia (1) December 11, Canberra, and E.M. Alexia, Groom (1991) Anonymous, Maritime Boundaries, Dordrecht: Martinus Nijhoff.

UNGA (1970), Third World in a General Assembly Resolution 2749 (XXVIII) 17 December ...

—International Conventions, General Assembly Resolution 3281 XII (XXIX), 12 December

2

Natural Resource Development (Oil and Gas) and Boundary Disputes

Rodman R. Bundy

Introduction

The following analysis focuses on the issues arising when natural resources are found in areas where either no international boundary has been delimited or where the reservoirs containing those resources straddle existing international frontiers. These issues can be highlighted by posing two hypothetical problems:

1 An oil company has a production sharing agreement covering an off-shore area where oil and gas have been found. The field straddles a delimited international boundary and oil has been produced normally on both sides of the boundary for some time. Due to unforeseen circumstances, whether *force majeure* or a decision to curtail production as part of a quota or price support plan, production is dramatically cut on the other side of the line. What, if any, legal obligation does the company have to follow suit, ie, to cut its own production?
2 An oil company is operating in an area which has been allocated pursuant to a valid permit by a Ministry of Petroleum. While carrying out exploratory drilling, it receives a warning from a neighbouring State asserting that the area in which the company is operating forms part of its territory or, in the case of off-shore areas, is under its jurisdiction. The company is reluctant to stop, not only because of the commercial interest of the acreage in question, but also because it has important exploration commitments and has already committed substantial funds to the project. What should the company do?

These hypothetical situations arise from actual events which we have encountered in working with State and private oil companies, and it is suggested that the responses to each situation depend on both legal considerations and practical factors.

Oil Fields which Straddle International Boundaries

Take the first hypothesis. Figure 2.1 shows the existing maritime delimitations in the Persian Gulf. If one focuses on the Iran–Abu Dhabi boundary, it can be seen that a large oil field (the Sassan or Abu al Bukoosh – ABK field) sits right on the median line separating the maritime jurisdictions of the two States.

Prior to the Iranian Revolution, the Iranian side of the field was producing some 200,000 barrels per day (b/d), and the Abu Dhabi side about 50,000b/d. When the Revolution broke out, disruptions in the Iranian oil sector resulted in the complete shut-down of production from the Iranian side for several months. Later on in 1979 oil production recommenced, but was cut back once more in September 1980 due to the outbreak of the Iran–Iraq war which resulted in Iranian oil installations becoming prime targets for Iraqi air raids. In April 1988, it was the United States Navy that finished the job: it destroyed the Sassan producing complex, in apparent retaliation for the USS *Samuel Roberts* hitting a mine in the Persian Gulf, and thus halted all production from the field on a near-permanent basis. This incident is the subject of a case before the International Court of Justice (ICJ).

Because of the petrophysical characteristics of the Sassan field, Iran's shut-down resulted in a substantial migration of oil to the Abu Dhabi side of the field, where production continued. Iran thus lost significant quantities of crude. In the circumstances, did Abu Dhabi have an obligation to curtail its own production or to reimburse Iran?

The answer was clearly no, and this for essentially two reasons. Unlike fresh water resources, to which concepts such as the right of a riparian State to a 'fair and equitable share' of the resource, and the prohibition against causing appreciable harm to other riparian States can be said to represent emerging trends of customary international law, the exploitation of international oil and gas reserves is still based largely on the law of capture. This means that, in the absence of an agreement to the contrary, a State or international oil company is free to maximise production from its side of the boundary line notwithstanding the policies of neighbouring States which share the same field.

In the Abu Dhabi–Iran example, what actually happened was that Abu Dhabi *increased* its production from the ABK field when Iran's production was shut down. Indeed, even when Abu Dhabi curtailed its overall production in compliance with OPEC (Organization of Petroleum Exporting Countries) quotas, it made a deliberate decision to exclude the ABK field from any prorated decrease. Clearly, this exacerbated the migration problem from Iran's point of view. Yet Iran had no cause of action against Abu Dhabi under international law.

It should be pointed out that in this specific example, Iran and Abu Dhabi had foreseen the possibility that a hydrocarbon deposit might straddle their boundary and had thus agreed to some fairly rudimentary

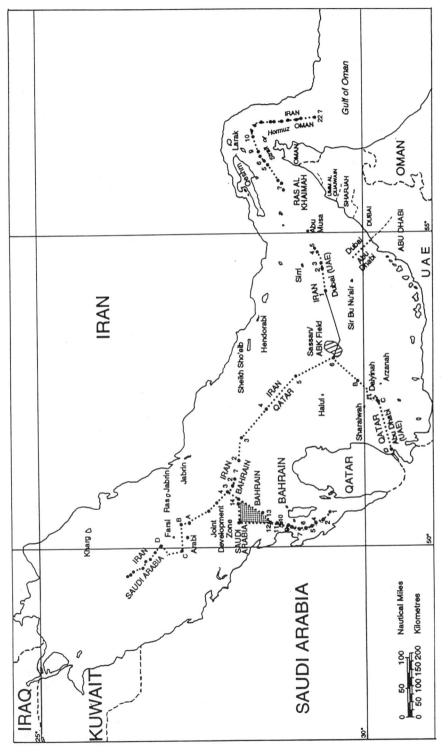

Figure 2.1 The Sassan/Abu al Bukoosh (ABK) Oil Field, Persian Gulf

provisions to deal with such a situation. In essence, their delimitation agreement, like others entered into by Iran with its Persian Gulf neighbours, provided that where a single geological petroleum structure or field extended across the boundary line, neither State would drill within 125m of the boundary without the agreement of the other. Both States also agreed to 'endeavour to reach agreement as to the manner in which the operations on both sides of the boundary could be co-ordinated or unitised' (see, for example, Article 2 of the Iran–UAE Agreement of 13 August 1974).

It is clear that this was scarcely a very vigorous obligation – the Parties had absolutely no obligation to reach agreement or to co-ordinate production; they only had to *endeavour* to do so. In practice, only a modest amount of co-ordination was achieved. Prior to the Iranian Revolution, a joint committee was established primarily as a conduit for the exchange of technical information relating to the field, but this line of communication broke down after the Revolution and remained so during the Iran–Iraq war.

The point is that Iran had no cause of action against Abu Dhabi for the oil it had lost due to migration, and Abu Dhabi had no legal obligation to reduce its production.

At present, it is difficult to envisage the adoption of a rule of international law requiring an 'equitable apportionment' of oil and gas resources which straddle international boundaries. For one thing, it would be difficult to argue that a State is geographically disadvantaged *vis-à-vis* its neighbours in the exploration and exploitation of hydrocarbon reserves in the same way as States may be disadvantaged in their access to fresh water resources. Obviously, up-stream users of fresh water have a geographical advantage over the down-stream users – they get to use the resource first. Disadvantaged States thus require some measure of protection so as to guarantee for themselves an equitable share. But the same cannot be said of a State which owns part of an oil field since that State is, in theory, just as able to develop the field as its neighbour. By the same token, why should a State be obligated to reduce its production in the name of equity simply because its neighbour has chosen a different production policy. Whether, in such circumstances, there still remains some lesser duty of *co-operation* between the States is a matter which will be discussed below.

The Problem Where There is No International Boundary

The second situation – where drilling takes place in areas where no boundary exists – arises with increasing frequency and often gives rise to serious problems.

In the early 1980s, we were involved in two large cases involving the delimitation of the continental shelf between Libya, Tunisia and

Malta where no boundary had previously been agreed. The problems were complicated by the fact that all three States had granted oil and gas concessions in the disputed area.

Throughout the 1970s, a series of protests and counter-protests was exchanged over each side's petroleum activities in these areas. For practical purposes, both Libya and Malta eventually agreed to a 'no drilling' understanding covering the disputed area pending resolution of the matter by the International Court of Justice.

For reasons which need not be discussed here, Malta abrogated the 'no drilling' agreement in 1980 by dispatching a drilling rig to one of its concessions in the disputed area. This led to a forceful protest from Libya including a visit from the Libyan Navy to the personnel on board the rig. Not surprisingly, drilling ceased and the rig was withdrawn. Happily, however, Libya and Malta went on to settle their differences peaceably before the ICJ, although not before the matter was first brought before the UN Security Council.

Much the same situation occurred between Libya and Tunisia, and indeed similar confrontations have arisen in many areas around the world, including the Middle East and the South China Sea, where concessionaires have been warned by neighbouring States not to proceed with petroleum operations because the areas in question lie in disputed boundary zones.

So what does one do in these circumstances? The answer largely depends on whether you are the concession holder, the host government or the protesting State.

For the concession holder, the situation can be extremely awkward. On the one hand, a company naturally tends to pay attention when a State tells it to stop doing something. In several cases in which we have been involved, initial warnings to stop operations were followed by visits from the protesting State's armed forces.

Perhaps the obvious reaction for the concession holder is to leave it to the two countries to sort out by invoking *force majeure* and suspending its contractual obligations. The problem with this approach is that whether *force majeure* can be successfully invoked to excuse the fulfilment of exploration or development commitments depends very much on the contractual provisions contained in the concession agreement, the nature of the threat received, and the attitudes of the host State.

Suffice it to say that the host State may take an entirely different view of the situation by considering that the threats are more political than real, and that absent some event that actually *prevents* performance, *force majeure* cannot be invoked, especially if the particular kind of threat in question was not foreseen and identified as such in the contract. In short, the host country has to decide how far to hold its concessionaires' feet to the fire.

In the two examples referred to above, the disputes between the contesting States became wholly intractable, leading to serious problems in their bilateral relations and, in one case, to a complaint before the Security Council, as has already been mentioned. Fortunately, at the end of the day good sense prevailed and the disputes were successfully litigated before the ICJ.

While much depends on the circumstances of each case, what can be said is that a State which issues ultimatums to its neighbours to cease operations, but then *refuses* to negotiate in good faith or to submit the dispute to international arbitration or adjudication, risks seeing its position on the international plane deteriorate. There are limits under international law to the ability of a State to blow hot and cold at the same time.

In most cases, the end result is likely to be frustration for the concession holder and, to a lesser extent, for the host country as well. For if the stakes are raised, and the dispute becomes a major bone of contention between the contesting States, or if it goes to litigation, there is often little that the concessionaire can do but to sit back and await the outcome.

This does not mean that lawyers, businessmen and diplomats alike should not seek to find some other kind of solution pending resolution of the dispute. Alternatives do exist and have been used with varying success in many parts of the globe.

One alternative that was tried in the Libya–Malta case was to create a 'no drilling' zone within a band 15 miles wide on either side of a hypothetical median line. This effort failed largely because Malta's position had always been based on a median line boundary (while Libya argued for a boundary significantly further north). Libya considered that it could not afford to accept any proposal which revolved around the median line because it might suggest tacit acceptance of the equidistance principle as the basis for the ultimate boundary. However, in other cases it may well be possible to agree on a limited area of dispute so as to allow development to proceed elsewhere.

Joint Development Zones

There are many other forms of co-operation which have increasingly found favour in recent years. These vary from mere undertakings not to drill within a certain distance of an established boundary line, as in Iran's agreements with its neighbours, to the Treaty between Australia and Indonesia on the Timor Gap Zone of Co-operation signed in December 1989 which, with its annexed model production sharing agreement and Petroleum Mining Code, runs to over 100 pages and covers virtually all aspects of joint production within the shared area.

Space does not permit the examination of all these agreements in detail here. However, it may be useful to discuss briefly a few representative examples to highlight some of the principal legal and practical issues that co-operation agreements can give rise to.

NORTH SEA: UNITED KINGDOM–NETHERLANDS (1993)

The United Kingdom (UK) has entered into several agreements relating to cross-boundary fields in the North Sea, the most recent of which is with The Netherlands. Figure 2.2 shows the location of various maritime boundaries in the North Sea. The section between the United Kingdom and The Netherlands was delimited in 1965. In a separate agreement signed that same year, the Parties also agreed that they would seek to reach an accord as to the manner in which any oil or natural gas structure extending across the boundary line could be most effectively exploited, and costs and proceeds shared.

Subsequent drilling resulted in the discovery of gas from a field known as the Markham Field, which straddles the international boundary. These developments led the two Governments to agree in May 1992 to a program of joint development of the field. The agreement came into force on 3 March 1993. In essence, the Markham Field agreement requires the groups of licensees on both sides of the boundary to form an agreement amongst themselves to regulate the exploitation of the field. In particular, the licensees are required to nominate a single licensee to act as the Unit Operator. The Unit Operator is charged with submitting to the two Governments a proposal setting forth the position and extent of the field and details as to how the petroleum from the field should be apportioned between the two groups of licensees on each side of the boundary. The Governments must then approve this proposal, and a system of referral to a neutral expert is provided for in the event that agreement is not reached.

The determination by the Unit Operator of the apportionment of the field serves as the basis on which tax and royalty payments are calculated. For purposes of this calculation, it is irrelevant where the actual producing platforms or wells are located. The controlling factor is the petrophysical characteristics of the field and its apportionment to the licensees on each side of the boundary.

As can be seen, the primary aim of the UK–Netherlands agreement is two-fold:

1 to obligate the licence holders on both sides of the boundary to agree on a joint unitisation and development plan to be carried out by a sole operator; and
2 to establish a mechanism whereby a determination can be made as to the limits of the field and an apportionment of petroleum to each side of the boundary.

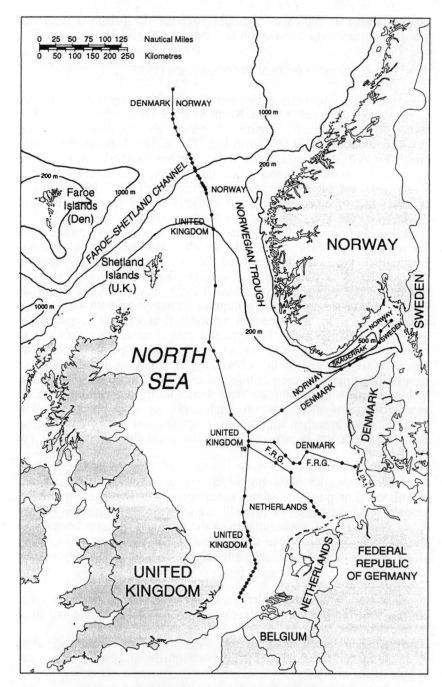

Figure 2.2 Maritime Boundaries in the North Sea

Where possible, the onus in terms of operations and planning is transferred from the States concerned to the licensees. It is therefore the Unit Operator who submits the plan for the development of the reservoir and keeps this plan up-dated. The plan and any amendments are then subject to the oversight of a joint Government body known in this case as the Markham Commission.

Obviously, this kind of agreement, by which petroleum is shared on the basis of a technical assessment of how much lies on each side of the boundary, is only possible where the boundary has already been delimited.

THAILAND–MALAYSIA

Turning to a second example (Thailand–Malaysia) – where no boundary has been agreed – the situation is very different. Figure 2.3 shows that in the Gulf of Thailand there are no agreed boundaries, but plenty of claims (by Thailand, Malaysia, Cambodia and Vietnam). Recognising the oil and gas potential of this area, and unable to agree on more than a relatively short segment of their offshore boundary (some 50km), Thailand and Malaysia signed a Memorandum of Understanding in 1979 designating a triangular area as a Joint Development Area.

While the idea of creating joint development zones in areas where no agreed boundary exists is on the face of it an attractive one, in reality a host of practical problems need to be addressed in order to make such a system work. In the Thailand–Malaysia case, it took the Parties 11 years to transform their Memorandum of Understanding into a full-fledged Joint Development Agreement (which was only signed in 1990). Foremost amongst the stumbling blocks was the fact that Malaysia favoured a production-sharing type of contract with its foreign partners while Thailand had already granted licences in the area modelled on the concession type of agreement. These differences had to be ironed out. In addition, Article 3(2) of the original 1979 Memorandum of Understanding provided that the creation of a Joint Authority by the two States with responsibility for petroleum development within the joint development zone would 'in no way affect or curtail the validity of concessions or licenses hitherto issued or agreements or arrangements hitherto made by either party'. It is not difficult to imagine the resultant difficulties in trying to reconcile the terms of existing concession agreements with the newly-created powers of the Joint Authority and with the production sharing type of framework that was provided for by the 1990 Agreement.

Unlike the UK–Netherlands agreement, the Thailand–Malaysia agreement provides for the *equal* sharing of production after deduction of royalties and production costs. This appears to be the normal rule of thumb for inter-State agreements creating joint development zones. For

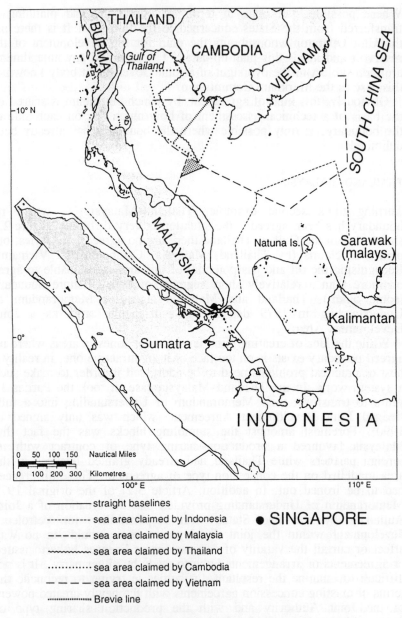

straight baselines
- - - - - - - sea area claimed by Indonesia
- - - - - - sea area claimed by Malaysia
〜〜〜〜 sea area claimed by Thailand
· · · · · · · · · sea area claimed by Cambodia
— — — — sea area claimed by Vietnam
··········· Brevie line

● SINGAPORE

The sea area claimed by Singapore cannot be represented on this map

Boundaries according to the opinion of the respective governments

Figure 2.3 Maritime Claims in the Gulf of Thailand

example, in the Bahrain–Saudi Arabia joint development zone (Figure 2.1), while Saudi Arabia retains the right to develop the oil resources of the joint area as it chooses, half of the net resource derived therefrom goes to Bahrain (Bahrain–Saudi Arabia, 1958). Similarly, the Abu Dhabi–Qatar agreement provides that whereas the boundary passes through the location of a well in the Al-Bunduq Field (Point B), and whereas this field is to be developed by Abu Dhabi, Qatar nonetheless retains a right to an *equal* share of royalties and profits therefrom (Abu Dhabi–Qatar, 1969).

If we move to other parts of the globe, both the France–Spain delimitation agreement of 1974 (Figure 2.4) and the Japan–Korea agreement (Figure 2.5) provide for variations on the same theme.

AUSTRALIA–INDONESIA ZONE OF CO-OPERATION

The last example, mentioned earlier, is the Zone of Co-operation created by the Australia–Indonesia Treaty of 11 December 1989 (for figure, see Chapter 5, Figure 5.2). Its genesis may be said to date back to the 1971 and 1972 boundary agreements between the two countries which stipulated that each would seek to reach agreement on the manner in which the joint deposits would be most effectively exploited and equitably shared. The Parties have been unable to agree on a continental shelf boundary in the Timor Gap, and this has given added impetus to the need to arrive at practical arrangements for oil and gas development in the disputed area.

The Zone of Co-operation covers some 61,000km^2 and is divided into three areas: Area A is the zone of joint development, whilst Areas B and C are under the sole jurisdiction of Australia and Indonesia, respectively. Each country retains an interest in the other's area of sole jurisdiction to the extent of 10% of the gross tax revenues arising from petroleum production in that area. But it is in Area A that the benefits of production are to be shared equally and it is also there that the most exploitable reserves are thought to be.

The Treaty creates a Joint Authority, but with powers that are more limited than those of the Joint Authority provided for in the Malaysia–Thailand agreement. Its functions are essentially administrative and it operates subject to a Petroleum Mining Code, annexed to the Treaty. Decision-making power is retained by a Ministerial Council. Although the Joint Authority is granted the power to enter into contracts, the actual form of contract – a model production sharing agreement – is annexed to the Treaty; variations to the model can only be made with the approval of the Ministerial Council (Article 6(1)(c)); and the conclusion and termination of production sharing contracts also requires Ministerial Council approval (Article 6(1)(d) and (e)). Further, it is the Ministerial Council which approves the distribution of production revenue between the States, approves the Joint Authority's

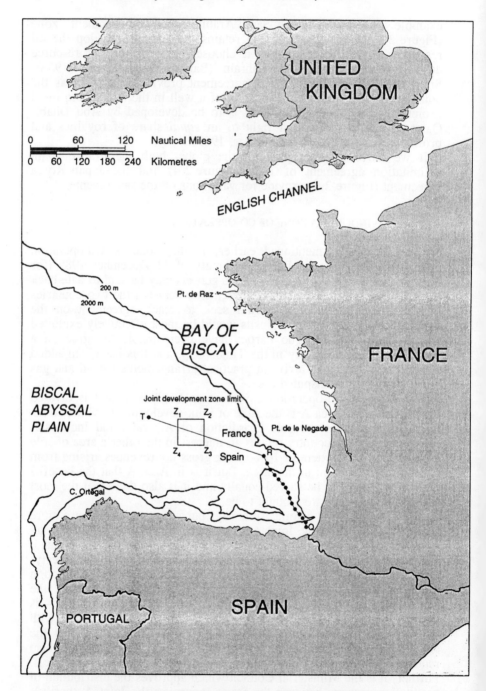

Figure 2.4 France–Spain Joint Development Zone

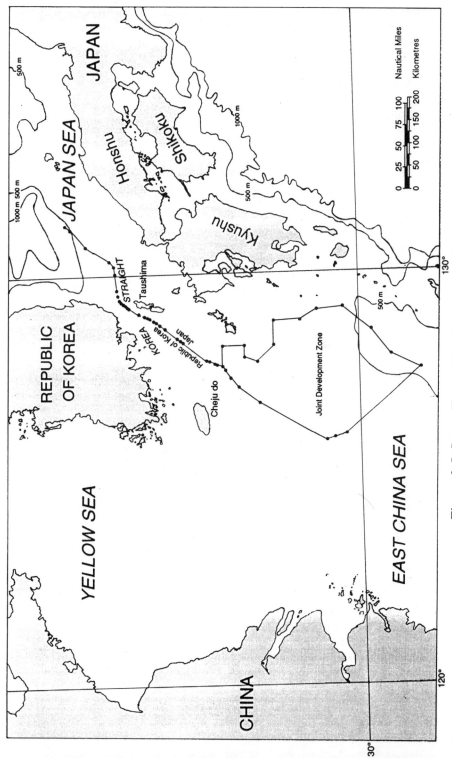

Figure 2.5 Japan–Korea Joint Development Zone

budget and establishes its regulations. Contractors must submit tax returns in both countries and receive a 50% rebate in each. The tax legislation of each country otherwise operates normally.

Attempts at Codification of the Law

Turning to the state of the law, there are two issues that warrant discussion:

1 what attempts have been made on the international plane to codify a series of legal principles covering shared oil and gas resources?
2 to what extent does the State practice discussed in this chapter reflect an emerging duty on States to co-ordinate and co-operate in the joint development or unitisation of shared oil and gas resources?

As already stressed, the natural starting point of the legal analysis is the law of capture which means that, ordinarily speaking, oil and gas resources found within a State's territory may be produced by that State without restriction, even if they straddle an international boundary.

That being said, it is significant that in the very first continental shelf delimitation case submitted to the ICJ in 1969 (the North Sea Continental Shelf Cases), the Court drew attention to the unity of deposits lying on both sides of the boundary line as one of the relevant factors that the parties should take into account in delimiting the continental shelf between them.

In his separate opinion in the case, the American judge, Judge Jessup, delivered a strong plea for increased international co-operation in the development of shared mineral resources. Nonetheless, he was the first to admit that concepts such as the doctrine of co-relative rights (so prevalent in domestic US practice) and the mandatory unitisation of petroleum reservoirs do not rise to the level of emerging rules of international law.

On 13 December 1973, the UN General Assembly adopted Resolution 3129 on 'Co-operation in the field of the environment concerning natural resources shared by two or more States'. The Resolution contained little in the way of positive obligations, but it did draw attention to the need to establish 'adequate international standards for the conservation and harmonious exploration of natural resources common to two or more States'. It also provided that co-operation between countries 'must be developed on the basis of a system of information and prior consultation' (UNGA 1973).

This is not the place to go into the thorny question whether General Assembly resolutions are binding under international law. However, at the least Resolution 3129 reflected a growing awareness amongst States of the importance of the issue. As such, it represented a tentative first step towards articulating a series of principles governing the exploitation of natural resources shared by two or more neighbouring States.

On 12 December 1974, the General Assembly adopted the Charter of Economic Rights and Duties of States by a vote of 120 for, six against and ten abstentions (Resolution 3281). Article 3 of the Charter echoed some of the themes introduced by Resolution 3129, providing that:

> In the exploitation of natural resources shared by two or more countries, each State must co-operate on the basis of a system of information and prior consultations in order to achieve *optimum use* of such resources without causing damage to the legitimate interests of others (UNGA 1974).

Furthermore, Article 30 of the Charter sounded an environmental theme by providing that,

> All States have the responsibility to ensure that activities within their jurisdiction or control do not cause damage to the environment of other States (UNGA 1974).

A definition of what constitutes 'optimum use' is not easy to agree. Indeed, in one case we handled, each side was effectively trying to define what 'optimum use' was in the context of oil and gas production. The question revolved around the meaning of a contractual term calling for the production of petroleum from a reservoir such as could be 'economically extracted' over the term of the concession – a kind of 'optimum use' formula. Several eminent economists testified that as long as the revenue achieved from production exceeded the cost of production by even as little as one cent per barrel, it was 'economical' to continue production. One can imagine how the host State reacted to this argument, which suggests that the contract in question required maximum production of the host State's most valuable, non-renewable resource at a margin of one cent (or even US$1) per barrel. The point is that 'optimum production' and 'optimum use' are concepts that are not always easily tailored to the different interests of oil companies and producing States.

Following the actions of the UN General Assembly in the early 1970s, the task of formulating more detailed principles fell to the UN Environmental Program. In 1978 it issued a series of Draft Principles which included the following elements:

1 States were encouraged to co-operate in the field of the environment concerning shared natural resources in a manner that was consistent

with the concept of the 'equitable utilisation' of those resources – a term that was not precisely defined.

2 States were also encouraged to endeavour to conclude agreements amongst themselves to regulate the utilisation of shared natural resources and to consider establishing joint commissions for consultations on environmental problems relating to their use.

3 Principle 3 stated:

'States have in accordance with the Charter of the United Nations and the principles of international law, the sovereign right to exploit their own resources pursuant to their own environmental policies, and the responsibility to ensure that activities within their jurisdiction or control do not cause damage to the environment of other States or of areas beyond the limits of national jurisdiction.'

In this context, the draft principles stated that:

'... it is necessary for each State to avoid to the maximum extent possible and to reduce to the minimum extent possible the adverse environmental effect beyond its jurisdiction of the utilisation of a shared natural resources...' (UNEP 1978).

4 States were also encouraged to make environmental assessments (impact statements) prior to engaging in any activity which might entail environmental risks, and to exchange information with their neighbours on environmental issues.

5 Finally, States were warned that they would be liable in accordance with applicable international law for environmental damage resulting from violations of their international obligations caused to areas beyond their jurisdiction.

As might be expected, one of the main controversies surrounding the Draft Principles was whether they created, or purported to express, binding obligations under international law. The Explanatory Note to the draft tried to allay concerns that new law was being created by stating that the draft had been drawn up simply for the 'guidance' of States, and that the principles were aimed at 'encouraging' States sharing a natural resource to co-operate on environmental issues. The Explanatory Note went on to say that the language used in the draft was not intended to prejudice whether, or to what extent, the conduct envisaged by the principles was already prescribed by existing rules of general international law. As such, the draft principles should probably only be viewed as *recommendations* which do not create any new rules of international law, nor necessarily even express existing rules.

It was also in 1982 that the United Nations Convention on the Law of the Sea was finalised. While it deals with a broad range of maritime issues, some of its provisions deserve brief mention here in so far as they relate to the exploitation of offshore natural resources. The main issue to which attention should be drawn concerns the different treatment given in the Convention to the exploration and exploitation of 'continental shelf resources' – ie, mineral resources found in the shelf itself – compared to the exploration and exploitation of Exclusive Economic Zone resources – ie, fish. With respect to the continental shelf, the Convention provides that the coastal State exercises sovereign rights for the purpose of exploring the shelf and exploiting its natural resources. These rights are exclusive in the sense that if the coastal State does not exercise them, no one else may do so without that State's express consent. No limitations are placed on the State's ability to exploit such resources in terms of the quantity extracted or the method of extraction.

The provisions relating to the Exclusive Economic Zone are quite different. While the coastal State has the sovereign right to exploit these resources, it has a corresponding duty to *conserve* and *manage* the resources as well. In particular, the coastal State is charged with controlling over-exploitation and promoting 'optimum utilisation' of the resource. No such obligation arises from the provisions of the Convention governing mineral resources.

Conclusions

While international law thus remains relatively undeveloped with respect to the exploitation of shared oil and gas resources, it is possible to perceive an emerging trend amongst States to deal with these issues on a bilateral level. In view of these developments, a fairly strong argument can now be made that there is a customary duty placed on States at least to consult with neighbouring States over the exploitation of jointly shared oil and gas reserves and perhaps to notify such States of new developments, even if a full-fledged duty to unitise and jointly develop such resources does not yet exist.

Bibliography

Abu Dhabi–Qatar (1969) 'Abu Dhabi–Qatar agreement', *Limits in the Seas* 18, 29 May (1970).

Australia–Indonesia (1989) 'Timor Gap Treaty', *International Legal Materials* XXIX: 469.

Bahrain–Saudi Arabia (1958) 'Bahrain–Saudi Arabia Joint Development Zone', *Limits in the Seas* 12, 10 March (1970).

UNEP (1978) 'Draft Principles' United Nations Environment Program; *International Legal Materials* XVII: 1098.

UNGA (1973) 'Co-operation in the field of the environment conerning natural resources shared by two or more states', United Nations General Assembly Resolution 3129; *International Legal Materials* XIII: 232.

UNGA (1974) 'Charter of Economic Rights and Duties of States' United Nations General Assembly Resolution 3281; *International Legal Materials* XIV: 251, 261.

3

Oil and Gas Reservoirs Across Ownership Boundaries: The Technical Basis for Apportioning Reserves

Richard E. Swarbrick

Introduction

Hydrocarbon reserves are those volumes of oil and gas which exist in reservoirs in subsurface traps. Once a discovery has been made it is necessary to assign volumes to the oil and gas field and to respective portions of the field if it straddles ownership boundaries. Implicit in any agreement to apportion hydrocarbon (oil and gas) reserves across ownership boundaries, including international boundaries, however, is the reliability of the estimation of the reserves. Sadly the technical basis for reserves estimation is often seriously constrained, especially in the early stages of the appraisal and development of a new field. In particular the definition of subsurface structure from which the extent of the productive reservoir is calculated and the calculation of the fluid volume contained therein are often highly speculative.

Although agreement to the apportionment of reserves may ultimately be a political and/or commercial decision, the basis is almost always initiated by technical considerations. This chapter aims to explain the nature of the technical basis for reserves calculations and to expose the uncertainty in the estimation.

Oil and Gas Reservoirs

An oil or gas reservoir is a portion of the earth's crust where interconnected pore space exists from which hydrocarbons can be brought to the surface. Since producable oil and gas are less dense than, and hence will float on water, the basal surface which bounds the oil (oil–water–contact (OWC)) or gas (gas–water–contact (GWC)) is almost always horizontal. The upper surface, the seal, is an impervious rock which prevents upwards migration of the oil and gas, now effectively trapped in the subsurface.

The volume of hydrocarbons in a reservoir in a subsurface trap is a function of the rock volume between the upper and lower surfaces, the percentage of the rock which is pore space (ie, not solid rock) and the proportion of the fluid which is hydrocarbons, as opposed to water or non-hydrocarbon gases. Where does the information come from to determine the volumes, and how reliable is it?

STRUCTURE MAPS

Total rock volume is determined from reservoir structure maps combined with available drilling information. To create a structure map requires imaging of the rocks in the subsurface, ie, their orientation and dip, and any discontinuities including faults which exist. Conventionally the structure is ascertained from interpretation of seismic reflection data, a technique which involves downgoing energy from a surface source reflected back from rock interfaces below the ground. The upcoming reflected energy is measured and also the time it has taken from source to receiver. The subsurface geology is thereby imaged (Figure 3.1), but the unit of measurement is time rather than depth. Hence the next step is to work out the velocity of each of the layers through which the energy rays have passed to convert the time taken into an estimated depth. This step, known as depth conversion, is prone to large errors, especially where there is little or no drilling data and where there are large changes in velocity, eg, where salt or volcanic rocks are present.

A network of seismic lines across an oil or gas field allows definition of the strongly reflecting rocks. The closer the spacing of the lines, the less uncertainty. Optimum definition is attained with a three-dimensional seismic survey. The reflectors which can be mapped may or may not be the hydrocarbon-bearing reservoir section. If the latter is not imaged directly there may be uncertainty as to the relationship between the reservoir and the nearest reflecting layer which must be considered in the geometric description of the reservoir structure. Additionally, seismic data quality varies and may not be uniform across the field, hence the reliability of any reservoir maps will change. Seismic data resolution is itself limited to one-quarter of the wavelength of the seismic wavelet, normally between 20m and 50m on conventional data at typical reservoir depths (say 2–4km below surface). Seismic data is not therefore imaging individual beds of rock, which rarely reach thicknesses of 20m, but rather interfaces bounding packages of rocks.

The structure maps defining the reservoir intervals are then combined with knowledge from the boreholes. The geographical extent of the oil or gas field is determined from the depth of the fluid contacts superimposed on the structure maps and yields the *area of closure* (Figure 3.2). Additionally the area of closure combined with the average thickness of the reservoir between OWC/GWC and topseal yields the *reservoir rock volume*. Uncertainty is a product of quality of the structure maps, and the distribution of fluids within the reservoir

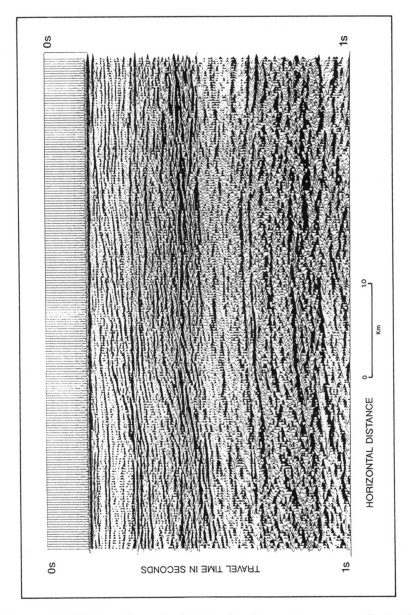

Figure 3.1 High quality seismic data shot from a boat at sea. Each of the continuous reflectors (trails of black adjoining wave peaks) is interpreted as a rock interface with contrasting rock properties which reflect the downgoing energy wave back to the surface. The vertical scale is the travel time for the energy wave to go down from the source and back to a receiver.

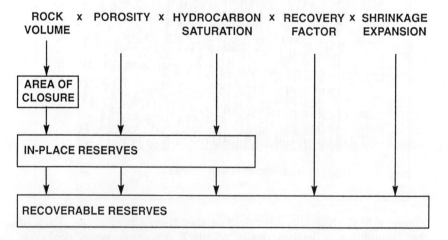

Figure 3.2 The input parameters required to compute hydrocarbon reserves in a trap. Area of closure, in-place reserves and recoverable reserves are all used in different cases to apportion reserves across ownership boundaries.

based primarily on borehole information. Sometimes the GWC at the base of a gas-bearing reservoirs can be seen imaged directly on seismic data.

Area of closure can be used as a basis for determination of reserves across ownership boundaries. It has the advantage of being one of the simplest formulae, relying solely on structural definition of the reservoir. The percentages of the total area of closure apportioned to each party would be applied to all volumes of hydrocarbons produced. Where a moderately uniform structure exists with boundaries passing close to the crest or high-point of the structure this method of determination is fair and should be pursued. Where ownership boundaries pass through the edge areas the method favours those with only the marginal portions of the field and is disadvantageous to those with the crestal area where the greatest average reservoir thickness exists.

FLUID VOLUMES

To determine the volumes of oil and gas in the reservoir from the total rock volume, knowledge of the rock porosity and the hydrocarbon saturation must be acquired from available borehole information. Porosity is a function of the type of rock and its burial history, involving compaction and cementation, and is measured directly only from large pieces of rock, ie, where the rock has been cored during drilling. These porosity values are moderately accurate but they record only the quality of the rocks drilled at the borehole site and the intervals for which core is available. At all other depths porosity is determined from a range of borehole geophysical measurements taken after drilling has stopped. Each method is relatively accurate but only under ideal borehole conditions. Calibration to porosity determined from core is always preferable.

Porosity can change dramatically across a reservoir, principally where there is a change in character of the rock linked to the original environment of deposition. For example sandstones deposited in a deltaic environment are focused along channel pathways and the volume and quality of the sandstones diminish away from the channels. Porosity measurements within the channels are therefore unrepresentative of the other rock-types at the same level in the reservoir. In contrast a reservoir comprising sand dunes is likely to be relatively continuous across a field area with similar porosity values at the same depth across the entire structure. In carbonate rocks dramatic changes in porosity can result from differences in the amount of cementation (infilling of the pore space by new mineral phases after deposition), largely controlled by the movement of fresh water and sea water during the early stages of burial.

Hydrocarbon-bearing rocks in reservoirs have a coating of the original formation water around all the grains lining the pore spaces. Borehole geophysical measurements are the prime source of information about the fluid content of the reservoir at depth, since the act of drilling disturbs the fluids within the vicinity of the borehole by forcing some mud filtrate into the adjacent rock. The fluid content in any cored material is strongly influenced by the drilling. The principal technique to determine fluid saturation is by means of a suite of instruments measuring either resistivity or conductivity. The tools focused far away from the borehole edge yield the most accurate information of the true reservoir saturation. The hydrocarbon saturation is calculated knowing the resistivity of the reservoir interval, the porosity (see above), and the resistivity (a function of the saltiness) of the water.

In a high porosity, clean reservoir interval the hydrocarbon saturation is moderately accurately determined and likely to remain constant to within a short distance (less than a metre) from the OWC/GWC. However where the reservoir is very fine-grained, and/or contains a large amount of secondary clays giving the rock a low permeability (ability to flow), capillary pressures will allow high water saturations to persist well above the OWC/GWC. In low permeability reservoirs the calculation of hydrocarbon saturation is much more difficult and hence prone to inaccuracy.

Combination of the reservoir rock volume with porosity and hydrocarbon saturation yields the *in-place reserves* in the field (Figure 3.2), a frequently used basis for the determination of reserves across ownership boundaries.

PRODUCIBLE FLUIDS

Hydrocarbons in the reservoir may not flow to the surface in the same proportions as they are distributed throughout the reservoir. To estimate the volumes of hydrocarbons which can be recovered at the surface two additional factors must be determined. Firstly a *recovery factor*, a function of the behaviour of the fluid in the reservoir and the reservoir engineering design for the field must be assigned. Secondly there will be volume and compositional changes when fluids are brought up from the high temperatures and pressure found in the reservoir and stabilised at surface temperatures and pressure.

The recovery factor of an oil or gas field is very difficult to determine prior to production from the field. The main considerations are the interconnectedness of the reservoir intervals and hence the ability of the trapped fluids to reach the borehole. A highly variable reservoir will require many more wells to drain it than a moderately homogeneous reservoir. Of equal importance is the method of drainage, an engineering consideration based on the geometry, quality and continuity of the reservoir. For example a simple structure without faults and with a thick, high quality reservoir could potentially be drained by a single producing well, perhaps augmented by a well injecting water below the OWC or GWC to maintain reservoir pressure. Alternatively a highly faulted reservoir with poor transmittability of fluids across the faults will require a large number of wells to drain the field and there may be considerable uncertainty as to the exact position of the faults and the reservoir behaviour prior to production experience. During later stages in the development of a field, observation of pressure decline resulting from a period of sustained production can provide a relatively accurate assessment of the likely volume of producible hydrocarbons which can be drained by each well in the field.

At reservoir depth oil can contain large volumes of dissolved (associated) gas. Oil will therefore shrink in volume from reservoir to surface as the dissolved gas comes out of solution. Conversely gas will expand greatly in volume as it is brought to the surface, eg, one volume of gas at about 4 km burial will expand to about 45 volumes of gas at standard temperature and pressure (STP). It is commonplace to estimate the relative proportion of fluids and gases at surface conditions and to model their behaviour in order to adjust subsurface volumes to surface conditions. Collecting samples at reservoir conditions is not straight forward and can lead to erroneous assumptions of reservoir fluid behaviour, especially during the pre-production phase of the field.

Combination of a recovery factor and volume changes with in-place reserves yields perhaps the most complicated and poorly verifiable basis for determination of reserves, ie, *recoverable reserves* (Figure 3.2). Nevertheless volumes produced and measured at the surface installation will ultimately be the historical basis for the apportionment of reserves and has the advantage that a cash value can be attached directly if the commodity prices are known. The determination can be made more complex, however, if non-technical factors are considered, eg, commerciality of recoverable reserve. Other methods of determination could include combining factors such as transport costs, marketability of products and taxation/royalty with the recoverable reserves. At this stage the purely technical basis for apportionment of reserves has been surpassed.

Definition of Field Reserves

A useful threefold subdivision of recoverable reserves is frequently used where an oil and gas field discovery has been made. The uncertainty of hydrocarbon volume recovery increases from the proven to possible category, reflecting less geological, geophysical and engineering data control.

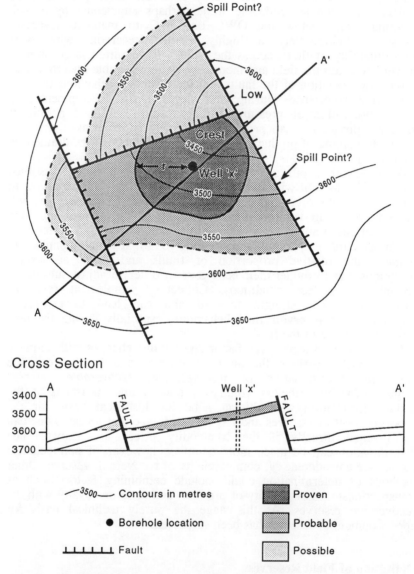

Figure 3.3 Subsurface structure map of a reservoir interval, and the
location of Well 'X' which has proved the existence of hydrocarbons in
the reservoir there. Proven, probable and possible reserves can be
assigned to different parts of the structure depending on the likelihood
of reserves being present and quantifiable.

(Published with the kind permission of Schlumberger Geco–Prakla and Texaco UK Ltd)

PROVEN RESERVES

Hydrocarbon volumes known to be present which can be produced at current prices using existing technology.

This category of reserves is auditable (ie, the geological and geophysical basis can be verified) and forms the basis for company assets attributed to unproduced oil and gas.

PROBABLE RESERVES

Hydrocarbon volumes whose likelihood of being present are high but where there is more uncertainty as to the range of possible volumes than in the proven category.

POSSIBLE RESERVES

Hydrocarbon volumes which are generally not tested by drilling but whose probability of existing is based on geological/geophysical understanding of the likely distribution of hydrocarbons in the area.

An example of how the allocation of reserves could be assigned to each category is illustrated using Figure 3.3. Well 'X' has been drilled near the crest of a structure which is compartmentalised by a number of faults. The well encountered hydrocarbons throughout the reservoir section, ie, the depth of the OWC/GWC is not known. At this stage the proven reserves might be assigned as the hydrocarbon volume found at the same structural elevation as the reservoir in the borehole, and upwards to the crest of the structure, but limited to a defined radius (r) from the borehole location (Figure 3.3). Probable reserves might include the remaining volume in the same fault compartment as the well, whilst possible reserves would be an estimation of the remaining potential of the gross structure and include areas not tested by the well (Figure 3.3). There is increasing uncertainty in the volumes of hydrocarbon volumes in each category; indeed there is no certainty of any hydrocarbon fluids in the possible category! Subsequent drilling would enable reserves to be moved from possible and probable categories into the proven category. Allocation of reserves in each category will be a function of the complexity of the reservoir, and will necessarily be somewhat subjective.

Conclusion

Apportionment of reserves is based on technical considerations which can be highly uncertain, especially in the early stages of the development of an oil or gas field. Reservoir volumes can be highly variable depending on a number of geological and engineering factors. Early apportionment of reserves across ownership boundaries should acknowledge this uncertainty in reserves estimation. Subsequent appraisal and development of the oil or gas field will permit verification of earlier assumptions and provide the technical basis for redetermination of the original split of reserves. Optimisation of reserves on the basis of non-technical considerations will always be an important feature of equity determination, but the uncertainties of the technical data should not be forgotten.

Bibliography

Chierici, G.L. (1994) *Principles of Petroleum Reservoir Engineering,* Volume 1, Springer Verlag.
Dake, L.P. (1978) *Fundamentals of Reservoir Engineering,* Elsevier.
Society of Petroleum Engineers (1987) 'Definitions for Oil and Gas Reserves', *Journal of Petroleum Technology* 39, 25: 577–8.

4

Offshore Petroleum Joint Development Arrangements: Functional Instrument? Compromise? Obligation?

Ian Townsend-Gault
William G. Stormont

Introduction

An offshore petroleum joint development arrangement is typically one where two or more countries enter into a formal agreement for the co-operative development of and the sharing of revenues derived from oil and gas activities within a given offshore area, by pooling their sovereign rights with respect to that area. This definition excludes other types of co-operative resource management arrangement with which joint development is sometimes (unaccountably) confused.[1] It also suggests, first, the existence of a treaty which will govern the undertaking, and second, that the states concerned are indeed possessed of the relevant rights to the area in question.

There are at least six such offshore petroleum joint development arrangements in the world today.[2] This is not exactly an overwhelming statistic taken in relation to the theoretical total number of maritime boundaries world-wide, but yet the subject has generated an enormous literature of comment, analysis, and advocacy.[3] Contributors in the last mentioned category enthusiastically advocate joint development as a total or partial solution to a whole range of maritime jurisdictional problems, mostly where two or more countries cannot agree on the course of an ocean boundary. The general argument runs something like this: if the boundary dispute in question is intractable, that is, is not susceptible to solution in the foreseeable future, but yet parties wish to commence offshore development in or around a boundary area, then a joint development arrangement provides for a ready solution to their mutual problems. What could be more logical than the establishment of a co-operative regime which, whatever its shortcomings, will at least allow development to proceed? 'Something for everyone', in fact.[4]

Another, related, view suggests that there is now a 'model' for joint development, and the Timor Gap Agreement has been selected by at least two distinguished commentators for this honour (Onorato and Valencia, 1990). But in what way can an arrangement which is very much the product of the need of two distinct countries, facing a common issue at a particular time in their mutual relations, be considered to be a 'model'? The answer is not difficult if the conditions precedent for the Timor Gap Agreement are common to all such situations, and if the aims of that arrangement are similarly shared by other states facing such a situation. In other words, the degree of commonality should be pronounced. Again, it is pertinent to ask if, in the circumstances, sufficient information is available to justify such an optimistic conclusion.

These are perhaps the benign views of the possibilities offered by offshore joint development arrangements. A subtly different approach is taken by those who either suggest, or come very close to doing so, that the conclusion of such an arrangement is an obligation on the part of the states concerned. This line of argument suggests that international legal norms are sufficiently well developed in such a way as to offer a concrete alternative to boundary delimitation stalemate. Accordingly, countries either 'must' or 'should' enter into a joint development arrangement, particularly if they are unwilling to abide by any third-party means of boundary dispute settlement. The argument here is that unwillingness to adopt any third-party means of resolving a boundary dispute obligates either the refusing state, or both states, to proceed to agree on a co-operative arrangement in the interest of ensuring that the appropriate environment exists for investment and development. The assumption is, of course, that such third-party mechanisms abound, and it is tantamount to perversity for countries to refuse to use any of them.[5]

To our mind, there is something peculiarly insidious, not to say dysfunctional and dangerous, about this latter view. To be fair, its advocates often adopt it when the alternative appears to be armed conflict, but it is at least arguable that such a threat is not sufficient for the coercion of countries into a meretricious arrangement which may promise a lot, but in the final analysis will fail to deliver anything. This is because a joint development arrangement is not a mechanical process, but rather a highly complex and complicated result of a series of dealings between the countries concerned over a range of issues, some of which may have little or nothing to do with the ostensible subject of the exercise. It should not be suggested lightly, and cannot take the place of any true mutuality of understanding between the two states. In other words, the conclusion of any form of joint development arrangement, in the absence of the appropriate level of consent between the parties, is merely redrafting the problem and possibly complicating it further. Such a result would likely have a deleterious effect on other aspects of the bilateral relationship between the countries concerned.

This is not to suggest that joint development arrangements do not have an important role to play in furthering ocean development. The indicators – such as they are – suggest that they do. But it must be remembered that these indicators are slight, not to say minimal, in international terms. To put the matter simply, we do not have a great deal of state practice with respect to joint development. Although there are at least six schemes in existence, only three of them appear to be worthy of serious attention. Again, set against the theoretical number of offshore boundaries in the world, this is not a particularly significant statistic. But that statistic is not necessarily a deterrent. Every new idea, especially those which are challenging and innovative, must surely be given the chance to make its mark and contribution, to be developed, and possibly adopted further. No rule of international law has avoided this process. But it is precisely because this process must be undergone that objection may be made to the inordinately optimistic, not to say irresponsible, nature of the advocacy of joint development arrangements in situations where the only qualifying characteristic justifying its application is that there is an apparently intractable offshore boundary dispute. It is our contention that this requirement is simply not sufficient.

The argument is therefore that joint development arrangements are applicable because nothing else would appear to have any chance of succeeding. But this in turn suggests that joint development is a 'last gasp' solution. This in turn obscures the functional nature of the arrangement, which is a legal mechanism for the attainment of the production of natural resources, *not* the solution to a jurisdictional problem. A moratorium, after all, would serve the latter purpose admirably and with far fewer complications. 'Do nothing' is a time-honoured response to a problem. But if a joint development arrangement is to be implemented, the question is, given all the relevant circumstances between the states concerned, *can* it succeed? What are the positive reasons in favour of joint development for its own sake?

One of the areas much in demand by those wishing to illustrate the efficacy of joint development arrangements is that of the South China Sea and Gulf of Thailand. Here we have the area of complex maritime disputes *par excellence*. The South China Sea is semi-enclosed, and the spider's web of boundary claims, already sufficiently complicated, is further complicated by the presence of two disputed groups of islands and reefs, those of the Spratly and Paracel archipelagos. In the Gulf of Thailand, a comparatively restricted area is claimed by four states, the fact that two of them have, until recently, been virtually absent from the international arena, has tended to complicate the issue to a further degree.

The object of this paper is twofold. First, we will examine some of the necessary preconditions for the establishment of a joint development arrangement, based on experience and practice to date. Second, we will consider the impact of state practice in this area on public international law, with specific reference to the potential content of any obligation for the establishment of such an arrangement. These remarks will be placed in the context of the ongoing jurisdictional disputes in the South China Sea and the Gulf of Thailand, prompted as they are by work being undertaken by the writers and their colleagues in Canada and other parts of South-east Asia in these two areas. No attempt is made to analyse the substantive content of the various agreements: the literature referred to in the notes offers a sufficient choice of papers which do, and the present volume offers further valuable contributions.[6]

International Law Considerations

Few new branches of international law have attracted as much attention from non-lawyers as has the law of the sea. This is not particularly difficult to understand or account for: the law of the sea is but a part of the more important and comprehensive topic of marine affairs. The only difference is that the ostensibly non-technical language of international law appears to be more accessible to non-lawyers, unlike, for instance, discussions of bio-mass, total allowable catch, resource economics, and the like. The result is that law of the sea concepts have entered what amounts to the vernacular of marine affairs, and are discussed, and advocated, even by those who may have but an imperfect knowledge of their meaning or interpretation. Furthermore, such commentators may also be unaware that the process of ascribing meaning to, and the interpretation of, legal instruments, are themselves technical issues of some subtlety. To the non-lawyer, this may appear to be the irascible comment of the specialist whose field is invaded by an impious laity, but that is not at all the case. There is no reason why non-lawyers should be in thrall to the doctrine and tenants of the law of the sea; but it is surely desirable that those who wish to use this information are aware of its appropriate application and limitations; in other words, that they have some idea of what exactly they are doing in making free with concepts drawn from a discipline of which they may know nothing. This much is surely common sense, but the extent to which these fairly elementary precepts are ignored is always surprising.

This seeming accessibility of the language of the international law of the sea is one of the reasons which explains the enormous literature on the subject in general, and also on joint development. But matters do not end there: the joint development of offshore petroleum resources is a subject that sits at the intersection of a number of disciplinary areas, and even a number of areas of the law, including the law of the sea and natural resources law. It should not be assumed that individuals well versed in the one are equally well versed in the other. All of this may account for the cavalier way in which law of the sea terminology is used, or abused.

This argument gains greater force with the imminent entry into force of the Law of the Sea Convention. Since that treaty was signed in December 1982, it has achieved an almost mythic status among adherents and detractors alike. This is due in part to the enthusiastic advocacy of numerous individuals who were active during the negotiation of the Convention at the Third United Nations Conference on the Law of the Sea, and who subsequently adopted the cause of the treaty, in some cases as a personal crusade. One result of this process has been the adoption of the language of the Law of the Sea Convention as a sort of ocean management vernacular, where concepts are used without a very clear idea of their possible meaning, particularly their legal meaning.

The dangers of this process will soon be apparent. The Law of the Sea Convention is many things to many people, but as of November 1994, it will also be a treaty in-force between at least 60 countries, subject to the rules of international law pertaining to such agreements, and requiring implementation and development through state practice, all of which will have important *legal* effects. Thus, a consideration of the meaning of provisions of the convention relating to delimitation, and, more importantly in the present context, interim measures pending a delimitation, will assume a commanding importance. This is because the majority of potential marine boundaries in the world have yet to be delimited. It is therefore increasingly likely, particularly between states party to the convention, that there will be increased emphasis on the need to enter into interim measures. A joint development arrangement is only one example of an interim measure, but the extent to which such an arrangement is likely to be 'interim' (meaning, arguably, short-term) is open to debate.

THE LEGAL FOUNDATION FOR JOINT DEVELOPMENT

The legal basis of the six joint development zones which have been established are similar: within the areas concerned, the respective states exercise sovereign rights for the purposes of the exploration for and exploitation of natural resources, *inter alia* of the seabed and its sub-soil. The allusion to sovereignty connotes exclusivity, and furthermore, exclusivity of a nature which appertains solely to states. A true joint development zone requires the pooling of the rights of the respective states, which rights are then exercised in common on a basis which should ideally be specified by the treaty in unambiguous terms. Problems arise, of course, when the states concerned purport to create a joint development arrangement for an area over which they do not exercise rights in international law. When in 1976 the Governments of Japan and South Korea considered a joint development arrangement in their adjacent offshore, the Government of the People's Republic of China (PRC) objected on the grounds that at least part of the zone covered areas which they regarded as appertaining to the PRC. The joint development zone established by Malaysia and Thailand in the Gulf of Thailand may infringe on the rights of Cambodia, whose government was not consulted when the arrangement was concluded. To our knowledge, the Government of the Kingdom of Cambodia has yet to take an official position on this matter, but it has declared that any and all arrangements of this sort entered into by governments or regimes in Cambodia since 1956 are void. A similar problem may exist with regard to the Timor Gap Agreement, in that the arrangement is valid only if Indonesia's claim to sovereignty over East Timor is accepted. For those who do not accept the authority of Indonesia to dispose of marine areas offshore East Timor, either *de facto* or *de jure*, the arrangement has no effect.

International law assumes that rights to seabed and sub-soil natural resources extending either to 200 nautical miles from the base line or to the edge of the continental margin, whichever is greater, are divided between the coastal states of the world. This is so because continental shelf rights arise *ipso jure*, that is, without any express claim being made.[7] The process of delimitation is therefore one of discovering the course of boundaries which are presumed to exist, given the exclusive nature of the rights which arise over the seabed and sub-soil, pursuant to the doctrine of the continental shelf. This point needs to be stressed because the point of departure for many suggestions with respect to joint development arrangements are the claims to jurisdiction made by the countries to a particular dispute. Where the dispute involves more than two countries, and yet the arrangement focuses on two alone, then the probity and utility of the joint development zone is at least open to question. At worst, the conclusion of such a zone is a violation of the rights of a third state, and therefore contrary to international law.

The problem with accepting the unilaterally declared position of a party to a maritime boundary dispute as the presumptive limit to a joint development zone, is that this claim may have little or no validity as it stands, and therefore to attach significance to it would be to encourage countries to make claims of increasing extravagance. This point is rather difficult, because it is in the nature of states to make the best possible case for jurisdiction, to claim as much ocean space as possible, and therefore to negotiate from a position of assumed strength. As discussions continue, the extravagant claim can be modified, bringing to the two countries closer and closer together. This is precisely the process which Indonesia and Vietnam are currently engaged in the area offshore Minh Hai Province and north of the Natuna Island group in the south-western South China Sea.

The problem here lies in the uncritical acceptance of countries claims as a starting point, rather than subjecting those claims to some sort of assessment. International law with respect to maritime boundary delimitation is not settled or codified, but nor is it disorganised and random. It is perfectly possible to subject state claims to a critical assessment based on readily ascertainable criteria, applied or sanctioned by the International Court, and more importantly, given the force of law through state practice. In other words, countries party to a maritime boundary dispute may have radically different views on the course of their boundary, and have used wholly different criteria to produce a line, conceptually wholly different from that of their neighbours. If we can be forgiven for using an example close to home, Canada and the United States had radically different ideas as to what criteria should be applied to draw their maritime boundary in the Gulf of Maine. In the event, the Chamber of the International Court in its decision (ICJ 246) produced a compromise, but one which appears to have been the result of the criteria chosen by Canada rather than the United States. In the view of the Court, the criteria used by the United States had less saliency than those employed by Canada. Similarly, the Court of Arbitration established by Canada and France to determine their maritime boundaries offshore of the islands of Saint Pierre and Miquelon was forced to choose between two radically different conceptions, both of which, however, were firmly based on international law. Again, the claims by Canada and the United States in the Beaufort Sea, the northern continuation of the Alaska–Yukon land boundary, are wholly dissimilar, with the United States applying equidistance, and Canada preferring a line based on historical claim.

Arguably, then, it is possible to adopt a critical position with respect to claims whereby the various criteria identified in continuous state practice and by the International Court or courts of arbitration can be deployed. But this process can be taken too far. The International Court has stated that the purpose of maritime boundary third-party settlement is to produce an equitable result, and it would appear from state practice that countries, in their discussions, have a similar objective in view. The issue of equity arises in a very different way *vis-à-vis* a joint development zone. The area covered by the zone must appear, to at least some extent, to be equitable, viewed from both sides. Or, rather, equally inequitable from both points of view. Perhaps the appropriate course is to consider whether the positions of the two parties can be supported according to the readily ascertainable criteria of international law, or some other stated criteria agreeable to the countries concerned. By discarding inappropriate criteria, the difference in the position of the two states can be narrowed to a point where the surrender of sovereignty would appear to prejudice/benefit both states equally.

THE QUESTION OF LEGAL OBLIGATION

It is axiomatic in international law that limitations on the sovereignty of states cannot be lightly presumed. Accordingly, it is impossible to deduce that there is an obligation to enter into any form of interim measures pending delimitation or a joint development arrangement in the absence of a positive legal rule. For states party to the Law of the Sea Convention, this matter will be settled once the Convention enters into force as between them. For non-parties, the situation is more complicated, hinging as it does on the status of this requirement in customary international law. What then does customary international law have to say on the subject of the presence of an obligation to enter into an interim arrangement pending final delimitation?

We would argue that the starting point is to reiterate the principle laid down in the Lotus Case; restrictions on the sovereignty of states should not be lightly presumed. In theory, states are free to enter into interim arrangements, or not, as they choose. Where then is the source of any obligation to the contrary? There can only be one answer; state practice. Furthermore, such practice should be constant and uniform, and the states concerned should be seen to act in accordance with a perceived legal obligation.

Applying these criteria to state practice on interim measures indicates that it would be difficult to argue the existence of a custom or usage with respect to interim measures, far less the existence of a rule of customary international law. Most states party to a maritime jurisdictional dispute appear to prefer for circumstances to provide an opportunity for a successful delimitation agreement. This issue is bound-up with a more complex one, which has to do with coastal states' behaviour as regards ocean boundary making. Why do countries conclude ocean boundary agreements? Why have some countries been enthusiastic promoters of boundary making with their neighbours, while others have done little or nothing? One of us has argued elsewhere (Johnston and Saunders, 1988: 204) that ocean boundary making is a highly functional act, in keeping with the highly functional nature of the law of the sea itself. States rarely enter into boundary agreements for abstract reasons. They do so because they need to have the boundary determined, usually for the purpose of resource planning and management. It is no accident that the majority of ocean boundaries in the world today involve important petroleum producing countries, such as Indonesia, the Arabian Gulf states, and the North Sea. It is true that the latter two regions mentioned are very much enclosed, and therefore the room for manoeuvre for many countries is not particularly large. But it is also true that they are important hydrocarbon producing areas, and it was no accident that the most important continental shelf boundary in the North Sea, that between Britain and Norway, was concluded just after domestic legal regimes were put in place governing exploration and production by the two countries and the ratification of the Convention on the Continental Shelf by the UK, nor was it particularly surprising that the boundary was negotiated in what today would appear to be extraordinary haste.

Even the most cursory analysis of ocean boundary-making behaviour from 1958 until the present day shows that the majority of the existing boundaries were concluded in a comparatively short time frame, but the rate of settlement began to decline in the early 1970s, just as recourse to third-party settlement began to rise. This can be attributed to a number of factors: the rapid rise in the world price of oil after the Middle East war of 1973, and the gradual acceptance of the concept of the exclusive economic zone. Thus, petroleum resources became ever more valuable, and the ocean jurisdictional stakes were raised immeasurably.

But if bilateral agreement was retarded by these developments, it might have been logical to expect that third-party settlement and the adoption of interim measures would have been heavily favoured in proportion. While there have been further developments on both fronts, it can hardly be said that the coastal states have turned to these alternatives with whole-hearted enthusiasm, looking to them for solutions to their jurisdictional problems. One swallow does not a summer make: half-a-dozen joint development arrangements does not evidence consonant, uniform state practice as to the existence of an obligation to adopt interim measures pending a delimitation.

At this point, it is appropriate to consider a different but related question: *should* there be an obligation to enter into an interim arrangement? Or, to put the matter another way, if two states are unable to reach an agreement on the course of their ocean boundary, and one wishes to proceed with petroleum development but the other does not, is the latter state under any obligation at all?

International law obliges states to resolve their difference via negotiation in good faith. Applying this to a process of negotiation with respect to an offshore boundary gives us two opposing hypothesis. The first would be that the reluctant state, by refusing to negotiate, is preventing its neighbour from enjoying its sovereign rights over the continental shelf for the purpose of exploration and exploitation of natural resources. The opposing view is that the state wishing to proceed is forcing its neighbour into a process which it may not wish to engage in, and which it may not be well equipped to engage in, given the highly technical nature of boundary negotiations and decision making.

As with so many issues in the law of the sea, the best approach to such questions is to consider the matter by considering the underlying principles of the law of the sea. As we have said before, the international law of the sea is a highly functional body of principles and rules. It has little to do with abstracts, and everything to do with providing a framework governing the mutual rights and obligations of states with regards to ocean space. Law of the sea developments up to the mid-1960s tended to emphasise unilateral rights and the phraseology of the doctrine of the continental shelf, with its emphasis on 'sovereign rights for the purposes of exploration and exploitation,' tends to emphasise this. But this concept must now be read together with that of interdependence and sustainable development, including optimum conservation and the balancing of interests in the oceans. Part 5 of the Law of the Sea Convention, relating to an exclusive economic zone, provides such a balance of rights and duties. It is true that most states have focused on the question of rights, but it is no longer seriously doubted that optimum ecosystem management requires these to be balanced with obligations, and not only on a sector by sector basis. At the domestic level, then, ocean management requires a degree of functional integration between the maritime sectors, but in such a way that each area of activity is able to proceed, but without danger of adverse impacts on the others.[8] But this process must be repeated at the sub-regional, regional, and then inter-regional level. Any one of the countries in the South China Sea region is free to determine its policies with respect to fishing, petroleum, navigation, environmental protection, and so on. But domestic decisions on each of these matters would have a profound impact not only on their immediate neighbours, but on distant states. For instance, it has now been proved that significant schools of tuna migrate between the waters of the South China Sea and the South Pacific. Tuna harvesting policy undertaken by any Melanesian state could impact adversely on Vietnam, the Philippines, Malaysia, or Brunei. The emerging principles of large ecosystem management are developing to recognise the regulatory and policy-making imperatives which arise from this state of affairs. Put another way, international law does not recognise exclusive coastal state jurisdiction over ocean space simply to gratify the wish of states to exercise governmental power in the oceans, but because coastal states are the most effective custodians of that ocean space and its resources. The concept of obligation was therefore implicit in the development of the law of the sea from the time that the international community determined that it was appropriate to extend jurisdiction beyond the limits of a three nautical mile territorial sea. Those opportunities and constraints exist to this day. It is arguably inappropriate, dysfunctional, and pointless to consider ocean management questions divorced from these seminal principles.

Applying those principles to specific cases suggests that the posture of the reluctant state may be the most problematic, in that it is effectively standing in the way of optimum ocean management in ocean space over which it has both a direct and indirect interest. It cannot exercise the full range of its own responsibilities if it does not know the extent of its boundaries, and it is preventing its neighbour from doing likewise. It is probably too much to say that international law requires positive acts on the part of states with respect to ocean management. It is, after all, implicit in the law of the sea that if a country does not want to exploit its marine resources, it does not have to, and no other country should take this as an opportunity to step in. But the limitations of this approach, based as they are on the spatial sector as the optimum area for ocean management, are not fully apparent. If it is true that coastal states are under an obligation to co-operate in ocean management, then the duty to negotiate and resolve differences becomes all the stronger. That duty becomes part of the general obligation to facilitate optimum management, as opposed to a more abstract decision as to whether or not to engage in negotiations.

Accordingly, it is impossible to conclude that there is an obligation at international law, either to adopt interim measures pending a delimitation or to conclude a joint development arrangement (which, after all, is only one of the possible interim measures). But there most certainly is an obligation to engage in negotiations for a boundary in good faith. While the continuation of a boundary stalemate may appear to be dysfunctional, if not totally contrary to the argument advanced above, then state practice forces one to the reluctant conclusion that stalemate appears to be totally palatable to the majority of members of the international community. When pressed on this point with respect to Chinese claims in the South China Sea, an official from Beijing once said that China was prepared to wait '1,000 years, if necessary' for other countries to come around to the Chinese way of thinking. Other countries may possibly adopt a shorter time frame. It is worth remembering that Canada and the United States negotiated for almost 20 years before submitting the matter of their Gulf of Maine boundary dispute to third-party settlement.

Political and Security Considerations

Where either political or economic considerations are brought into play, resource issues, the ostensible object of the exercise, may be relegated in importance, and prospects for the successful conclusion of a joint development agreement may be diminished. But resource management between states is obviously highly political, and it is pointless to examine the phenomenon of joint development without considering the overall context in which agreements are concluded, and within which the arrangements they establish must operate. The first issue for examination under this heading is that of political will.

A term much used, seldom explained, and open to a wide degree of interpretation, political will is nonetheless the single most important ingredient in the successful conclusion *and* continuation of any joint development agreement. The conjunction should be stressed: it should be remembered that the time-frame here can be measured in decades if oil or gas is discovered in commercial quantities. But what exactly is meant by 'political will'? It is not sufficient to say that, because two or more countries have signed a treaty establishing a joint development agreement that this is evidence of, or a substitute for, the political will to carry it out. Only the most obdurate legal mind would seriously claim that reliance on the maxim *pacta sunt servanda*[9] is a sufficient foundation for a complex bilateral undertaking.

An overriding consideration for the prospective parties to a joint development agreement is that the arrangement must be able to withstand domestic upheavals such as a change in government, or internal strife, in either state. In the case of a democracy such as Canada, a government entering into a controversial arrangement, for example the North American Free Trade Agreement (NAFTA) negotiated by the government of Prime Minister Mulroney, needs a parliamentary majority to support the initial deal. Such a government would also consider whether or not the arrangement could affect its chances of re-election. In this connection, it should be noted that the Government of Australia was criticised at home and abroad for entering into the Timor Gap Agreement, but clearly concluded that, on balance, domestic forces were more markedly *pro* rather than *con*.[10] In countries which enjoy other forms of government, the arrangement must satisfy the (sometimes heterogeneous) wishes and imperatives of the power elite, whether civilian or military. Recent Russian history indicates this dynamic well.[11]

So much for the decision to enter into the agreement in the first place. But there must also be a tacit understanding that the arrangement will survive the vicissitudes inevitable in any bilateral relationship. States must be able to depend on the word of other states, and it is in this context that *pacta sunt servanda* is an appropriate principle to adduce; the means whereby states give their word takes the form of a treaty, whose interpretation and application is governed by the rules of international law. However, as has already been said, it cannot be assumed too easily that the conclusion of a treaty disposes of a matter. Treaties can be renegotiated, or their implementation delayed without the state responsible seeming to break the terms of the agreement. The French *de facto* withdrawal from the European Community in 1967 provides an excellent example. It would not be difficult for a state party to a joint development agreement to delay decisions, or to take a variety of measures which would bring the activity to a virtual standstill, if it wished to show its displeasure to its partner. There can be no guarantee that this will not happen: but if oil and gas production from the disputed area enjoys the unmistakable support of the two states, then it is less likely. But if the arrangement has some other real purpose, then that lack of commitment to the ostensible enterprise may well prove fatal.[12]

The saga of the negotiations between Malaysia and Thailand to amplify the 1978 Memorandum of Understanding (MOU) into a complete regime was bedevilled by various factors: changes in governments with differing priorities than their predecessors and, in the case of Thailand, uncertainty regarding the stability of the regime. Agreement to proceed was finally reached, but it remains to be seen how strong the commitment is to this endeavour in the light of the claims of Vietnam and, to a lesser extent, Cambodia, in the Gulf of Thailand.

A joint development agreement lays a foundation for a mutually beneficial activity, but it is crucial that there is an immediate and effective translation into co-operation *at all levels*, and such co-operation must continue, maybe for decades. Failure will result in a dysfunctional mechanism responsible only for a proliferation of red tape without realising benefits for any of the contracting parties *(Business Times,* 1989). This, in turn, will alienate the oil industry, on whom, one imagines, the states concerned propose to rely. The conditions precedent for an effective bilateral regime include trust, or at least mutual confidence. For many states, these are already present in their everyday relations. But where the states concerned have a history of enmity, to consider joint development before implementing confidence-building measures is to court trouble. However, the joint development agreements examined in this paper were all concluded on the strength of a mutuality of interest and in the case of Thailand–Malaysia as well as Norway–Iceland, on the basis of a history of co-operation: ASEAN membership in the former case, and NATO membership and the 'Nordic solidarity' factor in the case of the latter. The question of confidence building most definitely arises in more problematic and complicated scenarios, such as in the South China Sea. That issue will be discussed later in the paper. At this point, we propose to examine some political and security issues which have arisen in connection with the existing arrangements.

JAN MAYEN

The Jan Mayen Agreement resulted from a dispute over fisheries in the vicinity of Jan Mayen Island. Norwegian vessels were reporting large catches in the area which led to the Norwegian government declaring a 200 nautical mile exclusive economic zone (EEZ) around the island. When Iceland countered with the claim that, under international law, Jan Mayen did not warrant an EEZ or continental shelf, and subsequently claimed that Jan Mayen was located on Iceland's continental shelf, the seeds of conflict were sown. While Norway's claim was a strong one, it nonetheless agreed to share hydrocarbons in an area primarily located on the Norwegian continental shelf (Ostreng, 1983: 14). Norway resorted to joint development because it was the best option to avoid further conflict with a close friend and neighbour.

There were also security considerations. Iceland is strategically situated in the middle of the Greenland–Iceland–UK gap (GIUK), through which the Soviet northern fleet would have to pass to gain access to the world's oceans. Iceland's Keflavik base was used by NATO to observe the movements of the USSR fleet and to monitor the entire Norwegian Sea and therefore was an essential link in NATO's defence capability (Ostreng, 1983: 16). Both Norway and NATO were anxious to avoid the eventuality of Iceland playing its 'Keflavik card', as it had been so ready to do in the so called 'Cod War' with the UK in the mid-1970s. The Keflavik card meant that Iceland would threaten to withdraw from NATO and cancel the Keflavik base arrangement with the USA. The danger of such a move would have potentially far reaching consequences for NATO defence strategy. Additionally, such a move on Iceland's part would pose domestic difficulties for Norway and jeopardise its delicately balanced policy of both reassurance and deterrence toward the USSR. If Jan Mayen were to be used as an alternative in the event of Keflavik closing, as was suggested in some quarters, Norway's attitude towards the USSR might have been interpreted as relying more on deterrence than reassurance, and thus appearing more aggressive (Ostreng, 1983: 18–9). However, the unsuitability of Jan Mayen as a NATO base, at least on the scale of Keflavik, meant that this option could not be seriously entertained, and thus increased the urgency of satisfying Iceland, and hence increased the pressure on Norway to settle.

The need for an agreement in the Jan Mayen area was sparked by two disputes, over fisheries and jurisdiction over the continental shelf, and hence hydrocarbon exploitation, fuelled by broader considerations of security, and domestic concerns. Perhaps most important to the successful establishment of the Jan Mayen joint development zone was the common identity, culture and history of the Norwegians and Icelanders, and the overriding political desire to preserve this atmosphere (Ostreng, 1983: 24). Little exploration has been done in the area: it is not considered as having major petroleum producing potential. It is worth noting however, that the 'Norwegian Petroleum Activity Fact Sheet' for 1994 identifies Jan Mayen as an area for future exploration (MIE, 1994: 43).

GULF OF THAILAND

The decision by Malaysia and Thailand to establish a joint development zone was a major step. However, the adoption of the 'agreement in principle' technique as represented by the memorandum of understanding, perhaps reveals something of the tentative nature of the support for the arrangement. Circumstances such as a change in government in both countries in the midst of negotiation may have served to impede the conclusion of an agreement due to the fact that the new Prime Ministers had different approaches and priorities to their predecessors who signed the MOU (Valencia, 1991: 40).

Private interests in Thailand may also have played a role in obstructing the conclusion of a complete agreement. Sentiments that Thailand deserved a larger area, or that the area should simply be divided, seem to have coloured the debate. As Mark Valencia points out, the latter view rests on the fact that the lion's share of the discovered gas deposits are on the Thai side of the equidistance line.

The view of Thai industrialists further complicated the settlement of a maritime boundary between the two countries (Valencia, 1991: 40). They felt that they could more readily benefit from this area as there is no large-scale industry in northern Malaysia to immediately draw on the natural gas.

There were further considerations; Vietnam, for instance, claimed part of the joint development area, and this may have contributed to Bangkok's hesitancy to move ahead. More importantly, government change and instability may have prompted an abrupt volte-face on the idea of joint development arrangements. Joint development arrangements, it must be remembered, are rare and risky ventures. There is an element of surrender in making such a deal; the other side of this coin is the triumph of neighbourly co-operation! Ideally, both are present; it depends which aspect is in the ascendant at any given time, and how this links to ancillary factors, such as fisheries or pollution co-operation. In the final analysis, the decreased gas production from the Erawan field may have been the determining factor forcing Thailand to press forward with joint development. In spite of these attendant difficulties and complicated negotiations, the conclusion of a successful agreement between Thailand and Malaysia was hailed as a sign of co-operation between two ASEAN stalwarts. Indeed, in an apparent allusion to the boundary disputes in the South China Sea, the agreement between Malaysia and Thailand has recently been hailed by Prime Minister Mahatir as a model for the settlement of 'similar overlapping claims where there are riches to be extracted' *(South China Morning Post,* 1994). As was pointed out earlier, the same claim has been made for a very different joint development arrangement in the Timor Gap between Australia and Indonesia.

TIMOR GAP

After initially refusing to recognise the annexation of East Timor following the departure of Portugal, the former colonial power, Australia announced in 1979 that it would accept Indonesia's sovereignty over the territory. Prior to Indonesia's annexation, Australia had tried and failed to negotiate an agreement with Portugal over what became known as the Timor Gap.[13] After lengthy negotiations, the Timor Gap Treaty was signed in 1989.[14] The Australian desire to conclude an agreement with Indonesia may have been partially due to the feeling that getting something was better than getting nothing (Onorato and Valencia, 1990: 21–2). This sentiment of political pragmatism coupled with economic objectivity was shared by the Indonesians. Joint development between the two countries was the best way to serve their mutual interests, and bring an end to wrangling over the Timor Gap boundary question. A cable sent by the former

Australian Ambassador to Indonesia, Dick Woolcott, supports this view:

> We are all well aware of the Australian defence interest in the Portuguese Timor situation, but I wonder whether the department has ascertained the interest of the Minister of the Department of Minerals and Energy in the Timor situation. It would seem to me that this department might well have an interest in closing the present Gap in the agreed sea border, and this could be much more readily negotiated with Indonesia than with Portugal or independent Portuguese Timor. I know I am recommending a pragmatic rather than a principled stand, but that is what national interest and foreign policy is all about.[15]

Australia's geographic location, and thus strategic concern for access to oil reserves, certainly played a role in the decision to come to terms on the Timor Gap. This geostrategic reality, coupled with the fact that production from the Bass Strait was declining, and the prospect of large hydrocarbon deposits in the disputed area, taken together, provided sufficient impetus for Australia to enter into the Agreement, thereby recognising the Indonesia annexation of East Timor (and paying whatever political price had to be paid for so doing), and abandoning its original jurisdictional claim in the Timor Gap.

FUNCTIONAL RESPONSES OR BILATERAL FENCE-MENDING?

In all three of the aforementioned cases, common ground existed which facilitated joint development. This was constituted by factors such as economic or security considerations, or appeals to close political and cultural ties such as ASEAN and 'Nordic solidarity'. The general atmosphere was thus conducive for the successful conclusion of an agreement. Most importantly, the primary prerequisite of joint development, political will, existed. None of these prerequisites are present or shared among the disputant countries in areas such as the South China Sea. It may be too soon for a functional instrument which confronts resource-sharing issues head-on. What is therefore required in that particular area is a foundation for developing a degree of trust and confidence which are themselves the prerequisites for the evolution of political will. The Indonesian–Canadian confidence-building initiative, described below, is attempting to lay that foundation.

The three cases examined above also show that continuing trust is a vital component to any joint development agreement, and, of course, its implementation. Parties to the agreement must have faith that their opposites will live up to the terms and spirit of any arrangement entered into, and that they are as one on the degree of commitment to the achievement of the goals of their project.

The high degree of political will required for the establishment and maintenance of any joint development agreement is intensified when attempting to move from the bilateral arrangements examined in this paper to the inevitable problems of consensus building in a multilateral scheme. While disputing countries may, in a general way, wish to resolve jurisdictional issues, the absence of the necessary degree of political will mitigates against progress. Countries with a history of good and long-term relations continue to find resource issues to be challenging and divisive. This appears to be the nature of the beast. As David Ong (1992: 221) has suggested:

the possibilities for joint development or any other arrangements of a co-operative nature will depend very much on certain factors, not the least among them recognition of the need for a clearly defined political will toward such an arrangement by the governments concerned.

To date, this atmosphere is notably absent in the South China Sea. In many cases, the area of the disputed Crestone concession off the coast of Vietnam being the most obvious, joint development is proposed merely to gain legitimacy for a particular claim. For example, China's offer to jointly develop the Crestone area appears at first glance to be a generous offer and an olive branch held out to the Vietnamese. Should the Vietnamese accept the offer it would only serve to legitimise China's right to grant concessions in an area regarded by Vietnam as part of its continental shelf. To some in Vietnam, accepting China's offer would reward an ambitious claim, pugnaciously asserted.[16] Should such a policy succeed, the implications for boundary making in other parts of the world would be considerable.

PROSPECTS FOR JOINT DEVELOPMENT IN THE SOUTH CHINA SEA

The jurisdictional dispute in the South China Sea appears to be truly intractable. It is not so much that there are conflicting claims to maritime jurisdiction, but also over islands. There is no shortage of rhetoric. Furthermore, the respective claims are based on radically different grounds. The claim advanced by China/Taiwan is based on historic usage. The Philippine position, in so far as it has been articulated officially, is based on treaty lines more than 100 years old, part of the legacy inherited by the modern independent government of that country. The Malaysian claim, based on equidistance, has been articulated only semi-officially, and that by Brunei not at all. The Vietnam claim tends to focus on sovereignty over the Paracel and Spratly archipelagos, using this as a basis for claims to maritime jurisdiction.

A number of non-judgmental comments can be made about the *status quo* in the South China Sea. First, there is a studied lack of precision in the positions advanced by some of the claimant states. The claim advanced by China, for instance, is broad, but ill-defined. There are no co-ordinates, and the maps published to accompany the claim – or at least those which the authors have been able to obtain after requests to Chinese officials – are somewhat imprecise, to say the least. It is doubtful whether the Philippines has officially articulated its claim; at a workshop convened in Manila, in February 1994, by the Bureau of Agriculture and Fisheries of the Philippines, supported by the Oceans Institute of Canada and funded by the Canadian International Development Agency, numerous speakers took the opportunity to berate government officials for failing to articulate the Philippine position on the Palayan–Spratly group, and so on.

There is no shortage of ideas of potential avenues for resolution of this dispute, and joint development is only one of the solutions advocated. But the question must be asked: the joint development of what, exactly, and why? One of the characteristics of virtually all the claims to jurisdiction of the South China Sea is extravagance. Each claimant state seems compelled to cast its net as widely as possible. Furthermore, constant flows of rhetoric from national governments have tended to reinforce already entrenched positions, and it is for this reason that many commentators have concluded that the jurisdictional dispute is not subject to resolution in the immediate future. Third-party settlement is inimical to the traditions of these countries, and will in any event produce 'winners' and 'losers'.

The project 'Managing Potential Conflicts in the South China Sea' was initiated to attempt to provide a neutral forum for discussing possible avenues for co-operation.[17] The premise of the project is that the jurisdictional dispute is not susceptible to solution in the near future, but also that the South China Sea area is being used, and abused, in a way which is at odds with the interest of the coastal states. There is little or no surveillance over polluters, overfishing, or other illegal uses of the oceans. The very considerable effort expended by the littorals on pressing their claims and defending the islands they occupy takes up much of their time and attention, to the detriment of proper management of the sea and its resources. Accordingly, the project, taking Article 123 of the Law of the Sea Convention as its starting point, suggests an alternative approach, based on the need to undertake joint action in the interests of management of the South China Sea ecosystem. The work of the Project, which includes research, workshops and technical working group meetings on issues such as marine scientific research, environmental protection, resource assessment, navigational safety, defence and security issues, and institutional mechanisms for co-operation, is therefore focused on regional co-operation. This is two-track diplomacy in action, or resource and environmental diplomacy in the interests of co-operative security.

Joint development is obviously one of the many suggestions which the states of the South China Sea must deal with. And, because the dispute tends to focus on the island sovereignty question, creating a joint development zone around the Spratly archipelago has been suggested. But is this suggestion feasible, or even desirable?

The first question concerns the size of the 'Spratly area'. One logical answer suggests that this zone is bounded by lines drawn an appropriate distance from the outermost islands of the group. But what exactly are the 'islands' of the group? Many maps suggest that the Spratlys are a large group of sizeable islands, but such is not the case. The majority of named features in the Spratly group are not islands in any sense of the term, legal or dictionary. Adopting the test of Article 121(1) of the Law of the Sea Convention thins the ground quite considerably. Then there is the question of the application of Article 121(3). It is open to doubt that any of the Spratly islands would pass this test; at most one or two might, if a liberal view was taken.

Is this the appropriate foundation for a joint development zone? A conservative view suggests that a half-dozen or so features would generate a 12 nautical mile territorial sea and none would generate an EEZ or continental shelf. Would not the best solution be to enclave these features, and deny them any role in the delimitation of the South China Sea between its opposite and adjacent states?

If this approach is taken, then another issue must be faced: the existence of a zone beyond national jurisdiction (at least for the purposes of the EEZ) in the South China Sea. Some recent research suggests that 200 nautical mile limits drawn from either archipelagic baselines, or other baselines established in keeping with the Law of the Sea Convention, do not always require opposite, but only adjacent boundaries. If this is indeed the case, then some form of co-operative authority for this area might be appropriate. But it is by no means clear that the littoral states cannot sustain claims to continental shelf which would require the conclusion of opposite continental shelf boundaries. One solution might be for these states to pool their rights over the area beyond 200 nautical miles, and establish a management commission in keeping with Article 123 of the Convention.

It goes without saying that all littoral states world-wide have an interest in what happens in the South China Sea, especially as regards developments in ocean law and policy. It is also clear that the jurisdictional dispute over the Spratly Island group and, to a much lesser extent, the Paracel Island group, is complicating the issue to an inordinate degree. Matters are not helped by a constant stream of wholly uninformed press comment referring to the 'oil-rich Spratlys'.[18] To dispose of this issue, it need only be said that while the geology of part of the Spratly area is promising, so far as is known, there is no evidence of the presence of a commercial accumulation of hydrocarbons. It should also be said that the current low price of oil world-wide, coupled with the inherent uncertainties of investment in this area, tend to mitigate against significant investment by oil companies and financial institutions in petroleum production in the South China Sea.

Conclusions

It seems difficult and dangerous to argue that joint development arrangements are applicable to a given situation because nothing else appears to have any chance of being accepted by the parties concerned. The question is, would a joint development arrangement work *ab initio,* given all relevant circumstances between the states concerned? Joint development is too complex a subject to be viewed as a last gasp solution, nor is it the tidy conclusion to a deadlocked situation. The arrangement has a life of its own. What, therefore, are the positive reasons in favour of joint development for its own sake? The point is, joint development is applicable when two countries wish to undertake co-operative offshore petroleum development. Precisely *why* might they wish to do this? We suggest the following tentative list:

1 Where both countries wish to develop the petroleum resources of a given area, and this wish outweighs other considerations, such as 'winning' a boundary dispute, and other bothersome items on the bilateral agenda, then join development is a functional and useful solution to their problem.
2 Where two countries either enjoy close relations, or wish to establish them, co-operation in the production of petroleum offers almost unparalleled opportunities for the display of trust, amity and friendship, provided the conditions laid down in the first point are satisfied.
3 Where one of them lacks capacity with petroleum management, both may gain, in that the more advanced state can sell or offer its expertise (as with Iceland and Norway with the Jan Mayen arrangement). Again, the conditions laid down in the first point must be satisfied.
4 Where both lack management capacity, then a joint development arrangement enables them to pool what will probably be scarce human and technical resources, assuming petroleum development is the paramount aim of any co-operative venture.

As to conditions which are prerequisite for a joint development arrangement, we suggest the following:

1 The states concerned must accept that they are pooling their sovereign rights over the area concerned. If either or both enter into

an agreement with the view that, in the last resort, they are sharing 'their' resources with their neighbour on a voluntary basis (which, by implication, may be revoked at any time), the agreement may be in trouble from the very beginning.

2 The states concerned must be *ad idem* on all major policy matters *ab initio*, or be very close to complete agreement on area, term, management, applicable law/regime and issues of similar import.

3 The states concerned must never loose sight of the paramount objective of the arrangement: exploring for and producing oil and gas.

THE QUESTION OF A 'MODEL' FOR JOINT DEVELOPMENT

Finally, we turn to the issue as to whether any of the existing arrangements is, or can be, a model for joint development. Arguably, there is insufficient state practice on these arrangements for any definitive statement to be made one way or the other. Not only are there very few agreements, but all have yet to be tested fully. Such a test would arise if there were a serious difference of opinion on a major matter, and especially once a commercial find has been announced.

The research project on joint development undertaken by the British Institute of International and Comparative Law culminated, *inter alia*, in a model agreement for joint development (Fox, 1989). The document deserves much attention and discussion, but in light of the paucity of state practice, cannot be measured or assessed except on somewhat abstract grounds. In all events, it presents a highly sophisticated 'check list' of issues which must be addressed, in one way or another, by parties to a joint development agreement.

The Timor Gap Agreement is perhaps the most highly sophisticated instrument devised by two experienced petroleum producing states with the express purpose of providing a stable regime for investment in an offshore area. Indeed, the elaboration of the regime provides a wealth of detail which might be regarded as the norm from the viewpoint of the petroleum industry, and nothing exceptional. The exception arises over the placement of this detail in treaty form.

But is the wealth of detail desirable? Since 1965 or so petroleum lawyers can attest to the shifting sands of legal certainty in the terms attached to petroleum production licences, whether promulgated in contractual or legislative form. The events of 1973 prompted drastic changes in licences, and the ebb and flow of price and availability have contributed to continuing uncertainty to the point where flexibility is the norm, and fixed long-term contracts exceptional. Circumstances change: the law changes with it. This is only meeting the requirements of the functional nature of natural resource law-making.

Was it therefore advisable to place so much detail in the Treaty and its Annexes? Any changes thereto will require the consent of both states, and treaties are rarely revised on an *ad hoc* basis, if at all. This is neither the time nor place to pass judgement on the appropriateness of the Timor Gap regime, or its potential longevity. But it is apposite to state that this degree of detail is exceptional, and that other states should be absolutely certain of what they are doing, and fully aware of the consequences of their actions, before they attempt something of the sort.

At this point in the global experience with offshore petroleum joint development, we see at least two bilateral arrangements which may provide models for other countries. Successful natural resource regulatory regimes are highly functional and responsive in nature. The primary responsiveness should be to the need for optimum utilisation of the resource. Malaysia and Thailand on the one hand, and Australia and Indonesia on the other, are confident that they have launched their respective ventures on the best possible footing, and that they are bound to succeed. Those countries considering whether or not to follow their example have two excellent prototypes to observe; the first real tests of the efficacy of international offshore joint development are now under way.

Acknowledgements

The authors would like to acknowledge the research assistance of Kelly Lowe, Class of 1994, University of British Colombia Faculty of Law, and Lynda Cheng, Faculty of Law, University of Melbourne.

Notes

1   Thus defined, joint development is wholly distinguishable from unitisation, the technique used to develop *inter alia* the Frigg gas field in the North Sea, or where countries agree to divide net revenues from a field being administered by one of them, as with the Bahrain–Saudi Arabia arrangement of 1958.
2   To date, six offshore joint development arrangements have been concluded: France–Spain 1974; Japan–Korea, 1974; Iceland–Norway, 1981; Thailand–Malaysia, 1979; Sudan–Saudi Arabia, 1974; Australia–Indonesia, 1990.
3   A sample of the recent or significant literature would include: *Australian Year Book of International Law* (1988-9); Townsend-Gault (1988); Valencia (1985); Valencia (1986); Wilde (1990); and the important two-volume study undertaken by the British Institute of International and Comparative Law under the direction

of Lady Fox, the second volume of which includes papers and commentaries by numerous authorities on the subject (Fox, 1989).

4 The most persuasive articulation of this argument is advanced by Mark Valencia in his article 'All For Everyone'. With respect, we would argue that the title offers more than the solution can deliver.

5 This view is abetted, probably unwittingly, by those who insist that international legal rules on maritime boundary delimitation are clear and precise, and their application predictable.

6 The second volume of the study conducted by the British Institute of International and Comparative Law (Fox, 1989) offers the most recent and convenient survey of the agreements, as well as further discussion, and is especially recommended.

7 Convention on the Continental Shelf, Article 2(2); UNCLOS, Article 77(2); see also ICJ (1969: 69).

8 The advantage of this approach is that each sector trades limitations on its freedom of action in return for certainty of being able to act within the mutually agreed limits. The alternative is a series of *ad hoc* policy advances and reversals. The manifest disadvantage of this approach is well illustrated by the unhappy saga describing the experiences of Texaco Canada Ltd when it attempted to exercise its rights with respect to exploratory drilling in the Gulf of Maine following the maritime boundary decision.

9 Literally, 'agreements are sacred'. This maxim expressed the international legal assumption that a treaty, as the highest form of international obligation, cannot be unilaterally abrogated, and its provisions will be carried out by all parties.

10 As of May 1994, Portugal (the colonial power, and, according to the United Nations, the true sovereign over East Timor), is pursuing litigation against Australia before the International Court of Justice, and two sets of litigation are in progress before the courts of Australia.

11 Some commentators have noted that the Chinese armed forces are notably more bellicose *vis-à-vis* the South China Sea than, for instance, the Ministry of Foreign Affairs in Beijing.

12 In more ways than one: such a lack of commitment will be communicated to the oil industry in various ways; company enthusiasm will falter, as will that of the financial backers of the operation, and the project will grind to a halt, with further corporate commitment somewhat unlikely.

13 The Timor Gap is so-called because prior to the joint development agreement, Australia had concluded continental shelf boundary agreements with Indonesia in respect of marine areas between the former and the provinces of Timor Barat (West Timor), and Irian Jaya (and the island lying west of New Guinea). There was

therefore a 'gap' in the continental shelf boundary between Australia and the Indonesian archipelago.

14   See note 2 above.

15   Cable from the Australian Ambassador to Indonesia to the Department of Foreign Affairs, (17 August 1975) reprinted in 'Documents on Australia Defense and Foreign Policy 1968-1975' (1981) 197, as cited by Wilde and Stepan (1990).

16   Leszek Buszynski puts the issue this way: 'China's idea of settlement is one that endorses China's claims; the Chinese conception of 'joint development' is foreign participation in the exploitation of China's resources' (Buszynski, 1992: 94).

17   The project was initiated in 1989 by Ambassador Hasjim Djalal and Professor Ian Townsend-Gault, and has been supported by a series of grants from the Canadian International Development Agency. Copies of the reports of the various workshops and technical meetings are available from the authors. For more information on the project, see Townsend-Gault (1994: 16); and Stormont (forthcoming).

18   The most recent of these references known to these authors is *Manchester Guardian Weekly* (1994).

Bibliography

Australian Year Book of International Law (1988–9) 'Incorporation of territory – East Timor and Indonesia – Timor Gap seabed boundary negotiations – views of Portugal', *Australian Year Book of International Law* 13, 288.

Business Times (1989) 'Long awaited Thailand–Malaysia gas, oil pact', *Business Times* 8, August.

Buszynski, L. (1992) 'ASEAN security dilemmas', *Survival* 34: 94.

Cable from the Australian Ambassador to Indonesia to the Department of Foreign Affairs, (17 August 1975) reprinted in 'Documents on Australia Defence and Foreign Policy 1968–1975' (1981) 197, as cited by Stepan

Fox, H. (1989) *Joint Development of Offshore Oil and Gas*, Vols.1 and 2, London: British Institute of International and Comparative Law.

Johnston and Saunders, (eds) (1988) *Maritime Boundary Making: Regional Issues and Developments,* New York: Croom Helm.

Manchester Guardian Weekly (1994) Le Monde section, 10 February.

MIE (1994) 'The Norwegian petroleum activity fact sheet, 1994', Oslo: The Royal Ministry of Industry and Energy.

Ong, D. (1992) 'Alternative joint development regimes: a comparison between the Malaysia/Thailand Joint Development Agreement and

the Australia/Indonesia Timor Gap Zone of Co-operation Treaty',
Oil and Gas Law and Taxation Review 10, 8, London: Sweet and
Maxwell.

Onorato, W.T. and Valencia, M.J. (1990) 'International co-operation
for petroleum development: the Timor Gap Treaty', *ICSID Review:
Foreign Investment Law Journal* 5: 1.

Ostreng, W. (1983) 'The Norway–Iceland arrangement for Jan
Mayen', paper given at the second workshop on the Geology and
Hydrocarbon Potential of the South China Sea and Possibilities of
Joint Development 22–6 August, Honolulu, Hawaii.

South China Morning Post (1994) 'Malaysia, Thailand in historic oil
and gas deal', *South China Morning Post* (Weekend Edition), 30
April.

Stormont, W.G. (forthcoming) *1994 Marine Policy.*

Townsend-Gault, I. (1988) 'Joint development of offshore mineral
resources – progress and prospects for the future', *Natural
Resources Forum* 12: 275.

Townsend-Gault, I. (1994) 'Testing the waters – making progress in
the South China Sea', *Harvard International Review* Spring: 16.

Valencia, M.J. (ed.) (1990) *Geology and Hydrocarbon Potential of the
South China Sea and Possibilities of Joint Development*, London:
Permagon Press.

Valencia, M.J. (1986) 'Taming troubled waters: joint development of
oil and mineral resources in overlapping claim areas', *San Diego
Law Review* 23: 661.

Valencia, M.J. (1992) *Malaysia and the Law of the Sea,* Malaysia:
Institute of Strategic and International Studies (ISIS).

Wilde, D. and Stepan, S. (1990) 'Treaty between Australia and the
Republic of Indonesia on the Zone of Co-operation in an area
between the Indonesian province of East Timor and Northern
Australia', *Melanesian Law Journal* 18: 18.

LEGAL REFERENCES

[Australia–Indonesia, 1990] Treaty on the Zone of Co-operation in the
Area Between the Indonesian Province of East Timor and Northern
Australia, *ILM* 29: 469.

[France–Spain, 1974] Convention between the Government of the
French Republic and of the Spanish State on the delimitation of the
continental shelves of the two states in the Bay of Biscay 29 January,
Limits in the Sea 83.

[Iceland–Norway, 1981] Agreement on the Continental Shelf between
Iceland and Jan Mayen, Oslo, 22 October in *ILM* 21: 1227.

[ICJ 1969] 'North Sea Continental Shelf Cases (Denmark v. Germany,
Netherlands v. Germany)', *ICJ Reports* 3: 69.

[ICJ 1984] Gulf of Maine case (Canada v. United States of America) *ICJ Reports* 246.

[Japan–Korea, 1974] Agreement between Japan and the Republic of Korea Concerning the Joint Development of the Southern Part of the Continental Shelf Adjacent to the Two Countries, Seoul, 5 February, reprinted in *New Directions on the Law of the Sea* IV: 117.

[Sudan–Saudi Arabia, 1974] Agreement between Sudan and Saudi Arabia relating to the Joint Exploitation of the Natural Resources of the Sea-bed and Sub-soil of the Red Sea in the Common Zone, reprinted in *New Directions on the Law of the Sea* V: 393.

[Thailand–Malaysia, 1979] Memorandum of Understanding between The Kingdom of Thailand and Malaysia on the Establishment of a Joint Authority for the Exploitation of the Resources of the Sea-Bed in a Defined Area of the Continental Shelf of the Two Countries in the Gulf of Thailand, Chiang Mai, 21 February.

[UNCLOS] United Nations Convention on the Law of the Sea.

5

South-east Asian State Practice on the Joint Development of Offshore Oil and Gas Deposits

David Ong

Introduction

This paper will discuss some of the latest developments in South-east Asian state practice on the joint development of offshore oil and gas deposits. The discussion will focus on three bilateral arrangements involving Malaysia and Thailand, Indonesia and Australia, and Malaysia again, this time with Vietnam, over offshore oil and gas deposits which are present within areas of overlapping continental shelf claims made by these countries in the South-east Asian marine region.

The question being put forward in relation to these agreements for the joint exploitation of shared hydrocarbon deposits is whether the example of co-operation which they embody provides some support for the contention that a duty to co-operate in a similar manner may now be imputed in respect of similar situations arising in the South-east Asian – South China Sea region? A wider issue arising from the subject of this paper is how far these agreements may be held to contribute to the development of rules of international law in respect of shared natural resources between states?

Background

In the case of Malaysia–Thailand, the specific area of dispute arose from overlapping continental shelf claims in the south-western part of the Gulf of Thailand, off the east coast of peninsular Malaysia, and adjacent to the end-point of the common land border between these two countries (Figure 5.1). In 1972, Thai and Malaysian negotiators were able to agree on a lateral continental shelf boundary in the south-western part of the Gulf of Thailand up to approximately 29 nautical miles offshore (Thailand–Malaysia, October 1979). But the negotiations subsequently broke down because of disagreement over the use of Ko Losin, a rock 1.5m (5 feet) above high tide, 39 nautical miles offshore, by Thailand as a base-point to extend the boundary line southwards at the expense of Malaysia. From the nearer point (29

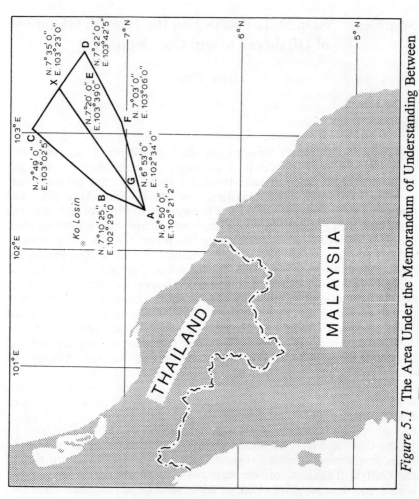

Figure 5.1 The Area Under the Memorandum of Understanding Between Thailand and Malaysia

Source: The International Journal of Estuarine and Coastal Law

nautical miles) offshore, their respective boundary claims diverge north and south. Further maritime boundary negotiations brought no results, due to both parties' apprehension concerning the natural gas potential in the area of overlap. Indeed, the later discovery of major deposits of natural gas in this area contributed much to the lack of continuity in the negotiations and lack of success in the settlement of the final maritime boundary between the two countries, even after the signing of the Memorandum of Understanding (MOU), which purported to commit both countries to joint exploitation of the non-living natural resources in the area (Malaysia–Thailand, February 1979). The 1979 Memorandum of Understanding was, however, hailed at the time as being yet another example of the close co-operation between the two countries, engendered by the prevailing feelings of goodwill and neighbourliness which exists between them. Both countries are of course also members of the Association of South East Asian Nations (ASEAN).

The MOU however merely set down the broad principles for joint development of the 'Defined Area'. Negotiations continued on the exact institutional arrangements to put into effect these principles but were stymied by several factors, the foremost among these being the problem of previously granted concessions. This problem was only resolved in the late 1980s, resulting in the signing of the 30 May 1990 Agreement establishing the Constitution of the Malaysia–Thailand Joint Development Authority (Malaysia–Thailand, 1990).

The Australia–Indonesia Timor Gap Zone of Co-operation Treaty was agreed in 1989 to fill in the gap between the maritime boundaries of the respective countries which were delimited by agreements in 1971 and 1972 (Australia–Indonesia, 1971 and Indonesia–Australia, 1972). The existence of this gap was due to the fact that at the time of the earlier maritime delimitation agreements between Australia and Indonesia the land territory to which this gap appertained, ie, East Timor, was controlled by Portugal. In 1975 however, Indonesia invaded East Timor and formally annexed it on 17 July 1976. This legally dubious action had a stalling effect on the negotiations for the resolution of the Timor Gap because of Australia's initial reluctance to recognise Indonesia's incorporation of East Timor. But declining production from Australia's major oilfields in the Bass Strait, coupled with the promisingly large potential for exploitable hydrocarbons in the Kelp structure in the north of the Timor Gap area, resulted in Australia granting *de jure* recognition of Indonesian sovereignty over East Timor in 1979.[1] Negotiations resumed, culminating in a Joint Statement by the two Foreign Ministers released on 25 October 1988 which, *inter alia* established a Zone of Co-operation in the Timor Gap in respect of petroleum exploration and exploitation (see Figure 5.2). This Joint Statement was followed up, slightly more than a year later, by the definitive Treaty signed on 11 December 1989 (Timor Gap Treaty 1989).[2]

The Malaysia–Vietnam case also concerns a disputed area of the continental shelf in the Gulf of Thailand which is subject to overlapping claims by both countries. This area is located off the north-east coast of peninsular Malaysia and the south-west of Vietnam. Although no exact co-ordinates for this overlapping claim area have been provided to date, an examination of the respective countries' overlapping continental shelf claims in this area would seem to point to a long sliver of sea-bed just south-south-east of the designated Malaysia–Thailand Joint Development Area (as determined by Article 1 of the 1979 Memorandum of Understanding). On 5 May 1992 a Memorandum of Understanding between Malaysia and Vietnam was signed in Kuala Lumpur, ostensibly in order to provide a framework under which the nominees of the respective governments (Petronas for Malaysia and Petrovietnam for Vietnam) can enter into a commercial agreement for the purpose of exploring and exploiting the petroleum resources (Ong, 1993). The MOU entered into force by way of the signing and exchanging of Diplomatic Notes to this effect in Kuala Lumpur on 4 June 1993.[3]

The International Legal Regime for Co-operation over Shared Natural Resources

This section will discuss the points of departure for a legal analysis of a possible obligation to co-operate over shared natural resources between two or more countries.

UN GENERAL ASSEMBLY RESOLUTIONS

Without needing to comment extensively on the issue of UN General Assembly (UNGA) Resolutions as a source of binding international obligation, it is important however to note that some General Assembly Resolutions are arguably more obligatory than others in their legal character. In particular, UNGA Resolutions that are passed by an overwhelming majority of UN member states, and are not objected to by a significant group of states, may be held to indicate the willingness of the international community of states to be guided by the principles embodied by that Resolution, even if they cannot be held to be legally bound by them. Viewed in this way, General Assembly Resolutions can be said to be a statement of intention by the states concerned regarding their course of conduct on the subject of the Resolution.

On the subject of co-operation over shared natural resources, as seen from the perspective outlined above, it is imperative to point out that Article 3 of the 1974 UN Charter of Economic Rights and Duties of States provides that:

in the exploitation of natural resources shared by two or more countries, *each state must co-operate on the basis of a system of information and prior consultations in order to achieve optimum use of such resources without causing damage to the legitimate interests of others* [emphasis added] (UNGA 3281).

Although this UNGA Resolution did not find agreement with a majority of the industrialised Western countries, which either abstained or voted against it[4]; it is clear from the debate which ensued that the main difficulty concerned the provision for the expropriation of foreign or multinational company assets under the guise of nationalisation[5] rather than the above Article exhorting co-operation in the exploitation of shared natural resources.

From an environmental perspective, the need to 'co-operate in the conservation and harmonious utilisation of natural resources shared by two or more states' has also been recognised by the UN Environment Programme's Governing Council (Nordquist and Simmonds, 1980: 82–5), and approved by a UN General Assembly Resolution (UNGA 213). Principle One of the Principles of Conduct in the Field of the Environment for the Guidance of States in the Conservation and Harmonious Utilisation of Natural Resources Shared by Two or More States, which the UNEP's Governing Council adopted by consensus on 19 May 1978, assumes that states sharing natural resources will have to 'co-operate in the equitable utilisation of shared natural resources', as well as in the protection of the environment from the adverse effects of such utilisation.

The 1982 UN Convention on the Law of the Sea (UNCLOS 1982)[6] also provides for practical provisional arrangements to be entered into by states finding themselves in dispute over ownership to common sea-bed areas. Such arrangements should be entered into with a spirit of understanding and co-operation. Articles 74(3) and 83(3) of the 1982 Convention further provide that the states shall make every effort not to jeopardise or hamper the reaching of a final agreement over the disputed area.

INTERNATIONAL CASE LAW

In the North Sea Continental Shelf Cases (1969), the International Court of Justice (ICJ) held that joint exploitation agreements were 'particularly appropriate when it is a question of preserving the unity of a deposit' (ICJ 1969: 52, paragraph 99). In a Separate Opinion, Judge Jessup held that the principle of joint exploitation may have a wider application in agreements reached by the parties concerning the still undelimited but potentially overlapping areas of the continental shelf which have been in dispute (ICJ 1969: 52, paragraph 82).

The Conciliation Commission set up in 1980 to deal with the fisheries and continental shelf dispute between Iceland and Norway around the island of Jan Mayen recommended a single dividing line for both the continental shelf and the Exclusive Economic Zone. But it also stated that the petroleum resources in an overlapping area claimed by both states should be jointly developed (Conciliation Commission 1981)[7]. This principle was later set down in the 1981 Iceland–Norway Treaty on the Continental Shelf between Iceland and Jan Mayen (Iceland–Jan Mayen, 1981).[8]

In the aftermath of the 1982 Tunisia–Libya Continental Shelf Case (ICJ 1982: 18), the dispute between these two countries appears to have been settled amicably in the Gulf of Gabes area at least, in favour of a joint exploitation agreement in August, 1988 (Fox *et al*, 1989: 64). A joint exploration zone, which is divided into two parts by a line running close to that indicated by the ICJ decision in the above case, has been established (Fox *et al*, 1989: 64). In this case it is interesting to note that the Dissenting Opinion of Judge Evensen in 1982 envisaged a similar system of joint exploitation of petroleum resources to the scheme established in 1988 (ICJ 1982: 321).

Furthermore, in the 1984 Gulf of Maine (ICJ 1984: 246) decision by the Chamber of the International Court of Justice, it was pointed out that the delimitation of a maritime boundary is not necessarily a panacea for disputes over offshore resources because even successful delimitation may still require a degree of close co-operation if opposite or adjacent States are rationally to exploit transboundary resources (ICJ 1984: 246).[9]

It may be concluded from these recent international law cases that co-operation towards some form of joint exploitation is increasingly being contemplated as a legally viable alternative to the usual methods of maritime boundary delimitation. These judicial opinions also provide some authority for the proposition that the scope of the general rule in international law requiring co-operation extends to include international common deposits situated in areas of overlapping claims, and does not only pertain to deposits which have been found to straddle previously agreed international boundaries.

South-east Asian Regional and Bilateral Agreements for Co-operation in the Exploitation of Shared Natural Resources

In the context of the wider South-east Asian region, recent developments have served to break the political impasse that had hitherto existed between the avowedly non-communist ASEAN and the predominantly communist Indo-Chinese countries, particularly Vietnam, since the fall of Saigon in 1975. The process of *rapprochement* has culminated with the accession by the Socialist Republics of Vietnam and Laos to the 1976 ASEAN Treaty of Amity and Co-operation in Manila, the Philippines on 22 July, 1992.[10] Significantly for the purposes of this paper, Chapter III (comprising Articles 4–12) of the Treaty prescribes co-operation in all fields of activity which are of common interest to the High Contracting Parties, and Chapter IV (Articles 13–7) commits the High Contracting Parties to the peaceful settlement of disputes between them through friendly negotiations and refraining from the threat or use of force.

Within the context of the ASEAN sub-region itself, which to date comprises six nations – Brunei, Indonesia, Malaysia, the Philippines, Thailand and Singapore, Article 19 of the 1985 ASEAN Agreement on the Conservation of Nature and Natural Resources provides that:

> Contracting Parties that share natural resources shall co-operate concerning their conservation and harmonious utilisation, taking into account the sovereignty, rights and interests of the Contracting Parties concerned in accordance with generally accepted principles of international law (ASEAN 1985).

At the bilateral level, it is important to point out at least one salient legal factor that may have been instrumental to the willingness of the parties in both the Malaysia–Thailand and Australia–Indonesia disputes to contemplate co-operating in the joint exploration and exploitation of the hydrocarbon resources in their respective overlapping claim areas. This legal factor relates to the inclusion of the so-called 'straddle deposit' clauses in many of the bilateral maritime boundary delimitation agreements concerned, both between themselves and with other neighbouring countries in the region. This trend towards acceptance of the need for co-operation in shared natural resources in the form of oil and gas deposits is much in evidence in maritime delimitation agreements concluded between South-east Asian nations and their neighbours (Kittichaisaree, 1987: 69–70).

For example, Article 4 of the 1969 Agreement between Indonesia and Malaysia relating to the delimitation of the continental shelf between the two countries in the Straits of Malacca and the South China Sea provides for the two Governments to seek an agreement as to the manner in which any single geological petroleum or natural gas structure which extends across the straight boundary lines drawn up so that part of such a structure which is situated on one part of the said lines is exploitable, wholly or in part, from the other side, shall be most effectively exploited (Indonesia–Malaysia, 1969). Article 3 of the 1971 tripartite agreement between Indonesia, Malaysia and Thailand, establishing a common tripoint for their respective maritime boundaries (Indonesia–Malaysia–Thailand, 1971), Article 2 of a related agreement between Thailand and Indonesia partially delimiting a continental shelf boundary between the two countries in the northern part of the Straits of Malacca (Indonesia–Thailand, 1971), and Article 2 of yet another agreement between Thailand and Indonesia relating to the delimitation of the sea-bed boundary between the two countries in the Andaman Sea (Indonesia–Thailand, 1975), all make exactly the same provision regarding any petroleum structure which extends across the boundary line, ie, that the governments concerned 'shall seek to reach agreement as to the manner in which that structure shall be most effectively exploited'. A further, and to this writer's mind more stringent, requirement of co-operation between states in order to effectively exploit such straddle deposits is manifested in the maritime delimitation agreements involving Australia. For example, in both the initial 1971 Agreement and the 1972 Supplementary Agreement between Australia and Indonesia establishing sea-bed boundaries on either side of the Timor Gap in the Timor and Arafura Seas, Article 7 provides that:

> ... the two Governments will seek to reach agreement on the manner in which the accumulation or straddle deposit shall be most effectively exploited and on the equitable sharing of the benefits arising from such exploitation (Australia–Indonesia, 1971 and Indonesia–Australia, 1972).

The contemporary significance of these 'straddle deposit' clauses cannot be too highly emphasised. The impact of these provisions on bilateral state practice in the region may be discerned from the fact that in at least two situations where such straddle deposits were either known to exist, or suspected of existing, the states concerned have each time sought to reach an agreement in just such a manner as that envisaged by these provisions. Significantly, in relation to the Malaysia–Thailand dispute, this requirement of equitable sharing of both the expenses incurred and the benefits derived from the exploitation of such a straddle deposit is also set down in Article 4 of the 1979 Memorandum of Understanding between the two countries which delimited the small section of continental shelf boundary in the Gulf of Thailand that was agreed upon before the negotiations broke down over Thailand's use of Ko Losin as a base-point. This provision is also present in Article 3(6) of the 1979 Memorandum of Understanding establishing the Joint Authority, thus further testifying to its usefulness in promoting and facilitating the co-operation of the states involved.

Indeed, it may be argued that a legal principle enjoining states to co-operate now exists between states in respect of offshore oil and gas deposits that are either found to straddle already delimited boundary lines, or are situated in overlapping claim areas of the continental shelf between two or more countries. This may be discerned from the now almost universal inclusion of such 'straddle deposit' provisions in maritime delimitation agreements which usually call for negotiations leading to a further agreement as to the manner in which such deposits may be most effectively exploited. It is the extent of this duty to co-operate which is now at issue rather than whether or not there is a duty.

Bilateral Agreements for the Joint Development of Offshore Oil and Gas Deposits in South-east Asia

Three case studies of bilateral agreements form the basis of the following discussions:
1979–90 Malaysia–Thailand Joint Development Agreement
1989 Australia–Indonesia Timor Gap Zone of Co-Operation Treaty
1992 Malaysia–Vietnam Memorandum of Understanding

INSTITUTIONAL AND ADMINISTRATIVE ARRANGEMENTS

The Malaysia–Thailand and Australia–Indonesia joint development agreements have established Joint Authorities with almost identical functions, that is to assume responsibility for the exploration and exploitation activities in their corresponding joint development zones. For the 1979–90 Malaysia–Thailand Joint Development Agreement, this includes the whole area of overlapping claims which is now designated as the Joint Development Area, under Article 1 of the 1979 Memorandum of Understanding. Under Articles 3 and 8 of the Australia–Indonesia Timor Gap Treaty however, the Joint Authority's ambit extends only to Area A of the designated Zone of Co-operation. Under Article 4, the other two Areas – B and C, come under the jurisdiction of the State Party nearest in distance to them. Area B thus comes under Australian jurisdiction and Area C under the jurisdiction of the Republic of Indonesia.

The Malaysia–Thailand Joint Authority differs slightly in that initially at least it assumed rights and responsibilities over all the 'non-living natural resources' of the sea-bed and subsoil of the Joint Development Area, under Article 3(2) of the 1979 Memorandum of Understanding. This phrase was amended by Article 2(1) of the later 1990 Agreement to the effect that 'the purpose of the Joint Authority shall be the exploration and the exploitation of the non-living resources, *in particular petroleum,* in the Joint Development Area' (emphasis added).

By contrast, the Australia–Indonesia Joint Authority is only responsible for the development of the *petroleum resources* in Area A under Article 8 of the Timor Gap Treaty. This limitation of the Timor Gap Zone of Co-operation Treaty to the regulation of activities pertaining only to petroleum resources has certain implications for the obligations of each Party to the Treaty should other non-hydrocarbon minerals be found within the Zone. It is arguable that the exploitation of such minerals will be outside the jurisdictional and operational ambit

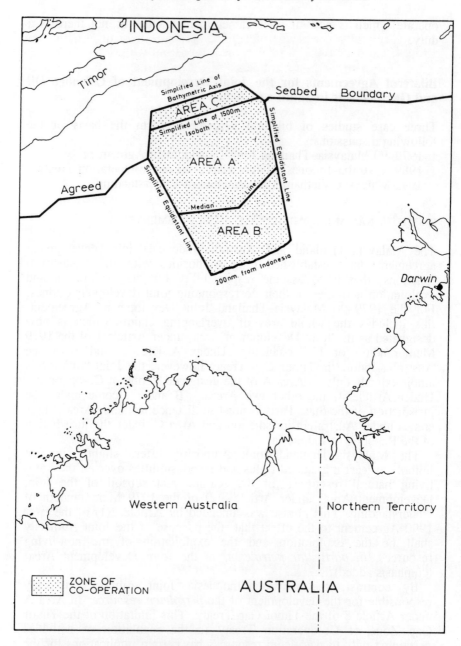

Figure 5.2 Australia–Indonesia Timor Gap Zone of Co-operation
Source: International Journal of Coastal Law

of this Treaty. Therefore, should a similar kind of dispute occur with regard to a non-petroleum type mineral deposit situated within the Zone of Co-operation, particularly if it is located within Area A of this Zone, the respective governments might find themselves having to negotiate another co-operative agreement in order to exploit this non-petroleum deposit jointly.

Furthermore, the Malaysia–Thailand Joint Authority ostensibly, at least, retains control over all aspects of policy and decision-making for the exploration and exploitation of the non-living natural resources in the Joint Development Area, whereas the Australia–Indonesia Timor Gap Treaty created an hierarchical, two-level arrangement composed of a Ministerial Council and a Joint Authority. The Ministerial Council has been given the overall responsibility for petroleum-related activities in Area A of the Zone of Co-operation, under Article 6. It is therefore the principal policy-making body. The Joint Authority is subordinate to the Ministerial Council, and is responsible to the Council for the day to day management of the petroleum activities in Area A, under Articles 7(3) and 8.

Nevertheless, the Joint Authority has been given juridical personality and more particularly, a contractual capacity for the performance of its functions (Timor Gap Treaty 1989: Article 7(2)). The most important contractual function which the Joint Authority is likely to perform relates to entering into production-sharing contracts (PSCs) with corporations for the extraction of petroleum. In this, however, the Joint Authority is subject to at least two constraints: First, it can only enter into such contracts subject to the Ministerial Council's approval (Timor Gap Treaty 1989: Article 8(b)). Second, the production-sharing contracts for Area A have been formalised and annexed to the Treaty; any variation of their provisions can again only be made subject to the approval of the Ministerial Council, under Article 8(o). [11]

An inspection of the powers vested in the Malaysia–Thailand Joint Authority under the 1990 agreement also yields some interesting observations concerning exactly who would have the final say in case any major authoritative decisions need to be made regarding important aspects of the joint development project: the Joint Authority, or the respective governments of Malaysia and Thailand? This uncertainty may be discerned from an intuitive interpretation of the wording of Article 7 of the Constitution, which is sub-titled 'Power and Functions'. Article 7(1) states that:

The Joint Authority shall *control* all exploration and exploitation of the non-living resources in the Joint Development Area and shall be responsible for the formulation of policies for the same [emphasis added].

The use of the word *control* only, instead of the words *development, control and administration* as in the parallel Article 3(2) in the Memorandum of Understanding; and the fact that responsibility for the formulation of policies by the Joint Authority is limited in its scope to the Joint Development Area alone may be seen as an attempt by the two governments to retain some higher authority which would enable them to be the final arbiters of any policy-making dilemma with respect to the whole scenario of joint development in the area. In other words, the two governments have ensured that they have the final say in the overall policy-making with respect to operations of the Joint Authority. We can conclude from this that although the Joint Authority has been given a juridical personality of its own, under Article 1(1) of the Constitution, which allows it both policy-making and administrative powers, under Article 7(1) and Article 7(2)(d), as well as the power to enter into contracts relating to the exploration and exploitation of the non-living resources of the Area, under Article 7(2)(e); nevertheless, the Joint Authority will not be able to proceed in either the domestic and especially not the international arena, without prior approval from both governments. Thus, the legal competence accorded to the Joint Authority does not extend to enable it to have independent relations with other outside entities, except of course those of a strictly commercial nature. Even these transactions or contracts, it must be noted, are subject to the approval of the Governments, under Article 7(2)(e). This conclusion would also seem to be appropriate when we bear in mind that both state parties had evinced a marked reluctance to providing the Authority with such a high degree of autonomy[12] as perhaps was envisaged under Article 3(2) of the Memorandum of Understanding.

Within this context of institutional problems in these two earlier agreements, it is significant to note that the latest example of an agreement to co-operate in an area of overlapping continental shelf claims, between Malaysia and Vietnam, apparently eschews any institutional- or regime-building tendencies and is obviously intended merely to facilitate the already nominated national oil companies in their efforts to secure investment partners in the search for oil and gas. The general principles of the earlier agreements may be seen to underpin the present agreement. These are as follows:

First, that such co-operation between the two parties for the exploration and exploitation of petroleum resources in the overlapping claim area has been agreed pending final delimitation of the area and is without prejudice to the position and claims of either country; (cf Article 2 of the 1979 MOU)

Second, all costs and benefits derived from the exploration and exploitation of the 'Defined Area' (*sic*) shall be borne and shared equally by both Parties; (cf Article 3(5) of the 1979 MOU)

Third, in keeping with the provisional nature of the agreement, the duration of the MOU is for 40 years subject to any extensions and reviews that both Parties may agree at a relevant juncture (cf 50 years under Article 3(1) of the 1979 MOU).

THE PETROLEUM DEVELOPMENT REGIME AND THE PROBLEM OF PREVIOUSLY GRANTED CONCESSIONS

Both these agreements seek to implement for their respective Joint Development Areas a similar kind of petroleum development regime based on the production-sharing concept.[13] In the Malaysia–Thailand case, the decision to opt for a production-sharing system for petroleum development was not arrived at without considerable difficulties. In fact, this issue had been a major bone of contention between the two countries during the negotiation period and is an important reason for the delay – more than 11 years – between the signing of the 1990 Agreement, and the 1979 Memorandum of Understanding. As Fox *et al* note, the ultimate shape of the Joint Authority was dependent upon agreement on the type of production framework for the Area (Fox *et al,* 1989: 135), whether it be the production-sharing system favoured by Malaysia, or the concession system of licensing which Thailand was more familiar with. Apart from the different licensing regimes advocated by the two governments, Thailand also experienced severe difficulties in respect of petroleum concessions awarded to American oil companies in the early 1970s which included within their 'Effective Concession Areas', parts of the then disputed area of overlapping continental shelf claims which has, since 1979, become the Joint Development Area. These problems were exacerbated by the explicit undertaking in Article 3(2) of the 1979 Memorandum of Understanding that:

... The assumption of such rights and responsibilities by the Joint Authority shall *in no way effect or curtail the validity of concessions or licences hitherto issued or agreements or arrangements hitherto made by either party* [emphasis added].

This undertaking made it very difficult for the two countries to re-negotiate terms with the concessionaires. There is an inherent incongruity in Article 3(2) which, on the one hand, grants the Joint Authority all exploration and exploitation rights on behalf of both state parties, but on the other hand, does not affect the validity of concessions hitherto issued, thus bringing into immediate conflict disparate interest groups. This was agreed upon by both state parties at the time, notwithstanding their knowledge of the fact that valid concessions were still effective in the Joint Development Area.

An interesting observation that can be made at this point about the Memorandum of Understanding is the absence of any clause which is similar to that of Article 8(1) of the 1972 Supplementary Agreement between Australia and Indonesia which states that:

> Where the Government of the Commonwealth of Australia has granted an exploration permit for petroleum or a production licence for petroleum ... over which the Government ceases to exercise sovereign rights by virtue of this agreement, and that permit or licence is in force immediately prior to the entry into force of this Agreement, the Government of the Republic of Indonesia or its authorised agent shall, upon application by the registered holder of the permit or licence, ... *be willing to offer and to negotiate a production-sharing contract under Indonesian law to explore for and to produce oil and natural gas in respect of the same part of the seabed on terms that are not less favourable than those provided under Indonesian law in existing production-sharing contracts in other parts of the seabed under Indonesian jurisdiction* [emphasis added].

In retrospect and with hindsight, we can see that a similarly worded clause would have been of great value in the Malaysia–Thailand example to avoid much of the legal wrangling between Thailand and her concessionaires in the Joint Development Area. On the other hand, however, neither the 1989 Zone of Co-operation Treaty[14] nor the 1990 Joint Development Agreement incorporate such a clause concerning previously granted concessions in the (then) disputed area. It would appear, therefore, that the question of the legal validity of such concessions, once the area becomes part of a joint development zone, still needs to be addressed (Townsend-Gault, 1990a: 171–86; and 1990b: 104–7).

In the 1992 Malaysia–Vietnam MOU, this ambiguity as to the status of previously granted concessions which are still valid at the time of the agreement is (rather inexplicably given the extended difficulties caused by this clause in the 1979 Malaysia–Thailand MOU) repeated, thus providing that the validity of concessions or licences issued or arrangements made by either party pertaining to the exploration and exploitation of resources shall not be adversely affected.

Marine Environmental Protection in the Joint Development Zones

In the Malaysia–Thailand case, there are no specific provisions relating to the protection of the marine environment in the Joint Development Area, under either the 1979 or 1990 Agreements. Under Article 4(1) of the 1979 Memorandum of Understanding, however, it was agreed that the rights concerned or exercised by the national authority of either Party over the prevention and control of marine pollution were to be extended to include the joint development area. This includes all powers of enforcement related thereto. In respect of Malaysia, these rights and powers are set down in the 1984 Exclusive Economic Zone Act (Malaysia, 1984)[15]. It remains to be seen whether these provisions can be enforced within such an area of joint jurisdiction.

The impact of petroleum-related activities on the marine environment is catered for under the Zone of Co-operation Treaty. In particular, Article 18 obliges the Contracting States to provide assistance to the Joint Authority with regard to pollution prevention measures, equipment and procedures in Area A. Furthermore, should the pollution in Area A spread beyond that Area, the Contracting States are required to co-operate in taking action to prevent, mitigate and eliminate such pollution (Article (18)(1)(b)). Within Area A itself, the Joint Authority is empowered to issue regulations to protect the marine environment, and is required to establish a contingency plan for combating pollution from petroleum operations in this Area (Article (18)(2)). Article 19, on the other hand, specifically provides for the liability of contractors for damage as a result of pollution from petroleum operations in Area A. Although such liability would seem to be in respect of damage arising out of petroleum operations only, this apparent limitation is nullified by the significantly broad definition of what constitutes 'petroleum operations' under Article 1(1)(j) of the Treaty.

Under the 1992 MOU between Malaysia and Vietnam, both Parties have undertaken to ensure that the development of petroleum resources in the 'Defined Area' (*sic*) shall be conducted with due regard to the protection of the marine environment. No further elaboration as to the extent of this undertaking has been forthcoming.

Conclusions

On a broad international front, the Malaysia–Thailand Joint Development Agreement, along with the Australia–Indonesia Zone of Co-operation Treaty, and other co-operative arrangements with respect to shared natural resources such as the Torres Strait Treaty between Papua New Guinea and Australia, may be held up as examples heralding a new trend toward a broader-based, more comprehensive style of ocean resource management in the near future. Such a trend represents a welcome departure from the more legalistic and hence more confrontational approach which has dominated ocean boundary-making in the past. The idea of a more functional approach to maritime boundary agreements which emphasises the management aspects of such an agreement and eschews the stricter, more rule-based approach towards boundary-making is not, of course, a new one. What is perhaps more significant is the fact that recent state practice in the Asia–Pacific region, especially in respect of joint exploitation agreements of common offshore oil and gas deposits, have echoed those which can be found in both the North Sea and the Persian Gulf regions. It is submitted here that when all these agreements are taken together, coming as they do from many disparate areas all over the world, the conclusion that may be arrived at, at least in respect of such straddle deposits of oil and gas, is that many of the countries that were involved in such disputes have embraced the functional approach towards their resolution, which in turn advocates the need for co-operative agreements based upon the mutual sharing of the costs incurred and benefits derived from the joint exploitation of the resource in question.

Comparing the two agreements which actually set up Joint Development Authorities, it can be said that the 1989 Australia–Indonesia Treaty is far more comprehensive in its treatment of the various legal issues arising from the concept of joint development. However, bearing in mind the fact that the respective governments in both these agreements have allowed themselves a great degree of flexibility and discretionary powers in order to quickly overcome any implementation problems, the success or failure of either of these two agreements ultimately turns upon whether the requisite political will can be maintained to see them through to their successful implementation.

Going from the above summation, the question of whether there now exists a duty under international law to co-operate towards joint development, may be answered in the negative, at least in respect of a duty existing under customary international law. Nevertheless, it is possible to impute a lesser type of international legal obligation upon states to co-operate when faced by similar problems arising from shared natural resources, over which the sovereign right to exploit is disputed. The precise extent of this new type of obligation in the international arena cannot as yet be determined, though its presence is readily ascertainable.[16] It remains to be seen, therefore, what effect it will have on future state practice involving disputes over shared natural resources, especially within the South-east Asian – South China Sea region.

Notes

1   The legality of this annexation and consequently the right of both Indonesia and Australia to enter into any agreement over the exploitation of hydrocarbons in the continental shelf area pertaining to East Timor is now the subject of a case brought before the International Court of Justice by Portugal on 22 February 1991. See Scobbie (1991).

2   The treaty came into force on 9 February 1991. See also Fox (1990).

3   Communication between the author and the Ministry of Foreign Affairs of Malaysia (26 July 1993).
4   The Charter was adopted by 120 votes to six, with 10 abstentions. The countries voting against the Charter were Belgium, Denmark, the (then) Federal Republic of Germany, Luxembourg, the UK and the USA. The abstaining states were Austria, Canada, France, Ireland, Israel, Italy, Japan, The Netherlands, Norway and Spain.
5   A separate vote was taken on Article 2(2)(c) which allowed the nationalisation or expropriation of foreign property. The majority in favour was 104 to 16, with six abstentions. See Harris (1991: 526).
6   Coming into force on 16 November 1994.
7   See Fox *et al* (1989: 63).
8   Entered into force 2 June 1982.
9   See also Fox *et al* (1989: 38).
10   At the Twenty-Fifth ASEAN Ministerial Meeting in Manila, 21–2 July 1992.
11   Annex C to the Treaty contains the Model Production Sharing Contract between the Joint Authority and contractors on the basis of which production sharing contracts for Area A are to be included concluded. Under Article 1(o), Annexes A, B, C, and D are included within the meaning of the 'Treaty'.
12   This was especially true in respect of the licensing powers of the Authority. See Fox *et al* (1989: 135 and 235). See also Ariffin (1985: 534–5).
13   Article 3 of the Zone of Co-operation Treaty states that 'Petroleum operations in Area A shall be carried out through production-sharing contracts' and Article 8(1) of the Malaysia– Thailand Joint Development Agreement states that 'any contract awarded... for the exploration and exploitation of petroleum in the Joint Development Area shall... be a production-sharing contract'.
14   Article 34(1)(b) of the Treaty, entitled the 'Rights of Contractors', only deals with the rights of contractors *vis-à*-vis the Joint Authority if and when the Treaty ceases to be in force.
15   This Act provides that the unlicensed discharge of substances containing either oil or any other pollutants into the Exclusive Economic Zone is an offence and the person(s) responsible shall be liable to a fine not exceeding one million Malaysian Ringgit (approximately US$330,000) (under Section 10 of the Act). It is questionable whether this provision can be a law which gives effect to applicable international rules and standards, as required under 220(3) of the 1982 Law of the Sea Convention.
16   This type of lesser international obligation has mainly arisen from joint statements, communiqués, and other forms of Declarations which were initially concerned with the protection of human

rights and the environment and are now increasingly evident in the international law on shared natural resources. See the excellent article by Hiram Chodosh (1991) on the evolution and place of this type of declarative international law in the hierarchy of international obligations between states.

Bibliography

Ariffin (1985) 'The Malaysian philosophy of joint development', in M. Valencia (ed.) 'Geology and hydrocarbon potential of the South China Sea and possibilities of joint development', *Energy – Special Issue* (March/April): 533–8.

Chodosh, H.E. (1991) 'Neither treaty not custom: the emergence of declarative international law?', *Texas International Law Journal* 26, 1: 87–124.

Fox, H. *et al* (1989) *Joint Development of Offshore Oil and Gas,* Vol.1 London: The British Institute of International and Comparative Law.

Fox, H. (ed.) (1990) *Joint Development of Offshore Oil and Gas*, Vol.2, London: The British Institute of International and Comparative Law.

Harris, D.J. (1991) *Cases and Materials on International Law*, 4th edn, London: Sweet and Maxwell.

Kittichaisaree, K. (1987) *The Law of the Sea and Maritime Boundary Delimitation in South-East Asia*, Oxford: Oxford University Press.

Nordquist and Simmonds (1980) *New Directions in the Law of the Sea,* Documents, Vol.X, New York: Oceana Publications; London: The British Institute of International and Comparative Law.

Ong, D. (1991) 'Thailand/Malaysia: The Joint Development Agreement 1990', *International Journal of Estuarine (now Marine) and Coastal Law (IJECL)* 6, 1: 57–72.

—— (1993) 'Malaysia: international agreements – continental shelf', News Section: National Reports, *Oil and Gas, Law and Taxation Review* 3, D–21.

Scobbie, I. (1991) 'The East Timor case: the implications of procedure for litigation strategy', *Oil and Gas, Law and Taxation Review* 9: 273–81.

Townsend-Gault, I. (1990) 'The impact of a Joint Development Zone on previously granted interests' in H. Fox (ed.) *Joint Development of Offshore Oil and Gas,* Vol.2, London: The British Institute of International and Comparative Law: 171–86

—— (1990) 'The Malaysia/Thailand Joint Development agreement', in H. Fox (ed.) *Joint Development of Offshore Oil and Gas,* Vol.2, London: The British Institute of International and Comparative Law: 102–8.

LEGAL REFERENCES

ASEAN (1985) Agreement on the Conservation of Nature and Natural Resources, signed at Kuala Lumpur, Malaysia on 9 July (but not yet in force).

[Australia–Indonesia 1971] Agreement between the Government of the Commonwealth of Australia and the Government of the Republic of Indonesia Establishing Certain Seabed Boundaries, signed at Canberra on 18 May, 1971.

[Conciliation Commission 1981] Report of the Conciliation Commission on Jan Mayen, 20 ILM 251 (1981).

[Iceland–Jan Mayen 1981] Agreement of the Continental Shelf between Iceland and Jan Mayen, 22 October. Entered into force: 2 June, 1982. 21 ILM 1222 (1982).

[ICJ 1969] *International Court of Justice Reports*: 52, para. 99.

[ICJ 1982] *International Court of Justice Reports*: 18.

[ICJ 1984] *International Court of Justice Reports*: 246.

[Indonesia–Australia 1972] Agreement between the Government of the Republic of Indonesia and the Government of the Commonwealth of Australia Establishing Certain Seabed Boundaries in the Area of the Timor and Arafura Seas, Supplementary to the Agreement of 18 May 1971 signed at Jakarta on 9 October, 1972.

[Indonesia–Malaysia 1969] Agreement between the Government of the Republic of Indonesia and the Government of Malaysia Relating to the Delimitation of Continental Shelves between the Two Countries, signed at Kuala Lumpur on 27 October 1969. See *Limits in the Seas Series* (1970) No.1, 'Indonesia–Malaysia continental shelf boundary', 21 January, Washington DC: Department of State, Office of the Geographer, Bureau of Intelligence and Research.

[Indonesia–Malaysia–Thailand 1971] Agreement between the Government of the Republic of Indonesia, the Government of Malaysia and the Government of the Kingdom of Thailand Relating to the Delimitation of the Continental Shelf Boundaries in the North Part of the Straits of Malacca, signed at Kuala Lumpur on 21 December, entered into force on 16 July, 1973. See: *Limits in the Seas Series,* (1978) No.81, 'Maritime Boundaries: Indonesia–Malaysia–Thailand', 27 December, Washington DC: Department of State, Office of the Geographer, Bureau of Intelligence and Research.

[Indonesia–Thailand 1971] Agreement between the Government of the Republic of Indonesia and the Kingdom of Thailand Relating to the Delimitation of the Continental Shelf Boundary between the Two Countries in the Northern Part of the Straits of Malacca and in the Andaman Sea, signed at Bangkok on 17 December. In *Limits in the Seas Series,* (1978) No.81, 'Maritime Boundaries: Indonesia–Malaysia–Thailand', Enclosure No.2, 27 December, Washington

DC: Department of State, Office of the Geographer, Bureau of Intelligence and Research.

[Indonesia–Thailand 1975] Agreement between the Government of the Republic of Indonesia and the Government of the Kingdom of Thailand Relating to the Delimitation of the Sea-bed Boundary between the Two Countries in the Andaman Sea , signed at Jakarta on 11 December. See: *Limits in the Seas Series,* (1981) No.93, 'Continental shelf boundaries: India–Indonesia–Thailand', 17 August, Washington DC: Department of State, Office of the Geographer, Bureau of Intelligence and Research.

[Malaysia–Thailand 1979] Memorandum of Understanding between Malaysia and The Kingdom of Thailand on The Establishment of The Joint Authority for the Exploitation of the Resources of the Sea Bed in a Defined Area of the Continental Shelf of the Two Countries in the Gulf of Thailand, signed at Chiang Mai, Thailand on 21 February, 1979. See Ong (1991: 61–3).

[Malaysia–Thailand 1990] Agreement between the Government of Malaysia and the Government of the Kingdom of Thailand on the Constitution and Other Matters Relating to the Establishment of the Malaysia–Thailand Joint Authority. See Ong (1991: 64–72).

[Malaysia 1984] Laws of Malaysia, Act 311. Gazetted on 31 December 1984.

[Thailand–Malaysia 1979] Memorandum of Understanding between the Kingdom of Thailand and Malaysia on the Delimitation of the Continental Shelf Boundary between the Two Countries in the Gulf of Thailand (24 October 1979).

[Timor Gap Treaty 1989] Treaty between the Australia and the Republic of Indonesia on the Zone of Co-operation in an Area between the Indonesian Province of East Timor and Northern Australia, signed at Canberra on 11 December, 1989; came into force on 9 February, 1991.

Treaty of Amity and Co-operation (1976) in South-East Asia, signed at Denpasar, Bali, Indonesia on 24 February 1976.

[UNCLOS 1982] UN Convention on the Law of the Sea, Montego Bay, 10 December, 1982. Coming into force on 16 November, 1994. 21 ILM 1245 (1982).

[UNGA 213] (1982) *United Nations General Assembly Resolution* 213 (XXXVII), 20 December 1982.

[UNGA 3281] (1974) *United Nations General Assembly Resolution* 3281 (XXIX), 12 December, 14 ILM 251 (1975).

6

A New Regime for International Pipelines from Central Asia

Jeremy Carver
Greg Englefield

Introduction

The potential for growth of oil and gas production from land-locked frontier regions, particularly in Russia and Central Asia, has raised the prospect of an increasing proportion of the world's oil and gas having to be transported across the *land territory* of a number of states. This need for land transboundary movement of hydrocarbons presents a number of problems, particularly in Central Asia and Transcaucasia, where political instability and differences between the various states have hindered the construction of an efficient transport system for the export of these resources to world markets.

Pipelines are the most efficient means of moving large quantities of oil and gas over long distances across land. Recent industry estimates suggest that over 28,000 miles of large diameter oil and gas pipeline will be built throughout the world over the next two years at a projected cost of over $30 billion. Major projects include pipelines between Russia and Central Europe, across Central Asia, between North Africa and Europe, in South-east Asia, and between the Middle East and India (Pipeline and Gas Journal, 1993; Pipeline Industry, 1993 and 1994). However, international pipelines are vulnerable to abuse by states across which they are built; a pipeline can be cut, or the flow of oil and gas can be stopped or diverted. In Central Asia, the lack of agreement on the course of an interstate pipeline is due in part to political differences between the various states, compounded by uncertainty over Russian, Turkish and Iranian ambitions in the region. Russia, having lost power since the collapse of the Soviet Union, is particularly keen to maintain a strong influence in Central Asia and Transcaucasia, and over any development of resources in these regions – whether so as to benefit from its growth, or to discourage too much competition for its own domestic resources. A lack of consensus has stunted the development of a workable plan to construct an oil and gas transport system between Central Asia, Transcaucasia, and world energy markets.

Until a legal regime is developed that will protect international pipelines from regional instability, the full potential of the hydrocarbon resources of Central Asia and Transcaucasia will remain unrealised. In this paper, we argue that establishing an international pipeline authority to build and manage a major oil and gas pipeline network between Central Asia and the Black Sea or Mediterranean Sea, with a legal personality independent of the states across which the pipeline system is built, is the best means of overcoming these problems.

Central Asian Oil and Gas Developments

The newly independent states in Central Asia and Transcaucasia are attracting increasing attention from Western oil and gas companies eager to identify new sources of hydrocarbons, as well as to develop the existing petroleum industry. The two states which have been identified as having the greatest potential are Azerbaijan and Kazakhstan. However, Turkmenistan, Uzbekistan and parts of southern Russia also have considerable oil and gas resources for both domestic use and for export. These states have been involved in detailed negotiations with Western companies over the past two years. In October 1993, the Azerbaijan Government signed an agreement with a large group of Western companies to exploit offshore resources in the Caspian which followed long and often difficult negotiations. In Kazakhstan, Chevron is developing the huge Tengiz field in the west of the country. On 3 December 1993, Kazakhstan signed an agreement with a consortium of six Western companies allowing exploration for oil and gas in a 100,000km² area of the north-east Caspian Sea. In September 1993, Uzbekistan launched its first bidding round for foreign companies to take stakes in both oil and gas fields.

The present method of exporting these resources, using the existing Soviet-built pipeline network, together with railway tankers, is inadequate to support current production let alone predicted growth. A much more efficient way of transporting hydrocarbons would be through a new pipeline system to a coastal terminus either on the Black Sea, the Mediterranean or the Arabian Sea.

In order to reach the Mediterranean Sea, a transport route must be established either directly from Central Asia and Transcaucasia through Turkey, to its southern coast; or to the Black Sea across either Russia or Georgia, and then through Turkey to the Mediterranean. This may be either by ship through the narrow Turkish Straits, or by land. However, political instability in Georgia, and the conflict between Azerbaijan and Armenia over Nagorno-Karabakh since 1988, present serious problems for such a route through Transcaucasia. A pipeline between Azerbaijan and Turkey would have to be constructed either across Georgia, Armenia or Iran. A more northern route through Russia avoids these potential problems, but would still require a logistically and politically difficult exit from the Black Sea through Turkey, as well as dependence by producer states on Russia. Though states in the region have attempted to improve bilateral relations in order to encourage investment in pipeline projects, it is still very unclear what the value of such measures is to the development of transnational pipelines in the region,[1] and whether bilateral agreements between a chain of neighbouring states would be sufficient to allow a pipeline system to be built across two or more international boundaries in the region.

A second possible route exits across Iran to either the Arabian Gulf or the Indian Ocean, or west to Turkey and the Mediterranean Sea. Although these routes would have the advantage of avoiding volatile parts of Transcaucasia and Central Asian reliance on Russia, a major infrastructure investment in Iran is unlikely to attract capital investment easily, particularly from the West.

Proposed Pipeline Projects

Various proposals have been made for an oil pipeline running west from Central Asia and Transcaucasia to either the Black Sea or the Mediterranean (see Figure 6.1 and Table 6.1). The most active to date is the Caspian Pipeline Consortium (CPC), established in 1992 by agreement between the governments of Kazakhstan and Oman acting through the Oman Oil Company Limited, and more recently Russia. The CPC has proposed a route from Kazakhstan across Russia to the Black Sea port of Novorossiysk. This scheme would make use of an existing Soviet-built pipeline between Tengiz and Grozny, and oil loading facilities at the Russian port of Novorossiysk. The aim of the project would be to transport up to 75 million tons per year of crude oil. Initial cost estimates are in excess of $1.5 billion. The pipeline would be 1,300 miles in length: the 800 mile 40-inch diameter pipeline between Tengiz and Grozny is almost complete, and a further 500 miles of new pipeline linking Grozny to Novorossiysk would have to be built. A southern extension linking Azerbaijan oil fields around Baku with Novorossiysk has also been proposed. Though this scheme has received considerable publicity, it is fraught with political as well as commercial problems. The periodic changes in the relationships between Russia, Kazakhstan and Azerbaijan have done little to encourage the confidence of private sector interests, particularly Chevron which is developing the Tengiz oil field and would be a major user of a pipeline system. The proposed division of ownership of the pipeline has been a particular source of disagreement. Chevron has argued that such a large pipeline project must adhere to a series of principles (Petroleum Economist, 1993: 38):

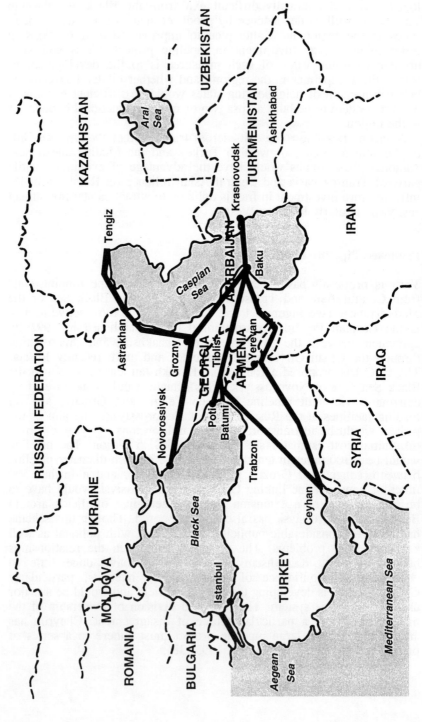

Figure 6.1 Prospective Pipelines from Central Asia and Transcaucasia

1 ownership of the pipeline should be in proportion to resources contributed by each participant in the project;
2 risks and rewards should be shared in proportion to resources contributed;
3 shippers should have non-discriminatory access and tariffs;
4 tariffs should provide a reasonable rate of return;
5 there should be protection against political risk.

Chevron would like a share in the ownership of the pipeline, as well as responsibility for raising capital for the project. However, CPC was established by inter-governmental agreement, and does not provide full ownership rights to private sector firms using the pipelines.

Until such issues are resolved, it seems unlikely that the project will receive the level of investment required. This plan, and other alternative routes to the Black Sea, also face the problem of access from Novorossiysk by oil tanker to the Mediterranean through the Turkish Straits. Though unhindered passage for all merchant ships traversing the Bosphorus and the Dardanelles is guaranteed by the 1936 Montreux Convention, Turkey has argued that a major increase in oil tanker traffic through these Straits could not be managed safely. The collision on 13 March 1994 between the *Nassia*, a Greek–Cypriot registered oil tanker, and another cargo vessel in the Bosphorus has provided support for Turkey's position (Brown, 1994). Reports published recently by the International Maritime Organisation (IMO) Sub-committee on Safety of Navigation have also highlighted the problems of transporting large quantities of oil through the Straits. It has been estimated that up to 100 million tons of oil per year might have to be transported through the Straits by 2005 (IMO, 1993a and b). Inevitably there would be serious congestion if the CPC project were to be built, or indeed any other pipeline from Central Asia to the Russian Black Sea coast. A traffic separation scheme through the Straits, as proposed by Turkey (IMO, 1993a), was discussed at the May 1994 meeting of the Maritime Safety Committee of IMO, and was instituted in July 1994 (MEED, 1994). Such a scheme will have the effect of limiting the volume of tanker traffic through the Straits, putting further strains on any possible alternative route to the Black Sea.

Other plans exist to build a pipeline from Central Asia through Transcaucasia, to either the Black Sea or the Mediterranean, avoiding Russian territory. Two main variations exist:

1 Baku to the Black Sea Coast of Georgia either at Poti or Batumi; with a possible extension on to the south coast of Turkey;
2 Baku to the Mediterranean coast of Turkey, probably to the existing terminus of the Iraq–Turkey oil pipeline at Ceyhan.

Table 6.1 Prospective international oil and gas pipelines from central Asia and Transcaucasia

| | | Transcaucasia | | | Central Asia | | Surrounding States | | | | | |
		Armenia	Azerbaijan	Georgia	Kazakhstan	Turkmen-istan	Russian Federation	Turkey	Iran	Bulgaria	Greece	Oman
Caspian Pipeline Consortium	Tenzig–Novorossysk		(x)		x		x					x
	Baku–Novorossysk		x		(x)		x					x
Botas – Route supported by Turkey	Baku–Ceyhan	(x)	x	(x)				x	(x)			
	Baku–Georgia–Ceyhan		x	x				x				
Kazakhstan Pipeline Co.	Kazakhstan–Baku–Ceyhan	(x)	x		x	x		x				
Black Sea Mediterranean	Kiyikoy–Ibrikbana							x				
	Zonguldak/Samsun/Trabzon–Turkey							x				
Southern Gas Route	Turkmenistan–Iran–Turkey					x	(x)	x	x			
Southern Oil Route	Kazakhstan–Iran				x	x			x			
	Turkmenistan–Iran					x			x			
Western Route	Burgas–Alexandroupolis						x			x	x	

(x) Pipeline route might cross territory of state   x Pipeline route would cross territory of state; known direct involvement in pipeline construction and management

An eastward extension could be built from Baku across the Caspian Sea to link Kazakhstan and other Central Asian states to one of these pipeline routes. The Turkish state-owned pipeline company, Botas, has been lobbying for a pipeline route through Turkey. Discussions have taken place with the State Oil Company of Azerbaijan (SOCAR) and the principal Western companies involved in developing Azerbaijan's hydrocarbon resources. However, identifying a route between Azerbaijan and Turkey is difficult. A pipeline along the Araks River valley would be the most logical route; however, such a pipeline would have to be built either through areas of Azerbaijan occupied at present by Armenian forces, or through Iran. It would also have to cross Kurdish areas of eastern Turkey. A route through Georgia would also be possible, however conflict within Georgia has made such a route less attractive to investors, and would involve either export across the Black Sea, or a relatively expensive extension of the pipeline across Turkey to the Mediterranean.

One method of avoiding the hazards of oil tankers passing through the Turkish Straits would be to construct a pipeline across Turkey linking the Black Sea to the Mediterranean, either in the east of the country,[2] or west of Istanbul between the Black Sea and the Aegean. However, while such a pipeline might help to resolve the logistical problem of transporting oil from the Black Sea to the Mediterranean, it would still require co-operation between Turkey and Russia, as well as the producing states, and it is far from clear whether this is likely in the near future. An alternative route announced in June 1994, would involve the construction of a pipeline across Bulgaria and Greece, thus bypassing Turkey completely (Petroleum Intelligence Weekly, 1994). Though this might solve the problem of transport through the Bosphorus, it is unlikely to be popular with Turkish authorities.

In April 1994, a Turkmen government spokesman announced that agreement had been reached between Turkmenistan, Iran, Turkey and Russia, to build a gas pipeline between Turkmenistan and Turkey across northern Iran, avoiding Transcaucasia and the Black Sea (Kynge, 1994). The scheme was heralded as a possible precursor to an oil pipeline network linking Central Asia with Iran and Turkey. However, no timetable for developing such a scheme has been agreed, and it would have the disadvantage of involving Iran, a disincentive to Western investment.

A stalemate appears to have been reached, with no project emerging as a clear favourite, largely because of political instability throughout the region and competition between the various states. Despite the clear economic advantages which will flow from the construction of a working transportation network, little real international progress seems to have been made on any of the routes outlined. It is reasonable to assume that technical obstacles, however complex, can be overcome; and even that the finance required for construction can be found – but only when the basic plan has been agreed by all parties, offering a degree of political security. The difficulty then seems to lie in achieving this fundamental consensus to develop an international transportation system. If states are reluctant to commit their natural resources to the territories of near or far neighbours, how much more nervous would be the banks and investors without whose funds no pipeline can be built.

To date, the proposals which have been put forward suggest an essentially *national* proposal, or – at most – a *bilateral* approach. Yet a pipeline through the Caucasus or Russia with access to the Mediterranean is an *international* vehicle; and should be approached as such. This, in turn, suggests the need for *international* mechanisms to achieve the objective, and for these an *international* institution would be required. Though international oil and gas pipelines have traditionally been constructed by bilateral agreement between the States across whose territories the pipeline passes, and operated on a national level in each territory, such a regime seems unlikely to succeed in the present context, despite the pledge to co-operate in transboundary movement of oil and gas resources made by all states concerned in the European Energy Charter.[3] Therefore, it may be to other forms of international co-operation that we should look to find a way to overcome the inevitable caution – even, suspicion – that would impede direct participation by states in a major transit pipeline project involving three or more different sovereignties.

How then should such an international vehicle be created, and what models can we use? The answer would seem to be an international organisation, created with legal personality separate from its member states, with capacity to make agreements with states, oil companies, contractors and banks. Such an organisation would be capable of achieving results which no single state could do acting individually.

International organisations with a degree of independence from states began to develop in the 19th century, as international relations advanced from reliance on bilateral treaties and conventional diplomatic contact between states to other forms of co-operation. The Congress of Vienna in 1815 introduced a new era of international conferences and multi-national treaties which developed international administrative unions for political and economic purposes; for example, the international postal union, various international commodity unions and international river commissions. It is clear that international organisations can be created with independent legal personality, and may have the legal capacity to make agreements with states and other organisations, and to have certain privileges and immunities. Of importance is the fact that an international organisation can have certain rights as well as responsibilities, on the international plane, independent of states.

One of the most durable means of achieving co-operation in international transportation is to be found in relation to international waterways. As well as the development of the idea of freedom of navigation along international rivers, they have also been the subject of a number of public international bodies established in the 19th and early 20th centuries to organise their maintenance and manage their use. The analogy between international rivers and pipelines may seem odd: a river has a more or less certain course, whereas a major obstacle to laying an international pipeline affects the decision over its course. However, the experience of international river management, and the River Commissions established during the 19th and early 20th centuries provide useful precedents for designing a modern international organisation to manage an international oil or gas pipeline.

The first steps towards the principle of free traffic on international rivers was taken at the beginning of the 19th century. The Final Act of the Congress of Vienna, in June 1815, provided that navigation was to be free for all nations on the Rhine. At that time, the Rhine flowed through a host of different and contending sovereignties, some now absorbed within modern Germany. Though it was not until 1868 that a full International Commission for the Rhine was instituted by the signature of the Convention of Mannheim, the idea was considered sufficiently successful by 1840, to provide a model for the regime needed to ensure international stability for the Danube: similar problems, but different states.[4] While it would be false to suggest that the waters of either the Rhine or the Danube have flowed unperturbed since then, river traffic has continued with relatively minimal interruption despite the turbulent relations between the states through whose territories the rivers flow. Along the Danube two commissions were created: the European Danube Commission formed by seven states, including non-riparian states, for the limited purpose of clearing the mouth of the Danube for international transport; and the Danube Commission made up of riparian states for the long term operation of navigation of the waterways. The European Danube Commission was further refined in 1865 by regulations signed at Galantz, and the Commission was formed as an independent organisation with an international character offering protection to its staff and facilities and having its own flag. After the First World War, an International Commission was established to administer the upper waters of the Danube, whilst the European Danube Commission controlled the lower Danube from Braila to the Black Sea. The Treaty of Paris, signed in July 1921, provided clear powers to the European Danube Commission for the management of the river, including the power to forbid certain acts by riparian states if they were detrimental to navigation (Article 14), to organise the policing of the river (Article 24) and establish a Secretariat and other services independent of the riparian states (Article 27). The property of the Commission and the person of the Commissioners were entitled to diplomatic privileges and immunities, and the Commission could fly its own flag on its buildings and vessels (Article 37). The jurisdiction of the European Commission over the

Danube was supported by the Permanent Court of International Justice in an Opinion issued in 1927 in response to a challenge by one of the riparian states, Romania (Hudson, 1969: 140). Though the Danube Commissions were in effect abolished as a result of the start of the Second World War, a Commission was re-established in 1948 by the riparian states,[5] and has continued to manage, albeit in a rather more limited way, the river since then.

The European experience in managing the Rhine and Danube as international rivers has influenced regimes in place elsewhere. Such river commissions share certain common features:

1 each has separate juridical personality, and is thus constitutionally independent of each constituent member state;
2 each has allocated to it certain specific functions, for which it – and not any member state – is responsible;
3 member states meet, and address their national concerns, within the constitutional framework of the Commission;
4 in resolving such issues, each member has only the influence (whether by an agreed voting system or other mechanism) to which it has agreed with the other members in the constituent treaty, as it may from time to time be amended.

A similar experience in building international co-operation is to be seen in the rapid growth of telegraphic and telephone communication during the second half of the 19th century. The tendency to create international bodies for the purpose of regulating and operating particular telecommunication lines was transformed into the International Telegraphic Union (ITU), established in 1865. Although its rights within the territories of member states were inevitably limited, the mutual incentives which all members had in permitting the ITU to retain overall responsibility for regulating international communications were considerable (Verzijl, 1970: 274–81). The International Sea Bed Authority (ISBA) proposed in the United Nations Convention on the Law of the Sea (UNCLOS), to come into force in November 1994,[6] is another example of an international organisation designed to manage resources and negotiate independently with different states. The ISBA will have clear aims, the ability to raise capital, commission work to exploit resources, and will distribute the income from such exploitation to states.

In exploring how to translate these experiences into the different context of an international pipeline, there will be many differences. Many of these, however, are differences of function, dictated by the operational needs of constructing and maintaining a pipeline. As such, they are well understood by the oil and gas industry. The key difference in approach lies in creating the *international institution*, independent of all its members, which will carry out these functions without the need to concern itself with the day to day affairs of the states across whose territories the pipeline will pass. Of course, such a body cannot be ignorant of the concerns of its members; and it will have to deal with the internal authorities of each member at various points in its management of the pipeline. These relations however, should be defined in the constituent treaty, and any other agreed operating by-laws developed as need requires. Moreover, the agreements must incorporate effective means of resolving disputes by fair and efficient procedures, accessible and well understood by all.

Another advantage of creating an international body lies in its ability to enter into the numerous and complex agreements with private sector interests for the construction, financing, maintenance and use of the pipelines. For every such contract to have to be undertaken separately for each territorial jurisdiction is a recipe for confusion, delay and waste of resources.

For each of the states involved in the pipeline, whether as producers of the hydrocarbons flowing through it, or merely as hosts for the physical extent, the primary concern is and will be to maximise their respective revenue from the operation. Here in particular, an international pipeline body can perform a vital role by reason of its independence. The financial arrangements will have to be spelt out with sufficient certainty when the body is created, or according to some formula which can be applied uncontroversially as the course of the pipeline is decided, and its costs become known. Once defined, it is better that each member can look to the body – their mutual creation – to discharge those financial obligations: impartially, in accordance with the agreed mechanisms set in place. When that same body has responsibility for raising, and servicing, the capital needed to build a pipeline, it can more efficiently account for the revenue engaged and more readily meet its financial obligations, without need to call upon members save in preordained circumstances.

It is clear that the states of the region must be the primary architects of any international organisation to establish and run a pipeline system. Initially, such a pipeline system would have one clear aim: to transport hydrocarbons from producing areas to the Black Sea or the Mediterranean, for onward shipment to world energy markets. The international body running the pipeline system could avoid the inevitable complications of integrating its pipeline system with those of the states across which it operates. Membership of such a body could include the states of the region, and interested international organisations (for example, the World Bank, or the European Bank of Reconstruction and Development). Such an international organisation, created by international treaty, with initial financial support from member states, international funding organisations and the private sector, would then have to negotiate with the various states for permission to construct a pipeline network, and with funding agencies and private sector capital to finance the construction. Of critical importance is that such an organisation is independent of the various states across which its pipeline will pass. The organisation would need to agree financial arrangements with 'host' states, and its liability for the pipeline once constructed.

Though all states in the region could be involved in the creation and management of such an organisation, it might be established initially by a smaller group of states. Other states could join later, spreading the pipeline network, and therefore reducing the risk of one state controlling the activities of the organisation. Such an organisation could undertake the construction of a number of pipelines reflecting commercial and technical realities and maximising the economic benefits flowing to its member states. A pipeline system operated by an independent international body could provide the means of unlocking the considerable resources of these states, and the present impasse which blocks their development.

Notes

1   International agreements have been signed between Azerbaijan and Russia (12 October 1992) and Azerbaijan and Georgia (3 February 1993) in which the signatories guarantee the transport of goods through pipelines. Armenia, Azerbaijan, Kazakhstan, Russia, Turkey, Turkmenistan, Ukraine and Uzbekistan signed the European Energy Charter on 17 December 1991, and all these states have ratified the 1985 Multi-Lateral Investment Guarantee Agency Convention.

2   One possible route would link the Black Sea port of Trabzon to the existing export terminal at Ceyhan on the Mediterranean coast of Turkey.

3   All the states concerned, except Iran, are parties to the European Energy Charter, signed at The Hague on 17 December 1991.

4   See Whiteman (1964); Colombos (1967); Verzijl (1970: 103–219); Oppenheim (1992: 574–88).

5   Convention concerning the regime of navigation on the Danube (with annexes and supplementary protocol). Signed at Belgrade, on 18 August 1948; Bulgaria, Czechoslovakia, Hungary, Romania, Ukraine Soviet Socialist Republic, USSR and Yugoslavia. *United Nations Treaty Series* 33: 195–225.

6   See Part XI and Annexes III and IV of the 1982 United Nations Convention on the Law of the Sea.

Bibliography

Brown, J.M. (1994) 'Collision raises Bosphorus question', *Financial Times*, 15 March.

Colombos, C.J. (1967) *The International Law of the Sea,* 6th edition, London: Longmans.

Hudson, M.O. (1969) *World Court Reports II (1927–32),* Oceana.

IMO (1993a) *International Maritime Organisation* document MSC 62/Inf.10, 26 March.

—— (1993b) *International Maritime Organisation* document NAV 39/3/10, 7 June.

Kynge, J. (1994) 'Turkmenistan in new oil and gas pipeline projects', *Reuters News Service*, 6 April.

MEED (1994) 'New Bosphorus rules spark row', *Middle East Economic Digest* 17 May.

Oppenheim (1992) *Oppenheim's International Law,* Vol.1, 9th edition, London: Longman.

Petroleum Economist (1993) July: 38.

Petroleum Intelligence Weekly (1994) 33, 25: 3.

Pipeline and Gas Journal (1993) August: 12–3.

Pipeline Industry (1993) November: 21.

—— (1994) January: 33.

Verzijl, J.H.W. (1970) *International Law in Historical Perspective* III, Sithoff.

Whiteman, M.M. (1964) *Digest of International Law* 3, US Department of State: 875–920.

LEGAL REFERENCES

Convention concerning the regime of navigation on the Danube (with annexes and supplementary protocol). Signed at Belgrade, on 18 August 1948; *United Nations Treaty Series* 33: 195–225.

Multi-Lateral Investment Guarantee Agency Convention (MIGA) (1985) *International Legal Materials* 24: 692.

Montreux Convention (1936) Convention regarding the regime of the Straits, with annexes and protocols, signed at Montreux, 20 July; *League of Nations Treaty Series* 173: 213–39.

Treaty of Paris (1921) Convention instituting the definitive Statute of the Danube, signed at Paris, 23 July; *League of Nations Treaty Series* 26: 174–99.

United Nations Convention on the Law of the Sea (1982) *United Nations,* 1983, E.83.V.5.

7

The Dead Sea:
A Case for Transboundary Mineral Exploitation

Gideon Biger

The Dead Sea, called in Hebrew the 'Salt Sea' and in Arabic *Bahar Lut* (the lake of Lot) is divided today by the boundary line between Israel and Jordan. In the near future another Arab country, Palestine, may join the two others in controlling and ruling this mineral-rich lake. The aim of this chapter is to examine the recent exploitation of the Dead Sea minerals, and the necessity and potential for future transboundary co-operation in this area.

Geographical Setting

The Dead Sea covers the deepest continental depression in the world. Its water level today is about 400m below sea level. This figure however is subject to frequent changes (Klein, 1961). After a series of drought years it may drop by 5m or more and may rise again after prolonged rain. In 1820 it was –402m, in 1896 it was –391m. In 1963 it stood on the –398.5m line, while in 1992 it stood at –404m. It is assumed that tectonic movement at the bottom of this sea has also influenced the water level (Nir, 1968). The Dead Sea is fed by various sources: underground salt water wells, the Jordan river, and flood waters. In the early 1960s the lake was about 80km (48 miles) long and 16km (10 miles) wide at its greatest breadth. Its maximum depth is about 400m (1,310 feet) but its southern extremity is shallow, and it is separated from the principal basin by a low-lying peninsula called *al Lisan* (the tongue). The level of the Dead Sea began to fall rapidly when Israel and Jordan began using the water of the Jordan and the Yarmuk rivers as well as that of the Sea of Galilee (Lake Tiberias) for agriculture and other applications. The shallow southern basin dried out rapidly and the Dead Sea proper retreated north (Figure 7.1).

The water of the Dead Sea, like that of other inland lakes with no outlet, has become increasingly saline. Today it registers the highest salt content in the world – over 26% near the surface of the southern basin and 33% at depth (Karmon, 1978) while ocean salinity averages about 3.5%. Every unit of water contains about 13.3% magnesium chloride (MgCl$_2$), 8.55% sodium chloride (NaCl), 3.46% calcium chloride (CaCl$_2$), 1.17% potassium chloride (KCl) and 0.59% magnesium bromide (MgBr$_2$). The estimated mineral reserves of the Dead Sea are 22 billion tons of magnesium chloride, 12 billion tons of sodium chloride, six billion tons of calcium chloride, two billion tons of potassium chloride and one billion ton of magnesium bromide.

The Boundaries in the Dead Sea

The British, who were awarded the mandate to govern Palestine after World War I, created Transjordan as a separate entity. The boundary between Palestine and Transjordan was established in 1922 placing it along a line drawn from 'a point two miles from Akaba, through the centre of the Wadi Araba, the Dead Sea, and the River Jordan to its junction with the River Yarmuk' (Palestine, 1922). No explanation was given concerning the crossing of the Dead Sea by the boundary but it seems that the British wanted to enforce some kind of co-operation between the future Jewish state in Palestine and the future Arab state to be established in Transjordan (Biger, 1994). The line at that time was merely an administrative border between two administrative units under one authority, that of the British High Commissioner for Palestine and Transjordan. International recognition of this boundary rested upon a memorandum concerning the amendment of those paragraphs of the mandate that referred to Transjordan. The boundary was delineated in a general way on maps, but no attempt was made to survey the Dead Sea in order to determine the exact location of the median line of the water body.

In 1946, following the granting of independence to Jordan, the administrative boundary was now to be an international boundary but only a small section, near Akaba, was demarcated. The exact delineation of the boundary in the Dead Sea was not decided.

The establishment of the State of Israel and the armistice agreement between Israel and Transjordan placed a new line in the Dead Sea (Rosental, 1983). A line was drawn from a point on the shore of the lake, north of the oasis of Ein Gedi to the middle of the sea. From there it was drawn congruent with the former line to the south coast of the sea. By this, Transjordan acquired about three-quarters of the Dead Sea. Again the line was not the product of accurate survey measurement and was in effect simply copied from earlier maps.

The 1967 war created the 'Cease Fire Line' between Jordan and Israel, placing the line on the former mandatory boundary, again only delineated on maps without any survey. The future of a permanent, accurately surveyed boundary line between Israel and Jordan in the Dead Sea still waits for formal agreement in the wake of the Israeli–Jordanian peace talks.

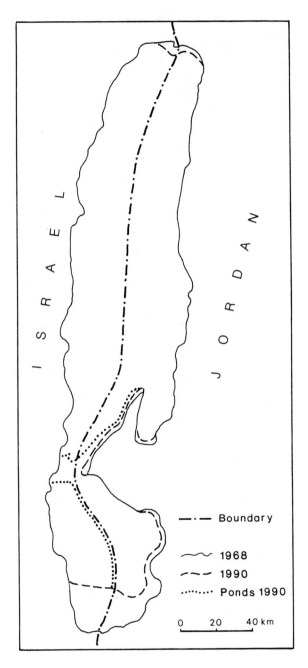

Figure 7.1 The Dead Sea 1968–90

Exploitation of the Dead Sea Mineral Resources

From the beginning of this century the huge potential mineral wealth of the Dead Sea was known. A licence for exploiting the Dead Sea mineral resources was granted by the British authorities only in 1929 to the Palestine Potash Company, founded by British and Jewish–Palestinian partners, its board including an Arab member (Bentwich, 1946). The company set up a factory at Kallia in 1931 at the northern end of the Dead Sea, on the Palestinian side of the lake and Transjordan had an equal share with British Palestine in the royalties. The extraordinary evaporation possibilities of the area, where the temperature rises to about 40°C in the summer, and an annual average rainfall of only 50mm, were used to concentrate the brines in evaporation pans. It was soon found that the terrain of the northern end of the Dead Sea was unsuitable for the construction of very large evaporation pans and in 1934 the company added auxiliary installations at Sedom, at the south-western end of the Dead Sea where more space was available. By 1947 the two plants were producing about 100,000 tons of potash and the bromide unit was producing about 1,000 tons per year. In the 1948 war the Kallia works were utterly destroyed by the Arab Legion and remained in Jordanian territory, unrepaired to this day. The Sedom works were enlarged by Israel, a bromide company was founded, and from 1955 both companies were integrated into the Dead Sea Works. Of the minerals contained in the water of the Dead Sea, potash (potassium chloride) and bromides are being won for industrial processes, and table salt is produced as a sideline (Orni and Efrat, 1971). Without going into details concerning the extraction of the salts from the Dead Sea waters, a crucial factor determining production levels is the area available for evaporation pans. From near shore pans, for example, about 188,000 tons of potash were produced in 1963–4. In 1963 works began on installation of new pans by building a dam about 11m high and 22km long along the Israel–Jordan border in the southern part of the Dead Sea. Many kilometres of small dams were built to protect the pans and to separate them from the open parts of the Dead Sea. The area of the pans is about 13,000ha (32,000 acres). As the Dead Sea receded from the pond areas, a 12km canal was built to ensure a reliable, steady flow of water into the pans area (Amiran and Karmon, 1964). Every year, 300 million m³ of Dead Sea water is pumped into the ponds where it evaporates using the heat of the sun. The network of ponds is one of the world's largest for the exploitation of solar energy. In 1955 the production of potash in Israel was about 15,000 tons while in 1993 it was 2,182,00 tons. Virtually all of it is used for fertilisers. Other products in 1993 included 57,800 tons of table salt, 47,500 tons of magnesium chloride chips (mainly as a de-icer for roads and for various industrial applications), 267,000 tons of industrial salt and 1,500 tons of bath salts. The 1993 bromide output was about 140,000 tons, supplying about one-third of world production. Total sales in 1993 were worth about US$700 million (Dead Sea, 1994). A magnesium metal plant, scheduled to be completed by the end of 1995, will initially produce 25,000 tons of magnesium and magnesium alloys a year.

The production of mineral resources by Jordan started more recently. The northern, original works in Kallia, were never rebuilt. Jordan started to produce potash separately only during the 1980s. The main obstacles were the capital needed and the rough hilly terrain in which transportation was difficult. Only after the construction of a totally new road between the Dead Sea and Akaba were the Jordanians able to use their part of the lake. In 1982 production was about 9,000 tons, but it rose in 1987 to about 660,000 tons while in 1992 the total production of potash in Jordan was about 1.1 million tons. The same procedure of evaporation of water from the Dead Sea in large ponds, is operated there. A Jordanian processing plant operates on the south-eastern side of the lake. As the water level falls, the Lisan peninsula and the large Israeli dam are blocking the southern part of the Dead Sea from the north, helping it to become a large evaporation pan. As with the Israeli works, water from the northern part is pumped into the large pans, to be evaporated there (Figure 7.2).

As things stand today, two totally separate establishments are working with the same procedures in the same area, producing the same products. Jordan has to send all its production to Akaba for export, while Israel sends some of its products to Eilat, nearby to Akaba via a road parallel to the Jordanian one. Another way of exporting the Israeli products is to transfer them to the Mediterranean ports of Ashdod and Haifa which the Jordanians cannot use. The only source of sweet water in this area is situated on the Jordanian side, in the Wadi Zarka springs, near Safi, while Israel has to bring fresh water overland from the north. Both countries have to build separate networks of dikes and ponds, pump the water from the northern part of the Dead Sea and send exports via their own transport systems. All of this is done some hundred metres apart, as a boundary separates these two countries which until recently were officially hostile to each other. Transboundary co-operation between the two countries could clearly benefit both of them.

As these lines are written the future of this area is not clear. The Arab Palestinians, demanding their independent state in the area of the former 'West Bank' would like to have a share of the Dead Sea area. They could possibly re-establish the works in Kallia, which might be in their area but the changes of water level might cause difficulties for the works there. Jordan and Israel would not like to have a 'third partner' in the Dead Sea and only future agreement can solve the problems of the small, but very important, Dead Sea.

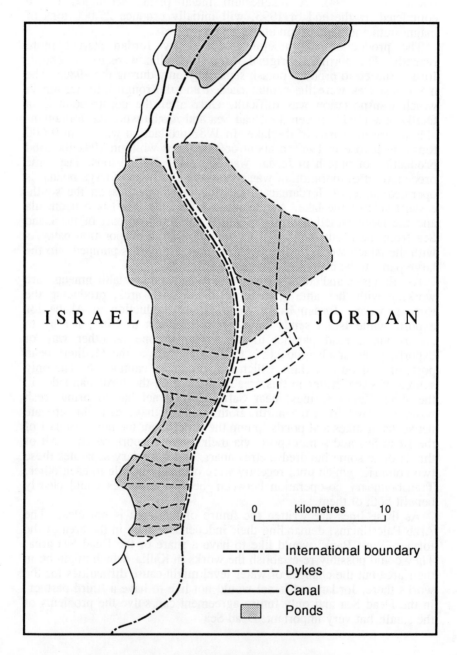

Figure 7.2 Dead Sea Works 1990

Bibliography

Amiran, D.H.K. and Karmon, Y. (1964) 'The expansion of the Dead Sea works', *Tijdschrift voor economische en sociale geographie* 55: 210–23.

Bentwich, N. (1946) *Palestine,* London: Ernest Benn.

Biger, G. (1994) 'The lacustrine and riverine boundaries of Israel', in C.H. Schofield and R.W. Schofield (eds) *The Middle East and North Africa: World Boundaries,* Vol.2, London: Routledge: 98–112.

Dead Sea (1994) *Managers Report for the Dead Sea Works to 31.12.1993,* April 1994, Dead Sea Works.

Karmon, Y. (1978) *Israel – Geography of the Land,* Tel Aviv: Yavne.

Klein, C. (1960) 'On the fluctuations of the level of the Dead Sea since the beginning of the 19th century', *Hydrological Paper* 7, Jerusalem: Water Commission Hydrogical Service, Ministry of Agriculture.

Nir, D. (1968) *Bibliography on the Dead Sea,* Jerusalem: Israel Academy of Sciences.

Orni, E. and Efrat, E. (1971) *Geography of Israel,* Jerusalem: Israel University Press.

Palestine (1922) *Official Gazette,* 1 September, Government of Palestine.

Rosental, Y. (1983) *Document on the Foreign Policy of Israel, December 1948 – July 1949,* Vol.3, Jerusalem.

Water

8

Shared Waters and International Law

Dante A. Caponera

The Concept of International, Shared or Transboundary Waters

The concept expressed by the words 'international', 'shared' or 'transboundary' water resources is synonymous. The expression may refer indifferently to atmospheric, surface or underground waters shared between two or more States. There are in the world more than 240 international river basins and an indeterminate number of aquifers whose waters are shared by two or more sovereign States. Any substantial interference by one country on the waters of such basins or aquifers may have effects – beneficial or detrimental – on the territory of another upstream or downstream State.

International law of water resources, as part of international law, regulates State relationships with respect to the utilisation of 'shared', 'common' or 'transboundary' water resources.

A river may be 'international' geographically and legally: geographically, if it flows through or between the territories of sovereign states; legally, if a State ceases to have all the powers over the waters of that river. Historically, an international river had to be navigable.

According to Article 38 of the Statute of the International Court of Justice (ICJ), which is competent to adjudicate disputes between sovereign States, the sources of international law are:

1 international conventional law, or the law of treaties;
2 international customary law, or State practice;
3 the general principles of law recognised by 'civilised nations';
4 judicial decisions, or international case law, and the teachings of the most qualified publicists as subsidiary sources.

INTERNATIONAL CONVENTIONS AND TREATIES

Where a treaty or treaties, whether multilateral or bilateral, are in existence, the provisions relating to water constitute the law applicable among the signatories. In earlier times, rivers were considered 'international' when 'navigable'; these rivers could be either *successive* or *contiguous*, depending on whether they crossed or separated two or more States. Major concerns were:

1 The delimitation of the boundary in the case of contiguous rivers. This could take place:

   at the banks, the water being *res comunis omnium*, ie, common to everybody;

   at one of the banks, in the case that the whole of the river belongs to one State;

   on the *median line*, ie, the imaginary line equidistant from either embankment, or

   on the *thalweg*, a German word meaning deepest navigable channel;

2 The principle of freedom of navigation on these rivers. A large number of bilateral treaties were signed concerning these questions.

The internationalisation of shared rivers and lakes for navigation purposes was initiated in 1815 at the Congress of Vienna when the Rhine Commission was established; successively, the Oder and Niemen, 1918, the Elbe, 1921, and the Weser, 1923, were declared international for the purpose of navigation. In 1856 the Treaty of Paris internationalised the Rhine and Danube rivers. The Act of Berlin of 1885 extended internationalisation to African rivers (Congo, Niger, Zambesi, etc). The Treaties of Versailles of 1919 and the 1921 Barcelona Convention finalised this process. Later, the development of hydropower led to the 1932 Geneva Convention relating to the development of hydropower affecting more than one State.

During the last 50 years, the development of international water uses for purposes other than navigation and hydropower generation and, in particular, for consumptive uses such as irrigation and water supply, has caused a number of other water treaties to be signed on several international or shared water resources.

These treaties are still limited in number, scope and regard, for instance, the Nile, Senegal, Gambia and Kagera rivers, as well as the Lake Chad in Africa; the Mekong, Indus, Kosi, and Ganges basins in Asia; the Rio Grande/Colorado, the boundary rivers between Canada and the United States and the Rio de la Plata in the Americas. A number of treaties have been entered into also in Europe. Among these, we may quote treaties concerning the Rhine and Danube rivers.

A number of potential or actual conflicts have emerged among States sharing international inland waters.

INTERNATIONAL CUSTOMARY LAW (OR STATE PRACTICE)

When there are no binding treaties, international customary law provides some important rules for the use of shared waters:

1 the duty to co-operate and to negotiate in good faith with a genuine intention of reaching an agreement;
2 the prohibition of management practices likely to cause substantial and lasting injury to other States, on the basis of the Latin principle *sic utere tuo ut alienum non laedas* (do not act in such a way as to cause injury to others);
3 the duty of prior consultation;
4 the principle of equitable utilisation of shared water resources. This is one of the key principles recognised by the international community.

GENERAL PRINCIPLES OF WATER LAW (DERIVING FROM LEGAL SYSTEMS)

Always in the case of the lack of written agreements, the general principles of water law, as expressed by the national legislation of different legal systems, apply. These include:

1 that the use of water resources by one country should not impair the rights and interests of other countries;
2 that the rights are not to be abused;
3 that co-basin States should promote good neighbourly relations; and
4 that the internal water laws of each basin State should be formulated and applied in such a way that they will not cause disputes.

INTERNATIONAL CASE LAW

The ICJ, some arbitral tribunals and decisions of inter-State courts in federal countries have also developed certain principles, usually limited to the resolution of specific disputes. These decisions are binding upon the states concerned. Some of these principles relate to 'equitable sharing' or 'equitable uses' or of 'equitable apportionment' of shared water resources.

THE DOCTRINAL BASIS

Earlier, the doctrinal basis included the legal theories:

1 of *absolute territorial sovereignty*, according to which a State has an absolute right to do as it pleases with the water in its territory. This doctrine, known as the 'Harmon doctrine', was introduced by the Attorney General of the United States in the late 19th century, in a dispute with Mexico concerning irrigation rights;

2 of *absolute territorial integrity*, according to which the riparians have an absolute right to the natural flow, unimpaired in quantity and in quality.

These two theories are no longer recognised in view of their extremism and their impracticability, ie, because they tend to protect the rights of one state only.

New theories include those of the 'community of interest' among riparian States and of 'limited territorial sovereignty' over shared water resources, in order to ensure each riparian a reasonable and equitable share in the use of the waters.

International Groundwater Law

International groundwater is underground water of interest to two or more States, either because it is situated in the territory of such States, or because, even if located entirely within the territory of only one State, it is connected to an aquifer or to a stream located in the territory of another State.

Activities carried out in the territory of one State may have negative repercussions within the territory of another State. For instance, the diversion of water of a surface stream recharging an underground aquifer situated in another State can cause the exhaustion of that aquifer or, vice versa, the overpumping of underground water recharging a surface watercourse flowing entirely within the territory of another State can reduce the flow of that watercourse.

SOURCES OF INTERNATIONAL GROUNDWATER LAW

The sources of international groundwater resources law are the same as those of international law (Article 38 of the Statutes of the ICJ).

Very few international conventions, generally particular, ie, regarding a specific case, refer to groundwater. As regards the second and the third sources, the same principles applying to international water resources in general are to be considered. Decisions by the ICJ and arbitral awards apparently have not been rendered in this field. Conversely, judicial decisions at the national level exist.

Attention should therefore be paid to the practice of federal countries in the solution of inter-State disputes. Three trends may be mentioned:

1 conclusion of inter-State agreements;
2 the exercise of a federal power of the States;
3 decisions of federal courts.

Recent Doctrine

Doctrine has evolved through the work of:

1 the Institute of International Law (1919 Madrid and 1961 Salzburg Declarations);
2 the 7th International Conference of American States (1933 Declaration of Montevideo);
3 the Inter-American Bar Association (1957 Declaration of Buenos Aires);
4 the Asian African Legal Consultative Committee (1964 New Delhi Declaration);
5 the work of the Council of Europe (1967 European Water Charter);
6 the International Law Association (the Helsinki Rules of 1966 and subsequent rules); and
7 the work of the AIDA, International Association for Water Law.

Finally, the International Law Commission of the United Nations has been requested and is currently proceeding to codify the rules concerning the use of non-navigational uses of international water courses.

Latest Trends and Guiding Principles

The academic community concerned with the development of international water resources law (Institute of International Law, International Law Association, AIDA, etc) have introduced the new concepts of:

1 international drainage basins or river systems as an aggregate of surface and groundwaters flowing into a common terminus;
2 the doctrine of equitable utilisation, according to which each basin or system State is entitled to a reasonable and equitable share, to be determined on a case-by-case basis according to relevant factors, in the beneficial uses of the shared water resources;
3 the consideration of the management of water resources as an integral part of rational management of all renewable natural resources.

These concepts are being elaborated by the International Law Commission of the United Nations.

Conclusion

The UN Water Conference of 1977 recommended that member States carry out integrated planning of their water resources, making sure that the users fully participate in this planning. The same Conference recommended that each country make the effort to bring about a genuine co-ordination among all institutions responsible for water, taking the drainage basin as the unit for rational management of water resources and their utilisation. The Conference also expressed the wish that governments and international organisations encourage the study of water law.

These recommendations have been confirmed in the course of the Conference on Water and the Environment, held at Dublin in 1992, and, finally, in Agenda 21, which was produced during the United Nations Conference on Environment and Development (UNCED), held in Rio de Janeiro the same year.

9

Sustainable Use of Shared Water Resources: the Need for a Paradigmatic Shift in International Watercourses Law

Ellen Hey

Introduction

The International Law Commission's (ILC's) fifth Special Rapporteur on the topic of the Law of the Non-Navigational Uses of International Watercourses, Robert Rosenstock, when comparing the draft articles adopted on first reading (UNGA A/46/405, hereinafter 'draft articles')[1] to the product of the United Nations Conference on Environment and Development (UNCED),[2] the Convention on the Protection and Use of Transboundary Watercourses and International Lakes and the Convention on Environmental Impact Assessment in a Transboundary Context reached the following conclusion: 'that nothing in these instruments requires fundamental change in the text of the draft as it stands after completion of the first reading' (Rosenstock, 1993: para. 4). In strict legal terms this conclusion is correct. The documents referred to do not require in law, explicitly[3] or implicitly,[4] that a set of articles be adopted with a different purport than the present draft articles.

However, on the basis of legal-policy considerations, I have come to the conclusion that fundamental changes are required in the draft articles, if these articles are to facilitate instead of hamper the implementation of Chapter 18 of Agenda 21. In the International Law Commission the view was also expressed that recent developments, including Chapter 18 of Agenda 21, require the reconsideration of the draft articles (ILC, 1993: para. 359). The changes which are required, I submit, would involve a paradigmatic shift of emphasis from the discretionary role of states to the functional role of states in international watercourses law. What is needed is a shift of emphasis from states being bound by international law only at their own discretion to states having the responsibility to develop and implement international law in order to further interests of humankind, ie, of individuals and collectivities of both present and future generations.[5]

The draft articles emphasise the discretionary role of states and could hamper, rather than facilitate, implementation of Chapter 18 of

Agenda 21. This is especially true in relation to three objectives which have a prominent place in Chapter 18. These objectives are:

1 securing access to safe and sufficient water-supplies, or at least water-supplies to meet the basic drinking and food-growing requirements, for all peoples;
2 enhancing public participation and management at the lowest appropriate level (subsidiarity); and
3 attaining integrated development and management of water resources.

Firstly, Chapter 18 reasserts the premise which was commonly agreed at the 1977 United Nations Water Conference that 'all peoples, whatever their stage of development and their social and economic conditions, have the right to have access to drinking water in quantities and of a quality equal to their basic needs' and provides that 'safe water-supplies and environmental sanitation are vital for protecting the environment, improving health and alleviating poverty' as well as 'crucial to many traditional and cultural activities' (Agenda 21: 18.47).[6] Secondly, Chapter 18, in numerous places, identifies public participation and subsidiarity as prerequisites for attaining the sustainable use of water resources.[7] Thirdly, Chapter 18 provides that integrated water resources planning, or development, and management 'must cover all types of interrelated freshwater bodies, including both surface and groundwater, and duly consider water quantity and quality aspects' (Agenda 21: 18.3) and that 'integrated water resources management... should be carried out at the level of the catchment basin or sub-basin' (Agenda 21: 18.9). These objectives emphasise the functional role of states. Attaining each of them will require a fundamental modification of the prevailing theory of state sovereignty as reflected in the draft articles.

The Functional Versus the Discretionary Role of States

If the functional role of states is taken as a point of departure (Dupuy, 1991: 201–4), states should facilitate the establishment of mechanisms which will enable all peoples to have access to safe and sufficient water-supplies, public participation and subsidiarity, and integrated development and management to be realised. In that case, international multilateral law on water resources should address both certain minimum requirements for the water management policies of individual states and minimum requirements for any co-operative mechanisms to be adopted by states.

Ensuring that all peoples have access to safe and sufficient water-supplies entails the development of mechanisms which recognise that states owe a minimum standard of care towards their nationals and residents. Public participation and subsidiarity require enhanced transparency of policies regarding water resources, devolvement of responsibilities for water management on local governments and other local entities, and the development of mechanisms which enable the public and local entities to participate in the formulation and implementation of policies regarding water resources. Attaining integrated development and management requires the establishment of mechanisms whose geographical scope of competence transcends political boundaries, including international boundaries, and whose material scope of competence entitles them to link water policies to other related policies. In the case of shared water resources, the establishment and implementation of such mechanisms will require substantial co-operation among states.

International law can facilitate co-operation among states by at least clearly defining the minimum duties resting upon states individually and jointly. However, the prevailing theory of sovereignty reflected in international law emphasises the discretionary powers of states (Wildhaber, 1986: 425–52). It results in a limited capacity of international law to impose an obligation on a state without its consent and a lack of position for actors other than states in international law. As a result the theory of states as having functional powers for purposes of furthering the interests of individuals and collectives is often disregarded (Johnston, 1988: 3–60). The emphasis is on the state as a subject of international law, instead of on the state as subject to international law. The work of the International Law Commission on the non-navigational uses of international watercourses is no exception. It does not impose upon states minimum requirements for the management of water resources, and, in the case of shared water resources, it leaves states a wide margin of discretion in determining whether they establish co-operative mechanisms, as well as in determining the nature of any co-operative mechanisms which they establish.

This paper analyses the dichotomy between, on the one hand, the work of the International Law Commission on the non-navigational uses of international watercourses,[8] which emphasises the discretionary powers of watercourse states,[9] and, on the other hand, providing access for all peoples to safe and sufficient water-supplies, public participation and subsidiarity, and integrated development and management, as included in Agenda 21 – which emphasises the functional powers of states. It means that the analysis will concentrate on the role of general principles and procedures of international water resources law, instead of on the specific measures (eg, emission limits, water quantity regulations, water quality standards) required for water management. In order to attain the objectives of Chapter 18 specific measures of course are essential. However, these rules, in the case of international watercourses, are best developed through co-operation among watercourse states and in the case of non-international watercourses, by individual states.

In this paper the following questions will be addressed. To what extent do the draft articles offer instruments for facilitating access for all peoples to safe and sufficient water-supplies? To what extent do the draft articles provide instruments for enhancing public participation and subsidiarity in the management of shared water resources? To what extent do the draft articles offer instruments for ensuring integrated development and management of shared water resources? The overall conclusion will be that the draft articles, instead of facilitating the attainment of these three objectives, might hamper their attainment. As a result, the question arises as to the role of international law at the multilateral level in the case of watercourses law.[10] This question will be addressed in the last section of this paper.

Securing Access for All Peoples to Safe and Sufficient Water-Supplies

> One in three people in the developing world still lacks these two basic requirements [ie, safe drinking-water and sanitation, E.H.] for health and dignity (Agenda 21: 18.47).

This quotation from Chapter 18 illustrates that all peoples are, in practice, far from having access to safe and sufficient water-supplies. The fact that international drainage basins constitute some 47% of the earth's land area, excluding Antarctica, and that for Africa and Latin America this percentage amounts to almost 60% (Biswas, 1991: 20, cited in McCaffrey, 1992–3: 17), brings home the point that securing access to safe and sufficient water-supplies in many cases will involve the waters of shared water resources.

In international law, the right of all peoples to access to safe and sufficient water-supplies, or at least to water-supplies to meet their basic drinking and food-growing requirements, has not attained the status of a human right.[11] Incorporating the right of all peoples to access to safe and sufficient water-supplies into international law would involve recognising that states are under obligation to the people living within their jurisdiction to secure such access. Furthermore, in the case of international watercourses it would involve recognising that, as a minimum requirement, watercourse states have a duty not to frustrate this right in their mutual relationships. At a higher level of abstraction, it means, in line with developments in human rights law, that the attainment of these standards becomes a legitimate concern of international law. Clearly, in this context, the functional role of states would prevail over their discretionary role.

Instituting the right of all peoples to safe and sufficient water-supplies requires the development of both substantive and procedural law. The former aspect will be addressed in this section; the latter aspect in the next section. Admittedly, it is extremely difficult to precisely define what a safe and sufficient water-supply is in quantitative terms. However, Chapter 18 illustrates that governments, at the policy level, have been able to agree on certain limited quantified minimum goals.[12] I suggest that such quantifications, at the multilateral level, should have the role of policy guidelines and, at least, at this stage, should not be incorporated into multilateral legally binding texts. This is especially because, beyond the minimum amount of water that each individual requires to live, what is an adequate supply of water depends on the specific circumstances of the availability of water. International law, in so far as the substantive aspect is concerned, should formulate the basic right to access to safe and sufficient water-supplies.

Given that a human right to access to safe and sufficient water-supplies is at the most an emerging right and that the object of the International Law Commission clearly has not been to draft such a human right, one is unlikely to find it among the draft articles. In fact, the draft articles only address watercourse states in their mutual relationships and not the relationship between a watercourse state, or states, and the persons living within its, or their, jurisdiction.[13]

The draft articles, however, do address factors relevant to equitable and reasonable utilisation (UNGA A/46/405: Article 6) and the relationship between uses (UNGA A/46/405: Article 10). Short of drafting a human right to safe and sufficient water-supplies, these provisions could have been used to determine that access to safe and sufficient water-supplies is a use which has priority over other uses.[14] This route was not followed. Instead, Article 6 lists a set of non-prioritised factors to be taken into account for purposes of determining equitable and reasonable utilisation. These factors do not include an explicit reference to safe and sufficient water-supplies, or similar wording. However, according to the commentary on Article 10(2), requirements of vital human needs are to be understood as being included in Article 6(1)(b) – 'the social and economic needs of the watercourse States concerned' (ILC, 1991: 180). Assuming this to be the case, the object of Article 6 seems to be to leave it to the discretion of watercourse states to weigh vital human needs against other social and economic requirements, as well as other factors listed in Article 6.

Article 10 half-heartedly concedes some limited priority to the requirements of vital human needs. Article 10(2) provides as follows:

> In the event of a conflict between uses of an international watercourse, it shall be resolved with reference to the principles and factors set out in Articles 5 to 7, with special regard being given to the requirements of vital human needs.

At first sight and on its own this provision seems to render a priority position for the requirements of vital human needs, which as the commentary clarifies includes 'providing sufficient water to sustain human life, including both drinking water and water required for the production of food in order to prevent starvation' (ILC, 1991: 180). Upon reading Article 10(2) together with Article 10(1) and the commentary to the two provisions it becomes clear however, that in principle no priority position is given to water requirements of vital human needs. Article 10(1) provides that 'in the absence of agreement or custom to the contrary, no use of an international watercourse enjoys inherent priority over other uses', thereby clarifying:

1 that in case there is no agreement or custom between watercourse states all uses are equally important; and
2 that watercourse states are free to give whatever use they wish priority through agreement or custom.[15]

Requirements of vital human needs would thus only prevail in case of conflict among uses and in the absence of an agreement or custom providing some priority of uses.

In addition to the above, the threshold included in Article 10(2) – water for the 'requirements of vital human needs' or, as provided in the commentary, water 'to sustain human life' and 'to prevent starvation' – in many cases will not be sufficient to meet the requirement that safe and sufficient water-supplies be accessible for all peoples. That is, of course, unless one holds that sustaining human life and survival is all that people are entitled to.

In conclusion, the draft articles, by not qualifying safe and sufficient water-supplies as a priority use provide watercourse states with legal arguments supporting the contention that other uses may be given priority and may infringe upon that use. As a result, the draft articles may hamper, rather than facilitate, the implementation of those parts of Chapter 18 which seek to further access of all peoples to safe and sufficient water-supplies. The argument that the draft articles only deal with international watercourses, and not non-international watercourses, does not justify the approach reflected in the draft articles. For if states are to have a responsibility in securing access to safe and sufficient water-supplies for all peoples within their jurisdiction, attaining equitable utilisation for all watercourse states on an international watercourse would mean, at least, that this use should be protected in their mutual relations. This is regardless of whether access to safe and sufficient water-supplies is to be considered a human right. Furthermore, adopting such an approach would support the contention in Principle 1 of the Rio Declaration that 'human beings are the centre of concerns for sustainable development'.

Public Participation and Subsidiarity and International Water Resources Law

Chapter 18 of Agenda 21 identifies full public participation, including that of women, youths, indigenous people, local communities, and delegation of water resources management to the lowest appropriate level (subsidiarity), as keys to attaining the sustainable use of water resources.[16] Enhancing public participation implies that public participatory techniques need to be developed and implemented.[17] Such techniques would include enhanced transparency of government policies, the possibility for the public to have their opinions heard and taken into account in the formulation and implementation of policy regarding a water resource, and the possibility for individuals and collectivities to recover any damages suffered. It involves providing all peoples with the necessary instruments to secure access to safe and sufficient water-supplies. Enhancing subsidiarity implies that local government institutions and community institutions need to be strengthened and empowered.[18]

In the case of international watercourses, the attainment of the above mentioned aims would entail the development of transparent procedures enabling transnational co-operation. For, if responsibilities are devolved on the lowest appropriate level of government or on communities, such entities on either side of an international boundary are likely to have a need for intensive contact. International watercourse law could play an important role in this process by providing the minimum requirements to be met by states involved in establishing co-operative arrangements and by indicating the role these other entities may have in international watercourse management. The draft articles, however, provide no incentives, let alone obligations, for the development of participatory mechanisms or for transnational forms of co-operation.

With the exception of one provision, the draft articles do not refer to the individuals and collectivies in whose interest, ultimately, the management of international watercourses takes place. As also emphasised in the previous section of this paper, the draft articles address watercourse states in their relationship to other watercourse states and do not make the interests of individuals or collectives the object of their concern. In addition, even the one article, Article 32, on non-discrimination, possesses a fundamental problem.

Article 32 provides as follows:

> Watercourse States shall not discriminate on the basis of nationality or residence in granting access to judicial and other procedures, in accordance with their legal system, to any natural or judicial person who has suffered appreciable harm as a result of an activity related to an international watercourse or is exposed to a threat thereof.[19]

The article clearly does not impose upon states a duty to develop adequate administrative and judicial procedures to secure public participation in the formulation and implementation of policy and for obtaining redress of damages suffered. Instead, the object of the article is to avoid discrimination between persons residing in the state where the source, or likely source, of the harm is located and persons residing in the state where harm is suffered or may be suffered, as well as between nationals and non-nationals residing in the state where the source of harm is located. Thus, if a watercourse state does not provide adequate procedures to protect the interests of its own nationals, that same inadequate level of protection will be accorded to nationals and residents of other watercourse states as well as to its residents.

Article 32 reflects the barest minimum that may be expected in the form of public participation in the management of international watercourses.[20] More substantive rules requiring that eg, access to information, public hearings, and prompt and adequate recourse to administrative and judicial procedures be made available in the transnational context would be required, if an effective level of public participation is to be attained.[21] The draft articles are thus unlikely to facilitate the goals of public participation and subsidiarity contained in Chapter 18 and in other chapters[22] of Agenda 21. They instead emphasise the discretionary powers of states and deny the functional role of states in securing proper management of a watercourse in the interests of the individuals and collectives who depend on that watercourse.

In the context of the above criticism, the set of articles on implementation proposed by the fourth Special Rapporteur on the topic, Stephen McCaffrey (1990: 57–65), are relevant. The intention of the Special Rapporteur was to incorporate these provisions in an Annex to the draft articles with the object of facilitating the implementation of the draft articles. These provisions contained several 'overarching principles' (McCaffrey, 1990: para. 37) which would have provided a basis for participation by individuals and collectivities. The provisions included the duty not to discriminate between adverse effects in another watercourse state and adverse effects in the state where the activities are, or may be, taking place (McCaffrey, 1990: Article 2); the requirement that prompt and adequate recourse be available to natural and judicial persons suffering appreciable harm in a watercourse state other than the state where the activities are taking place (McCaffrey, 1990: Article 3(1)); that watercourse states co-operate in the implementation of existing international law and towards the further development of international law on responsibility and liability (McCaffrey, 1990: Article 3(2)); the right of equal access to judicial and administrative procedures for the redress and prevention of transboundary harm (McCaffrey, 1990: Article 4); the duty for watercourse states to take appropriate measures to provide information to persons in other watercourse states who are exposed to significant risk of appreciable harm and to designate authorities which shall receive and disseminate this information (McCaffrey, 1990: Article 5). A bi-annual Conference of Parties would take palce which would review implementation of the articles and which, unless one-third of the Parties object, would be open to observers from

(a) international agencies or bodies, either governmental or non-governmental, and national governmental agencies and bodies; and

(b) national non-governmental agencies or bodies which have been approved for this purpose by the State in which they are located (McCaffrey, 1990: Article 7).

All that remains of what was a substantial step in the direction of enabling public participation is Article 32 referred to above. The provisions, proposed by McCaffrey, would have gone a considerable way towards emphasising that states have functions to fulfil towards individuals and collectivities.

Integrated Water Resources Development and Management and International Watercourses Law

Attaining the objectives and implementing the activities contained in Chapter 18, and in particular Part A on integrated water resources development and management, in fact requires that the geographical extent of the competence of management bodies is not defined by political boundaries. Instead the natural boundaries and sub-divisions of the water-system should be used (Agenda 21: 18.9). As mentioned above, in the case of international water resources, this would entail the establishment of management bodies whose geographic scope of competence transcends international boundaries.[23] As a result, international, or transnational co-operation becomes imperative. States, if regarded as functional entities which form part of the international community, have a responsibility to establish, at least, the framework within which such co-operation is to take place. Chapter 18 of Agenda 21, however, only half-heartedly concedes this point. Paragraph 18.4, for example, provides that:

Transboundary water resources and their use are of great importance to riparian States. In this connection, *co-operation among those States may be desirable* in conformity with existing agreements and/or other relevant arrangements, taking into account the interests of all riparian States. [emphasis added by E.H.]

Furthermore in those cases where international co-operation is mentioned as a route to be pursued, the advice is qualified by the term 'where' or 'as appropriate'.[24]

A similar reluctance is found in the work of the International Law Commission. While the commentary to the draft articles on numerous occasions refers to the need for co-operation among, and the expediency of joint action by, watercourse states,[25] the articles themselves, as will be illustrated below, do not to impose legally binding obligations to this effect.

Although Article 8[26] formulates a duty to co-operate, it entails a duty for watercourse states to negotiate in good faith and not a duty to take collective action.[27] This approach, if accompanied by specific minimum requirements that states must meet individually and jointly, can be regarded as a practical approach in a politically divided world. However, the draft articles do not provide such requirements.[28] It is thus that two further questions arise:

1 what other obligations to undertake collective action do the draft articles entail; and
2 what does the object of the duty to negotiate in good faith – optimum utilisation – entail?

The following mechanisms involving some form of collective action are referred to in the draft articles: watercourse agreements (UNGA A/46/405: Article 3); joint management mechanisms (Article 26); harmonisation of policies for purposes of preventing pollution (Article 21(2)); the development of a common list of substances the inputs of which should be prohibited, limited, investigated or monitored (Article 21(3)); exchange of data and information on the status of the watercourse (Article 9); exchange of information and consultation on the possible effects of planned measures (Article 11); and notification and consultation on planned measures with possible adverse effects (Article 12–9). It is beyond doubt that each of these mechanisms, as such, would facilitate integrated development and management of an international watercourse. However, this is not the issue at stake. Rather, the issue at stake here is whether the relevant provisions impose obligations on states or whether they merely indicate desirable behaviour and, in case obligations are imposed, whether these have been sufficiently developed to be able to further integrated development and management. If this standard is applied, each of the mechanisms mentioned is deficient.

THE DUTY TO NEGOTIATE IN GOOD FAITH

The draft articles do not require that states adopt watercourse agreements; joint management mechanisms; and lists of substances whose input into a watercourse are to be prohibited, limited, investigated or monitored. The duty imposed instead is that states, at the request of any one of the watercourse states, negotiate in good faith or consult with a view to adopting such mechanisms. This leaves a large measure of discretion to states as to whether or not they engage in negotiations and whether they actually adopt such mechanisms. In practice this also means that states are not under the obligation to establish a mechanism by way of which they jointly assess the effects of uses and the combined effects of different uses. Moreover, Article 26, on joint management mechanisms, does not require that a holistic ecosystem approach be adopted, instead it only refers to the watercourse as such.[29]

Furthermore, Article 3, on watercourse agreements, does not refer to the need, let alone require, that watercourse states adopt an agreement which covers the whole of the international watercourse in question. Provided the agreement does not 'adversely affect to an appreciable extent', or as proposed by the present Special Rapporteur 'adversely affect to a *significant* level' (emphasis in the original text) (Rosenstock, 1993: paras. 12–3),[30] the uses of third watercourse states, other watercourse states may adopt agreements for a part of the watercourse, or for a particular project, programme or use. The possibility of adopting subsidiary agreements to an overall framework agreement covering the whole of the international watercourse in question is essential for practical purposes. However if integrated development and management is to be pursued, the obligation to conclude an agreement covering the full extent of the watercourse would be desirable. Furthermore, attaining integrated development and management would seem to require that inter-state relations with respect to a particular watercourse be based on the assumption that all watercourse agreements may affect the uses of all other watercourse states and that all watercourse states, in principle, should be entitled to participate in the negotiation of agreements related to such uses and become parties to the agreements. Alternatively, third watercourse states, at least, should be entitled to be informed of the negotiations and participate therein as observers, if they so wish. However, as Article 4(2) of the draft articles illustrates, a third watercourse state is entitled to participate in such negotiations and agreements only if its use may be affected to an appreciable extent by the agreement.[31] As is evidenced by the commentary to Article 4, it is up to the third watercourse state in question to show that its use may be so affected by the agreement.[32] Whether third watercourse states are to be informed of negotiations depends on the interpretation given to the term 'measures' in Article 11. While the commentary suggests that a broad interpretation should be given to the term (ILC, 1988), it remains unclear whether negotiations about possible measures come within these terms.

Another lacuna in the provisions on watercourse agreements, joint management mechanisms and lists of substances is that they do not specify what is to occur if consensus is not reached during the envisaged negotiations or consultations. The draft articles do not contain a reference to third party involvement at this stage of the process. The draft articles, in fact, do not contain any references to dispute settlement mechanisms.[33] Although the former Special Rapporteur submitted draft articles on dispute settlement, these were never considered by the International Law Commission, due to lack of time (McCaffrey, 1990: 66–79). The present Special Rapporteur also found that the inclusion of fact-finding and dispute settlement provisions in the draft articles would be an important contribution for the International Law Commission to make (Rosenstock, 1993: para. 8). The reactions in the Commission, however, were mixed (ILC, 1993: paras. 351–7). It thus remains to be seen if and how the Commission will deal with the subject of dispute avoidance and settlement.

NON-SPECIFIC DUTIES AND NO CONSEQUENCES IN CASE OF NON-COMPLIANCE

The draft articles impose three clear obligations on watercourse states to undertake collective action involving all watercourse states.[34] These are the duty to exchange data and information on the condition of the watercourse, the duty to exchange information and consult on planned measures and the duty to harmonise pollution prevention policies.

None of these mechanisms, however, are further developed by the draft articles. It is not specified, for example, what information is to be exchanged and what the harmonisation of pollution prevention policies entails. In addition, each of the provisions has certain weaknesses which make them of limited value for purposes of facilitating integrated development and management.

Article 9[35] requires the regular exchange of available technical data and information related to the hydrological, meteorological, hydrogeological and ecological nature and forecasts of the watercourse. It does not require, however, that watercourse states collect data, nor that data be processed. In addition, no consequences are attributed to non-compliance with the obligation to exchange information.

Article 11[36] requires the exchange of information and consultation on the possible effects of planned measures on the condition of the watercourse. The strength of this article is that it requires that *all* possible effects of *all* planned measures are to be the subject of the exchange of information and consultation among all watercourse states. Through such consultations the assessment of possible effects of planned measures can become a joint effort of all watercourse states. This would indeed provide an effective mechanism for furthering integrated development and management. However, in view of the inclusion of provisions on notification and consultation on planned measures with possible adverse effects – a limited category of planned measures – which do impose, albeit deficiently, certain duties upon states, it must be assumed that one may not lightly conclude that specific duties, such as the duty to conduct joint assessments of planned measures, ensue from Article 11. Furthermore, as is the case with Article 9, the draft articles do not attribute any consequences to non-compliance with the obligations contained in Article 11.

The fact that the draft articles do not attribute any consequences to non-compliance with Articles 9 and 11 is all the more regrettable as these articles would secure a basis – information – from which to develop an integrated development and management policy for a watercourse. In addition, the information exchanged on the basis of these articles, within the framework of the draft articles, presumably would be an important element in triggering a request by a watercourse state for the negotiation of a watercourse agreement, a joint management mechanism, and a list of substances whose inputs are to be prohibited, limited, investigated or monitored; as well as a request to be notified, envisaged in Article 18.

The obligation to harmonise environmental protection policies, although vague in the sense that the exact purport of the obligation to harmonise policies remains unclear, nevertheless clarifies that having separate national environmental policies is not enough for attaining adequate protection of an international watercourse. It imposes a duty to engage in some form of co-operation in order to bring the different policies in tune with one another. In so far as integrated development and management are concerned, the article, however, remains deficient. Firstly, the draft articles do not attribute any consequences to non-compliance. Secondly, the article only concerns pollution prevention and not other uses of a watercourse. The latter would need to be considered if integrated development and management are to become a fact.

A NOTIFICATION AND CONSULTATION PROCEDURE WHICH EMPHASISES DISCRETION

Articles 12–9 of the draft articles contained a notification and consultation procedure applicable to planned measures which may have an appreciable adverse or significant adverse effect for other watercourse states. The procedure envisaged is to take place, not between all watercourse states, but between the state planning the measure and other watercourse states which may be adversely affected by the measure. The main aim of the procedure, as envisaged in the draft articles, was not to further integrated management, optimum utilisation or equitable and reasonable use, but rather to facilitate the implementation of the duty not to cause appreciable harm contained in Article 7 of the draft articles.[37] However the proposal put forward by the present Special Rapporteur, with respect to Article 7, might affect the aim of the notification and consultation procedure.[38] This proposal received a mixed reaction in the International Law Commission (ILC, 1993: paras. 396–404 and 410–1). However, if they were to be accepted they would make equitable and reasonable use the threshold for determining state responsibility, except in the case of pollution where appreciable or significant harm[39] would remain the applicable threshold. It would seem logical that these changes, if adopted, would also be reflected in envisaged notification and consultation procedure making equitable and reasonable use the aim of the consultation procedures. Such an amendment, in my view, would bring the consultation procedure a step in the direction of facilitating integrated development and management because it would require the weighting of different uses during consultation.

Other drawbacks of the procedure as contained in the draft articles, are as follows:[40] it is left to the notifying state to assess whether there is likely to be an appreciable or significant adverse effect and which other watercourse states may be among those so affected and thus need to be notified; that the notifying state has the obligation to submit only 'available' technical data and information, instead of relevant data and information, eg, an environmental impact assessment; that the procedure does not apply to adverse effects on the watercourse as such but only to adverse effects on other watercourse states; that no legal consequences follow from a failure of the notified state to reply to the notification; and that a state which wishes to be notified has to show that it has 'serious reason to believe' that the planned measure may have an appreciable or significant effect upon it. These drawbacks mean that the notification and consultation procedure is not a mechanism which, through the joint assessment of planned measures, would further integrated development and management. It is instead a procedure which seeks to leave as much as possible to the discretion of individual states, both the notifying and the notified state. The absence of dispute settlement provisions underscores this appraisal.

OPTIMUM UTILISATION, A GOAL TO BE PURSUED WITHOUT CONCOMITANT DUTIES

As stated above, the object of the envisaged co-operation among watercourse states, according to Article 8, is the optimum utilisation of the international watercourse in question. In light of the lack of specific legal obligations following from the duty to co-operate as such, the question arises whether the envisaged goal adds any new elements which might strengthen that duty.

At the onset it needs to be stressed that the attainment of optimum utilisation is not an obligation resting upon watercourse states, but that it is a goal to be pursued by watercourse states. In other words, it is not an obligation which a watercourse state, or watercourse states jointly, owes or owe to the international community or to the members of that community, ie, it is not an obligation *erga omnes*.

Leaving aside the question as to the desirability and status of obligations *erga omnes* in international law,[41] it is a fact that obligations which seek to protect interests which extend beyond those of the immediate states concerned (obligations *erga omnes*) and which are dependent for their realisation on co-operation with other states have been incorporated in international law. Examples of such obligations include the duty of coastal states to secure the conservation and optimum utilisation of transboundary and inter-dependent stocks located in the exclusive economic zones of two or more states,[42] as well as the obligation of states to protect and preserve the marine environment (UNCLOS: Article 192). Optimum utilisation as contained in the draft articles, being a goal to be pursued by watercourse states instead of an obligation resting upon watercourse states, would seem to belong to a different category. The inclusion of the word 'adjust' in Article 3 of the draft articles also suggests that the draft articles contain only obligations which watercourse states owe each other, and which they may amend through agreement among themselves.[43]

What then is the significance of the goal of optimum utilisation as contained in the draft articles? The draft articles link optimal utilisation to the doctrine of equitable utilisation. Article 5(1)[44] expresses this link as follows:

> Watercourse States shall in their respective territories utilise an international watercourse in an equitable and reasonable manner. In particular, an international watercourse shall be used and developed by watercourse States with a view to attaining optimal utilisation thereof and benefits therefrom consistent with adequate protection of the watercourse.

Equitable utilisation entails 'both the right to utilise an international watercourse in an equitable manner, and the obligation not to exceed its right to equitable utilisation' within its own territory (ILC, 1987: 70). It thus encompasses a right and a duty which each watercourse state is entitled to and must observe within its own territory. What constitutes equitable utilisation in a given case, of course, depends on specific circumstances and requires the taking into account of all relevant factors, including those listed in Article 6 (ILC, 1987: 72–3). Ultimately, it involves balancing the different rights and interests of watercourse states. It is this balancing of interests which, on the basis of the commentary to Article 5(1), seems to form the essence of optimum utilisation.

The commentary to Article 5(1) provides that the implication of optimum utilisation is that of 'attaining maximum benefits for all watercourse States, and achieving the greatest possible satisfaction of all needs, while minimising the detriment to, or unmet needs of each' (ILC, 1987: 70). In addition, optimum utilisation is not to be 'pursued blindly but must be consistent with adequate protection' (ILC, 1987: 71). Obviously, from a practical point of view, these goals, given the intense use of most international watercourses, cannot be attained without some form of co-operation among watercourse states.

Article 5(2) also links the duty to attain optimum utilisation to the duty to co-operate. The last phrase of Article 5(2), however, provides that such co-operation shall take place 'as provided in the present articles' and thereby weakens the legal significance of this link. This phrase, as also emphasised in the commentary to Article 5(2), refers to Article 8 (ILC, 1987: 72). We have thus come full circle: back to the obligation to negotiate in good faith.

In conclusion, the draft articles express the desirability of watercourse states co-operating in the use of an international watercourse with the object of attaining the optimum utilisation of the watercourse in question. They, however, do not impose on watercourse states a concomitant duty to use their functional powers to assure the attainment of this goal. Given the fact that some members of the Commission referred to the need to incorporate into the draft articles the concept of sustainable development and the so-called holistic approach to protection of the environment, integrating economic and social conditions with environmental issues (ILC, 1993: paras. 359 and 388), the present Special Rapporteur may yet develop provisions which will facilitate integrated management and development.

An Evaluation

The dichotomy described in this paper raises the question as to the role of international law at the multilateral level in the case of watercourses law. Firstly, it is clear from the mandate, given to the International Law Commission by the General Assembly in 1970, that it was not the intention that the Commission concern itself with watercourses law in general but rather with international watercourses law. Secondly, the 'framework approach' as applied by the International Law Commission raises questions as to the normative character of the result of the work of the Commission on international watercourses law. Both elements are exponents of the theory of sovereignty which emphasises the discretionary role of states.

The mandate of the International Law Commission is 'to take up the study of the law of the non-navigational uses of international watercourses with a view to its progressive development and codification' (GAOR, 1970), thus limiting the work of the Commission to international watercourses. Although that approach might have been warranted in 1970, today it no longer is. The issues with which international law may legitimately concern itself within a state's territory have expanded, especially where the minimum rights of the peoples living within that territory are concerned and where the interests of the international community as a whole are concerned. An example of the first type of concern is of course human rights law and includes the right to life as well as certain procedural rights to which all human beings should be entitled if their rights are or may be encroached upon. Examples of the latter type of concern are the conservation of biodiversity and the protection of the environment. Both types of concerns are relevant in case of watercourses in general and provide a justification for amending the mandate of the International Law Commission so that the Commission will be able to include minimum standards within the draft articles, minimum standards applicable to both international and non-international watercourses.

The framework approach was described, in 1980, as entailing the following: the preparation of a set of draft articles that would contain 'basic rules applicable to all international watercourse systems' and which would be 'complemented by other agreements which, when the States concerned choose to conclude them, will enable States of a particular watercourse system to establish more detailed arrangements and obligations governing its use' (ILC, 1980: para. 95). So far the understanding of the framework approach seems to accord with what is generally understood by this approach (Handl, 1990: 5–7). However, the International Law Commission went on to explain that it felt that:

> what was needed was a set of draft articles that would lay down principles regarding the non-navigational uses of international watercourses in terms sufficiently broad to be applied to all international watercourse systems, while at the same time providing the means by which the articles could be applied or modified to take into account the singular nature of an international watercourse system and varying needs of the States in whose territory part of such a system were situated (ILC, 1980: para. 95).

It is this latter part of the understanding of the framework approach, and especially the word 'modified', which gives rise to questions as to the normative status of the draft articles. The term 'adjust' in Article 3 of the draft articles underscores this concern.[45]

Is the understanding of the framework approach and its reflection in Article 3, to be taken to mean that the articles, even if included in a multilateral treaty, will not be legally binding upon the states party to that treaty, if watercourse states of a particular watercourse agree to deviate therefrom? (Bourne, 1992: 65–6). For example, will the states party to such a multilateral treaty, by agreement among themselves, be free not to implement the limited public participation referred to in Article 32 and will they not be bound to protect and preserve the ecosystem of an international watercourse, as provided in Article 20 of the draft articles? If this is the intention of the draft articles, then the discussion conducted in the Commission as to the eventual legal status of the articles is a rather theoretical one. For, whatever the legal status of the articles, they could be altered by states through agreement among themselves.

The alternative is that if the approach adopted is to be understood as an attempt of the Commission to adopt a dynamic and flexible approach to international law making, then other essential elements of that approach, such as flexible procedures for review and dispute avoidance procedures, should be included in the text.[46] Although the latter approach inevitably leads to 'a significant degree of indeterminacy of the normative landscape' (Handl, 1990: 6), its intention is not to create treaties which are devoid of normative character. The intention rather is to create continuous inter-action between developments in technology, policy and law (Gehring, 1990: 35–56). Flexible procedures for review and dispute avoidance seek to secure such inter-action and mitigate the drawbacks of the indeterminacy of the normative landscape. If this is what the International Law Commission intended to embark on when it adopted its framework approach, the Commission should reconsider its assessment of whether Agenda 21, and especially Chapter 18 thereof, does not warrant a fundamental reconsideration of the draft articles as adopted at first reading. The progressive development of international law as reflected in the general mandate of the Commission and in its particular mandate with respect to international watercourses would seem to warrant such a reassessment.

The considerations presented in this section of the paper would entail a thorough revision of the draft articles and would require the International Law Commission to address the question of the relationship between legally non-binding texts and legally binding text. From a legal-policy point of view, such a revision is desirable both if the work of the Commission on the international law on watercourses is to make a positive difference to the implementation of Chapter 18 of Agenda 21, and if the International Law Commission is to play a significant role in the development of a body of international law which is to further sustainable development' (Caron, 1992: 269–71). The result of the work of the International Law Commission on watercourses may prove to be a test case for determining whether the Commission will play a role in the development of international law for furthering sustainable development or whether this will take place through other forums. The development of effective international law for furthering sustainable development will certainly require a paradigmatic shift of emphasis from the discretionary role of states to the functional role of states.

Notes

1   For a general overview of the draft articles see McCaffrey, 1992: 17–29.
2   For the texts of the Rio Declaration and Agenda 21 see United Nations Publication, Sales No. E.93.I.11.

3   The documents do not contain an explicit requirement that states develop international legally binding obligations which enable the implementation of the goals expressed in these documents.

4   The documents do not impose legally binding obligations on states which can only be implemented through the adoption of legally binding obligations of a certain content at the multilateral level.

5   For a discussion of the functional versus the discretionary role of states see 'The Functional Versus the Discretionary Role of States', below.

6   Also see Part E on Water and Sustainable Urban Development and Part F on Water for Sustainable Food Production and Rural Development of Chapter 18, Agenda 21.

7   See for example Agenda 21: 18.9(c); 18.12 (i), (m) and (n); 18.19; 18.22; 18.34(d); 18.45; 18.50 (b) and (c); 18.54; 18.59 (c) (ii) and (iii), and (d); 18.65; 18.68 (b) and (d); 18.72; 18.76 (a)(iv), b(iv), and (e)(iii) and (iv); 18.81(b).

8   'International watercourse' for the purposes of the work of the ILC is defined in Article 2(a) as 'a watercourse, parts of which are situated in different States' and a 'watercourse' is defined in Article 2(b) as 'a system of surface and underground waters constituting by virtue of their physical relationship a unitary whole and flowing into a common terminus'. The Special Rapporteur in his 1993 Report proposed the deletion of the phrase 'flowing into a common terminus' and indicated a preference to include within the scope of the definition unrelated confined groundwater (Rosenstock, 1993: para. 11). The reactions of other Commission members to these suggestions were mixed (ILC 1993: paras. 363–71).

9   Article 2(c) defines a 'watercourse State' as 'a State in whose territory part of an international watercourse is situated'. The Special Rapporteur did not foresee any amendments to this provision in his 1993 Report (Rosenstock, 1993: para. 11).

10   The present Special Rapporteur commented on the question whether the draft articles should form the basis for a framework agreement or should ultimately have the status of model rules. He expressed no preference, but indicated that he believed it desirable for the Commission to take a position on this question (Rosenstock, 1993: paras. 6–7). The reactions in the International Law Commission were mixed, but most members expressed a preference for continuing to work on the basis of assumption that a framework agreement would be the result (ILC, 1993: paras. 344–50).

11   For further information see McCaffrey, 1992–3. Several non-governmental forums, however, have stipulated the fundamental

human right to an environment adequate for health and well-being. See eg, WCED (1987: Article 1). The commentary to Article 1, however, contains the following sentence: 'It cannot be said that the fundamental human right to an adequate environment already constitutes a well-established right under present international law', (p.40). For further information on human rights law and environmental law see Alfredsson and Ovsiouk (1991: 19-27).

12 See eg, Agenda 21: 18.58.
13 Also see section on public participation below.
14 Also see Hunt (1992: 282-3).
15 The commentary to Article 10(2) provides that
    within the meaning of the article, therefore, a 'conflict' between uses could only arise where no system of priorities governing those uses, or other means of accommodating them, had been established by agreement or custom as between the watercourse States concerned (ILC, 1991: 180).
16 See note 7.
17 Eg, Agenda 21: 18.12(n) and (p); 18.19; 18.50(b)(ii) and 18.59(d).
18 Eg, Agenda 21: 18.20; 18.50(c) and 18.59(e).
19 In his 1993 Report the Special Rapporteur did not submit any remarks on this article.
20 For comments on Article 31 see Caron (1992: 276-9); Hunt (1992: 288-94); Vinogradov (1992: 249-55).
21 See eg, WCED (1987: articles 6 and 20). Article 6 concerns the provision of timely information, access and due process to persons in the case of a use which may significantly affect their use of a natural resource, irrespective of whether that natural resource is transboundary or not. Article 20 concerns the provision of remedies – both the obligation to provide remedies and the obligation to refrain from discrimination in providing those remedies – for persons who have or may be detrimentally affected by a transboundary interference with their use of a transboundary natural resource.
22 Especially Agenda 21, chapters 23-32 on 'Strengthening the Role of Major Groups'.
23 For an analyses of natural ecosystem boundaries and sovereignty see Byers (1991: 65-76).
24 See for example Agenda 21: 18.10; 18.12(o)(iii); 18.73.
25 See eg, the commentary to the following draft articles: Article 3 (former Article 4, ILC, 1987: 57-66); Article 5 (former Article 6 ILC, 1987: 69-82) and Article 26 (ILC, 1991: 182-6).
26 The text of Article 8 reads as follows:

Watercourse States shall co-operate on the basis of sovereign equality, territorial integrity and mutual benefit in order to attain optimal utilisation and adequate protection of an international watercourse.

27   When the text of what is now Article 8 was discussed in the ILC there was considerable debate as to whether international law imposes on states a general duty to co-operate. This debate led Special Rapporteur, McCaffrey, to express the following:

Co-operation in the meaning of Article 10 [present Article 8] denotes a general obligation to act in good faith with regard to other States in the utilisation of an international watercourse. ... The obligation to co-operate was quite clearly an obligation of conduct. What it involved is not a duty to take part with other States in collective action but, rather, a duty to work towards a common goal. (ILC, 1987: para. 98).

28   The generality of Article 8 and the rest of the draft articles was also pointed-out by several members of the International Law Commission and the present Special Rapporteur in his 1993 Report. The Special Rapporteur also indicated that he would:

continue to reflect on ways of making Article 8 more precise without detracting from the ability of the draft as a whole to serve as a framework relating to the many varied situations (Rosenstock, 1993: para. 26).

29   This is irrespective of the fact that Article 20 does reflect such an approach through the introduction of the ecosystem approach. It is the ecosystem of the watercourse and not only the watercourse as such which is to be protected and preserved. On this point see Hunt (1992: 284–7).

30   The reactions to this suggestion in the International Law Commission varied (ILC, 1993: paras. 377–87). On the approaches to the threshold between permissible and non-permissible harm in the case of the pollution of international watercourses see Nollkaemper (1993: 33–9).

31   As pointed out by the present Special Rapporteur replacing the term 'appreciable' by the term 'significant' in Article 3 would require a similar change in Article 4(2) (Rosenstock, 1993: para. 13).

32   ILC (1987: 68), where it is provided that the third state 'should only be required to establish that its use may be affected to some appreciable extent'.

33   On the desirability of developing dispute avoidance and dispute settlement mechanisms see: Agenda 21: Chapter 39, on 'International Legal Instruments and Mechanisms', and, in particular, paragraph 39.10 which refers to the need to develop

mechanisms for the avoidance and settlement of disputes; Caron (1992: 271–3).

34 The normative character of these obligations, however, would be subject to the meaning of the term 'adjust' in Article 3 of the draft articles, see the 'Evaluation' below.

35 The present Special Rapporteur in his 1993 Report recommended no changes to this article (Rosenstock, 1993: 11).

36 The present Special Rapporteur did not consider this article in his 1993 Report.

37 On the relationship between the no appreciable harm rule and the equitable utilisation rule see Bourne (1992: 72–92); Handl (1992: 129–33); McCaffrey (1989: 508–10).

38 The Special Rapporteur proposed the following new text for Article 7:

> Watercourse States shall exercise due diligence to utilise an international watercourse in such a way as not to cause significant harm to other watercourse States, absent their agreement, except as may be allowable under an equitable and reasonable use of the watercourse. A use which causes significant harm in the form of pollution shall be presumed to be an inequitable and unreasonable use unless there is: (a) a clear showing of special circumstances indicating a compelling need for *ad hoc* adjustment; and (b) the absence of any imminent threat to human health and safety.' (Rosenstock, 1993: para. 25)

39 Amending Article 3 to refer to significant, instead of appreciable, harm would also affect Article 7 (Rosenstock, 1993: para. 13).

40 For comments on the notification and consultation procedure see Bourne (1992: 66–72); Handl (1992: 124–9); Székly (1992: 99–100).

41 On the nature and desirability of applying the concept of *obligations erga omnes* in international law see Schachter (1991: 208–213). For criticism of the development of *obligations erga omnes* see Weil (1983: 431–3).

42 Although the United Nations Convention on the Law of the Sea (UNCLOS) does not offer other states or the international community effective remedies, it is clear from the text of Article 63(1) *juncto* Article 61 and 62 that coastal states are not relieved of the duty to ensure the conservation and optimum utilisation of such transboundary fish stocks if their negotiations pursuant to the duty to co-operate (also a duty to negotiate in good faith) are not successful. For further information see Lagoni (1992: paras. 7–30); Hey (1989: 47, 53–7 and 122–4).

43   On the possible implications of the term 'adjust' in Article 3 see
      the 'Evaluation' below.
44   No changes to Article 5 were recommended by the present Special
      Rapporteur in his 1993 Report.
45   The need for clarification of the term 'adjust' was raised by a
      member of the International Law Commission during the last 1993
      session of the Commission (ILC, 1993: para. 348).
46   For information on this type of regimes see Gehring (1990: 35–
      56).

Bibliography

Alfredsson, G. and Ovsiouk, A. (1991) 'Human rights and
    environment', *Nordic Journal of International Law* 60, 1/2: 19–27.
Biswas, (1991) 'Water for sustainable development, a global
    perspective', *Development and Co-operation* 5: 20.
Bourne, C.B. (1992) 'The International Law Commission's draft
    articles on the Law of International Watercourses: principles and
    planned measures', *Colorado Journal of International Environmental
    Law and Policy* 3: 65–92.
Byers, B. (1991) 'Ecoregions, state sovereignty and conflict', *Bulletin
    of Peace Proposals* 22: 65–76.
Caron, D.D. (1992) 'The frog that wouldn't leap: the International
    Law Commission and its work on international watercourses',
    Colorado Journal of International Environmental Law and Policy 3:
    269–79.
Dupuy, R.-J. (1991) 'Humanity and the environment', *Colorado
    Journal of International Environmental Law and Policy* 2: 201–4.
Gehring, T. (1990) 'International environmental regimes: dynamic
    sectoral legal systems', *Yearbook of International Environmental
    Law* 1: 35–56.
Handl, G. (1992) 'The International Law Commission's draft articles
    on the Law of International Watercourses (general principles and
    measures): progressive or retrogressive development of international
    law?', *Colorado Journal of International Environmental Law and
    Policy* 3: 123–34.
Handl, G. (1990) 'Environmental security and global change: the
    challenge to international law', *Yearbook of International
    Environmental Law* 1: 3–33.
Hey, E. (1989) *The Regime for the Exploitation of Transboundary
    Marine Fisheries Resources*, Martinus Nijhoff Publishers.

Hunt, C.D. (1992) 'Implementation: joint institutional management and remedies in domestic tribunals (Articles 26–8 and 30–2)', *Colorado Journal of International Environmental Law and Policy* 2: 281–94.

Johnston, D.M. (1988) 'Functionalism in the theory of international law', *Canadian Yearbook of International Law* 26: 3–60.

Lagoni R. (rapporteur) (1992) *Principles Applicable to Living Resources Occurring Both Within and Without the Exclusive Economic Zone or in Zones of Overlapping Claims,* International Law Association.

McCaffrey, S.C. (1989) 'The Law of International Watercourses: some recent developments and unanswered questions', *Denver Journal of International Law and Policy* 17: 505–26.

—— (1992) 'Background and overview of the International Law Commission's study of the non-navigational uses of international watercourses', *Colorado Journal of International Environmental Law and Policy* 3: 17–29.

—— (1992–3) 'A human right to water: domestic and international implications', G*eorgetown International Environmental Law Review* 5: 1–24.

Nollkaemper, A. (1993) *The Legal Regime for Transboundary Water Pollution: Between Discretion and Constraint*, Graham and Trotman/Martinus Nijhoff Publishers.

Schachter, O. (1991) *International Law in Theory and Practice,* Martinus Nijhoff Publishers.

Székly, A. (1992) '"General Principles" and "Planned Measures" provisions in the International Law Commission's draft articles on the non-navigational uses of international watercourses: a Mexican point of view', *Colorado Journal of International Environmental Law and Policy* 3: 93–101.

Vinogradov, S.V. (1992) 'Observations on the International Law Commission's draft rules in the non-navigational uses of international watercourses: "management and domestic remedies"', *Colorado Journal of International Environmental Law and Policy* 3: 235–59.

WCED (Expert Group on Environmental Law of the World Commission on Environment and Development) (1987) *Environmental Protection and Sustainable Development*, Graham and Trotman/Martinus Nijhoff Publishers.

Weil, P. (1983) 'Towards relative normativity in international law?', *American Journal of International Law* 77: 413–42.

Wildhaber, L. (1986) 'Sovereignty and international law', in R.St.J. Macdonald and D.M. Johnston (eds) *The Structure and Process of International Law: Essays in Legal Philosophy Doctrine and Theory*, Martinus Nijhoff Publishers.

LEGAL REFERENCES

Agenda 21 (and the Rio Declaration) (1993) United Nations Conference on Environment and Development, Rio, UN Publications Sales No. E.93.I.11.

Convention on Environmental Impact Assessment in a Transboundary Context (1991) adopted at Espoo, Finland on February 25, *International Legal Materials* 30: 800.

Convention on the Protection and Use of Transboundary Watercourses and International Lakes (1992) adopted at Helsinki, Finland on March 17, *International Legal Materials* 31: 1312.

GAOR (1970) Res. 2669 (XXV), December 8.

ILC (International Law Commission) (1980) 'Report of the International Law Commission on the work of its thirty-second session', *United Nations General Assembly, Official Records,* thirty-fifth session, Supplement No. 10(A/35/10).

—— (1987) 'Report of the International Law Commission on the work of its thirty-ninth session', *United Nations General Assembly, Official Records,* forty-second session, Supplement No. 10(A/42/10).

—— (1988) 'Report of the International Law Commission on the work of its fortieth session', *United Nations General Assembly, Official Record,* forty-fifth session, Supplement No. 10(A/43/10).

—— (1991) 'Report of the International Law Commission on the work of its forty-third session', *United Nations General Assembly, Official Records,* forty-sixth session, Supplement No. 10(A/46/10).

—— (1993) 'Report of the International Law Commission on the work of its forty-fifth session', Official Records, forty-eighth session, Supplement No. 10(A/48/10) United Nations General Assembly.

McCaffrey, S.C. (Special Rapporteur) (1990) 'Sixth report on the Law of the Non-Navigational Uses of International Watercourses', United Nations General Assembly, Doc. A/CN.4/427 and Add.1, in *Yearbook of the International Law Commission*, II, 1.

Rosenstock, R. (Special Rapporteur) (1993) 'First report on the Law of the Non-Navigational Uses of International Watercourses', United Nations General Assembly, Doc. A/CN.4/451.

United Nations Convention on the Law of the Sea (1982) *International Legal Materials* 21: 1261.

UNGA (1992) 'Law of the Non-Navigational Uses of International Watercourses: Draft Articles' *United Nations General Assembly* Doc. A/46/405.

10

World Bank Policy on Projects on International Waterways in the Context of Emerging International Law and the Work of the International Law Commission

David Goldberg

This article deals with the legal aspects of the World Bank's policy[1] on projects on international waterways. It should be made clear that this presentation is intended only as a basic synopsis of the subject with the emphasis on drawing pragmatic conclusions. The Bank's policy, which is set forth in Operational Directive (OD) 7.50, an internal policy document approved by the Executive Directors of the Bank, is applicable to all projects which are on an international waterway, which are defined to include any:

1 river, canal, lake or any similar body of water which forms a boundary between, or any river or body of surface water which flows through two or more states, whether members of the Bank or not;
2 any tributary or any other body of surface water which is a part or a component of any waterway described in (1) above; and,
3 bays, gulfs, straits or channels, bounded by two or more states or, if within one state, recognised as necessary channels of communication between the open sea and other states, and any river flowing into such waters.

Projects on international waterways require special handling, because they may affect relations not only between the Bank and its borrowers but also between countries, whether members of the Bank or not. The Bank recognises that the co-operation and goodwill of riparians is essential to the most efficient use and exploitation of international waterways for development purposes. The Bank, therefore attaches the utmost importance to having riparians enter into appropriate agreements or arrangements for the efficient use of the entire waterway system, or any part of it, and stands ready to assist in achieving this end. When differences remain unresolved, the Bank, prior to financing the project, will normally urge the country proposing the project to offer to negotiate in good faith with other riparians to reach appropriate agreements or arrangements. The Bank will not finance projects on international waters that would cause appreciable harm to other riparians.

What are the legal underpinnings to the provisions of OD 7.50? First and foremost, it must be said that OD 7.50 approaches the subject from the standpoint of an international co-operative institution which, pursuant to Article III, Section 4(v) of the Articles of Agreement of the Bank (a similar provision exists in the International Development Association (IDA) Articles of Agreement), has 'to act prudently in the interests both of the particular member in whose territories the project is located and of the members as a whole'. In this context the Bank, in formulating its policy, has taken cognisance of the international law in this field, to the extent that it is relevant to the Bank's role as a lending agency.

What are the sources of international law on this subject? Article 38 of the Statute of the International Court of Justice of The Hague (which is part of the UN system) enumerates, in order of precedence, the sources of international law which the Court must utilise, as follows:

1 the law of treaties, that is the body of treaties and conventions ratified by governments;
2 customs;
3 generally accepted principles;
4 decisions of the judiciary and doctrines of qualified authors.

As it happens, the law on international waterways is one of the most unsettled areas of international law, although a significant amount of work has been undertaken by various international law groups, in particular the International Law Association, and by the International Law Commission (ILC) of the United Nations, pursuant to a General Assembly Resolution in 1970. The work of these bodies draws heavily on the sources of international law mentioned above.

In essence, two substantive principles have been developed which appear to command the greatest acceptance in international law circles and are reflected in several bilateral and multilateral treaties. The two principles are:

1 the principle of prohibition against appreciable harm by way of deprivation of water rights, pollution or otherwise; and,
2 the principle of the right of each riparian of an international waterway to a reasonable and equitable share in the utilisation of the waterway.

The first principle, that of prohibition against appreciable harm, derives from an age-old Latin maxim: *sic utere tuo ut alienum non laedas* meaning 'so use your own property as not to injure your neighbour'. This principle has been acknowledged as one that seeks to facilitate good-neighbourly relations between states in that it reserves the right of each state to use waters in its territory in accordance with its needs, provided that it does not infringe in an appreciable manner on the rights of other states. It is embodied in Article 7 of the draft Articles of the International Law Commission on 'The Law of the Non-Navigational Uses of International Watercourses' (McCaffrey, 1990). This substantive principle, strengthened and safeguarded by a number of procedural requirements having a particularly important role in the emerging international law on this subject, is the back-bone of the Bank's policy under OD 7.50.

It should be noted that the prohibition is not against causing *any* harm but harm which is appreciable, ie, not trivial or inconsequential. The report of the fortieth session of the International Law Commission (ILC, 1988: 85) comments as follows:

> As explained in the commentary to Article 4, the term 'appreciable' embodies a factual standard. The harm must be capable of being established by objective evidence. There must be a real impairment of use, ie, a detrimental impact of some consequence upon, for example, public health, industry, property, agriculture or the environment in the affected State. 'Appreciable' harm is, therefore, that which is not insignificant or barely detectable but is not necessarily 'serious'.[2]

The second substantive principle, that of the equitable utilisation of the international waterway, means that each riparian of such a waterway has an equality of right with every other co-riparian to utilise the waters in a reasonable and beneficial manner. Equality of right does not mean in this context the right to an equal division of the waters but rather that each riparian has an equal right to the division of the waters on the basis of its needs, consistent with the corresponding rights of co-riparians. This principle is also reflected in several treaties, particularly bilateral and multilateral treaties of a regional character, and is featured in Articles 5 and 6 of the draft Articles of the International Law Commission. The Indus Waters Treaty between India and Pakistan of 19 September 1960 (UNTS 419) is perhaps the most well known of such bilateral treaties.

The report of the fortieth session of the International Law Commission (ILC, 1988: 77) describes the factors relevant to equitable and reasonable utilisation as follows:

> Utilisation of an international watercourse [system] in an equitable and reasonable manner within the meaning of Article 6 requires taking into account all relevant factors and circumstances, including:
> (a) geographic, hydrographic, hydrological, climatic and other factors of a natural character;
> (b) the social and economic needs of the watercourse State concerned;

(c) the effects of the use or uses of an international watercourse
     [system] in one watercourse State on other watercourse States;
(d) existing and potential uses of the international watercourse
     [system];
(e) conservation, protection, development and economy of use of
     the water resources of the international watercourse [system]
     and the costs of measures taken to that effect;
(f) the availability of alternatives, of corresponding value, to a
     particular planned or existing use.

It is important to note that whereas the injunction of not causing
appreciable harm is stated as an imperative prohibition in absolute
terms, the right to an equitable sharing, although at times described as
'complementary', is less readily conceived as self-standing inasmuch as
the practical result in each case must first be determined by an
agreement between the parties or an award of a competent tribunal. It
is clear that the right in question, ie, to a reasonable and equitable
sharing, involves a judgement taking into account and evaluating
numerous relevant factors, and has no practical conclusion unless and
until determined in such a manner. This distinction is reflected in the
Bank's approach under OD 7.50. Whereas the 'no appreciable harm'
principle is firmly embodied in the OD, no comparable expression is
given to the equitable sharing principle. It must be made very clear,
however, that the Bank does not take a position adverse to this
principle, but in the absence of an agreement between the parties or the
judgement of a competent tribunal, either of which the Bank would
respect, the right of each party to an equitable sharing is inchoate and
the Bank is not vested with the authority to take upon itself the
function to adjudicate such rights.

Before alluding to issues which have arisen since the adoption of the
policy in OD 7.50, it might be appropriate at this point briefly to
summarise its main provisions. As already stated, the OD applies to
varying types of international waterways, including rivers, canals and
lakes which flow through two or more states whether Bank members
or not, as well as tributaries of such waterways. It should be noted,
however, that it does not as yet extend to groundwater.

The most important procedural provision of the OD is that it
requires Bank staff, as early as possible during the identification stage
of the project cycle, to advise the prospective borrower that, if it has
not already done so, it should formally notify the other riparians of the
proposed project. If the prospective borrower wishes the Bank to give
notification on its behalf, the Bank will do so, but if the prospective
borrower objects to any such notification to other riparians of the
international waterway concerned, the firm rule is that the Bank will
discontinue further processing of the project. The notification should
contain, to the extent available, sufficient technical and other necessary
specifications and data which would enable the other riparians to

determine as accurately as possible the potential for appreciable harm by way of deprivation of water rights, pollution or otherwise. It may be noted here that the concern is twofold, namely that the project does not adversely affect the interests of other riparians and that it will not be adversely affected by plans for use of the waters by other riparians. A reasonable period of time normally not to exceed six months is allowed for the recipient state to respond.

There are two exceptions to the requirement for notification. First, where the proposed project involves additions or alterations by way of rehabilitation, construction or otherwise to any ongoing schemes and, in the judgement of the Bank, such a project will not adversely change the quality or quantity of water flows to other riparians, nor will it be adversely affected by uses of the water by other riparians, notification in the manner described is not required. Second, if the proposed project is a water resource survey or feasibility study, notification is not required but the terms of reference for such survey or study should include an examination of any potential riparian issues. However, in all cases, Bank staff are advised to ascertain whether any agreements or arrangements exist among the riparians for the development of the waterway concerned and to make efforts to secure compliance with such agreements or arrangements.

The OD provides that senior management be kept informed of developments, in particular in those cases where other riparians have raised objections. In the case of receipt of objections, the OD requires a memorandum, prepared by the region in consultation with the legal department, to be sent to senior management detailing, *inter alia*, the nature of the issues raised; the Bank staff's assessment of the objections and whether the project will cause appreciable harm or be harmed by uses that other riparians might make of the waters of the waterway concerned; whether the Bank should urge the parties to resolve their differences through amicable means; and whether the objections are of such a nature that it would be advisable to obtain an opinion from independent experts. With respect to the experts, it should be noted that a roster of eminent persons with knowledge of international water systems and international law is maintained by senior management. Should the Bank decide to proceed with the project despite the objections of other riparians, the Bank will inform those riparians of its decision.

It is very relevant in this context to note that in the equivalent text of the International Law Commission (Article 12 onwards) a system of prior notification is only triggered by the criterion that the contemplated measures may, as perceived by the state planning the project, have an 'appreciable adverse effect' on other watercourse states. The planning state must, therefore, in each case undertake its own assessment of the impact of the project on other states using the watercourse, and only if it concludes that there will be such an adverse effect does it need to provide notification. (If it does not provide notification, any other watercourse state learning of the plans in some other way may request the planning state to apply the provisions of Article 12). Thus it may be observed that the Bank's current notification standards are, in fact, more rigorous than those contemplated by the International Law Commission.

In one important respect OD 7.50 goes beyond the concepts of emerging international law in focusing, as has already been indicated, not only on the appreciable harm which the proposed project may cause to other riparians but also on the potential harm which others may cause to the project. This rule is clearly derived from quite different considerations than the precepts of international co-operation, goodwill and legal practice; rather it flows from the self-interest of the Bank not to provide funding for a project which may not be viable or produce the expected economic benefits because of lack of certainty as to the quantity or quality of water flows needed for the success of the project. In fact, the application of this rule produced the most interesting developments in the case of the proposed Baardhere Dam Project in Somalia.

Briefly, this proposed project involved the construction of a dam, power generation installations and irrigation works on the Juba River which stems from an upper basin in Ethiopia. Another important tributary flows into Kenya. Somalia requested the Bank to notify the two riparians on its behalf. The Bank did so and provided the two governments, Kenya and Ethiopia, with the necessary project details. The Government of Kenya responded by requesting more information, whereas the Bank received a reply from Ethiopia raising objections to the proposed project on the grounds, *inter alia,* that Ethiopia intended to utilise the flow of the entire river for irrigation and had plans for development of a hydroelectric scheme on the river.

Bank staff took the view that appreciable harm to the project from Ethiopia was improbable, but owing to the uncertainty relating to Ethiopia's plans for the future, an opinion was requested from the panel of independent experts from the roster maintained by the Bank. A panel of three experts, including an international legal expert, was selected to review all riparian issues related to the proposed project. The report of the panel supported the assessment which had been made by Bank staff. This is the first case in which Bank management found it expedient to use the independent expert mechanism.

Questions have arisen with respect to the notification requirement in cases where an agreement exists between the riparians of the international river concerned or where an institutional framework has been established to deal with the utilisation of the international waterway concerned. In such situations the OD itself states clearly that Bank staff should make efforts to secure compliance with the requirements of such agreements or framework arrangements.

Questions have also been raised about the length of time that should be given to other riparians to respond to a notification from a prospective borrower. The OD provides that riparians should be allowed a reasonable period of time which should normally not exceed six months. Obviously, the amount of time actually needed will vary according to the nature of the proposed project – for instance, a simple project may require a shorter time-frame because the project details may not be so complicated for the riparians to determine the possible effect of the project, while a complex hydroelectric or irrigation scheme may require more time. It should be noted that the six months' outer time-limit is consistent with the time-limits to be found in notification provisions in most international agreements and, in fact, the International Law Commission has stipulated the same time-limit. We have also found that in many cases where the Bank has a local office, the representative has played a useful role in obtaining as prompt a response as possible.

On the whole, I believe OD 7.50 has to date served the interests of the Bank and its members very well. While, as with any new policy, there was some resistance to carrying out its provisions in the beginning, I believe the principles contained in the OD are now well understood throughout the Bank and in member countries where riparian issues are recurrent. It has also served to maintain a Bank policy which is generally in line with the most recent developments in international law.

On this latter subject, however, there has been criticism, as previously indicated, to the effect that Bank rules are inherently biased against upstream riparians, who are obviously most prejudiced by the 'no appreciable harm' rule without being able to receive any offsetting relief under the 'equitable utilisation rule'. Whilst this charge may on the face of it appear to have some validity, the result is not because of bias introduced by the Bank rules, but rather the relative impact and interplay of the two principles under international law, as discussed earlier in this paper. In short, in the absence of an agreement by the parties or a determination by a competent tribunal of the respective rights of the riparians, in practical terms the Bank cannot resolve or enforce equitable sharing rights. Of course this may create great difficulties in certain cases for upstream riparians who have traditionally under-utilised the waters in question but the resolution of this problem lies outside the jurisdiction of the Bank. I should re-emphasise, of course, that OD 7.50 in outlining the Bank's basic policy approach makes it clear that:

The Bank, therefore, attaches the utmost importance to riparians entering into appropriate agreements or arrangements for the efficient utilisation for the entire waterway system or any part of it, and stands ready to assist in achieving this end. In cases where differences remain unresolved, the Bank, prior to financing the project, will normally urge the state proposing the project to offer to negotiate in good faith with other riparians to reach appropriate agreements or arrangements.

The agreements or arrangements so contemplated would be expected to be based upon and give force and effect to the 'equitable utilisation rule', taking into account all relevant factors and circumstances, including those listed in Article 6 of the International Law Commission's draft Articles, and mentioned earlier in this paper.

Unfortunately, from the perspective of crystallising international law on this subject, the members of the International Law Commission have not as yet been able to fully resolve the interplay between draft Articles 5 and 6 dealing with 'equitable utilisation' and draft Article 7 dealing with 'no appreciable (or significant) harm'. Thus the Report of the International Law Commission (40th Session) 1988, comments as follows:

> A watercourse State's right to utilise an international watercourse [system] in an equitable and reasonable manner finds its limit in the duty of that State not to cause appreciable harm to other watercourse States. In other words – *prima facie,* at least – utilisation of an international watercourse [system] is not equitable if it causes other watercourse States appreciable harm ... Thus, a watercourse State may not justify a use that causes appreciable harm to another watercourse State on the ground that the use is 'equitable', in the absence of agreement between the watercourse States concerned.

This important issue of the interplay between the two dominant International Law Commission principles is discussed by Professor McCaffrey, then Special Rapporteur of the International Law Commission, in his article 'The law of international watercourses; some recent developments and unanswered questions' (McCaffrey, 1989). After referring to the approach of the International Law Commission (as already cited) he remarks:

> First, the ILC's approach affords a measure of protection to the weaker state that has suffered harm. It is not open to the stronger state to justify a use giving rise to the harm on the ground that it is 'equitable'. A second, and related, point is that it is far simpler to determine whether the 'no harm' rule has been breached than is the case with the obligation of equitable utilisation. Thus, primacy of the 'no harm' principle means that the fundamental rights and obligations of states with regard to their uses of an international watercourse are more definite and certain than they would be if governed in the first instance by the more flexible (and consequently less clear) rule of equitable utilisation. And, finally, the 'no harm' rule is preferable in cases involving pollution and other threats to the environment. While a state could conceivably seek to justify an

activity resulting in such harm as being an 'equitable use', the 'no harm' principle would – at least *prima facie* – require abatement of the injurious activity.

The International Law Association, on the other hand, leans more to the view that the controlling principle is that of equitable utilisation. Although its Water Resources Committee has not taken a formal position on this for purposes of commenting to the new Special Rapporteur of the International Law Commission on the latter's draft Articles, the Chairman and several other prominent members of the Water Resources Committee have written very strongly in favour of such a position. Furthermore, the whole matter has been thrown into further doubt and confusion by the recommendation of the new Special Rapporteur of the International Law Commission (at its forty-fifth session in the summer of 1993) to modify draft Article 7 on 'no appreciable harm' so that in effect it should, except in the case of pollution, give precedence to an equitable and reasonable use of the watercourse (ILC, 1993). This recommendation faced a good deal of opposition, with the result that the drafting Committee of the International Law Commission has deferred action on draft Article 7.

The proponents of either side of this debate appear to proceed from the same starting point, namely, that draft Articles 5 and 7 are fundamentally inconsistent and that one principle must give way to the other.

It is argued that either draft Article 7 precludes a balancing of interests as contemplated by draft Article 5, or is redundant if one presumes that usage causing appreciable harm is, *ipso facto*, unreasonable and inequitable. But what is the added-value of draft Article 7 if it is entirely subordinated to draft Article 5 (which specifically includes among the list of factors to be considered the effects of usage in one watercourse State on other watercourse States)? Such subordination would render draft Article 7 entirely nugatory because no reliance could be placed upon it without first reaching a dispositive conclusion under draft Article 5.

Furthermore, it could be expected that granting outright priority to draft Article 5 would cause great uncertainty and in practice would enable an upper watercourse State to cause massive harm to its downstream neighbours by altering or cutting off existing flows at will, based upon its own interpretation of equitable utilisation. It might also be mentioned that potential financiers of major projects affecting an international watercourse would be hard-put to determine, on the basis of this principle, whether their involvement is warranted on practical or legal grounds, in the absence of agreement between the parties or other binding determination of their respective riparian rights.

On the other hand, it is argued that granting outright priority to draft Article 7 would inevitably freeze the *status quo* and benefit the more highly developed downstream riparians.

Rather than veering from one extreme to the other, we may wish to consider whether there is not a sensible way to reconcile all the articles in question in a manner which gives full meaning to each. To achieve this we must, in considering draft Article 5, place the accent on 'agreement' or 'adjudication', whilst in the case of draft Article 7 place the accent on 'action', in fact unilateral action by the party (or parties) changing the *status quo*.

Let us start with draft Article 5 which establishes the principle of equitable utilisation and draft Article 6 which explains how this principle should be implemented.

Draft Article 5 is a very broad principle, the application of which to any particular watercourse must hinge upon a determination which takes into account *all* relevant factors and circumstances, *including* those listed in draft Article 6. Draft Articles 5 and 6 do not provide a clear-cut formula for determining entitlements, but instead present a large array of variables, the cumulative effect of which will lead to a different result depending upon the relative weight which may be attached to each factor or circumstance in the subjective viewpoint of whoever is assessing the application of the principle to the particular situation. Draft Article 6(2) *explicitly* recognises that equitable utilisation cannot be implemented without 'consultations in a spirit of co-operation', or, more plainly, some form of agreement between the watercourse States concerned. An alternative mode of resolution would be a decision of the International Court of Justice or some other dispute-resolution procedure selected by the parties. It follows that where an agreement or judicial decision eventuates this creates its own binding force, and any problems that may arise thereafter would likely be of an interpretative nature in respect of the terms of the agreement or judicial decision.

It should be stressed that in the process of determining the respective rights of each riparian to a reasonable and equitable share of the waters pursuant to draft Articles 5 and 6, existing uses by any riparian is only one of the relevant factors to be considered, and its relative importance will depend upon the circumstances of the case.

The fundamental dilemma that is not addressed by draft Article 5 is how to provide a viable standard of conduct in the absence of an agreement or a judicial decision. This is surely the practical role of draft Article 7, ie, in the absence of, or pending, an agreement or other binding determination of such rights, no riparian may unilaterally change the *status quo* in such a manner as to cause appreciable harm to other riparians. This elemental protection to downstream riparians afforded by draft Article 7 counterbalances, at least to some extent, the physical control in the hands of an upper riparian, and provides a mutual stimulus to seeking an agreed solution. It also provides the minimum measure of certainty and stability for financial investment in developmental activities.

It is submitted that this reconciliation of draft Articles 5 and 7 should satisfy the extreme critics on both sides. Those who advocate the strengthening of draft Article 5 should be satisfied with a framework which recognises the primary objective of achieving agreement based on equitable utilisation. Those who favour draft Article 7 should appreciate the protection it grants while an agreement is being worked out, but may not rely on it to avoid the duty to co-operate, consult and negotiate in good faith. It is further submitted that the energies currently being devoted to the debate between extreme positions on draft Articles 5 and 7 could usefully be re-directed towards achieving consensus on some dispute-resolution procedures in the draft Articles, which is of critical importance for enforcement of the principles.

To bring this approach into sharper focus by a concrete illustration, I would like to follow up on an example described by Professor Thomas Naff (1993) in his article 'International Riparian Law in the West and Islam'. He writes:

The Nile River offers a good case in point. Egypt, for whom any sustained, significant reductions in the flow of the Nile could spell disaster, has taken a narrow view of the no appreciable harm proposition and argued that this principle should be the standard legal reference rather than equitable utilisation. Supposing, hypothetically, Ethiopia, as part of its economic development and recovery program were to build a high dam (significantly above 15m) on the Blue Nile – a major feeder of the main stem of the river – and use the captured water in-country. That would reduce the flow of the Nile to Egypt by a certain amount annually. Supposing further that the Egyptians decided to adjudicate the issue rather than to settle it by the superiority of their arms; they would certainly invoke the principle of no appreciable harm, narrowly construed, and reject Ethiopian arguments based on rights conferred by equitable utilisation and upper riparian status. If the principle of appreciable harm prevailed, either by a court judgement or imposed by military force, equitable utilisation would be negated, but at the same time, Ethiopia would be denied the legitimate right of economic development, thus causing it appreciable harm.

Let us take a closer look at this analysis, proceeding from the assumption made by Professor Naff that Egypt would decide to adjudicate (or negotiate) the issue. Clearly Egypt would be entitled in this process to rely heavily on the aspect of potential harm to existing uses of the water. This is expressly contemplated by draft Article 6 as a relevant factor in determining rights of reasonable and equitable utilisation. But, it is submitted, this factor cannot be the sole determinant of riparian rights if draft Articles 5 and 6 are to be considered in any meaningful way so as to respect the principle of equitable utilisation. Sudan would doubtless lay emphasis on its social and economic needs. The adjudicator would have to consider the availability of alternatives of corresponding value to the particular planned or existing use, and other relevant circumstances. Draft Article 7, on the other hand, would serve to prevent Sudan from taking any unilateral action based on its own definition of equitable rights, so that a fair solution could only be reached through the process of adjudication (or negotiation).

If all of this could be achieved, the end result would, it is suggested, match rather harmoniously with the framework adopted by the Bank under OD 7.50.

Finally, as was pointed out at the beginning of this paper, OD 7.50 does not apply to groundwater. Considering that groundwater constitutes 97% of the fresh water on Earth (excluding ice-caps and glaciers) this is obviously an omission which needs to be addressed. The Bank has already determined that since some aspects of groundwater are not well understood, the Bank will promote the acquisition of knowledge concerning internationally shared groundwater to provide a basis for establishing guidelines governing the Bank's activities. But what might these guidelines be?

Once again the status of emerging international law is unsettled. The draft Articles of the International Law Commission include groundwater, but only to the extent that it is connected to surface water, ie, 'flowing into a common terminus'. Efforts to remove this latter limitation at the 45th Session of the International Law Commission, in the deliberations of its drafting Committee, were unsuccessful. There seems to be no good reason why the Bank, assuming it has reasonable access to the relevant data, should not go at least as far as the International Law Commission by extending OD 7.50 to connected groundwater. Should it go further and include also isolated aquifers, which may be of considerable importance (eg, like the one stretching across the Sahara desert from the Libyan Jamahiriya to the Atlas mountains)? Whilst this whole matter needs very careful consideration with particular emphasis upon the Bank's capacity to reach sound and defensible decisions based upon currently available data, and with a view to keeping in step with the rules of international law currently being formulated, it is conceivable to consider drawing a distinction between rechargeable aquifers on the one hand and non-rechargeable (or minimally rechargeable) aquifers on the other. In their classic work on the Bellagio Draft Treaty on Transboundary Groundwaters by Professors Hayton and Utton (1989: 706[3]) they make the following observation:

> The very nature of the finite stock of water in a non-rechargeable basin compels a modification of the traditional concept ... Each appropriator, subsequent to the initial appropriation, reduces in amount, and in time of use, the supply of water available to all prior

appropriators, with the consequent decline of the water table, higher pumping costs, and lower yield.

One possible approach, therefore, would have the Bank decide that OD 7.50 should indeed apply to all groundwaters but with the explicit presumption that in the case of non- or minimally rechargeable aquifers any new extraction will in fact cause appreciable harm to other riparians. This would require their concurrence, or non-objection at least.

Notes

1   The World Bank has played, and is continuing to play, a major role in water resources development in developing countries. Development of projects on international waterways is a complex subject. This article deals with the legal aspects of the World Bank's policy on projects on such international waterways, and its contribution to emerging international law, with particular reference to the work of the International Law Commission.
2   It may be noted that at its 45th Session (from 18 June to July 1993) the Drafting Committee of the International Law Commission recommended that the term 'significant harm' be used in place of 'appreciable harm', following a suggestion by the new Special Rapporteur that the latter term may have an alternative meaning which would lead to ambiguity. As will be noted later, the International Law Commission has not yet taken action upon the recommendations of its Committee. In any event, there is no real difference between 'significant harm' and 'appreciable harm' as used in OD 7.50.
3   Quotes New Mexico Supreme Court, Mathers v Texaco, 77 NM 239 (1966): 239; 243–4; 421 para. 2d; 771; 775.

Bibliography

Hayton, R.D. and Utton, A.E. (1989) *Transboundary Groundwaters: The Bellagio Draft Treaty,* Albuquerque: International Transboundary Resources Center.

ILC (1988) 'Report of the International Law Commission on the work of its fortieth session', *United Nations General Assembly, Official Records,* forty-fifth session, Supplement No.10(A/43/10).

—— (1993) 'Report of the International Law Commission on the work of its forty-fifth session', *United Nations General Assembly, Official Records,* forty-fifth session, Supplement No.10(A/48/10).

McCaffrey, S. (1989) 'The Law of International Watercourses: some recent developments and unanswered questions', *Denver Journal of International Law and Policy* 17: 505–26.
—— (Special Rapporteur) (1990) 'Sixth report on the Law of the Non-Navigational Uses of International Watercourses', United Nations General Assembly, Doc.A/CN.4/427 and Add.1, in *Yearbook of the International Law Commission* II, 1.
Naff, T. (1993) 'International riparian law in the West and Islam', in Proceedings of the International Symposium on Water Resources in the Middle East; Policy and Institutional Aspects, Urbana, Illinois, USA, October.
UNTS 419 'Indus Waters Treaty between India and Pakistan of 19 September 1960', *United Nations Treaty Series* 419: 125.

11

The Effects of War on Water and Energy Resources in Croatia and Bosnia

Mladen Klemencic

Introduction

This paper may not appear to be very optimistic regarding transboundary co-operation but it is rooted in real life and experience. After the break up of Yugoslavia the character of relations between former republics changed significantly. As they had successfully undertaken many joint ventures during the 'Yugoslav' period, the former republics, today's successor states, should have had their earlier co-operation redefined on a new basis. But peaceful resolution of those issues was blocked by the crises and war caused by Greater-Serbian ambitions in Croatia and Bosnia-Hercegovina. In this situation of permanent tension, transboundary co-operation and management of shared natural resources appear to be marginal questions. The depth of conflict overshadowed not only these, but many other vital issues.

However, there are some positive cases in the area. Slovenia and Croatia have reached an agreement regarding the only ex-Yugoslav nuclear power plant at Krsko. The power plant was built in Slovenia in the 1970s as a joint venture. The energy produced was equally shared between Croatia and Slovenia and co-operation has been continued on the same basis under the new circumstances for the benefit of both sides.

But there are many more examples showing completely different effects of the crises and war on transboundary co-operation. In most cases there has been no co-operation at all. Moreover, there are examples showing that originally-shared resources have become a particular bone of contention where geographic conditions have been favourable. The case studies in this paper give evidence on the variable, but mostly negative, effects of the war on transboundary management in and between Croatia and Bosnia-Hercegovina (Figure 11.1).

1 ZRMANJA
2 CETINA
3 TREBISNICA

Figure 11.1 Position of River Systems

The Zrmanja River

The hydro-power and water-supply system on the Zrmanja river in northern Dalmatia (Figure 11.2) was not originally of a transboundary character. All installations, as well as the drainage area of the river, are within the boundaries of the Republic of Croatia, but after the war broke out the area was found to be on the 'other side of the line'. In particular it is on the cease-fire or dividing line between rebel Serbs and regular forces of the Republic of Croatia. The main installations of the Zrmanja system, including a reversible hydro-power plant, the Stikada reservoir, and the Dolac pumping stations are on territory controlled by the irregulars. The cease-fire line divides those

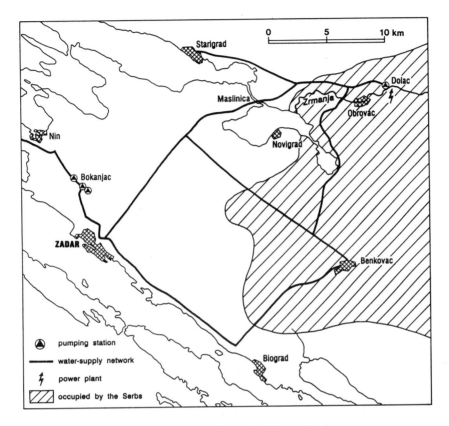

Figure 11.2 The Zrmanja River System

installations from the main consumption area, namely the town of Zadar.

During three years of war and fragile cease-fires no agreement has been reached upon exploiting the water resources. The consequences of the break up of the original power transmission network are experienced not only by the population of the town of Zadar, but by the population of the whole region of Dalmatia. Reductions in the power supply were sharp enough to paralyse the entire economy of the region. A regular electricity supply was provided only after alternative sources of energy, such as expensive liquid-fuel plants, were installed.

The break up of the supply system caused the greatest problems concerning water consumption in Zadar. The town was without a regular and sufficient supply of water for months. Water from the Zrmanja river was substituted by reactivation of former pumping stations in the neighbouring area of Bokanjac, but the alternative could not provide sufficient quantities of water. The water shortage was especially acute during the dry summer months when minimal demands were ensured only by special shipments of fresh water from other areas.

The case of the Zrmanja river shows how water resources can be mis-used, or can be used as part of a war campaign. It is surprising how inactive the UN peacekeeping forces were, although their mandate included the re-establishment of all means of communication. In spite of repeated warnings and requests by the Croatian authorities, the peacekeeping forces have done nothing to force rebels to co-operate in order to at least partially alleviate shortages in Zadar, and the coastal area around it.

The Cetina River

The Cetina river system (Figure 11.3) is an interesting case of transboundary co-operation in a karst area, quite apart from the questions raised by the war. The river's drainage area covers 3,725km^2, but only 38% (some 1,440km^2) of it is within the orographical limits of the river valley in Croatia. Around 61% of the drainage area embraces the karst *poljes* of south-western Bosnia and the mountain area around them. Such a huge and water-rich drainage area provided good conditions for the building of a complex water-power and water-supply system. The power plant of Kraljevac on the Gubavica waterfall was built as early as 1912, the first big power plant in Croatia. After the Second World War the power plants of Peruca, Zakucac 1 and 2, and Djale were constructed in the Cetina river valley, as well as that of Orlovac supplied by water coming from the Busko lake in Bosnia-Hercegovina. The Busko lake is the central reservoir for waters collected from the karst *poljes* of Livno, Duvno, Glamoc, and Kupres and is connected with the Cetina river valley by a subterranean tunnel through the Kamesnica mountain. The water-power system of Cetina is therefore a transboundary one because the power plants are in Croatia, but they depend completely, or partially, on inflow from Bosnia. Both former-Yugoslav republics, today independent states, participated in the building of the installations for the system.

Joint management of the system, which constitutes 42% of Croatia's hydroelectric capacities, was stopped by the war. It was encouraged by the fact that the area around Busko lake in Bosnia-Hercegovina is inhabited mostly by Croats and during the war it has stayed under their control. But the war caused problems in the part of the system within Croatia, on territory controlled by rebel Serb forces. The upper part of the Cetina valley, including another huge reservoir of Peruca, together with the dam and power plant of the same name, stayed out of legal Croatian control. Since 1991 the installation has not been functioning as part of the integral power network of Croatia. The Peruca dam and

Figure 11.3 The Cetina River System

power plant are situated in an area designated a 'pink zone' since the United Nation's Protection Force (UNPROFOR) deployment in Croatia. Although they were for some time under Serbian control, according to the so-called Vance peace plan, pink zones are not part of the UN Protected Area (UNPA) in Croatia. UNPROFOR's original task was to demilitarise the area and to look after the re-institution of legal authorities, but that task has never been fulfilled. Moreover, during 1992 the Peruca dam was subject to continuous threats. The Serbs, who controlled the area, persistently kept the water level in the lake above the tolerance level. Moreover, they laid mines in the dam, and therefore threatened downstream areas with an ecological catastrophe. Mines laid in the dam were finally activated on 28 January

1993. The dam was sabotaged after the Serbs were militarily and politically forced to withdraw from the area. The explosion, fortunately, did not cause a sudden catastrophe. The dam was seriously damaged but Croatian experts prevented a catastrophe in time.

The Trebisnica River

The Trebisnica river system is situated mostly within Bosnia-Hercegovina (Figure 11.4), but an important installation, the Dubrovnik power plant, is in Croatia. Water from Trebisnica is partially diverted towards the Croatian coast through a tunnel. There is a power plant as well as a pumping station only a few kilometres south-east of the town of Dubrovnik. The pumping station was built to serve the water supply system of the Dubrovnik coastal area, as well as the Bay of Kotor in Montenegro. Therefore, three republics of the former Yugoslavia participated originally in water management of a single river basin.

During the war the Serbs, who controlled the valley of the Trebisnica river, blocked the tunnel and prevented operation of the power plant. Nevertheless, during 1992 an agreement was reached among local authorities upon resumption of both water-power and water-supply systems. An agreement was reached at local level, separate from the main peace negotiations. According to the agreement

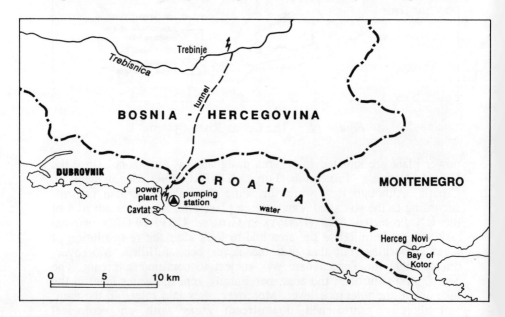

Figure 11.4 The Trebisnica River System

the Serbs enabled the inflow of water through the tunnel for the Dubrovnik power plant, while the Croatian side guaranteed the water supply for the Bay of Kotor. Therefore, a sort of tripartite agreement was signed and transboundary co-operation concerning water resources was renewed. The agreement was based on the vital interests of the local population and it was not subject to political solutions discussed within the main negotiations.

Conclusion

The case studies examined by this paper provide evidence of the different effects of war regarding water resources. The cases of the Zrmanja and Cetina rivers bear witness to the development and significance of dividing lines within Croatia. The cease-fire line between Croats and Serbs appears to be more of a barrier against co-operation than the international boundary between Croatia and Bosnia. Moreover, the Serbs did not hesitate to target water facilities directly instead of keeping them out of combat. In both cases the UN peace-keeping forces failed to establish normal conditions. UNPROFOR did not prevent sabotage on the Peruca dam although the Serbs openly threatened it long before they actually sabotaged the dam. The third case, that of Trebisnica river, is a more optimist one. A compromise was reached because both sides had an interest in achieving a peaceful and reasonable solution.

In the future, theoretically, water resources as well as other transboundary resources and facilities might be a means of confidence building in the region. However, it is still not clear whether certain aspects of transboundary co-operation can precede political resolution or whether co-operation will come only as a consequence of future political resolution. As far as past developments show, local conditions will remain for some time probably the most important decisive factor. Such a situation can generate some good solutions for particular cases, but on the other hand it cannot guarantee long-term peaceful management in the area as a whole.

12

Development of the Slovak–Hungarian Section of the Danube

Miroslav B. Liska

The idea of utilising the enormous energy of the Danube dates back to the beginning of this century, but it took nearly another 50 years, until progress in science and technology was ready for the implementation of such projects. During the fifties and sixties the complex utilisation of the Váh and Vltava rivers was the main task, but studies of the development of the short Czecho–Slovak stretch of the Danube were already under way, accompanied by necessary surveys and research.

The same approach can be witnessed in the upper section of the Danube, where in Austria there are nine river-steps in operation and the tenth (Freudenau) is under construction. Germany has also built a whole cascade of river-steps and recently accomplished the historical dream of connecting the North and Black Seas by the Rhine–Main–Danube Canal.

The development of the Danube was not limited to the more developed countries of Western Europe. Former Yugoslavia and Romania built the Iron Gate Project on the lower Danube, overcoming the biggest navigation obstacle – the Danube Cataracts – and installing a huge electrical capacity of 2,050MW, producing nearly as much electric energy as all nine Austrian river-steps.

Preparation of the Gabčíkovo–Nagymaros (G–N) System of Projects

After intensive studies and elaboration of preliminary designs in 1961, 1964, and 1967 (every time in more detail), towards the end of 1960s there was a period of hesitation, because of the large financial resources required. Eventually, three impulses pushed the G–N System from the stage of study into implementation:

1 large and catastrophic floods, in Hungary in 1954 and in 1965 in Slovakia, and the request of the inhabitants of the endangered region for flood-protection and economic development of the region;
2 the recommendation of the Danube Commission to improve the parameters of the Danubean waterway between Bratislava and

Budapest, which the governments of Czechoslovakia (ČSFR) and Hungary (HR) accepted; and
3 the oil crisis in 1973, which showed the importance of developing domestic and renewable sources of energy.

Brief Description of the Gabčíkovo–Nagymaros System

The mutually agreed upon solution consists of the following parts and structures (Figure 12.1):

1 a reservoir containing 243 million m³ of water, having a surface of 60km², reaching up to Bratislava (rkm1,868[1]), created by the Dunakiliti weir situated on Hungarian territory at rkm1,842 and by peripheral dams on both sides of the Danube;
2 a diversion canal 25km long, enabling the control of flood peaks and the bypassing the gravel fords and narrows constituting serious obstacles to navigation, and creating the head-water of the hydroelectric power station (HPS);
3 the Gabčíkovo canal-step, situated at km17 of the canal, comprising two ship-locks (34 x 275m) and a peak HPS equipped with eight Kaplan turbines (gross head: 16–23m) and generators with a total installed capacity of 720MW and an average output of 3 billion kWh/year, two-thirds of peak capacity;
4 the Nagymaros river-step situated at rkm1,696, containing a weir with seven taintor gates (24 x 8m – the same as Dunakiliti) and two ship-locks (size as in Gabčíkovo), but a smaller run-of-the-river HPS with six horizontal turbines (gross head: 3–10m), producing on average one billion kWh/year;
5 flood levees reconstructed into lateral dams along the Danube and its tributaries, with seepage canals and pumping stations;
6 deepened sections of the Danube downstream of Palkovičovo and downstream of Nagymaros; and
7 protective measures in the old Danube channel, along the diversion canal (rkm1,842 to rkm1,810).

The 1977 Treaty Concerning Construction and Operation of the Gabčíkovo–Nagymaros System (Treaty 77)

The bilateral 'presidential' treaty of highest rank was signed in 1977 and ratified by the parliaments of both countries. Because the system was asymmetrical, with a larger portion of structures on Slovak territory (and with a significantly larger occupation of land) – the Treaty was deliberately conceived as unilaterally unrevocable. The main structures: the Dunakiliti weir, the diversion canal, the Gabčíkovo canal step and the Nagymaros river-step were considered

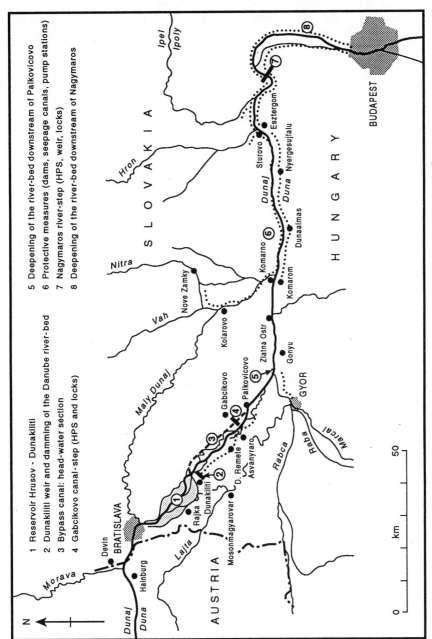

Figure 12.1 General Layout of the Gabcikovo–Nagymaros System

mutual property. All the costs and energy produced were – or in the case of energy should be – divided equally, in spite of significant differences in the schedule of implementation. The Treaty involved no change of borders, which remained 'in the present (1977) main navigation line' (Treaty, 1977: Article 22).

Progress and Delays of Construction Works

The construction of Gabčíkovo started in 1978. The first unit was to be put into operation in July 1986 and the construction of the whole G–N Project was scheduled for completion at the end of 1990. However, in the early eighties, following a Hungarian request, the possibility of temporary suspension of work was negotiated, with the result of the signing of a Protocol amending the Treaty 77, prolonging the construction time and delaying the date of operation by four years.

In 1984, the Hungarian Republic signed an agreement with Austrian firms concerning the financing and construction of the Hungarian share of the work. As a result, Hungary proposed the shortening of the construction time of Nagymaros by 15 months. After starting work on Nagymaros in 1988, the amendment to the Treaty 77 was accepted in the form of a Protocol, signed in February 1989 – only three months before Hungary, without any notice and previous consultation, suspended work on Nagymaros and later also stopped the implementation of its share of the work on Gabčíkovo.

Obstacles in Accomplishing the Gabčíkovo–Nagymaros Project

The official reason for the suspension and later termination of work was the threat of an environmental catastrophe. At first however, the completion of the Gabčíkovo Project was not contested. The offer of a common completion of Gabčíkovo was, in fact, officially submitted by the Hungarian side in November 1989, but was withdrawn in January 1990, after the preliminary studies of the temporary solution on Slovak territory were stopped.

However, the background to these events was of a political character, as the reports of Hungarian authors revealed. Protests against the communist regime in the form of political demonstrations were severely suppressed, but environmental protests were tolerated. As one of the largest investments, all the difficulties of the country could be related to Nagymaros: mainly impact on the environment and a burden on the state. The public was not informed that Austrian firms had taken over not only the construction of two main structures – the Dunakiliti weir and the Nagymaros river-step – but also their financing, with the prospect of repayment through part of the Hungarian share of electric energy produced.

In addition, the arguments were 'enriched' by a national dimension. Nagymaros was said to spoil the view on the Danube bend at Visegrad, considered to be part of the national heritage. Austrians were accused of the eco-exploitation of neighbouring countries, and Slovaks of an attempt to separate Hungarians living along the Danube and to concretise the borders, ie, to fix the border definitely in the Danube bed, according to the decision of the Trianon peace treaty of 1920. This treaty was considered by many Hungarians to have been forced upon their country after the fall of the Austro-Hungarian Empire, reducing Hungary significantly in size. The borderline in a region of mixed population was drawn so that about an equal number of 400,000 Slovaks remained in Hungary, and Hungarians in Slovakia. After half-a-century, during which the Hungarian army occupied the south of Slovakia three times, the number of Slovaks in Hungary fell to about 10,000, while the number of Hungarians in Slovakia grew to over 560,000. But illogically, the Slovaks were accused of an attempt to assimilate the Hungarians. As the 1977 Treaty contains a voluntarily signed confirmation of the Trianon border line, some groups of Hungarians strove to abrogate it by all possible means.

In an attempt to preserve good neighbourly relations, ČSFR used every opportunity to negotiate, with the aim of discovering the reasons for the unilateral abandonment of work. It reviewed all the potential environmental impacts of the G–N Project and studied all possibilities for their mitigation.

On the other hand, the Hungarian side, violating the Treaty (the validity of which it did not contest at the time), gradually brought the activities of the Joint Expert Group to a standstill and also reduced the meetings of plenipotentiaries under various pretexts. Thus communication on a professional level was stopped and no possibility remained of verifying accusations and of finding a solution to the disputed problems.

The offer of the plenipotentiary of the ČSFR Government, to address a joint request for assistance to the European Community in the frame of the PHARE[2] programme, to study the most serious of the possible impacts on groundwater levels, was rejected by the Hungarian side in October 1990. On the basis of all the evaluations carried out thus far, taking into account all possibilities, including the proposed abandonment of the Project, in January 1991 the governments of the ČSFR and of the Slovak Republic decided to continue the preparation of the temporary solution within the territory of the ČSFR. The economic damage resulting from the abandonment would reach a sum of over 100 billion Crowns, which represents (in purchase value) about US$10 billion.

The government delegations met, after long delays, in April 1991, nearly two years after the unilateral stoppage of work. After violating the obligation to notify and to consult on the matter prior to taking unilateral action, the Hungarian side also disrespected the 'obligation

to negotiate with the aim of reaching a solution of the dispute',
prescribed by international customary law. By a resolution of its
parliament of April 1991, the Hungarian government was authorised to
negotiate only the abrogation of the Treaty, and the restoration of the
'original state of the territory' which was clearly impossible by that
time. Therefore, all talks on a professional level were conditional upon
the acceptance of an ultimate request to discontinue work fulfilling the
Treaty also on the ČSFR side.

Under these limitations, the second round of negotiations between
the government delegations in July 1991 could not, and did not,
contribute anything to the solution of the dispute. At the end of July,
the governments of the Slovak Republic and the ČSFR decided to
implement the temporary solution to put the Gabčíkovo Project into
operation. Preparatory work started in November 1991.

The Temporary Solution of Operation of the Gabčíkovo Project

The aim of the temporary solution (called variant 'C', because variant
'A' was the completion of the whole G–N Project according to the
Treaty and variant 'B' the completion of Gabčíkovo in co-operation
with Hungary) was to diminish the size of the reservoir by one-third,
in order to limit it to Slovak territory and to replace the function of the
Dunakiliti weir (Figure 12.2).

The temporary solution consists of the following structures:

1 a lateral dam, 5–7m high, 11km long, leading along the left bank of
   the Danube from the right dam of the canal to Čunovo – the final
   closure of the Danube bed at rkm1,851.75;
2 the Čunovo system of weirs, replacing the function of Dunakiliti,
   contained in the first phase: a bypass weir with four taintor gates
   (18 x 5.1m), an inundation weir with 20 taintor gates (24 x 3.6m),
   an intake into the Mosoni Danube with a connection canal, and dams
   connecting the structures with lateral right side dams;
3 structures of the second phase: a weir with three taintor gates
   (24 x 8.5m), enabling the passage of bottom sediments and ice-
   blocks, an auxiliary lock for recreational vessels, divisible into two
   sections 24 x (125 + 50.5) and a HPS with a capacity of 52MW,
   which can serve to discharge a minimum sustainable flow of up to
   400m³/sec into the old Danube channel in order to secure the
   survival of its aquatic environment.

The first phase of the variant 'C' structures was put into operation by
closing the Danube bed at the end of October 1992, and following the
partial filling of the reservoir and the canal, the experimental operation
of the Gabčíkovo HPS was also started.

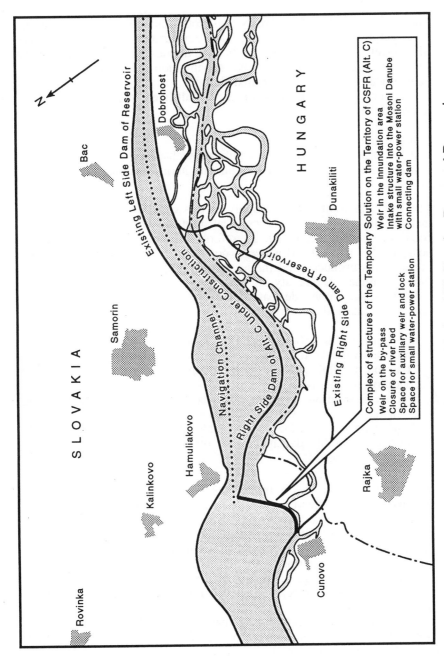

Figure 12.2 Temporary Solution (Variant 'C') Showing Decreased Reservoir

Legal Aspects of the Dispute

The validity of the 1977 Treaty was not contested by the Hungarian side, yet Hungary has suspended and terminated its fulfilment since May 1989. It is beyond any doubt that treaties are to be kept *(pacta sunt servanda),* if the civilised cohabitation of nations is to be maintained, especially in a unified Europe.

Of course, there are cases when non-fulfilment of a treaty could be tolerated:

– if it is impossible to fulfil it;
– if the basic conditions have significantly changed;
– if its fulfilment would cause significant harm or damage.

The first condition does not apply to this case. The second does not include the change of the political regime while other (physical) conditions have not changed. Therefore, only the third condition could possibly be applied. However, no new evidence about expected impacts was produced and the acceptable mitigation of these has been foreseen in the 1977 Treaty.

In any case, if one side feared that some of the known impacts could seriously damage the environment, it would be obliged to:

– inform the partner about its fears or suspicions;
– produce evidence that the fears are substantiated, and that there exists no possibility of mitigation of the impacts under the existing conditions of the treaty;
– propose a solution, together with its technical documentation and estimated costs, and with an evaluation of its consequences;
– if the proposed solution is acceptable only to one side, but would cause considerable damage to the other side, a fair compensation should be proposed.

When one side violates a treaty, the other has the right to stop its fulfilment – but in this case the damage was caused by interruption of fulfilment and such a countermeasure would only worsen the situation. A countermeasure taken (eg, stopping of fulfilment of the treaty), cannot logically justify the previous breach or a subsequent termination of the treaty. Countermeasures not connected with the treaty (eg, blocking of the passage of trucks or ships, as threatened by Hungary) would only worsen the relations between the two states, but would not diminish the damage.

In the case of significant damage caused by a unilateral breach of the treaty, measures not foreseen by the treaty are admissible and justified, but only under certain conditions:

- measures should be temporary, to force the partner to fulfil its obligations; therefore, if successful, the measures should be withdrawable;
- measures should diminish significant damage by partly fulfilling the goals of the treaty;
- measures must not be inhuman or damaging to the partner or to third parties.

If Hungary in this case were to claim that the provisional solution of putting the Gabčíkovo part of the Project into operation causes significant harm, it can be easily proved that:

- the temporary solution, diminishing the size of the reservoir and limiting it to Slovak territory, has a lower impact on Hungarian territory than the mutually agreed original solution;
- if the planned measures had been implemented, the impact of the operation would have been beneficial.

Effects of Operation of the Gabčíkovo Project

Improved flood-safety has been achieved in the whole Gabčíkovo section of the Danube, on both banks of the river. Nearly half of the volume of a 100-year flood ($10,600 m^3/sec$) can pass through the canal, thus relieving the hydraulic load on the deteriorated subsoil of the levees.

The navigation parameters in the section of the Danube between Bratislava and Palkovičovo have been improved in accordance with the recommendations of the Danube Commission.

In its first year of operation the Gabčíkovo hydroelectric power station produced nearly two billion kW-hours of electric energy – but only of the basic quality of run-of-the-river power. Generation of peak power and the ability to take on a regulatory role in the national grid (for example servicing sudden energy demands whilst thermal power stations work up to full capacity) has been impossible without the stilling basin of Nagymaros, and energy from this section remains undeveloped.

Problems of flood protection and navigation improvement downstream of Palkovičovo have remained unsolved.

Environmental Impacts of the Gabčíkovo Project

The impounding of Danube water and the slowing down of the high velocity of its current has definitely stopped the erosion of the river-bed, with all its detrimental consequences. The harbour in Bratislava is again fully accessible and the branches of the Malý and Mosoni

Danubes were salvaged from a sewer-like state and transformed into rivers with a permanent flow, gradually improving their environments.

The groundwater level in all relevant sections of the Danube has been raised – by 3–4m downstream of Bratislava and about 50cm at Dunajská Streda; this rise has also beneficially increased the dynamics of the underground flow. The drainage effect of the tailrace canal and of the old river-bed affected only a very limited part of the adjacent area. This influence has been compensated for by the filling of all the branches of the Danube with water, improving the situation even beyond the pre-dam state.

Since the early eighties, the quality of the Danube water has constantly improved. Since 1993, the urban waste water of Bratislava has been treated at the town on the right side of the Danube. Several sewer systems with purification plants have also been constructed in the villages along the Danube. Analyses of sediment show no dangerous organic matter and older deposits are trapped in fine sediments, not affecting the groundwater quality. The asphalt-concrete lining of the canal does not influence quality. The possibility of eutrophication of water in the lower part of the reservoir and in the canal will not become dangerous until a sufficiently large flow is maintained.

. The quality of groundwater either has not changed or has even been improved (enriched oxygen content). As expected, the increased seepage nearly exclusively feeds the upper, very polluted layer of groundwater, dilutes it, and slowly flushes the polluted water into the lower situated Malý and Mosoni Danubes.

The conditions of the aquatic life and wildlife have been largely improved by the abundance of water in the inland delta of the Danube, which has been returned to much better conditions, like those that existed decades ago. An area free from the passage of vessels is also planned for the future.

Intervention of the International Court of Justice and the State of the Dispute

Both sides agreed to present their dispute to the International Court of Jusctice in The Hague. Only the temporary water-management regime is under discussion. The Treaty of 1977 provided for the discharge of a minimum flow of 50m³/sec in winter and up to 200m³/sec in the growing season into the Danube, which left 81% of the average run-off for electricity production. The Slovak side proposed, as a fair compromise, to temporarily raise (until the decision of the Court) the minimum sustainable flow several times, to a level of 100–500m³/sec, which would leave the power station about 65% of the average run-off.

The Hungarian side requested the maintenance of about two-thirds of the run-off in the Danube, which would dramatically reduce the output and worsen the economy of Gabčíkovo, without gaining significant environmental effects. On the contrary, from the ecological point of view, in such a case erosion would continue in the old Danube channel, as would the danger of eutrophication of water in the reservoir. Much better effects can be obtained by the proposed underwater dams and other previewed measures.

The monitoring results prove that, after implementation of the correct measures, the resulting environmental impacts are prevailingly beneficial. Therefore, the next step should be the filling of all the branches on the Hungarian side with water, which would eliminate practically all adverse impacts. Close monitoring and its evaluation would then enable the proposal of necessary improvement measures.

The dispute has never been a dispute between Slovaks and Hungarians, but rather between those who were familiar with all the facts and those who either used the issue to gain some political influence, or who uncritically accepted unsubstantiated opinions or various half-truths out of context. Co-operation with Hungarian colleagues in the framework of the 1977 Treaty was very good and the idea of returning to the treaty conditions is backed up also by Hungarian independent experts – professors of the technical universities of Budapest, Karlsruhe, and Milwaukee. As soon as the matter is given to professionals to settle, and the influence of politicians is eliminated, a mutually acceptable solution will be found.

Notes

1   rkm refers to locations on the Danube measured upstream in kilometres from the mouth of the river.
2   The PHARE Programme is an environmentally oriented programme, financed by the European Union, originally as the Poland and Hungary Aid for Research of the Environment, but now utilised for all East European countries.

13

Building a Legal Regime for the
Jordan–Yarmouk River System:
Lessons from Other International Rivers

N. Kliot

Introduction

The water resources of the Jordan–Yarmouk river, an international river with very small amounts of water, are a continuous source of dispute between Israel and the other co-riparians of the basin: Syria, Lebanon, and the Hashemite Kingdom of Jordan (see Figure 13.1). More recently, the groundwater resources of the Occupied West Bank have become a source of conflict between Israelis and Palestinians. According to Mandel (1991) there are three theoretical sources of conflict over international (transboundary) rivers:

NON-CO-OPERATIVE SETTING

In the case of the Jordan–Yarmouk this is expressed by a history of 'war in rounds' between Israel and her Arab neighbours since it became independent in 1948. The hostility among the riparians of the Jordan–Yarmouk embraces all the levels of relations between states, and when states are involved in disputes over issues of 'high politics' they are disinclined to co-operate in issues of 'low politics' such as the development of water resources in a shared basin (Lowi, 1993). Though American mediator Eric Johnston tried, in the 1950s and 1960s, to negotiate an agreement among the riparians of the Jordan–Yarmouk he did not succeed and, except for Israel and Jordan who agreed to the water allocations of the Johnston Plan, no other riparian consented to it, and no agreement has been reached.

ENVIRONMENTAL IMBALANCE

The second source of conflict over international river basins is the environmental imbalance. This refers to the perceived growing scarcity of usable water and perceived growing inequality in the distribution of usable water. Within the Jordan–Yarmouk river basin the Hashemite

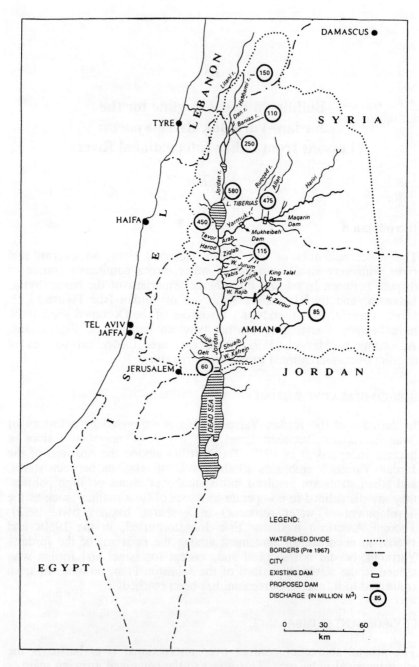

Figure 13.1 Hydrology, Geomorphology and Geography of the
Jordan–Yarmuk Basin

Kingdom of Jordan is already facing a growing scarcity of water and a growing inequality in the distribution of usable water. Syria (and to a lesser extent, Israel) have expanded their use of the Yarmouk waters to such an extent that Jordan has been left with only a small amount of water. Israel would not agree to the construction of a storage dam (the Maqarin Dam) on the Yarmouk (a project which could expand the water supply of Jordan) unless her riparian rights in the river were acknowledged – a situation unacceptable to Syria.

POWER ASYMMETRY AMONG NATIONS

Finally, the power asymmetry among nations which are reluctant partners to an international river basin, also serves as a source of conflict. Israel is perceived as the hegemon in that river basin and, as there is absolutely no restraining reciprocal interdependence among the riparian nations, there is no pressure on Israel (or Syria) to resolve their differences and reach a settlement.

In 1979 Israel signed a Peace Treaty with Egypt, and in 1994, at the time this paper is being written, negotiations over a regional peace settlement are taking place between Israel, the Palestinians, and the Arab states. This long overdue and dilatory process will also impel the adversaries to discuss common water resources.

AIMS

This paper aims to present possible regimes for the Jordan–Yarmouk river based on international regimes, as reflected by treaties and agreements in other international rivers – particularly those rivers where there is overt conflict, and in which the regime or institutional arrangement deals with consumptive water uses such as irrigation. The regimes which will be discussed in detail are the Colorado (USA and Mexico); the Indus (India and Pakistan are the major disputants although there are other riparians to the river); Lake Chad (Cameroon, Chad, Niger and Nigeria), and the Niger (Benin, Burkina Faso, Ivory Coast, Guinea, Cameroon and Chad). There are legal and hydrological principles which lie beyond these regimes.

Basin-wide development is advocated by planners, economists and even jurists. This notion is based on the concept that, as a river drainage basin constitutes one geographical unit which does not recognise any international borders, the development of the water resources of such basins should be integrated, ie, the whole river should be developed as one unit in order to maximise the benefits of such development to all the co-riparians of the basin. The legal norms of customary international law as expressed by the Helsinki Rules and International Law Commission (ILC) rules provide the legal support for this approach.

The most important articles of the International Law Association (Helsinki Rules) and ILC set of rules for international rivers stipulate the necessity for equitable and reasonable utilisation and participation in international water courses, and;

The obligation not to cause appreciable harm, namely to abstain from measures which change the quality and quantity of water available for other riparians. Under the 'community of property' model for water sources, a drainage basin is jointly developed and managed as a unit without regard to international borders, with an agreed sharing of the benefits of the river (Teclaff, 1967). Although the full realisation of such an approach is still a rare event, there are good reasons for believing that the practice of nations will move in this direction (Dellapenna, 1993: 16). None of the treaties and agreements discussed in this paper belong to this category but the Treaty for Amazonian Co-operation is a good example of this trend. Dellapenna (forthcoming) classifies the institutional arrangements adopted in the various treaties and agreements as 'measures short of allocating the water between the states' and 'measures allocating water between states'. In this paper we shall examine the utility and chances for implementation of both measures for the Jordan–Yarmouk basin.

Measures Short of Allocating the Water between the Riparians to an International Water Course

Both the ILC and Helsinki Rules stipulate the need for co-riparians to exchange information about any existing or planned project in a specific basin. ILC Rules make exchange of data and information mandatory. Also, every state that is partner to an international river basin is entitled to participate in negotiations, and to become a party to any water course agreement that applies to the entire water course. Examples can be seen in the rivers Niger, Lake Chad and Colorado.

The Act of Niamey 1966, which established the regime for the river Niger, stipulated that the riparian states will undertake to establish close co-operation concerning the study and execution of any project likely to have an appreciable effect on the river and its tributaries. To this end, it envisaged the establishment of the Niger River Commission, to be entrusted with the task of co-ordination. The riparian states, by the terms of the Agreement, undertook to inform the Commission at the earliest stage of all studies and works, and to abstain from carrying out on portions of the river and its tributaries any works without adequate notice to and prior consultation with the Commission. Since 1980 when the Niger Basin Authority replaced the Commission, this body was assigned the responsibility for this function (Ofosu-Amaah, 1990; Teclaff, 1991). The Lake Chad Basin Commission provisions require prior consultation before the initiation of measures likely to have an appreciable effect on water quantity or quality in the basin (Sand, 1990; Agoro, 1966). The legal regime of the river Indus states that the parties, India and Pakistan, are bound to prior notification of proposed water works. The permanent Indus Commission has extensive authority which includes the initiation of hydrological studies and undertaking tours of inspection (Rauschning, 1990; Baxter, 1967).

None of the above measures prevail in the Jordan–Yarmouk basin. When the American mediator Johnston tried to negotiate an agreement on water allocation for the partners in that basin he was confronted with the problems of lack of data, partial data and contradictory data in relation to the water resources of the basin (Kliot, 1994). The co-riparians of that basin never exchanged any data and neglected their duty to notify the other riparians of any water works that were being planned or implemented. The outcome is that Syria, Israel and Jordan embarked on separate development projects of the water resources of the basin, causing appreciable harm to each other and creating water wastage and inefficient and expensive water delivery systems (Kliot, 1994).

Lack of information and limited or no access to scientific data on the underground water resources of the West Bank impede Palestinian researchers who need this data in order to evaluate the water resources available for the West Bank. A decision to establish a data bank and measures for information and scientific research exchange between Palestinians, Israelis and other researchers was taken in a recent conference (which convened in Urbana-Champaign, Illinois, USA). It is quite clear that exchange of data and mandatory consultations must be the first essential step in any negotiations among the co-riparians of the Jordan–Yarmouk water course and the mountain groundwater resources of the West Bank. The scarce water resources of this basin must be utilised with the greatest care and this task is impossible in the absence of any co-operation among the reluctant partners of the basin.

Measures for Allocation of Common Water Resources

THE LEGAL REGIME OF PARTITION OF THE INDUS

It is crucial to differentiate between the Indus and other international river basins presented in this paper, because there is no integrated development of the water resources of this basin, except for a consent between the partners to utilise its water and to divide the water resources as equitably as possible. As partition of water may be a solution for the Jordan–Yarmouk basin it is necessary to explore, in depth, the regime and agreement for this basin.

The Indus River basin became an international river when India and Pakistan re-emerged as independent states after 1947. The Indus basin drains an area of 1,000,000km² and flows for 2,970km from the Tibetan plateau to the Arabian Sea near Karachi. Its principle tributaries are the Kabul, the Jhelum and the Chenab, the Sutlej, Beas and Ravi. The co-riparians are therefore, China, Nepal, Afghanistan, India and Pakistan, but only the two latter states utilise its waters. During the period of British rule the area between the tributaries in Punjab was the first to be developed. The 1947 boundary of partition cut across the Indus basin in such a way that of the 13 canal systems of the basin in pre-partition Punjab, 10 were in Pakistan and two in India, and one canal was divided between the two countries (Rauschning, 1990: 216). East Punjab (India) discontinued the water supply to West Punjab (Pakistan) in two of the canals and a conflict between the newly created states became a heated dispute.

The International Bank for Reconstruction and Development (World Bank) proffered its good offices in order to facilitate negotiations among the co-riparians. The World Bank first suggested a basin-wide integrated development plan for the Indus based on functional co-operation between India and Pakistan but both countries were unwilling for such broad co-operation (Baxter, 1967; Lepawsky, 1963). After some years of negotiations, mediated by the Bank, the Indus Water Treaty was signed on 19 September 1960 by India, Pakistan and the World Bank (UNTS, 1962, vol. 419: 125). The Treaty assigned all the waters of the eastern tributaries of the Indus (Sutlej, Beas and Ravi) to India and the western tributaries (Jhelum and Chenab, and main channel of the Indus) to Pakistan (see Figure 13.2).

A transition period of 10–13 years was established during which Pakistan was to receive waters from the eastern rivers (from India) and took upon itself to construct and bring into operation a system of canals which will divert water from the western tributaries to the irrigated areas of Western Punjab.

India also agreed to make a contribution of £62 million towards the cost of the above work. The World Bank granted Pakistan a loan, and raised development funds for Pakistan to cover its expenses in developing a separate irrigation system. The Treaty also contained provisions for co-operation, declaration of intention to prevent undue water pollution and measures for settlement of disputes (Rauschning, 1990). A permanent Indus Commission, consisting of two commissioners appointed by India and Pakistan respectively, was assigned. Authority was given to establish and maintain co-operation arrangements for the implementation of the Treaty and to promote co-operation between the parties (Baxter, 1967: 47).

We may pose the question as to what are the ramifications of the Indus Treaty to the body of customary international law, and what are the lessons to be learned from it which will apply to the Jordan–Yarmouk basin?

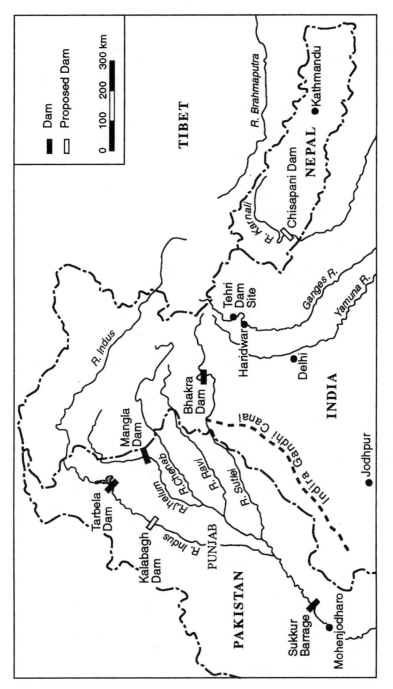

Figure 13.2 The Partition of the Indus

RAMIFICATIONS FOR THE JORDAN–YARMOUK BASIN

Article XI of the Indus Water Treaty states expressly that the parties (India and Pakistan) did not intend to establish any general principle of law or any precedent. But the practice and implementation of the Treaty point to some important principles of international law. India gave up its upper stream sovereignty and belief that it could utilise the resources of the upper tributaries however it wishes.

The second principle of international law which was applied by the Indus Treaty is the principle of equitable apportionment of the water of that basin.

However, the Indus basin manifests some similarities to the Jordan–Yarmouk basin. First, India and Pakistan have had a tradition of hostility since their independence and, with specific respect to Indus River basin issues, a mutual atmosphere of 'suspicion and bitterness' prevailed, in which separate sovereignty rather than shared interdependence was the norm (Mehta, 1986: 11; quoted in Mandel, 1991: 23). Since the partition of the Indian subcontinent, India and Pakistan have engaged in three full-scale wars as well as numerous other skirmishes. Yet in each instance they did not target water facilities or interfere in the operations of the Joint Indo-Pakistani Indus Commission (Dellapenna, 1993: 5). Also relevant to the Israeli–Arab context of conflict is the power asymmetry between the riparian states India and Pakistan. India was in a position to enforce any arrangement on Pakistan and there was little restraining reciprocal interdependence between India and Pakistan. Israel is perceived as the most powerful state in the Jordan–Yarmouk basin and was able to disrupt any Arab water projects which it felt were harmful to its water supply.

Following the Indus precedent, a partition of the Jordan–Yarmouk water resources may evolve along the following lines: the Jordan resources Dan, Hasbani and Banias would be assigned to Israel together with the side-tributaries and Lake Tiberias drainage basin. The Dan, with a total water supply of 250 million m^3 originates in Israel and all of its drainage basin is within Israel. The sources of the Hasbani (125–130 million m^3) are located in Lebanon and some of it is used by the local Lebanese farmers – the rest flowing into Israel. Israel could pay Lebanon an annual rent for the use of these waters. The Banias, the third of the tributaries of the Jordan, was located within Syrian territory before 1967. Its water supply amounts to 130 million m^3 and it also flows to Israel. Unlike the Hasbani, it was not utilised before 1967, because the geomorphological and geological structure of the spring and the topography of its surroundings are difficult, and pumping the water to the areas where it is needed is both difficult and expensive. Israel could compensate Syria for the benefits it receives from the Banias. Both Syria and Lebanon would have to waive their riparian rights to these two tributaries.

The Yarmouk and its tributaries would be assigned to Syria and the Kingdom of Jordan. Most of the drainage basin of the Yarmouk and most of its water resources, which total some 450–475 million m³ of water, originate in Syria. Syria at this time, is using about 200 million m³ of the Yarmouk's waters, whereas Jordan is left with only 120–130 million m³ for its use. Israel is utilising some 70–100 million m³ – mostly winter flow stored in Lake Tiberias (Kliot, 1994; Lowi, 1993). A plan to partition the water of the Yarmouk must include Israel waiving its riparian rights to the Yarmouk. Syria and Jordan could co-operate in the construction of the Maqarin Dam on the Yarmouk thus expanding water supply to Jordan and hydro-electricity to Syria. However, the construction of the Maqarin is dependent on Syria's curtailing of its water use of the Yarmouk. As stated before, it is already using nearly 200 million m³ of water in the upper stream parts of the Yarmouk. Because of this extensive use, the above mentioned Maqarin Dam cannot store more than 50–100 million m³ of water for Jordan. Syria and Jordan will have to compensate Israel for the rights in the Yarmouk, which it is giving away. It is also important to note that Jordan and Syria most probably will have to apportion some of the Yarmouk waters to the Palestinian entity of the West Bank, which is also a partner to the river. In conclusion, a partition of the water resources of the Jordan–Yarmouk drainage basin will divide these scarce and precious resources as follows:

Syria 160–180 million m³ of water (Yarmouk)
Jordan 150–180 million m³ of water (Yarmouk)
Israel 400 million m³ of water (Upper Jordan)
The Palestinians – between 50– 70 million m³ (Yarmouk)

It should be noted that this type of partition reduces the contact between the adversaries to a minimal level of co-operation and preserves the present separate development projects of Syria, Jordan and Israel.

Partition of the water of the Jordan–Yarmouk does not allow for enlarging the quantity of water which will be available for the co-riparians to a large extent, and does not necessarily represent the most efficient method of water utilisation within this basin, and also encourages waste. Most of the integrated plans envisaged for the Jordan–Yarmouk depicted Lake Tiberias as a common storage with two canals parallel to the Jordan River conveying water by gravity to areas on both sides of the river. When there is partition of the water none of these plans can be realised. Examples from other regions (Lake Chad, Niger) show that even conflicting parties could agree on co-operation rather than on partition of scarce water resources.

OTHER LEGAL REGIMES OF CO-OPERATION

The Colorado

A genuine co-operative regime for a river basin includes a commission which manages the river as a common property, avoiding projects which may cause harm, and developing projects designed for the benefits for all the co-riparians. The Colorado river was the subject of heated controversy between its co-riparians within the USA, and between the USA and Mexico. The Colorado River, 2,400km long with a water supply of 17.5 billion m³, drains an area of almost 624,000km² in the USA, but only 3,300km² in Mexico. The river serves as the border between the US and Mexico for about 33km and its waters are used for irrigation in Mexico's Baja-California (Mexicali Valley).

The Colorado Water Treaty between the US and Mexico was signed in 1944. The treaty allotted Mexico a minimum of 1.8 billion m³ of water and a maximum of 2.04 billion m³. Mexico had to construct and pay for a diversion structure to be located in the Colorado river below the international boundary, and the Morales Dam was built for that purpose. The USA constructed, at its own expense, the Davis Dam and reservoir for partial use in regulation of water delivered to Mexico (Meyers, 1967). The 1944 treaty had guaranteed Mexico a specific water quota, but the agreement said nothing specific about water quality. A controversy with Mexico on the quality of Colorado waters delivered to Mexico developed in 1961, when the average annual salinity of the flow crossing the border almost doubled. Resulting crop losses in Mexico evoked a loud outcry and Mexican officials accused the US of violating the 1944 treaty and threatened to take the issue to the International Court of Justice (Hundley, 1990: 38-9). The Americans took steps to alleviate the problem. Fresher water was released from the American dams and a canal was constructed in 1965 to divert saline drainage water around the Mexican intake. The two nations sought a negotiated settlement and on 30 August 1973 they signed an agreement known as Minute 242 of the International Boundary and Water Commission.

The agreement promised Mexico water that would have an average annual salinity of no more than 115ppm over the salinity of the water going to the Imperial Valley. The agreement obligated the US to all the costs necessary to maintain the agreed-upon salinity levels. Also, the US took upon itself the financial responsibility for the installation of the drains in the Mexicali Valley (Mexico's Baja California) and the funding of any other rehabilitation measures necessary to eliminate the 'salinity problem' there. In June 1974 the Colorado River Basin Salinity Control Act was approved by the US Congress. The measure authorised upstream salt-control projects in Nevada, Utah and Colorado and one of the world's largest desalination plants near Yuma, Arizona. (This plant was not functioning in the summer of 1994.)

It is important to note that the setting between Mexico and the USA was only mildly non-co-operative (Mandel, 1991). Although there are significant economic and socio-cultural differences between Mexico and the USA, the two countries maintain good relations. But the Mexican American inequality in usable water during the dispute was pronounced and became an emotional issue tied to Mexican nationalism (Bath, 1981: 183; Le Marquand, 1977: 30–1). Although the power disparity between the two countries was enormous, the USA behaved as a responsible riparian and took steps to solve the problem in a neighbourly manner.

The Niger
Other river regimes which may be helpful for the Jordan–Yarmouk basin come from Africa: Niger and Lake Chad. The Niger rises in the Futa Jallon highlands in Guinea and flows through Mali and Niger, forming the border between Niger and Benin – and then flows into Nigeria. The river has a drainage basin of 2.2 million km² and nine riparian states share its drainage basin. In descending order of their share in the basin the co-riparians are Mali, Nigeria, Niger, Algeria, Guinea, Cameroon, Burkina Faso, Benin, Ivory Coast and Chad. The Niger is 4,290km long and is navigable in its upper course in Mali and in its lower course in Niger and Nigeria. The Act of Niamey which entered into force on 1 February 1966 (but was signed in October 1963) was adopted by the co-riparians in order to regulate navigation and economic co-operation. The Act of Niamey stipulated that navigation on the river and its tributaries is entirely free for all nations. The riparian states may use the river for agricultural and industrial uses, and collect the products of its fauna and flora (Godana, 1985). Riparian states undertook to establish close co-operation concerning the study and execution of any project which is likely to have an appreciable effect on the river and its tributaries. To this end, it envisaged the establishment of the Niger River Commission to be entrusted with the task of co-ordination and solving disputes between the riparian states regarding the interpretation or application of the Act. The co-riparians have to inform the Commission, at the earliest stage of all studies and works, and must abstain from carrying out on portions of the river and its tributaries any works likely to pollute the waters or to have an adverse environmental impact, without adequate notice to and prior consultation with the Commission. The Commission was replaced by the Niger Basin Authority in 1980 and it has competence over water control and utilisation, infrastructure development, environmental monitoring and preservation, co-ordination of planning and statistical compilation (Ofosu-Amaah, 1990: 247–9). The co-operation in the Niger basin is noteworthy because some of the states have urgent water needs and a severe water scarcity and they chose co-operation over competition and conflict.

Lake Chad

Lake Chad, on the other hand, manifests an acute conflict over its scarce, ever diminishing water resources. In 1973, the lake was divided into two separate parts, the northern one, which no longer received any river inflow and in 1976 went completely dry, and the southern part which continued to shrink and by 1986 had become a series of disconnected pools (Sand, 1990). The four major riparian states, Nigeria, Niger, Chad, and Cameroon, signed an agreement to recognise the existing national boundaries on Lake Chad. But in the wake of the recent droughts, sovereignty disputes arose over newly emerged unmarked islands, leading to serious military confrontations between Chad and Nigeria in April and May 1983, which focused on the question of the permanent border demarcation and security.

The Chad Basin Convention and Statute was signed in 1964 and was mostly similar to the Niger Basin Treaty provisions. But navigation in Lake Chad is open only to the riparian states. The Lake Chad Statute requires prior consultation before the initiation of measures likely to have an appreciable effect on water quantity or quality in the basin. The Lake Chad Basin Commission may act as a dispute settlement body. The Commission's major role is the joint management of surface and groundwater resources in the basin, and it serves as a general forum for regional co-operation among riparians, on a wide range of issues. The Commission assisted in solving the border dispute between Chad and Nigeria, and monitors all military activities in the area. The Commission's work, especially in relation to the drought and water scarcity in the lake, is assisted by the United Nations Environment Programme, which initiated the preparation of a regional development plan for the Lake Chad basin. Lake Chad basin exemplifies a basin in which conflict is almost inevitable because of the scarce water resources and the complex sharing of a lake with constantly changing borders and decreasing water volume. With the help of UN bodies, and the Organisation for African Unity (OAU), co-operation is maintained in the basin.

IMPLICATIONS FOR THE JORDAN–YARMOUK BASIN

The implications of these various legal regimes to the Jordan–Yarmouk basin are many. First, it was found that even in basins where water scarcity is acute and an overt conflict prevails, a co-operative management of the common property is maintained. It seems that the Israeli–Arab conflict setting of the Jordan–Yarmouk is not exceptional, and if the other basins were able to work out arrangements for the benefit of all riparians, the partners of the Jordan–Yarmouk could also succeed.

Co-operation and common management of the Jordan–Yarmouk basin would fulfil a number of roles. First, it would enable the co-riparians to manage water resources in a more efficient way and avoid wastage. For example, if water storage is established in Lake Tiberias and the Maqarin (when it is constructed), and perhaps a new storage in the Hula Valley constructed, then the co-riparians would be able to develop a storage capacity for drought years. This is extremely important because the region is rapidly advancing to an era in which all the fresh good quality waters will be diverted to the consumption of domestic (municipal) use, whereas farming will have to utilise only secondary and treated waters.

Examples for more conventional water projects which could save money and water are a canal to divert the Jordan water using gravity instead of the present Israeli water carrier which pumps water from Lake Tiberias and uses large amounts of electricity, a desalination plant which could treat the saline water which Israel dumps in the lower Jordan and also the saline water resources located in the lower Jordan Valley near Jericho.

On a larger scale, and probably with the assistance of the World Bank, UNEP and other international organisations, a total water management of Israel, Jordan, the Palestinians and perhaps Syria could be envisaged. Total management would include two or three large-scale desalination plants for sea water which may be located in the Rift Valley of the Jordan, thus taking advantage of the relative difference in heights between the Mediterranean Sea and the Rift Valley in order to produce cheap energy which could be utilised for desalination. This location is also accessible for potential consumers in Jordan and the West Bank. In addition, all the domestic effluents of Israel, the West Bank and Gaza would be treated and recycled to be used in agriculture. The common commission which would have the authority for the co-operative development and management of the shared water resources would also handle the common groundwater resources of the West Bank allocating the best quality groundwater located west of the Jordan to both Palestinians and Israelis at a quota of $100m^3$ per person – an amount that is considered proper for domestic use.

Finally, a common Israeli–Arab commission for the Jordan–Yarmouk could offer Lebanon the project of selling the Litani waters to Israel, the Palestinians and Jordan. The waters of the Litani could be delivered at a low rate, utilising gravity to the Jordan channel, and distributed to consumers from there. It is estimated that the various projects may expand the total water supply of Israel, Jordan and the Palestinians by at least 1.0 billion m^3. Expansion of water supplies and a more efficient water use is urgently needed for the Middle East, and it seems that measures of common management constitute, in the long run, a better solution to the water-scarce societies of the Middle East, especially in comparison to the partition of the water resources which would not change the current amount of water.

Conclusions

This paper proposes joint management co-ordinated by a common commission for the Jordan–Yarmouk basin and for the shared underground water resources.

Based on treaties and agreements in other international river basins it is clear that even in areas of acute water shortages, and problems with water quality, co-operative solutions could be envisaged. Founded on customary international law, it is possible to share common water resources in a rational and equitable manner and co-riparians can abstain from causing appreciable harm to the water resources available to other riparians. Co-operation makes sense in the Jordan–Yarmouk basin because of advantages involved in economy of scale. Only management of all the available water resources and using the benefits of a large market, may reduce the cost of producing good quality water for the consumers who, in the year 2010, may number 15–20 million people (in Jordan, Israel, West Bank and Gaza). Water scarcity in this region is so severe that 'water wars' are not going to solve them – only co-operation and co-operative management of these resources will benefit the whole region.

Bibliography

Agoro, I. (1966) 'The establishment of the Chad Basin Commission', *ICLQ* 15: 542.

Agreement Concerning the Niger River Commission and its Navigation and Transport on the River Niger of 25 November 1964 (1967) *UNTS* 587: 19–33.

Bath, C.R. (1981) 'Resolving water disputes', *Proceedings of the Academy of Political Science* 34: 181–8.

Baxter, R.R. (1967) 'The Indus Basin' in A.H. Garretson, D.R. Hayton and C.J. Olmstead (eds) *The Law of International Drainage Basins,* New York: Oceana Books: 443–85.

Dellapenna, J. (1993) 'Institutional building', paper given at the Israeli–Palestinian First Conference on Water Resources, Zurich, Switzerland, January.

—— (forthcoming) 'Treaties as instruments for managing internationally-shared water resources: restricted sovereignty vs. community of property', in *Middle East Water: The Potential and Limits of Law.*

Godana, B.A. (1985) *Africa's Shared Water Resources. Legal and Institutional Aspects of the Nile, Niger and Senegal River Systems,* London: Frances Pinter.

Hundley, N. (1990) 'The West against itself: the Colorado River – an institutional history' in G.D. Weatherford and F.L. Brown (eds)

New Courses for the Colorado River, Albuquerque: University of New Mexico Press: 9–50.

Kliot, N. (1994) *Water Resources and Conflict in the Middle East,* London: Routledge.

Le Marquand, D. (1977) *International Rivers: The Politics of Co-operation,* Vancouver, BC: The University of British Columbia.

Lepawsky, A. (1963) 'International development of river resources', *International Affairs* 39: 533–55.

Lowi, M. (1993) *Water and Power,* Cambridge: Cambridge University Press.

Mandel, R. (1991) 'Sources of international river basins disputes', paper presented at the Annual Meeting of the International Studies Association, Vancouver, Canada.

Meyers, C.J. (1967) 'The Colorado Basin', in A. Garretson *et al* (eds) *The Law of International Drainage Basins,* New York: Oceana: 487–603.

Ofosu-Amaah, G. (1990) 'Niger river regime', in R. Bernhardt (ed.) *Encyclopedia of Public International Law* 12: 247–9, North Amsterdam: Holland.

Rauschning, D. (1990) 'Indus water dispute', in R. Bernhardt (ed.) *Encyclopedia of Public International Law* 6: 214–8, North Amsterdam: Holland.

Sand, P.H. (1990) 'Lake Chad' in R. Bernhardt (ed.) *Encyclopedia of Public International Law* 12: 213–6, North Amsterdam: Holland.

Teclaff, L. (1967) *The River Basin in History and Law,* The Hauge: Martinus Nijhoff.

——— (1991) 'Fiat or custom: the checkered development of international water law', *Natural Resources Journal* 45: 31–56.

UNTS (1962) 'Indus Water Treaty 1960', 419, 125: 233–5.

14

Water Resources in the Middle East: Boundaries and Potential Legal Problems, Using Jordan as a Case Study

Ewan W. Anderson

Introduction

Boundaries and legal problems associated with the Tigris–Euphrates, Nile and Jordan drainage basins are well known (Starr and Stoll, 1988). However, in the context of the Middle East as a whole, the total area of these three catchments is relatively limited and the water problems of the remainder of the region have rarely been addressed. Clearly, there are other examples of perennial surface flow, but the hydrological emphasis throughout most of the region is upon groundwater and temporary flows (Blake *et al,* 1987). These are also likely to generate boundary and legal problems. To illustrate the issues, Jordan, which exhibits a potential for all of the problems, is taken as an example.

Jordan enjoys a range of sources and potential sources of water. Both the Jordan and the Yarmuk rivers present obvious cases of boundary and transboundary surface water flow over which there will need to be legal agreement. Even in the relatively straightforward case of the Jordan drainage basin, several countries could be involved: Lebanon, Syria, Israel and, probably, Palestine. If agreement is to be reached on the distribution of water within the entire Jordan system, all riparian countries would be implicated.

However, if the entire water budget of Jordan is examined, there are many more sources, the list of neighbouring states involved is increased and there is a great variety of potential legal problems. In this short paper, an attempt is made to relate possible international legal requirements to the hydrology of Jordan.

Sources of Water

SURFACE FLOWS

The key surface flows are permanent and are all related to the Jordan system. For the Jordan as a whole, a large number of schemes for the sharing of the water have been devised (Kliot, 1994), but the Johnston Plan remains the most influential (Naff and Matson, 1984). However, water is so vital that statistics are treated as confidential and therefore while the Plan offers guidelines, these cannot be implemented in any precise fashion. Furthermore, the Plan itself was constructed at a time of enhanced flow and, over the last few years, there has been considerably less water available for allocation. A key legal issue will therefore be a determination of water allocation between the riparians: Lebanon, Syria, Israel and Jordan, calculated to take account of discharge fluctuations. A further point concerns quality of water. Increases in the area irrigated result in increased return flow and a decline in quality downstream. This factor would obviously require compensation.

Jordan has no direct control over the three headwater streams of the river, but, obviously, should any changes occur to them, the water supply for the country would be influenced. At present, there is joint monitoring with Israel in the lower reaches of the major tributary, the Yarmuk. This allows Jordan some jurisdiction over the abstraction for the East Ghor Canal. On the other hand, if Syria is drawn fully into the peace negotiations, the situation could change and Syria, rather than Israel, would then be the co-riparian on the lower Yarmuk. Finally, it must be remembered that surface flow contributes to groundwater recharge and therefore any changes on the surface will affect subsurface storage.

Only a relatively small area of Jordan contributes runoff to the River Jordan system. Most of the country experiences only temporary flow through wadis. The discharge involved may be very large, but flow is likely to last only a matter of days. Given its violence and irregular occurrence, wadi flow is particularly difficult to measure with any accuracy. However, it is vital, not only for grazing animals and short term crop production, but particularly for the recharge of the major aquifers of eastern Jordan. It is clear from meteorological evidence, that a high proportion of such wadi discharge is generated by rainfall falling outside the borders of Jordan (Agnew and Anderson, 1993). Thus, the wadis constitute temporary transborder water flow and are therefore the concern of international law. In particular, the construction of recharge dams throughout the Middle East is likely to have a major effect upon wadi flow. For example, from analysis, it seems that at least half the flood peaks attained by Wadi Ruwaishid cannot be correlated with local rainfall and must be the result of precipitation in Iraq. Therefore, should Iraq construct a dam to hold back Wadi Ruwaishid and to replenish its own aquifers, the aquifers of eastern Jordan would lose a key source of input. With regard to temporary surface flow, therefore, agreement needs to be reached with Syria, Iraq, and Saudi Arabia.

Should the West Bank achieve independence as part of a reconstituted Palestine, then Jordan would need to negotiate not only over the surface flow of the River Jordan, but also over the temporary flows from wadis, which sustain the river in its lower reaches.

SURFACE STORAGE

The regulator of the River Jordan system is Lake Kinneret (Anderson, 1991) and, although Jordan is not a riparian, the water budget of the lake must be a prime concern. Any hydraulic activity in the lake basin can only reduce the amount of water available downstream for Jordan.

The other major area of surface water is, of course, the Dead Sea and the use of this for mineral abstraction is a major Jordanian concern. Therefore, legal agreements need to be reached with Israel and, probably Palestine, now that the Jericho area is being developed as part of the new state.

Should general agreement within the basin be reached, then there must be a possibility that the Maqarin Dam will, at last, be built. This would provide another legal issue in that the lake impounded would stretch along the border between Syria and Jordan. Thus issues, not only of water supply and flood control, but also of, possibly, power generation, fishing and tourism might be raised.

In parallel with surface flow, there is also temporary surface storage. A typical element of the landscape of eastern Jordan is the *ga'a*,[1] a pan on which runoff collects. With inputs from wadis and neighbouring slopes, the surface of the *ga'a* rapidly seals and a temporary lake forms. In time past, inhabitants have dug *mahafir*,[2] from which they could extract freshwater. This use of temporary surface storage is likely to be of increasing importance as the Badia is developed (Agnew and Anderson, 1993). Legal issues are bound to arise as a considerable number of *ga'a* straddle Jordan's borders with Syria, Iraq and Saudi Arabia.

GROUNDWATER

For most of Jordan, the only permanent source of water is from aquifers. Shallow aquifers, either in wadi gravels or in the limestone or other sedimentary rock immediately beneath the surface, offer a supply accessible to even relatively primitive hand-dug wells. Again, it is obvious that what is abstracted in one country is no longer available for its neighbour. Thus, the question of water codes, national water law and the licensing of well construction is raised.

However, deep aquifers are, in the long term, likely to pose greater legal problems in that they may well offer a larger and more long-term supply of water (Anderson, 1992). Like the shallow aquifers, they frequently extend across international boundaries, but, unlike shallow aquifers, their geology is somewhat conjectural. It cannot yet be proved that what is extracted in one country necessarily diminishes the supplies of a neighbour. At depths of 1,000m and more, the transmissivity of rocks is greatly reduced and water movement is extremely slow. Furthermore, there may not be hydrological connections between various parts of what is classified as one sedimentary aquifer.

In the case of fractured aquifers, the hydrology may well be somewhat simpler. Also, the exact location of the key fractures can be accurately ascertained. Thus, in the Jordan Basin there are several major fractures, extending southwards from the mountains of southern Turkey and Lebanon. Since these seem to offer a promising source of additional water, as yet untapped, their development is important. Unlike sedimentary rock aquifers, the disposition of fractured rock aquifers effectively compels co-operation between neighbouring states and therefore legal agreements are necessary.

ATMOSPHERIC WATER

The occurrence of precipitation and dewfall (Anderson, 1988) depend upon the humidity of the prevailing air mass. In Jordan, air masses moving from the Mediterranean tend to be humid, whereas those from the East are significantly drier. A deliberate lowering of the relative humidity of an air mass could clearly deprive a country of precipitation. This is, in effect, what happens as a result of cloud seeding, which is known to have been practised in Israel (Agnew and Anderson, 1992). Clouds with a relatively high humidity, but one which is insufficient to result in viable precipitation, are injected with chemicals so that rainfall can be induced. The result must be that as the air mass moves on, its humidity has been lowered. Cloud seeding in some form has been practised for a long time, but its exact effects are still somewhat conjectural. Thus, it is possible that seeding in one country may result in rainfall with adverse effects in a neighbour. International law has yet to be brought to bear upon this subject, but it is clearly not without interest in the case of Jordan.

SEAWATER

As Jordan develops, it may be necessary to install desalination plants along the coastline of the Gulf of Aqaba. All of the key desalination techniques require a water input free from pollutants and therefore legal issues might arise over the question of coastal pollution.

TRANSBORDER PIPELINES

With the parlous state of the Jordanian water budget, a number of other solutions have been suggested, including the import of water by pipeline. The latest suggestion concerns a pipeline, bringing seawater to be desalinated in Jordan. The pipelines present a particularly complex field for international lawyers, with regard to their control, maintenance and security.

Conclusion

The water budget of Jordan is already complex (Kliot, 1994) and the potential for other sources would only add to the complexity. Jordan enjoys shared surface flow, both temporary and permanent, surface storage, both temporary and permanent, groundwater, both shallow and deep, and the coastline of a small, semi-enclosed gulf. There are also transborder sources, on the surface and below the surface. Finally, actions taken in neighbouring countries may well influence water supplies to Jordan. Thus, there is a vast range of potential legal problems, several of them as yet to be addressed by international law in general.

Notes

1   Saltlake or playa.
2   Excavations in the *ga'a* into which water can flow for later abstraction.

Bibliography

Agnew, C.T. and Anderson, E.W. (1992) *Water Resources in the Arid Realm,* London: Routledge.

Agnew, C.T. and Anderson, E.W. (1993) 'Water resources in the Badia: initial study', Jordan: British Institute in Amman for Archaeology and History.

Anderson, E.W. (1988) 'Dew measurements: eastern *Prosopis sp* belt in the Wahiba sand sea', *Journal of Oman Studies,* Special Report No 3: 201–12.

Anderson, E.W. (1991) 'The Middle East and hydropolitics', *World Energy Council Journal* December: 35–8.

Anderson, E.W. (1992) 'Water conflict in the Middle East – a new initiative', *Jane's Intelligence Review* 4, 5: 227–30.

Blake, G.H., Dewdney, J.C. and Mitchell, J.K. (eds) (1987) *The Cambridge Atlas of the Middle East and North Africa,* Cambridge: Cambridge University Press.

Kliot, N. (1994) *Water Resources and Conflict in the Middle East,* London: Routledge.

Naff, T. and Matson, R. (eds) (1984) *Water in the Middle East – Conflict or Co-operation,* Boulder, Colorado: Westview Press.

Starr, J.R. and Stoll, D.S. (1988) *The Politics of Scarcity,* Boulder, Colorado: Westview Press.

15

Sharing of Transboundary Rivers:
The Ganges Tragedy

M. Asafuddowlah

Introduction

The rivers have played a vital role in the history and economy of
Dacca District ... Along them, since time immemorial, have
travelled both warriors and traders: witness, for example, the
histories of Sonargaon and Dacca ... located along their courses ...
still today, they are bustling with activity, their channels thronged
with busy motor launches, stately steamers and the eternal slow
procession of said boats, big and small. Fish they provide and
domestic water supplies, too ... their annual floods water the land
and determine the harvests that will be reaped.

If rich blessings they bring, then tragedies also they bring –
calamitous high floods which wash away dwellings, livestock and
crops; changes in course which erode settlements and fertile
cropland, or close arteries of trade; and sudden storms which
overtake boatmen, puny against the rivers' might. So, into all parts
of the people's lives – their history, their culture, their economy,
their very way of life – have the rivers entered.

In the vast basins of the Ganges, the Brahmaputra and the Meghna
which join in Bangladesh before entering the Bay of Bengal, a rapidly
growing population, already close to 500 million, a monsoon of heavy
summer rains and a long post-winter dry season, make water
management a central element in economic planning and development.
These basins drain an area of 1.75 million km² of which only 7% lies
within Bangladesh. In few other situations does mankind have to deal
directly with the raw power of nature as it does in Bangladesh.

Bangladesh is an overpopulated small country located in the South
Asian region. The country is riverine with 54 rivers including the
Ganges, Brahmaputra, Meghna, Teesta, etc, flowing in from
neighbouring India. The flows of these rivers, over the centuries, have
shaped the country's civilisation, cultural pattern, agro-ecological

system and production structure. The Ganges is the most important among those 54 transboundary rivers draining through Bangladesh.

Dispute Over Sharing of Water Resources of the Ganges

THE GANGES

The Ganges is one of the largest transboundary rivers flowing through the South Asian region. Its basin spreads over China, India, Nepal and Bangladesh. The river originates from the southern slopes (at 7,000m) of the Himalayas and empties into the Bay of Bengal through Bangladesh after traversing a distance of 2,527km. The flow of the Ganges is highly seasonal. The three trans-Himalayan tributaries, the Karnali, Sapt Kosi and Sapt Gandaki emanating from Nepal provide 71% of the total dry season flows and 41% of the annual flows of the Ganges at Farakka in India. Floods during the monsoon and scarcity of water during the dry season are the two extreme characteristics of the Ganges flow. Whilst during the monsoon the peak flood flow of this river often touches the 70,750m³/s mark at Farakka causing catastrophic floods in Bangladesh, the flow dwindles to a mere 1,560–1,700m³/s during the dry season, resulting in scarcities of water.

DEPENDENCE OF BANGLADESH ON THE GANGES

The life of about one-third of the population of Bangladesh living in the south-western region revolves around the Ganges. This river plays the most crucial role in the sustenance of life and living of more than 40 million people of the country. It provides water for agriculture, domestic and municipal use, fisheries, industries, forestry, navigation, and maintenance of the delicate ecological balance in the south-western region where the Sundarbans, the largest mangrove forest of the world is located. The freshwater flow through the Gorai, the only distributary of the Ganges in Bangladesh, flushes down the salinity which intrudes from the Bay of Bengal in the south-western region. There is no other major source of water in this region to cater to these needs during the dry season in particular. The dependence of millions of Bangladeshis on the Ganges is thus total. Any variation in the flow pattern of the Ganges in Bangladesh, therefore, tells significantly on the agro-socio-economic life of the people.

CONFLICT OVER SHARING OF THE GANGES

India constructed a barrage across the Ganges at Farakka only 18km upstream of the Bangladesh border and commissioned it in 1975 for the ostensible purpose of diverting more than 1,130m³/s of dry season flows of this river into the Bhagirathi-Hooghly river of West Bengal to flush silts for improving the navigability of the port of Calcutta. It was agreed in 1974 at the summit between Bangladesh and India that the Farakka Barrage would not be put into operation before an agreement was reached for sharing the dry season flows of the Ganges between the two countries. In 1975 India told Bangladesh that she needed to test the feeder canal of the Farakka Barrage. She sought Bangladesh's permission to divert 310–450m³/s of Ganges flows from Farakka over the 10-day period from 21 April to 31 May 1975. Bangladesh, in good faith, accorded her consent. India used this advantage to commission the Farakka Barrage and continued unilateral diversions of the Ganges flows beyond the stipulated period and throughout the dry season of 1976. The Farakka Barrage was thus put into operation by India without reaching any agreement on the sharing of the Ganges flow with Bangladesh. This act constituted a tragic betrayal that led to a crisis of confidence and gave rise to the problem of sharing the flows of the Ganges between Bangladesh and India, which with the passage of time became the most contentious issue in their relationship.

NEGOTIATIONS ON THE GANGES

The issue of the Ganges first came into focus when, on 29 October 1951, the then government of Pakistan (including the area that now includes Bangladesh) drew the attention of the Indian government to reports of a scheme for diverting large amounts of dry season flow from the Ganges to resuscitate the Bhagirathi river in West Bengal. India replied in 1952 that the project was only under preliminary investigation and described Pakistan's concern over possible effects as purely hypothetical. Thus began the long history of negotiations on the sharing of the waters of the Ganges, which even after 40 years remains unresolved. In the years up to 1970, the governments of Pakistan and India discussed the issue of sharing the Ganges many times at different levels, starting from experts to the heads of governments. India, in the meantime completed the construction of the Farakka Barrage in 1970.

After independence in 1971 the government of Bangladesh took up the Ganges issue in earnest with the Government of India. The Indo-Bangladesh Joint Rivers Commission (JRC) was constituted in 1972. The Prime Ministers of Bangladesh and India, in a Joint Declaration of 16 May 1974 expressed their determination that before the Farakka Project was commissioned they would arrive at a mutually acceptable allocation of the waters available during the periods of minimum flow in the Ganges. But in April 1975 India commissioned the Farakka Barrage capitalising on the good faith of Bangladesh. India continued unilateral withdrawals of the scarce dry season flows of the Ganges throughout 1976 causing serious adversities in Bangladesh. Failing to dissuade India from such acts, Bangladesh took the issue to the United Nations. On 26 November 1976 the UN General Assembly adopted a consensus statement which *inter alia* directed India to sit with Bangladesh urgently at Dhaka to negotiate a fair and expeditious settlement of the problem. Several rounds of discussions followed and on 5 November 1977 the two countries signed an agreement for sharing the dry season flows of the Ganges available at Farakka for a period of 5 years (1978–82). In October 1982 the two sides signed a Memorandum of Understanding (MOU) for sharing the Ganges flows during 1983 and 1984. There was no sharing of Ganges flows in 1985 in the absence of any understanding or agreement. The two countries signed another MOU in November 1985 for sharing the Ganges flows for three years from 1986 to 1988. In the face of such *adhocisms* in terms of sharing, Bangladesh had so far not been able to undertake any concrete steps towards the more meaningful and optimal utilisation of the Ganges waters in different sectors in vast areas of the south-western region.

In all the negotiations, India always tried to make the sharing contingent upon augmenting the dry season flows of the Ganges. India persistently pressed Bangladesh to agree to its proposal of transferring 2,830m³/s of dry season flows of the Brahmaputra to the Ganges for augmenting the latter's flows through a link canal seven times bigger than the Suez Canal cutting across Bangladesh's north-western part. Bangladesh maintained that the dry season flows of the Ganges at Farakka could easily be augmented by harnessing the vast water resources available on an annual basis in the Ganges basin itself, through storage of the monsoon runoffs in the upstream regions. Further, Bangladesh pointed to the fact that the dry season Brahmaputra flow by itself was not enough to meet the present and future needs of the Brahmaputra basin. Moreover, intensive studies revealed that the Indian link canal proposal was technically unsound, economically unwise, socially unacceptable and ecologically disastrous for Bangladesh.

Since the dry season of 1989 there has been no instrument operative for sharing the flows of the Ganges. Consequently India is making massive unilateral diversions of the scarce dry season flows of this river causing drastic reductions in the Ganges flow in Bangladesh. As a result Bangladesh received only 260m³/s of water in the Ganges at Hardinge Bridge in March 1993, in place of 1,980m³/s which used to flow through this point in the same month during the pre-Farakka years. This has caused havoc to the bio-diversity of more than one-third of the area of Bangladesh. Incessant requests by Bangladesh and negotiations at all levels between the two countries failed to break the deadlock. India has always stalled discussions on substantive issues. In May 1992 during the meeting of the Prime Ministers of the two countries, the Indian Prime Minister categorically assured that every possible effort would be made to avoid undue hardships to Bangladesh by sharing the flows of the Ganges at Farakka on an equitable basis. Since then there have been two ministerial level meetings and two secretarial level meetings between the two countries. No sharing agreement, however, has emerged. The Prime Ministers met again in April 1993, but the fulfilment of the promise of the Indian Prime Minister to avoid undue hardships to Bangladesh remains as elusive as ever. In order to reach a permanent settlement of the issue in the interest of peace and good neighbourliness, Bangladesh showed all the friendly gestures and made progressive sacrifices, even at the cost of her own economy. India however, never reciprocated.

The Resultant Crisis in Bangladesh

EFFICACY OF THE FARAKKA BARRAGE

The Farakka Barrage was constructed by India for diverting $1,130m^3/s$ of dry season Ganges flow into the Bhagirathi-Hooghly river to improve the navigability of Calcutta Port. The efficacy of diversion of water from the Ganges for flushing silt from the Hooghly had been questioned in the past by many, including many Indian experts. They comprehended that such diversions would only be a waste of the scarce dry season flow of the Ganges. Over the last 18 years since the commissioning of the Farakka Barrage, India has on average diverted $850-1,130m^3/s$ of dry season Ganges flow every year into the Hooghly from Farakka. At times, when there were no sharing arrangements, India diverted more than $1,130m^3/s$ through the feeder canal of the Farakka Barrage. The navigability of the port of Calcutta, however, did not improve and nor would it ever. The prestigious Indian fortnightly, *India Today,* concluded in its 16 February 1981 edition, 'Farakka or no Farakka, Calcutta Port is doomed'. On 2 July 1993, *The Telegraph* of Calcutta commented, 'it is time the authorities acknowledged that Calcutta Port is doomed to extinction. The Calcutta Port is 190km up the river. It needs to face the grim truth that it has outlived its utility'.

ADVERSE IMPACTS OF THE FARAKKA BARRAGE ON BANGLADESH

While the Farakka Barrage failed to improve the plight of the port of Calcutta, it certainly played havoc with Bangladesh. India does not talk of the needs of Calcutta Port any more – she now raises the issue of increasing demands on the Ganges waters for irrigation in the upstream regions like Uttar Pradesh, Bihar, and so forth. The massive withdrawals of dry season Ganges flows by India have caused serious impacts on every sphere of life in the Ganges-dependent areas of Bangladesh. The flow of the Ganges in Bangladesh nowadays, turns almost to a trickle during the dry season. This man-made hazard has inflicted crippling blows to the entire south-western region of the country.

The hydrological and morphological characteristics of the Ganges and its distributaries in Bangladesh have been severely impaired. The flow reduction in the Ganges has caused excessive siltation, a rise in river beds and consequent reduction of the conveyance capacity of the river channels, resulting in aggravated floods during the monsoon. The offtake of the Gorai, the main distributary of the Ganges in Bangladesh, gets choked every year as early as January, making this important river high and dry throughout the dry season. The once effluent Ganges now turns influent during lean periods.

Due to the total stoppage of the dry season freshwater supply through the Gorai, saline intrusion from the Bay of Bengal into the south-western region has advanced further inland affecting both surface and groundwater over about 25,900km². The river water salinity level of the Khulna recently exceeded 29,000micromhos/cm compared to that of 5,000micromhos/cm during pre-Farakka days. The soil salinity is also increasing in the process. The phenomenon of increased salinity is causing deleterious effects on agriculture, domestic and municipal water supply, industry and public health in vast areas of the region. The most devastating effect of salinity has, however, been on the Sundarbans, the largest mangrove forest. The whole forest is now facing serious decay due to increased salinity. The large variety of wildlife inhabiting the forests is also being endangered.

Agriculture has been the worst hit sector. The drastic fall in water level of the Ganges has seriously impaired the operation of the pumping plant of the Ganges-Kobadak Project, the largest irrigation scheme in the area, which has more than 121,410ha under its direct command. The pumps of this project are forced either to remain idle or operate with drastically reduced capacity due to acute scarcity of flows in the Ganges. Besides, severe stress in soil moisture, soil salinity and non-availability of fresh groundwater are affecting the agricultural productivity of the entire south-western region during Rabi and Kharif-I seasons, depriving the farmers of millions of tons of crops. Scarcity of water in the main Ganges and its distributaries has disturbed the flow pattern, velocity, turbidity, total dissolved solids (TDS) and salinity levels on which fisheries thrived. The Gangetic water system supports over 200 species of freshwater fish and 18 species of prawns in the area. Fish catches have dwindled in the region. Thousands of fishermen are consequently now out of a job.

The Ganges flow reduction has hit the navigation sector as well. More than 320km of major and medium navigable waterways have now been rendered inoperative during the dry season. As a result hundreds of boatmen have been thrown out of their occupation.

The groundwater in the region underwent depletion with the level falling in most places by more than 3m due to the lowering of river stages. The water quality also degraded due to increased concentrations of TDS, chlorides, sulphates, etc, affecting the agriculture, industry, domestic and municipal water supply, and the soil itself, over a large area. People are now forced to drink water of 1,200ppm although the World Health Organisation's prescribed limit for drinking water is only 500ppm. This is aggravating the overall public health situation.

The environment of the entire south-western region is now under grave threat. Increased salinity both in soil and water, massive siltation of the river beds, alarming lowering of groundwater tables, quick depletion of soil moisture, diminishing potentials of the Sundarbans mangrove ecosystem, and changes in water quality are all threatening the delicate ecological balance of the region. Desertification is gradually creeping in, taking advantage of land degradation and prolonged arid conditions on the northern side of the Ganges in Bangladesh.

The withdrawal of the precious dry season water resources of the Ganges by India over the years has forced Bangladesh to incur massive losses in the fields of agriculture, fisheries, forestry, industry, navigation, water supply, etc. Estimates of direct damages caused to Bangladesh in these sectors indicate a total loss amounting to about US$3 billion. If indirect losses are taken into account, this amount would increase significantly. Further, being deprived of her legitimate share of the Ganges flows, Bangladesh is losing the benefit of an additional crop yield exceeding 3 million tons worth more than half a billion US$ annually.

THE CRISIS AND THE VULNERABILITY OF REGIONAL PEACE AND STABILITY

Indian interventions in the natural flow of the Ganges is pushing a big part of the Bangladeshi population to the threshold of poverty and destruction. This is nothing but a gross violation of human rights and justice. To put it simply, the economic structure of Bangladesh is now faced with disaster. Water is a very precious resource. When there are millions of people dependent on it for their survival, no country, using the plea of being an upper riparian, has the right to unilaterally control this vital resource and deny millions in Bangladesh their right to live. India's assurance not to create undue hardships to Bangladesh has to be proved beyond rhetoric and can only be demonstrated by restoring a legitimate share of the Ganges flow to Bangladesh. The present situation cannot be allowed to persist any longer as the very survival of a nation is at jeopardy. The Ganges issue had been a major irritant in Indo-Bangladesh relations over the last two decades. The crisis over the Ganges has now attained such dimensions that it is threatening the peace and stability of the region. Further inaction on the part of India would, therefore, have disastrous implications for millions living in this part of the globe.

In the close future, conflicts over water will increasingly come into focus as the world's growing population increases demand on this scarce resource. Between 1940 and 1980 global water use doubled. It is expected to double again by the turn of the century. Currently, 214 of the world's major river systems are shared by two or more countries. Of these, Africa has 57, Asia 40, Europe 48, North and Central America 33 and South America 36. There are nine river and lake basins that are shared by six or more countries.

Legal Inadequacies *vis-à-vis* Transboundary River Water Sharing

In terms of geophysical compulsion, the issue of sharing of international river basins is something which is of great concern for Bangladesh. River basin management has a spatial dimension because it involves the sharing of a scarce resource among neighbours. An upstream country feels scanty obligation to augment the flow for the downstream country. The lower riparian is thus denied its required volume of water, which disturbs the ecological equilibrium, and slowly the degradation of the entire ecosystem sets in. It is a pity that few people outside the affected region seem to appreciate the gravity of this creeping process of degradation which is both real and far-reaching.

There is no global convention that lays down agreed laws on international watercourses. In fact, there is not even a globally accepted definition of an international watercourse. The World Bank, for the purpose of its project operation, recognises 'a river, canal, lake or similar waterbody, which forms a boundary between or flows through two or more countries' as an international waterway. The work of some international bodies and jurists have helped evolve the basic features of environmental equilibrium in international river basins by establishing the principle that each state has a duty not to cause appreciable harm to others that share the river basin. The International Law Association, in 1966, adopted the Helsinki Rules on the Uses of International Rivers where co-basin states were specifically prohibited from doing anything to cause pollution in international rivers. The principles formulated by the International Law Association are now included in the Helsinki Convention on the Use of Transboundary Watercourses, signed in 1992. This convention stresses the obligation of the upper riparian to use its water in such a manner as not to cause adverse transboundary impact on the lower riparian.

It has been years since 1970, when the United Nations entrusted the International Law Commission (ILC) with the job of formulating and codifying the Laws of Non-navigational Uses of International Watercourses. It is not known how many more years the ILC will take to complete its assignment. At the current rate it looks never-ending.

In Article 20 of Part IV of the Draft Report on the Law of Non-navigational Use of International Watercourses prepared by the ILC, it was stated:

> Watercourse States shall, individually or jointly, protect and preserve the ecosystems of international watercourses.

In Article 21 it was elaborated:

> Watercourse States shall, individually or jointly, prevent, reduce and control pollution of an international watercourse that may cause appreciable harm to other watercourse States or to their environment, including harm to human health or safety, to the use of the waters for any beneficial purpose or to the living resources of the watercourses. Watercourse States shall take steps to harmonise their policies in this connection.

Indian actions with regard to the flow of the Ganges have already caused substantial harm to the environment, including harm to human health in Bangladesh. Detrimental alterations of the water quality in terms of salinity, TDS, etc, have caused progressive deterioration of public health in Bangladesh. The environment of a region of the country has undergone such deterioration that the existence of the natural flora and fauna are threatened with extinction. Land has been degraded to such an extent in some areas that it has lost its productivity, making the poorest people on earth still poorer.

Article 20 imposes an obligation on the upper riparian to protect and preserve the ecosystem of the international watercourses.

In Article 4 of Part I of the Draft Report on the Law of the Non-navigational Uses of International Watercourses by the ILC during its 43rd Session in 1991, it was stated:

> i) Every watercourse State is entitled to participate in the negotiation of and to become a party to any watercourse agreement that applies to the entire international watercourse, as well as to participate in any relevant consultations.

> ii) A watercourse State whose use of an international waterway may be affected to an appreciable extent by the implementation of a proposed watercourse agreement that applies only to a part of the watercourse to a particular project, programme or use is entitled to participate in consultations on, and in the negotiation of, such an agreement, to the extent that its use is thereby affected, and to become a party thereto.

India has entered into bilateral agreements with Nepal in 1991 and 1992 to undertake projects on the rivers Karnali, Pancheswar, Saptkosi and Buri Gandaki, all tributaries of the Ganges. These projects are going to intervene with the natural flow of these rivers downstream, to the detriment of the interest of Bangladesh which is the lowest riparian of the Ganges. Bangladesh has unfortunately been left out of these Indo-Nepal bilateral negotiations which essentially should be multilateral and include Bangladesh as a necessary partner.

India is taking full advantage of the absence of any codified law on the non-navigational uses of transboundary rivers and Bangladesh is suffering day after day, year after year. The ILC, therefore, should wake up and complete the task of codification of the laws relating to uses of international watercourses as early as possible, for the sake of humanity and save lower riparian countries like Bangladesh from impending disaster.

Conclusion

The sharing and management of an international river course is a matter of international concern – because it is a transboundary environmental resource, and the environment is basically global. Countries sharing a river basin should co-operate among themselves to ensure equality and sustainability. When that does not happen naturally, some international impetus is needed. It is sterile to argue that when two States share a river basin, management issues should be strictly bilateral in the event of any conflict. When the environment of one country is adversely impacted by the actions of another country, the international community cannot, and should not, look the other way. It is the collective obligation of mankind to protect environmental resources – and that includes international river basins. It is acknowledged that enforcement is the biggest hurdle of international law. But there are also examples of enforcement. In conflict resolution among States or resource utilisation, all parties should submit themselves to the processes of negotiation, mediation and international arbitration. International law has successfully regulated many economic, technical and social issues. Environmental issues emanating from international river basin utilisation can also be approached within a similar framework. In the long term, a mechanism has to be evolved to enforce the rules for preventing/mitigating transboundary environmental damages in international river basins, and the United Nations should have the mandate to perform such functions so that the free and bountiful gift of God can be enjoyed equally by all in an environment that guarantees equity and harmony – the way it was meant to be shared.

16

On the Question of Fresh Water Management in South Asia

R.C. Sharma
Suparna Nag

Introduction

Water constitutes the most basic of man's resources. The accelerating demand for this fixed reserve of water for the expansion of agriculture, operation of industrial units, development of low-cost inland waterways for transporting industrial and agricultural products, and for domestic and drinking purposes weighs heavily on the quality of life and the environment. The growing pollution due to discharge of industrial wastes, the excessive use of fertilisers and pesticides and so forth may have disastrous long-term effects. Therefore, a comprehensive plan for water resource development and management is essential to ensure maximum benefits. This can be ensured through the implementation of a plan benefiting entire drainage basins, covering the co-riparian states.

Problems may, however, arise when individual basin states pursue their own priorities, regardless of the consequences for the other basin states. This phenomenon of water resource politics is especially conspicuous in South Asia, where seasonal variations control the bulk of the fresh water supply. Since it is a vital resource, shaping the lives and well-being of the population of this region, it is essential to look into the policies of water resource management and the underlying politics shaping its development.

Sources of Water

Not only India, but a large part of South Asia is dependent on the vagaries of the monsoon, which constitutes one of the predominant sources of water supply in the region. This supply is available not only in the form of fresh water from the land but from other elements of the hydrological cycle as well. These have been broadly classified into the tangible and potential resources; the former connotes all water resources available through direct pumping or by obstructing its free circulation while the latter refers to those resources which are not easily accessible in most instances and their utilisation depends on other factors. A notable classificatory scheme was propounded by C.S. Fox (1952).

The present state of technology plays an important role in the utilisation of this renewable resource, presently much below its optimal potential. The limited availability of this resource has necessitated its development in a manner ensuring its optimum utilisation through proper planning, management and conservation. However, its limited nature and uneven geographical distribution, especially of freshwater resources, give rise to political implications on a national or international scale, involving a debate over its equitable allocation between or amongst states or nations. It is in this light that a brief study of the river basins of one of the resource-rich nations, India, will set the stage for an insight into the politics of water resource management (Table 16.1).

India, as well as much of South Asia, being dependent on agriculture, relies heavily on the often unpredictable monsoons for irrigation. In India, especially, where about 75% of the working population, either directly or indirectly, relies on agriculture, one is prompted to highlight one of the major uses of fresh water – irrigation. This also entails optimum utilisation of water to ensure maximum benefits. Dagli (1971) has estimated that of the total of 1,665,225 million m^3 of surface water resources of the country, merely 555,075 million m^3 is available for utilisation. Thus, to ensure an adequate supply of water for irrigation, prudence must be exercised to conserve the resource by constructing irrigation projects, both large and small, which will accrue maximum benefits. This has been fulfilled often through the initiation of 'Command Area Development' (CAD) projects.

The demand for irrigation facilities is accelerating rapidly in much of South Asia, especially in India, Pakistan and Bangladesh, and on a smaller scale in Sri Lanka and Afghanistan. This is in order to meet the needs of growing populations and to ensure an increase in the productivity of crops for both domestic consumption as well as for export. A case study of the irrigation scenario of Bangladesh reveals that it was always an irrigation-poor part of even undivided India. Its principal problem revolved around a drastic increase in demand for water during the dry months coupled with disastrous floods during monsoons. This entailed a proper water management programme with the purpose of conservation of the scarce water resources. Thus, the Water and Power Development Authority was established in 1959, charged with carrying out a Master Plan (the drawing up of which was completed in 1964) with a 20-year perspective. It identified a number of projects, including barrages across the Ganga, Brahmaputra and the Megna, to provide flood protection and

Table 16.1 Major, Medium and Minor River Basins of India

Name of Rivers	Area (km²)	Annual average discharge (million m³)
Major Rivers		
Indus	468,068*	207,800*
	321,289	41,955
Ganga	1,050,000*	
	861,404	493,400
Brahamputra+	580,000*	
	187,113+	510,450
Barak	70,895	
Sabarmati	21,674	3,200
Mahi	34,842	8,500
Narmada	98,796	40,705
Tapi	65,145	17,982
Subarnarekha	19,296	7,940
Brahmani	39,033	18,310
Mahanadi	141,589	66,640
Godavari	312,812	105,000
Krishna	258,948	67,675
Pennar	55,213	3,238
Cauvery	87,900	20,950
Total	2,575,949	1,405,945
Medium Rivers		
East Flowing	133,682	20,570
West Flowing	79,984	74,965
Flowing into other countries	25,636	16,676
Total	239,302	95,535
Minor Rivers	96,510	60,080
Desert Rivers	99,432	9,912
Grand Total	**3,011,193**	**1,571,472**

* Represents the total annual average discharge, whether in India or outside India. Same applies for its catchment area.

Source: K.L. Rao (1979) Table 4.3 (p.47), Table 4.4 (p.49) and Table 4.5 (p.50)

irrigation facilities and enable Bangladesh to achieve agricultural self-sufficiency. In 1966, the World Bank reviewed the project and suggested the development of smaller, short-term projects. Furthermore, the success of the larger projects were dependent on an international understanding with India which controlled 56 of the 57 rivers flowing into Bangladesh. However, in spite of these factors, by 1984–5 Bangladesh had extended irrigation facilities over an area of 2.44 million ha and by the year 2000 aimed to bring 3.75 million ha under irrigation, with a maximum potential of 4.45 million ha. Simultaneously Bangladesh also aims to improve its flood control measures. At present, even though 2.6–3.0 million ha are flooded annually during the peak discharges of the Ganga and Brahmaputra, a potential area of 8.28 million ha is susceptible to floods. Flood control measures brought 32% of this area under protection by 1984–5 and by 1991 this figure increased to 42%.

In India however, the area susceptible to floods is 27.5 million ha within the Ganga and the Brahmaputra–Barak basins alone, of which merely 5.8 million ha are under flood protection schemes. In the field of irrigation however, India is relatively advanced. This is exemplified by the fact that by 1984–5, 70 million ha were under irrigation involving an investment of Rs898.78 *crore*.[1] Still, much remains to be done in the field of irrigation to improve overall agricultural productivity through efficient harnessing of the country's water resources.

In Pakistan, the main source of irrigation is the Indus River and its six main tributaries. It irrigates an area of about 15 million ha and in many areas old inundation channels have been replaced by modern irrigation channels. However, because the Indus flows through parts of India as well, its water is shared by the two states. After the conclusion of the Indus Water Treaty, the areas of some of the tributaries were connected to others by means of link canals, in spite of which Pakistan receives 165,845 million m³ of water annually from the Indus. Link canals have also been constructed to transfer water from the Jhelum, Chenab, Ravi and Sutlej rivers into Pakistan.

The Need for Water Resource Management

The core of the water resource management problem is water's uneven geographical distribution. Water resource management is therefore essential for the development of irrigation, flood control and provision of water to all sections of the population.

The issues of major concern may be loosely classified into professional or public issues, the former based on science and the latter on politics. It is noted that the public issues are areas of conflict, arising out of the expression of public opposition, usually having a strong base at the local political level (Lowe *et al,* 1986).

Once it surfaces, it becomes a professional issue, conditioned by prevailing political policies. It has been observed that most of the public issues stem from a combination of three situations:

1 growing awareness of global and regional disparities in water resource availability endangering increased expectations and bringing about a change in the water demand;
2 the maintenance of the existing level of water resource utilisation becoming difficult on the same resource base or pricing structure;
3 resource utilisation, abuse or disregard by one group or nation, threatening to cause damage to the other.

The magnitude of these problems may be either applicable to a single basin or may be evident on a global scale.

One of the distinguishing features of international rivers especially, is the politics over their use and management. This can be attributed to the differing demands for this resource in the basin countries depending on variables such as population growth, level of economic development, cultural practices, foreign policy objectives and the availability and accessibility of other domestic water sources.

Furthermore, in areas where an internal political structure exists in the form of a federal government, a considerable degree of regional autonomy is granted to the region with regard to its water resource utilisation in areas within its jurisdiction. However, when the resource is of an inter-provincial or international nature, it exerts a different impact altogether. Nationalist tendencies are observed to exert a modifying impact on the regional political structure and, therefore, on water resource regionalisation. In the Third World, the regional political structure often becomes diffused and the control of water is strongly tied to social organisations at the local level.

Since international rivers constitute a significant proportion of the region's supply of water, much attention is given to them to supplement the national supplies and meet the needs of economic development. Therefore, if each country is reviewed as an economic unit, the physical effects generated in one are passed on to its neighbour, giving rise to external influences. Thus, this entire array of problems requires an understanding of the water resource management issues, since it includes issues of environmental management as well. It is also noted that conflicts of the past reflect interests similar to those of today, though the rationale behind early projects was more economic than political.

Approaches to Water Resource Management

The efficient management of water resources entails a process of decision-making centred on its allocation and use. Water management is the process by which the resource is defined and put into use in combination with other resources. At the national level, water management is concerned with the utilisation of the nation's water resources as a whole and its relationship to other management systems. This approach to water resource management is defined as the *holistic approach,* which revolves around the management of the total resource as an instrument of public action. Thus, this approach gives direction to the process of creating a national policy as well as individual microactivities. Other notable approaches include cost studies, which evaluate the impact upon the water quality standards which are being adopted and enforced throughout the nation.

The various approaches to resource management especially of water can be illustrated with the help of a model as shown in Figure 1.

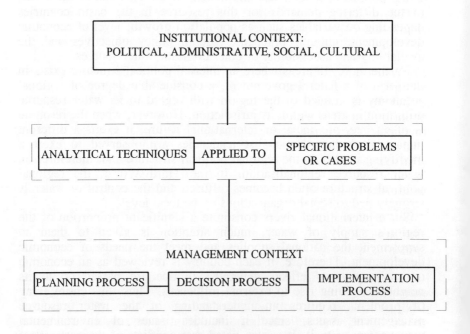

Figure 16.1 Conceptual Model For Application of Analytical
Techniques
Source: Hufschmidt (1982: 20)

The formulation of the project entails the identification of the need for action, determining the size, scope and the components of a desired change and selecting a preferred set of actions from a list of alternatives. Proper formulation of the project is critical in determining the magnitude of success or failure of a project. However, political considerations often play a dominant role in altering decisions from the ones which were originally formulated. Thus, the policy decisions and welfare motives are often intricately related to political factors. After the implementation of the project, using appropriate management techniques, the evaluation of the project forms a notable phase, involving a cost-benefit analysis of the framework of the project and its concepts, and measures of valuation. Attempts have also been made to use the safe minimum standard for judging the trade-off between preservation of certain natural systems and development activities, thereby establishing a valuable nexus between ecologists and economists.

The implementation of these approaches to resource management entails the adoption of efficient techniques of management which yield beneficial results in the long run. The most prevalent techniques are:

Environmental Impact Analysis (EIA): This involves not only an identification of the impact but a description of the existing system, including an awareness of the existing problems and the available opportunities. It is essentially 'used in the development of objective functions, decision criteria weightages, performance measures and analysis of the incidence of environmental quality benefits and costs' (Hufschmidt, 1982). Though its use is restricted, it provides a baseline in environmental planning in the absence of other adequate measures.

Cost-Effectiveness Analysis: An effective and useful method of estimating least cost for achieving specific targets and is used in situations where the benefits cannot be expressed in monetary terms.

Cost-Benefit Analysis: An efficient technique used in water resource management to address a single objective of economic efficiency (like GNP or the national income) under conditions when benefits exceed the cost. The 'cost' reflects the consumption of the resource that could have been used in alternative ways and its present value is calculated to a common point of time for comparison.

Risk-Benefit Analysis: This technique is used in decision-making on alternative energy systems involving different types of risk. It involves the 'benefit function' or the economic value of the output and the 'risk function' which is substituted for the cost function.

Multiple-Objective Analysis: Used in formulating and evaluating projects with multiple objectives or for the management of specific resources under alternative development plans.

Systems Analysis and Optimisation Models: Systems analysis is more of a process than a technique dealing with large, complex problems. It is useful in resource management planning (Holling 1978) taking into account the problem as a whole (Churchman, 1968) with interdependence amongst the parts of the system. This is achieved through collection, organisation and analysis of data in a comprehensible form.

Optimisation models on the other hand are conducted through linear programming, for the maximisation or minimisation of an objective function, subject to a set of constraints.

Input-Output Analysis: This technique is applied at the regional or national level, capturing indirect production effects. It comprises a set of sectoral outputs, using inputs in strictly defined proportions within a matrix where the total input co-efficient and the final set of demands are all measured in monetary terms.

Trade and Investment Models: This technique traces out the environmental impact of economic activities in less developed countries (Pearson and Pryor, 1978), besides estimating the global supply and demand of renewable and non-renewable raw material.

Other Techniques: All the management systems are tested for their consequences in terms of their service objective (like flood control, water quality control, etc) and recreation or socio-economic and organisational objectives (like income distribution effects, cost-allocation issues, repayment, etc).

Each project is considered individually and formulated to achieve one or a set of objectives. Besides, some techniques have also sought to integrate projects to increase their physical and economic efficiency.
Certain constraints, however, affect the application of these techniques significantly. The use of a particular technique may be limited when, for instance, the political context weighs in favour of development or when the project is fully planned. Conversely, the technique is of greater use in situations where the aid agency requires a system of economic analysis of environmental aspects of the project or where the agencies emphasise the identification of the consequences in the project planning process.

It has been observed that due to variations in the institutional context and variations in the management setting, no particular technique can be universally applicable to all the cases, rather, the adaptability of specific techniques to different contexts would need to be examined before their implementation.

Water Resource Management Programmes

Water resources constitute an important subject for illustrating the conflicting interests brought about by their alteration and the cause-effect phenomena which may have biological implications. Thus, in order to balance these effects, a multi-resource planning approach is essential for efficient resource management. Environmental issues are also gaining ground rapidly, particularly in South Asia. This is associated with the concept of sustainable development, gaining importance amongst national governments as well as amongst donor nations and international lending agencies. Thus, the success of a water management project may weigh heavily on aspects of safeguard and compensatory action, the costs and benefits of which are built into the programmes. Therefore, most of these projects have drawn the critical attention of environmentalists in view of considerations like submergence, displacement of population, loss of forests and cultivable land and the ecological effects of damming rivers, questions of dam safety, salinity and waterlogging, sedimentation, floods, health impacts and the sharing of costs and benefits.

In addition, other factors like ignorance, hasty decisions, lack of co-ordination, poor management and implementation, bad maintenance, lack of experience, inappropriate technology, corruption and other factors often inhibit the optimal benefits from a project. However, in order to ensure optimal benefits, it is suggested that eco-fundamentalism be avoided and reasonable environmental safeguards and EIA be implemented, substantiated with a continuous re-valuation of the project in terms of cost-benefit analysis over time, space and even across national boundaries, ensuring sustainable development.

However, one of the major issues of concern pertains to the increasing pollution of water resources (rivers). This is exemplified by the accelerating rate of pollution of the river Yamuna, which, within its 48km stretch through Delhi, gets increasingly polluted every day by sewage, industrial and other wastes. A study by the Water Research Institute (1986) revealed that prior to entering Delhi it contains 75 coliform organisms per ml of water, but after receiving 200 million litres of untreated sewage every day, it leaves Delhi with 24 million coliform organisms per ml of water. Besides, it also picks up 20 million litres of industrial effluents including 500,000 litres of DDT wastes every day while flowing through the national capital.

Thus, the concept of contemporary water resource management does not solely revolve around the implementation and evaluation of the project but simultaneously sheds light on the environmental implications of implementing or not implementing the project.

The Politics of Water Resource Management

The politics of water resource management forms a notable component of management projects, with conspicuous implications, both favourable and unfavourable, on the implementation of the projects. Most of the issues of these politics are interlinked to the problems of equitable sharing of international or national water resources, which include international waterways, lakes and river basins shared by more than one state or nation. The dilemmas of equitable sharing have long been apparent in regard to the use of rivers and lakes, common between two or more states or nations. Criteria of prior use, historic rights and relative needs have been advanced as equitable standards, involving numerous controversies between or amongst the states or nations.

It has been observed that even though navigational issues dominated freshwater politics initially, recently agricultural and industrial use of water has caused political debate. This is due to increased demands for water, a reduction in its supply due to natural and man-made causes and a decline in its total volume. Thus, the potential scarcity coupled with the new technological developments in agriculture and industry have given rise to the question of equitable sharing and the emergence of freshwater management politics.

Marquard (1978) conducted a study on the politics of international river basin co-operation and management, in which he identified four types of issue which are responsible for generating controversies on the international plane. These include:

Public Goods: these include goods over which both the countries have equal access and enjoy benefits equitably. It also implies the right to free and open transit. An example of such an issue relates to navigational agreements concluded between nations.

Common Pool Resources are similar to public goods, except that their use by one country diminishes the benefits to the other(s). Problems arise especially in the case of a boundary river or lake, when one country sharing it disposes of waste into it or withdraws some of the water resources, thereby affecting the other country.

Integrated Development Opportunities: the integrated development of a river can increase the benefits from its use to the basin countries over the benefits from the national development of the river. This often gives rise to economies of scale. The regulation of the river may often lead to externalities from the upstream to the downstream country. Conflicts may arise over the equitable division of costs and benefits between them, varying with the water management scheme.

Upstream–Downstream Conflict: this takes place when the upstream country uses the international river to the detriment of the downstream country, the latter having no reciprocal power over the upstream country, which often has no incentives to alter its behaviour.

These four situations illustrate that international river agreements are more concerned with problems revolving around the sharing of a resource than with the reinforcement of territorial claims, generating incentives or disincentives for international co-operation. However, these situations are equally relevant in the generation of water resource management disputes on a national scale between two or more states.

Inter-State River Disputes

An in-depth study of the inter-state river disputes taking place within the Indian sub-continent serves to exemplify the dimensions of freshwater resource politics prevailing within the regional framework of South Asia. Amongst them, the notable ones which have attracted the attention of the Government of India are as follows:

Narmada Water Dispute The 1,300km long Narmada river, constitutes an important river of peninsular India. This river includes the construction of a high dam at Navagam to irrigate large tracts of Gujarat, the Luni Valley or Rajasthan and a part of Madhya Pradesh, through which it mainly flows, as well.

Krishna Water Dispute The river Krishna too is an important peninsular river, draining an area of 258,948km², of which 26.8% lies in Maharashtra, 43.8% in Karnataka and 29.4% in Andhra Pradesh. With the reorganisation of the basin states in 1953 and 1956, demands for fresh allocations of its water resource emerged. In 1963, under the Ministry of Irrigation and Power several new projects were sanctioned by all the basin states based on the interim allocations. However, Maharashtra and Karnataka wanted the matter to be referred to an Inter-stated Tribunal under the Inter-state Water Disputes Act, 1956. The Tribunal was set up in 1969, and made its recommendation in 1973 allocating 16,000 million m³ and 19,680 million m³ respectively to the two states.

Godavari Water Dispute The river Godavari, the largest of the peninsular rivers, drains an area of 312,812km², of which 48.6% lies in Maharashtra, 23.8% in Andhra Pradesh, 20.7% in Madhya Pradesh, 5.5% in Orissa and 1.4% in Karnataka. In 1951 the Planning Commission allocated its water amongst the states through a number of new projects. The agreement was ratified by all the states

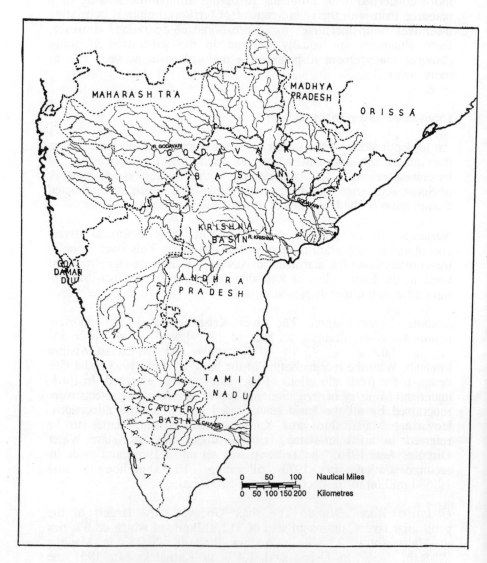

Figure 16.2 Inter-State Basins of Peninsular India:
Prospects of Water Sharing

present, except Orissa, which was not invited to the conference. This questioned the validity of the agreement.

In 1953 and 1956 the reorganisation of the states once again raised the question of the allocation by the Planning Commission. The states wanted the dispute to be referred to a tribunal which was set up in 1969 to settle the allocation of water amongst Maharashtra, Karnataka and Andhra Pradesh in the upper reaches of the main Godavari. These states later resorted to bilateral negotiations to arrive at a mutual settlement of the dispute.

Cauvery Water Dispute The river Cauvery has been in the spotlight for a considerable period with regard to the dispute for the apportionment of its water resources between Karnataka and Tamil Nadu. Rising in the state of Karnataka, the river drains an area of 87,900km², of which 55.5% lies in Tamil Nadu, 41.2% in Karnataka and 3.3% in Kerala. In 1924 an agreement was concluded between Karnataka and Tamil Nadu, over the construction of dams across the river. The present disputes, however, revolve around the interpretation of the 1924 Agreement. The two governments are still at loggerheads over the fact that, in spite of 75% of the drainage area of the Cauvery lying in Tamil Nadu, it utilises much less water. This has prompted it to appeal for a redressal of the Agreement, which has been opposed by Karnataka.

Water disputes of this nature are evident on a larger geographical plane within the South Asian region. International water disputes of this nature have been highlighted in this study, with special emphasis on the Indo-Bangladesh Ganga water dispute, which has attracted considerable global attention in the present decade.

International River Disputes in South Asia

Innumerable instances of water disputes are evident within the geographical and political framework of South Asia, but the study of a few isolated cases will no doubt shed light on the inter-nation co-operation and the conflicting issues facing states in sharing these valuable resources. The case studies presented here attempt to focus on some of the disputes.

INDO-BANGLADESH GANGA WATER DISPUTE

A study of the Ganga river system reveals that the lives and well-being of a significant section of the populations of India and Bangladesh are tied to it. In Bangladesh itself, the well-being of one third of the population in the south-west part of the country is

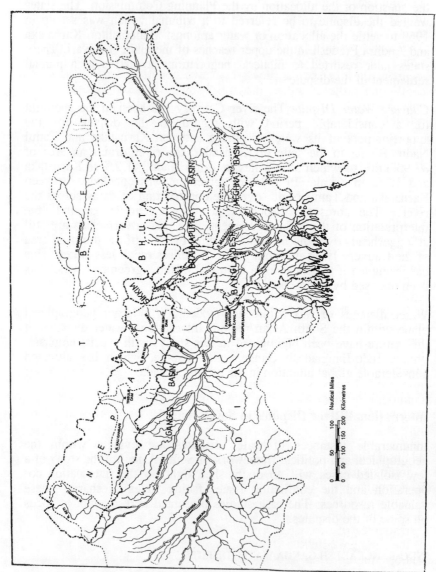

Figure 16.3 Ganges–Brahmaputra Basin: Prospects for Water Sharing

intricately associated with this river system. However, the dramatic seasonal variation in the flow of this river has resulted in a considerable reduction in its dry season flow (November to May). Though it has been estimated that Bangladesh and India require a total of 282,471.5 million m³ of water from this river by the year 2000 to meet their annual requirements (the countries require 59,812.415 million m³ and 221,733.96 million m³ respectively), the actual supply is much below this estimated flow. Thus, in order to augment the dry season flows these two countries have put forward conflicting projects, rather than resorting to bilateral co-operation to ensure a relatively steady supply of water and establish a neighbourly relationship.

The dispute was sparked off in 1962 when India took a unilateral decision to establish the Farakka Barrage across the Ganga, about 18km from the Indo-Bangladesh border, which was vehemently opposed by Bangladesh. The barrage was designed to divert 1,132m³/s of Ganga water into the Bhagirathi–Hooghly system to clear the silt deposited in the Hooghly, for the efficient functioning of Calcutta Port. This water was especially essential to India during the dry season for flushing more water into the Hooghly, but its diversion would, however, have heavy consequences on Bangladesh, threatening a further reduction in its dry season flow.

In 1951, the then East Pakistan government, in anticipation of the adverse effect of the Farakka Barrage, protested against the plan – protests which led to a series of negotiations between the two nations at technical and official levels even after the construction of the barrage, but failed to reach any constructive conclusion. Following the independence of Bangladesh, both nations established the Indo-Bangladesh Joint Rivers Commission in March 1972, to undertake a joint study and harness the water resources of the international rivers common to them. The Commission established a forum for maintaining a liaison between the participating countries with a view to:

1 Ensuring maximisation of benefits to both the countries through joint efforts.
2 Formulating flood control works and recommending implementation of joint projects.
3 Studying flood control and irrigation projects so that the water resources of the region could be utilised on an equitable basis for their mutual benefits.
4 Formulating proposals for co-ordinated research and studying the advance-warning systems of floods and cyclones.

The Commission was also required to perform such functions as would be entrusted to it by mutual consent of the two governments. However, the issue of sharing the Ganga waters between them remained beyond the purview of the Commission. It was proposed to leave the issue to the mutual decisions of the Prime Ministers of the two countries. At a ministerial meeting held in July 1973 in New Delhi, the two sides agreed to draw up a mutually acceptable solution before operating the Farakka Barrage. This was later confirmed by India's External Affairs Minister in February 1974, during his visit to Dacca. In May 1974 the Prime Ministers of both nations agreed that:

1 During the dry season flow in the Ganga there might not be enough water to meet the needs of the Calcutta port or those of Bangladesh.
2 Augmenting the dry season flows of the Ganga to meet the requirements for both the port and Bangladesh. Therefore, the Indo-Bangladesh Joint Rivers Commission was entrusted with the task of studying the issue and making appropriate recommendations. The recommendations proposed that the allocation of the Ganga waters would be made obligatory between the two nations before commissioning and operation of the Farakka Barrage.

Based on the ministerial level talks between the two nations in April 1975 in Dacca, a trial operation of the Farakka Barrage was proposed by India, to which Bangladesh agreed. An agreement was therefore reached to run the feeder canal from 21 April to 31 May 1975, with a discharge of 311.3–452.8m³/s over a 10-day period. Without renewing this agreement India continued to divert the Ganga waters from Farakka even after 31 May 1975 to the full capacity of the feeder canal. This had disastrous effects in Bangladesh during the 1975–6 dry season. The discharge at the Hardinge Bridge reached a record low of 656.56m³/s on 29 May 1975, compared to the average of 1,839.5m³/s during the same period averaged over the previous seven years. The Gorai, the main distributory of the Ganges, dried up on 20 March 1976, affecting not only the agricultural activities of Bangladesh, but fisheries, forestry, navigation, industry, health and ecology as well. It resulted in saline water intrusion up to 150km inland.

After diplomatic exchanges between the two nations Bangladesh put forward the issue to the United Nations. The General Assembly of the UN adopted a consensus on 26 November 1976, as a result of which the parties agreed to meet at Dacca at the ministerial level to expedite a settlement and maintain the principles of international law governing the use of water from international rivers.

The negotiations held between the two countries on 16 December brought about no solution however. On 18 April 1977 an agreement was reached which was manifested in the signing of the Ganges Water Agreement on 5 November 1977. This agreement involved the following conditions:

1 The two sides would find a long-term solution and devise means for the augmentation of the lean season flow of the Ganges.
2 The dry season availability was recorded from the flow of the river between 1948–73 on the basis of 75% availability. The shares of India and Bangladesh in the flow over 10-day periods were fixed, shares in the last 10-day period of April (the leanest month) being 580m³/s and 976m³/s respectively, out of a total availability of 1,556m³/s during the period.
3 The point of sharing would be at Farakka. In order to ensure a just share to Bangladesh at Farakka, provision was made to ensure that it did not fall below 80% of the stated share during a particular period.
4 The agreement was initially valid for a period of five years but could be extended with mutual consent.

This agreement has been considerably successful in apportioning the Ganga flow between the two countries, though the dry season flow expectations are difficult to meet. This demand for the Ganga water especially between January to May can be met, given the existing technology and patterns of use, if the flow can be augmented.

Therefore, both the countries have prepared two separate schemes to serve this purpose. India has proposed the transfer of 2,830m³/s of water from the Brahmaputra to the Ganga through a 209 mile-long link canal to meet its requirements of 1,132m³/s in contrast to the present availability of 580m³/s. One-third of this flow would pass through Bangladesh and join the Ganges at a point above Farakka. This would involve the construction of a barrage at Jhogighopa in Assam. In order to meet the water shortages in the Brahmaputra basin due to the proposed diversion, India has proposed the construction of three dams in the upper reaches of the Brahmaputra during the subsequent phases.

Bangladesh rejected this proposal and instead proposed a joint venture with Nepal, to which India raised objections on the grounds that it is a bilateral issue and therefore should be resolved between the two countries.

The proposed link canal project was therefore an obvious failure especially because Bangladesh felt threatened that not only would the river flow come under the physical control of India with the construction of the Jhogighopa dam, but if the lean flow of the Brahmaputra was further reduced, it would affect Bangladesh in particular. Besides, the project was technically, economically and ecologically designated as inviable by Bangladesh.

The completion of the project would not only raise the same problems evident by deviating the water from the Ganges, extending the salinity front during the dry season, but would also involve the displacement of a significant section of the population and submergence of valuable agricultural land. However, no understanding has been reached so far on this issue, though the Ganges Water Agreement, 1977, has provided the foundation for a long-term settlement of the dispute.

INDO-NEPAL WATER DISPUTES

Though the Ganga water dispute between India and Bangladesh has received international attention and is an issue of global concern, the proposals of the third co-riparian state, Nepal, are equally important in drawing a successful plan for optimum utilisation of the Ganga waters. Nepal showed keen interest in the proposal for the construction of storage dams in the state across the Ganga as it could evolve as a major exporter of hydroelectric power to India and Bangladesh. Besides, being a land-locked state, it would provide Nepal access to the sea through the Ganga and its tributaries.

This proposal was feasible only through a consensus amongst the three co-riparian states through a tripartite treaty on free navigation. However, it did not materialise since India publicly and officially rejected the Barcelona Convention and Statute on the Regime of Navigable Waterways of International Concern on 17 March 1956. Furthermore, with the completion of the Farakka Barrage in 1975, Nepal's proposal for free navigation received a serious setback. In the light of this problem, King Birenda of Nepal pointed out in December 1977 that only a joint effort through regional co-operation could resolve the conflicting issues and harness the optimal benefits from the Ganga to the advantage of the region as an integrated unit.

However, besides this issue, other projects undertaken after 1951 by India and Nepal were not completely in favour of the latter. This was conspicuous especially in the cases of the Kosi river project (1954) and the Gandak river project (1959).

The Kosi, one of the most important left-bank tributaries of the river Ganges, originats in Nepal with its three major arms – the Sun Kosi, the Arun and the Tamur. It has a total catchment area of 74,500km^2 of which 11,000km^2 lie within India. Of the total volume of water, the Sun Kosi contributes 44%, the Arun 37% and the Tamur 19%. The significance of the Kosi lies in the fact that it offers a vast potential for the development of hydroelectric power and irrigation facilities, whilst on the other hand the river has always remained a potential threat because of the devastating floods it can inflict in its lower basin, especially because of its lateral movement, as is the case of the Hwang Ho (Yellow River) in China. This can be attributed to its heavy loads of silt coupled with a steep gradient prompting its course to shift sideways. Thus, in about 200 years, the river has moved 112km laterally from Purnea district in Bihar to its present position.

Several schemes have been considered from time to time since 1893 to find a feasible solution to this problem. It was, however, only in 1953, when a devastating flood highlighted the urgency of the matter, that a tangible scheme was formulated. The scheme was prepared by the Central Water and Power Commission and was sanctioned by the Government of India in December 1953. The project was primarily intended as a flood protection device, but it also proposed to simultaneously construct irrigation canals to irrigate large tracts on its eastern bank.

During the Third Five Year Plan (1961–6) the new schemes incorporated in the project included:

1 establishment of a hydroelectric power station on the main canal to generate 20,000MW of power;
2 the construction of the Rajpur branch canal, branching off from the eastern main canal, and intended to irrigate an area of 897,000 acres in Saharsa district of Bihar;
3 the Western Kosi canal system with the Western Main Canal branching off from the barrage, to irrigate an area of 803,000 acres in the district of Darbhanga in Bihar and a part of Nepal;
4 extension of the eastern and western flood embankments; and
5 construction of water courses of considerable capacity.

Besides the generation of irrigation facilities, Nepal received 10MW of hydroelectric power and was permitted to construct a bridge over the barrage, opening an important west-east transit route in the country, though the total cost of the project was borne by India.

The project, however, remained far from meeting the expectations of India, since she had always intended to take up a project of a much larger magnitude than the one formulated. Amongst the various measures being considered, effective flood management would be possible through the construction of storage reservoirs in the basin. The Barakshetra gorge through which the Kosi flows before emerging into the plains has always been considered an ideal site for the building of a high storage dam. The Kosi High Dam had been conceived in the late thirties, and was investigated by the then Central Water, Power, Irrigation and Navigation Commission (CWINC) in India. The preliminary project report envisaged the construction of a 239m high dam to form a reservoir with a gross storage capacity of 85,000 million m³, which would moderate a peak flood of 680m³/s to a more manageable 160m³/s. Moreover, it would have a potential to generate 1,800MW of hydroelectric power. With an estimated cost of Rs177 *crore* the project was expected to provide significant irrigation benefits downstream in both Nepal and in Bihar.

The Kosi High Dam Project proposal was however dropped, anticipating the birth of another Bhakra Nangal in the eastern region and the difficulty in finding a market for the hydroelectric power generated. Hence, the search for a more modest scheme was instigated, focusing on the immediate needs of flood moderation and preventing the lateral movement of the river. This project, completed within a decade, failed to solve the flood problems entirely though it did serve the limited objective of arresting the meandering of the river. This, over time, prompted the revival of the Kosi High Dam Project. The revised feasibility report prepared by the Indian Central Water commission in 1980 presented the following features:

Barakshetra Dam, Kosi
Dam height: 269m
Storage capacity: 135,000 million m³ (gross)
                 94,000 million m³ (live)
Installed power generation capacity: 3,000MW
Annual energy potential: 2,590 million kWh.

With the construction of a storage dam in Nepal, Bangladesh revealed considerable interest in the proposal. It primarily revolved around the feasibility of augmenting the Ganga flow by means of storage facilities in the Nepal Himalayas. Bangladesh expressed its ideas in 1983, updating its proposals through the Indo-Bangladesh Joint River Commission. It listed seven storage dams whose original proposed heights had been further increased. The Kosi High Dam, being a component of Bangladesh's proposal, had been envisaged with an increased height of 269m from the original proposed height of 239m. The Kosi High Dam and the other six dams (Chisapani, Kali–Gandaki I, Kali Gandaki II, Trisul–Ganga, Seti and Pancheswar) were estimated by Bangladesh to increase the dry season flow in the Ganga by 70,000 million m³. However, this proposition was rejected by India as well as by Nepal due to a number of causes.

Amongst them, the environmental implications assumed great importance, more so in the case of a large water management project. The proposed Kosi High Dam project thus offered a vast scope for debate focusing on environmental concerns.

The joint study and investigation for the Kosi High Dam is likely to be completed by 1995. Meanwhile the Ganga Mukti Andolan, Bhagalpur and the Human Rights Organisation of Nepal (HURON) have pointed out to the Nepalese Government the seismic hazards which the dam may be exposed to, advocating a series of smaller projects in the Kosi basin instead. Unless the joint study and investigation report on the Kosi High Dam is completed, the assessment of the human impact on the environment is not possible.

Therefore, the underdevelopment of the water resources common to Nepal and India could be attributed mainly to the political relationship between the two neighbouring states. A number of debatable propositions vitiated political attitudes on both sides. This posed an obstacle to Indo-Nepal riparian co-operation which was inhibited or reduced to periodic formal reiterations. The consequence has been decades of delay in the implementation of this project and a host of other important projects. The Kosi High Dam which was first contemplated in 1950 has been periodically buried and revived in accordance with the prevailing political climate. The economic viability of the different projects hinges on India's import of the surplus power from Nepal. One estimate shows that if the proposed Karnali project had been started in the 1960s and been completed in the 1970s, it could have accrued an additional revenue of Rs1,000 *crore* annually to Nepal. Moreover, it could have saved India billions of dollars' worth of oil imports especially after the hike in oil prices. Until recently, all the proposed projects faced political hesitancy from Nepal.

In 1982, Nepal proposed to take up the Mulaghat Multipurpose Project (60MW) on the Tamur, an arm of the Kosi. But India objected on the grounds that the Mulaghat Dam would be submerged, if the Kosi High Dam, in which it had once again revealed interest, was constructed. Nepal was, however, reluctant to discuss the Kosi project and the entire exercise reached an impasse. Similarly, two proposed mega-projects on the Karnali (at Chisapani) and the Mahakali (at Pancheswar) rivers failed to make a breakthrough due to differences in opinion on both sides.

Nepal has always visualised itself as a smaller partner, fearing that it would always be a minor beneficiary in transboundary river projects. Hence, in a number of basin studies conducted in Nepal, Indian involvement has been deliberately avoided. For instance, Nepal got the Karnali basin study conducted by the Nippon Koei team of Japan in 1962. In 1968, the Snowy Mountain Authority of Australia reviewed two of the 10 best hydroelectric power station sites identified in the basin. This was further reviewed and a report was prepared for the Chisapani (Karnali) Dam by Narconsult AS and Electrowatt of Norway in 1977. Similarly, a Japanese firm conducted a study of the Kosi Basin.

However, after the restoration of democracy in Nepal, Mr G.P. Koirala visited Delhi in December 1991 and provided a concrete shape to the proposal on the basis of the spadework done earlier by the high level task force. Thereafter, Nepal dropped the idea of parallel investigations and a joint study for the Kosi High Dam was agreed upon.

But the democratic restoration in Nepal has seen some potential impediments between the two neighbours in riparian co-operation. During the election campaign, Nepal's communist parties and others adopted a strong nationalist stand criticising the development of rivers common to both Nepal and India. This led to a major procedural impediment, based on a provision in the kingdom's new constitution, that agreement on natural resources must be ratified by a two-thirds majority of the National Panchayat. Even so, the conducive political climate has provided evidence of goodwill and the determination to work for mutually beneficial projects.

Resolution to National and International Water Disputes

An analysis of the river water disputes, both on a national and an international plane depicts that many of the conflicts are attributed to the apportionment and conflicting uses of the water resources. Many of these conflicts have failed to reach a constructive resolution. Interference from international agencies has intensified the existing dilemma in some instances, since most international law is devised on the basis of the experience of developed societies and not practical solutions to Third World problems.

Though most international water disputes depend on the successful conclusion of bilateral negotiations and regional co-operation amongst the co-riparian states, national level disputes can be resolved through the implementation of appropriate plans and policies.

International water disputes originating within South Asia demand a system of regional co-operation amongst the co-riparian states to resolve the issues and enable optimal utilisation of water resources. This, however, involves a number of technical and economic considerations:

1 All the co-riparian states should have equal access to international water resources and each nation should benefit from their development without diminishing the benefits of any other riparian. This can be achieved through navigational agreements for boundary lakes and rivers, for instance.
2 There should be opportunities for integrated development amongst co-basin states.
3 The water use by the upper riparian state should not reduce its availability or adversely affect its quality in the lower riparian state, when the latter does not have a reciprocal power over the upper riparian. Instances of this situation arise when withdrawal of waters for upstream use, or use of a river for waste disposal by the upper riparian, affects the lower riparian.
4 However, even when the natural inducement to co-operate is minimal, economic and political incentives to co-operate may be overpowering. This is evident when the project is capital-intensive and prompts a financial collaboration of the riparian states of the basin. Alternatively, international funding agencies may fund the project only with prior approval of the basin states of the region.
5 Natural or economic incentives may sometimes be reflected in the desire of a basin state to project an international image, important for pursuing a good neighbourly relationship with the other co-basin states.

Thus, these factors may sometimes comprise a crucial factor to prompt the individual basin states to co-operate in developing and utilising the water resources of the basin, in spite of the persistence of diverse problems amongst themselves. This may solve much of the politics and conflicting relationships between and amongst the nations of South Asia in the light of sharing their international water resources within the region.

Notes

1   *Crore* is a Hindu term meaning ten millions.

Bibliography

Arogyaswamy, R.N.P. (1971) 'The evaluation and utilisation of water resources' in V. Dagli (ed.) *Natural Resources in the Indian Economy,* Bombay: Vora and Co Publishers: 68–77.

Barik, N. (1984) 'River water disputes in South Asia: a comparative perspective', unpublished M.Phil. dissertation, CIPOD, SIS, JNU, New Delhi.

Biswas, A.K. (1983) 'Some major issues in river basin management for developing countries', in M. Zaman *et al* (ed.) *River Basin Development*, Dublin: Tycooly International Publishing: 17–27.

Bruce, J.P. and Maastand, D.E.L. (1968) 'Water resource research in Canada', Special Study No.5, Government of Canada Science Secretariat, July.

Butrico, F.A. *et al* (1971) *Resource Management in the Great Lakes Basin,* Lexington, Massachusetts: Health Lexington Books.

Choudhury, G.R. and Khan, T.A. (1983) 'Developing the Ganges basin', in M. Zaman *et al* (ed.) *River Basin Development*, Dublin: Tycooly International Publishing: 28–39.

Dayal, G. (1994) 'In troubled waters', *Rashtriya Sahara,* January: 100–1.

Everson, W. (1973) 'The hope we have', in C.R. Goldman *et al* (ed.) *Environmental Quality and Water Development,* San Francisco: W.H. Freeman: 12–25.

Gyawali, D. (1989) 'Water in Nepal', Occasional Paper No.8, Hawaii: East–West Environment and Policy Institute.

Falkenmark, M. (1986) 'Fresh waters as a factor in strategic policy and action', in A.H. Westing (ed.) *Global Resources and International Conflict,* Oxford University Press: 85–113.

Fano, E. (1977) 'The role of international agencies', in A.E. Utton and L. Teclaff (eds) *Water in a Developing World – The Management of a Critical Resource,* Boulder, Colorado: Westview Press: 219–30.

Fleming, W.M. (1982) 'Environmental and economic impacts of watershed conservation on a major reservoir project in Ecuador', in M.M. Hufschmidt and E.L. Hyman (eds) *Economic Approaches to Natural Resource and Environmental Quality Analysis,* Dublin: Tycooly International Publishing: 292–9.

Fox, I.K. (1973) 'Some political aspects of the relationships between large-scale inter-basin water transfers and environmental quality', in C.R. Goldman *et al* (ed.) *Environmental Quality and Water Development,* San Francisco: W.H. Freeman: 413–24.

Goldman, C.R. (1973) 'Environmental impact and water development', in C.R. Goldman *et al* (ed.) *Environmental Quality and Water Development,* San Francisco: W.H. Freeman: 1–11.

Hufschmidt, M.M. (1982) 'New approaches to economic analysis of natural resources and environmental quality', in M.M. Hufschmidt and E.L. Hyman (eds) *Economic Approaches to Natural Resource and Environmental Quality Analysis,* Dublin: Tycooly International Publishing: 2–30.

Jain, S.K. (1971) 'Fruitful use of India's enormous water resources', in V. Dagli (ed.) *Natural Resources in the Indian Economy,* Bombay: Vora and Co Publishing: 61–7.

Jain, S.N. *et al* (1971) *Interstate Water Disputes in India,* Bombay: N.M. Tripath.

Joy, J.L. and Everitt, E. (eds) (1976) *The Kosi Symposium,* Sussex: Institute of Development Studies.

Le Marquard, D. (1978) 'Politics of international river basin co-operation and management', in A.E. Utton and L. Teclaff (eds) *Water in a Developing World – The Management of a Critical Resource,* Boulder, Colorado: Westview Press: 147–65.

McDonald, A. and Kay, D. (1988) *Water Resources – Issues and Strategies,* Longman Scientific and Technical and New York: John Wiley and Sons.

Milliken, J.G. (1977) 'Alternative strategies for closing the supply/demand gap', in V.P. Nanda (ed.) *Water Needs for the Future – Political, Economic, Legal and Technological Issues in a National and International Framework,* Boulder, Colorado: Westview Press: 257–75.

Miller, M.L. *et al* (1987) 'Natural resource management systems', in M.L. Miller *et al* (ed.) *Social Science in Natural Resource Management Systems,* Boulder, Colorado: Westview Press: 3–32.

Nanda, V.P. (1977) 'Emerging trends in the use of international law and institutions for the management of international water resources', in V.P. Nanda (ed.) *Water Needs for the Future – Political, Economic, Legal and Technological Issues in a National and International Framework,* Boulder, Colorado: Westview Press: 15–38.

Pradhan, B.K. (1986) *Opportunity Costs of Delay in Development of the Himalayan Water Resources – A Nepalese Perspective,* Kathmandu.

Rao, K.L. (1979) *India's Water Wealth,* New Delhi: Orient Longman.

Rodosevich, G. (1977) 'Global water law systems and water control', in V.P. Nanda (ed.) *Water Needs for the Future – Political, Economic, Legal and Technological Issues in a National and International Framework,* Boulder, Colorado: Westview Press: 39–58.

Schachter, O. (1977) *Sharing the World's Resources,* New York: Columbia University Press.

Sharma, C.K. (1988) *Water and Energy Resources of Himalayan Block,* Kathmandu.

Sharma, V.K. (1985) *Water Resource Planning and Management,* Bombay: Himalaya Publishing House.

Shah, N. (1971) 'Natural resources in the Indian economy', in V. Dagli (ed.) *Natural Resources in the Indian Economy,* Bombay: Vora and Co Publishing: 13–36.

Siddiqui, M.F.A. (1983) 'Management of river systems in the Ganges and Brahmaputra basins of the Indian sub-continent for development of water resources', in M. Zaman *et al* (ed.) *Water Resource Development,* Dublin: Tycooly International Publishing: 137–49.

Smith, S.C. (1974) 'Economics and economists in water resource development', in L.D. James (ed.) *Man and Water,* Kentucky: The University of Kentucky Press: 81–101.

Upadhyay, S.N. (1991) *Nepal's Trans Boundary Resources, New Perspectives in Co-operation,* USA: International Trans Boundary Resources Centre.

Varhese, B.G. (1990) *Waters of Hope,* Oxford and New Delhi: IBH Publishing.

Water Resources Ministry, Nepal (1985) *Water Resources Development in Nepal,* Kathmandu.

Watt, K.E.F. (1968) *Ecology and Resource Management – A Quantitative Approach,* New York: McGraw Hill Book Company.

White, G.F. (1974) 'Role of geography in water resources management', in L.D. James (ed.) *Man and Water,* Kentucky: The University of Kentucky Press: 102–21.

Zaman, M. (1983) 'The Ganges basin development: a long-term problem and some short-term options', in M. Zaman *et al* (ed.) *Water Resource Development,* Dublin: Tycooly International Publishing: 99–109.

—— (1983) 'Institutional and legal framework for co-operation between Bangladesh and India on shared water resources', in M. Zaman *et al* (ed.) *Water Resource Development,* Dublin: Tycooly International Publishing: 185–94.

17

Management of Transboundary Water Resources:
A Case Study of the Mekong

Prachoom Chomchai

Introduction

Use of the transboundary water resources of the Mekong basin has been characterised largely by a virtual absence of hard and fast rules derived from international law, though, with the arbitrary drawing (in 1957) of the demarcation line between the upper Mekong (with China and Myanmar as riparian states) and the lower Mekong (with Thailand, Laos, Cambodia and Vietnam as riparian states), this situation has changed slightly. The year 1957 witnessed the establishment of the Mekong Committee to 'co-ordinate' the use of the waters of the lower Mekong and major proposals to abstract them by riparian states go through the formality of approval by the Committee. The requirement of consensus in all decision-making has helped to stabilise the situation. Nevertheless, despite certain joint statements of principles, the Mekong Committee does not possess supra-national authority and member states are not compelled to submit to the committee all their proposals to abstract or otherwise use Mekong waters. Furthermore, if disputes should occur, there is no ready mechanism for adjudication.

On the other hand, in the time-hallowed traditional irrigation systems of northern Thailand, whenever disputes in water use broke out, there was a ready mechanism of adjustment. Moreover, kinship and family ties also exerted a moderating influence.

It is otherwise with regard to the international use of the Mekong. This is particularly true of the whole of the Mekong basin where an 'open-access' system seems to prevail. While riparian states of the lower Mekong have made frantic efforts to 'co-ordinate' their use of the river, little or no formal rapport exists between the upper and the lower basins. The newly-established Mekong Development Research Network (MDRN), which fosters technical and scientific co-operation among all six riparian states of the Mekong currently constitutes the only link between the two basins. In the meantime, China has proceeded to dam the river upstream, its first dam (Man Wan) having started to generate hydropower in 1993. While the ecologic and other consequences of such a move by China remain to be ascertained, it has thrown the Mekong

Committee's planning for the lower basin out of gear and has enhanced the need to foster basin-wide co-operation to treat the basin as an integrated planning unit.

Treaties have been signed between Siam (as Thailand was called in the old days) and France (on behalf of its protectorates in Indo-China); but they have regulated largely the navigational use of the Mekong. In any case, the upper Mekong remains a virtual 'no man's land'. Claims that customary international law exists to regulate the joint use of the Mekong have been called into question by China's unilateral damming of the river. Either there exists a customary international law calling for consultation with downstream riparian states and China has chosen to ignore it or such a law does not exist. There is a strong presumption in favour of the latter; for the downstream riparian states have apparently not openly protested against such a move by the uppermost riparian state.

Resolution of Domestic Water Disputes: A Case Study Of Northern Thailand

Based on the experience of northern Thailand (Surarerks, 1986), it can be said that disputes occur often, especially between water users at the canal head and those at the canal end. Most disputes are caused by water shortages at the beginning of the rice growing season and during the dry season and by the selfishness of the farmers at the head of the canal. Other reasons are that the water delivery schedule did not coincide with the timing or period that the crops need and that the water distribution between farmers at the head and tail of the canal or project is not fair or just.

The solutions of these water disputes are generally either found by the administrators of the project, such as the weir committees or *amphoe* (district) officers, or by group decision, such as in water-users meetings and by co-operation of officers of the *amphoe* with weir committees and water users. Frequently the *kamnan,* head of the *tambon* (sub-district) and *phuyai ban,* village head, would participate in the group for solving water use disputes, especially for warning and compromising dispute parties and even calling for a fine.

It is to be noted that, in the people's system, water problems are generally solved by individuals, while in the national system principles and regulations are more important. In the people's system all administrators agreed that in solving the problems of water theft and water disputes, the ability and integrity of the individual administrators responsible for the system are of paramount importance. Water disputes are solved because the water users trust and respect the *huana muang fai* (water head man) and the *phuyai ban* (head of the village) or even *kamnan* (head of the *tambon*). The percentage of 'others' in both systems in the above in fact mostly meant that water disputes were solved by the head of *tambon* or both of them helped the weir committees or *huana muang fai* in finding solutions. However, in the national system more than half of the administrators disagreed with this view saying that the resolution of problems in water management depends on principles rather than individuals.

In general, water conflicts in both people's and national systems are easily solved because of the kinship and family relationships between the members and through belief in the leadership of the conciliator. Culture and tradition are other important factors in solving problems of water conflicts.

Another point to make is that irrigation laws or irrigation acts still have loopholes, especially in the people's system where water users have their own rules or principles, known as *sanya muang fai* or *muang fai* (weir) agreement. For this reason better law and order are greatly needed.

The experience of northern Thailand should give lessons for the resolution of the international water conflicts dealt with below.

Unregulated Use of Water Resources

In parallel with the case of aquifers, the unregulated use of international resources like an international river can result in either or both of two types of 'social dilemma'. First, over-exploitation typical of 'common-pool' resources (CPRs), defined by their characteristics of subtractability and high cost of exclusion of potential beneficiaries from exploiting them (Young, 1993: 2; Ostrom, 1990: chapter 1) can result. Common-pool problems arise when individually rational resource-use decisions bring about a result that is not optimal when considered from the perspective of the exploiters as a group. In their joint use, each individual is driven by an immutable logic to withdraw more of the resource units (or invest less in them) than is optimal from the perspective of all the users (Gardner *et al*, 1990: 335). Typically, there are many appropriators or users withdrawing the resource. The roots of the problems associated with such resources are found in the inadequate economic and institutional framework within which they are exploited. In other words, they have been utilised within an open access framework so that resource ownership is according to the rule of capture. When ownership rights are not defined, users tend towards over-exploitation (Young, 1993: 2).

The second type of social dilemma frequently associated with the unregulated use of international water resources is the imposition of negative externalities (Buchanan and Stubbebine, 1962) on third parties who do not themselves benefit from the exploitation activity. These are largely negative technological – as opposed to pecuniary – externalities: they arise through technologies. For fishing trawlers to operate efficiently, they need to travel over a large 'domain'. Fixed nets operating in the same territory increase the operating costs for both trawlers and fixed-net users. Similarly, if one group of fishermen use dynamite in their fishing efforts, the costs for other fishermen rise as a result of this production technology. These technological externalities could be both reciprocal and unidirectional in nature (Dasgupta, 1982: 31). There arise reciprocal externalities when, as in the case of riparian states scrambling to tap the same aquifer through pumping, each imposes costs on all the others and each experiences costs imposed by others. Unidirectional negative externalities arise when a riparian state imposes a negative externality on another or others but not vice versa. Both the failure to conserve common-pool resources and the imposition of negative externalities on others are phenomena which could usefully be addressed, given the right legal and institutional framework in which the resources are exploited.

For the sake of clarity, it is important, even at the risk of introducing come repetition, to elaborate further on common-pool resources (CPRs). They are defined to be *sufficiently large* natural or man-made resources from whose use it is costly (but not necessarily impossible) to exclude potential beneficiaries from obtaining benefits (Gardner *et al*, 1990: 335). The dimensions of such a resource are presumably judged in relation to the use expected to be made of it and have to be viewed dynamically. Though this definition differs somewhat from what has been quoted from Young (1993: 2) above, CPRs partake of the nature of public goods. Nevertheless, because of the subtractability of their units they are not public goods strictly so-called.

It is important to determine precisely how common-pool resource dilemmas come about. According to Gardner *et al* (1990: 336–7), there are four necessary (and sufficient) conditions to produce a CPR dilemma: resource unit subtractability, multiple appropriators, suboptimal outcomes and constitutionally feasible alternatives.

First, there must be, as has been noted, resource unit subtractability. This is defined as the presence of a resource that makes available, over time, a flow of resource units that are subtractable in the sense that a resource unit withdrawn or harvested by one individual is not fully available to another individual. Because of this characteristic, common-pool resources are not, strictly speaking, public goods. Examples of common-pool resources and their corresponding resource units given by Gardner *et al* (1990) are a groundwater water basin and cubic metres of water extracted; a fishing ground and tons of fish caught; and an oil field and barrels of oil pumped.

It is important, in the interest of analytical clarity, to distinguish between the resource as a *stock* and the harvested or withdrawn use – units as a *flow* (Blomquist and Ostrom, 1985). This distinction is especially useful in connection with *renewable* resources, where one can find a natural replacement rate such that, as long as the withdrawal rate does not exceed the natural replacement rate, a renewable resource will not be exhausted. On the other hand, when a resource has no natural replacement (an *exhaustible* resource), then any withdrawal rate maintained over time will lead eventually to exhaustion.

The second in the set of necessary and sufficient conditions for the generation of a CPR dilemma is the existence of multiple appropriators already discussed. In other words, more than one individual or team of individuals, known as appropriators (Plott and Meyer, 1975) are withdrawing or harvesting resource units from the resource.

The third condition in the set is, as has also been noted, the fact that suboptimal outcomes characterise the joint use of the resource. Given the particular configuration of the physical system, technologies, rules, market conditions and attributes of the appropriators, their strategies in the use of the resource lead to suboptimal outcomes from the global perspective of the appropriators. Individuals or parties jointly using a common-pool resource are presumed to face a tragic situation in which their individual rationality leads to an outcome that is not rational from the perspective of the group as a whole.

The fourth and final condition – often overlooked – in the set is the presence of constitutionally feasible alternatives. Given the existing institutional and 'constitutional' arrangements, at least one set of co-ordinated strategies exists that is more efficient than current decisions and is 'constitutionally' feasible, a co-operative surplus being thereby generated. In other words, a set of strategies exists in which total discounted benefits exceed total discounted costs including production, investment, governance and transaction costs; and given existing rules for institutional change, there exists a necessary consensus for such a change. A sufficient (but not necessary) condition for such a set of feasible alternatives would be the existence of a pareto-optimal set of co-ordinated strategies that are individually advantageous to all appropriators or potential appropriators.

The first two conditions (resource unit subtractability and multiple appropriators) and the definition of a CPR as a sufficiently large resource coupled with the high costs of exclusion of potential beneficiaries from obtaining benefits from their use are necessary to create what Gardner *et al* (1990) call a CPR *situation*, which approximates to, but is not a public good situation (Musgrave, 1959) of course, the presence of condition one distinguishes a CPR situation from a public good one.

The presence of the third and forth conditions (suboptimal outcomes and constitutionally feasible alternatives) serve to distinguish a CPR *dilemma* from a simple CPR *situation*. If suboptimal outcomes (according to the third condition) are not produced for at least one combination of the physical system, technology, rules, market conditions and attributes of the appropriators, there is nothing problematic in the situation. Similarly, if no alternative set of constitutionally feasible strategies (given discounted benefits and costs) would produce a better outcome for the appropriators or for the group of current or potential appropriators (according to the forth condition), there is no dilemma.

Among the precious natural resources, water stands in a curious position from the point of view of analysis with the help of concepts measured per unit of time and, in as much as it originates from solar energy, is renewable, though there is no visible *stock* from which it is derived. Water withdrawn from a river is also a flow, though it is not extracted from a given *stock*. It is true that a particular river may be fed by man-made as well as by natural lakes whose stored water could be said to constitute a *stock*, at any rate of a temporary nature. Of course, ultimately the *stock* of water, which is the source of river water, is the constant quantity of water contained in the hydrologic cycle. The extent to which a particular river basin can capture its share from the constant hydrologic cycle depends, however not on how river water is withdrawn but on how the watershed resources, which are *exhaustible,* are conserved. Thus, deforestation, an excessive use of an exhaustible resource, will affect the amount of rainfall a river basin can expect to secure from the hydrologic cycle.

With their peculiar characteristics, the CPR condition of resource unit subtractability does not apply exactly to surface water resources found in rivers and streams. Moreover, the CPR as defined by Gardner *et al* (1990) does not exactly fit such characteristics. Despite these reservations, however, thinking on CPRs appears to shed light on the use of international water resources.

In the absence of an international agreement among riparian states on the use of the Mekong, a major international river, each riparian state's water rights are not defined. The current use of the Mekong thus resembles the discussed model of exploitation of common pool resources with all the undesirable consequences that come with it. From the global viewpoint of all the Mekong riparian states, it is thus likely that the river is now suffering from suboptimal outcomes in its largely unco-ordinated use by riparian states. Of course, these could be avoided, and optimal outcomes arrived at if all the riparian states could get together to co-ordinate their individual use of the river, as some of them have done under the aegis of the Mekong Committee. Unregulated use of the Mekong by a riparian state could also impose negative externalities – both reciprocal and unidirectional – on other riparian states.

Without clearly defined water rights, however, it is unlikely that the Coase Theorem (Coase, 1960) and its various ramifications can usefully be applied to the current Mekong situation either. Moreover, without well defined water rights, the transaction costs of getting together – not to mention those involved in subsequent political bargaining – would be prohibitive. Failing a Hobbesian intervention (Hobbes, 1651) by an impartial third party, only a serious deterioration in the situation exemplified by pollution of the river's water or destruction of riverine fisheries would compel these riparian states sooner or later to come together. Of course, it would be better if they did not have to wait until things had come to a head: long-term planning, as has been attempted under the Mekong Committee, would be better than crisis management.

As the water rights of each riparian state are not defined, it may be more useful, in the process of negotiation, to rely instead, as suggested by Calabriesi and Melamed (1972) on the concept of entitlement.

Resolving Conflicts in the Joint Use of Natural Resources: A Case Study of the Mekong Committee

It was fortunate that, before the foundation of the Mekong Committee in 1957 by Cambodia, Laos, South Vietnam and Thailand, there had been no open conflicts in the riparian countries' joint use of the Mekong waters which – if experiences in other international river basins could serve as a guide – could have led to the same outcome in terms of basin organisation. The relatively underdeveloped state of the riparian countries of the lower Mekong has turned out to be a blessing in disguise.

In general, it could be said that competitive pressure for tapping the water resources of the Mekong has been comparatively recent, as the region's inhabitants blessed with abundant natural resources relative to their numbers have not, until comparatively recently, been faced with the pressing need to do so. For instance, life in the ancient Khmer Empire which flourished from the 9th to the 12th century and which centred on present-day Siem Riep and Angkor Wat with its highly fertile fields and fisheries associated with the neighbouring Great Lake, could be said to typify easy subsistence in the lower Mekong area until possibly the latter half of the 19th century, by which time the modern boundaries of the four riparian countries had begun to take shape.

With the advent of the latter half of the 19th century, population pressure on the natural environment began to make itself felt. As a consequence, the Korat Plateau in north-east Thailand (which coincides roughly with the lower Mekong basin in north-east Thailand) began to lose its forest cover and its sustainable fertility in the face of growing rice cultivation. At the same time, growing cities and towns across the north-east, in a wave of urbanisation, began to extend their commercial and economic influence into the surrounding countryside, thereby accentuating the pressure on natural resources and the environment.

The turn of the century witnessed not only an increase in such pressure but also the emerging demand for electricity, irrigation and transport. Moreover, in the aftermath of the Second World War, the concept of 'development' as a desirable goal in its own right was introduced into the region, one of the most backward in the country. With this wave of modernisation efforts, not entirely untinged by paternalism, a desire to help meet 'merited' wants at the grass-roots level and political canvassing for votes, the limits to growth began to be felt. As a result largely of international paternalism and altruism, attention was naturally turned to the Mekong river system which had been left largely untapped except for navigation and possibly fisheries. Establishment of the Mekong Committee in 1957 was therefore timely.

Apart from a relatively low level of development of the riparian countries, the requirements of a huge investment of resources and expertise confined the existing use of the Mekong to that for navigation, which, at a low level of development, relied mainly on maintaining the river largely in its natural state. Except for French-built facilities for transhipment at Khone Falls on the Laos–Cambodian border, such development efforts to remove natural obstacles to navigation as rock-blasting and construction of river ports and ramps dated from the Mekong Committee days only. Moreover, as far as navigation is concerned, it has been restricted largely to the satisfaction of domestic needs in Cambodia, Laos and Vietnam, though treaty provisions from colonial days still govern the international aspects of navigation on the Mekong.

While the foundation of the Mekong Committee was favoured by the initial advantage of not being constrained by open conflicts in the existing use of the Mekong, a potential source of future conflict lies in the riparian countries' *different perceptions* of the use to which the waters of the Mekong could be put.

While all riparian countries of the Mekong share the autarchic aim of self-sufficiency in energy and food, they appear to need or to perceive different basic roles for the river. Cambodia needs to tap the Mekong system not only for irrigation and hydropower generation to meet export and domestic requirements but also for navigation to link it with the external world. With its vast hydropower potential Laos is particularly well placed and disposed to exploit it for export as well as for developing agriculture, forestry and agro-industry. As a land-locked country, Laos – like its Chinese counterpart, Yunnan province further upstream – uses the Mekong as its main transport artery for maintaining contact with the external world. Thailand, with its booming economy, needs water, particularly from the mainstream, for developing irrigation in its handicapped north-east and power to propel its energy-intensive growth. Finally, Vietnam's requirements appear to centre on increasing dry-season flows to combat saline intrusion into the delta and more fully develop its agriculture for home as well as for export markets. Of the four riparian states both Cambodia and Laos have found themselves to be in unique positions *vis-à-vis* development of the lower Mekong: as most of the two countries lie within the lower Mekong basin area, the development of their natural resources could be conceived almost entirely in terms of the development of the lower Mekong basin.

If the proposed expansion of the Committee's jurisdiction is accepted, the interests of Myanmar and China in the upper basin will also have to be added to the boiling pot. China, for its part, expects to use the Mekong both for hydropower generation and for navigation. The potential transport link between its Yunnan province and countries in the lower basin through the Mekong seems to be particularly valuable. This is borne out by the fact that, in recent months, Chinese vessels of 50 and 60 tons capacity have made an effort to explore possibilities by successfully travelling down from Yunnan to Luang Prabang and Vietiane and back.

Such differing perceptions and needs among riparian states of the lower Mekong reflect the riparian countries' varying stages, priorities and strategies of political and economic development, divergent endowments and geographical situations with regard to the river, though they may be no more than differences in emphasis. Turning such heterogeneity in their thinking and conditions into potent cohesive forces does pose a great challenge to the Committee which has to rely on the Executive Agent and his Secretariat for generation of ideas of the common good. It is believed that such differences are ultimately reconcilable and that co-operation in the development of the river is thus possible.

Whatever differences in the attitudes of riparian countries to the Mekong river there may have been, one *overriding need* is common to all. This is for the basic data which are indispensable for rational planning and the operation of water resources projects. The exploitation of water resources could hardly be contemplated unless all the relevant facts are known about rainfall and run-off, not just for one or two years but for decades, and not just within national boundaries but for the whole basin; otherwise resources would be wasted on reservoirs that might never fill up or dams that might just be washed away. This is why the central co-ordinating and clearing-house role of the Mekong Committee has been found to be indispensable.

Apart from interdependence in data-gathering for planning and development, there appears to exist the possibility of an *integrated approach to basin development.*

The search for a lasting formula can be traced back to 1969 when the Mekong Committee organised the Fifth Economic and Social Seminar having 'Legal and Administrative Aspects of Lower Mekong Development with Special Reference to Initial Mainstream Projects' as its theme. It was seen from the outset that many of the potential projects in the basin, in particular those on the mainstream, are such that, although they may be located in a given riparian country, their benefits in the form of electric power, flood control and irrigation water are available to all the riparian countries. A number of perplexing problems arise in determining how to share these outputs or benefits and how to apportion the costs of providing them. If, for instance, a price is set on electric power in such a way as to make it easy to clear the market, there arises the question as to whether each riparian country is entitled to take as much power as it wants at that price or whether some rationing scheme should operate. A case can be made for sharing the power supply on the basis of such things as past rates of electric power consumption, the rate of growth of consumption and the size of the population. Obviously, considerations of economic equity and political feasibility will enter into the calculations which should lead to different quota systems. Similarly, it can be asked whether the cost of a project should be shared in exact proportion to the sharing of the benefits or whether some other rule should apply. Faced with such questions the Seminar felt that institutional arrangements for the construction, operation and administration of initial mainstream projects should take into account three principles, namely, integrated basin development, equitable sharing of costs and benefits and respect for the rights of sovereign States. It was recommended that, on the basis of these principles, the following three-step approach be implemented:

1 a basic agreement among the four riparian states to establish governing principles upon which the proposed development would proceed;
2 a special agreement between the states in whose territory the works are to be constructed; and,
3 the establishment of an authority empowered to construct and administer the enterprises.

This recommendation was endorsed by the Indicative Basin Plan of 1970.

Indeed, a Mekong Authority along the lines of the Tennessee Valley Authority (TVA) appears to be an attractive long-term solution to the problem, and it could also raise development funds on its own account in the world's capital markets. Of course, the acceptability of the concept depends very much on Thailand, which, in the last analysis, will be asked to guarantee loans, as it is the most creditworthy of all the four riparian countries.

Opportunities for power exchange become more obvious when it is realised that Thailand's energy demand, currently estimated at 7,000MW per annum, constitutes 88% of the total demand of the lower Mekong basin. Moreover, it is growing at the average annual rate of 15%. It is being met partly by Laos, which has 51% of the lower Mekong basin's hydropower resources. Such an exchange has been made possible by an integrated power grid existing between Thailand and Laos, and possible expansion of such a grid can also be envisaged with a broader horizon of power exchange.

Integrated planning in the area of navigation also looks feasible, especially in the corridor linking the upper and the lower Mekong. The volume of cargo transported on this reach of the river appears to have grown at the high rate of 20% per annum over recent years. Use of the Mekong especially to transport exports from Yunnan down to countries in the lower Mekong basin presents a more economic alternative to their carriage by rail to the port of Canton.

An important approach to such integrated development can be detected from arrangements made between two riparian neighbours, Thailand and Laos. They began with the Nam Ngum hydropower dam which was completed in 1991, as a result of a Mekong Committee-sponsored effort, and the original installed capacity (30MW) has been expanded to 150MW. This has been a sub-regional project *par excellence,* as it was built in one country (Laos) for the express purpose of serving the need of another country (Thailand).

To this end Thailand and Laos entered into agreements, under the Mekong Committee's auspices, whereby Thailand consented not only to buy power from the project but also to loan power and cement to Laos for its construction with repayment in power after it was completed. Under one such agreement a special transmission line was built across the Mekong to implement the power exchange, and it has now become the Mekong Committee's property. An inter-connected grid has, since 1971, facilitated sub-regional power integration by enabling surplus power in Thailand to be re-exported back to Laos in order to save transmission costs over sparsely-populated areas in Laos.

Under similar arrangements, Thailand has also more recently imported surplus hydropower from the Xeset project (45MW) in southern Laos. In view of the growing demand for power in Laos as well as that in Thailand, construction of similar export-oriented dams on Nam Theun as well as further upstream in Nam Ngum is being investigated, though their economic feasibility would appear to depend on Thailand's long-term commitment to purchase the substantial additional power that would be made available.

While such an approach towards sub-regional integration in the field of hydropower has been made possible through a combination of multilateral arrangements and *ad hoc* bilateral agreements, more rigorous and widespread integration would seem to require the establishment of the mentioned Mekong Basin Authority, though this may still be a long way off. Pending the establishment of such an authority the Mekong Committee does provide a joint mechanism with or without basin-wide integration. Even if it turns out that the riparian states eventually prefer an arrangement of individual projects without provision for integration, special agreements would still be helpful in elaborating an accepted set of operating principles which regulate the various facilities. Of course, as compared to the Mekong Basin Authority, such arrangements would reduce the total beneficial effects within the basin and be less flexible. With changing circumstances, agreements would have to be re-negotiated over and over again, and the process could be time-consuming.

While the general realisation of the immense potential of the Mekong had come rather late in the day, the issue of sustainable development, at the practical if not at the intellectual level, was raised quite early in the exploitation of water and related resources of the basin. In the Khmer Empire rice agriculture was based on terrace soils lying to the north of the Great Lake in what is now Cambodia's Siem Reap province. Somehow or other, this agriculture was located beyond the zone of flooding and depended on gravity-flow irrigation systems to divert water from the neighbouring rivers which constitute part and parcel of the

Mekong system. The location of major Cambodian towns and cities, with the exception of Phnom Penh, just beyond the zone of flooding is believed to suggest that agriculture and the associated political power were based outside the Cambodian flooding zone for many centuries. However, the high agricultural productivity that supported the construction of Angkor proved not to be sustainable and today the soils of the Sime Riep area, as a result of pressure put upon it the Khmer Empire, are some of the worst in Cambodia.

The importance of conserving the natural resources and the environment in the Mekong basin in order to protect the viability of the watershed cannot be overestimated. Yet it has to be realised that conservation efforts can be made only at a cost. For instance, it is not easy to feed the people and at the same time avoid using available natural resources which have sustained their livelihood for as long as they can remember. It has to be admitted that, in order to survive, the rural masses tend to over-exploit forests and marginal lands. The pressure to do so is particularly compelling when they see what the 'good life', led generally by the urban elite, could bring them.

The struggle for survival of the rural masses and the pressure this puts on the available natural resources are no less intense elsewhere. Brazil, with its vast resources of rain forests, constitutes an interesting case study. This country's massive foreign indebtedness could become a drain on its natural resources, if it takes an easy way out. While Brazil's debt may be said to have resulted from past efforts to solve national problems, it could well see the rain forest as a way out of its current indebtedness. In consequence, there could be further destruction which could cripple the country's resource base and thwart the efforts made by future generations at sustained development. Because of global inter-dependence, this might go so far as cripple the resource base of the entire world.

If it is true, as had been argued, that the poor of the developing world, in their efforts to ensure short-term survival, and big business, in order to reap windfall profits, over-exploit natural resources and thereby threaten the ecology of the globe, then they have to be persuaded to change their behaviour. The crucial distinction between long-term sustainable development and short-term survival and gain has to be brought home to them. In other words, they should be made to realise that conservation of the watershed is vital for the production of hydropower, which is a source of clean, competitive and fully renewable energy and the only sustainable long-term alternative to the fossil and nuclear options. This will not be easy to achieve, as it represents a classic case of an appreciable discrepancy between private and social costs leaving the field wide open for exploitation for private gains. Moreover, alternative sources of income will also have to be found for the people affected by this.

The point is that, thus far, problems including conflicts over resource use have arisen within national boundaries of the riparian countries in the lower Mekong basin; but it will not be long before they spill over into the transboundary sphere. As there are intimate linkages between national and regional arrangements; ultimately national policies in resource use including forestry and fishery will have to be harmonised with such regional mechanisms as have been developed by the Committee to facilitate an exchange of information, consultation and joint planning that could avert transboundary conflicts over resource use.

In fact, conflicts, potential or actual, over resource use, particularly in international river basins, are not peculiar to the Mekong basin but can be seen in any region of the world, developing and developed alike. For instance, the United States and Mexico may soon have to face a situation of conflicting aspirations in California and Mexico. Their position *vis-à-vis* each other reflects a true contrast, that of a developed society like the United States confronted with a developing one like Mexico. This is not surprising, as a great deal of transboundary complications in water resources do arise between geographical areas with a wide disparity in economic and political power and this makes it all the more difficult to unravel. Again, the protracted war between Iran and Iraq could be traced to conflicts over water use, while the more recent Gulf war could be said to be basically over a precious resource, ie, oil.

The Mekong Committee, which has been set up to develop the water related resources of the lower Mekong basin, has made strenuous efforts to elaborate ground rules to conserve natural resources. It has also implemented a number of pre-investment and investments projects to enhance the productivity of these resources. Its pre-investment projects have been designed to provide information to enable rational investment decisions to be made. Investigations have been made, for instance, into such areas of agro-industries as the possibility of using kenaf for paper pulp and the possibility of establishing vegetable oil-cum-livestock processing as an integrated complex in order to take advantage of the inherent complementaries of activities. On the other hand, its investment projects have consisted essentially in constructing such water-related infrastructure as multi-purpose dams, regulators, fish ponds and river ports. Inputs from these projects could, of course, be taken into account in further investment decisions, and the Committee's investment activities should be indicative of follow-up investment opportunities generated in its member countries.

In the past, successful cases of private investment known to have been induced by work of the Committee have relied partly on using information generated by the Committee's pre-investment investigations or on forward linkages generated by the Committee's provision of essential production inputs. An example of the first category is large-scale paper pulp manufacture in the north-east of Thailand. It began on the basis of the locally available supply of kenaf but its source of raw material has now been diversified to include such things as sugar cane bagasse and bamboo. The second category is exemplified by canning activities also carried out in north-east Thailand. As it has turned out, irrigation facilities made available by the Huai Mong project in north-east Thailand generated the growth of such vegetables as tomato and mushroom, the plentiful supply of which has led to their canning for domestic as well as overseas requirements.

An examination of the Committee's activities suggests that, apart from its role in averting conflicts over resource use and stimulating investment, other roles which are complementary are emerging. These include monitoring of water quality and laying down of standards for pollution control. Of course, in order for enforcement to be effective, co-operation among riparian countries is indispensable.

Mention has already been made of the beneficial impact of the Committee's pre-investment studies and investment activities on follow-up investment in the private sector. In fact, one could indeed go further to spell out the more pervasive, albeit less palpable, impact of the Committee's activities on the investment climate and consequently on development in general. The first bridge across the lower Mekong, due for completion in 1994, should indeed make for further economic integration of parts of the lower Mekong sub-basin, and this should in principle mean, *inter alia,* a potentially larger market which is a positive factor for the investment climate and development.

Again, the whole of the development-oriented programme of the Committee should inspire confidence among potential investors in the future growth path of the lower Mekong sub-basin. Indeed, the most potent incentive for investment is the Committee's crucial role in ensuring that the lower Mekong sub-region will be free from conflicts over resource use and that it will continue to enjoy constructive co-operation which will pave the way for peace and stability, pre-requisites *par excellence* for investment decisions.

Conclusion

In a climate where international water law is still not hard and fast it is interesting to speculate on the future of collaboration in water resources use in the Mekong.

For its part, in its 36 years of existence the Mekong Committee has developed, alongside an emerging legal infrastructure with the help of the unanimity rule and consensus-building, positive roles *vis-à-vis* the management of conflicts over the joint use of the lower Mekong. This has, in a way, approximated the international Mekong situation to a domestic one exemplified by irrigation systems in northern Thailand. These favourable factors and its complementary roles in monitoring water quality and laying down of standards for pollution control have depended on the co-operation of riparian states for their effectiveness. Likewise, and integrated approach linking major projects, particularly on the mainstream, would seem to require, with the riparian states' co-operation, the future transformation of the Mekong Committee into a

Mekong Basin Authority that is able to undertake autonomous development of the basin. With long years of co-operation, a 'Mekong spirit' has also evolved, and it is hoped that this, together with other cohesive factors including their joint stake in the development of the river, will stand the riparian countries of the lower Mekong in good stead in the years to come.

In the long run, the interdependencies between the upper and the lower Mekong would seem to require integrated basin-wide planning. Whatever success has been achieved in fostering co-operation in the lower reaches of the river should be implanted on to the whole basin. MDRN and an expanded Mekong Committee are two possible instruments to achieve such ends.

Bibliography

Blomqist, W. and Ostrom, E. (1985) 'Institutional capacity and the resolution of a common dilemma', *Policy Studies Review* 5: 383–93.

Buchanan, J.M. and Stubbebine, W.C. (1992) 'Externality', *Economical* 29, November: 347–75.

Calabresi, G. and Melamed, A.C. (1972) 'Property rules liability rules and inalienability: one view of the cathedral', *Harvard Law Review* 85, April: 1089–128.

Coase, R.C. (1960) 'The problem of social cost', *Journal of Law and Economics* 3, 1.

Dasgupta, P. (1982) *The Control of Resources,* Cambridge, Massachusetts: Harvard University Press.

Gardner, R., Ostrom, E. and Walker, J.M. (1990) 'The nature of common pool resources', *Rationality and Society* 2: 335–58.

Hobbes, T. (1651) *Leviathan,* C.B. Macpherson (ed.) 1968 edition, Harmondsworth: Penguin.

Musgrave, R.D. (1959) *The Theory of Public Finance,* New York: McGraw-Hill.

Ostrom, E. (1990) *Governing the Commons: Evolution of Institution for Collective Action,* Cambridge: Cambridge University Press.

Plott, C. and Meyer, R.A. (1975) 'The technology of public goods, externalities and the exclusion principle', in E.S. Mills (ed.) *Economic Analysis of Environmental Problems,* New York: National Bureau of Economic Research.

Surarerks, V. (1986) *Historical Development and Management of Irrigation System in Northern Thailand,* Chiengmai: Chiengmai University, Thailand.

Young, R.A. (1993) 'Managing aquifer over-exploitation: economics and policies', in I. Simmers (ed.) *Aquifer Overexploitation, Selected Papers 3,* 23rd International Congress of the International Association of Hydrogeologists, Hanover: Verlag Heise Publishers.

18

New Challenges for US–Mexico
Water Resources Management

Stephen P. Mumme

Few serious observers of the US–Mexico water management regime would dispute the fact that binational management of common water resources is presently in a state of flux. In fact, it may be fair to say the binational water management regime is undergoing its most serious transformation since the present treaty based regime was consolidated by the United States–Mexico Water Treaty of 1944. The present state of flux is a product of two basic trends affecting the border region. It is first a function of the shifting demands on border water resources brought about by the rapid pace of urbanisation and industrialisation between the two countries. It is second a function of the accelerating pace of economic integration between the two countries, particularly as these trends affect the border region. The two trends are, of course, integrally related. The fact that economic integration has received a considerable boost with the recent signing of the North American Free Trade Agreement is of no mean consequence in directing greater attention to water management problems in the border area and, thus, must be taken as a distinct dimension of influence on recent developments in transboundary water management.

This paper provides an overview of the way these developments are shaping a more complex water management regime along the US–Mexico border. In the first part, this paper identifies a number of trends that are altering public demands on the water management regime. The second and third parts set out the main lineaments and assumptions of the old water management regime, centring around the role and functions of the International Boundary and Water Commission (IBWC), and the transitional regime in place over the past decade. The fourth part identifies the important new institutional developments currently reshaping border water management. The concluding part summarises the changes underway and draws out the principal policy implications of the new water management regime as well as such lessons as the US–Mexico experience provides other border regions confronting similar processes of rapid development, economic integration, and urbanisation.

The Dynamics of Change in Border Water Management

The changes affecting a transformation of water management practices along the US–Mexico border are the result of well known processes of secular economic development in play in any number of regions around the globe. Since 1950 – a useful demographic baseline – the US–Mexico border region has been fundamentally transformed from a preponderantly rural, agricultural region to one exhibiting a considerable degree of urban dynamism. It has also been transformed from a region whose water based economy was primarily domestically centred to a region whose economic processes are much more integrated. This demographic and economic transformation has influenced patterns of water use. Again, since 1950, demands on water resources have gradually but steadily shifted from agricultural uses towards urban uses, with a concomitant shift in public concern from quantitative to qualitative problems.

These trends are readily seen in standard demographic materials on the US–Mexico border region. Table 18.1 shows that average population density on the Mexican side of the border increased from 3.9 persons per kilometre in 1950 to 16.7 persons in 1990. On the US side densities increased from 11.6 in 1950 to 30.7 in 1990. In other words, the population densities in the border region quadrupled in Mexico and nearly trebled in the United States from 1950 to 1990. This increase in human population generally is seen in the urbanisation of the border area. Table 18.2 shows the combined populations for the eight largest twin cities located on the border. In 1950 the combined US–Mexico twin city population was 1,019,056 according to official census data. In 1990 the population was 4,869,379, an increase of 470%.

The pronounced urbanisation of the border region during this period substantially exceeded the rate of corresponding growth in agriculture. Table 18.3 shows that irrigated acreage in Mexican border states increased from 2,900 thousand acres in 1950 to 3,848 thousand acres in 1990, an increase of 33%. On the US side, irrigated acreage decreased from 14,936 in 1949 to 13,499 in 1987, a net loss of 10%.

Table 18.1 Population density in US–Mexico border states (per km)

	1950	1990
USA total	11.6	30.7
Mexico total	3.9	16.7

Source: D. Lorey, *United States–Mexico Border Statistics Since 1900: An Update* (1993).

Table 18.2 Combined population of eight largest twin cities along US–Mexico border

1950	1990
1,019,056	4,869,379

Source: D. Lorey, *United States Mexico Border Statistics Since 1900:*
An Update (1993).

Table 18.3 Irrigated acreage on the border (thousands of acres)

	1950	1987/1990
USA. total	14,936	13,499
Mexico total	2,900	3,848

Source: D. Lorey, *United States Mexico Border Statistics Since 1900:*
An Update (1993).

Figures such as these are only indirect indicators of shifting patterns of water consumption. Most water in the border region, in excess of 80%, continues to be used in agriculture. What the figures do suggest is that net urban demand on water resources has risen at a much more rapid rate than demand in agriculture, which has by and large peaked and is currently subsiding in overall importance. It is this trend towards urbanisation that is driving changes in the water management regime (Sepulveda and Utton, 1982; Eaton and Anderson, 1987).

As the demographics and economics of water utilisation in the border region have shifted, so too has the politics of water management. Urban centres have successfully laid claim to a greater proportion of available waters in the transboundary watersheds, to the detriment of agricultural interests. Nowhere is this better seen than in the Colorado River basin, where downstream cities like Mexicali and Tijuana have taken an increasing share of the water allocated to Mexico under the 1944 Water Treaty that governs allocation between the two countries; similarly, cities like San Diego, California and the Arizona cities of Phoenix and Tucson have absorbed an ever larger share of the water allocated to those states under the existing allocation regime. These allocative changes are expressed in water pricing increasingly less favourable to traditional agricultural practices.

Moreover, since the mid-seventies, the politics of water quality has challenged the politics of allocation for the lion's share of public concern and a place on the government's policy agenda. Nowhere is this more evident than at the International Boundary and Water Commission (IBWC), the binational agency created by the 1944 Treaty for the purpose of administering the international treaties establishing the old binational water regime. Some exposition of these arrangements is necessary in order to better understand the implication of the new arrangements that have recently been adopted to improve the management of transboundary waters along the border.

The Old Regime

What might be called the 'old regime' in US–Mexico border water management was created over the course of nearly a century, beginning with the Treaty of Guadalupe Hidalgo in 1848. This regime, set out in successive conventions and treaties including the 1889 Boundary Convention, the 1906 Water Treaty, the 1933 Boundary Rectification Treaty, the 1944 Water Treaty, and 1970 Boundary Agreement, took as its topmost priorities the allocation of transboundary water resources, the adjustment of territorial claims, and the prevention of physical damages arising from the unregulated flows and flux of the principal international watersheds, the Rio Grande/Rio Bravo and the Colorado.[1] The development of this regime is well covered in the literature and need not be recapitulated here, except to point to its most important features, which are these:

The Old Regime was Fundamentally Allocative. It responded to the needs of an expanding rural population in a frontier setting whose primary goals, whether US or Mexican, were harnessing existing water resources for productive use through irrigation, hydropower, or both. These concerns naturally brought the two nations into conflict over the appropriation and use of the water assets of the borderlands, conflicts that were gradually adjusted through diplomacy during the first half of the 20th century.

The Old Regime was Territorially Defensive. It sought to secure the territorial dominion of each country in so far as that was possible through diplomatic initiative. Because the two great rivers formed the land boundary for substantial distances and because both rivers tended to meander according to the vagaries of flood and drought, the securing of territorial boundaries was complicated. Thus, a great deal of attention focused on riparian containment and the development of diplomatic formulae for boundary adjustment where containment was not technically or politically feasible or cost effective.

The Old Regime was Exclusive, that is, limited to a narrow range of public actors and participants concerned with managing the assets and behavioural features of the watersheds in accordance with the values set out above and the rules generated on their behalf by the two countries. In practice, this meant channelling issues related to water management through a narrow range of institutions, most prominently the IBWC, which was created for that purpose. The IBWC was given an exclusive jurisdiction which it chose to interpret very narrowly in geographic and functional terms. The Commission from its modern inception in 1945 sought to distinguish itself from other domestic agencies with water management functions. It did so by narrowing its functional scope and cultivating close ties to an elite tier of water managers at the state and national level in each country, downplaying its policy independence and authority and defending the core values of its clientele in each country. In the process it gained an extraordinary degree of functional autonomy for an agency of its type.

The Old Regime was Distributive. By this, I mean that the old regime sought to resolve problems in so far as possible by limiting its regulatory role in water management and providing substantive benefits to the communities – particularly the US communities – that comprised its basic constituency along the border. This was particularly true of the IBWC, which preferred to leave regulatory problems and enforcement to the domestic agencies of each government.

These values dominated binational water management until fairly recently and it is wise to understand their appeal. First and foremost they secured the economic development of the border region. They did so not by providing equity in allocating transboundary resources, rather by providing security. In an arid region where water is scarce, security is a trump value for water management. Second, they produced a stable institutional foundation for achieving security, one that had the consent of all 'the powers that be' in basin-wide water management. This is not to say that allocative issues did not simmer and erupt from time to time and do not continue to do so. However, the so-called 'law [and we might say 'politics'] of the river' supplied a predictable, reliable foundation to which various claimants on the resource could turn to resolve allocative conflicts. Within the reach of its mandate, the IBWC has been a core part of this 'law of the river(s)'. Finally, the resolution of binational problems arising under treaty tended to be resolved by the provision of concrete benefits to border constituencies, thus enabling border water managers – particularly those in the United States – to maintain a strong measure of political support.

The adequacy of this old regime for managing a broader range of urban-environmental and ecological problems was seriously tested in the mid-1970s as burgeoning environmental consciousness and the mobilisation of environmental actors coincided with an increasing number of water quality problems arising from rapid urbanisation and growth and overutilisation of the stock of water available for a range of purposes. Under the 1944 Water Treaty certain non-allocative functions were anticipated; the IBWC, for example, was assigned primary jurisdiction for all binational sewage and sanitation problems.

This mandate was tacked on *ad hoc,* largely owing to the unavailability and disinterest of other domestic agencies in shouldering what seemed to be a very minor burden in the grand scheme of things. Other 'ecological' concerns were simply not anticipated – certainly they were not mentioned. To take just one instance among many, the 1944 Water Treaty's order of priority for water allocation treats ecological and species preservation in the water course as its least valuable priority – that function is covered in a catch-all clause designating 'any other beneficial uses which may be determined' as the lowest allocative priority.

The Transitional Regime

Emerging challenges to the old regime generated what might be called a 'transitional regime' beginning in the late 1970s. This transitional regime took the form of greater elaboration of the non-allocative powers of the IBWC and the insertion of other agencies in response to multiplying demands for environmental change. In 1979, Minute 261 of the IBWC interpreted Article 3 of the 1944 Water Treaty – by which the two governments 'hereby agree to give preferential attention to the solution of all border sanitation problems' – to extend to a broad range of sanitation and sewage problems along the border and increase the priority given these problems by the two governments (Mumme, 1980). In 1983, the two governments signed a landmark executive agreement, the US–Mexico Border Environmental Co-operation Agreement, better known as the La Paz Agreement, which established a framework for regular monitoring, consultation, and negotiation to resolve a comprehensive range of transboundary environmental problems (TIAS, 1983). Implementation of the La Paz Agreement was entrusted to the respective environmental ministries of the two countries, with formal recognition of the IBWC as the lead agency for dispute resolution in the area of water resources. Under the La Paz Agreement five new Annexes were signed over the past decade, respectively addressing sanitation, air pollution, and hazardous waste problems along the border. In 1991, responding to criticism, the two countries undertook a joint planning exercise, the Integrated Border Environmental Plan (IBEP), whose first stage recommendations were officially adopted in February 1992 (EPA, 1992). Under this arrangement, which fits within the La Paz framework agreement, the two countries went to considerable lengths to identify extant environmental problems and outline a set of priorities for funding. The Salinas administration, with help from multilateral banks, committed US$450 million to the development of border infrastructure, most of this dedicated to sewage and sanitation projects.

Notwithstanding the upgrading of priorities, this 'transitional regime' proved inadequate to demands placed upon it. Environmentalists found fault with its *ad hoc,* diplomatic approach to problem resolution, its lack of action-forcing mechanisms, and its failure to generate greater opportunities for public education and participation in transboundary environmental management.[2] The IBWC, with its leading role in transboundary water management, continued to be a lightning rod for public criticism for its exclusive mode of diplomacy and lack of responsiveness to the new environmental constituencies emerging along the border. Such criticisms of the IBWC, the La Paz framework agreement, and the IBEP found a timely venue in the recently concluded debate over the North American Free Trade Agreement (NAFTA). By hitching concerns for transboundary environmental management to the powerful engine of trade, the environmental community was successful in generating a 'new regime' which promises to reshape the character of binational water management for a long time to come.

The New Water Management Regime

The new regime for binational water management is an outgrowth of the NAFTA agreement, particularly the supplemental side agreements on environmental management. These side agreements, three in number, deal respectively with trilateral environmental policy and enforcement, financing border infrastructure, and co-ordination and review of binational investments associated with the new funding mechanism (Office of the President 1993a; 1993b). Three new institutions, a Commission on Environmental Co-operation (CEC), a North American Development Bank (NADB), and a Border Environment Co-operation Commission (BECC) have been created for this purpose.

Before discussing the role each of these new institutions will play in binational border management it must be said that the new institutions do not at all replace the existing agreements and mechanisms found in US–Mexican water management. All the previously mentioned institutions continue to stand and guide binational diplomacy in this area. The new institutions add significantly, however, to the ability of the two countries to actually use the old agreements and implement old, new, and future commitments in water management in the border region. The defining effect of these new agreements is to create a multi-tiered, nested set of functionally differentiated institutions with greater incentive to co-ordinate with each other and enhanced capacity and means to address the range of contemporary problems found in the border community. Specific to water management, the net effect is to augment binational capacity to manage the full range of water quality problems found along the border, from salinity on the one hand, to sewage, industrial pollution, and water threatening hazardous wastes on the other. It will also modestly increment binational capacity to address certain types of ecological problems related to water supply.

With this in mind, let us review the three recently created institutions that augment the border water management regime (see Table 18.4). The first of these, the CEC, provides a trinational administrative forum for assuring the enforcement of domestic environmental legislation in each country. The CEC is the first truly *supranational* body in North America created for purposes of environmental administration. It is comprised of a Council – comprised of the environmental ministers of the three subscribing nations (Canada, Mexico, the United States) – and supplemented by a Secretariat – whose mandate it is to monitor and review environmental management in the three countries and investigate complaints brought to it by the governments and non-governmental parties – and a Joint Public Advisory Committee of 15 members apportioned equally among the three governmental parties. Complaints will be heard by impartial review panels who will make recommendations to the Council. The Council, in turn, by a two-thirds majority, has the power to decide the question and impose penalties in the nature of fines and trade sanctions to achieve compliance with its rulings. The Secretariat will also function as an information warehouse on environmental conditions in the three countries and produce reports and data of benefit to the environmental community.

The practical effect of this system on transboundary water management is to provide a hitherto unavailable forum to governmental and non-governmental bodies to hold the parties accountable for the enforcement of their environmental laws. Several benefits are immediately ascertainable. First, the focus on domestic environmental enforcement better integrates international policy objectives with domestic objectives, a linkage that has heretofore been rather weak. Second, environmentalists have an institutional mechanism designed to be more responsive to their interests. The CEC mechanism must hear their complaints and investigate if evidence is compelling. Further, it must acquire and make publicly available environmental data – to include water related qualitative data, hazardous and toxic substances and disposal data, and data on ecological conditions affected by water supplies – that will facilitate monitoring of border water quality and water related conditions. Third, it has an action forcing mechanism – sanctions – that reinforces the arsenal of domestic regulatory devices available in each country. Fourth, it guarantees private access to judicial remedies by interested parties, reinforcing the potential use of these mechanisms to achieve enforcement of domestic environmental laws. In general, then, the CEC provides a badly needed international regulatory umbrella that will supplement the extant international and domestic enforcement regime for all three countries.

Table 18.4 NAFTA Environmental Institutions Compared

	Mandate	Constitutive Elements	Meetings
Commission on Environmental Co-operation (CEC)	Foster protection and improvement of the environment in the territories of the Parties for the well being of present and future generations; promote sustainable development; increase trinational environmental co-operation; support NAFTA's environmental goals; avoid creating trade distortions; strengthen co-operation in regulation in the trinational area; enhance compliance with, and enforcement of, environmental laws; promote transparency and public participation; promote economically efficient environmental measures; promote pollution prevention politics and practices.	Council (3 members, environmental ministers or deputies). Secretariat (headed by Executive Director). - Executive Director serves three year term, renewable for an additional term. - Executive Director's post rotates among parties. Joint Public Advisory Committee (15 members, 5 per party).	Council meets at least once a year. JPAC meets once a year concurrent with Council, more often if necessary.
North American Development Bank (NADB)	Raise and disburse capital for community adjustment needs related to NAFTA implementation; advise the President regarding implementation of community adjustment and investment program; identify adjustment needs; also provide advice on 'any matter' requested by the President; review community adjustment program on a regular basis. Border Environment Finance Facility will focus specifically on the US-Mexican border (100 miles each side of the border).	NADB Board of Directors (9, each party appoints 3). NADB Advisory Board (9 US Members). Border Environment Finance Facility (6 members; 3 Mexico; 3 US) - Facility Manager (3 year term, renewable).	At least once annually.
Border Environment Co-operation Commission (BECC)	To help preserve, protect and enhance the environment of the border region in order to advance the well being of the people of the US and Mexico; to co-operate as appropriate with the Border Environment Finance Facility and other national and international institutions, and with private sources supplying investment capital for environmental infrastructure projects in the border region	Board of Directors (6 members equally drawn from the US and Mexico representing localities, states, and public, plus 4 ex-officio members from IBWC and environmental ministries. Public Advisory Board (9 US; 9 Mexico drawn from all border states).	Meets quarterly at minimum.

The remaining NAFTA environmental institutions are directed more specifically to the US–Mexican border. The first of these, the NADB, is designed as a quasi-autonomous appendage to the present Inter-American Development Bank (IADB). The NADB is designed to capture and direct financial resources at development problems arising from implementation of the NAFTA accords, with emphasis on poverty and economic adjustment along the border and in the Mexican interior. Within the NADB, a new Border Environment Finance Facility is endowed with initial capitalisation of roughly US$3 billion, and empowered to raise additional capital from private and governmental sources for purposes of funding badly needed environmental infrastructure along the border. Various estimates have been given of present infrastructural needs of border communities, but most range from a low of US$7 billion to a high of US$20 billion (US Council, 1993). The existence of a funding agency is a much needed device that will greatly increase the availability and flexibility of funding sewage and sanitation projects along the border.

The second institution, the BECC, is closely articulated with NADB insofar as BECC has the authority to identify and authorise projects for NADB funding. Applications for assistance in financing border infrastructure projects are to be directed through the BECC which is empowered to determine their desirability and feasibility, seek available financing from NADB and other sources, and authorise and co-ordinate projects. BECC's Board of Directors is comprised of six individuals, three from each country, supplemented by four *ex officio* members, to include the national commissioners of the IBWC and the administrators of the respective national environmental protection agencies or their delegates. The six regular directors represent US and Mexican border states, localities, and the general public and must have 'expertise in environmental planning, economics, engineering, finance, or related matters'.[3] The Board is assisted by a General Manager and Deputy General Manager to be appointed for renewable terms of three years. The Board is also assisted by an 18-member Advisory Council consisting of nine members apiece from the US and Mexico, each serving a renewable term of two years. The BECC and the IBWC are instructed to 'cooperate with each other in planning, developing, and carrying out border sanitation and other environmental activities'.[4]

The net effect of these two new border mandated agencies is:

1 to greatly improve the prospects for funding water and sanitation infrastructure along the border,
2 to take the policy monopoly on border sanitation projections away from the IBWC and disperse it between the IBWC and the BECC,
3 to amplify the range of water quality management activities along the border, and

4 to significantly improve the accessibility, responsiveness, and accountability of the water management agencies to a broadened constituency along the US–Mexican border.[5]

The new regime, in short, responds directly to the criticisms levied at existing institutions while leaving intact those aspects of the old and transitional regimes that cannot easily be changed (the 1944 Water Treaty) or which may continue to usefully serve the United States and Mexico as they seek to resolve a wide range of extant and potential environmental problems in the border region.

The new institutional mechanisms, it should be said, are essentially additive to the present water management regime, though they do redistribute some management responsibilities, as noted above. Yet it is also true that certain types of water related problems are not addressed, or addressed indirectly by these institutional changes. At the top of the list are apportionment problems. At present, a number of lesser surface streams and all transboundary groundwater aquifers remain unapportioned. The resolution of these problems is not affected by the new institutional infrastructure and is most likely to be resolved within the architecture of the old and transitional regimes, which is to say, by bilateral diplomacy through the IBWC under the aegis of the La Paz Agreement. The new institutions may have some positive effect in a related issue-area, that of ecosystem and endangered species management where water supply is critical to that end. Currently, for example, the Colorado River estuary and upper Gulf of California suffers from reduced surface water discharge and heavy contamination by effluent brine from upstream irrigation districts. The pending operation of the world's largest reverse osmosis desalination plant will have further adverse impacts on this ecosystem (Van Der Werf, 1994). Mexico recently designated the region – which supports two endangered species of porpoise – a national protected area, thereby increasing the priority attached to ecosystem protection (Defenders of Wildlife, 1993). The estuary and wildlife reserves along the lower Rio Grande are also potentially affected by surface water flows (Pendleton, 1993). In these cases and others it may be possible for environmentalists to use the new CEC and BECC mechanisms to require domestic governments to alter current patterns of water use to better manage these resources; it may also be possible to use these institutions to generate information and binational co-operative initiatives to improve ecosystem management. The potential exists; whether these institutions are used for this type of purpose remains to be seen. Finally, the CEC and BECC may be used in tandem to address binational water contamination problems, including groundwater pollution, arising from hazardous and solid waste disposal and pesticide use in the border region. It is important to note, however, that the division of labour between the two organisations is such that regulation and enforcement is dominated by the CEC, extant bilateral agreements, and domestic legislation, whereas the BECC may be mobilised to provide needed infrastructure to ameliorate or prevent such health hazards.

Conclusion

The recent amplification of the US–Mexican water management regime is certainly the most far reaching and consequential reform of bilateral water management practices since Minute 261 and the La Paz Agreement ushered in a broader awareness of the need for comprehensive environmental management along the border more than a decade past. In many ways these changes represent the culmination of half a century of institutional change in managing binational water problems. Interestingly, this process has been an incremental, cumulative process, not a case of radical reform or rejecting previous management models for new ones. Instead, new layers of functions have been created to address new problems, and new institutions have been adopted that supplement, rather than replace, old ones.

The new institutional structure recognises the limits of functionalist expansion within the mandates of old agencies and the need to layer on new bodies that are more responsive and capable of dealing with social needs and demands only dimly envisioned by the architects of treaties and agreements in the first half of the 20th century. These treaties and agreements, aimed at allocating and appropriating water resources, still command considerable public support within the border community and are difficult to change. On the other hand, the old treaty language proved functionally inadequate to manage the qualitative concerns of an increasingly urbanised border community. Thus, the new institutions are designed to meet these demands directly and to do so in a more comprehensive, more inclusive way.

This new, nested, approach to binational water management is certainly not optimal or efficient in orthodox management terms. Contemporary agencies – to include those generated from the NAFTA process – share management authority with each other and require considerable inter-agency co-ordination to effectively execute their mandates. The nested institutional solution is, however, politically expedient, preserving those aspects of the old regime that continue to command political support and supplementing them with institutions that respond to newer constituencies and needs.

While the political logic behind the new management regime is most compelling, the functionalist logic also has great merit. Short of a comprehensive management authority with supra-national powers – the Holy Grail of many environmental advocacy groups – the system of nested institutions has considerable flexibility, particularly in a transnational setting. First, it accommodates to the *realpolitik* of national sovereignty in transnational resources management, preserving a measure of discretion to national governments as they approach problems of water resources management in an international context. Second, it provides flexibility, allowing national parties the option of addressing specific problems through one of several institutional pathways. Third, it accommodates a larger, if still differentiated, constituency for transboundary environmental management. While co-operation at the level of public support for binational solutions as well as inter-agency co-operation is not assured, it may be facilitated by the overlaying of institutional mandates, capacities, and decision-making forums.

What, then, does the US–Mexican experience suggest for the development of binational or multinational water management practices elsewhere? It seems to me the lessons are these. First, movement towards comprehensive transnational water resources management is likely to proceed incrementally, for both political and functionalist reasons. In those instances where institutions simply do not exist it may be possible to amplify the range of functions incorporated in a single agency, but such extension runs the risk of moving ahead of grass-roots constituency support. Second, care must be taken to fit management reforms, particularly the creation of new management agencies, to the political conditions that prevail at the time in each of the participating countries. This problem is aggravated where significant economic and political differentials are found among member countries. Third, where functionalist mandates are strongly embedded in older institutions, the creation of new institutions is likely to advance management reform in lieu of eliminating old ones.

In sum, the US–Mexican border water management experience, especially in light of recent innovations, provides ample fodder for support of an incrementalist, institutionally differentiated approach to water management, instead of a comprehensive, efficiency driven approach to institutional design often favoured by modern planners confronted with the need to manage resources in a transnational setting. These are lessons that can be useful to other countries sharing transboundary water resources in a rapidly urbanising environment.

Notes

1   For discussion see, Mumme (1993) and Ingram (1993).
2   For discussion of a number of critical assessments see Mumme (1992).
3   Agreement on Border Environment Cooperation Commission, Section 3.A.5.
4   *Ibid,* Section 6.C.
5   For commentary, see Kelly (1994); Ingram *et al* (1994) and Seligman (1994).

Bibliography

Agreement (1993) between the United States of America and the Government of the United Mexican States Concerning the Establishment of a Border Environment Co-operation Commission and a Border Environment Finance Facility, Washington DC: Office of the President, *ad referendum* text, 22 October.

Agreement (1983) on co-operation for the protection and improvement of the environment in the border area', 14 August. *United States and Mexico, TIAS* No. 10827.

Defenders of Wildlife (1993) *Mexico to dedicate Northern Gulf of California as Biosphere Reserve June 10, to Protect Porpoise,* press release, 8 June, Washington, DC.

Eaton, D.J. and Anderson, J.M. (1987) *The State of the Rio Grande/Rio Bravo*, Tucson: University of Arizona Press.

Ingram, H., Milich, L. and Varady, R. (1994) *Toward Better Policy Design in Transnational Environmental Management: Learning from the US–Mexico Example,* Tucson: Udall Center for Studies in Public Policy, University of Arizona.

Kelly, M. (1994) *Fullfilling Promises: Implementation of the Border Environment Cooperation Commission (BECC) and the North American Development Bank (NADBANK),* Austin: Texas Center for Policy Studies.

Lorey, D. (1993) *United States–Mexico Border Statistics Since 1900: An Update,* Los Angeles: UCLA Latin American Center Publications.

Ingram, H. (1993) 'Transnational water resources management: learning from the US–Mexico experience', fourth annual Abel Wolman Distinguished Lecture, The Water and Science Technology Board of the National Research Council, Washington, DC, 8 November.

Mumme, S. (1980) 'The background and significance of Minute 261 of the International Boundary and Water Commission', *California Western International Law Journal* 11: 223–35.

—— (1992) 'New directions in United States–Mexican transboundary environmental management: a critique of current proposals', *Natural Resources Journal* 32: 539–62.

—— (1993) 'Innovation and reform in transboundary resource management: a critical look at the International Boundary and Water Commission, United States and Mexico', *Natural Resources Journal* 33: 93–120.

North American Agreement (1993) on Environmental Co-operation Between the Government of the United States of America, the Government of Canada, and the Government of the United Mexican States, Washington, DC: Office of the President, final draft, 13 September.

Pendleton, S. (1993) 'NAFTA boom is threatening border ecology,' *The Christian Science Monitor* July 14: 9–11.

Seligman, D.A. (1994) 'NAFTA and green trade', *Environment* 36: 4.

Sepulveda, C. and Utton, A.E. (1982) *The US-Mexico Border Region: Anticipating Resource Needs and Issues to the Year 2000*, El Paso: Texas Western Press.

US Council of the Mexico–US Business Committee (1993) *Analysis of Environmental Infrastructure Requirements and Financing Gaps on the US-Mexico Border,* 14 July, Washington DC: US Council.

US Environmental Protection Agency and Mexican Secretaria de Desarrollo Urbano y Ecologia (1992) *Integrated Environmental Plan for the Mexican-US Border Area [First Stage, 1992-1994]*, Washington, DC: EPA.

Van Der Werf, M. (1994) 'Draining the budget to desalt the Colorado', *High Country News* 21 February: 1–13.

19

Chile–Bolivia Relations:
The Lauca River Water Resources

Monica Gangas Geisse
Hernan Santis Arenas

Introduction

In June 1939, Pedro Aguirre Cerda, then President of Chile, visited the port-city of Arica. During his visit he stated that the government, taking into account the requests of many entrepreneurs' associations and landowners of the River Azapa's valley, proposed the extension of the irrigated areas in that valley, in the vicinity of the port, making use of the waters of the high plateau's River Lauca to do so. The principal objective of this decision, it was stated, was to increase the production of fresh food for the population of the region and to reduce unemployment.

On 11 July 1939, the government of Bolivia communicated its reservations to the Chilean Government over the possible diversion of water via an irrigation channel from the River Lauca. The objection was raised because of the international character of the river, making the countries lying along the river subject to a juridical regime of rights and obligations. The Lauca river has its origin in Chilean territory, more or less at 18°10'S, 69°25'W, runs south-eastwards and crosses the Chilean–Bolivian frontier at approximately 18°35'S, 69°5'W. Within Bolivian territory the river continues its course south-east to its confluence in the Coipasas Lake, under the exclusive domain of Bolivia.

This brief description permits us to determine the rules of international law that should be applied to the use and exploitation of the waters of this river: it is a course of water starting its flow in Chile, successively crossing over the territories of this country and of Bolivia, being Chilean in its upper course and Bolivian in the lower course towards its outlet. Both governments have long known the juridical regime of shared river basins, having been represented on international conferences over this matter (Barcelona, 1921; Montevideo, 1933), and had differences in the case of the River Mauri and the concession Chile had given to a private enterprise there (1929).

When Chile made its announcement, Bolivia, as noted, expressed its reservations over a possible diversion from the River Lauca. Bolivia did, however, state at the time that it did not seek to promote any incident or ignore the right of the Chilean Government to exploit natural resources in its own jurisdictional territory.

The principal aim of this paper is to explore Chilean–Bolivian relations concerning the use of part of the flow of the River Lauca under Chilean jurisdiction. Interstate relations, after approximately 33 years, were broken off by the Bolivian Government, because of the exploitation of these resources. It was only in the period between 1975 and 1978 when the Chilean Government was prepared to discuss a possible transfer of territory, that Bolivia reopened diplomatic relations. Then, following the failure of these negotiations, because of the unexpected intervention of Peru, relations were again interrupted and reduced to consular level only.

To examine the topic of water resources of the River Lauca, the observations and analysis include a brief description of the events that ended with the diversion of a part of the Chilean flow of the river towards the valley of Azapa and the break off of diplomatic relations on the part of Bolivia. By way of introduction, a short description is included to locate this area that causes such curious politics when a state decides to use part of the flow of a shared river basin. We also include an account of the problem by a renowned Bolivian historian. Each one of these sub-themes is the result of research into, and reflection on the peaceful management of resources of shared river basins possible in this part of the planet.

The Lauca River Basin: General Aspects

The River Lauca is an international river of continuous course that originates in Parinacota's marsh, which is fed by the neighbouring small lake of Cotacotani. From its source to its confluence with the lake of Coipasa the river measures approximately 225km, 75km in Chilean territory and 150km in Bolivian territory. Its springs are located at about 4,400m above sea level, while the confluence with lake Coipasa is located at about 3,760m above sea level.

As shown in Figure 19.1, 21 tributaries join the river in Chilean territory before it crosses the Chilean–Bolivian frontier, at Macaya, at a height of 3,892m above sea level.

During the studies related to the diversion project, hydrometrical gauging at a point close to the frontier gave as a mean flow of the river in low water the figure of 2.6m³/sec. In flood this flow increases to 5–8m³/sec. The overall area of the river basin is 12,956km². For the basin as a whole, the average flow in the low water period is 8m³/sec as compared to a figure of 16m³/sec in flood.

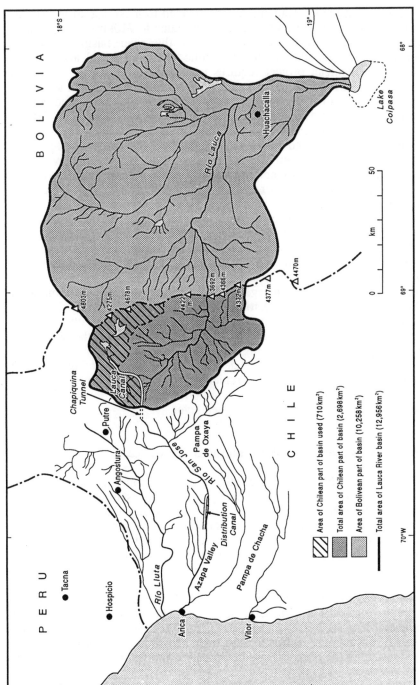

Figure 19.1 Hydrology of the River Lauca and the Azapa Valley Region

The area that the Chilean authorities decided to make use of to provide water resources to divert to the west, amounts to 710km². Such an area represents 25% of the overall area of the river basin in Chilean territory. The capacity of the hydraulic works designed and built to satisfy the Chilean project requires and could make use of 46.7% of the overall flow of the River Lauca prior to entering Bolivian territory.

The sources of the River Lauca are located in the orographic heights of Parinacota's snowy mountains, Quimsachata and Puquintica. On the western slopes of these snowy mountains is Lake Chungara, without visible drainage, and also the lagoon of Cotacotani that feeds Parinacota's marsh from which the River Lauca flows. Many creeks also converge on the River Lauca in Chilean territory. Further sources originate from the slopes of the volcano Guallatiri and from Puquintica and Arintica's hills.

In general, the climate of the area appears dominated by the high steppe. As Koeppen (1931) indicates, the high steppe is characterised by relatively abundant summer rainfalls of convective type – the high plateau winter – combined with high temperatures. During the astronomical winter, dry season, the temperature drops below 18°C, which impedes significant agricultural activity. During the months of August, September and October strong winds blow from the west, conveying dust and sand. Incomplete rainfall observations and registers refer to an annual mean between 320 and 350mm, with the months of December to March having higher rainfall.

These conditions favour the development of a zone of pasture and steppe vegetation. It should be remembered that the mean height in the high plateau in this area is about 4,000m above sea level, while the snow level is about 5,500m above sea level.

Purposes of the Public Work on the River Lauca

The Chilean authorities, concerned with irrigation and the generation of hydroelectricity, developed many public works in the area. These included a diversion dam, a canal of 33km, and a tunnel of 4.5km to cross the Chapiquiña saddle. At the exit of the tunnel, the diverted waters use the dry bed of Chusmiza's Creek, and the bed of the River San Jose (Azapa) for approximately 60km. At the end of this course a diversion dam was built, from where water is introduced by canal to the agricultural zone of the Azapa valley.

At the exit of the tunnel-crossing of the Chapiquiña the waterfall was used to establish a hydroelectric plant. The plant has an installed potential of 10,200kW, generating 36,722,000kWh in the 1980s. Energy production is directed to Arica and there it joins the national grid reaching the port of Iquique, 350km to the south.

General Conditions of the Land in the River Azapa's Valley

When President Aguirre Cerda took the decision to set up an irrigation project in the Azapa valley, the area had about 4,000ha with a strong agricultural potential, only 500ha of which was irrigated. The water for this irrigation was obtained from springs, because of the disappearance of surface flow about 65km inland. The subtropical climate of the lower course, together with the quality of soils, made a development plan based on the transference of water resources from the River Lauca to the River Azapa viable. Furthermore, in the 1940s and 50s the increase in the population of both the port-city, and the Chilean northern zone as a whole, created a strong local demand for fresh food at acceptable prices.

At that time Chilean development efforts were based upon agricultural expansion in order to satisfy the demands of a growing population, to break from poverty and diversify an economy with a strong dependency on mining exports.

Moreover, although in the receiving basin of the diverted water resources people were scarce, Arica and the Azapa Valley experienced chronic unemployment particularly for manual labour. The administration of Aguirre Cerda therefore planned economic and social development. The idea was to help increase irrigated areas in the Azapa valley and this was included into the development proposals just mentioned. In addition, the population politics of that administration aimed to settle people particularly in border areas, with the purpose of promoting integral development.

To many analysts – Chilean and foreign – the administration of Aguirre Cerda signalled the beginning of import substitution policies and the acceleration of forms of economic dependency; for others, it was the moment at which Chilean society was wakened from its mining-dominated culture of the 19th century and sought to acquire speedily characteristics typical of the 20th century with all its technologies and scientific development.

The Lauca River Affair, 1939–62

It was stated early in this paper that in 1939 Pedro Aguirre Cerda visited Arica and made a public declaration concerning the irrigation of the dry lands of the Azapa valley to produce food for the people of the zone and to provide manual employment, using part of the water resources of the high plateau River Lauca to do so.

The mere announcement of the project was enough for Bolivia to formulate a reservation over a possible diversion of the River Lauca in a note from the Ministry of Foreign Affairs and Culture, La Paz, dated 11 July 1939. In this note, Bolivia stated that the objection was made neither with an intention to promote any incident over this matter, nor ignoring the right of the Chilean Government to carry out works to profitably employ its national wealth. The following month (August) Bolivia renewed its reservations. This was the moment at which the Chilean ambassador in La Paz, Benjamin Cohen, stated that the project was not a *diversion* of the River Lauca, but only a natural *use* of its waters; furthermore the intake would be made in the upper part of the river; and finally that the water to be harnessed amounted to less than 10% of the flow that the River Lauca receives from its Chilean tributaries. The Chilean note gave a reassurance that the project was in accordance with the Statement of Montevideo, 1933, adopted by the Seventh Pan-American Conference, and the conclusions adopted by the International Right Institute in 1911, at its session in Madrid. In September, Ambassador Cohen renewed the idea of 'canalisation' and not 'diversion' of the flow of the River Lauca, repeating in November the notion of natural use of the waters of the river.

A review of this issue in the archives of the Ministry of Foreign Affairs of Chile, included in the Chilean 'White Book' (1963), shows a prolonged silence on the part of Bolivia. In 1947, Bolivia broke its silence and the clamour raised over the use of the waters of the River Lauca for Chile did not cease until 1962.

In December 1947, Bolivia established its position on this matter. A Chilean–Bolivian Committee was created to address the River Lauca issue. Long and bureaucratic comings and goings among chancelleries and ambassadors, and among these and the secretaries related to public works, meteorology, hydrology, agriculture and other connected topics were initiated. Finally, in August 1949, the Chilean–Bolivian Committee proposed a diversion of 2.75m³/sec of flow to irrigate 2,000ha. When this was agreed, three months was given for the parties to present observations. At the beginning of December 1949, this period expired, but these three months were in fact the beginning of four years of Bolivian silence on the topic.

In December 1953, during the government of Carlos Ibañez, the Chilean public electrical company presented a project to use the diversion canal by building a hydroelectric plant beyond the Chapiquiña saddle. At that moment, the Bolivian government renewed its reservations.

The Chilean Government repeated, in a note of 10 March 1954, that the history of the matter clearly showed that Bolivia had not presented any objection or observation in the internationally stipulated terms under the negotiations of 1949. Curiously, after this Chilean note, the Bolivian government renewed its silence on the subject, between 1954 and 1958.

Subsequently, in a note of 24 June 1958, the Bolivian government reminded Chile that the two countries had not arrived at an adequate agreement and having explained the reasons for this from the Bolivian point of view, they made a fresh proposal: the Chilean government should give Bolivia technical information of the precise details and modifications introduced in previous years to the works on the River Lauca in Chilean territory, so that Bolivia could judge the significance of the works. On this basis, it was stated, the Chilean and Bolivian governments could reach a definitive and mutually acceptable agreement.

From the Chilean perspective, as recorded in the Chilean White Book, all the diplomatic communications between the Chilean and Bolivian governments, from 1939 to 1960, had the objective of finding a procedure to permit Bolivia to determine the significance of the intake works and to investigate if these works would affect its interests as one of the countries lying along the River Lauca.

Another proposal made by Bolivia, perhaps with greater perseverance, has been to establish a convention with Chile over the use of the international waters of the River Lauca. However, careful analysis of Chilean–Bolivian relations could well lead to another hypothesis, that is, that Bolivia through these difficulties intended to raise the topic of its status as a land-locked state.

From 1960 Bolivia apparently sought to bring the issue before the court of the Council of the Organization of American States (OAS). Bolivia accused Chile of committing an aggressive act against Bolivia threatening American peace, and it stated that a Consultative Meeting of Ministers of Foreign Affairs should be called to restrain the aggression and to apply sanctions to the aggressor. On 24 May 1962, 18 countries – excluding Chile and Bolivia – unanimously adopted a resolution rejecting the Bolivian claims.

The OAS limited its action discreetly hoping that both governments would normalise their diplomatic relations as soon as possible, and formulated a friendly call for both parties to resort to one of the means of peaceful solution that the Inter-American System has. Bolivia systematically refused to resort to a juridical means of solution. To accept such a form of resolution Bolivia demanded a condition which Chile deemed unacceptable: Chilean suspension of the diversion of the River Lauca.

On 6 December 1962, the Bolivian government made a request to the XI Inter American Conference that the 'Port aspirations of Bolivia' should be included as the next point on the agenda. The theme of the River Lauca has certainly been a vehicle Bolivia has used to make people aware of its land-locked state problem. In pursuing this policy, Bolivia has had to sacrifice diplomatic relations with a neighbouring country. It is necessary to bear in mind that between 1975 and 1978, when the Pinochet administration was disposed to negotiate territorial access to the sea, the government in La Paz reopened diplomatic relations. These were broken again when the position of Peru was heard. From 16 April 1962, when Bolivia again broke off its relations with Chile, the topic of the River Lauca was replaced by the maritime aspirations over the Chilean littoral.

The River Lauca Affair from a Bolivian Perspective

V. Abecia Baldivieso, a Bolivian historian, whilst studying international relations and the history of Bolivia, has written about the affair. Two chapters of his book are 'Arica and the diversion of River Lauca' and 'The diversion of River Lauca and the negotiations over the port' (Abecia Baldivieso, 1979).

Abecia Baldivieso wrote that Chilean opposition to the River Lauca project emerged because the project implied a deepening in the 'Chileanisation' of Arica. This strategy, according to Bolivian politicians, consisted of an attempt to reduce, as far as possible, the dependence of Arica's port on Bolivian commerce.

In light of this, in 1943 the Bolivian government asked the USA for its co-operation to peacefully obtain a solution to the Bolivian landlocked state problem. When it was consulted over this affair, the Chilean government stated its willingness to study and consider the Bolivian proposal which sought to improve the transit regime through Chilean territory, on condition that there were no unresolved territorial claims and that there was no possibility of territorial cessions. In 1944, a new Chilean government manifested a disposition to consider any direct negotiations tending to the solution of the port problem, which was corroborated again in November 1946.

Clearly, the author interweaves the promises of a port with the diversion of the River Lauca's waters, illustrating that the real purpose of the complex Bolivian attitude concerning the river was intended to further revision of the Treaty of Peace and Friendliness of 1904, resulting in the Chilean transfer of territory to Bolivia so that the latter extends to the coast.

The offer of negotiations for the concession of a port on the Pacific by the Chilean government was interpreted as a delaying action, while the Chilean government was busy speeding up the beginning of the works on the River Lauca. The Chilean government fixed two important premises to begin the negotiations: the exclusion of territorial compensation for Bolivia and a confirmation to the government of Peru fulfilling the obligations of the Treaty of 1929, which led to an end to the controversy over Tacna and Arica.

The President of the USA, Harry Truman, appeared on the scene agreeing with the President of Chile, Gonzalez Videla, over some general ideas of Peruvian–Bolivian–Chilean development, using the water resources of Lake Titicaca. The Bolivian historian says Chile sought to dominate all the water resources, utilising the protective mantle of the Washington government. What the author does not explore is the revolution in Bolivia at the beginning of the 1950s and how the Lauca affair was submerged into obscurity and emerged only to exacerbate nationalism with respect to a port in the Chilean littoral.

The author maintains that the use of waters of the Lauca is only an aggressive act by Chile against Bolivia, and that Bolivia appealed to the regional organisations in search of protection and justice for its position.

Some Final Considerations

It is not easy to analyse and to consider these kind of themes in the context established by the International Boundaries Research Unit with respect to shared water resources. But this is a case study that brings our attention to the kind of difficulties that nations must face when intending to use their own natural resources, which are in shared river basins.

The negative result of the relations between both states is worrying. As we have analysed in other papers and contributions, a territorial solution to the complex problem of Bolivia as a land-locked state is impossible. On the positive side, Bolivia has shown signs in the 1990s of understanding the value of bilateral economic co-operation.

It is complicated, too, to use the topic of shared water resources to conceal other international political purposes. States, such as Chile for example, are sensitive to pressures and extortion. Similarly, diplomatic behaviour through time should be always equal, so as to facilitate debate with the certainty of fair play. We think now is the time to indicate that research on these topics should be objective, rigorous and systematic. Bolivian and Chilean colleagues probably do not agree with the methodology of this paper.

However, the important thing is to examine these case studies relating to the negative and positive uses of shared resources in borderland zones. It seems possible that in the next century states may be disposed to lower a little the profile of their opaque frontiers to become, instead, translucent frontiers. Could it be possible in this context for Chile and Bolivia to renew suspended relations and reach a realistic solution to the affair of the River Lauca?

Notes

This paper stems in part from projects Fondecyt No. 1215/86, DIUC No.015/90 and DTI C3020/9013, C3020/9223 and C3020/9333.

Bibliography

Abecia Baldivieso, V. (1979) 'Las relaciones internacionales en la historia de Bolivia', *Los Amigos del Libro,* La Paz, Bolivia: Academia Nacional de Ciencias de Bolivia.

Bolivia, MRREE (1962) 'La desviación del río Lauca. Antecedentes y Documentos', La Paz: Ministerio de Relaciones Exteriores República de Bolivia.

Chile, MRREE (1963) 'La Cuestión del Río Lauca', Santiago: Ministerio de Relaciones Exteriores República de Chile.

Espinoza Moraga, O. (1964) 'La cuestión del Lauca', *Nascimento, Santiago.*

Gangas-Geisse, M. and Santis-Arenas, H. (1993) 'Overcoming difficulties for promoting and improving development in borderlands with Peru and Bolivia: the Chilean case in the northern areas', paper given at International Conference on Regional Development: The Challenge of the Frontiers, Ben-Gurion University of the Negev, Beer-Sheva, Israel, 28–30 December.

Koeppen, W. (1931) *Grudiss der Klimakunde,* Berlin: Walter De Gruyter and Co; translated into Spanish (1948) *Climatología,* Mexico and Buenos Aires: Fondo de Cultura Económica.

Environment and Conservation

20

Poseidon's Trident:
Biological Diversity Preservation,
Resource Conservation and Conflict Avoidance
in the South China Sea

Glen Hearns
Peter Tyedmers

Introduction

An area of the South China Sea known to many, and not only
mariners, as 'dangerous ground' refers to a group of unmarked reef
features which have presented hazards to marine navigation for
centuries. In more recent times there has been substantially more cause
to support this title. These seemingly innocuous features have become
the focus of much political and military tension in the region as they
are currently claimed, either entirely or in part, by six littoral states:
the People's Republic of China, Taiwan, the Philippines, Malaysia,
Vietnam, and Brunei Darussalam. In recent years, as none of the
claimant states appears prepared to abandon its claim to sovereignty,
the atmosphere surrounding them has been defined by naval clashes
and the seizure of commercial fishing vessels. Unfortunately, as a
result of this ongoing military activity, irreplaceable mid-ocean reef
habitat is being lost.

Although the reasons for the conflict are complex and date back
centuries, one impetus for it is clear: all claimants want access to the
area's resources, both existing and potential. As the quest for
resources, both living and non-living, increases throughout the region
over time, tensions will continue to escalate in the disputed Spratly
area.

In response to the rising tension in the area, over the last four years
a series of annual informal meetings have been held, with participants
from ten regional countries coming together to search for ways in
which the dispute might peacefully be resolved.[1] In one such recent
meeting, a proposal for the establishment of a Spratly marine protected
area was advanced. Such an endeavour, the authors argue, would serve
not only to preserve the valuable biological diversity associated with
the reef system, but also to support the development of a sustainable

regional fishery. Moreover, such a park would defuse the existing volatility over the reefs, and reduce the potential for future violence in the region which could result from a dearth of living resources as a consequence of unregulated exploitation.

Physical Setting

The area in question, which shall be referred to as the Spratly reefs[2] for the remainder of this paper, is composed of over 500 unmarked reefs and cays spread out over a 240,000km[2] area in the southern half of the South China Sea. The vast majority of these features are below sea level, and lie atop a series of extension block-fault bound ridges which run almost parallel to the Palawan and Borneo mainlands. Upon these ridges, calcareous sediments of up to Tertiary age have been deposited (Valencia, 1991: 67). The entire Spratly reefs area is surrounded by deep troughs,[3] and is therefore independent of – and should therefore not be regarded as an extension of – any adjacent state's continental shelf. Indeed, the area is so characterised by block faulting that between the features themselves depths of 3,015m below sea level are reached.

Historical Setting

The reefs have been used for centuries by both Chinese and Vietnamese fishermen, as seasonal fishing bases (Valero, 1993: 17). More recently, during the early part of this century (1917) the islands were exploited by numerous countries for their fisheries and valuable guano resources (*ibid:* 18). In 1933 the French annexed the Spratly reefs to their adjacent Indo-Chinese colonies (Haller-Trost, 1991: 40). However, as the Second World War approached the French departed and the reefs were subsequently occupied by the Japanese between 1939 and 1945 (Valero, 1993: 17).

As a result of the San Francisco Treaty of Peace with Japan, in 1951 the territories which had been occupied by Japan during the war were repatriated to various states. However, the issue of the repatriation of the Spratly reefs was never properly addressed. In spite of the fact that at the time, although both Vietnam and the Philippines claimed the features, neither claim to sovereignty was recognised. In addition, although the People's Republic of China and Taiwan also claimed sovereignty over the Spratly reefs, it was unclear at the time who should officially represent China and neither was invited to the treaty negotiations (Haller-Trost, 1991: 40).

A more recent period of activity in the Spratly reefs commenced in 1956 when the Filipino entrepreneur, Tomas Cloma, claimed a large portion of the Spratly reefs as his own 'freedom-land' (Kalayaan). In response, Taiwan immediately occupied the largest of the features, Itu Aba (Hornik, 1991) and South Vietnam occupied Spratly Island proper along with the Paracel Islands in the northern South China Sea.

This level of occupation remained more or less the *status quo* until the mid-1970s, when the international oil shock brought the issue of sovereignty over the Spratly reefs to the fore once again. As part of the global rush to secure energy resources, oil exploration throughout South-east Asia increased and interest in the oil potential of the Spratly area was born. As a result, South Vietnam[4] and the Philippines[5] leased exploration concessions to foreign and domestic oil companies and a new wave of military involvement began in the area as countries attempted to assert their claims of sovereignty and jurisdiction. As a result, China, Vietnam,[6] Malaysia, and the Philippines all established or re-established military installations in the area (FEER, 1992).

Throughout the early and mid-1980s there was relatively little military activity amongst the reefs. This changed, however, in 1987 with the establishment of new Chinese[7] and Malaysian[8] military installations on several previously unoccupied reefs. Once again, these moves initiated a period of intensified entrenchment and military deployment by all the claimant states which culminated in March 1988 when Chinese forces sank at least two Vietnamese vessels, with the resulting loss of over 70 lives (FEER, 1992). A few weeks after the sinking of the Vietnamese vessels, Malaysian gun boats seized three Filipino fishing vessels in waters claimed by both countries (*Asiaweek,* 1988).

Although there have been no recent military conflicts in the Spratly reefs, the situation in the area is far from tranquil. Military installations continue to be strengthened, while a variety of commercial ventures have been initiated in various parts of the area. As the region experiences increasing pressure on both its living and non-living resources, control of the Spratly reefs will become increasingly desirable and military clashes are virtually inevitable.

One option which could forestall future military conflict in the area is the establishment of some form of marine protected area. The remainder of this paper will consider some of the potential benefits that would result from the creation of such a protected area in the Spratly reefs.

Biological Diversity Preservation

The establishment of a marine protected area in the Spratly reefs would go a long way towards safeguarding the valuable and irreplaceable biological diversity which exists on and around the coral reefs of the South China Sea. The loss of biological diversity might be entirely academic if it were not for our inherent dependence upon living organisms. The biological diversity of the earth has provided us with food, medicines and a host of raw materials from which we draw our livelihoods. The well-being of these ecosystems, and their inherent diversity of biological material, is integral to human survival, and thus we must take measures to provide for their continuity. The marine environment in general is of particular interest and importance as it is currently the least understood. As humans are a land based species, we have paid much less attention to the marine environment than to our terrestrial habitat.

Many important human medicines are currently derived from terrestrial plants and fungi which have developed potent chemical deterrents to protect themselves from predators, parasites and other competitors (Farnsworth, 1988: 83).[9] In the marine environment, not only are there plants and fungi, but also sessile animals which have developed comparable chemical deterrents (Thorne-Miller and Catena, 1991: 18). As a result, there is likely to be a vast array of biochemical compounds available from marine organisms. If their terrestrial counterparts are a guide, these biochemical compounds could provide enormous humanitarian and financial benefits.[10] For example, arabinosides, derived from some sponges, have led to treatments against herpes. In addition, many promising potential medicinal compounds have already been extracted from a number of other marine organisms including, *inter alia,* seaweed, algae, corals, and worms (Norse, 1993: 19, 21).

Although the oceans are generally believed to host fewer individual species than the terrestrial environment, the genetic diversity in the marine environment can be said to be greater. Genetic diversity is often associated with speciation. This, however, can be quite misleading, especially when one considers that it is at the higher levels of taxonomic classification where the largest variation in genetic material is seen, and not simply at the species level. With this perspective in mind, it is likely that there is far more potential variation in biochemical compounds in the marine environment then in the terrestrial environment. This becomes apparent when examining the distribution of phyla in the animal kingdom. Of the 33 animal phyla known to exist, 32 occur in the oceans, 15 of which are exclusively marine. Put another way, while over 95% of all animal phyla exist in the marine environment, only a little over 50% are found in the terrestrial environment. From this one could conclude that the marine environment has the potential to provide a vast array of useful genetic material which has to date been over-looked.

With regard to biological diversity, the Spratly reefs are paragons. They lie in some of the most biologically diverse waters in the world and are host to a plethora of species. Like its terrestrial counterpart species diversity in the oceans increases with decreasing latitude. However, in the oceans there is also a variation with respect to longitude, and species diversity is at a maximum in the Indo-Pacific region. This longitudinal disparity in diversity is exemplified when looking at the world-wide distribution of corals: the tropical waters of the Caribbean are host to only 20 genera of coral, whereas the waters of South-east Asia contain approximately 70 genera (McMannus, 1994).

In addition to lying in some of the most biodiverse waters in the world, the Spratly reefs present a relatively unique preservation opportunity because they are in relatively pristine condition, when compared to other coastal reefs in South-east Asia. For example, a study carried out in the Philippines in 1982 revealed that of the 632 coastal reefs surveyed, over 70% had been negatively impacted to such an extent that they had less than 50% live coral cover remaining. Unfortunately, this level of degradation is the rule rather than the exception for the majority of coastal reef systems in South-east Asia (Geoffery *et al,* 1990).

Even though the Spratly reefs have witnessed human activity for centuries, historically most of this activity has taken the form of seasonal fishing which has a relatively minor impact. More recently, however, the presence of military installations and personnel has had an enormous impact on the ecological integrity of the system. Not only are reef structures being modified and destroyed through dredging and construction, but the day to day activity of several hundred people living on the fragile systems is endangering many species. Moreover, idle troops hoping to earn a little more money on the side have been known to engage in such harmful activities as dynamite fishing (McMannus, 1994).

The creation of a marine protected area in the Spratly reefs would therefore not only safeguard the marine biological diversity in the region but would also preserve some of the most spectacular mid-ocean reef systems known. An obvious potential economic spin-off from this could come in the form of low impact eco-tourism. For comparison, it has been estimated that tourist activities on the Great Barrier Reef in Australia result in an annual direct expenditure of approximately US$1 billion (Hudloe, 1990) and that the consumer surplus (the amount tourists are willing to pay above and beyond the existing actual fares and other costs involved in seeing the Great Barrier Reef) exceeds AUS$6 million annually (Spurgeon, 1992).

Resource Conservation

SUSTAINABLE FISHERIES

Apart from bringing in revenue through tourism, a marine protected area in the Spratly reefs could have a major positive impact on the long term viability of marine capture fisheries in the region. The ongoing collapse of many of what were once perceived as the world's inexhaustible fish stocks, such as the Peruvian anchovy and, more recently, the Grand Banks Atlantic cod stocks off Canada's east coast is slowly forcing fisheries experts to reconsider previous management strategies. The unfortunate reality is that, from a global perspective, the outlook for the world's fisheries is not bright. Approximately 85% of the world's total fish catch currently comes from the oceans, and that catch peaked at 86 million tonnes in 1989. Since then there has been a steady decline in the world's marine capture fisheries production despite ever-increasing levels of effort and technology (*Economist,* 1994).

The tragedy of this situation is emphasised when one considers that only 10% of the world catch is currently taken from international waters, with the rest coming from within some states' 200 nautical mile jurisdictional limits (*ibid:* 13). This implies that even in areas where some form of management is in place, over-fishing is occurring. Therefore, in an area where no clear jurisdiction exists, such as the Spratly reefs, there is even greater potential for rampant over-exploitation.

This has enormous potential implications for the developing littoral states of the South China Sea, where the majority of animal protein consumed is derived from marine sources (Thorne-Miller and Catena, 1991: 17). The South China Sea is one of the most heavily fished areas in the world. The regional catch has increased from 6.6 million tonnes in 1986 to 8.3 million tonnes in 1989, and comprises an estimated 9.6% of the total world catch (Mansor Mat Isa, 1993). This high level of fisheries production is even more alarming when one is confronted with the fact that, as early as 1985, most demersal fish stocks in the area were already heavily exploited (*ibid*). Considering the current and growing pressures being exerted on the fish populations of the South China Sea, it is likely that regional fisheries production will follow the global trend and begin to decline, probably sooner rather than later. A Spratly reefs marine protected area could provide a partial solution to this impending dilemma.

Studies have shown that marine refugia can be highly useful in increasing fish populations of certain species in adjacent fishing areas (Alcala and Russ, 1990). As fecundity of many fish species increases almost exponentially with size, areas where species are left undisturbed in their natural abundance produce far more larvae than do fished areas. As a result, significant spillover can occur both through active migration of adult fish and as a result of the passive diffusion of fish from areas of high natural densities within refugia to adjacent areas of low fish densities outside the refugia.

Moreover, as many fish species have pelagic larval stages in their development, ocean currents may well transport these larvae by passive dispersal to distant waters. In the case of the Spratly reefs, transportation by passive dispersal is likely to be to the coastal zones of some of the littoral states of the South China Sea. Due to the physical geography[11] and the shifting monsoonal weather patterns of the South China Sea a complex cyclical current regime exists (Chou Loke Ming and Aliño, 1992: 9).[12] These cyclical current patterns suggest that over the course of several months larvae of both benthic and pelagic species, produced in the Spratly reefs, may be passively dispersed to the coastal zones of Vietnam, the Philippines, China, Malaysia and even Indonesia, depending on the predominating monsoon. These dispersed larvae would therefore help to reinforce local littoral populations which are under increasing pressure from artisanal fishing, and where local reproduction is relatively low or infrequent (McMannus, 1994). As the reefs are important spawning grounds for coastal tuna (one of the most sought after pelagic species in the region, Mansor Mat Isa, 1993) and many economically important reef species, the refugia-induced effects of spillover and passive dispersal of larvae on the regional fisheries could be enormous.

Although the South China Sea current dynamics are not fully understood and the effect of larval dispersion on the regional fisheries has not been assessed, in light of the declining trend occurring in fisheries production around the world, a precautionary approach to fisheries stewardship in the region is clearly advisable. This is particularly relevant in the case of the Spratly reefs, which are currently in relatively pristine condition and where fish populations are still healthy. Indeed, a marine protected area in the Spratlys could well serve as a foundation for an integrated regional marine conservation and fisheries management system.

Finally, the establishment of a marine protected area in the Spratly reefs would not only enhance the potential for maintaining sustainable fisheries throughout the adjacent littoral areas; it would also reduce the potential for a 'tragedy of the commons' phenomenon (Hardin, 1968)[13] occurring through over-fishing in the region. As long as uncertainty exists with regard to the disposition of jurisdictional claims, opportunities remain for wanton and exploitative behaviour, from both claimant and non-claimant nations. It is not that fishers intentionally despoil the basis of their livelihood; it is simply that if one attempts to conserve a common stock by purposely limiting your own catch, there is no reason to believe that future benefits will be realised because there is no guarantee that the fish which are left will not be seized by someone else.

NON-LIVING RESOURCES

In general, the creation of a marine protected area would undermine one of the fundamental issues currently driving the conflicting claims to the Spratly reefs. A totally, or even partially, protected area would diminish the acute aggression surrounding the question of access to both living and non-living resources. As has been discussed, the overall benefit of an enhanced sustainable regional fishery would likely far exceed any short term costs resulting from decreased access to Spratly reef fishing areas. Similarly, in terms of non-living resources, particularly the potential for oil and gas, these would not be lost should a marine protected area be established, but merely banked for possible future exploitation should they be needed. An agreement similar to the Madrid Protocol of the Antarctic Treaty, could be applied, whereby a 50-year moratorium on resource extraction is imposed, at the end of which the question of whether to explore and exploit could be revisited and a new decision made. In the short term, all claimant countries could thus rest assured that they would not be left behind in a race to ascertain and develop resources, as the race would, at least temporarily, be called off.

Furthermore, by establishing a Spratly marine protected area, not only could the extreme biological and financial costs associated with resource exploration be eliminated or redirected, but the millions of dollars which are currently being spent to maintain the various military installations in the area could be put to other, potentially more humanitarian, purposes in the respective countries. For example, for a country such as Vietnam, maintaining the *status quo* presents a significant challenge in that it can ill afford the financial burden of maintaining its military presence, and yet politically cannot afford simply to abandon its claim.

Conflict Resolution and Avoidance

Ultimately, a marine protected area in the Spratly reefs would address the fundamental problem which exists in the geopolitical setting of the South China Sea, namely the ongoing conflicts over sovereignty and jurisdiction. Such an endeavour would require an enormous degree of co-operation and collaboration on the part of the claimant states. In addition, the endorsement and support of non-claimant states in the region would be required thereby helping to unify the region as a whole. Establishing a park would likely also result in increased communication and technology transfer between the various states. For a country such as Vietnam, this could facilitate the transition from pariah to full participant in the region and allow it to take advantage of other developments occurring in and around the region. Finally, the process of co-operatively establishing a marine protected area could foster co-operation in other sectors.

The concept of establishing parks as a means of resolving conflicts in disputed areas is not new. For example, the 'Si-A-Paz' binational complex of protected areas in the lower San Juan Valley of Central America has successfully alleviated the border tension between Costa Rica and Nicaragua (Hamann *et al,* 1993). To date, however, no park exists anywhere in the world on the political and spatial scale of the Spratly reefs.

Conclusions

Conflicts over access to resources, of one kind or another, have occurred throughout human history. However, the world is currently entering an era in which the widespread scarcity of renewable resources will likely result in violent confrontation on a scale, and of a quality, previously unattained. Research suggests that the future social and political turbulence set in motion by changing environmental conditions will likely follow different patterns to those of previous resource-centred conflicts (Homer-Dixon *et al*, 1993). Indeed, it is believed that the future scarcity of renewable resources will have an insidious and cumulative effect on the social integrity and stability of populations. As groups of people become aware that not only is their basic livelihood being extinguished but that their very survival is being challenged and there are no new pastures to roam, drastic demographic changes are likely to occur. This will most likely be particularly acute in small and densely-populated developing countries, where such events have already been seen to result in ethnic clashes and insurgency. The creation of a marine protected area to enhance and promote a sustainable regional fishery would thus help to reduce the potential for conflicts resulting from a scarcity of fish in the South China Sea.

Clearly, a marine protected area in the Spratly reefs would be a significant step towards securing the long term stability of the region, in terms of both biological diversity preservation and resource conservation. Moreover, a marine protected area could play a notable role in the areas of conflict resolution and conflict avoidance in the region, as well as enhancing collaboration and co-operation more generally.

Notes

1   These meetings are the essence of the 'Managing Potential Conflicts in the South China Sea' project which was initiated in 1990. They are hosted by the Indonesian government and are funded primarily by the Canadian International Development Agency (CIDA). The meetings have been organised and facilitated principally by the Centre for Asian Legal Studies, at the University of British Columbia, and by the Ministry of Foreign Affairs in Indonesia.

2   Although the common English name for the region is the Spratly
     Islands, as the vast majority of the features lie below sea level,
     and as it is the reefs which are of primary importance both
     biologically and economically, the authors feel that the name
     Spratly reefs is more appropriate. This position is supported by an
     interpretation of Article 121 (the Regime of Islands) of the United
     Nations Convention on the Law of the Sea.

3   The reefs are separated from the islands of Palawan and Borneo
     by the Palawan trough, whose minimum depth is 1,000m. To the
     north and north-west of the Spratly reefs lie the abyssal depths of
     the South China Sea, where depths of over 5,000m are achieved.

4   In 1973 South Vietnam leased offshore concessions to several
     American companies. See *Asiaweek,* 1988.

5   Between 1975 to 1980, Swedish (Salen), American (Amoco),
     British (London and Scottish Marine Oil Ltd), and Filipino oil
     companies held interests and drilled exploration wells off Reed
     Bank in the northern part of the Spratly reefs. The results,
     however, were not encouraging, and all of the exploration wells
     were plugged and abandoned. Some governments and companies
     remain interested in the oil potential of more remote, deeper water
     parts of the Spratly area, and, as a result, perpetuate the
     unsubstantiated claim of vast oil reserves in the region.
     Unfortunately, this has only served to intensify the aggressive
     disposition of the claimant states. See Valencia, 1991: 73–4.

6   After the fall of Saigon in April 1975, and the unification of
     North and South Vietnam, the new Vietnam adopted all the claims
     of the former South Vietnam.

7   Under the auspices of setting up a UNESCO-funded weather
     station, which UNESCO subsequently denied, the People's
     Republic of China occupied several reefs in the central portion of
     the region (Fiery Cross and Cuataron reefs), and then
     springboarded to Louisa reef, one of the most southerly features,
     only 270km from the coast of Brunei and 124km from the
     Malaysian-held Shallow reef . See *Asiaweek,* 1988.

8   The Malaysians ensconced themselves on three additional features
     (Dallas, Mariveles and Barque Canada reefs). See *Asiaweek,*
     1988.

9   Approximately 25% of all prescriptions filled in North America
     contain active chemical compounds derived from higher plants.

10   It has been estimated that treatments for cancer and viral diseases
     could bring in over US$1 billion/annum, and as 78 extractions
     from a single tunicate ascidian were found to be toxic to cells the
     potential for an anti-tumour drug increases as the biochemistry of
     the marine environment is explored.

11 The South China Sea may be regarded as a semi-enclosed sea. Although at its deepest the sea reaches 5,559m, it is bordered by relatively shallow passages to adjacent marine areas all of which are less than 50m deep, save the Luzon Strait connecting the sea to the north-west Pacific. Within this semi-enclosed vessel a complex system of surface currents evolves throughout the year which are dependent upon monsoonal wind patterns.

12 The period between December and February is dominated by the north-east monsoon promoting an anti-clockwise system of currents, while the south-west monsoon between June and August create a slight reversal in direction.

13 Strictly speaking the situation that Hardin envisioned is not a tragedy of a 'commons' (which, when properly functioning, are mutually regulated, limited access, common property resources), but rather a despoilment of an unregulated public access resource.

Bibliography

Alcala, A. and Russ, G.R. (1990) 'A direct test of the effects of protective management on abundance and yield of tropical marine resources', *Journal de conseil International sur l'exploration de la mer,* 46: 40–7.

Asiaweek (1988) 'Another Spratly spat', 20 May: 26–7.

Chou Loke Ming and Aliño, P. (1992) *An Underwater Guide to the South China Sea,* Times Editions Pte.

Economist (1994) 'The catch about fish', and 'Tragedy of the oceans', 19 March: 13: 21–4.

FEER (1992) 'Treacherous shoals', *Far East Economic Review* 13 August: 14–7.

Farnsworth, N.R. (1988) 'Screening plants for new medicines', in E.O. Wilson (ed) *Biodiversity*, National Academy Press: 83–97.

Geoffery, L., Hinrichsen, D. and Markham, A. (1990) *Atlas of the Environment,* New York: Prentice Hall Press.

Haller-Trost, R. (1991) 'The Spratly Islands: a study on the limitations of international law', Occasional Paper 14, University of Kent.

Hamann, R., Ankersen, T., Gonzalez, M. and Bloom, J. (1993) 'Binational management of the San Juan River Basin: from war to co-operation', Mesoamerican Biodiversity Legal Project Round Table Discussion, University of Miami, 26–8 October.

Hardin, G. (1968) 'The tragedy of the commons', *Science* 13 December: 1243.

Homer-Dixon, T., Boutwell, J. and Rathjens, G. (1993) 'Environmental change and violent conflict', *Scientific American* February.

Hornik, R. (1991) 'The Spratly spat', *Time* 24 June: 30–2.

Hudloe, T.J. (1990) 'Measuring the value of the Great Barrier Reef', *Australian Parks and Recreation* 26, 3: 11–5.

Mansor Mat Isa (1993) 'The state of fisheries in the South China Sea', in *Proceedings from the First Working Group Meeting on Marine Scientific Research in the South China Sea,* Manila: Appendix J.

McMannus (1994) 'The Spratly Islands: a marine park', submitted to AMBIO, 3 February.

Norse, E. (1993) *Global Marine Biological Diveristy,* Island Press.

Spurgeon, J. (1992) *The Marine Pollution Bulletin* 24, 11: 529–36.

Thorne-Miller, B. and Catena, J. (1991) *The Living Ocean,* Island Press.

Valencia, M. (1991) *Malaysia and the Law of the Sea,* Malaysia: Institute of Strategic and International Studies.

Valero, G.M. (1993) *Spratly Archipelago: Is the Question of Sovereignty Still Relevant?,* Philippines: UP Printery.

21

The Bacalar Chico Reserve
A Case Study in Government and NGO Collaboration
in Conservation Projects

A.R. Harborne
P.J. Mumby
P.S. Raines
J.M. Ridley

Introduction

Belize, a small country bordering Guatemala and Mexico, boasts sovereignty over the world's second largest barrier reef system. With approximately 200,000 visitors a year, a large proportion of whom utilise the coastal zone in some way, effective coastal zone management is a major priority of the Government of Belize. The Belize Coastal Zone Management Unit (CZMU), established in 1990 as part of the Department of Fisheries, aims to develop a country-wide management strategy for the entire coastal zone. A key component of this programme is the provision of marine protected areas, of which there are two already in existence; Glovers Atoll and the Hol Chan Marine Reserve at San Pedro.

The town of San Pedro is the largest tourism development associated with the barrier reef. San Pedro lies at the southern most end of Ambergris Cay, which is connected to Mexico's Yucatan Peninsula to the north (Figure 21.1). The vast majority of Ambergris Cay is undeveloped. However, several comprehensive development proposals have been submitted which, if authorised, could lead to a proliferation of tourist amenities such as golf courses and hotels.

Bacalar Chico

The Bacalar Chico region encompasses barrier reef, seagrass beds, mangrove wetlands, lagoons and higher cay forest. It also contains a narrow, partly man-made channel that forms a natural border between Belize and Mexico. The area is home to many of Central America's rarest fauna and flora. At Rocky Point, the barrier reef merges with

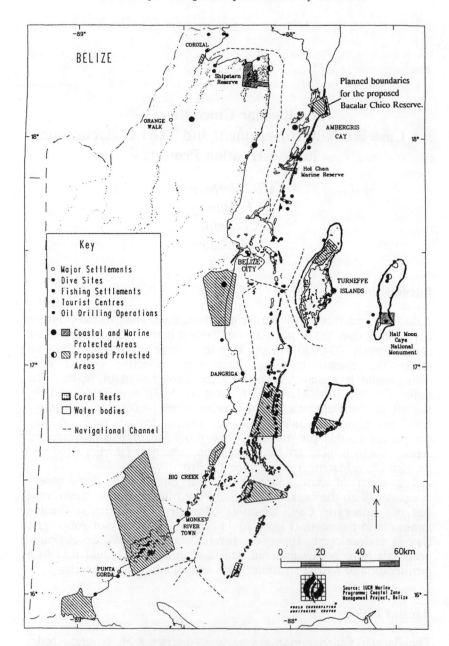

Figure 21.1 Map of Belize Showing the Position of Ambergis Cay and the Planned Boundaries for the Proposed Bacalar Chico Reserve
Source: World Conservation Monitoring Centre

continental mainland, thus forming an unusual raised reef of exposed Pleistocene coral. Rocky Point is also an important spawning area for the nassau grouper (*Epinephelus striatus*) and yellowfin grouper (*Mycteroperca interstitialis*) (Perkins, 1983).

The reef itself has luxuriant coral growth, and the back reef lagoon possesses extensive seagrass beds and patch reefs. The entire stretch of beach is one of the most important nesting sites in the country for loggerhead and green turtles (*Caretta caretta* and *Chelonia mydas*).

Mangrove wetlands and lagoons provide nursery areas for many marine organisms, including commercially significant species. Wetlands also provide vital habitats for many species of wading birds and for manatees (*Trichechus manatus*) and crocodiles (*Crocodylus* spp).

Mayan archaeological sites are located in the higher forested areas. The site of San Juan has been excavated, but many others have not been studied. The higher forest exhibits a rich fauna and flora that includes the jaguar (*Panthera onca*), ocelot (*Felis pardalis*) and unique plant communities. Indeed, Bacalar Chico is thought to be an important corridor allowing jaguars to move between Mexico and Belize.

Bacalar Chico is clearly an ecologically sensitive region and therefore, given the current development pressures, the Government of Belize considers it to warrant urgent protection.

Collaborative Efforts Towards the Bacalar Chico Reserve: A Model of Co-operation

NON-GOVERMENTAL ORGANISATION COLLABORATION

In order to protect Bacalar Chico, the European Community (EC) is currently funding a collaborative endeavour between three non-governmental organisations (NGOs): Coral Cay Conservation (CCC), the International Tropical Conservation Foundation (ITCF) and the World Conservation Union (WCU).

CCC has recruited volunteers that will be trained to undertake the marine element of the baseline survey work. CCC will also extend its existing programme of training in SCUBA diving, resource assessment and tropical marine ecology for Belizeans associated with the programme and produce educational and training material. Consultants hired by the ITCF through the CMZU will carry out terrestrial surveys and the ITCF will provide the materials to construct a field station and assist the Government of Belize in the implementation of the reserve. Belizean staff will be recruited and will be attached to the San Pedro headquarters of the Hol Chan Marine Reserve at the southern tip of Ambergris Cay, whose remit will be extended to cover management of Bacalar Chico. IUCN will supply policy and management advice to the CZMU.

The collaborative nature of the project will require data to be integrated from a variety of sources. For example, marine data (CCC) and terrestrial data (ITCF) can be used to classify remotely sensed imagery, the results of which are then manipulated within a geographic information system (GIS). GIS plays a central role in the resource management planning process in Belize (Mumby *et al*, forthcoming).

Close collaboration between the NGOs and the Government of Belize will result in the following:

1 A designated reserve at Bacalar Chico, together with a management plan, preliminary reserve infrastructure, equipment, and scientific monitoring and survey programmes. A GIS database will be created to form the basis of the management plan.
2 Technical support for the establishment of an overall policy framework and supporting documents for a national coastal zone management programme for Belize, in co-operation with the GEF/UNDP coastal zone management programme.
3 Education and interpretive materials, aimed at both tourists and the local community.
4 Expansion of SCUBA training programmes for marine reserve personnel.

INTER-DEPARTMENT COLLABORATION WITHIN THE GOVERNMENT OF BELIZE

In addition to NGO/Government of Belize collaboration, the Bacalar Chico project will serve to enhance inter-departmental co-operation within the Government of Belize. Bacalar Chico is likely to become the first joint marine/terrestrial reserve in Belize and, as such, falls under the auspices of both the Fisheries and Forestry Departments. To ensure the reserve's success, these departments are working closely together and thus establishing mechanisms for joint conservation efforts in future.

INTER-GOVERNMENT COLLABORATION

The Bacalar Chico Reserve offers an excellent opportunity for collaboration between the Belize and Mexican governments. At this stage, plans for the reserve are restricted to the Belize side of the border and thus represent a 'Type 9' park in McNeil's classification (McNeil, 1990). It is possible that the Bacalar Chico Reserve could be extended into a true transboundary park given appropriate inter-governmental mechanisms and co-operation. IUCN has produced guidelines for the management of transboundary parks, which include the following important points (IUCN, 1990):

Formulate Co-operative Agreements for Integrated Management of Border Protected Areas. Detailed measures for co-operative management allow harmonious and effective management of the reserve. It is anticipated that the management plan for the Belizean area will be completed within two years and it would be prudent to adopt similar principles on the Mexican side, for example with regard to zoning criteria. Similarly, enforcement of management initiatives should be co-ordinated in a consistent manner between the two countries. The guidelines suggest that this may necessitate a working-level consultative committee which may initially consist of NGOs in order to pave the way for government links.

Identify Practical Management Activities in Border Parks to Facilitate More Effective Conservation. This guideline particularly concerns consistent warden and reserve personnel activity, which can be attained through standardised training. This may be achieved by running training courses at the Marine Research Centre on the Turneffe Atoll, a new facility established jointly by the Government of Belize, University College of Belize and Coral Cay Conservation.

Design Joint Visitor Use Facilities and Programmes. The Bacalar Chico reserve will naturally attract a large number of tourists. However, to make optimum use of the reserve, it would be important to establish joint marketing programmes and complementary facilities and access.

Formulate Co-operative Research Programmes and Share Results. It is hoped that both Mexican and Belizean scientists, plus visiting researchers, will work together in this unique area. These collaborations will be able to draw on a wide range of disciplines, expertise and equipment.

Prepare Joint Nominations of Border Parks Meriting Inclusion on the World Heritage List. Currently only two of the sixteen natural World Heritage properties found on international boundaries were jointly inscribed. The Belize barrier reef is already under consideration for inclusion on the World Heritage list and the possibility of including a transborder component to this application could be considered.

Conclusion

The concept of transboundary co-operation is not new to Belize. The 'Mundo Maya' (or 'La Ruta Maya') concept unites Belize, Mexico,

Guatemala, Honduras and El Salvador in a joint effort to facilitate tourism relating to Mayan archaeology. Belize, Guatemala and Mexico are also working towards a 'Tri-National Park' system that would lead to a biosphere reserve encompassing the three adjacent protected areas of Blakmul (New Mexico), Maya Biosphere (Guatemala) and the Rio Bravo Conservation Area (Belize). Elsewhere, transboundary parks are often used to foster relationships between countries. In this case, the Bacalar Chico project is serving to unite the NGO community, NGOs with the Government of Belize, and departments within the Government of Belize. As the importance of managing resources by natural units is well understood (McNeil, 1990), it is ecologically desirable to encourage co-operation at the inter-Government level and establish Bacalar Chico as the first transboundary reserve, with a marine component, in Belize.

Acknowledgements

The authors wish to acknowledge Programme for Belize for its help in supplying background information for this paper. Coral Cay Conservation would also like to acknowledge the support of the Belize Centre for Environmental Studies, the Coastal Zone Management Unit, the EC DGVIII and the British Government's Darwin Initiative. Sue Wells is also thanked for her editorial comments.

Bibliography

Gray, D.A., Mumby, P.J., Gibson, J., and Raines, P.S. (forthcoming) *Geographic Information Systems: A Tool for Integrated Coastal Zone Management in Belize*.
IUCN (1990) 'Promoting effective management of transfrontier parks and reserves guidelines', in J.W. Thorsell (ed.) *Parks on the Borderline: Experience in Transfrontier Conservation*, Cambridge: IUCN.
McNeil, R.J. (1990) 'International parks for peace', in J.W. Thorsell (ed.) *Parks on the Borderline: Experience in Transfrontier Conservation*, Cambridge: IUCN.
Perkins, J.S. (1983) *The Belize Barrier Reef Ecosystem: An Assessment of its Resources, Conservation Status and Management*, New York: New York Zoological Society.

22

La Ruta Maya:
A Transfrontier Ecocultural Tourism Circuit
in the Yucatan Region

Héctor Ceballos-Lascuráin

Introduction

Ecocultural tourism has demonstrated in many developing countries that it constitutes an important instrument for socio-economic development as well as for conservation of natural and cultural heritage. Its proven potential to attract foreign exchange to Third World countries should make this type of tourism a top priority in areas where severe economic difficulties necessitate the search for imaginative and practical solutions. It can also contribute to raising the ecological awareness and environmental education of local and national populations.

Based on these considerations, the governments of Mexico, Guatemala, Belize and Honduras, in collaboration with international institutions concerned with the conservation of the world's natural and cultural heritage, are taking the first steps to constitute a multinational ecocultural tourism circuit known as La Ruta Maya (Figure 22.1). This project has great potential for stimulating socio-economic development and the preservation of the natural and cultural wealth of the Maya region, a unique area which is presently facing destruction of its natural environment, sacking of its archaeological heritage, and loss of cultural identity. Enlightened, environmentally sound and creative management of the Maya region will provide a model for multinational co-operation in utilising local assets to solve political, economic, and environmental problems.

Background

The idea of establishing a multinational tourism circuit in the Maya region goes back as far as the 1960s, when the Organisation of American States (OAS) and the International Development Bank (IDB) showed interest in developing and funding a project with these characteristics. However, at that time, Mexico (the country with the

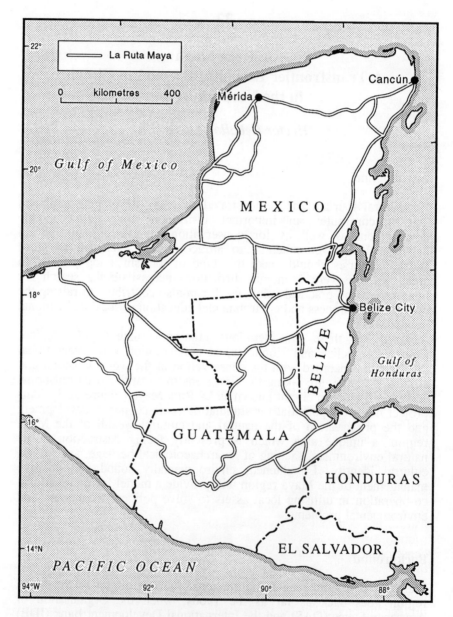

Figure 22.1 La Ruta Maya

most developed tourist industry of the Maya region) opted to develop along the lines of the more traditional commercial tourism resort approach. Thus, Cancún and other beach resorts were born, receiving an enormous financial boost and international promotion, which has undoubtedly brought a considerable amount of foreign exchange to Mexico, but also serious ecological damage and imbalances to the socio-economic structure due to the explosive and uncontrolled growth of these tourism poles.

A more encouraging development took place in 1976 when the Mexican Ministry of Public Works expressed interest in assessing the ecological and cultural attractions of some of the national parks and other protected areas (including archaeological sites) of the Maya area, and commissioned a preliminary inspection of the area for that purpose. Unfortunately, due to the end of a presidential term, no continuity was given to the project.

In 1987, Wilbur E. Garrett, editor of *National Geographic,* presented the preliminary proposal for developing a four-nation tourism circuit also called La Ruta Maya, which has created great interest among the governments of the countries involved and the international conservation community.

Recently the European Community offered important funding to the four countries of the Maya region to develop a joint five-year European marketing/promotion action programme for an ambitious tourism project also named La Ruta Maya.

The Concept of Ecotourism

Ecological tourism, or ecotourism, is a relatively recent phenomenon. We may define ecotourism as tourism that consists of travelling to relatively undisturbed or uncontaminated natural areas with the specific purpose of studying, admiring, and enjoying the scenery and its wild plants and animals, as well as any existing cultural manifestations (both past and present) found in these areas. In these terms, ecotourism implies a scientific, aesthetic, or philosophical approach, although the ecological tourist need not be a professional scientist, artist, or philosopher. The main point here is that the person who practises ecotourism has the opportunity of immersing him or herself in the natural environment in a way that most people cannot enjoy in their routine, urban existence. That person will eventually acquire a consciousness and knowledge of the natural environment, together with the cultural one, that will convert him or her into somebody keenly involved in conservation issues (Ceballos-Lascuráin, 1987).

Nature travel to the tropics fits in well with world-wide initiatives to protect biological diversity and find nonconsumptive uses of wildlife and other natural resources that generate economic returns. Ecotourism in Third World countries would bring many advantages. It would stimulate greater awareness of the conservation of the natural and cultural environment and aid in preventing further deterioration, destruction, and pollution. It also implies the rational use of high potential tourist resources in areas with few options for other modes of development, generating new work opportunities and fostering an economic spillover to local populations.

It is important to recognise the potential of ecotourism for generating foreign exchange. Several countries have discovered this and their governments have encouraged this type of tourism over the last few years. In Kenya, for instance, the tourist industry (mainly ecological in character) is the largest single earner of foreign currency. In 1992 earnings from tourism totalled US$480 million, of which a third was provided by seven national parks. In Costa Rica, the tourist trade (also predominantly nature-oriented) ranks second, after coffee growing, as a source of foreign exchange. The variety and close proximity of natural habitats protected by Costa Rica's national park system have made that country extremely popular for nature tourism groups. In the Khumbu area of Nepal (which includes Sagarmatha (Mt Everest) National Park) tourism, the principal source of cash income, accounts for 90% of the region's income (Bjonnes, 1980).

The Maya region is one of many areas around the world offering a combination of attractive natural features and magnificent archaeological remains, creating a double appeal to the visitor. Each year more and more people in industrialised countries are developing more profound interest in nature and 'exotic' cultures, and travel abroad in search of experiences not found in their own countries. The World Tourist Organisation (WTO, 1993) estimates that in 1992 there were 450 million foreign tourist trips worldwide. Preliminary estimates are that around 10% were nature-motivated.

Needless to say, strict regulation must exist in order to avoid negative environmental impact due to tourist activity. An important aspect to be considered in the physical planning is the need for a new approach in architectural design and building technology. Almost by definition ecotourism occurs in areas which are relatively isolated and characterised by a fragile and delicate ecological balance, and it is important that all building facilities, roads, and services provided must be designed in such a way that environmental impact is minimised and that a certain level of functional self-sufficiency is attained. The use of what may be loosely termed as 'ecotechniques' in the physical planning and construction of facilities must be encouraged. These ecotechniques include the use of solar energy, capture and utilisation of rainwater, recycling of waste material, natural cross ventilation (instead of air conditioning), a high level of self-sufficiency in food generation (through orchards, 'ecological farms', aquaculture, etc), the use of locally available building materials and native technology, and the blending of the architectural shapes with the natural environment. Accommodation for nature tourists should be modest but comfortable, clean but unpretentious. This gives an added advantage to ecotourism over conventional leisure tourism, the cost of an ecological tourism centre being about four times lower per room unit than a four-star hotel (although, in spite of this, many ecotourists are willing to pay room rates comparable to those of luxury hotels). The experience that an ecotourist seeks when he comes to a natural and exotic place is the opportunity of communion with nature and native cultures, of getting away from the concrete jungle and the commodities of modern urban life (Ceballos-Lascuráin, 1984).

The Natural Heritage of the Maya Region

Projecting northward into the Gulf of Mexico like a giant thumb, between North and South America, lies the Yucatán Peninsula, which comprises the Mexican states of Yucatán, Campeche, and Quintana Roo. This area includes a major portion of the land of the Maya, which stretches south to also include the eastern parts of the Mexican states of Tabasco and Chiapas, the entire countries of Guatemala and Belize, and the north-western corner of Honduras. Towering mountains of volcanic origin (Mount Tajumulco, at 4,210m is the highest) lie along the Pacific slopes. The soil is cultivated from sea level to about 3,000m. This whole area is characterised by deep valleys and pine- fringed mountains. The western slopes are generally dry but to the east the climate is much wetter. It was in this highland zone that the Maya found volcanic stone to make the *metate* for braying corn; they also found obsidian (volcanic glass) used in mirrors, knives, and razors, and from the streams came jade, as important to the Maya as life itself. In the high cloud forests are the famed resplendent quetzal birds that yielded the jade green tail feathers which decked the headgear and cloaks of the chieftains, and the endemic horned guan, the size of a small turkey, with a remarkable red knob stemming from its head.

In the lowland areas is El Petén, where rainforests alternate with seasonal swamps called *skalches* or *aguadas*, and high bush with alternating savannahs of tall grass. These jungles which constitute the western hemisphere's northernmost rainforests (which are severely threatened), are rich in wildlife. The avifauna is truly astonishing: more than 750 species of birds are found here (greater than the combined total of the USA and Canada), including the endemic ocellated turkey, the extremely rare Harpy eagle, the endangered scarlet macaw, the great curassow, several species of quail, parrots, woodpeckers, and many songbirds. Many endangered animals like the jaguar, the tapir, the howler monkey, and the crocodile are still to be found here, as well as a multitude of tropical butterflies, many of them endemic and very rare. The rainforest includes giant cedars which were fashioned by the Maya into outsized canoes 25m long for navigation on the Caribbean, mahogany, *Lignum vitae,* the zapotillo or chewing gum tree which yields a fine tasting fruit as well as the chicle sap, the brazilwood which was used for dyeing Maya cloth, and many more.

The tropical jungles graduate into the 'thumb' proper. In Yucatán, the northern part of the peninsula is characterised by a zone of low, flat limestone. Unlike the land further south, lakes and streams are scarce. The only available drinking water is provided by the *cenotes,* which are circular sink holes, some of great size, formed by the collapse of underground caves, perennially filled with water percolating through the limestone. These natural wells necessarily have served as the focal points for native settlements since the first occupation of the land. The lowland climate is hot, uncomfortably so towards the close of the dry season. The rains usually come in May and last until October.

The coastal areas include extensive wetlands and marshes, abounding in waterbirds, both resident and migratory. The Caribbean coast, with fine white sand and waters characterised by amazing hues of blue and turquoise, also contain the second largest coral barrier reef in the world, which hosts a myriad brightly coloured tropical fish. These waters are considered among the best in the world for snorkelling.

All in all, the Maya region constitutes the area of greatest biodiversity in Middle America but its continuing destruction by uncontrolled human settlements, land clearance for cattle grazing, and logging, is cause for deep concern among conservationists.

The Cultural Heritage of the Maya Region

The Mayas possess one of the greatest civilisations of the western hemisphere. Their culture dates back to at least 600 BC. During a long formative period, the Mayan farmers made simple pottery and built low platforms for their temples and houses. Between 300 and 900 AD (the Classic Period) priests developed an amazing knowledge of astronomy and calendrics, mathematics (including the concept of zero), and the utilisation of hieroglyphics. They supervised the building of great religious centres, where the arts flourished. Architectural achievements were extraordinary, in particular the use of the corbelled vault their great stone temples and palaces. For reasons not totally explained, Maya civilisation in the south disintegrated around 900 AD. In northern Yucatán it merged with post-classic Mexican culture only a century before the Spanish arrived.

The Maya territory is divided into three major areas: the highlands bordering the Pacific slope; the central lowlands stretching along the Usumacinta River basin through the Petén to Honduras; and the northern lowlands, including the whole of the Yucatán Peninsula. The rulers of the Maya city states were autonomous, but they did enjoy intercommunication and co-operation across a vast territory which totalled about 325,000km².

The number of Mayan archaeological ruins remaining today is remarkable. In the Mexican state of Yucatán alone, 1,117 sites have been officially recorded by the National Institute of Anthropology and History (INAH, 1980). Throughout the Maya area, many archaeological sites remain unexplored and even unknown to this day, hidden under the lush vegetation.

Only a minority of these sites are presently accessible to the average traveller. In the highlands the best known of these are Zacaleu, Mixco Viejo, Utatlán, Iximché, and Kaminaljuyú, all in Guatemala. In the central lowlands, the most important sites are (in Mexico) Palenque, Yaxchilán, Bonampak, Comalcalco, Chincultic, and Toniná; (in Guatemala) Tikal, Uaxactún, Quiriguá, Yaxhá, Seibal, Dos Pilas, El Mirador, and Río Azul; (in Belize) Altun Ha, Xunantunich, and Caracol; and (in Honduras) Copán. In the northern lowlands the best known sites are Uxmal, Chichén, Itzá, Cobá, Tulum, Sayil, Labná, Xlapak, Kabah, Edzná, Dzibilchaltún, Becán, Chicanná, Xpuhil, Río Bec, Calakmul, and Kohunlich (Kelly, 1982).

The degree and quality of communications, transport, and tourism infrastructure varies considerably across the Maya region. A few limited areas, especially in the northern part of the Yucatán Peninsula, area easily visited by national and international travellers, but most of the region lacks adequate facilities and services, and there has been little promotion of its unique cultural and natural assets. Charming highland and lowland villages, still inhabited by a predominantly Mayan population, are to be found throughout the area. Here Indian folklore lives on and there is a flourishing handicrafts industry. Finally, there are marvellous examples of Spanish colonial architecture in different localities of this region, both religious and civil, adding yet another attraction for the visitor.

Description of the Ruta Maya Project

Initial support for a multinational ecocultural tourism circuit in the Maya region has been given by International Union for the Conservation of Nature-US, the Wild Wings and Underhill Foundations, *National Geographic,* and the Mexican Secretariat of Tourism. The proposed project, due to its complexity, interdisciplinary nature, and multinational characteristics, should have a duration of at least four years. Four phases have been outlined for the project:

PHASE I: PRELIMINARY STUDIES (first year)

Collection and Processing of Relevant Information

1 Identification and classification of an inventory of ecocultural tourism attractions of La Ruta Maya.
2 Survey of the present supply of tourism services.
3 Survey of the demand for ecocultural tourism services.
4 Survey of the supply of ecocultural tourism services in other tropical countries.
5 Information on local legislation, government participation and promotion, involvement of NGOs and local populations.
6 Definition of itineraries and interpretative programmes.

Preparation of a Regional Plan

1 Zoning and integration of protected areas in regional land use programmes.
2 Ecological guidelines.
3 Identification of different tourism routes.
4 Communications and transportation.
5 Localisation of main ecocultural tourism attractions.
6 Localisation of existing tourism facilities.
7 Site plans and design guidelines for physical facilities.

Setting up of a Management Plan for La Ruta Maya

1 Guidelines for agreements, mechanisms, and actions (intersectoral and international).
2 Realisation of a master management plan and local management plans.

Design of National and International Promotion Campaigns

1 Design awareness campaign in the four countries involved.
2 Design of international promotion campaign.

PHASE II: ESTABLISHMENT OF NATIONAL AND MULTINATIONAL AGREEMENTS AND STRATEGIES IN PREPARATION FOR INFRASTRUCTURAL AND OPERATIONAL PHASES (second year)

1 Discussion and approval of Phase I documents by authorities of the four countries involved.
2 Signed agreement between the heads of state of the four countries involved, in which the participation of government agencies is

clearly defined (Ministries of Tourism, Environment, Public Works and Communications, Education, Agriculture, etc).

3 Co-operation agreements with international development agencies and NGOs (International Development Bank, World Bank, Organisation of American States, MAB-Unesco, United Nations Environmental Programme, European Union, US-AID, World Wildlife Fund, International Union for the Conservation of Nature, etc) in order to initiate the following two phases.

4 Establishment of contacts with private groups (travel and tourism agencies, hotel entrepreneurs, architectural designers, building contractors, local communities, universities, national and local NGOs in the fields of natural and cultural heritage conservation, etc).

5 Formulation of marketing, publicity, and advertising strategies.

6 Shortlist of immediate management plans in protected areas.

PHASE III: SITE PLANNING (third year)

1 Planning basic physical infrastructure for La Ruta Maya: highways, roads, trails, petrol stations, airports, landing fields, docks, facilities for visitors in national parks and other protected areas.

2 Contracting, financing, and involvement of private entrepreneurs in the building of hotels, restaurants, and other facilities for ecocultural tourists, with local government supervision.

3 Setting up of management offices (both government and private) for administering the operational phase of La Ruta Maya.

PHASE IV: INITIATION OF OPERATIONAL ACTIVITIES (fourth year)

1 Marketing, publicity, and advertising campaigns.

2 Active involvement of all participating parties in operational activities: government agencies, travel agencies, hotel and restaurant operators, local communities, conservation agencies, local communities and NGOs.

3 Inauguration and operation of initial facilities: communications, transportation, hotels, restaurants, etc.

4 Preliminary evaluation of these operational activities.

The preparation of a physical master plan will consider the following issues:

Roads
The new roads that would be required by La Ruta Maya should have a low impact on the environment. They should be made as narrow as possible (7m wide at the most), either paved with asphalt or improved all-weather gravel with an established maximum speed of 80km/hour

and a specified load limit. They should be exclusively for ecocultural tourists (not mass tourism) and closed to heavy commercial traffic (including big buses, freight, and lumber trucks). It is suggested that in some cases these ecocultural tourism roads run parallel to existing heavy traffic highways (bypassing the bigger settlements), since existing highways are increasingly becoming characterised by heavy traffic and a degraded landscape with roadside deforestation, litter, a proliferation of buildings – many with a slum appearance – and even traffic jams in some of the bigger towns. This way the tourist would have a more interesting experience and be more in contact with the natural environment as he or she travels. Roadside development would be kept to an absolute minimum.

Transportation
Traditional big tourist buses with air conditioning and onboard toilet facilities already service many of the main highways of portions of the Maya region but they would be inappropriate for use on the ecocultural tourism roads used to connect the more isolated natural areas and archaeological sites. Instead, it is suggested that traffic be restricted to minibus or van-type vehicles, a policy which has the additional advantage of discouraging mass tourism. A shuttle-type circuit service with established schedules is also a possibility (with a Eurail-type ticket made available). Private cars and campers would also be encouraged and proper facilities for servicing them made available.

Hotels, Dining
At present there are many localities in the Maya region which do not have adequate hotel and dining facilities. In the protected areas, needless to say, strict regulations must exist in order to minimise negative environmental impact due to tourist activity. As was mentioned earlier, a new architectural and building technology approach is needed, in order to minimise environmental impact and provide a certain level of functional self-sufficiency.

Parks
In the Maya region there are presently several national parks and other protected areas (including archaeological sites). Unfortunately, in many cases the 'protected status' is more theoretical than practical and many areas are undergoing an alarming process of deterioration which must be stopped. The promotion of transfrontier ecocultural tourism through a project like La Ruta Maya is one such means of doing so.

Conclusion

Many problems will be encountered in the development of La Ruta Maya: poor international relations (especially between Guatemala and Belize), political unrest and even guerrilla warfare, problems with land tenure and invasion in protected areas, intense logging and other deforestation activities, opposition from influential local leaders, diverse practices of law-breaking and corruption, and increasing narcotics traffic to name but a few.

But there are also grounds for optimism: the awareness of all four countries involved regarding the importance of conserving the rich heritage of the area; the recognition that ecocultural tourism may contribute in attaining that goal; the importance that the tourist trade in general has attained in many parts of the Maya area, creating a strong touristic tradition and infrastructure; the consciousness acquired (especially in recent years) by many local groups and communities that the preservation of the cultural and natural heritage is both a matter of pride and a motor for socio-economic development as well as a means of improving the quality of the environment; and the great initial interest that many international development agencies and conservation organisations have shown in environmental projects in developing countries in general, and in the Maya areas in particular.

Bibliography

Bjonnes, I.M. (1980) 'Ecological conflicts and economic dependency on tourist trekking in Sagarmatha (Mount Everest) National Park, Nepal: an alternative approach to park planning', *Norsk Geografisk Tidsskrift* 34: 119–38.

Ceballos-Lascuráin, H. (1984) 'Ecotechniques applied to urban development and housing: SEDUE's ECODUVI Project', in *Proceedings of the International Conference on Passive and Low Energy Ecotechniques,* Mexico City, 6–11 August, Mexico: Pergamon Press.

Ceballos-Lascuráin, H. (1987) 'Ecological and cultural tourism in Mexico as a means of conservation and socio-economic development', in *Proceedings of the International Forum Conservation of the Americas,* Indianapolis, 18–20 November, Washington DC: Partners for Livable Places.

Garrett, W.E. (1988) *La Ruta Maya: A Proposal,* Washington DC: National Geographic Society.

INAH (1980) *Atlas Arqueológico del Estado de Yucatán,* Mexico: Instituto Nacional de Antropologia e Historia.

Kelly, J. (1982) *The Complete Visitor's Guide to Mesoamerican Ruins,* Norman, Oklahoma: University of Oklahoma Press.

MacKinnon, J., MacKinnon, K., Child, G. and Thorsell, J. (1986) *Managing Protected Areas in the Tropics,* Gland, Switzerland and Cambridge: IUCN.

WTO (1992) *World Tourism Statistics,* Madrid: World Tourist Organisation.

tение and conservation, protected areas, timber logging, and other
non-subsistence activities, opposition from influential local factors
degree revenues of investment log and corruption, and the casino
reacting on the tolerance of the law.

But there are also grounds for optimism. Awareness of all four
countries involved regarding the importance of conserving the rich
heritage of the past, the recognition that ecotourism cannot may
contribute to sustaining that and the importance that the tourist trade in
general has pushed to many parts of the Maya area, creating a strong
cultural tradition and infrastructure that conservation, turned
especially in recent years, for many local groups and communities, the
the preservation of the cultural and natural heritage is both a matter of
pride and a motive for socio-economic development as well as an issue
of improving the quality of the environment, and the great many
active international non-governmental agencies and community-based
organisation has assisted in environmental projects in developing
countries in general, and in the Maya area in particular.

Bibliography

Boniface, J.M. (1965). Ecological conflicts and economic development
on tourism in Manu Biosphere. Journal of Tourism (eds) National Park.
Anon (n.d.). an alternative approach to area planning. *Town Country*
Planning 59(1) 10-30.

Gaballa, J.Lawrence, R. (1994). Three ways to market an urban
development and housing. SEDUE's ECODUL Project, the
appropriateness of the informal cooperation on tourism aspects in
developing countries. Mexico. Chetumal, Quintana Roo, Mexico.
Permanent Press.

Campbell, Lincoln, E. (1993). Ecotourism: the central tension in
Mexico because or limits of conservation and preservation in
development. Paper presented at the International Tourism
Environments the Interface, Minneapolis, 18-20 November
Massachusetts MA. Harvard, Tropical Forest.

Garrett, Wilburn, (1989). La Ruta Maya. National Geographic, Washington, DC
National Geographic Society.

INAH (1988). *Zona Arqueológica, Estado de Estudio de Yucatan, Mexico.*
Instituto Nacional de Antropología e Historia.

Kelly, J. (1982). *The Maya from Idea*, a guide to ruins, *Mexican Antiquity*.
Norman, Oklahoma: University of Oklahoma Press.

Munro-Clark, Rosa M., Johnson, R., Child, G., and Thorsell, J. (1986).
Managing Protected Areas in the Tropics. Gland, Switzerland and
Cambridge: IUCN.

WTO (1992). *World Tourism Statistics.* Madrid, World Tourist
Organisation.

23

Environmental Jurisdiction on the High Seas:
The Special Case of the Arctic Ocean

William V. Dunlap

Economic development and global warming are indirectly posing new threats to the health and viability of the Arctic Ocean, threats that the current legal regime is ill-equipped to counter. This, therefore, is a proposal for a new legal regime for the environmental protection of the Arctic Ocean. The proposed regime is purely functional – directed solely at the prevention of vessel-source pollution. It is based on a recognition of the ecological and geographical unity of the Arctic seas and of some significant differences between them and the waters of the world oceans to the south. This paper presents the outline of an argument that such a regime is both desirable and feasible.

Introduction

Even if the present legal regime for the world's oceans is sufficient to protect them against serious injury from vessel-source pollution (I am inclined to think that it is not, but that is an issue not addressed by this paper), the Arctic Ocean is much more sensitive and considerably more vulnerable to pollution damage than are the others. The international community has recognised this, by granting to coastal states the right to prescribe and enforce maritime laws and regulations for the prevention of vessel-source pollution in ice-covered areas of the exclusive economic zone (EEZ). This was achieved in Article 234 of the 1982 United Nations Law of the Sea Convention (LOSC, 1982: Article 234), which is due to come into effect in November of this year.[1]

As the exclusive economic zone can extend as far as 200 nautical miles offshore, the authority granted by Article 234 appears to be generally regarded as sufficient to permit coastal states to protect their own environmental interests. In other parts of the world, this may very well be true, as the biodegrading properties and the sheer volume of the world oceans tend to digest and dilute oil spills on the high seas before they can inflict serious damage upon coastal and estuarine environments (Karrick, 1977: 225–6; ZoBell, 1969: 317). The Arctic

Ocean, however, differs in several important respects from the world's other oceans in ways that render the 200-mile buffer inadequate and, over the very long haul, perhaps almost meaningless.

First, the Arctic is a mediterranean ocean, enclosed by land along much of its circumference (Figure 23.1). It is not so enclosed as the Mediterranean Sea, but its exchange of water with the Atlantic and Pacific is greatly restricted by the high submarine ridges across the connecting straits, reducing its ability to dilute pollution and cleanse itself through ordinary processes (Rey, 1982: 31–8; Sugden, 1982: 154; Foster, 1978: 122).

Second, the water is very cold, the temperature of the surface layer ranging between 3°C and −1.8°C (Treshnikov, 1977). At these temperatures, oil tends to congeal, making it more difficult to disperse (Karrick, 1977: 227),[2] and the biological processes that can be relied upon to combat spilled oil naturally in other oceans are either absent or greatly retarded (Puskas *et al,* 1987: 510; Atlas, 1986: 63; Clark and MacLeod, 1977: 134; Karrick, 1977: 286).

The third difference is ice: more than 80% of the surface of the Arctic Ocean and its coastal waters is permanently covered by ice, and the rest is ice-covered for several months every year (CARC, 1984: 5).[3] Furthermore, the lower reaches of the Arctic Ocean and its adjacent seas fester with large and small segments of another kind of ice in the form of icebergs (Petersen, 1977: 326–8). The presence of ice has two very general effects: not only does it increase the risk that an accident will occur through collision, but the permanent ice cover tends, in a variety of ways, to magnify the effects of the pollution: by retarding the natural degradation processes (Payne *et al,* 1992: 639, 659), by making it more difficult to clean up an oil spill, and by helping to shape an ecosystem that is more sensitive to outside interference and thus susceptible to greater damage.[4]

Ice complicates the cleanup procedure by trapping and hiding the oil. The underside of sea ice is extremely rough; oil that gets underneath stays there and is difficult to locate and recover (Hibler, 1989: 55–8). The thicker the ice, the more difficult it becomes to clean up the spilled oil (Sydnes, 1992: 613). In addition, oil spilled on top of ice reduces its albedo and hastens the melting process, and the resulting exposure of the underlying sea water to sunlight tends to prevent refreezing (Sydnes, 1992: 613; Clark and MacLeod, 1977: 142–3; Ramseier, 1974: 7).

The ice tends to create a more sensitive ecology in a number of ways. It reduces the photosynthetic potential of the water by blocking the penetration of light into the sea. It also dilutes the surface layer by leaching out salt, which sinks. When the ice melts in the spring, it creates a stable surface of lighter, less saline water, which discourages upwelling or vertical exchange of water, which in turn keeps supplies of nutrients such as phosphates, nitrates, and silicates low (Dunbar, 1985: 10). Nevertheless, an intense growth of plant cells, mainly

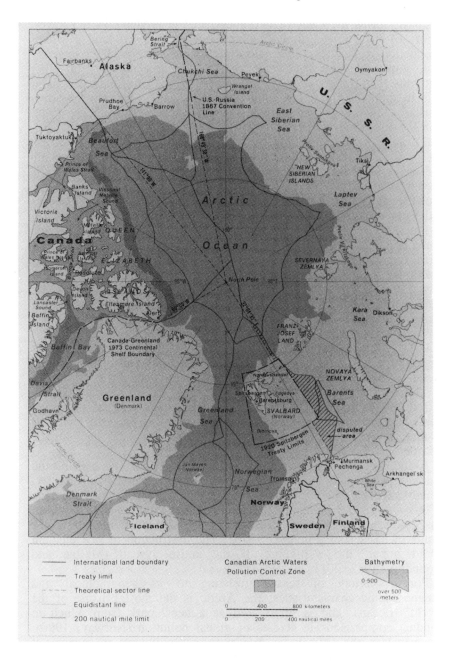

Figure 23.1

Source: Central Intelligence Agency (1978) *Polar Regions Atlas*

diatoms, forms the basis of two specialised ecosystems in the lowest layers of the ice – a summer production in floe ice, and a winter production in fast ice. These flora are adapted to low light intensity and, partly because the water column contains far less of other nutrients than the water in the other oceans, the flora play the major role in supporting a complex but specialised fauna, including worms, crustacea, fish, birds and mammals (Dunbar, 1985: 12; Sugden, 1982: 145–7), for which the ice then provides a platform for feeding, rest, and transportation (Alexander and Niebauer, 1990: 206; Petersen, 1977: 327). Damage to these diatoms by the accretion of oil beneath the ice could severely impair the primary production of the Arctic Ocean and, because of the key role that the polar seas play in the global ecological system, the primary production of the world oceans (Alexander and Niebauer, 1990: 206).

Finally, there is the movement of the ice. The interminable drift and the consequent deformation of the ice are among the Arctic ice cover's most dominant features (Hibler, 1989: 47). The movement of the Arctic ice pack is characterised by two major patterns, the Transpolar Drift Stream, carrying ice from East Siberia west across the Arctic Basin south of the Pole, and by the Amerasian Gyre, a clockwise flow largely in the Beaufort Sea but affecting the movement of ice throughout the ocean (Hibler, 1989: 48–55; Clark and Finley, 1977: 460–1). There is no reason to suppose that oil spilled in the high seas region of the Arctic Ocean and retained by the ice will not eventually reach the EEZ and perhaps even the territorial waters of one or another of the coastal states. (The same is true of oil or other pollution introduced in the EEZ, territorial waters or even internal waters of coastal states; what any state does, or allows to be done, with its waters will eventually have a direct effect on its Arctic neighbours (Harders, 1987: 285).)

Arctic ecosystems are characterised by a low diversity of plant and animal species and by slow growth and low reproductive capacity, which suggests slow recovery from serious environmental damage (Clark and Finley, 1977: 462). Taken together, all these factors help to shape a delicately balanced ecosystem that survives 'literally at the limits of existence' (Sprague, 1973). The destruction of one element could impair the well-being of the entire system (McRae and Goundrey, 1982: 201).

For a variety of reasons relating to its geographical and oceanographic characteristics, the Arctic is the most pristine of the world's oceans, and is often used as a benchmark from which to conduct comparisons in studies of global pollution (Norway, 1990). Nevertheless, the water is far from pure, and pollutants are entering it daily, primarily from landbased sources but also from vessels and from airborne particles (Perkins, 1986).

Until now (and even now) the threat from vessels has not been terribly great. The presence of ice year-round in much of the ocean, and for a large part of the year in the remainder, discourages shipping, as well it should. Furthermore, the major Arctic coastal states, ie Canada and the Soviet Union (now Russia) have exercised fairly strict controls over navigation in the ice-covered regions off their coasts and have provided excellent and sophisticated auxiliary services, in the way of ice forecasting and spotting, weather forecasting, ice-breaking, and pilotage (Frolov, 1991: 44; Walker, 1992: 163–4; Hamnes, 1993: 52).

Now, however, a number of concurrent but not necessarily related developments are increasing the likelihood that commercial navigation, particularly by oil tankers, will increase substantially over the next few decades, thus greatly increasing the risk of incidents that could seriously, perhaps catastrophically, damage the health of the Arctic environment. Among these are: the introduction of large and powerful icebreakers, capable of operating anytime and anywhere in the polar sea, alone or leading a convoy of tankers (Pullen, 1984; Brigham, 1985: 133; Walker, 1992: 163; Frankel, 1988: 109, 111–3); plans for the development of submarine oil tankers that could navigate under the polar ice cap (CARC, 1984: 131–2; Pullen, 1984: 131; Frankel, 1988: 110–1); the decision of the Soviet Union (apparently endorsed and encouraged by the new Russian government), to open the Northern Sea Route (the shipping lanes along Russia's Asian Arctic coast between the White Sea and Vladivostok) to international commercial shipping (Brigham, 1993; Armstrong, 1993; Østreng, 1991, 1992; Dunlap, 1991);[5] and efforts by the petroleum industry to open the Northwest Passage to the shipment of oil from the Beaufort Sea to the Atlantic coast (Lamson and Vanderzwaag, 1988: 3–4; Stuart and Lamson, 1988: 130; McRae and Goundrey, 1982: 199–200). Behind all of these, to one extent or another, lies the ongoing exploration for and exploitation of hydrocarbon resources in Arctic waters off the Alaskan, Canadian, Norwegian, and Russian coasts (Caron, 1993: 381). Finally, there is the possibility that global warming will reduce or weaken the polar ice cap sufficiently to allow not only longer shipping seasons in the straits and coastal shipping lanes but also routine navigation across the Arctic Basin, providing significantly shorter routes between North Atlantic and North Pacific ports (Wadhams, 1992: 28; Jansson, 1990). There has already been a substantial increase in the Arctic tourist trade, including voyages through the North-east Passage and even to the North Pole in Russian nuclear icebreakers that have been converted to cruise ships.[6]

With an increase in navigation, an increase in accidents is inevitable. In the century before the Titanic was sunk by an iceberg, 19 collisions with ice were reported. In the 80 years afterwards, there were 37 reports. Both records are probably incomplete (Parnell, 1992). As most of these incidents are attributable to human error in the form of misjudgements in respect to ice, even the availability of large icebreakers and sophisticated warning systems does not guarantee safety. During the freezeup of October 1983, for example, more than

50 vessels were trapped in ice in the East Siberian and Chukchi Seas, and one sank (Schmemann, 1983; Armstrong, 1984).

National laws and regulations have been put in place to prevent inadequately ice-strengthened vessels and unqualified masters from operating in the ice-infested areas and to proscribe certain activities, such as dumping of oil, in areas under national jurisdiction (eg AWPPA 1970; ASPPR 1972; NSR 1990). Under international law, these rules do not apply to ships outside national jurisdiction, and ships that have left national jurisdiction are not subject to coastal state jurisdiction for infractions committed while within the national jurisdiction (LOSC 1982: Article 92(1)).[7] It is a cardinal rule of international law that ships on the high seas, and for most purposes the exclusive economic zone (LOSC 1982: Article 58(1),(2)), are subject only to the jurisdiction of their own flag state,[8] with certain narrow exceptions involving piracy (LOSC Articles 100–7 and 110(1)(a)), slave trading (LOSC Articles 99 and 110(1)(b)) and illegal broadcasting (LOSC Articles 109 and 110(1)(c)).

Given this peculiar sensitivity and vulnerability of the Arctic Ocean, already recognised by the international community in Article 234, and in light of political and technological developments that are leading, probably inexorably, to a marked increase in Arctic shipping, the thesis of this paper is that someone – preferably the international community or a broad consortium of Arctic states and states with Arctic interests – needs to establish rules for the use of the Arctic Ocean and, just as important, be prepared to enforce them. If this seems a bit premature, given the rather tenuous nature of some of the developments just enumerated, the point is that it needs to be done before trans-Arctic shipping begins in earnest. The inspiration for much of today's international regulation of maritime pollution can be traced back to the *Torrey Canyon* disaster of 1967 (Sand, 1988: ix; Clark and Finley, 1977: 421–7). Would it not make more sense to look ahead – to a whole class of accidents that might yet be averted? This was the essence of Canada's position in the late 1960s[9] when it was preparing to extend its maritime jurisdiction into the high seas of the Arctic Ocean.[10] (Even in Canada, however, the effort never gained any real momentum until, three years after *Torrey Canyon*, the Liberian tanker *Arrow* dumped 20 tons of oil into Nova Scotia's Chedabucto Bay (Cowan, 1970; Clark and Finley, 1977: 432–7).)

The Proposal

The establishment of a legal jurisdiction over shipping on the high seas of the Arctic could at the very least permit the establishment and enforcement of substantive DCEM (design, construction, equipment, manning) regulations and rules of operation on the high seas of the Arctic. The precise content of the rules would, of course, be decided by whatever organisation or group of nations took upon itself the task of legislating for the Arctic Ocean. At a minimum, the rules ought to adopt the standards of Canada's Arctic Waters Pollution Prevention Act (AWPPA 1970) and the regulations (ASPPR 1972) promulgated pursuant to it. In addition, they might provide for the following: enforcement in the economic zone or elsewhere of violations that occurred on the high seas; enforcement in the high seas of rules violated in a zone of national jurisdiction; and even civil jurisdiction, in the courts of the Arctic coastal states, over allocation of liability for pollution incidents. As the substantive content of any new legal regime will depend to a great extent on the way in which the regime comes into being, it seems preferable to discuss the latter first.

THE CHOICE OF FORUM

The more inclusive the decision-making forum, the better, both for purposes of assuring international acceptance of this particular regime, and for the future of law-making, regime-formation and international co-operation in the Arctic region. While Canada is to be commended for going it alone with the Arctic Waters Act and leading the way to a new rule of international law, if the end can be achieved through negotiations within the international community that is the desirable course of action.

The most effective and most generally acceptable approach would be through a multilateral convention, probably drafted and opened for signature within the framework of the International Maritime Organisation (IMO), in which the world's maritime states would accede to regional or national enforcement in the Arctic high seas of standards laid down in the same convention or by a designated body, such as the IMO.

If the proposal were to be carried out on a regional basis, it would be far preferable if it were done at the invitation or under the auspices of a competent international organisation, such as the United Nations General Assembly or the IMO. Such prior international approval would avert much of the criticism and challenge that such an assertion of jurisdiction would inevitably face (eg Department of State, 1970b).

One possible analogy is the series of regional seas agreements initiated by the United Nations Food and Agricultural Organisation (FAO, 1974)[11] in the wake of the 1972 United Nations Conference on the Human Environment in Stockholm sponsored by the United Nations Environment Programme (UNEP).[12] These now cover the Mediterranean Sea (Barcelona Convention 1976), the Persian Gulf (Kuwait Convention 1978), the Gulf of Guinea (Abidjan Convention 1981), the South-east Pacific (Lima Convention 1981), the Red Sea (Jeddah Convention 1982), the Caribbean Sea (Cartagena Convention 1983), the Indian Ocean (Nairobi Convention 1985), and the South-west Pacific (Noumea Convention 1986). In addition, there are other regional conventions concerning the marine environments of the North Sea (Bonn Agreement 1983; Copenhagen Agreement 1971), the north-east Atlantic (Oslo Convention 1972) and the Baltic Sea (Helsinki Convention 1974), and an action plan and agreements are in preparation for the South Asian seas.

In a real sense, however, these offer no precedent or support at all. They are regional agreements to institute Action Plans, which entail environmental assessment, environmental management, legal agreements on co-operation and institutional and financial arrangements (Sand, 1988: 11; Abecassis and Jarashow, 1985: 128). None of them attempts to impose duties on non-signatories or to abridge the traditional maritime freedoms of the high seas.

The absence of an Arctic regional organisation is not a drawback. All the conventions of the Regional Seas Programme provided for regular conferences of the state parties to function as the policy-making authority. In most cases, the secretariat functions were assigned to pre-existing organisations, either an office of UNEP[13] or an intergovernmental organisation in the region.[14] The exception, the Kuwait Convention for the Persian/Arabian Gulf, established the Regional Organisation for the Protection of the Marine Environment, with permanent headquarters in Kuwait (Kuwait Convention 1978: Article XVI). A number of proposals have been made for the creation of an Arctic Regional Council or other intergovernmental structure (eg Brubaker, 1993: UNEP regional sea programme; Pharand, 1992: Arctic Regional Council; McRae, 1987: 128–32: Arctic shipping regime; Harders, 1987: marine regionalism; Nelson and Needham, 1985: UNEP regional sea programme) but nothing has yet come of them. Given the geographically based sovereignty and jurisdiction of the present international system, it is hardly surprising that the proposals envisage a council that promotes regional co-operation rather than one involved in the governance of the region.

If the formal impetus is to come from the Arctic region rather than from an international organisation, the participation ought to be as inclusive as possible. The international community is unlikely to accept a unilateral assertion of jurisdiction by a few states, no matter how large and powerful. Participation by the five Arctic coastal states – Canada, Greenland/Denmark,[15] Norway, Russia, and the United States – would probably not be sufficient to avoid the suspicion that the region's states were acting in their own interest at the expense of other states with Arctic interests. At the very least it should include the other three states with Arctic or near-Arctic territory – Sweden, Finland, and Iceland – and other states with significant Arctic interests, for example Japan and South Korea (Friedheim, 1988: 493). It would be difficult as a matter of international politics and diplomacy to succeed without at least their acquiescence, if not their participation. Ideally, perhaps, the process should include all interested states. Consider, for example, the

Antarctic Treaty System, which is open to any state but which offers significantly greater input into the decision-making process from those states 'conducting substantial scientific research there' (Antarctic Treaty 1959: Article 9(2)).

Despite the precedent of the Arctic Waters Act, through which Canada, ultimately successfully, asserted a limited maritime jurisdiction over waters then regarded as high seas, any undertaking by one or two states would be highly dubious. It is nevertheless possible that this will prove to be the only way of moving the process forward. For example, though Canada is often given credit (largely because of the delay in proclaiming the Arctic Waters Act) for a commitment to a multilateral approach, 'it was only after the government had acted unilaterally that extensive multilateral negotiations were pursued' (M'Gonigle and Zacher, 1977: 119–20; Franckx, 1993: 87–8).[16]

If, as the threat of trans-Arctic navigation grows nearer and more menacing, the international community and the Arctic region refuse to act, it may require one Arctic state to take upon itself the task of breaking the ice, so to speak. One must not forget, however, that Canada exerted a great deal of time and energy in seeking international acceptance of the Arctic Waters Act. Its ultimate success was in no small part due to the fact that the Third United Nations Conference on the Law of the Sea (UNCLOS III) was just beginning its decade of deliberations. This provided a ready-made forum at which Canada could present its position, garner support among coastal states, and negotiate with the maritime powers which were resisting attempts to increase coastal state jurisdiction (M'Gonigle and Zacher, 1977: 138–46). Without such a forum, it would be very difficult indeed to achieve any international consensus on an Arctic maritime jurisdiction.

Consider the criticism levelled at the United States Senate in 1988, when it proposed that the United States and the Soviet Union unilaterally declare a moratorium on fishing in the Donut Hole and enforce it against vessels of all nations (Senate, 1988; Canfield, 1993: 269–74). The Donut Hole is a high seas enclave in the Bering Sea, completely surrounded by the economic zones of the United States and Russia. A large stock of pollock straddles the three zones. While the United States and Russia were able to conduct management programmes within their respective zones, and even co-operatively, there were no controls over the taking of resources in the high seas, and the area was being persistently overfished, with serious repercussions not only for fishing in the two economic zones but for the future of pollock in the entire region. Even though many scientists thought that the fishing should be managed on a regional basis (eg Wespestad, 1993), including the high seas, the senators' proposed assertion of jurisdiction was described as inconsistent with international law (Burke, 1988: 288) and was criticised for proposing unilateral action prior to multilateral negotiations for an international fishery management regime (Freidheim, 1988: 505; Burke, 1988: 288).

Taking part of the senators' advice, the United States and Soviet governments invited the four other nations whose ships regularly fished for pollock in the Donut Hole – China, Japan, Poland, and South Korea – to enter into negotiations over a management scheme. The negotiations have only recently reached a successful conclusion (Associated Press, 1994).[17] By adopting a more inclusive solution, the United States and Russia achieved an internationally acceptable regime, agreeable to all concerned states, with relatively little difficulty.

Another factor to be considered by any state – or even a consortium of all the region's states – contemplating a unilateral assertion of jurisdiction, is the response of the International Court of Justice, should the issue ever come before it. When Canada enacted its Arctic Waters Act, it simultaneously amended its acceptance of the jurisdiction of the International Court of Justice to exclude disputes 'in respect of the prevention or control of pollution or contamination of the marine environment in marine areas adjacent to the coast of Canada' (Canadian Declaration, 1970). Under the circumstances, wherein Canada was attempting to develop international law through state practice, 'the government viewed it as counterproductive to subject itself to the judgment of the conservative World Court' (M'Gonigle and Zacher, 1977: 118–9).[18]

The Court can have great influence on the outcome of debates over whether a state practice constitutes a breach of international law or represents the cutting edge of a developing norm.[19] How the Court would deal with this would depend to some extent on the manner in which it was promulgated. An international convention is unlikely to be challenged before the Court. A broad-based regional initiative would face a much stronger chance of acceptance than would a unilateral assertion, especially in view of the strong emphasis that the international system in general (see United Nations Charter: Articles 33 and 52), and the law of the sea in particular (LOSC 1982: Article 197),[20] place on the regional solution of regional problems. Canada clearly knew what it was doing when it withdrew from the Court's jurisdiction after deciding to impose its maritime regulations unilaterally, but public opinion and international politics can impose a high cost on such tactics.

THE SCOPE OF THE PROPOSAL

The present state of international law falls short of satisfactorily protecting the Arctic Ocean from vessel source pollution in two ways. First, there are no adequate binding standards for navigation in the Arctic. Second, even if there were, they would not be enforceable on the high seas except by the flag state of the vessel concerned (LOSC

1982: ̄ Article 92(1)), and much of the problem with maritime oil pollution – operational as well as accidental – today can be traced to flag state permissiveness in enforcement of internationally binding standards (Abecassis and Jarashow, 1985: 98–9). Canada solved the first problem by promulgating its own binding standards and went a long way toward solving the second by unilaterally enforcing them on what at the time were regarded as the high seas. One of the assumptions underlying this proposal is that the states most likely to be adversely affected by the breach of shipping standards are likely to provide the most effective enforcement.[21]

The precise content of the rules is not important for this discussion and would be likely to change over time with the development of technology. A useful model, however, is the general approach adopted by Canada in the Arctic Waters Act and the Arctic Shipping Pollution Prevention Regulations, through which jurisdiction was to be exercised both preventively, by setting standards for navigation, and remedially, through a domestic liability and compensation scheme (M'Gonigle and Zacher, 1977; McRae and Goundrey, 1982; and McRae, 1987).

The act authorised the Governor-in-Council to 'prescribe as a shipping safety control zone an area of the Arctic waters' (AWPPA 1972: Section 11.(1); also see Figure 23.1) and to set construction, equipment and manning regulations for ships navigating in the zone (AWPPA 1972: Section 12.(1)(a)). Non-conforming ships could be prohibited from entering (AWPPA 1972: Section 12.(1)). For the high seas jurisdiction being proposed here, the delimitation and differentiation of zones is probably unnecessary. The relevant area is already defined by the intersection of the limits of national jurisdiction, and for the foreseeable future its ice conditions are equivalent to those of the most severe of Canada's 16 shipping safety control zones, from which all but the strongest vessels are banned in winter months, and certain classes of unstrengthened vessels throughout the year (ASPPR 1972: Section 16).

The Canadian act prohibits the deposit of waste in Arctic waters and subjects violators to fines of up to C$100,000 (Section 18.(1)).[22] Liability for pollution damage is absolute (no defences whatsoever, Section 7.(1)) and the legislation does not specify a limit of liability. By the time the regulations were issued in 1972, however, talks with members of the insurance industry had persuaded the Canadian government that unlimited liability was unworkable. Canada, as a coastal state with significant shipping, minerals and hydrocarbons interests, was unwilling to let the insurance industry effectively close down its Arctic shipping by withholding coverage (M'Gonigle and Zacher, 1977: 119–20; Smith, 1988: 205). The Arctic states may not have the same concerns regarding the use of the ice-covered high seas, and they may be willing to insist upon unlimited liability for clean-up costs and consequential damages.

While providing compensation to victims of marine pollution is a secondary objective of this proposal and of maritime-pollution law in general, it may, in the event, promote the primary goal of preventing pollution. Ship owners who know that they will be held liable for the costs of clean-up and of consequential damage can be expected to comply with rules against intentional discharge and to take greater care to avoid accidents that might result in accidental spillage (Churchill and Lowe, 1988: 264).[23]

Article 234 grants coastal states prescriptive and enforcement jurisdiction over navigation in ice-covered areas of the economic zone, but it does not address the issue of civil jurisdiction of courts to hear cases arising out of maritime damage claims and to apportion the liability (Abecassis and Jarashow, 1985: 94–8, 114). It leaves untouched the current law regarding the stoppage and arrest of ships for purposes of civil liability and the issues of personal, *in rem*, and subject matter jurisdiction when the forum state is not the flag state of the defendant vessel. These rules are now governed by a series of conventions – principally the 1952 Arrest Convention, the 1952 Collision Convention and the 1969 and 1984 Liability Conventions – and by disparate national rules which apply to the gaps in international law, which are many (Abecassis and Jarashow, 1985: 94–8). There has been some effort to co-ordinate national law on a regional basis. The 1968 Brussels Convention on Jurisdiction and Enforcement of Judgements (Brussels Convention 1968), for example, establishes a uniform system for the European Community, but there is no international uniformity.

The question then is: to what extent should this proposed plan for the Arctic high seas attempt to enhance the civil jurisdiction of the Arctic states concerning matters arising out of pollution incidents on the high seas? Inasmuch as the imposition of liability and the allocation of costs are secondary to the principal goal of preventing pollution, and because there is considerable pressure for the creation of a uniform world-wide set of rules, it might be regarded as prudent to restrict the scope of this proposal to regulatory jurisdiction, leaving questions of civil jurisdiction to the law as it now stands or as it will inevitably develop.

COMMENTARY

Although it abridges one of the fundamental principles of international law – that a ship on the high seas is generally subject only to the jurisdiction of its flag state (LOSC 1982: Article 92(1)) – this proposal is a relatively modest one. Having recognised an imminent threat to the Arctic environment, it identifies two ways in which international law falls short of protecting that environment from the particular threat in question, and then proposes modifying international law only to the extent necessary to eliminate most of the threat. First, it proposes the establishment of internationally binding standards governing navigation in the high Arctic. Second, it proposes making those rules enforceable on the high seas, but only in a very limited area of the rather remote Arctic Ocean enclave, which differs sufficiently from the world's other oceans to warrant this exceptional treatment.

This ought not to be viewed as an extension of national jurisdiction, another instance of the 'creeping jurisdiction' that made the development of the new law of the sea so unpalatable to many in the United States and other major maritime powers. However it may be established and administered, it envisages a regional or international jurisdiction, for the benefit of the entire region and, ultimately, of the entire world. It does not partition off or reserve resources to any state or consortium of states; rather, it is a strictly functional jurisdiction that goes no further than 'required to achieve the specific and vital purpose of environmental protection.' (Beesley, 1971: 7).[24]

Proposals for various political or legal Arctic regimes have been put forward over the past decade. Most of those concerned with legal regimes have not dealt with the high seas but with coastal waters. On the North American side are discussions of Canadian jurisdiction over the straits of the Canadian Arctic Archipelago (eg Pharand, 1988; McRae, 1987; Vanderzwaag and Pharand, 1983; Dellapenna, 1972; Head, 1962) or of the validity of the Arctic Waters Act and its 100-mile environmental zone (McRae, 1998; McRae and Goundrey, 1982). On the Eurasian side, the proposals are largely concerned with Soviet, and now Russian, jurisdiction over the Northern Sea Route and over the straits of the Northeast Passage and the Russian Arctic Archipelagos: Novaya Zemlya, Severnaya Zemlya, and Ostrova Novosibirsk (Kolodkin and Volosov, 1990; Vyshnepolski, 1952).

In recent years, Brubaker (1993), Friedheim (1988), Pharand (1992), McRae (1987), Nelson and Needham (1985) and Vanderzwaag *et al* (1987) have all proposed the creation of regional councils, new legal regimes, or new ways of approaching problem-solving and resource management in the Arctic. Many elements of their analyses of Arctic problems and solutions have helped shape this proposal. They all entail a broad new legal or political structure or a new attitude, none of which is likely to develop in the foreseeable future (although the Arctic Strategy (1991) and the Donut Hole Agreement (1994) are certainly hopeful signs). Those that could be effected as easily as this proposal, such as Pharand's proposal for the establishment an Arctic Regional Council (Pharand, 1992), do not contemplate assertions of maritime jurisdiction.

This proposal concerns only a small patch of ocean at least 200 miles from the nearest land and is directed at one very specific problem, vessel source pollution. Its underlying issue is narrow and mundane: who has the power to stop, board and detain vessels in the Arctic high-seas enclave for purposes of enforcing pollution regulations? The solution should be equally narrow and mundane. It is possible to achieve the goals set forth here within the current framework of international law and politics; the more the process resembles business as usual, the more likely it is that a new regime can be established before the Arctic becomes navigable and the first tankload of oil is spilled at the North Pole.

Theories of Sovereignty and Jurisdiction

Over the years, a variety of theories of Arctic sovereignty have been proposed that would justify unilateral or regional assertion of jurisdiction over navigation in the Arctic high seas. By and large, these have not gained international acceptance and appear to have no chance of doing so.

The 'sector theory' asserts the existence of national sovereignty over the area north of a state's territorial boundaries, establishing a series of pie-shaped wedges converging at the North Pole (Roth, 1990: 857; also see Figure 1).[25] To the extent that it is used to claim territory, the Sector Theory has little relevance to, or impact on, international law inasmuch as sovereignty over all known land in the Arctic has already been established on other grounds and, thanks to satellite technology, there is no reason to believe that there are any undiscovered islands in the region. The sector theory has also been put forward as a basis for claiming sovereignty over the sea, but never by a government – only by individual politicians and scholars (eg Machowski, 1992: 167; Vyshnepolski, 1952: 40).

As a justification for unilateral prescription and enforcement, the sector theory is not particularly useful. It would grant nearly half the high-seas segment of the Arctic to Russia, and divide the other half among Canada, the United States, Norway, and Greenland/Denmark, and perhaps even a little sliver for Britain. The difficulty is that the sectors create a series of boundaries across which offenders could escape and a variety of zones of national jurisdiction in which the substantive rules might well differ if, indeed, all the Arctic states chose to exercise jurisdiction in this manner. As a practical matter, the sector theory might work better as a legal foundation for the regional enforcement of regionally agreed standards, eliminating concerns about differing rules and routes of escape. Nevertheless, the sector theory has no generally recognised basis in international law, and this proposal is not meant to provide it with one.

Does the presence of a permanent ice covering on the Arctic Ocean affect its legal status and provide a basis for the exercise of coastal state jurisdiction over the high seas? Legal scholars have put forward theories advocating sovereignty claims over the ice adjacent to Arctic land territory (Breitfuss, 1928; Smedal, 1932: 41–5) but these have been widely rejected (McKitterick, 1939; Machowski, 1992; Dollot, 1949: 125; Auburn, 1982: 38; Balch, 1910: 256–66). The generally accepted view now is that the presence of a permanent ice cover – whether fast ice (ice attached directly or indirectly to the shore), or pack ice (floating ice detached from land) (Armstrong *et al*, 1973: 14, 31) – is largely irrelevant to the legal status of the sea beneath it. For purposes of this discussion of the Arctic high seas, the prevailing view is perfectly acceptable. For some other purposes, however, it may not be entirely satisfactory.[26]

Article 123 of the 1982 Law of the Sea Convention imposes a duty on states surrounding an enclosed or semi-enclosed sea to engage in regional co-operation to protect and preserve the marine environment. This is an appealing focus for environmentalists seeking to authorise, encourage or compel the Arctic states to establish a regional jurisdiction over the Arctic Ocean (Harders, 1987: 295). Nevertheless, even if the provision applies to the ocean and its coastal states, its language and the rights and duties to which it refers are so broad and vague as to be of little value in an effort to compel unwilling states to comply.

It is not at all clear that the provision does apply. Despite its mediterranean nature, the Arctic Ocean may not satisfy the legal definition of a semi-enclosed sea, which requires either that the sea be connected to another sea or the ocean by a narrow outlet, or that it consist entirely or primarily of the territorial seas and exclusive economic zones of two or more coastal states (LOSC 1982: Article 122). The second element is clearly not met, as the high seas segment takes up nearly half the area of the ocean.[27] There is some disagreement over the first, but a comparison of the Arctic with those seas that are recognised as semi-enclosed[28] suggests that it does not fall into that category (Harders, 1987: 295).[29]

Even if the Arctic Ocean were treated as a semi-enclosed sea, Article 123 merely imposes an obligation on its coastal states to co-ordinate their rights and duties. It does not alter the content of those rights and duties, and certainly does not authorise an extension of national jurisdiction beyond the economic zone into the high seas. In this respect, the approach resembles the UNEP Regional Seas Programme, which, as a basis of maritime jurisdiction, has already been discussed and rejected.

Possible Objections

Once all the Arctic states have established their economic zones and environmental zones and after all the maritime boundary delimitations have been worked out, the zones of national jurisdiction will completely surround the high seas segment of the Arctic (Figure 1). This could give rise to an argument that additional regulation of the high seas is unnecessary: the Arctic States (so the argument may go) already have prescriptive and enforcement jurisdiction in the economic zone, including authority to set design, construction, equipment, and manning standards. Because no ship can enter the high seas of the central Arctic without passing through one of these zones, the states already have the authority under international law to prevent inadequate ships and unqualified crews from entering the central Arctic by banning them from the ice-covered areas of the economic zones. This argument fails to take into account the difference between jurisdiction and effective enforcement. No regulation in the economic zone will be entirely effective, and once a vessel has passed out of the zone, it is beyond the reach of all but its own flag state. Moreover, even if the economic zone regulations were effective in limiting access to the high seas, they cannot regulate conduct there. It is the Donut Hole problem. Canada's prohibition of the discharge of oil is not effective on the high seas, and never can be as international law now stands.

On one level, the objection to establishing such a legal regime for the high seas is obvious: Article 234 was a step beyond international law as it then stood, but was in line with concurrent developments at UNCLOS III. This proposal is a giant step beyond Article 234. That so-called 'Arctic exception' was created by the same convention that recognised the exclusive economic zone and placed some aspects of it under the jurisdiction of the coastal state. Article 234 does not prescribe substantive regulations in the EEZ, but merely grants the authority to do so to the coastal state, which was simultaneously being granted a significant jurisdiction there. A relatively minor and strictly proscribed augmentation of coastal state jurisdiction within a newly created maritime zone represents a significantly less intrusive adjustment of rights and duties than does this proposal to modify the widely accepted historic rules of freedom of the high seas.

On another level, however, the protection afforded by the international law of the sea to the world's seas in general is not sufficient to protect the special circumstances of the Arctic Ocean and its ice-covered areas. The international community has now recognised, through Article 234, the special situation of these ice-covered areas, and this indicates that the whole of the Arctic Ocean, not just a 200-mile-wide belt around its perimeter, requires a special legal regime.

How likely is it that the Arctic states will adopt such a proposal? How much interest is there in changing the law to protect a sea across which few ships venture? Canada has consistently expressed its concern over pollution threats to the Arctic marine environment (see, for example, Secretary of State, 1985) and has acted on those concerns by seeking ways to strengthen its control over maritime activities in the Canadian Arctic.[30] Nevertheless, Canada still has not extended its Arctic pollution jurisdiction beyond the original 100 miles, even though Article 234 allows 200 miles.[31] Is it likely to attempt to impose a new regime on the high seas if it has not exerted the full measure of its permitted jurisdiction over its own coastal waters? Perhaps it is waiting for the Law of the Sea Convention to take effect in November 1994,[32] although that seems irrelevant as Canada has not yet ratified the Convention. It may be awaiting the outcome of negotiations to modify the elements of the Convention that were unacceptable to the United States, the United Kingdom, and other major shipping states. The negotiations will help to determine whether these maritime powers will sign and ratify the Convention, and this, in turn, may affect Canada's decision whether to ratify (Pitt, 1993; Charney, 1992; Mangone, 1993).

The United States has, in this century at least, jealously protected the freedom of the high seas (although it was the United States, in 1945, that began the movement toward the creation of coastal state jurisdiction over the continental shelf and nearby high-seas fisheries (Truman Proclamation 1945).[33] Under its Freedom of Navigation programme, the United States has, since 1979, regularly challenged maritime claims that it regards as inconsistent with international law, through diplomatic channels and 'nonprovocative' naval activity (Rolph, 1992: 146–52; Bureau of Public Affairs, 1988). The United States was willing to go along with the expanded jurisdiction over ice-covered areas, but this was in large part because Article 234 represented a series of compromises that encouraged Canada to drop its support of a provision that would have permitted a broader coastal state jurisdiction in a potentially large number of non-Arctic special environments (McRae, 1987: 109).[34] On the other hand, the new Donut Hole agreement, which still awaits ratification by the six states, indicates that the United States is concerned with protecting ocean resources in the high seas. It also suggests that, if the United States acts at all, it is likely to adopt the preferable approach of broad, multilateral negotiations, rather than unilaterally assert jurisdiction and risk encouraging other coastal states to begin restricting freedom of the high seas off their own shores.

Conclusion

Canada has been accused of being interested not in the environmental protection of the Arctic Ocean but in protecting and extending its sovereignty after the United States Coast Guard icebreaker *Polar Sea* and the United States oil tanker *Manhattan* traversed the Northwest Passage (M'Gonigle and Zacher, 1977: 280). There may be some truth in this, but it is evident from the public debate that preceded the Act that a driving force behind the desire for sovereignty was the need to protect the Canadian Arctic environment.

The imposition of Canadian-style regulation on the entire Arctic Ocean would probably be workable. If, in the event, the regime proposed here turns out to be so strict and costly as to price trans-polar shipping out of the market, then perhaps that is not entirely a bad thing. The world has managed so far without transpolar routes and is likely to continue to thrive without them. The cost of shipping and the price of goods are not the only economic factors to be reckoned with in ascertaining the feasibility of Arctic transport, and there are non-economic factors to be considered as well. As Prime Minister Trudeau told the Canadian Parliament when he announced the government's intention to introduce the Arctic Waters Act:

> We do not doubt for a moment that the rest of the world would find us at fault, and hold us liable, should we fail to ensure adequate protection of the environment from pollution or artificial deterioration. [We] will not permit this to happen either in the name of freedom of the seas, or in the interests of economic development.[35]

Notes

1   Guyana, on 16 November 1993, became the 60th state to ratify the convention. As a result, the convention will come into effect, as between the ratifying states, on 16 November 1994. See ILM (1994).

2   Karrick discusses the general relationship between temperature and abiotic reactions. There is some doubt, however, that low temperatures impede dispersal; see McRae and Goundrey (1982: 202).

3   Ice extent in the Arctic Ocean and marginal seas ranges from 14.8×10^6 km^2 in March to 7.8×10^6 km^2 in September (Parkinson *et al*, 1987). About half the sea ice occurs in the Arctic Basin and the Barents Sea (Hibler, 1989: 48). Ice thickness is not well known, but averages 1.5–2.5m in the Canada basin and 3.5–4.5m in the Transpolar Drift Stream near the Pole (Barry, 1990: 92).

4   In addition to the characteristics described in the text, ice and the snow that covers much of it have high absorptive capacities for many pollutants. This can help purify the seas, but it can also promote the long distance transfer of pollutants. See Roginko and Lamourie, 1992: 261; Buzuyev and Gudkovich, 1990: 102).

5   Also see Terence Armstrong's annual reports in *Polar Record* on activity and developments in the Northern Sea Route, the most recent of which are Armstrong (1992 and 1993a).

6   The first surface vessel to reach the North Pole was the Soviet nuclear icebreaker *Arktika,* on 17 August 1977. By 30 August 1993, 11 surface vessels had done so: seven of them, all Soviet or Russian nuclear icebreakers, carried tourists, an average of about 90 per voyage. Headland (1993).

7 An exception is made in the case of hot pursuit, which may be continued beyond national jurisdiction if begun within it (Article 111).

8 'Ships shall sail under the flag of one State only and... shall be subject to its exclusive jurisdiction on the high seas.' LOSC 1982, Article 92(1).

9 See P.E. Trudeau's statement to Parliament, quoted in part at the end of this paper.

10 The 200-mile economic zone has been so generally accepted that it is sometime difficult to recall that in 1970, when Canada legislated its own extended jurisdiction out to 100 miles, it was exceeding the internationally acceptable maximum limits by at least 88 miles. On the history of the breadth of the territorial sea, see Churchill and Lowe (1988: 65–8).

11 FAO has a tradition of promoting such regional agreements (Sand, 1988: ix).

12 See generally Sand, 1988: ix-xxvi. Each of the agreements consists of a regional convention, listed below, and one or more protocols, not listed, concerning co-operation in environmental protection.

13 Mediterranean, Caribbean, West/Central Africa, East Africa (Sand, 1988: xii).

14 Red Sea, South-east Pacific, South-west Pacific (Sand, 1988: xii).

15 Greenland, an external territory of the Kingdom of Denmark, attained internal autonomy on 1 May 1979. Denmark remains responsible for foreign relations (Europa, 1993: 947–50).

16 Cf Trudeau (1970), after the introduction of the Arctic Waters bill in Parliament:
   [W]here no law exists, or where law is clearly insufficient, there is no international common law applying to the Arctic seas, we're saying somebody has to preserve this area for mankind until the international law develops.
   See also Department of State (1970):
   Canada, perhaps more than any other country, played a very important lead role in achieving a commitment by the international community to resolve these [maritime claims] issues multilaterally.

17 See Canfield (1993) for background on negotiations and Dunlap (1994) for a description of the agreement (Donut Hole Agreement 1994).

18 Henkin appears to agree with Canada on this point: '[A]ny state which seeks to make new law cannot agree to litigate under old law' (Henkin, 1971: 132).

19 In the Anglo-Norwegian Fisheries Case (1951), for example, the Court upheld Norway's use of straight baselines, which had the effect of enlarging Norway's internal waters and extending

seawards the outer boundary of the territorial sea. The rules established by the court were taken up by the International Law Commission and later incorporated into the Territorial Sea Convention (Article 4) and eventually into LOSC (Article 7).

20   The Article states that 'States shall co-operate on a global basis and, as appropriate, on a regional basis, directly or through competent international organizations, in formulating and elaborating international rules, standards and recommended practices and procedures consistent with this Convention, for the protection and preservation of the marine environment, taking into account characteristic regional features.'

21   Enforcement, both preventive and penal, by other states is permitted, of course, but not on the high seas. Port states have authority to investigate and institute proceedings regarding violations on the high seas (LOSC 1982, Article 218(1)) and, if requested by a coastal state, regarding violations within that coastal state's jurisdiction (Article 218(2)). Flag states (Article 217), port states (Articles 218, 219, 220(1)), and coastal states (Articles 220–1) have varying degrees of jurisdiction, depending upon the circumstances, but only the flag state has jurisdiction to detain a vessel on the high seas for enforcement of pollution regulations.

22   In addition, the act authorises seizure and forfeiture of the vessel and its cargo (Section 24.(1)).

23   Nevertheless, the link between liability and greater care is not universally acknowledged. See Abecassis (1984). Liability as an incentive is an underlying assumption of the US Oil Pollution Act of 1990, which establishes a regime of strict liability for illegal oil spills in the US EEZ or other navigable waters and permits state law to impose unlimited liability for such spills (Oil Pollution Act 1990; Noyes, 1992).

24   Describing the AWPPA 1972; quoted in McRae (1987: 101).

25   For a reasonably detailed discussion of the sector theory, particularly as it applies to Canada, see Pharand (1988, 3–87).

26   For example, Canadian northerners use ice not only as a platform for fishing but also for hunting and transport, often without regard to what may lie beneath it. See Canada's reply to US criticism of the Arctic Waters Act, Canadian Note (1970). Does it necessarily follow that, because there is water underneath, foreign ships have the right to traverse it, thus ploughing up the ice and destroying transport routes and hunting domains? Cf McRae (1987: 99) ('[T]he area has never been perceived simply as water').

27   Many of the seas recognized as semi-enclosed are either entirely (Baltic Sea, Caribbean Sea, Mediterranean Sea, Persian Gulf, Red Sea, South China Sea) or largely (Bering Sea, 92%; Gulf of

Maine, 98%; Sea of Okhotsk, 97%) occupied by 200-mile coastal zones (Alexander, 1974: 158–9 (Table 1)).

28   The Mediterranean Sea is 99% enclosed by land; Baltic Sea, 97%; Black Sea, 99% (Alexander, 1974: 158–9 (Table 1)).

29   Lewis Alexander (1974: 157), applying geographical criteria, does regard the Arctic as a semi-enclosed sea. At least one legal scholar seems willing to entertain the possibility that the Arctic Ocean may be a semi-enclosed sea (Pharand, 1989: 163).

30   Besides AWPPA 1970 and ASPPR 1972, already discussed, Canada claimed a system of straight baselines, which, if ultimately validated under international law, will render the Northwest Passage internal waters and place it firmly under Canadian sovereignty. See Arctic Sovereignty (1985).

31   Canada has claimed 200-mile fishery conservation zones in the Atlantic and Pacific Oceans (Fishery Zones 1976).

32   The convention will not come into effect until November 1994. Like the visions relating to the EEZ and the marine environment, Article 234 was adopted by consensus and, arguably, has become customary law (Pharand, 1980: 465–6). On the other hand, as the United States has not signed the convention and Canada has not ratified it, it has been argued that Article 234 is not binding as between those states (McRae, 1987: 112). For a discussion of the mixture of customary, conventional, and consensual law in the convention, see Larson (1994).

33   The clamation asserted United States jurisdiction over 'natural resources of the subsoil and sea bed of the continental shelf' and to establish fishery conservation zones in the high seas contiguous to the coast well before these concepts of jurisdiction were incorporated into international law.

34   The other vision was eventually adopted as Article 211(6) of the LOSC 1982.

35   Prime Minister Trudeau's Throne Speech to Parliament, 24 October 1969, quoted in M'Gonigle and Zacher (1977: 200).

Bibliography

ARTICLES, BOOKS AND CHAPTERS

Abecassis, D.W. (1984) 'Liability for oil pollution from ships', in Mankabady (1984): 300–17.

Abecassis, D.W. and Jarashow, R.L. (1985) *Oil Pollution from Ships,* London: Stevens and Sons.

Alexander, L. (1974) 'Regionalism and the Law of the Sea: the case of semi-enclosed seas', *Ocean Development and International Law* 2: 151–186.

Alexander, V. and Niebauer, H.J. (1990) 'Arctic ecosystems, sea ice and global warming', in Kotlyakov and Sokolov 1990b: 206–11.

Armstrong, T. (1984) 'The Northern Sea Route, 1983', *Polar Record* 22, 137: 173–82.

—— (1992) 'Northern Sea Route 1991', *Polar Record* 28, 166 239–40.

—— (1993) 'The Northern Sea Route Project', *Polar Record* 29, 168: 60.

—— (1993a) 'Northern Sea Route 1992', *Polar Record* 29, 170: 245.

Armstrong, T., Roberts, B. and Swithinbank, C. (1973) *Illustrated Glossary of Snow and Ice*, Cambridge: Scott Polar Research Institute.

Associated Press (1994) 'Curb on Bering Sea fishing tentatively set', *The New York Times*, 14 February 1994, A8: 3.

Atlas, R.M. (1986) 'Fate of petroleum pollutants in Arctic ecosystems', in Bridgeo and Eisenhauer 1986: 59–67.

Auburn, F.M. (1982) *Antarctic Law and Politics*, London: C. Hurst.

Balch, T.W. (1910) 'The Arctic and Antarctic regions and the Law of Nations', *American Journal of International Law* 4, 4: 265–75.

Barry, R.G. (1990) 'Arctic sea ice and its variability', in Kotlyakov and Sokolov 1990a: 91–101.

Beesley, J.A. (1971) 'Rights and responsibilities of Arctic coastal states: the Canadian view', *Journal of Maritime Law and Commerce* 3: 7.

Breitfuss, L.L. (1929) 'Territorial division of the Arctic', *Dalhousie Law Review* 8, 4: 456–70.

Brigham, Commander L.W. (1985) 'New developments in Soviet nuclear Arctic ships', in *Proceedings, US Naval Institute* 111/12, 994, December.

—— (ed.) (1991) *The Soviet Maritime Arctic*, London: Belhaven Press and Scott Polar Research Institute.

—— (1993) 'Opening the northern sea route', *Polar Record* 29, 168: 60–1.

Bridgeo, W.A. and Eisenhauer, H.R. (eds) (1986) *Arctic Water Pollution Research: Applications of Science and Technology*, Oxford: Pergamon Press.

Brubaker, D. (1993) *Marine Pollution and International Law*, London: Belhaven Press.

Bureau of Public Affairs (1988) *US Freedom of Navigation Program*, Washington, DC: US Department of State.

Burke, W.T. (1988) 'Fishing in the Bering Sea donut: straddling stocks and the new International Law of Fisheries', *Ecology Law Quarterly* 16, 1: 285–310.

Buzuyev, A.Y. and Gudkovich, Z.M. (1990) 'Urgent problems in studying sea ice in the Arctic Ocean', in Kotlyakov and Sokolov 1990: 101–6.

[Canadian Note (1970)] 'Summary of Canadian note of April 16 tabled by the Secretary of State for External Affairs in the House April 17', reprinted in *International Legal Materials* (1990) 9: 607–15.

Canfield, J.L. (1993) 'Recent developments in Bering Sea fisheries conservation and management', *Ocean Development and International Law* 24, 3: 257–89.

CARC (1984) *Ocean Policy and Management in the Arctic,* Ottawa: Canadian Arctic Resources Committee, 46 Elgin St, Ottawa, Ontario K1P 5K6.

Caron, D.D. (1993) 'Toward an Arctic environmental regime', *Ocean Development and International Law* 24: 377–92.

Charney, J.I. (1992) 'The United States and the revision of the 1982 convention on the Law of the Sea', *Ocean Development and International Law* 24, 4: 279–303.

Churchill, R.R. and Lowe, A.V. (1988) *The Law Of The Sea,* Manchester: Manchester University Press.

Clark, R.C. Jr, and Finley, J.S. (1977) 'Effects of oil spills in Arctic and subarctic environments', in Malins (1977b): 411–76.

Clark, R.C. Jr, and MacLeod, W.D. Jr (1977) 'Inputs, transport mechanisms, and observed concentrations of petroleum in the marine environment', in Malins (1977a): 91–223.

Cowan, E. (1970) 'Oil tanker *Stern* sinks off Canada', *The New York Times*, 13 February 1: 8; 15: 1.

Dellapenna, J.W. (1972) 'Canadian claims in Arctic waters', *Land and Water Law Review* 7: 383–419.

Department of State (1970a) 'United States statement on Canadian fisheries closing lines announcement', US Department of State Press Release, No. 357, 18 December, reprinted in *International Legal Materials* 10: 441 (1971).

—— (1970b) 'Statement on Government of Canada's bills on limits of the territorial sea, fisheries and pollution', US Department of State Press Release No. 121 of 15 April, reprinted in *International Legal Materials* 9: 605–6 (1970).

Dollot, R. (1949) 'Le droit international des espaces polaires', *Recueil des Cours*, Academie de Droit International, 1949/II, Vol. 75: 125.

Dunbar, M.J. (ed.) (1977) *Polar Oceans,* Calgary: Arctic Institute of North America.

—— (1985) 'The Arctic marine ecosystem', in Engelhardt (1985): 1–35.

Dunlap, W.V. (1991) *Transit Passage in the Soviet Arctic Straits*, unpublished thesis, University of Cambridge (on file at Scott Polar Research Institute Library, Cambridge).

—— (1994) 'A Pollock-Fishing Agreement for the Central Bering Sea', *Boundary and Security Bulletin* 2, 2: 49–57.

Engelhardt, F.R. (1985) *Petroleum Effects in the Arctic Environment*, London: Elsevier Applied Science Publishers.

Europa World Year Book (1993) London: Europa Publications.

[FAO (1974)]. *Protection of the Marine Environment against Pollution in the Mediterranean*, FAO Fisheries Report No. 148, Annex I.

Foster, T.D. (1978) 'Polar oceans: similarities and differences in their physical oceanography', in McWhinnie (1978): 117–40.

Franckx, E. (1993) *Maritime Claims in the Arctic,* Dordrecht: Martinus Nijhoff.

Frankel, E.G. (1988) 'Arctic marine transport and ancillary technologies', in Lamson and Vanderzwaag (1988): 100–29.

Frolov, I. (1991) 'The 1987 expedition of the icebreaker *Sibir* to the North Pole', in Brigham (1991): 33–44.

Friedheim, R.L. (1988) 'The regime of the Arctic – distributional or integrative bargaining?', *Ocean Development and International Law* 19: 493–510.

Griffiths, F. (ed.) (1987) *Politics of the Northwest Passage,* Kingston and Montreal: McGill–Queens University Press.

Hamnes, H. (1993) 'ERS–1 satellite navigation brings access to the Arctic', *Sea Technology* 34, 18: 51–4.

Harders, J.E. (1987) 'In quest of an Arctic legal regime: marine regionalism – a concept of international law evaluated', *Marine Policy* 11, 4: 285–98.

Head, I.L. (1962) 'Canadian claims to territorial sovereignty in the Arctic regions', *McGill Law Journal* 9: 200–26.

Headland, R. (1993) 'Ships which have reached the North Pole (excluding submarines)', unpublished report, in archives of Scott Polar Research Institute, Cambridge.

Henkin, L. (1971) 'Arctic anti-pollution: does Canada make – or break – international law?', *American Journal of International Law* 65, 1: 131–6.

Herman, Y. (ed.). (1989) *The Arctic Seas,* New York: Van Nostrand Reinhold.

Hibler, W.D. III. (1989) 'Arctic ice-ocean dynamics', in Herman (1989): 47–91.

IAHR 1990 *The 10th Symposium on Ice*, 20–4 August, Espoo, Finland, Proceedings. Espoo: Helsinki University of Technology.

—— 1992 *11th International Symposium on Ice*, Banff, Alberta, 15–9 June, Proceedings. Edmonton: Department of Civil Engineering, University of Alberta.

[ILM (1994)]. 'Recent actions regarding treaties to which the United States is not a party', *International Legal Materials* 33, 1: 309.

Jansson, J. (1990) 'Global warming and Arctic shipping', in IAHR (1990) 3: 19–27.

Johnson, B. and Zacher, M.W. (eds) (1977) *Canadian Foreign Policy and the Law of the Sea,* Vancouver: University of British Columbia Press.

Karrick, N.L. (1977) 'Alterations in petroleum resulting from physico-chemical and microbiological factors', in Malins (1977a): 225–99.

Kolodkin, A.L. and Volosov, M.E. (1990) 'The legal regime of the Soviet Arctic – major issues', *Marine Policy* 14, 2: 158–68.

Kotlyakov, V.M. and Sokolov V.E. (1990a) *Arctic Research, Advances and Prospects, Vol. 1*, Moscow: Nauka.

—— (1990b) *Arctic Research, Advances and Prospects, Vol. 2*, Moscow: Nauka.

Lamson, C. and Vanderzwaag, D.L. (1988) *Transit Management in the North-west Passage, Problems and Prospects,* Cambridge: Cambridge University Press.

Larson, D.L. (1994) 'Conventional, customary, and consensual law in the United Nations Convention on the Law of the Sea', *Ocean Development and International Law* 25, 1: 75–85.

Lay, S.H., Churchill, R. and Nordquist, M. (1973) *New Directions in the Law of the Sea, Vol. 1,* Dobbs Ferry, New York: Oceana.

M'Gonigle, R.M. and Zacher, M.W. (1977) 'Canadian foreign policy and the control of marine pollution', in Johnson and Zacher (1977): 100–57.

McKitterick T.E.M. (1939) 'The validity of territorial and other claims in polar regions', *Journal of Comparative Legislation and International Law, Third Series,* XXI: 94.

McRae, D.M. (1987) 'The negotiation of Article 234', in Griffiths (1987): 98–114.

McRae, D.M. and Goundrey, D.J. (1982) 'Environmental jurisdiction in arctic waters: the extent of Article 234', *University of British Columbia Law Review* 16, 2: 197–228.

McWhinnie, M.A. (ed.) (1978) *Polar Research, to the Present, and the Future,* Boulder: Westview.

Machowski, J. (1992) 'The status of polar ice under international law', *Polish Polar Research* 13, 2: 149–75.

Malins, D.C. (1977a) *Effect of Petroleum on Arctic and Subarctic Marine Environments and Organisms, Vol. 1: Nature and Fate of Petroleum,* London: Academic Press.

—— (1977b) *Effect of Petroleum on Arctic and Subarctic Marine Environments and Organisms, Vol. 2: Biological Effects,* London: Academic Press.

Mangone, G.J. (1993) 'Negotiations on the 1982 Law of the Sea Convention', *The International Journal of Marine and Coastal Law* 8, 4: 530–41.

Mankabady, S. (1984) *The International Maritime Organisation,* London: Croom Helms.

Murthy, T.K.S., Sackinger, W.M. and Wadhams, P. (eds.). (1992) *Advances in Ice Technology,* Southampton and Boston: Computational Mechanics Publications.

Nelson, J.G. and Needham, R.D. (1985) 'The Arctic as a regional sea,' *Environmental Conservation* 12: 7–15.

Norway (1990) *State of the Arctic Environment, Draft Proposal for the Arctic Monitoring and Assessment Programme,* Norway: State

Pollution Control Authority (on file at Scott Polar Research Institute Library).

Noyes, J.E. (1992) 'The US Oil Pollution Act of 1990', *International Journal of Esturine and Coastal Law* 7, 1: 43–56.

Østreng, W. (1991) 'The Northern Sea route: a new era in Soviet policy?', *Ocean Development and International Law* 22: 259–87.

—— (1992) 'The geopolitics of the Northern Sea route', *International Challenges* 12, 1: 21–5.

Parkinson, C.L., Comiso, J.C., Zwally, H.J., Cavalieri, D.J., Gloersen, P. and Campbell, W.J. (1987) 'Seasonal and regional variations of northern hemisphere sea ice as illustrated with satellite passive-microwave data for 1974', *Annals of Glaciology* 9: 119–26.

Parnell, G.Q. (1992) 'Ship operations in ice: practical speed considerations', in Murthy *et al* (1992): 307–12.

Payne, J.R., McNabb, G.D. Jr and Clayton, J.R. Jr (1992) 'Oil-weathering behaviour in Arctic environments', *Polar Research* 10, 2: 631–62.

Perkins, E.J. (1986) 'The biological accumulation and monitoring of chemical wastes in Arctic waters', in Bridgeo and Eisenhauer (1986): 1–11.

Petersen, G.H. (1977) 'Biological effects of sea-ice and icebergs in Greenland', in Dunbar (1977): 319.

Pharand, D. (1988) *Canada's Arctic Waters in International Law*, Cambridge: Cambridge University Press.

—— (1989) 'Les problémes de droit international dans l'Arctique', *Études Internationales* 20, 1: 131–64.

—— (1992) 'The case for an Arctic regional council and a treaty proposal,' *Revue générale de droit* 23: 163–95.

Pitt, D.E. (1993) 'US seeks to "fix" mining provisions of sea treaty', *The New York Times*, 28 August 1: 3: 1.

Pullen, T.C. (1984) 'Arctic marine transportation: a view from the bridge,' in CARC (1984): 127–41.

Puskas, J., McBean, E. and Kouwen, N. (1987) 'Behaviour and transport of oil under smooth ice', *Canadian Journal of Civil Engineering* 14, 4: 510–8.

Ramseier, R. (1974) 'Oil on ice', *Environment* May: 7.

Rey, L. (1982) *The Arctic Ocean, The Hydrographic Environment and the Fate of Pollutants,* London and Basingstoke: Macmillan Press, Scientific and Medical Division.

Roginko, A.Y. and Lamourie M.J. (1992) 'Emerging marine environmental-protection strategies in the Arctic,' *Marine Policy* 16, 4: 259–76.

Rolph, J.W. (1992) 'Freedom of navigation and the Black Sea bumping incident: how "innocent" must innocent passage be?', *Military Law Review* 135: 137–65.

Roth, R.R. (1990) 'Sovereignty and jurisdiction in Arctic waters', *Alberta Law Review* 28, 4: 845–72.

Sand, P.H. (1988) *Maritime Environment Law in the United Nations Environment Programme, An Emergent Eco-Regime*, London and New York: Tycooly Publishing.

Schmemann, S. (1983) 'Soviet seeks to lay blame for ice crisis', *The New York Times*, 23 October 1983: 19: 1.

Smedal, G. (1932) *De l'Acquisition de Souveraineté sur les Territoires Polaires,* (translated from Norwegian by Pierre Rokseth), Paris: Rousseau et Cie.

Smith, B.D. (1988) *State Responsibility and the Marine Environment, the Rules of Decision,* Oxford: Clarendon Press.

Sprague, J. (1973) 'Aquatic resources in the Canadian north: knowledge, dangers and research needs', in CARC (1973): 170–1.

Stuart, W.J.H. and Lamson, C. (1988) 'Canadian arctic marine transportation: present status and future requirements', in Lamson and Vanderzwaag (1988): 130–52.

Sugden, D. (1982) *Arctic and Antarctic, a Modern Synthesis,* Oxford: Basil Blackwell.

Sydnes, L.K. (1992) 'Oil, water, ice and light', *Polar Research* 10, 2: 609–18.

Treshnikov, A.F. (1977) 'Water masses of the Arctic basin', in Dunbar (1977): 17–31.

[Trudeau (1970)]. 'Remarks of Prime Minister Trudeau to a press conference on 8 April 1970', reprinted in *International Legal Materials* 9: 600–4.

Vanderzwaag, D., Donihee, J., and Faegteborg, M. (1987) 'Towards regional ocean management in the Arctic: from co-existence to co-operation', *University of New Brunswick Law Journal* 36: 1–33.

Vanderzwaag, D. and Pharand, D. (1983) 'Inuit and the ice: implications for Arctic waters', *Canadian Yearbook of International Law* 21: 53–84.

Vyshnepolski, S. (1952) 'K probleme pravovogo rezhima arkticheskoy oblasti [On the problem of the legal regime of the Arctic region]', *Sovetskoye Gosudarstvo i Pravo* 7: 36–45.

Wadhams, P. (1992) 'Global warming: a polar approach', in IAHR Vol. 1 (1992): 23–40.

Walker, J.M. (1992) 'Some recent advances in Arctic shipping', *World Meteorological Organisation Bulletin* 41, 2: 160–4.

Wespestad, V.G. (1993) 'The status of Bering Sea pollock and the effect of the Donut Hole fishing', *Fisheries* 18, 3: 18–24.

ZoBell, C.E. (1969) 'Microbial modification of crude oil in the sea', in *Proceedings [of] Joint Conference on Prevention and Control of Oil Spills*, American Petroleum Institute and Federal Water Pollution Control Administration, New York: 317–26.

LEGAL REFERENCES

Abidjan Convention (1981) Convention for Co-operation in the Protection and Development of the Marine and Coastal Environment of the West and Central African Region, Abidjan, 23 March; in force 5 August 1984; *International Legal Materials* 20: 746 (1981).

Anglo-Norwegian Fisheries Case, [1951] ICJ Reports 116.

Antarctic Treaty (1959) Washington, DC, 1 December; in force 23 June 1961;. 402 UNTS 71.

[Arctic Sovereignty 1985]. 'Canada: Statement Concerning Arctic Sovereignty, in the House of Commons by the Secretary of State for External Affairs, 10 September 1985; *International Legal Materials* 34: 1723–8 (1985).

[Arctic Strategy 1991]. Arctic Environmental Protection Strategy, June 14, 1991, agreed by the eight Arctic states: Canada, Finland, Greenland/Denmark, Iceland, Norway, Sweden, Soviet Union, United States. Reprinted in *International Legal Materials* 30: 1624–69 (1991).

Arrest Convention 1952. International Convention Relating to the Arrest of Seagoing Ships, Brussels, 10 May 1952; in force 24 February 1956; *United Nations Treaty Series* 439: 193; *United Kingdom Treaty Series* 47 (1960); *American Journal of International Law* 53: 539.

[ASPPR 1972]. Arctic Shipping Pollution Prevention Regulations, *Canada Gazette*, Part II, Vol. 106, no. 20, 10 October 1972.

[AWPPA 1970]. Arctic Waters Pollution Prevention Act. Bill c–202, 2nd sess. 28th Parl., 18–19 Elizabeth II, c. 47 (1969–70), reprinted in *International Legal Materials* 9: 543 (1970). Assented to 26 June 1970. Proclaimed to enter into force 2 August 1972; *Canada Gazette* 106: 2072.

Barcelona Convention 1976. Convention for the Protection of the Mediterranean Sea Against Pollution, Barcelona 16 February 1976; in force 12 February 1978; *International Legal Materials* 15: 290 (1976).

Bonn Agreement (1989) for Co-Operation in Dealing with Pollution of the North Sea by Oil and Other Harmful Substances; Bonn, 13 September 1983; in force 1 September 1989; Cmnd. 9104.

Brussels Convention 1968. Convention on Jurisdiction and the Enforcement of Judgements in Civil and Commercial Matters, Brussels, 27 September 1968, in force 1 February 1973; *International Legal Materials* 8: 229.

[Canadian Declaration 1970]. 'Canadian Declaration Concerning the Compulsory Jurisdiction of the International Court of Justice, April 7, 1970', reprinted at *International Legal Materials* 9: 598–9 (1970). Rescinded on 10 September 1985; *International Legal Materials* 24: 1729–30 (1985).

Cartagena Convention 1983. Convention for the Protection and Development of the Marine Environment of the Wider Caribbean Region, Cartagena, 24 March 1983; in force 11 October 86; *International Legal Materials* 22: 221 (1983).

Civil Liability Convention 1969 and 1984 Protocol. International Convention on Civil Liability for Oil Pollution Damage, Brussels, 29 November 1969; in force 9 June 1975; *United Kingdom Treaty Series* 106 (1975). Protocol of 1984 to Amend the 1969 International Convention on Civil Liability for Oil Pollution Damage, London, 25 May 1984; not in force as of 1 May 1994.

Collision Convention 1952. International Convention for the Unification of Certain Rules Relating to Penal Jurisdiction in Matters of Collision or Other Incidents of Navigation, Brussels, 10 May 1952; in force 20 November 1955; *United Nations Treaty Series* 429: 233; *United Kingdom Treaty Series* 47 (1960); *American Journal of International Law* 53: 536.

[Donut Hole Agreement 1994] Convention on the Conservation and Management of Pollock Resources in the Central Bering Sea, initialed at Washington DC, 11 February 1994 by China, Japan, Korea, Poland, Russia and the United States; Signed at Washington DC, 16 June 1994 by China, Korea, Russia and the United States; not in force as of 1 August 1994.

[Fishery Zones 1976]. *Canada Gazette*, Extra No. 101, Vol. 110 (November 1, 1976). Reprinted in *International Legal Materials* 15: 1372 (1976). Unofficial map at p. 1375.

Helsinki Convention 1974. Convention on the Protection of the Marine Environment of the Baltic Sea Area, Helsinki, 22 March 1974; in force 3 May 1980; *International Legal Materials* 13: 546 (1974).

Jeddah Convention 1982. Regional Convention for the Conservation of the Red Sea and Gulf of Aden Environment, Jeddah, 14 February 1982; in force 20 August 1985.

Kuwait Convention 1978. Regional Convention for Co-operation on the Protection of the Marine Environment from Pollution, Kuwait, 23 April 1978; in force 1 July 1979; *International Legal Materials* 17: 511 (1978).

Lima Convention 1981. Convention for the Protection of the Marine Environment and Coastal Area of the South-East Pacific, Lima, 12 November 1981; in force 19 May 1986; U.N. Doc. UNEP/CPPS/IG.32/4.

[LOSC 1982]. United Nations Law of the Sea Convention, Montego Bay, 10 December 1982; in force 16 November 1994.

Nairobi Convention 1985. Convention for the Protection, Management and Development of the Marine and Coastal Environment of the Eastern African Region, Nairobi, 21 June 1985; not in force as of 1 May 1994; *Official Journal of the European Communities* 1986: C 253/10.

Nordic Agreement (1971) on Co-operation in Taking Measures Against Pollution of the Sea by Oil, between Denmark, Finland, Norway, and Sweden; Copenhagen, 16 September 1971; in force 16 October 1971; UNTS 822/324.

Noumea Convention 1986. Convention for the Protection of the Natural Resources and Environment of the South Pacific Region, Noumea, 25 November 1986; in force 22 August 1990; *International Legal Materials* 26: 38 (1987).

[NSR 1990]. Regulations for Navigation on the Seaways of the Northern Sea Route, 14 September 1990. English translation appears in Franckx 1993: 315–8 and in *International Challenges* 12: 121–6 (1992).

Oslo Convention 1972. Convention for the Prevention of Marine Pollution by Dumping from Ships and Aircraft, Oslo, 15 February 1972; in force 7 April 1974, U.K.T.S. 119 (1975); *International Legal Materials* 11: 262 (1972).

Oil Pollution Act (1990) Public Law No. 101–280, *Statutes at Large* 104: 484 (1990).

Paris Convention 1974. Convention on the Prevention of Marine Pollution from Land-Based Sources, Paris, 4 June 1974; in force 6 May 1978; *International Legal Materials* 13: 352 (1974).

[Secretary of State 1985]. Statement of the Secretary of State for External Affairs, 10 September 1985, in House of Commons, reprinted in *International Legal Materials* 24: 1723–8 (1985).

[Senate 1988]. Senate Resolution 396, 100th Congress, 2nd Session. *Congressional Record*, 21 March 1988 (daily ed.), p. S2621.

Truman Proclamation 1945. Proclamation No. 2667, 'Policy of the United States with Respect to the Natural Resources of the Subsoil and Sea Bed of the Continental Shelf', September 28, 1945, 10 Federal Register 12303; 3 C.F.R., 1943–48 Comp., 67; XIII *Bulletin*, Department of State, No. 326, September 30, 1945, 485, reprinted in Lay *et al* (1973: 106–7). Proclamation No. 2668, 'Policy of the United States with Respect to Coastal Fisheries in Certain Areas of the High Seas', September 28, 1945, 10 Federal Register 12304; 3 C.F.R., 1943–8 Comp., 68, reprinted in Lay *et al* (1973: 95–8).

24

The Gulf of Maine Action Plan

Melissa Waterman

Introduction

The Gulf of Maine is a remarkable marine ecosystem. With a watershed stretching into Quebec, and a water area bounded by Nova Scotia and Georges Bank, the Gulf of Maine is the central physical feature of northern New England. As an area where ecological zones overlap, the Gulf watershed hosts a remarkable diversity of plant and animal species. The high biological productivity and species diversity of the Gulf's marine waters have made it an internationally recognised water body.

Characteristics of the Gulf of Maine

The Gulf of Maine is a basin formed by glaciers, bordered on the northern and western sides by land and on the southern and eastern sides by Browns Bank, Georges Bank, and the Nantucket Shoals (Figure 24.1). The Gulf of Maine is situated between two distinct oceanographic regimes – the Gulf Stream to the south and the Labrador Current and the Gulf of St Lawrence outflow to the north. Plant and animal species found in the Gulf reflect these distinct oceanographic boundaries. The Gulf of Maine is a unique natural area, poised at a transition spot between the temperate and boreal or subartic regimes.

Four ecological zones may be found within the Gulf of Maine: Virginian, cool temperate, boreal, and subartic. An increasing proportion of boreal species and decreasing proportion of Virginian species exist along a gradient from Cape Cod to Cape Sable.

There are significant geographic variations in Gulf water temperatures during summer months. The western part of the Gulf, near Cape Cod, has temperatures between 15 and 18°C. The eastern area, including the Bay of Fundy, has cooler water, 12–15°C. The coldest Gulf water during summer occurs along eastern Maine and the Fundy Isles, at less than 12°C.

There is consequently a great diversity in species in the Gulf beginning with the phytoplankton which may be a mix of temperate and boreal species. Within the Gulf of Maine, Georges Bank has much

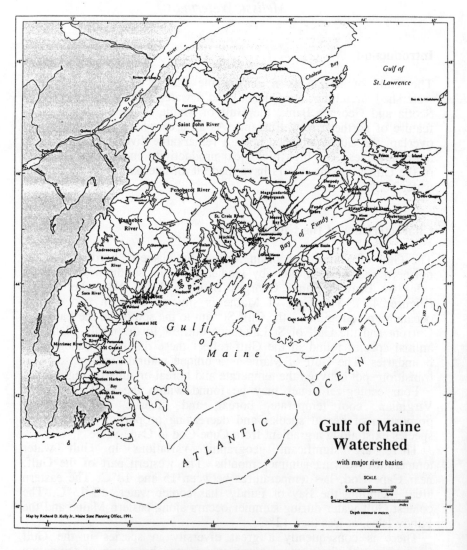

Figure 24.1 Gulf of Maine Watershed with Major River Basins

richer phytoplankton concentrations than elsewhere in the Gulf. It is also estimated that it has the highest annual primary productivity ($455gC/m^2$).

The geographic and seasonal patterns of phytoplankton in the Gulf are strongly influenced by tidal mixing. High phytoplankton biomass and production takes place throughout the spring and fall months in tidally-influenced areas of the Gulf (off south-west Nova Scotia, around Grand Manan, and around Georges Bank and the Nantucket Shoals).

It appears that plankton dynamics in the Gulf are influenced by the influx of nutrient-rich slope water through the north-east channel. Upwelling of this water occurs along the coast of eastern Maine. Some say that up to 44% of new nitrate entering the Gulf through the north-east channel upwells along eastern Maine. High primary productivity also occurs in areas where the influx of nitrogen interacts with the nearshore coastal current.

The greatest species diversity is found further up the Gulf food chain. In one location, Deer Isle, New Brunswick, the local archipelago features 836 invertebrate species, 96 fish species, 70 resident bird species, 20 mammalian species, and 223 species of terrestrial and aquatic plants. In the Passamaquoddy region alone, over 1,500 invertebrate species can be found.

High annual primary productivity attracts many migratory species of sea creatures to the Gulf. Endangered whales, such as the northern right whale, humpback, minke, finback, and the rare blue whale congregate in the Gulf during the spring and summer months for feeding and courtship activities. Migratory bird species make use of the offshore islands and extensive tidal wetlands in the region during their yearly migrations.

The Gulf of Maine is also known for its great stocks of groundfish. Cod, haddock, herring, hake, pollack, mackerel, redfish, and bluefish congregate in its waters. Scientists have analysed the distribution of groundfish species from Cape Hatteras to the Hudson Strait. From the conclusions of this analysis, the Gulf of Maine area is deemed quite complex in terms of groundfish species diversity. Scientists have called for increased emphasis on research relating to the interdependence of marine communities in the Gulf, and thus their vulnerability to human or natural disruptions.

The Gulf of Maine watershed, unlike the watersheds of Chesapeake Bay or the Great Lakes, enjoys a relatively low human population and, overall, its marine waters have not yet shown signs of serious environmental degradation. However, the same cannot be said for its living resources and certain estuarine habitats, in which there has been a phenomenal decline in groundfish stocks, almost certainly a result of intense fishing pressure. To take one example, the biomass of Georges Bank, while remaining comparable to 45 years ago, is now composed of markedly different species. Where once cod and haddock dominated, now skate and dogfish make up the majority of species found on Georges Bank.

Program Inception

During the 1980s, both Canada and the United States began to realise that proper management of the Gulf of Maine required mutual co-operation. As state and provincial natural resource managers began to comprehend the complexity of biological and oceanographic factors in the Gulf of Maine more fully, they began to look for ways to manage the Gulf as a single ecosystem, regardless of political boundaries.

In the late 1980s, Massachusetts, New Hampshire, Maine, New Brunswick, and Nova Scotia concluded that growing stresses upon the Gulf of Maine posed real threats to its well-being. The five jurisdictions perceived that their traditional cultural and economic ties led to a common interest in protecting and preserving the well-being of the enormously productive Gulf.

In 1989 the governors and premiers created the Gulf of Maine Program (Figure 24.2). In December of that year the five jurisdictions signed the Agreement on the Conservation of the Marine Environment of the Gulf of Maine, creating the Gulf of Maine Council on the Marine Environment. The Agreement makes clear the intent of the states and provinces with regard to the future of the Gulf:

> ... the Parties to this agreement recognise a shared duty to protect and conserve the renewable and non-renewable resources of the Gulf for the use, benefit and enjoyment of all their citizens, including generations yet to come...

The Council, comprised of two Cabinet representatives and one private individual appointed by each Governor and Premier, makes policy decisions affecting the scope and direction of the Gulf of Maine Program. The Gulf of Maine Working Group, which includes senior staff within members' agencies, monitors Program implementation and conducts long-range planning for the Program. The Council has created several committees with public and private members to implement key elements of the Gulf Program.

The Agreement specified that the Gulf Council develop a long-term natural resources action plan, which would contain both an assessment of the state of the Gulf and details of joint measures to prevent future degradation. In addition, the Council was directed to design a regional marine environmental quality monitoring plan which, when implemented, would provide both Canadian and United States' agencies with data on environmental trends in the Gulf.

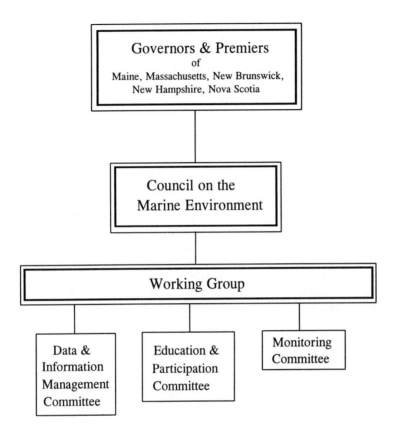

Figure 24.2 Gulf of Maine Program Organisational Chart

Creating the Action Plan

Development of the Action Plan was a long and painstaking process. Beginning in January 1990, members of the Council management committee, the Gulf of Maine Working Group, met to clarify the pressing environmental priorities of the Gulf region. A joint US–Canadian conference, entitled 'The Gulf of Maine – Sustaining Our Common Heritage', held in December 1989, provided important scientific information and, just as valuable, public direction for Action Plan development.

The structure of the Action Plan was based on the work of the United Nations Regional Seas Program and the US Environmental Protection Agency National Estuary Program. The stated priorities of myriad organisations, agencies, and research institutions were incorporated into the draft Action Plan, either explicitly or by reference. The Plan was released for public comment in 1991. Seventy five individuals, agencies, and organisations in the five states and provinces commented. In July 1991, the final draft was presented to the Gulf Council. The Council approved the document and presented it to the governors and premiers as directed.

Content of the Action Plan

The Action Plan is divided into five sections: Monitoring and Research; Coastal and Marine Pollution; Habitat Protection; Protection of Public Health; and Public Education and Participation. Each section has a clear goal, several objectives, and an assortment of actions to be taken under each objective. The objectives themselves are ranked by priority, with the highest-priority objectives initiated in the first three years of the Plan (1991–3). Re-evaluation of the entire document occurs in three year cycles, in order to reassess the effectiveness of the Plan's implementation, to incorporate new information or new environmental issues within the document, and to offer the opportunity for public comment.

Selected Gulf of Maine Program projects

Implementation of the Action Plan has progressed through the activities of Council member agencies and the efforts of Council committees. Funding for implementation, to date, has been compiled from various federal, state, and provincial funds; unlike other marine management efforts in the United States, the Gulf of Maine Program does not receive regular or consistent federal support.

Gulfwatch was initiated in 1991 as a pilot project of the Program's regional Marine Environmental Quality Monitoring Plan. *Gulfwatch* has two objectives: to determine if blue mussels are suitable as an environmental indicator species in the Gulf; and to determine if the three states, two provinces, and assorted federal agencies can work together on a regional scientific project. The project's success after three seasons is due largely to the amount of in-kind support provided by agencies around the Gulf: *Gulfwatch* operated with 48% cash support and 52% in-kind support during its first year.

Providing access to existing environmental databases around the region is another priority objective of the Gulf Program. The Gulf Program has begun a regional data management system, known as the *Gulf of Maine Environmental Data and Information Management System*, which is operated, as a prototype, by the University of New Hampshire. The Program's Data Committee, representing scientists, academics, and agency staff, conducted a regional user-needs survey to determine the precise requirements of such a system, and to determine the extent and format of available environmental databases. It is intended that, through this system, researchers, interest groups, and policy makers will be able to avail themselves of the abundant current and historic Gulf environmental data.

To determine the nature of pollutant inputs entering the Gulf from its 69,000 square mile watershed, a *point-source pollution inventory* was initiated to estimate the level of contaminants borne by waterways into the Gulf. The 'first cut' of this inventory provides a gross overview of pollutant inputs; refinement of that estimate will be required to discern priority pollutants and sources. The Environmental Protection Agency (EPA) and National Oceanic and Atmospheric Administration (NOAA) have taken a lead role in this process and are poised to provide technical assistance with the next stage of this project. Extending the work now underway by the three states, the Gulf Program intends to complement the point source inventory with similar non-point source pollution control efforts.

Protecting regionally significant habitats within the Gulf of Maine region is another key component of the Gulf Program. Drawing together the appropriate agencies and private organisations in the region, the Gulf Program has provided a locus for discussion of the Gulf as a bioregion, and for new co-operative ventures in habitat identification. The US Fish and Wildlife Service plays an important role in Gulf Program habitat efforts, through its education, technical assistance, and biological characterisation work.

Gulf Program public education and participation efforts take many forms. The Gulf Program hosted a workshop for invited educators and communicators from across the region to define specific educational needs and available materials unique to the Gulf region. Education activities thus far have focused on raising awareness of the Gulf as an interconnected system defined by currents and nutrient cycles and independent of political borders. A Gulf of Maine Watershed map and information poster has been distributed to educators and communicators throughout the five jurisdictions. A Gulf of Maine Information Kit is under development. Finally, a Gulf of Maine Trail Network signpost and guidebook project has begun, to provide better information for the several million annual visitors to the region of the Gulf's unique ecological and cultural features.

Effect of the Action Plan

While the Action Plan does not have the force of law, it is a document that represents the consensus of public agencies operating in the Gulf of Maine, in both Canada and the United States. As such it has proved to be extremely effective as a guide for agencies focusing on the Gulf of Maine. Through the Action Plan, the Environment Canada

Conservation and Protection branch has begun to realign its activities in the Gulf of Maine–Bay of Fundy region, with a commensurate increase in staff and financial support. The EPA and NOAA have joined forces to work together on an inventory of pollutant sources within the Gulf of Maine watershed, an activity that would not have occurred without the Action Plan.

Conclusion

The Gulf of Maine Program is genuinely international and offers a precedent-setting forum for the varied entities in the Gulf region to join forces to protect the well-being of a shared resource. The Gulf Program successfully acts as a broker between interests in the provinces and states, and contributes significantly to the pool of information about the Gulf of Maine. Through the creation of the ten-year Gulf of Maine Action Plan, the Gulf-wide Marine Environmental Quality Monitoring Plan, and the initiation of targeted projects, Canadians and Americans are working together in a shared marine water body with great effect.

The Gulf Program promotes multi-institutional, multi-disciplinary research and management of the Gulf of Maine environment. Since 1989, the Gulf of Maine Council on the Marine Environment has proven successful in forging partnerships that bridge many of the political and institutional boundaries in the Gulf, and has built a strong foundation for sustainable use of this valued international water body.

25

African Boundaries and National Parks

Ieuan Ll. Griffiths

Africa has about 50,000 miles (80,000km) of international boundaries which divide the continent into 50 separate pieces of territory: 46 sovereign states, Western Sahara, the exclave of Cabinda, and the two tiny exclaves of Spanish North Africa. The continent also possesses over 200 national parks, and game, forest or nature reserves (hereafter referred to collectively as national parks) where the local fauna and flora are conserved. The wildlife of sub-Saharan Africa constitutes one of the wonders of the modern world. But it is under enormous threat, both from poachers of ivory, skins and rhino horn and from pressure on its space from burgeoning rural populations who, for the first time in many parts of Africa, are experiencing shortage of land from which to earn a living. The location of the parks within African countries is of special interest.

Boundaries and national parks come together in a statistically close relationship. Almost 40% (76 out of about 200) of the national parks of Africa lie on international boundaries. Almost one-third of all African boundaries (35 of 109, 32.1%) have a national park on one or both sides. These figures have to be put into the context of only 30 of the 50 African territories (60%) having national parks of any description. National parks are confined to sub-Saharan Africa, and even there 12 territories have no national parks. Excluding boundaries between two countries neither of which has national parks the percentage of boundaries on which there are national parks rises to 36.8% (35 of 95).

National parks were mostly created for the purpose of conserving the natural fauna and flora of Africa. Areas selected for national parks within individual countries were often those best endowed with wildlife and least densely populated by human beings. Often the two characteristics went together, for wildlife areas are usually infested with tsetse fly and are not the easiest of human habitats.

South Africa's Kruger Park, in its earliest manifestation, the Sabi Game Reserve, claims to be the oldest established national park on the continent (Stevenson-Hamilton, 1937). The idea was first mooted in the *Volksraad* of the *Zuid Afrikaansche Republiek* (Transvaal) in 1889 when two areas, between Zululand and Swaziland and on the eastern Transvaal lowveld, were proposed as suitable areas. It was not until

March 1898 that legislation was passed formally setting up the Sabi Game Reserve which was to grow and develop into the Kruger Park. In its early days the Sabi Game Reserve was 1,800 square miles (4,660km²) in area between the Sabi and Crocodile rivers to the north and the south and between the Lebombo mountains to the east and the Drakensberg escarpment to the west. The Lebombo marked the boundary between the Transvaal and Portuguese Mozambique. Re-designated after the Boer war, the Sabi Game Reserve was manned by a white chief warden with two assistant wardens who trained a small army of Africans. Its African population was cleared and war was waged against African poaching. Hunting of game, by anyone, was strictly forbidden and a breakthrough in conservation came in 1903 when Stevenson-Hamilton, the chief warden who served from 1902–46, successfully pressed charges against a senior white police officer. In 1904 the conservation area was greatly increased in size when privately owned land between the Sabi and Oliphant rivers was placed under the supervision of Stevenson-Hamilton. In 1926 a National Parks Act, under which the Kruger National Park was constituted, was passed through the South African parliament. In 1928 the Park was opened to the public who were catered for by newly constructed roads, bridges and rest camps. A whole new form of tourism, the motor wildlife safari, was born. It has spread to all parts of Africa and gone from strength to strength. Facilities for tourists in the Kruger Park have steadily improved over the years and the numbers of visitors has increased almost annually.

The Kruger Park authorities have not lost sight of their priorities which are the preservation of the rich fauna and flora of the lowveld. The whole tourist industry that has grown up is a bonus, bringing in significant revenue which is put towards animal conservation, but also public support. The Park has been hugely successful in looking after its wild animal stock, preventing the demise of endangered species and protecting its vulnerable animal populations against the depredations of poachers and disease.

The present area of the Kruger National Park is 7,440 square miles (19,010km²), the equivalent of about 93% the area of Wales and over 170% that of The Gambia. Its borders extend for almost 600 miles (950km) of which over 210 miles (340km) make up the international boundary between South Africa and Mozambique, from the Crocodile River at Komatipoort to the Limpopo River. Over 80% of the Transvaal section of the boundary with Mozambique is made up by the Kruger National Park. The Park is on average about 38 miles (60km) wide and presents a strip of territory of that width west from the length of Mozambique boundary. For about 30 miles (48km) the Park's northern perimeter along the right bank of the Limpopo is part of South Africa's boundary with Zimbabwe (Figure 25.1).

In having an international boundary as a large part of its perimeter the Kruger Park set a trend which was to be followed by national parks

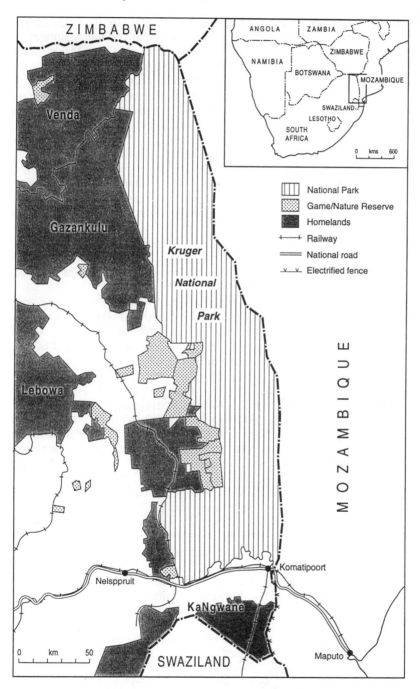

Figure 25.1 The Kruger National Park

in all parts of sub-Saharan Africa. For example, in East Africa the boundary between Kenya and Tanzania marks part of the perimeter of several national parks and game reserves. In Kenya the Masai Mara National Reserve, (645 square miles, 1,675km^2), and the vast Tsavo National Park (8,000 square miles, 20,750km^2) both have the boundary as part of their southern perimeter, whilst in Tanzania the 5,675 square mile (14,700km^2) Serengeti National Park and the Mkomazi Game Reserve also lie against the boundary. The Parks on either side of the boundary have a long common frontage and game moves freely across the international boundary. The Masai Mara forms the northern part of the Serengeti plains across which millions of wildebeeste, zebra, gazelles and other species of antelope with attendant predators migrate seasonally, oblivious of the straight line boundary. This part of the boundary also cuts across the traditional territory (culture group area) of the Masai people who ignore the straight line boundary with the same contempt as the migrating animals. Almost 30% of the 470 mile (750km) international boundary between Kenya and Tanzania is made up of national park or game reserve on one side or the other, or on both sides (Figure 25.2).

In West Africa the most impressive group of national parks and wildlife conservation areas is that clustered about *le Parc National du W du Niger* (Figure 25.3). It is an international national park which extends over parts of Niger (2,200km^2, 850 square miles), Burkina Faso (3,500km^2, 1,350 square miles) and Benin (5,020km^2, 1,950 square miles). The total area of the Park is 10,720km^2 (4,150 square miles), just a little less than the area of The Gambia. The Park takes its name from the 'W' configuration of the River Niger where it cuts through the Atakora mountain chain at the northern extremity of the Park in Niger. South of the Atakora mountains the Park mainly comprises a vast peneplain covered with savannah woodland which supports a large and varied wildlife. The *Parc de refuge du Moyen-Niger* was first set up in 1926, but it was not until 1954 that *le Parc National du W du Niger* was definitively constituted. To the south-west there are two further smaller national parks, *le Parc de l'Arli* in Burkina Faso and *le Parc de la Pendjari* in Benin which have a common frontage along the Pendjari river which makes up the international boundary. Clustered around the national parks, and greatly extending the conservation area, are various Animal Reserves, *Zones Cynegetique* and *Zones de Chasse*. All but 10km (97%) of the 335km (210 mile) boundary between Benin and Burkina Faso has national parks and Reserves to a depth of at least 10km on both sides of the frontier, a substantial buffer zone between the two countries which is traversed by only two minor roads. The whole complex represents an enormous block of wildlife conservation areas in the heart of West Africa. As a tourist attraction it has far less highly developed facilities than the Kruger National Park or, for that matter, the Kenyan and Tanzanian Parks but, like them, it also occupies a

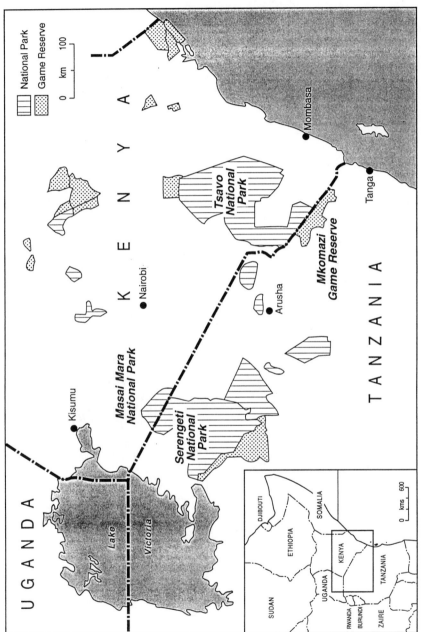

Figure 25.2 Parks on the Kenya–Tanzania Border

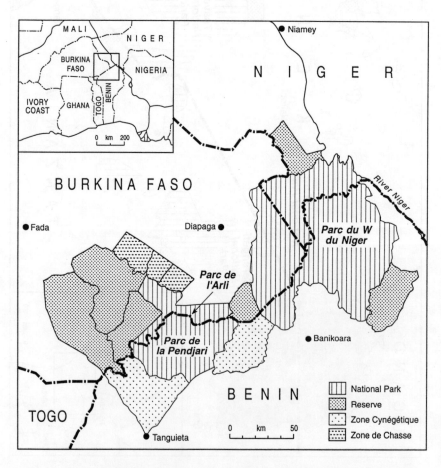

Figure 25.3 Parks on the Borders of Benin, Burkina Faso and Niger

cross-border area, with the Benin–Burkina Faso–Niger boundary tripoint near the centre of *le Parc National du W du Niger*. The international nature of the Park originally derives from the French colonial federation of *Afrique Occidentale Francaise* but has been maintained as an international co-operative enterprise since the colonies were separately given independence in 1960.

The national parks described seem to be straightforward attempts to conserve something very worthwhile: precious parts of Africa's environment uniquely rich in fauna and flora. In part they are a reaction to the sickening slaughter of the 19th and early 20th centuries (Methuen, 1846) when the wildlife of Africa was decimated by 'great white hunters', armed with the fire arms of ever advancing technology, roaming the plains with deadly abandon, some for gain, some for 'sport' (Bryden, 1936: 277). The location of national parks was largely determined by the distribution of the surviving wildlife when the new attitudes tending towards conservation began to make an impact and the first reserves were created. The wildlife areas were therefore largely residual, tracts of land that had not been taken into African cultivation or white settlement and in which wildlife survived. They were areas that were not inviting for human settlement and to some extent the very presence of wildlife made them less attractive. The connection between such areas and the tsetse fly and sleeping sickness has already been mentioned. The wildlife areas were also malarial, often low-lying swampy riverine areas of pestilential infestation, or sometimes not easily penetrated mountainous areas.

In pre-colonial Africa such areas frequently served as boundaries. They were unattractive to human settlement and had low densities of population. Such areas often conveniently separated one pre-colonial polity from another. An example of this may be seen in western Zambia. The pre-colonial Lozi kingdom along the upper Zambesi valley is separated from the rest of Zambia by a tract of land along the middle Kafue valley. This large area is covered with scrub woodland mainly developed on Kalahari sands. It is infested with tsetse fly and malarial mosquitoes and is overall an environment hostile to human settlement. It is rich in wildlife, not on the prodigious scale of parts of East Africa but rich enough, and is today constituted as the Kafue National Park (Figure 4). The Kafue Park area is a classical form of African pre-colonial boundary, a no man's land area rather than the precise linear boundary beloved of the European partition of Africa. Since the 1970s the Kafue National Park has been crossed by a paved road linking Lusaka with Mongu, the Barotseland capital.

Most national parks in Africa were set up after the European partition of Africa gave the continent its present mesh of boundary lines. Few modern boundaries were defined with areas such as the middle Kafue valley in mind, if only because European knowledge of Africa at the time of the partition was far too limited. The fact that so many sub-Saharan African boundaries are now adorned with national

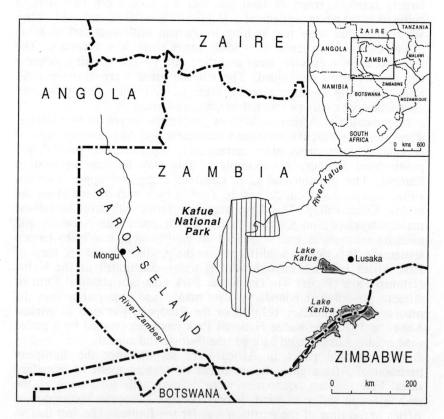

Figure 25.4 The Kafue National Park, Zambia

parks suggests that boundaries attract such areas. Boundaries tend to repel economic development. The other side of the same coin appears to be that they attract conservation areas, and lends credence to the claim that boundaries positively marginalise.

There has also been a realisation in recent years that a zonal boundary, such as a national park, can be more secure than a linear boundary unless the latter is given elaborate protection. A broad depopulated zone along a boundary is difficult to cross without attracting official attention, especially when that zone has a large population of sometimes fierce wild animals carefully watched by wardens trained and skilled in anti-poaching activities. The best example is the Kruger Park in South Africa which in effect 'guards' over 200 miles of the frontier with Mozambique. The South African boundary with Mozambique divides two of the most disparate standards of living of any two contiguous countries in the world (Griffiths, 1994). Average gross national product per capita is over 30 times greater in South Africa than in Mozambique. Even allowing for distortion of the average figures by the relatively high incomes of South African whites to which black Mozambicans do not aspire, South Africa attracts many immigrants to cross the border illegally. The apartheid state had two defences against this illegal traffic. One was a lethal electrified fence 'the snake' built along the Mozambique border from the Swaziland tripoint to Komatipoort. Northwards from Komatipoort the defence was provided by the Kruger Park itself. The illegal immigrants take up to twenty-four hours to cross the Park during which time they are a possible prey to wild animals. Reports of man-eating lions in the Park are too numerous to be totally discounted as merely propaganda designed to put off would-be migrants. The problem of illegal migration has not disappeared with the demise of apartheid, and whilst 'the snake' had its lethal current turned off in 1993, the Park continues to present its dangers to the unwary migrant.

The national parks of Africa are coming under increased pressure from a number of sources. The animals themselves, particularly elephants and rhinos, are endangered by large-scale poaching. Rich and ready markets for ivory and rhino horn were available in the Far East, and in Africa the multiplicity of wars saw many parts of the continent flooded with modern weaponry for mass slaughter. With the motivation and the means came the poachers: men often displaced by war, trained in the use of modern automatic rifles such as the Soviet AK-47, and hungry for the rich rewards to be gained from poaching.

Some African governments were unable to control poaching because the wildlife areas were outside their control. This was often due specifically to the peripheral location of national parks within states. In several African states the writ of central government does not extend to all border regions, which sometimes foster dissident groups (Richards, 1994). As national parks are often in border regions they suffer accordingly. Other governments put poaching control low on the political agenda or were unable to finance wildlife conservation. Some African political elites were themselves heavily involved in the poaching business.

In 1989 the Convention on International Trade in Endangered Species (CITES) passed, after much political in-fighting, a ban on trade in ivory and other elephant parts (Douglas-Hamilton, 1992). The ban was renewed in 1992 despite stiff opposition from some African countries, notably Botswana, South Africa and Zimbabwe. There, poaching of ivory has been controlled to the extent that culling of elephant herds is necessary to maintain a stable elephant population within the designated areas. When the elephants spread from these areas they can be especially destructive of crops in surrounding districts of human settlement. The southern African countries argue that ivory obtained in culls should be released on to the international market in a controlled way, the proceeds being ploughed back into wildlife protection and conservation. It is a long-running argument conducted passionately, with the total ban on ivory trade construed as being imposed on Africa by outside do-gooders who do not make reparation for the lost revenue which is borne solely by the African countries. On the other hand, a partial ban with quotas has not worked in the past especially where wildlife protection is less well organised, and that includes African states where border national parks are no-go areas for central governments.

National parks are also under pressure from the expansion of rural human populations. Occasionally this can work to the advantage of tourism as in the Serengeti, where human encroachment has concentrated the great wildlife migrations into a restricted area making them all the more spectacular (Sterry, 1992). But the juxtaposition of densely settled areas and national parks is perhaps best seen in South Africa where the design of 'grand apartheid' deliberately consigned 'homelands' to the same peripheral areas of the state as national parks. This seen in Figure 25.1 where parts of the 'homelands' of KaNgwane, Lebowa, Kazangulu and Venda in the eastern Transvaal all border the Kruger National Park. The road journey from Nelspruit into the southern (Pretorius Kop) section of the Kruger Park runs through the most densely populated part of the KaNgwane homeland. The obviously overcrowded and thickly settled hills abruptly give way to the Park where the human population is confined to the tourist and rangers' camps. The contrast is stark.

This particular case poses another major problem for the Mandela government. For rural black South Africans the greatest aspirations are for sufficient land to earn a living after decades of deprivation under the apartheid state. As in other African countries where a large proportion of the land was alienated by white settlers, for example Kenya and Zimbabwe, the new South African government will probably find that meeting the legitimate aspirations of the rural African will be difficult. National park land could well be threatened as it has been in parts of Zimbabwe. In the case of South Africa the problem is the more acute as national parks and 'homelands' compete for the same border lands.

Another use to which the Kruger Park was put during the later years of the apartheid regime is related to the geographically marginal position of the Park. The northern parts of the Park were used clandestinely as training camps for cadres of the Mozambique National Resistance (MNR) and supply centres from which the South African Defence Force fuelled the MNR-led civil war in Mozambique. The northern part of the Kruger Park was not only on the Mozambique border but was depopulated and well away from prying eyes. Access to the northern section of the Park could be legitimately restricted on grounds of the unsuitability of the wet season for tourists. Such restrictions are common to many other national parks in Africa, for example, *le Parc National du W du Niger where* there is a well defined tourist season. The short rainy season, from June to September, leads to the closure of the Park, which generally operns at the beginning of December when the trails can be used again. The legitimate and sensible restrictions on access during the wet season, or indeed for other reasons consistent with good conservation practice, can sometimes be used as a cover for clandestine nefarious activities by governmental agencies.

The great length of international boundaries in Africa is a strait-jacket on independent development. Also, vast areas of the continent are marginalised simply because they are crossed by the arbitrarily-drawn lines imposed by former colonial powers. The existence of many national parks in these border areas has been a lone bonus. National parks are in many ways perceived by central governments as the ideal land-use for national margins, even serving to strengthen control of the actual linear boundary by adding a traditional African frontier zone. Occasionally national parks have been abused by dubious central government activity and, elsewhere, border areas are sometimes beyond the control of central government. In both cases the peripheral location of national parks is a key element. National parks in Africa are under increasing pressure from poachers, civil war, rural population growth and land hunger. Will their location in the border regions of Africa assist their survival?

Table 25.1 Boundaries and National Parks in Africa

Countries which have Parks on boundaries	National Parks, etc, on boundaries	Boundary with:
Angola	Mucusso CP	(Namibia)
	Iona NP	(Namibia)
	Luiana CP	(Zambia)
Benin	W NP	(Burkina Faso)
		(Niger)
	Pendjari NP	(Burkina Faso)
	Pendjari ZC	(Burkina Faso)
	Atakora ZC	(Burkina Faso)
Botswana	Chobe NP	(Namibia)
	Gemsbok NP	(Namibia)
		(South Africa)
	Mashatu GR	(South Africa)
		(Zimbabwe)
	Sibuyu FR	(Zimbabwe)
Burkina Faso	W NP	(Benin)
		(Niger)
	Arli NP	(Benin)
	Arli RPF	(Benin)
	Pama RPF	(Benin)
	Kourtiagou RPF	(Benin)
Cameroon	Bouba Njida NP	(Chad)
	Campo R	(Equatorial Guinea)
Central Africa Republic	Bamingui-Bangoran NP	(Chad)
Congo	Mont Fouari R	(Gabon)
	Nyanga R	(Gabon)
Gabon	Mont Fouari R	(Congo)
	Nyanga R	(Congo)
Kenya	Masai Mara NR	(Tanzania)
	Tsavo NP	(Tanzania)
	Mount Elgon NP	(Uganda)
Lesotho	Sehlabathebe NP	(South Africa)
Malawi	Lengwe NP	(Mozambique)
	Kasungu NP	(Zambia)
	Nyika NP	(Zambia)
	Vwaza NP	(Zambia)
Mozambique	Niassa GR	(Tanzania)
Namibia	Skeleton Coast NP	(Angola)
	Kaudam GR	(Botswana)
	Caprivi GR	(Angola)
		(Botswana)
	Mahango GR	(Botswana)
Niger	W NP	(Benin)
		(Burkina Faso)
	Tamou RPF	(Burkina Faso)

Table 25.1 continued

Rwanda	L'Akagera NP	(Tanzania)
	Karisimbi	(Zaire)
Senegal	Niokolo-Koba NP	(Guinea)
South Africa	Kalahari Gemsbok NP	(Botswana)
		(Namibia)
	Royal Natal NP	(Lesotho)
	Giant's Castle GR	(Lesotho)
	Mzimkulwana NR	(Lesotho)
	Mzimkulu WA	(Lesotho)
	Kruger NP	(Mozambique)
		(Zimbabwe)
	Ndumo GR	(Mozambique)
	Tembe ER	(Mozambique)
	Richtersveld NP	(Namiia)
Sudan	Dinder NP	(Ethiopia)
Swaziland	Mlawula NR	(Mozambique)
	Malolotja NR	(South Africa)
Tanzania	Serengeti NP	Kenya)
	Mkomazi GR	(Kenya)
Uganda	Kidepo NP	(Sudan)
	Queen Elizabeth NP	(Zaire)
Zaire	Garamba NP	(Sudan)
	Virunga NP	(Uganda)
Zambia	Sioma Ngwezi NP	(Angola)
		(Namibia)
	Lower Zambesi NP	(Zimbabwe)
Zimbabwe	Hwange NP	(Botswana)
	Kazuma FR	(Botswana)
	Kazuma Pan NP	(Botswana)
	Chimanimani NP	(Mozambique)
	Dande SA	(Mozambique)
	Gonarezhou NP	(Mozambique)
	Mtarazi Falls NP	(Mozambique)
	Malapati GR	(Mozambique)
	Chewore SA	(Zambia)
	Mana Pools NP	(Zambia)
	Matetsi SA	(Zambia)
	Sapi SA	(Zambia)
	Urungwe SA	(Zambia)
	Zambesi NP	(Zambia)

Abbreviations: Coutada Publica (CP), Forest Reserves (FR), Game Reserves (GR), National Parks (NP), Nature Reserves (NR), Parks (P), Reserves (R), *Reserves Partielles de Faune* (RPF), *Reserves Totales de Faune* (RTF), Safari Areas (SA), Wilderness Areas (WA), *Zones Cynegetiques* (ZC)

Notes: The above listing is not exhaustive. Some Parks, etc, listed above are not operative because of wars.

Bibliography

Bryden, H.A. (1936) *Wildlife in South Africa,* London: Harrap.

Douglas-Hamilton, I. and O. (1992) *Battle for the Elephants,* London: Doubleday.

Griffiths, I.Ll. (1994 [in press]) 'Permeable boundaries in Africa', in P. Nugent and A.I. Asiwaju (eds) *African boundaries,* Edinburgh: Centre for African Studies.

Methuen, H.H. (1846) *Life in the Wilderness or Wanderings in South Africa,* London: Richard Bentley.

New Scientist (1990) Vol.125, 1701, 27. (Summary in IBRU (1990) *Newsletter No.3,* University of Durham: International Boundaries Research Unit.) Also subject of BBC-TV film narrated by Nadine Gordimer.

Richards, P. (1994) 'Videos and violence on the periphery', *IDS Bulletin* 25, 2, April: 88–93.

Sterry, P. (1992) *Wildlife Travelling Companion, East Africa,* Marlborough: Crowood.

Stevenson-Hamilton, J. (1937) *South African Eden: From Sabi Game Reserve to Kruger National Park,* London: Cassell.

Maps Consulted

Africa: *Cartes Routieres et Touristiques, Paris, Pneu Michelin, Echelle 1:4,000,000, 953 Afrique Nord et Ouest, 17e ed, 954 Afrique Nord-Est, 7e ed, 955 Afrique Centre et Sud, 18e ed,* 1991–2.

Botswana: Minimap, 1:4,000,000 and 1:860,000, Cape Town, Map Studio, 3rd edition 1992.

Ivory Coast: *Carte Routiere et Touristique, Paris, Pneu Michelin, Echelle 1:800,000, 975 Cote d'Ivoire, 17e ed,* 1990–1.

Kenya: Tourist Map, Masai Mara National Reserve, 1:125,000, Nairobi, Macmillan, 1988.

Kenya: Map of Tsavo West National Park, 1:250,000, Nairobi, Survey of Kenya, October 1983.

South Africa: Minimap, 1:3,300,000, Cape Town, Map Studio, 4th edition 1993.

South Africa: Tourist Map, Eastern Transvaal and Kruger National Park, 1:460,000, Cape Town, Map Studio, 4th edition 1992.

West Africa: *Carte Touristique: Parcs Nationaux des Pays de l'Entente (Benin, Burkina Faso, Cote d'Ivoire, Niger, Togo), 1:375,000,* Abidjan, Conseil de l'Entente; Paris, Institut Geographique National, 1984.

Zimbabwe: Minimap, 1:2,000,000, Cape Town, Map Studio, 1990.

Fisheries

26

The Role of the United Nations in Managing the World's Fisheries

Moritaka Hayashi

Introduction

The title assigned by the organisers of this Conference has such broad implications that some preliminary comments are warranted on the role that the United Nations proper plays in the world's fisheries. In fact, its role is a rather limited one: within the United Nations system there is a specialised agency having general competence in the management of fisheries world-wide, ie, the Food and Agriculture Organization of the United Nations (FAO).

Traditionally, the United Nations has been engaged only in the area of general multilateral treaty-making for regulating fisheries outside the territorial seas of coastal States. The first exercise of this kind was the elaboration of a draft convention by the International Law Commission and its adoption in 1958 as the Geneva Convention on Fishing and the Conservation of the Living Resources of the High Seas. The second example is the Third United Nations Conference on the Law of the Sea, which culminated in 1982 with the adoption of the United Nations Convention on the Law of the Sea (UNCLOS), containing a number of basic provisions regarding fisheries both within the exclusive economic zone (EEZ) and on the high seas.

In recent years, however, the United Nations has become involved in much broader activities in the field of fisheries. This was essentially caused by mounting global concerns, particularly from the environmental perspective, with the rapidly deteriorating condition of the living resources in the world's oceans. The concern regarding certain aspects of fisheries became so acute that it assumed too high a political overtone to be handled only by the FAO, a technical body normally comprised exclusively of fisheries experts. The forum thus chosen is the United Nations General Assembly, a highly visible political body appealing to environmental groups and national constituencies, as well as the general public.

The use of large-scale pelagic driftnets was the first such question brought to the General Assembly, which has adopted resolutions on banning such gear on the high seas. Another question similarly brought to the Assembly is the conservation and management of straddling fish stocks and highly migratory fish stocks.

The question of driftnet fishing has been the subject of numerous papers and discussions. This paper therefore will focus only on the latter, which is currently under discussion and negotiation at the United Nations Conference on Straddling Fish Stocks and Highly Migratory Fish Stocks. The main purpose of the paper is to analyse the salient issues being dealt with and the positions of participants in the Conference. Before doing so, however, a brief description of the types of fish stocks and the problems they face may be useful.

Straddling Fish Stocks and Highly Migratory Fish Stocks and Their Fisheries

STRADDLING FISH STOCKS

The term 'straddling stock' is not used in UNCLOS but it is understood to mean the kind of stocks referred to in its Article 63(2), ie, a stock or stocks of associated species which occur both within the EEZ of a coastal State and in an area of the high seas adjacent to the zone.

According to FAO experts, most of the species occurring in the high seas are found inside and outside the EEZ boundary, either at the same time or sequentially (eg, during the various phases of their life cycle) and could be considered 'straddling', at least from a purely biological point of view (FAO, 1993: 4). Straddling stocks may, therefore, be found in any part of the world's oceans and seas. Commercially important stocks, however, occur particularly in the following well-known areas in the Pacific and Atlantic Oceans.

In the North-west Pacific, there was an enormous biomass of Alaska pollock widely distributed particularly in and around the high-seas enclaves of the Bering Sea (the 'donut hole') and the Sea of Okhotsk (the 'peanut hole'). The total catch of the stocks in the North Pacific increased steadily from 300,000 tons in the 1950s to 6.7 million tons in the late 1980s. Catches in the donut hole, however, have dramatically decreased from 1 million tons in the late 1980s to 22,000 tons in 1992 (FAO, 1993: 20). In August 1992, the coastal States and the fishing States – China, Japan, Poland, the Republic of Korea, the Russian Federation and the United States – came to an agreement to suspend temporarily fishing for pollock 'on a voluntary basis' for the period of two years until the end of 1994.[1] These States have continued their consultations with a view to adopting a long-term conservation regime and succeeded on 11 February 1994 in adopting an international Convention on the Conservation and Management of Pollock Resources in the Central Bering Sea.

Pollock stocks in the peanut hole, according to the Russian Government, have sharply declined in recent years because of 'unregulated fishing', which led the Government to edict in 1993 a total ban on fishing in that high-seas pocket, not only by the Russian fleet but also by vessels from distant-water fishing nations (DWFNs) (UN 164/L.21: 2). The States concerned discussed the conservation and utilisation problems in May–June 1993 and recognised the desirability of taking interim measures, on a voluntary basis. While the Russian Federation proposed a moratorium on pollock fishing in the peanut hole, and Japan and the Russian Federation expressed their intention to continue temporary suspension of their fishing, China, Poland and the Republic of Korea expressed their intention to reduce their fishing efforts by 25% in comparison with the same period in 1992 (ICCMOS/3, 1993: reproduced in UN 164/INF/6).

In the South Pacific region, particularly in the extension of the Challenger Plateau beyond 200 miles off New Zealand, the fishery for the orange roughy, which matures at an age of 20–5 years and may reach 100 years, has been conducted initially by Australia and New Zealand since the 1980s and recently also by Japan, Norway, the Republic of Korea and the Russian Federation. The biomass and catch-rates of the species decreased rapidly in recent years and it is estimated that the current biomass is 20% of the pristine biomass (FAO, 1993: 21–2).

The Chilean jack mackerel is found extensively from New Zealand to the coasts of Chile and Peru. Harvested mostly by the former USSR as well as Chile and Peru, the total catch of this species increased more than 200 times from 17,000 tons in 1970–4 to 3.8 million tons in 1990. The status of the whole South Pacific stock is unknown (FAO, 1993: 22–3).

In the Atlantic Ocean, the most controversial stocks are cod and a mixture of other bottom fish, such as American plaice, redfish, witch flounder, Greenland halibut, yellowtail flounder, etc, which straddle the 200-mile Canadian zone off Newfoundland. These stocks have been exploited heavily both by Canadian vessels and DWFN fleets. The high seas fisheries in the region are managed by the Northwest Atlantic Fisheries Organization (NAFO), to which Canada and most of the DWFNs belong. A number of stocks in the area are now seriously depleted, and the ground fish stocks are generally in the worst condition in history. The decline of the cod biomass was so particularly severe in the last few years that local cod fisheries have been closed since 1992 by the Canadian Government.

In the South-west Atlantic, several important demersal stocks occur both within the EEZ of Argentina and the adjacent high-seas areas, including the areas off the Falklands Islands (Malvinas). These stocks include short-fin squid, hake and southern blue whiting which have been harvested by Argentina and Uruguay as well as DWFN fleets from Japan, Poland, the Republic of Korea, Spain, Taiwan (Province of China), and the former USSR. Total catches of the stocks of short-fin and common squid, occurring particularly in the Patagonian Shelf and Slope, increased steadily from around 100,000 tons annually in the early 1980s to 750,000 tons in 1987, but dropped to 550,000 tons in 1990. FAO considers that these stocks are now fully- to over-exploited in the Patagonian Shelf area (FAO, 1993: 28). The hakes, yielding around 425,000 tons per year in much wider areas, are also considered to be fully exploited (FAO, 1993: 29).

HIGHLY MIGRATORY FISH STOCKS

UNCLOS defines 'highly migratory species' by way of listing such species in the annex. The list includes nine tuna and 12 billfish species, two tuna-like species, four species of sauries, pomfrets, dolphin fish, oceanic sharks and cetaceans. They all move for long distances across the oceans, in and out of EEZs, disregarding their boundaries. 'Highly migratory fish stocks' as used in the United Nations Conference refer to these species, with the exception of marine mammals.

By far the most important highly migratory fish stocks are tuna, particularly the so-called 'principal market tuna species', which include bluefin, bigeye, yellowfin, albacore and skipjack.

The total world catch of the principal market tuna species has doubled since the early 1970s, from 1.4 million to 2.8 million tons per year. During the same period, the total annual catch of tuna and tuna-like species has increased from 1.9 million to 4.2 million tons (FAO, 1993: 8).

The current status of tuna species is summarised by FAO as follows: some species are still in good condition with relatively low to moderate exploitation rates such as for skipjack in all oceans, albacore in the Atlantic, and yellowfin in the Western and Central Pacific. Other stocks such as yellowfin in the Eastern Pacific and the Atlantic are under more severe pressure. Other stocks are exploited beyond their maximum sustainable yield (MSY), such as northern bluefin in the Eastern Atlantic and the Mediterranean Sea, albacore in the South Atlantic and, possibly, bigeye in the Atlantic. Some resources such as northern bluefin and southern bluefin in the Atlantic are considered depleted. The status of yellowfin in the Western Atlantic and northern bluefin in the Pacific is unknown, and the status of the remaining stocks can be classified as heavily to fully exploited (FAO, 1993: 10).

United Nations Conference on Straddling Fish Stocks and Highly Migratory Fish Stocks

BACKGROUND

Because of the grave situation facing Newfoundland fishermen in the North-west Atlantic, Canada began to raise the question of conservation and management of high seas fisheries in the United Nations in 1990, when it started to prepare for the United Nations Conference on Environment and Development (UNCED).

At the third session of the Preparatory Commission for UNCED in August 1991, Canada and some like-minded countries submitted a proposal on the conservation and management of the living resources of the high seas. The proposal was replaced in March 1992 by a revised paper (UN 151/PC, 1992). The revised paper covered not only straddling stocks but also highly migratory species, and the co-sponsors were accordingly expanded to include those States which were concerned with either or both of such stocks. The 40 co-sponsors included Argentina, Canada, Cape Verde, Chile, Kenya, Sri Lanka, Tunisia and the United Republic of Tanzania, as well as South Pacific Forum Fisheries Agency (FFA) countries like Fiji, New Zealand and Papua New Guinea.

The paper contained several 'principles', including the following:

States fishing a straddling stock or highly migratory species on the high seas must take all measures necessary to 'give effect to the special interest and responsibility of the coastal State' concerning the portion of the stock outside the 200-mile limit and in the highly migratory species while outside that limit';[2] and

high seas fishing must not have an adverse impact on the resources under coastal States' jurisdiction.

Initially the co-sponsors wanted the contents of their proposal reflected in draft Agenda 21, which the Preparatory Commission was drafting as a basic document containing action programmes to be adopted by UNCED (Agenda 21 (draft): 17.53-4; 17.83-4). However, since some of the elements in that proposal did not appear to receive consensus support, Canada and other co-sponsors advanced the idea of convening a conference under United Nations auspices to discuss questions relating to high seas fisheries. After intensive negotiations, a carefully crafted compromise was adopted by consensus in Rio de Janeiro containing the following four essential elements (UNCED: 17.49):

1 The conference should be convened as soon as possible under
United Nations auspices, but drawing, *inter alia*, on scientific and
technical studies by FAO;
2 The conference should be aimed at promoting effective
implementation of UNCLOS provisions on straddling and highly
migratory fish stocks;
3 The mandate of the conference is to identify and assess existing
problems related to the conservation and management of such fish
stocks, consider means of improving co-operation on fisheries
among States, and formulate appropriate recommendations; and
4 The work and the results of the conference should be fully consistent
with UNCLOS provisions, in particular the rights and obligations of
coastal States and States fishing on the high seas.

On the basis of the above-mentioned UNCED recommendations, the
United Nations General Assembly decided to convene the Conference
in 1993 and requested it to: identify and assess existing problems
related to the conservation and management of such stocks; consider
means of improving fisheries co-operation among States; and formulate
appropriate recommendations (UNGA, 47/192).

The Assembly further decided that the Conference should complete
its work before the forty-ninth session of the Assembly in 1994 and
requested that the work and results of the Conference should be fully
consistent with the provisions of UNCLOS (UNGA, 47/192).

The Conference has held three sessions so far, with the first one
devoted to organisational matters. On the basis of the discussions
during the second session in July 1993, the Chairman prepared a
negotiating text (UN 164/13). He issued a revised version of the text
(UN 164/13/Rev.1) at the end of the third session in March 1994. The
final session is scheduled for August 1994.

QUESTION OF FORM OF THE CONFERENCE OUTCOME

The mandate given to the Conference is to formulate 'appropriate
recommendations'. It is therefore up to the Conference to decide on the
form of the substantive document it may eventually adopt.

On this question a number of coastal States, notably Argentina,
Brazil, Canada, Chile, Colombia, Ecuador, Iceland, Mexico, Norway,
Peru, Sierra Leone and Sweden, made it clear that the Conference
should adopt a legally binding convention. A draft convention was
tabled by Argentina, Canada, Chile, Iceland and New Zealand (the
'Five-Power Draft Convention', UN 164/L.11/Rev.1). Another
comprehensive draft convention was submitted at the end of the third
session by Ecuador, merging a number of existing proposals (UN
164/L.44). On the other hand, some DWFN delegations like China,
Japan, Poland and the Republic of Korea stated that a non-binding

instrument containing a set of recommendations or guidelines would be more appropriate.

Several others stated that they were flexible on the final form of the document. These included the European Community, Morocco, the Russian Federation and the United States.

The question of the ultimate form of the document to be adopted by the Conference is still difficult to predict. While there appears to be widespread support for a binding instrument, the text prepared by the Chairman as the basis for negotiation and its revision are not in the form of a draft convention, and requires considerable amount of work if it is to be transformed into a convention during the two-week session in August.

GEOGRAPHICAL SCOPE TO BE COVERED

One of the most controversial issues permeating the entire range of topics being discussed at the Conference is the geographical scope of application of the document to be adopted. The question is whether it should apply only to the high seas, or it should cover also the areas under national jurisdiction, particularly EEZs, in as much as the two types of stocks under discussion occur on both sides of the EEZ boundary or migrate freely between the two zones.

Several coastal States stressed that in Agenda 21, Chapter 17, the recommendation to hold the Conference is placed under programme area (c), dealing with sustainable use and conservation of living resources of the *high seas*, and not programme area (d), which deals with living resources under national jurisdiction. Therefore the mandate of the Conference is limited to those portions of the straddling and highly migratory stocks which are found on the high seas. They also pointed out that Article 63(2) of UNCLOS provides that the coastal States and the States fishing for straddling stocks in an area beyond and adjacent to the EEZ shall seek to agree on the measures necessary for the conservation of these stocks *in the adjacent area*. They further reminded the Conference of the sovereign rights of the coastal State under Article 56(1)(a) of UNCLOS for the purpose of conserving and managing the living resources within their EEZ.

On the other hand, DWFNs, notably China, the European Community, Japan, Poland, the Republic of Korea and the United States insisted on the need to address the issues with respect to both high seas and EEZs, particularly since the stocks in question could only be meaningfully managed by looking at units of stocks throughout their biological range.[3] The United States emphasised the multi-species, ecosystem-oriented management, taking into account the relationship among species and their habitats (UN 164/L.3: Annex, para. 2; UN 164/L.15: I, para. 7). Japan pointed out that since highly migratory stocks in particular may have a range of migration covering the high seas and sometimes more than 10 EEZs, it would be wiser to adopt uniform measures throughout their migratory range, as it had already been done in some regional agreements on tuna fisheries (UN 164/L.28: para. 7).

The Russian Federation, while recognising the biological indivisibility and the 'principle of the unity and inseparability' of straddling stocks, cautioned that this argument should not be used to gain access to the stocks within EEZs (UN 164/L.25: 2–3).

These arguments were repeated many times in various contexts. In the revised negotiating text, the Chairman attempted to settle this question by inserting a provision at the beginning of the document, defining its scope of application. According to the text, the document is to apply to conservation and management of the two types of stocks on the high seas, except for those parts relating to precautionary approaches and the question of compatibility and coherence between national and international measures (UN 164/13/Rev.1: para. 2). Since there are still strong reservations on the part of several delegations about narrowing down the scope of the document, the Conference may still have to face difficulties in finding a satisfactory solution at the summer session.

NATURE OF CONSERVATION AND MANAGEMENT MEASURES

On the nature of conservation and management measures to be adopted through co-operation, particular attention was given to the precautionary principle/approach, the question of management reference point, and the collection and sharing of data.

Precautionary Approach
With regard to the concept of precautionary principle/approach, reference was frequently made to the following 'Principle 15' of the Rio Declaration adopted at UNCED:

> In order to protect the environment, the precautionary approach shall be widely applied by States according to their capabilities. Where there are threats of serious or irreversible damage, lack of full scientific certainty shall not be used as a reason for postponing cost-effective measures to prevent environmental degradation (UNCED: 6).

A number of delegations – especially those of coastal States – were of the view that the principle embodied in the Rio Declaration should be applied as widely as possible in fisheries management. The Five-Power Draft Convention would require Parties to 'apply appropriate precautionary measures', and further provides that where there are threats of serious or irreversible damage to the stocks in question, the lack of full scientific certainty shall not be used as a reason to postpone such measures.[4] The FFA countries stressed similar points and placed the burden of proof that fishing on the high seas was not adversely affecting the resources and the marine environment on the State fishing the stock.

Several other delegations, particularly DWFNs, stated that Principle 15 of the Rio Declaration was developed in the field of pollution prevention and therefore should not automatically be made applicable to fisheries management. In order to buttress this argument, they referred to the report of the FAO Technical Consultations of September 1992, which recommends caution in dealing with this issue, stating that the practical implications of precautionary management would have to be carefully examined to avoid unnecessarily restrictive measures (FAO, 1992: para. 67). Against this a coastal State responded that it had expressed reservations to that report.

After preliminary discussions, the Conference decided to set up at the third session a working group on the subject and asked FAO to prepare a background paper. The FAO paper (UN 164/INF/8) suggested that the difference between the precautionary 'principle' and 'approach' are more perceived than real and the confusion between the two has been due largely to the slack use of the terms and lack of guidance on their practical application. Stating that the most relevant expression of the precautionary approach for the Conference was the above-quoted statement in the Rio Declaration, the paper went on to discuss the various aspects in applying the precautionary approach to fisheries management, and offered practical guidance for management.

The Working Group on the Precautionary Approach worked on the basis of the Chairman's negotiating text. There was a large measure of support in recommending to the plenary that States shall apply widely the precautionary approach as follows:

1 States shall act so as to obtain and share the best scientific evidence available in support of conservation and management decision-making;
2 In managing fish stocks, States shall consider their ecosystems. They should develop data collection and research programmes to assess the impact of harvesting on the ecosystems, adopt plans to reduce bycatch to the extent feasible, and consider the protection of habitats of special concern;
3 The absence of adequate scientific information shall not be used as a reason for failing to take or postponing measures to protect target and non-target species and their environment;
4 The precautionary approach shall be based on the best scientific evidence available and include all appropriate techniques and be aimed at setting stock-specific minimum standards for conservation. When precautionary management reference points are approached, measures shall be taken to ensure that they will not be exceeded.

5 In cases where the status of stocks is of concern, strict conservation and management measures shall be applied and shall be subject to enhanced monitoring;

6 In the case of new fisheries, conservative measures shall be established as soon as possible in co-operation with those initiating the fishery, and shall remain in force until there are sufficient data to allow assessment of the impact of the fishery on the long-term sustainability of the stocks and their ecosystems (UN 164/WP.1).

The Chairman incorporated all these points in the revised negotiating text (UN 164/13/Rev.1: para. 4).

Management Reference Points

With respect to management reference points, UNCLOS requires States to take measures which are designed to maintain or restore populations of harvested species at levels which can produce the maximum sustainable yield (MSY), as qualified by relevant environmental and economic factors, including the special requirements of developing States (Articles 61(3) and 119(1)(a)). The MSY concept, however, was considered no longer adequate by some delegations. Several coastal States preferred the concept of 'optimum sustainable yield', as qualified by relevant environmental and economic factors.[5] Another example given was the formula adopted by the 1980 Convention for the Conservation of Antarctic Marine Living Resources (CCAMLR).[6]

Since the discussion of this question required highly technical knowledge, the Conference decided to set up at the third session an expert working group to consider it. Also on this question FAO was requested to prepare a background paper. The FAO paper (UN 164/INF/9) discusses a number of reference points that have been proposed in recent years and points out that these tend to focus on defining acceptable levels of fishing mortality and minimum spawning stock criteria rather than on catch and fishing effort criteria.

The Working Group on Reference Points for Fisheries Management prepared a set of technical guidelines on biological reference points (UN 164/WP.2), which made clear distinction between limit reference points and target reference points. Limit reference points set boundaries which constrain utilisation within safe biological limits and beyond which resource-building programmes are required. They are designed for conservation and warn against the risk of over-exploitation. Target reference points guide policy makers in resource utilisation and are designed to indicate when an objective is being approached.

The Guidelines recommend, *inter alia*, that MSY should be adopted as a limit reference point rather than as a target reference point, and for already depleted stocks the biomass which can produce MSY may serve as an initial rebuilding target. It is also recommended that for broad application of the precautionary approach to stock conservation, a minimum international standard for management should be agreed upon, and an appropriate standard is to apply MSY as a limit on fisheries.

From rather detailed Guidelines, the Chairman adopted five key paragraphs for inclusion as an annex to his revised negotiating text (UN 164/13/Rev.1: Annex 2).

Collection and Sharing of Data

With regard to the question of collection and sharing of data, UNCLOS contains only the following broad, general rules:

> Available scientific information, catch and fishing effort statistics, and other data relevant to the conservation of fish stocks shall be contributed and exchanged on a regular basis through competent international organizations...where appropriate and with participation by all States concerned (Article 119(2)).

It was generally recognised that current data collection and sharing with respect to high seas fishing is quite unsatisfactory. The Chairman attempted to give in his negotiating text, in addition to a set of basic principles, detailed lists of type of data and information to be collected and exchanged, as well as the procedures for such exchange. Although there was a consensus on the need to enhance the collection and sharing of such data and information and some coastal States and FAO were in favour of making such lists as comprehensive as possible, DWFNs generally doubted the inclusion of several items in the lists from the point of view of feasibility and practicability. Particularly resisted by Japan and other DWFNs was the requirement that various data on catch and efforts on high sea fishing operations be sent to the fisheries administrations of relevant coastal States without prior arrangement.

At the third session, Japan submitted an alternative text on data collection and sharing. The revised negotiating text has incorporated some of the concerns of DWFNs, including the requirement of reporting to coastal States.

PRINCIPLES OF INTERNATIONAL CO-OPERATION

Article 63(2) of UNCLOS provides that the coastal State and the States fishing for straddling stocks in areas of the high seas adjacent to the EEZ of that State 'shall seek...to agree upon the measures necessary for the conservation of these stocks in the adjacent area'.

With respect to highly migratory stocks, Article 64(1) states that the coastal State and other States fishing for such species in the region:

shall cooperate... with a view to ensuring conservation and promoting the objective of optimum utilisation of such species throughout the region, both within and beyond the exclusive economic zone.

Regarding fishing on the high seas in general, Article 117 lays down the basic obligation, stipulating:

All States have the duty to take, or to cooperate with other States in taking such measures for their respective nationals as may be necessary for the conservation of the living resources of the high seas.

Further, Article 118 provides that 'States shall cooperate with each other in the conservation and management of living resources in the areas of the high seas'. Article 118 further obliges States whose nationals exploit identical living resources, or different living resources in the same area, to 'enter into negotiations with a view to taking the measures' necessary for the conservation of such resources.

From these provisions it is clear that central to the UNCLOS regime on the two types of stocks in question is the duty of all States concerned to co-operate with a view to adopting necessary measures for the conservation and management of such stocks (UN Law of the Sea: 10, 25).

Such duty must be performed directly between the States concerned or through appropriate international organisations (Articles 63–4), which are typically regional fisheries bodies. If no such organisation exists, they are obliged to co-operate to establish one (Articles 64 and 118).

The Chairman's negotiating text contained several elaborations on these provisions of UNCLOS. One of them, on the duty to enter into consultations in good faith and to act in a manner that does not constitute an abuse of right, 'with due regard to the rights, interests and obligations of other States' appeared to be generally acceptable.[7]

The obligation of non-members of regional fisheries arrangements to co-operate with them and respect their conservation and management measures was generally endorsed. It was also generally agreed that regional bodies should be open to participation, on a non-discriminatory basis, by all interested States, and that non-members should be encouraged to join.

Several States argued that where no regional organisation or arrangement exists for straddling stocks or highly migratory stocks, States concerned are obliged to enter into agreement to ensure effective conservation and management of the stocks in question. Some others, however, stated that, though desirable, no such obligation should be imposed.

REGIONAL ARRANGEMENTS

In the negotiating text, the Chairman set out a number of measures to be taken by regional bodies to ensure sustainability of the two types of stocks in question. Among such measures, views of delegations were divided on the appropriateness of requiring regional bodies to adopt procedures for compulsory and binding settlement of disputes. While the idea was supported by a number of coastal States, DWFNs generally questioned it, pointing out the need to take into account the different characteristics of each body and special regional circumstances.

With regard to the activities of non-members of regional arrangements that undermine existing measures, the Chairman incorporated in his negotiating text a new paragraph taken from the recently-concluded Central Bering Sea Convention, to the effect that States participating in regional arrangements shall take measures, individually or collectively, which they deem necessary and appropriate to deter such activities (UN 164/13/Rev.1: para. 43).

With respect to particular seas characterised as enclosed and semi-enclosed seas, the Russian Federation, which made repeated references to the serious situation in the Sea of Okhotsk, suggested giving special rights to the coastal States, such as the right to establish the total allowable catch (TAC) for the straddling stocks. Several delegations voiced their objections to the suggestion, stating that it would go beyond what is provided for in Article 123 of UNCLOS.[8]

DUTIES OF THE FLAG STATE

The negotiating text enumerates a number of detailed measures to be taken by the flag States of fishing vessels to ensure that they comply with regional conservation and management measures for straddling and highly migratory stocks. Since the preparation of the negotiating text, an agreement covering the same subject applicable to all high seas fisheries was adopted by consensus in November 1993 under FAO auspices, ie, the Agreement to Promote Compliance with International Conservation and Management Measures by Fishing Vessels on the High Seas (the FAO flagging agreement). Several States, including both DWFNs and coastal States, indicated that general reference to the agreement should be made in the final document. Some of them preferred to replace the whole section by a mere reference to that agreement. Other States, however, were opposed to such idea, arguing that this agreement was not entirely satisfactory since it allowed the exclusion of vessels of less than 24m in length, which are abundant in certain waters such as the South Pacific. Some coastal States further doubted that not all DWFNs would become Parties to the agreement.

After the third session, the Chairman maintained the section on the flag State in his revised negotiated text. Among measures that must be taken by the flag State are, according to the text: control of vessels on the high seas by means of licences or other forms of authorisation; implementation of quotas and other control measures; establishment of a national record of fishing vessels; requirement for marking of vessels and gear for identification in accordance with uniform and internationally recognisable systems; requirements for catch verification; requirements for regular reporting of position; catch and effort information; and implementation of agreed inspection schemes and observer programmes (UN 164/13/Rev.1: para. 24).

COMPLIANCE AND ENFORCEMENT OF INTERNATIONAL MEASURES

There is no dispute in principle in requiring flag States to take measures for ensuring compliance by vessels flying their flag with applicable international and regional rules and standards for the conservation and management of the stocks under discussion, though some flag States expressed concerns with too detailed requirements of enforcement to be imposed on them.

Flag States alone, however, are not sufficient to ensure compliance of rules and regulations by vessels operating at a great distance from their coasts. Suggestions were made that coastal States should be given the power to enforce international rules on the high seas, including the right to arrest the violating vessels if necessary. This was strongly resisted by DWFNs as contrary to international law and going beyond the provisions of UNCLOS. In their view, States can exercise jurisdiction over vessels under foreign flags only through agreement among the States concerned. Regional arrangements thus play an important role for compliance and enforcement on the high seas.

The main focus of discussion on this issue was the procedure, within the framework of such regional arrangements, under which authorities of States other than the flag State may board, inspect and, if appropriate, arrest a vessel. In the revised negotiating text, the Chairman strengthened the requirements for States to 'seek to agree' on such procedures by obliging States to 'agree' on such procedures (UN 164/13/Rev.1: para. 31).

The negotiating text also contains provisions regarding exercising enforcement measures against stateless vessels or vessels which conceal their identity (UN 164/13/Rev.1: para. 33–4).

PORT STATE JURISDICTION

A number of coastal States tried to stress the rights, and even obligations, of the port State to inspect documents and catch on board foreign fishing vessels when such vessels are voluntarily in its ports.

They also asserted the rights of the port State to deny access to its ports by such vessels if necessary, and to detain a vessel until the flag State takes its control where there are reasonable grounds for believing that the vessel has contravened or otherwise undermined internationally agreed measures. Furthermore they urged States to enact legislation empowering their authorities to prohibit landings where the catch has been taken in a manner that undermines the effectiveness of such international measures.

On the other hand, several DWFNs were strongly against such views, pointing out that the port States are not given such power under international law. Since the provisions of UNCLOS on port State control are only for the purpose of pollution control, in their view the system cannot simply be transplanted to the field of fisheries. Particularly, detention of vessels is a serious matter and the port State should have no such power unless it is conferred by regional bodies or by agreements between the States concerned.

Some DWFNs referred to the FAO flagging agreement, which allows the port State with reasonable grounds for believing that a vessel has been engaged in an activity that undermines the effectiveness of international measures merely to 'promptly notify the flag States accordingly'. In order for the port State to conduct investigatory measures, the flagging agreement requires that the Parties make necessary arrangements among them (FAO flagging agreement: Article 5(2)). Since the revised negotiating text still maintains the reference to detention of vessels by the port State (UN 164/13 Rev.1: para. 38), it is still likely to create some problems at the August session.

SETTLEMENT OF DISPUTES

On the settlement of disputes relating to the conservation and management of straddling and highly migratory fish stocks, there is no objection to the applicability of various procedures set out in UNCLOS as between the Parties to it.[9] Suggestions were made that non-Parties to UNCLOS should also accept the same procedures.

The need for expeditious and binding procedures for settling fisheries disputes was universally recognised, particularly because of the seasonal nature of fisheries operations. Among various means, however, a clear preference for a regional approach was expressed by several delegations, including the European Community, Japan, Papua New Guinea and the United States (UN 164/L.15: I, para. 8).

Opinions were divided, however, as to whether the document to be adopted should contain the compulsory recourse to binding procedures, such as a special arbitration procedure annexed to the negotiating text. While DWFNs generally questioned the appropriateness of formulating such provision, a number of coastal States stressed the need for such a system. As pointed out above, DWFNs also doubted the wisdom of requiring regional bodies to adopt a compulsory and binding procedure for dispute settlement. An interesting observation was made by the United States that those which call for a compulsory binding system of dispute settlement are mostly States which would like to limit the application of the document only to the high seas.

COMPATIBILITY BETWEEN CONSERVATION AND MANAGEMENT MEASURES
WITHIN AND OUTSIDE THE EEZ

The question of how to ensure the compatibility and coherence between the conservation and management measures that a coastal State adopts for its EEZ resources and the measures taken by regional organisations or arrangements for the same or related stocks outside the EEZ has proved to be one of the most difficult issues.

At the heart of the issue is the argument of a number of coastal States that the coastal State has special interests or preferential rights, or even special responsibilities, with regard to the living resources, particularly straddling and highly migratory stocks, in the areas of the high seas adjacent to its EEZ.[10] Some coastal States went on to claim the supremacy of their rights over those of foreign fleets on the adjacent high seas in the sense that in case of a conflict, the rights of the latter would be subordinate to those of the former.

As justification for such claims of special or preferential rights, some coastal States put forward the following arguments:

1 Coastal communities are dependent on fisheries for their livelihood; DWFN fleets are 'nomadic' or highly mobile, and can move easily from one fishing ground to another, while coastal fishermen cannot;
2 Coastal States have the most to lose if resources collapse. They have the incentive, which is far less strong for DWFNs, and the best experience, to conserve stocks in certain areas;
3 Coastal States are in a better position to monitor compliance with the conservation and management measures;
4 UNCLOS (Article 87) provides that the exercise of freedom of fishing on the high seas is 'subject to the conditions laid down in section 2'. Article 116 (in section 2) stipulates that fishing on the high seas is 'subject to...the rights and duties as well as the interests of coastal States' provided for, *inter alia*, in Article 63, para. 2, and Articles 64–7, ie, provisions relating to straddling, highly migratory and some other species.

Against these arguments, DWFNs stated that no such special interest or preferential rights of the coastal State are provided for in UNCLOS.[11] Some of them also argued that it would be 'greatly unequal and unjust' to give the coastal State such extra rights after it has acquired through the UNCLOS regime on the EEZ approximately 95% of all marine living resources. They also recalled the unsuccessful attempts towards the end of the Third United Nations Conference on the Law of the Sea to introduce the notion of a 'special interest' or the right of the coastal State to extend its conservation measures to the high seas.[12]

Given the sharp confrontation between these two positions, the Conference had to explore possible approaches which would be acceptable to both sides. There was no disagreement on the need to achieve the compatibility and coherence between the conservation and management measures adopted within and outside the EEZ. The question was how to attain that goal in a mutually satisfactory manner.

On the basis of a heated debate on this question between the two opposing sides, the Chairman tried to draft several compromise formulas. For the revised negotiating text, he first proposed that States shall confirm the UNCLOS obligations to co-operate in reaching agreement on necessary conservation and management measures. He then proposed that in determining the manner in which compatible measures are to be achieved, and the nature and extent of those measures, States shall:

1. respect any measures and arrangements adopted by relevant coastal States in accordance with UNCLOS in the EEZ;
2. take into account the biological characteristics of the stocks, the relationship between the distribution of the stocks and the fisheries as well as the geographical particularities of the region;
3. take into account the relative dependence of the coastal States and the States fishing on the high seas;
4. ensure that the measures do not result in undue harmful impact on the living marine resources; and
5. ensure that the measures established in respect of the high seas are no less stringent than those established, in accordance with UNCLOS in the EEZ, in respect of the same stocks (UN 164/13/Rev.1: para. 7).

The Chairman further proposed that if States are unable to reach agreement, they shall resolve their differences in accordance with the dispute settlement procedures specified in the document. And until the settlement process is ended, States shall continue to observe relevant minimum international standards, and where the coastal State or States have adopted measures for the conservation and management of the stocks, States fishing on the high seas shall observe measures 'equivalent in effect to the measures applying' in the EEZ. On the other hand, if measures have been agreed in respect of the high seas, in the absence of national measures for the EEZ, the coastal States shall observe measures equivalent in effect to those agreed in the high seas (UN 164/13/Rev.1: para. 8).

While coastal States were generally in favour of these formulations of the Chairman, DWFNs indicated their dissatisfaction with the general thrust and in particular with points 1, 4 and 5 above, as well as the interim measures imposed on the high seas fisheries, pointing out that they were unbalanced.

Conclusions

Although the Conference has yet another session to complete its mandate, certain tentative conclusions could be drawn from the above examination of the current stage of the Conference.

Important work has been accomplished in order to identify and assess, in a comprehensive manner, existing problems related to the conservation and management of straddling fish stocks and highly migratory fish stocks.

It has strengthened the convictions of both coastal States and DWFNs that there is a need to enhance their co-operation in the conservation and proper management of such stocks. It hardly appears coincidental that three important multilateral conventions directly relevant to the subject were successfully adopted within a ten-month period after the first session of the Conference. These are: the Convention for the Conservation of Southern Bluefin Tuna between Australia, Japan and New Zealand; the FAO flagging convention and the Convention on the Pollock Resources in the Central Bering Sea. These three Conventions were negotiated with the participation of some of the most active delegations attending the United Nations Conference.

General agreement has been reached on a number of principles, guidelines and practical measures to be followed by States. If implemented faithfully by States, and through them by fishing vessels, these action standards would go a long way toward improving current fishing practices of some States.

However, on several important issues, the views of coastal States and DWFNs are still divided. Indeed, the division is so serious on some issues – including the crucial question of compatibility of the measures to be taken in the EEZ and on the high seas areas adjacent to it – that unless each side is ready to accept further compromise, the final document would contain little guidance that goes beyond the general provisions of UNCLOS on these issues if it is to be adopted by consensus.

Given the size of the document and the limited time between now and the August session, unless serious efforts are made by all key delegations during the inter-sessional period to reach a consensus, it is unlikely that the Conference will adopt a convention at its final session in August. It is more probable that the Conference will adopt a document of a non-binding nature. However, this does not mean that the United Nations General Assembly, upon consideration of the Conference outcome, will necessarily accept it as the final work on the subject. It appears likely that some kind of mechanism may be adopted in order to follow-up the results of the Conference. This may be a periodic review of States implementation, or re-convening of the Conference for drafting a convention, or, after several years, convening a new conference to elaborate a convention.

Notes

1   See the Joint Resolution of the Fifth Conference on the Conservation and Management of the Living Marine Resources of the Central Bering Sea, 14 August 1992 (text in Meltzer Research and Consulting, 1993: Appendix II).

2   It is recalled that at the Third United Nations Conference on the Law of the Sea, a number of coastal States attempted without success to include similar concepts of 'special interest' in areas beyond EEZs in the draft convention on the law of the sea. In 1982, Australia, Canada, Cape Verde, Iceland, Philippines, Sao Tome and Principe, Senegal and Sierra Leone tabled amendments to draft Article 63(2) of the Convention, spelling out the right of the coastal State in the event of failure to reach agreement on conservation measures within a reasonable time to bring the dispute to an appropriate tribunal. Such tribunal was to determine the measures to be applied in the adjacent areas of EEZs, taking into account those measures applied to the same stocks by the coastal State within its EEZ (UN 62/L.114). At the request of the President of the Conference, however, the sponsors of the proposed amendments did not press for a vote.

3   This concept was referred to by the European Community as 'the principle of the unity of the stock within the totality of its distribution area'. See UN 164/L.8: Annex I, para.2.

4   See UN 164/L.11/Rev.1, Article 5. The same Article makes reference to its Annex II containing a detailed list of measures to be taken under certain circumstances on the high seas.

5   See working paper submitted by Chile, Colombia, Ecuador and Peru (UN 164/L.14: II).

6   The Convention uses the concept of 'the greatest net annual increment' (Article II(3)(a)).

7   Similar provisions are found in UNCLOS, Articles 87(2), 116 and 300.

8   Article 123 urges States bordering an enclosed or semi-enclosed sea to cooperate with each other in exercising their rights and in performing their duties, and requires them to endeavour to co-

ordinate, *inter alia,* the management, conservation, exploration and exploitation of the living resources.

9   In addition to the formal judicial procedures, several practical and expeditious means of settling disputes are available under UNCLOS. Such means are: (1) procedures and mechanisms to be established under regional agreements (Article 282); (2) compulsory resort to conciliation (Article 297(3)(b)(i)–(iii)); (3) special arbitration procedure under Annex VIII; and (4) fact-finding procedures as a component of the special arbitration procedure under Annex VIII.

10   See, eg, Five-Power Draft Convention (UN 164/L.11/Rev.1: Article 4(a)(iii)); list of issues submitted by Argentina (UN 164/L.10: para. 1.4).

11   See, eg, list of issues submitted by Japan (UN 164/L.6: I, para. 2).

12   See note 2 above. See also UN Law of the Sea: 23–4.

Bibliography

Agenda 21 (draft) *United Nations* Doc A/CONF. 151/4 (PART II),

FAO (1992) 'Report of the technical consultation on high seas fishing', Rome, 7–15 September, *FAO Fisheries Report* 484, reproduced in UN 164/INF/2.

FAO (1993) 'World review of high seas and highly migratory fish species and straddling stocks', *FAO Fisheries Circular* 858, preliminary version.

ICCMOS/3 (1993) 'Joint report of the first session of the International Conference on the Conservation and Management of the Marine Living Resources in the High Seas of the Okhotsk Sea', Document ICCMOS/3, 1 June, reproduced in UN 164/INF/6.

Meltzer Research and Consulting (1993) 'Global overview of straddling and highly migratory stocks: the non-sustainable nature of high seas fisheries' (Paper prepared for the Government of Canada, 1993).

UN 62/L.114 (1982) *United Nations* Doc A/CONF.62/L.114, 13 April.

UN 151/PC (1992) *United Nations* Doc A/CONF.151/PC/WG.II/L.16 /Rev.1, 16 March.

UN 164/13* (1994) *United Nations* Doc A/CONF.164/13*, reissued for technical reasons on 23 November.

UN 164/13/Rev.1 (1994) *United Nations* Doc A/CONF.164/13/Rev.1, 30 March.

UN 164/INF/2 (1993) *United Nations* Doc A/CONF.164/INF/2, 14 May.

UN 164/INF/6 (1993) *United Nations* Doc A/CONF.164/INF/6, 26 July.

UN 164/INF/8 (1994) *United Nations* Doc A/CONF.164/INF/8, 26 January.

UN 164/INF/9 (1994) *United Nations* Doc A/CONF.164/INF/9, 26 January.

UN 164/L.3 (1993) *United Nations* Doc A/CONF.164/L.3, 1 June.

UN 164/L.6 (1993) *United Nations* Doc A/CONF.164/L.6, 8 June.

UN 164/L.8 (1993) *United Nations* Doc A/CONF.164/L.8, 1 June.

UN 164/L.10 (1993) *United Nations* Doc A/CONF.164/L.10, 12 July.

UN 164/L.11/Rev.1 (1993) *United Nations* Doc A/CONF.164/L.11/ Rev.1, 28 July.

UN 164/L.14 (1993) *United Nations* Doc A/CONF.164/L.14, 16 July.

UN 164/L.15 (1993) *United Nations* Doc A/CONF.164/L.15, 16 July.

UN 164/L.21 (1993) *United Nations* Doc A/CONF.164/L.21, 22 July.

UN 164/L.25 (1993) *United Nations* Doc A/CONF.164/L.25, 26 July.

UN 164/L.28 (1993) *United Nations* Doc A/CONF.164/L.28, 27 July.

UN 164/L.44 (1994) *United Nations* Doc A/CONF.164/L.44, 28 March.

UN 164/WP.1 (1994) *United Nations* Doc A/CONF.164/WP.1 21 March.

UN 164/WP.2 (1994) *United Nations* Doc A/CONF.164/WP.2 24 March.

UN Law of the Sea 'The regime for high-seas fisheries: status and prospects', *United Nations publication*, Sales No. E.92.V.12.

UNCED 'Report of the United Nations Conference on Environment and Development, Vol. I', *United Nations* Doc A/CONF.151/26/Rev.1 (Vol.I) and corrigendum.

UNGA 47/192 (1992) 'United Nations General Assembly resolution 47/192', 22 December.

27

Historic Prejudice and Invisible Boundaries: Dilemmas for the Development of the Common Fisheries Policy

David Symes
Kevin Crean

Introduction: Whose Seas are They Anyway?

The European Community would appear to present a unique situation whereby the territorial boundaries within the surrounding seas, have *in effect*, been dissolved in the creation of a communal exclusive fishing zone formed by the merging of the EEZs of nine member states. The existence of a Community zone has been further reinforced through the assumption of responsibility for management of the shared fish stocks by means of a Common Fisheries Policy (CFP). The words 'in effect' are quite crucial, for the legal underpinnings of the situation are open to interpretation (Churchill, 1987).

In reality, each member state is separately responsible for defining the maritime waters which come under its jurisdiction. The Commission of the European Communities has no powers to amend the maritime boundaries of its member states. However in 1976, at a time of contagious spread of EEZs throughout the North Atlantic, member states were enjoined 'by means of concerted action to extend the limits of their fishing zones to 200 miles off their North Sea and North Atlantic coasts ...' (Council Resolution of 3 November 1976). The Commission had also proposed that the Community should assume responsibility for negotiation of access rights with third countries and on International Commissions; it further proposed a draft regulation for the management of fisheries within the 200 mile limits of the member states and made recommendations for rationalisation of the Community's fishing fleets through a decommissioning scheme.

Although the proposals for a common management regime were to give rise to protracted and often bitter negotiations, the die had been cast. While the 200 mile limits were subject to the legislative authority of individual member states, the national benefit was immediately commuted by the Commission's assumption of responsibility for resource management and, in particular, by the precedence given to the concept of 'equal access', which has remained a political cornerstone of the CFP.

The origins of 'equal access', which is unique to fisheries policy and deeply contentious, also remain shrouded in the complexities of interpretation of the Treaty of Rome (Churchill, 1987). It is, however, made quite explicit in Article 2(1) of Regulation 101/76 which states:

Rules applied by each Member State in respect of fishing in the maritime waters coming under its sovereignty or within its jurisdiction shall not lead to differences in treatment of other Member States.

Member States shall ensure in particular equal conditions of access to and use of the fishing grounds situated in the waters referred to ...

Yet, as Churchill (1987: 124) points out, while national regulations must be non-discriminatory, this does not imply any harmonisation of those regulations. The only general concession granted to the coastal states over the issue of equal access was a derogation covering the 12 mile territorial zone, first given in 1972, renewed in 1982 and again in 1992 to last until the expiry of the CFP in 2002.

In principle, therefore, all stocks within the 200 mile zones of member states are Community stocks to be managed by the Community on behalf of all its fishermen irrespective of nationality and respecting the principle of non-discrimination. In practice, however, boundaries persist in national (and regional) administrative systems and are deeply embedded in the minds of Europe's fishermen. Concepts of common use rights and equal access have become entangled in perceptions of national resources.

But how, one might reasonably ask, have such perceptions of territoriality arisen when Europe's fishermen have never enjoyed exclusive rights to stocks and therefore never experienced the realities of a national exclusive zone? For UK fishermen those realities would have included the narrowness of geographical limits defined by median lines (see Figure 27.1), boundary disputes and the need for a common management strategy to conserve the 'shared stocks' of the North Sea, English Channel and Irish Sea. Why, then, has so strong a sense of grievance over 'lost rights' persisted and indeed strengthened over time? Several factors may be cited: reaction to the loss of fishing rights in distant waters and the expectation of full compensation in securing exclusive rights in home waters; arguments and promises implicit in the claims and counter-claims during renegotiation of the CFP from 1976 to 1982 (see Wise, 1984); the persistence of a strong and very vocal anti-EC political lobby; dismay at the outcomes of the CFP to date; and fears for the consequences of full accession for Spain and Portugal. Such concerns have been nurtured in an atmosphere of legal uncertainty, administrative complexity and political obfuscation.

Issues of 'invisible boundaries' and the reassertion of national prejudice are activated by any event or decision which is seen to erode

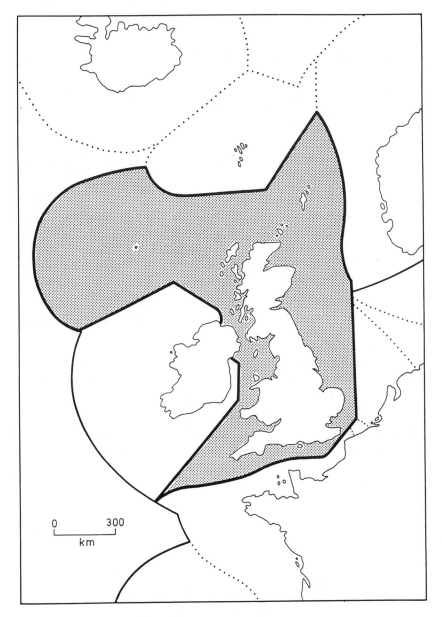

Figure 27.1 A Notional UK Exclusive Fishing Zone
(after Wise, 1984)

the putative rights of the fishermen, especially where these rights are put at risk by allegedly discriminatory actions. The fishermen tend to face in two directions: they oppose any curtailment of their rights of equal access to stocks in European waters and, at the same time, resist the invasion of their perceived national territories by foreign fishermen in pursuit of identical rights of access. Discriminatory action may be triggered either by Community policy or by decisions of individual member states, including their own government.

The aim of this paper is, therefore, to challenge the notion that the CFP has created a single (ie, common) system for managing shared stocks within EC waters. It argues that there is a fundamental difference between *policy formulation* (the framing of broad terms of reference for the CFP) which clearly is in the hands of the Commission and Council of Ministers, and *policy implementation* which is largely devolved to member states and 'regional governments' resulting in a diversity of management regimes. Through an analysis of current debates in the UK, the paper will attempt to demonstrate the insidious influence of historic prejudice and invisible boundaries in shaping the industry's response to policy measures. By way of conclusion, the paper asks, somewhat speculatively, whether it might not prove wiser to try and harness these centrifugal forces in establishing regional management systems for the Community's fisheries.

The Common Fisheries Policy: Community Fish Stocks v National Management Regimes

The underlying principles of the CFP – horizontality, non-discrimination and relative stability – have more to do with reinforcing the concept of European unity and co-operation than with effective management of a seriously depleted, highly sensitive and unstable resource. The CFP is a political statement, neatly aligned with the Community's general principles and designed to avoid rocking the European boat. It seeks, therefore, to reinforce economic and political stability within the Community – a precept which translates uneasily into a policy framework and regulatory system. As a result, the ensuing system is singularly ill-suited to the particular conditions of Europe's fisheries – mixed fisheries within which the component species exhibit different biological structures and characteristics and respond differently to specific regulatory measures.

In its search for politically neutral regulatory measures to maintain the *status quo,* the Commission opted for a system based on output limitations (Total Allowable Catches and quotas) set mainly with reference to the physical state of the stocks but also with an eye on maintaining continuity for the industry and its markets. TACs are a tried, tested and largely discredited device for controlling fishing effort, used initially by international commissions like the North East

Atlantic Fisheries Commission (NEAFC) and subsequently readopted, seemingly without question, by the Community. Technically they are widely recognised as inappropriate in multi-species fisheries where catch levels are set independently for each component species rather than for the aggregate stock. It is doubtful whether TACs can be regarded as anything more than a statistical notation of the target catch to be achieved through regulatory measures which directly limit fishing effort.

The CFP contains limited means for the delivery of TACs. Technical conservation measures, in the form of *gear regulations*, offer an important strategic device for moderating fishing effort. But when applied across the board through compromise horizontal regulations, they become poorly adapted to the regionally diversified mixed fisheries that make up Europe's resources. Inadequate mesh sizes, the reluctance to adopt square mesh panels, the absence of a one-net rule and frequent derogations hinder effective technical conservation. *Ground closures* are regarded as potentially discriminatory and there is, therefore, a reluctance on the part of the Commission to make widespread use of them in the protection of valuable nursery grounds. Moreover, the system of single species TACs and quotas, together with the minimum landing-size regulations intended to reinforce the technical conservation measures, have a pernicious side effect on catches, encouraging and indeed compelling fishermen to discard large numbers of fish at sea (Crean and Symes, forthcoming). Overall the policy framework, with its patent failure to prevent the downward spiral of the industry's fortunes, commands little respect from the fishermen.

Devolved Management: the UK–a Divided Nation?

Part of the thesis developed in this paper is that certain aspects of organisation of fisheries policy in the EC actually foster the development of nationalist rather than *communautaire* attitudes within the industry. This is held to be true both of the method for negotiating national interests in Brussels and of the persistence of national management systems for the implementation and monitoring of the CFP. In describing the relationships between the EC and the member states, it is first necessary to appreciate the distinction between the *Commission* (DGXIV) as the Community's civil service formulating a largely technocratic, apolitical, European view, and the *Council of Ministers* which provides the political arena within which vigorously contested negotiations are fought out, with each member state's fisheries minister expected to represent and defend national fishing interests in reaching the inevitable compromise. Success or failure in these negotiations is judged by the industry not on the significance of the decisions in tackling fundamental management problems but on how much of the national interest was preserved or conceded.

It is clear, however, that a significant measure of subsidiarity (whereby decision making is devolved to the lowest competent level) already exists in fisheries policy. Large areas of management and target achievement are devolved to the member states, including quota management, licensing, rationalisation of the fishing fleet together with monitoring, control and surveillance procedures.

The example of fleet restructuring can be used to illustrate this devolved management. The Multi-Annual Guidance Programme (MAGP), worked out in Brussels, sets detailed segmented targets for the reduction of national fishing effort. Although the Commission has indicated that 65% of the target reduction in the current MAGP should be achieved through the decommissioning of fishing vessels, it leaves the means of achieving the balance to the discretion of the member state. The UK government had introduced the opportunity for 'days at sea' restrictions into the provisions of the Sea Fisheries (Conservation) Act 1992, ostensibly as a direct means of effort reduction but palpably in the eyes of the industry as a means of 'decommissioning on the cheap'. The proposal was vigorously contested by the leading fishermen's federations on the grounds that it infringed the basic rights of fishermen to earn a living and discriminated against British fishermen. The methods of opposition chosen by the two major federations differed. The Scottish Fishermen's Federation (SFF) opted for a 'public awareness campaign'; the National Federation of Fishermen's Organisation (NFFO), representing interests in England and Wales, pursued a path of expensive litigation, achieving at least a temporary victory in the High Court when the case was referred to the European Court of Justice to test the extent to which the UK proposals satisfy the principles of the EC regulation. As well as demonstrating some of the complexities of devolved policy making through subsidiarity, the example also illustrates something of the organisational divisions within the UK industry.

Fisheries administration in the UK is highly fragmented. The historical provinces of England, Wales, Scotland and Northern Ireland which comprise the Kingdom are all represented in the administrative and policy-making machinery. However, the absence of autonomous regional government means that all decisions are ultimately made in Whitehall and endorsed by the UK parliament at Westminster. Concepts of territoriality are doubtless reinforced by the structure of decision making. Administration of the so-called 'British Seas' surrounding the UK require consultations between no fewer than seven government departments (Figure 27.2): the four provincial divisions of the UK; two British Crown dependencies situated within UK waters – the Isle of Man and the Channel Islands – whose position with regard to EC fisheries regulation is ambiguous (Churchill, 1987: 60–5); and

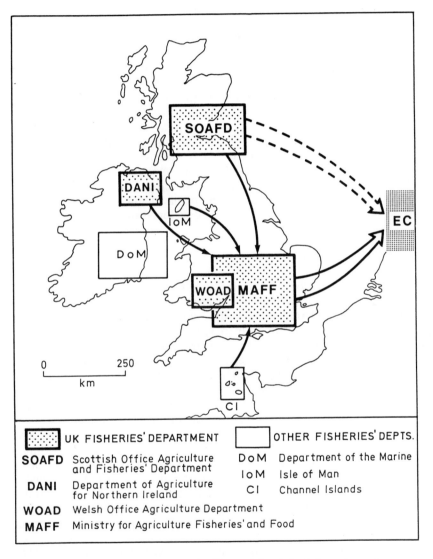

UK FISHERIES' DEPARTMENT   OTHER FISHERIES' DEPTS.

SOAFD Scottish Office Agriculture   **DoM** Department of the Marine
and Fisheries' Department   **IoM** Isle of Man

DANI Department of Agriculture   **CI** Channel Islands
for Northern Ireland

WOAD Welsh Office Agriculture Department

MAFF Ministry for Agriculture Fisheries' and Food

Figure 27.2 A Schematic Plan of the Administration of
the 'British Seas'

the Republic of Ireland which shares the administration of the Irish Sea. Power struggles are clearly evident in the formulation of a 'UK position' to be argued in negotiations within the Council of Ministers. At departmental level there is keen rivalry between MAFF and the Scottish Office over the assumption of *primus inter pares* status by MAFF as the department ultimately responsible for fisheries policy and challenged by the SO on the basis that well over half of the UK industry is based in Scotland. This rivalry is reinforced by the federations representing 'provincial' fishing interests in consultation with their respective departments. As a result rather different perspectives – not to say regional prejudices – tend to crystallise around the different structures and fishing systems prosecuted by the industry north and south of the border (Symes, 1994).

Rather more tangible differences can be observed between the 'English' and 'Scottish' fisheries administration in, for example, the absence of Sea Fisheries Committees responsible for the regulation of inshore waters from the Scottish and Northern Irish scene and in the separate Inspectorates charged with monitoring, control and surveillance of the industry. In effect, therefore, there are distinctive, though not essentially very different, management systems within the UK working to a common set of rules developed in Brussels.

How To Conserve 'Our' Fish

In recognition of their profound opposition to the 'days at sea' restrictions proposed by the UK government as part of the strategy for compliance with MAGP targets, the two major provincial federations were invited to submit proposals to MAFF and the SO that would form a coherent alternative to the government's own proposals. The federations chose to work independently rather than seek to reach a common position. Again this indicates not only the different fishing systems north and south of the border but also reflects deep-seated, historical divisions – a situation willingly exploited by the government in a 'divide and rule' approach to consultation within the industry.

Each federation chose to speak on behalf of the 'UK' industry and each cited a broadly similar range of counter-measures to those proposed by the government. But the style of the documents (SFF, 1993; NFFO, 1993) was significantly different. The NFFO presented a much more finely tuned, detailed and ultimately less controversial package of proposals 'emphasising the principle of conservation by selectivity' – a notion much less strongly evident in the Scottish submission.

On matters of technical conservation, the NFFO proposals are more closely argued with detailed recommendations covering different fisheries, fishing areas and gears. This reflects, in part, the more highly diversified fisheries and fishing systems deployed by the

'English' sector of the industry. Whereas the NFFO's proposals covered all of the 'British Seas' and had involved close consultations with some non-member regional associations, the Scottish proposals for demersal fisheries were confined entirely to the North Sea and west of Scotland which were treated essentially as a single entity. This in itself is significant for it reflects the greater mobility of parts of the English demersal fleets fishing all around the UK coast, compared with the greater concentration of effort by Scottish demersal fishermen in the northern North Sea and west of Scotland. Only in those sections of the SFF's submission which dealt with pelagic fisheries were detailed references made to areas off the English and Welsh coasts.

The NFFO's solution focused on more restrictive gear regulations, particularly with reference to the introduction of square mesh panels for towed demersal and nephrops gear, and upon detailed seasonal ground closures to protect spawning grounds especially in the Irish Sea. The most important technical disagreement between the English and Scottish submissions concerns the dimension of the square mesh panels with SFF preferring a 80mm panel to facilitate the whiting fishery, as against the NFFO's more restrictive 90mm recommendation.

The crucial difference between the two approaches is the more swingeing proposals, argued in less conciliatory language, within the SFF document. Most contentious is the proposal for a temporary moratorium on TACs, ostensibly to allow scientists a more realistic assessment of catches and the state the stocks. Such a proposal, virtually impossible to argue in Brussels, would seem to undermine the chances of success in gaining government approval for the package of proposed measures. Neither MAFF nor SOAFD have been quick to respond to the federations' submissions. It is hard not to regard this episode as an example of ritualistic behaviour between the government departments and the federations rather than as a basis for serious negotiations. The significance of the cases presented by the federations lies in their independent approaches and in exploring some of the options for greater regional sensitivity in the application of technical conservation measures.

Keeping The Others Out: the Evolution of Exclusion Zones in the British Seas

Rather more controversial, because it appears to take issue with the cornerstone principles of non-discrimination and equal access rights, is the establishment of fishery exclusion zones. Figure 27.3 demonstrates the complex array of exclusion zones covering a large part of the UK's 200 mile sector. Equal access is far from being the norm or indeed the only condition governing the orientation of resource exploitation in Community regulated waters. Also of importance is the condition

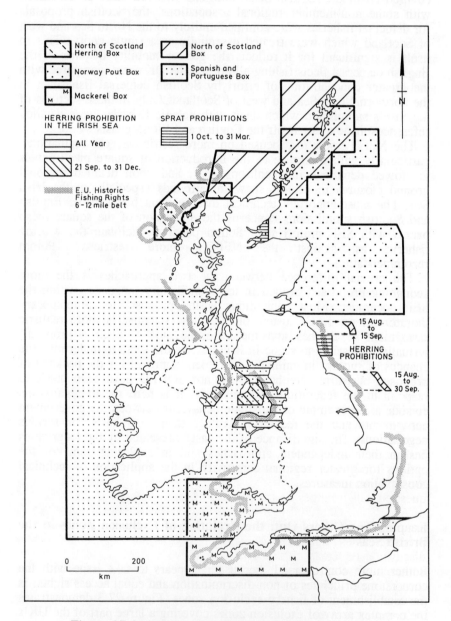

Figure 27.3 Access Arrangements and Closure Areas
in the 'British Seas'

referred to as 'right of establishment' (Wise, 1984) which favours one or more groups of users to the exclusion of others. In the fisheries context such rights would be established essentially through historic track records of participation in the fishery. Although the Commission has explicitly favoured the principle of 'equal access' in declarations of broad policy aims, it has often implicitly adopted a position closer to 'rights of establishment' in maintaining the precept of 'relative stability', especially in the negotiation of access conditions for new member states.

Three broad types of exclusion zone can be discerned: the 12 mile limit; seasonal closure areas; and the controversial 'boxes'. Prior to the establishment of the CFP, territorial limits for European fishing waters had been agreed by the European Fisheries Convention 1964. A two-zone system was introduced: an inner area (0–6 miles) where the coastal state held exclusive fishing rights; and an outer area (6–12 miles) where exclusive coastal state rights were moderated by the historic rights of foreign nations prosecuting fishing activities in the area. The EC's original intention of allowing equal access up to the shoreline clearly conflicted with the earlier condition of exclusive territorial limits and was contested by the new member states in 1972. A compromise in the Act of Accession provided for a derogation from 'equal access' in respect of the six mile zone surrounding all member states' coastlines and an extension to 12 miles in certain fishing dependent regions, including the whole of Britain and Ireland. The derogation is scheduled to last until the expiry of the CFP in 2002. Management of fisheries within the 12 mile zone is the direct responsibility of the member state. For England and Wales this responsibility is devolved, in part, to the 12 Sea Fisheries Committees, comprising equal representation for local (County) government and the fishing industry, with powers to enact by-laws for the protection of inshore fisheries within the six mile zone. In Scotland, management responsibility is vested in the Scottish Office under the provisions of Inshore Fishing (Scotland) Act 1984.

One unresolved issue relating to the 12 mile limits is whether they are intended to serve national or regional interests – again largely a question which hinges on the niceties of interpretation of the 1972 Act of Accession. Churchill (1987: 136) favours the regional interpretation arguing that it accords with the aims underlying derogation, namely to promote the interests of inshore fishermen particularly in disadvantaged areas. However Churchill also notes (1987: 163) the contrary views expressed privately by members of the Commission that the 12 mile limits represent a national zone. In practice this has certainly proved to be the case.

In theory, beyond the 12 mile limit, ground closures are not widely implemented because of their alleged discriminatory effects, though the initial impressions of Figure 27.3 would seem to cast doubt on this presumption. Where such 'closures' do occur they can provoke considerable antagonism not only between different member states but also within the initiating member states, for the notion of non-discrimination may be carried over from international to inter-regional and inter-sectoral contexts. Seasonal ground closures, where they are clearly intended to protect spawning or nursery stocks as in the case of the seasonal herring prohibitions in the North and Irish Seas, cause little animosity. Likewise the much larger Mackerel Box off the south-west coast of England, which seeks to protect juveniles of the western mackerel stock by the somewhat indirect means of restricting the amount of mackerel on board to 15% of the total catch except in the case of hand lining, has met with comparatively little opposition – although recently the Scottish pelagic industry has argued for the relaxation of some of the detailed conditions (SFF, 1993).

By contrast, the Norway Pout Box in the northern North Sea proved a highly contentious and fiercely debated issue from its inception as a temporary closure area at the UK's instigation in 1977 to the final acceptance of a more modest all-year-round exclusion zone in 1980. The UK's aim was to reduce the amount of industrial fishing, mainly by Danish vessels, for Norway pout over a large area of the North Sea used as a nursery ground for juvenile stocks of haddock and whiting which were eventually to be exploited by the UK industry and especially by the Scottish sector. Although the Norway Pout Box raised the question of preference between industrial fishing and fishing for human consumption and the problem of substantial by-catches of immature food fish (Holden, 1993), the debate also involved the principle of discrimination against a particular member state's interest. It remains a source of tension between British and Danish fishing interests.

If the principal argument underlying the Norway Pout Box was the conservation of juvenile haddock and whiting stocks, the same line of argument could not be applied to either the North of Scotland or the Irish Box. Both clearly flout the principle of equal access; they are intentionally discriminatory and cannot be fully justified on the basis of 'rights of establishment' – at least not in the North of Scotland example.

The North of Scotland Box represents the only concession granted to the UK in response to its demands for preferential access beyond the 12 mile limit at the time of the renegotiation of the CFP, 1976–82. In principle the main criterion for restricting access within the box was to grant preference to local fishing vessels; in practice, however, the limitation on vessels over 26m actually allowed free access to large numbers of UK vessels fishing out of non-local ports (as has subsequently been argued by Shetland fishermen in particular). Properly speaking the box is a Community fishing zone in the sense that licence allocations for vessels over 26m are managed by the Commission rather than by the UK authorities. At present 62 British, 52 French, 42 German and two Belgian vessels over 26m are permitted to fish the area at any one time. This attempt at the rationing of fishing effort for larger vessels is contested by the English middle-water fleet, where it is seen as an unwelcome example of 'regionalism' (Palfreman, 1993).

The latest development in the evolution of exclusion zones in the seas surrounding the British Isles is the Irish Box, established in 1986 at the time of Spain and Portugal's accession to the Community. This is by far the largest of the exclusion zones, covering a total of 70,000 square miles around the island of Ireland and thus enclosing parts of the UK's fisheries zone. Its purpose is quite simply to protect Irish fishing grounds and therefore the Irish fishing industry from encroachment by Spanish fishing effort. Outside the Box, but within Ireland's 200 mile limit, a list system is in operation to curb Spanish fishing effort: access to this outer area is limited to 300 vessels of which only 150 can fish at any one time and the numbers are further controlled by International Council for the Exploration of the Sea (ICES) Fishing Areas (23 in Area VI, 70 in Area VII and 57 in Area VIII). But both measures are only temporary expedients: they are scheduled to be replaced by normal EC access regulations in 1996. Both the UK and Irish industries are concerned at the likely impacts of relaxing access controls even though the concept of 'relative stability' will continue to be enforced through the allocation of TACs. Attempts are being made to have parts of the Irish Box redesignated on conservation grounds (*Fishing News International,* 1994).

Whatever the purpose of exclusion zones and no matter how successful they are in achieving their ultimate objectives, they certainly help to perpetuate the image of fish stocks as a national (or regional) resource. Concessions of this nature far outweigh the principle of equal access in the minds of most fishermen and so reinforce the historic prejudice and invisible boundaries. Where these prejudices are challenged by the threat of withdrawal of the concessions, the arguments can become quite extreme.

Repatriating 'Our' Fish: the Save Britain's Fish Campaign

Something of the strength of the UK fishing industry's dismay and despondency at the evident failure of the CFP to replenish stocks in European waters and to guarantee stability of employment and income may be judged from the 'Save Britain's Fish Campaign', which has enlisted fairly widespread support among certain sectors of the industry and is now endorsed by the Scottish White Fish Producers Association (SWFPA), the largest and most powerful member of SFF. The Campaign also enjoys some limited political support, notably from back bench, anti-Marketeer Labour MPs Austin Mitchell and Bryan Gould.

The basis of the Campaign's argument for the withdrawal of the UK from the CFP rests on four main points (Save Britain's Fish Campaign, 1993):

1 the illegality of the CFP, in that the Treaty of Rome makes no specific reference to fisheries as a distinct sector of the economy coming within the remit of the Community's authority;
2 the constitutional right to overturn earlier parliamentary decisions, which may appear to bind the UK to the terms of the Policy, through the fundamental democratic principle that 'no parliament may bind its successors';
3 the inequity of a doctrine through which 'all EC fishermen have equal rights of access irrespective of the contribution to waters and to fish stocks of their countries of origin ... which is unknown anywhere else in the world';
4 the threat that full accession of Spain will pose to the sanctity of 'relative stability' and the expectation that increased access for Spanish fishermen to the Irish and North Seas will be at the expense of British fishing rights.

Without commenting on the veracity or legitimacy of these claims, there is an argument being developed for the repatriation of the UK's exclusive fishing zone and for the uncoupling of Britain's participation in the CFP from the rest of her involvement with the EC. More importantly, the Campaign affords evidence of a significant body of UK fishermen who wish to reinstate national control over fisheries on the basis of historic prejudice and invisible boundaries.

But the Campaign is more than an expression of frustration at the failure of the CFP or irritation with systems of regulation imposed by foreign bureaucrats. The bid for a return to the *status quo ante* is seemingly based on the false premise that the harness of regulatory restraints imposed on fishermen's freedom of action can be unbuckled and that UK fishermen can once again find their own solutions to the inherent problems of uncertainty through strategic choices of action. A hidden agenda for the Campaign appears to be the reassertion of the fishermen's self-identity as independent, self-reliant and valuable contributors to the needs of society in place of the externally perceived image of the fishermen as a geographically peripheral, socially marginal and increasingly criminalised section of the population (Vestergaard, 1994). Protagonists of the 'Save Britain's Fish Campaign', however, choose to ignore the fact that restrictive regulation has become an endemic feature of politically contrived fisheries management systems, whether the architects are to be found in Brussels or Westminster. The Campaign has so far offered no prescription for the management of the repatriated stocks nor any indication of the mechanisms of co-operation with other coastal authorities, including the EC, in the management of transboundary stocks in the 'British Seas'.

Any attempt to assert independent control over fisheries management within a national exclusive fishing zone will be likely to result in legal disputes concerning the detailed definition of the UK's exlusive fishing zone. In particular, the status of the 200 mile limits surrounding Rockall claimed by the UK would come under scrutiny. Unchallenged at the time of the initial extension of fisheries limits in 1976, because it served to restrict access to non-EC member state fishing vessels without conferring any particular advantages upon UK fishing interests, the situation would almost certainly be contested by other members of the EC.

Future Challenge: Redrawing the Invisible Boundaries?

The remainder of the 1990s promises to be a stressful time for all involved in the exploitation of Europe's fisheries. Not only is there the threat of a deepening resource crisis and a very slow downward adjustment of fishing capacity, but a number of issues are likely to put added pressure on fisheries managers throughout the EC and to further intensify national prejudice. These issues would include *inter alia*:

1 the full accession of Spain and Portugal in 1996 and the abandonment of the exclusion zones designed to defend local fisheries against a Spanish armada;
2 the possible accession of Norway, adding considerably to the EC's resource base;
3 the development of potentially important deep-sea fisheries on the continental slopes, either just within or just outside the 200 mile national EEZs, but with biological characteristics (age class structures and reproduction rates) which render traditional management systems wholly inappropriate;
4 and, finally, the warning that the 'end of the CFP is nigh', at least in its existing form.

Before the turn of the century there will be a need to renegotiate the CFP entirely anew without preconditions and therefore without necessarily having the protective principle of 'relative stability' or the derogation on the fundamental principle of 'equal access' which reserves the 12 mile limit for coastal state fishing interests. In detail, the future options are innumerable. In reality, three strategic choices are open: firstly, to retain a system close to the *status quo* but with a formula which recognises Spain and Portugal's full accession; secondly, to return fisheries management to the sole responsibility of national governments while recognising the need for common action to resolve problems posed by transboundary stocks; and, finally, to derive a wholly new strategy based on devolved regional management.

The possible extent of the EC's exclusive fishing zones early in the next century, assuming the accession of Norway, Sweden and Finland and the creation of exclusive fishing zones within the Mediterranean, is awesome to contemplate. Its very size and internal diversity must challenge the logic of a remodelled common fisheries policy based on equal access, non-discrimination and the implementation of horizontal legislation covering all of the Community's fishing zone. The accession of Norway would further extend the concept of fishery dependent regions and add weight to The Hague preference principle of granting special concessions to disadvantaged fishing regions within the management regime. Broader concerns for the strengthening of the 'community of the regions' at the expense of centrally managed federalism could also lend support to the idea of regional fisheries management. Some of the arguments in support of the latter have been developed elsewhere (Symes and Crean, 1992; 1993) but the essential premise for regional management is that it will reduce the gap between the regulatory bodies and the resource user groups which has grown ever wider during the lifetime of the CFP. Only in this way can one hope to gain the willing compliance of industry with systems of management designed to strengthen the resource base for the benefit of those who, by reason of geography, are most dependent on it.

Conclusion

The experience of the EC suggests that the successful management of shared resources lies not so much in the drawing of effective boundaries as in the evolution of an effective management regime. Within the EC in the 1970s there were few substantive arguments concerning the extension of fishing limits and the creation of a Community exclusive fishing zone. However, weaknesses in the framing, administration and form of the management regime have led to the exposure of territoriality as an emerging issue in fisheries politics.

Despite the effective dissolution of national maritime boundaries within the EC, stocks have not proved any easier to manage, nor has it proved possible to rationalise the industry in accordance with available stocks. There has been – and no doubt will continue to be – a massive investment of resources in attempts to manage the stocks of the Community Pond. Yet the EC is no further forward in resource conservation, industrial restructuring nor in coping with the social 'fall-out' from the CFP. Confidence in the Policy, never very high, has slumped: voices raised against it have become ever more strident and their demands increasingly extreme. The approach of 2002 must surely concentrate the minds of administrators, politicians and fishermen alike in a positive rethink of the appropriate framework for the management of seriously endangered stocks in the heavily over-fished areas of the Pond. Our conclusion is that we should look to harness the tide of regionalism evident in the fishing industry (and in much wider circles) and redraw the 'invisible boundaries' of management not around national, bureaucratic institutions but along the lines of regional interest.

Note

Some of the issues and ideas referred to in this paper are being developed as part of an EC-funded research project on *Devolved and Regional Management Systems for Fisheries* AIR-2-CT93-1392, DG XIV SSMA.

Bibliography

Churchill, R.R. (1987) *EEC Fisheries Law*, Dordrecht: Martinus Nijhoff.

Crean, K. and Symes, D. (forthcoming) 'The discards problem: towards a European solution?', *Marine Policy*.

Fishing News International (1994) 'Ireland wants another "box"', *Fishing News International*, March.

Holden, M. (1993) *The Common Fisheries Policy: Origin, Evaluation and Future*, Oxford: Fishing News Books.

National Federation of Fishermen's Organisations (1993) *Conservation: An Alternative Approach, Report on Alternative Proposals to the Government's Sea Fish (Conservation) Act 1992*, Grimsby.

Palfreman, D.A. *et al* (1993) *The Fishing Industry in Yorkshire and Humberside – A Regional Study*, Goole: Blacktoft Publications.

Save Britain's Fish Campaign (1993) *The Common Fisheries Policy: Past, Present and Future*, Aberdeen.

SSF (1993) *UK Fisheries Conservation Policy: Proposed Alternative Strategy to the Government's Days at Sea Scheme*, Aberdeen: Scottish Fishermen's Federation.

Symes, D. and Crean, K. (1992) 'Alternative management systems for marine fisheries: prospects for the North Atlantic region', in J.L. Suarez de Vivero (ed.) *The Ocean Change: Management Patterns and the Environment*, Seville.

—— (1993) 'Regional self-management: towards a socially responsible fisheries policy?', paper presented to the Fifth Conference of the European Association of Fisheries Economists, Brussels, March.

28

Marine Boundary Enforcement from Space: Satellite Technology and Fisheries Jurisdiction

James E. Bailey
Laurel A. Muehlhausen

It is important ... that we have a feel for the accelerated time perspective that technological innovation in general, and fisheries technology in particular, have thrust upon us. We are *not* standing still and gazing on a calm, unchanging pastoral scene; we are aboard a fast train moving from the country into a city of undetermined size and complexity, and we should be prepared for the changing scene. (Jacobson, 1975)

Introduction

An irrefutable aspect of technological innovation is that it causes social change; indeed, in many instances technological innovation has forced social change. Such changes manifest themselves not only on the scale of nations but also in smaller, specialised societies that are more acutely affected by particular technological changes. One such specialised society is that of fishermen.

Perhaps more so than any other phenomenon, technological innovations have propelled changes in the way humans go about the business of harvesting fish. Typically, those technological innovations have aided fishermen in increasing the size of their catch. In fact, technological change has been so beneficial to fishermen that virtually every commercially valuable fish stock has become threatened with exhaustion.[1] That phenomenon has forced nations and international organisations to create legal regimes to limit the effectiveness of technological innovation.

This phenomenon of legal reaction to technological innovation is not unique to the fishing industry, nor does it take a unique form.[2] The legal regime selected is often either put into effect long after the effects of the technological innovation have manifested themselves or after the technology it proposes to address has itself become obsolete. Typically such legal regimes are aimed at rendering fishing operations less efficient rather than employing new technology to more efficiently regulate the fishing industry.[3]

The time lag between the date of widespread use of a new technology and legal reaction to that technology commonly results in the development of new technologies that either render the now-regulated technology obsolete (and therefore the regime regulating it) or enables the fisherman to legally circumvent the law which has been drafted to apply to a specific technology. Predictably, technological innovation in the fishing industry has thus resulted in a constant struggle between fishermen eager for technological innovations that increase their efficiency and their harvest and governments that seek to restrain technological innovation in order to preserve dwindling fish stocks.[4]

The collapse of commercial fisheries around the world has been documented elsewhere and will not be reviewed in detail here.[5] However, the cause of the various collapses has unquestionably been the inadequately regulated application of advanced technology in every phase of fishing: location, capture, processing, vessel construction and navigation (Jacobson, 1975). The introduction of revolutionary technology in the fishing industry is a familiar phenomenon in the history of fishing. In fact, the history of the law of the sea is more accurately described as the history of the interaction between law and marine technology.

Unfortunately, these technological innovations have frequently kept the ability of fishermen to harvest larger amounts routinely ahead of nations' efforts to regulate those activities. The result is a familiar pattern of legal reaction to new technologies that make fishing more efficient. That legal reaction has usually been inadequate and untimely.

Two things determine the effectiveness of any legal regime: its timeliness and the ability to enforce it. Legal institutions are, by their nature, reactive. As such, the recognition of novel social circumstances which dictate a change in an existing legal theory or legal regime is often delayed. A legal regime that fails to react adequately to new circumstances is, or will soon become, obsolete. Further, the effectiveness of any legal regime is determined by the technology available to enforce it. Until very recently the legal regimes adopted for regulating high seas fishing could not be effectively enforced because the technology for effective enforcement either did not exist or was not applied as part of the legal regime.

Enforcing Zones of Ocean Jurisdiction

THE NEED FOR ENFORCEMENT TECHNOLOGY

A particularly difficult legal problem has been the establishment and regulation of boundaries of fishing areas in both the national and international context.[6] Monitoring these boundaries and restricting the activities of fishermen on the open sea has, for the most part, been dependent on the number and speed of boats operated by the agencies charged with enforcing fishing regulations. Recently though, technological innovations in the area of satellites offer the possibility of rational regulation of both boundaries and fishing activities previously regulated either poorly or not at all.

Enforcement of coastal states' rights within the Exclusive Economic Zone (EEZ) rests almost entirely on the state of enforcement technology. Indeed, effective implementation of the EEZ regime described in the 1982 United Nations Convention on the Law of the Sea (UNCLOS) rests entirely on this technology. Article 73 of UNCLOS provides that a coastal State may, in addition to other measures, board, inspect, arrest and carry out judicial proceedings as necessary to ensure compliance. This implies an expectation that enforcement will typically take the form of arrest by a military vessel followed by an action *in rem* (Craven, 1985). Yet, the international law of hot pursuit, both according to custom and Article 111 of UNCLOS, requires that the arresting vessel 'have good reason to believe that the [arrested] ship has violated the laws and regulations of [the coastal State]' (UNCLOS, 1982; Convention on the High Seas, 1958). Thus, the prerequisite to enforcement is a technology of surveillance. However, the vastness of ocean areas within coastal state jurisdiction makes enforcement extraordinarily difficult as well as very expensive. Thus, any method of surveillance must ensure compliance and be cost-effective (Gulland, 1983).

There are three methods of surveillance: by vessel, by aircraft or by satellite. The weakness of vessel surveillance, however, is its random nature. Surveillance by an enforcement vessel must result from chance encounters for two reasons. First, the area to be patrolled is too large to keep under constant vessel surveillance.[7] Second, patrols and therefore observation of violations must be random because any logical pattern of patrol would permit violators to schedule their violations to avoid detection.[8]

Surveillance by aircraft is often more effective than by vessels for the obvious reason that an aircraft can observe a larger area by virtue of its speed and vantage point. However, weather conditions and cost are significant restraints on aircraft surveillance. Neither vessel nor aircraft surveillance promises to ever be an effective means of ocean boundary or marine resource enforcement.[9] Moreover, given that

developed nations such as the United States have considerable
problems enforcing their zones of ocean jurisdiction, the limited
resources of developing nations must render effective enforcement
virtually unattainable (Craven, 1985: 1152–3).

Surveillance by satellite offers the greatest potential for effective
enforcement; however, UNCLOS was not drafted with the appropriate
use of satellite surveillance in mind. Typically, satellite surveillance is
thought of as simply a higher flying aircraft with the added handicap of
its utility being dependent on the degree of cloud cover.[10] Such use of
satellites is no longer the best use of the available technology. In fact,
the most effective use of satellites in the enforcement of ocean area
boundaries does not entail photographic surveillance.[11]

ENFORCEMENT USING SATELLITES

For most purposes the two most important types of satellites are
geostationary and polar orbiting.[12] Geostationary satellites orbit
35,800km above the Earth's equator, which enables these satellites to
match the rate of the Earth's rotation and thereby remain in the same
location relative to a particular place on the Earth.[13] Obviously,
geostationary satellites, by design, only cover a fixed area of the
Earth.[14] Another characteristic of geostationary satellites is that
sending signals to these satellites requires a large, powerful
transmitter. Examples of geostationary satellites are GOES (USA),
Meteosat (ESA) and GMS (Japan) (Rao *et al*, 1990: 55). While
geostationary satellites provide considerable information useful in
fisheries management, polar-orbiting satellites are the most relevant to
enforcement of ocean areas subject to national jurisdiction.

Polar-orbiting satellites move in orbits crossing each pole at a
heights of around 850km and a rate faster than the Earth's rotation.
The combination of the polar satellites' speed and orbit enables them to
observe the entire surface of the planet in a short time.[15] How quickly
a survey of the entire planetary surface can be accomplished depends
on the number and speed of the polar satellites used. For example,
polar-orbiting satellites used by the United States' National Oceanic
and Atmospheric Administration (NOAA) cover a 5,000km wide path
and can observe a given point for about 11 minutes per satellite pass.
The US Global Positioning System (GPS) relies on a network of polar-
orbiting satellites that collectively provide constant global coverage.
The frequency with which a satellite passes a particular location is a
function of latitude; while polar-orbiting satellites cross the poles 14
times a day, they cross equatorial locations only twice in 24 hours
(Systems West, 1993: 2).

A distinct advantage of polar-orbiting satellites is that their relatively
low orbit permits communication with the satellite using small amounts

of energy and, therefore, very small transmitters are capable of using these satellite systems.

THE ARGOS SYSTEM

One of the most important location and data collection systems is the French Argos system carried by the NOAA/TIROS-N polar-orbiting satellites (Rao *et al,* 1990: 151). The Argos system combines data transmission combined with geolocation from users' platform transmitter terminals (PTTs) located world-wide (Muehlhausen and Vassal, 1992). This information is transmitted from the satellites, processed at one of Argos' two processing centres (either Landover, Maryland, USA or Toulouse, France), and accessed by users via computer networks (Muehlhausen and Vassal, 1992). In addition to providing access to a wealth of meteorological and oceanographic data (Rao *et al,* 1990: 153–4), Argos also enables users to track fishing vessels (Springer, 1993).

The flexibility and utility of the Argos system as a means of tracking and geolocation is amply demonstrated by its use in tracking wild birds. During a three-month period in 1989, Argos was used to track the migration and feeding patterns of albatrosses in the south-western Indian Ocean (Jouventin and Weimerskirch, 1990). Using transmitters weighing less than 2% of the birds' 12kg body weight, the study tracked the birds on numerous individual flights of up to 15,000km. Data from the satellites were stored at and retrieved from the Argos Processing Centre in Toulouse, France (Jouventin and Weimerskirch, 1990). The applicability of this system for monitoring the movements of fishing vessels is obvious. Furthermore, this technology is currently available for fisheries and boundary management.

Access to the Argos' data distribution system is available to anyone with a computer and modem linked to a telephone transmission system (Muehlhausen and Vassal, 1992: 363). Therefore, Argos data can be easily shared among several users around the world, provided that they have the access code to a given data set (Muehlhausen and Vassal, 1992: 366). While Service Argos, Inc at Landover, Maryland and CLS/Argos, Toulouse, France maintain the processing centres and computerised databases (Muehlhausen and Vassal, 1992: 363), PTT deployment and data collection is determined by individual users. The data collected for a user who has deployed the PTT is proprietary to that user and may only be released with their consent (Muehlhausen and Vassal, 1992: 364).

Argos can also be used to collect more information than simply vessel location. For example, a device about the size of a calculator can be programmed so that the observer or fisherman can answer pre-set questions about fishing effort and catch size. Following the transmission of this data by the PTT to the Argos system a regional fisheries office can access the processed data from the Argos computer networks. The data are available in a computer database within hours of reporting. The data transmitted is secure because it is transmitted in an encoded form and the individual user must release their individual access code before the data can be downloaded from the computer networks. Finally, the Argos system independently establishes the location of the PTT, and therefore the reporting vessel, at the time of the data transmission. Thus catch and location data cannot be misreported or altered by the observer or self-reporting fisherman.[16]

THE GLOBAL POSITIONING SYSTEM (GPS)

The 24-satellite GPS system was developed by the US military to aid aircraft, warships, and missiles to locate targets by providing precise co-ordinates of both the launch system and the target (Chien, 1988). No longer restricted to military use, GPS has wide civilian application.

Each GPS satellite uses radar tracking to determine the satellite's precise location and four atomic clocks keep precise time (Chien, 1988). Whenever a GPS receiver on Earth receives the GPS satellite's broadcast of the satellite's location and time, the receiver notes the precise time of signal reception, then calculates its distance from the satellite from the time lapse between the satellite broadcast and the receiver reception (Chien, 1988). The receiver then immediately repeats this calculation with two or three other satellites and triangulates to determine its own precise longitude, latitude, and altitude (Chien, 1988). Although the system can generally pinpoint locations to within 15m,[17] the Pentagon limits civilian users to Selective Availability mode with an accuracy of about 100m (Chien, 1988).

Anyone with a GPS receiver can immediately determine their location at any time anywhere in the world. Many commercially-available GPS receivers are hand-held instruments. User cost is approximately $500 for a receiver; the US government pays for all system costs so there are no usage charges (Chien, 1988).

Unlike Argos, GPS does not transmit position data from the Earth to the satellite. Thus, by itself, GPS does not permit remote monitoring of a user's location. However, GPS position data can be transmitted over other satellite systems like Argos or Inmarsat. Thus, GPS can be used alongside an existing system such as Inmarsat which would transmit vessel location back to the Inmarsat satellite and on to the agency monitoring the fishery. Adding a GPS to an existing Inmarsat-C terminal costs only a few hundred dollars.

APPLYING THE TECHNOLOGY

Merely knowing the location of those vessels engaged in fishing operations can be of great assistance to enforcement officials. Most obviously, the satellite signal indicates when vessels enter either regulated or closed fishery areas. Also, by noting successive locations of a vessel over time, enforcement officials can infer fishing effort from the time spent in the fishing grounds. Additionally, the speed of the vessel can be approximated by measuring the distance between successive location signals, thus enabling regulators to determine whether the vessel is in transit (higher speeds) or actually fishing (lower speeds) (Springer, 1993). Both the GPS and Argos systems can be used in this fashion.

For example, location data can be remotely collected by outfitting the vessels with an Argos PTT. Argos software then permits the regulator to plot large numbers of vessel locations on a gridded map of the ocean. Determination of the nature of the vessel's activity could be deduced as described above, and a patrolling vessel or aircraft could be sent to investigate as needed. Any interruption of vessel location transmissions, could be treated as either a distress call[18] or illegal tampering with the system, and depending on the circumstances, the vessel's fishing permit could be suspended.

Alternatively, fishermen could be required to self-report their locations as determined by the on-board GPS receiver. The vessels would then transmit this information by radio or Inmarsat at regular intervals. It would also be possible avoid self-reporting problems by linking the GPS unit to an automated transmission schedule over Inmarsat.

RECENT APPLICATIONS

In recent years satellite tracking has enabled various enforcement agencies faced with monitoring thousands of vessels spread over immense ocean areas. From 1989 through 1992, the US National Marine Fisheries Service (NMFS) used Argos to track several hundred fishing vessels from Japan, Korea, and Taiwan in an effort to enforce the ban on drift net fishing in the North Pacific (Springer, 1993). In monitoring foreign drift net operations NMFS used data generated from Argos to confirm that 21 Taiwanese and 17 South Korean vessels were fishing illegally 'in an area up to 75 nautical miles north of the legal boundary allowed by our bilateral drift net agreements. US Coast Guard ships and aircraft were dispatched to verify the violations' (Springer, 1993).

In addition to location monitoring, these systems can improve analysis of data on the two most chronically inadequately reported areas: catch and effort statistics (Gulland, 1983: 185). For example, in the US system, the vast majority of catch data is hand-recorded on paper charts, hand-delivered or mailed by the observer to a regional office, and then hand-tabulated or transferred to computer to make totals and summarise data. Eventually, the information is available for evaluation. Unfortunately, modern fisheries are under such pressure that responses to fishing activity may require an immediate reaction by the regulatory agencies. Satellite transmission systems will significantly reduce the time necessary to collect and analyse the data.

Additionally, satellites have been used to increase the co-ordination and efficiency of national fishing efforts. Several countries have nationalised their fishing efforts and created centralised data distribution centres.[19] For example, the Commonwealth of Independent States' fishing fleet receives data from the Space Information Service in Moscow, and data collected by satellite are combined with field data to reduce search time and improve fishing efficiency fleet-wide (Simpson, 1992: 11). Canada, Japan and France have similar programs (Simpson, 1992). Finally, United States programmes have shown that satellite data and field data can be combined to reduce search time by 50% for albacore tuna and swordfish fishermen.[20] Encouraged by these results, several nations have recently moved to enact comprehensive regulatory schemes that rely on satellites for their success.

Last year the New Zealand Ministry of Agriculture and Fisheries introduced a satellite tracking system for all foreign trawlers in New Zealand waters. The New Zealand regulation requires both domestic and foreign vessels of certain size or those operating in particular areas to carry a transmitter that relays information concerning the vessel's activity to a land-based computer system in New Zealand.[21]

On 31 March of this year NMFS issued final standards for a satellite-based fishing vessel monitoring system which will provide the positions of fishing vessels and real-time catch and environmental data (Federal Register, 1994). NMFS believes that this system may be the only practical way of preventing chronic over-harvesting within US fishing zones (Federal Register, 1994). However, while NMFS has endorsed the use of this system, it has left the decision of whether to implement such a system up to the individual Fishery Management Councils that supervise US fisheries. Due to the over-fishing problems off the New England coast, current plans are that this summer (1994) vessel monitoring equipment will be required on every fishing vessel operating in the New England and Mid-Atlantic fisheries.[22]

Currently, installation of a satellite tracking system is being considered by the European Union for all vessels over 10m that remain at sea for more than 24 hours at a time (Independent, 1993). At the moment, no decision has been reached on whether a Eutelsat system, Argos or a GPS/Inmarsat combination will be used. Finally, Article XI of the recently completed Convention on the Conservation and Management of Pollock in the Central Bearing Sea requires vessels operating in the area to use real-time satellite position-fixing transmitters.

Conclusion

The use of satellites to track vessels, monitor ocean boundaries and enforce fisheries management regimes offers a legitimate hope that fisheries management can move away from the traditional mode of legislation designed to undermine technological innovations that make fishing operations more efficient. Satellite tracking systems, in combination with dockside observers and marine patrols, will provide the means of using the latest technology to regulate and encourage the most technologically efficient fisheries.[23]

That is the technological potential; it can only be fulfilled by the implementation of an appropriate legal regime. Currently, international law barely addresses the use of satellites. And in those institutions that discuss international law of the sea issues, satellites pass unnoticed.[24] Of far greater immediate utility than a legal regime regulating the seabed is an international regime that co-ordinates fishing activity and requires all fishing vessels to be equipped with vessel monitoring devices. Alternatively, coastal nations should consider enacting national fisheries regimes that require every vessel operating within their fishing zones to carry a vessel monitoring device.

The eve of the 21st century is certainly the time for the international community to acknowledge that the traditional method of vessel recognition, flying a flag off the vessel's stern, is hardly more than a quaint custom with little relevance to a world whose future may depend on rational management of food from the seas.

Notes

1   See, for example the *Guardian* (1994).
2   See, for example, the observations of Jon Jacobson: 'First, in the Continental Shelf Convention it seems clear that the unworkable 'exploitability test' for delineating the seaward boundary resulted from a failure of the framers to grasp the reality of a rate of technological change that would, within a little more than decade, make sea-bed resource recovery beyond the 200-meter isobath a practical feasibility. More than any other shortcoming of the 1958 Conference, this failure led to the felt need for another conference as early as 1973.
     'Second – and more pertinent to the present discussion – the 1958 High Seas Convention, by codifying 'freedom of fishing', continued to treat ocean fishes as common property, as 'free

goods', at a time when over-fishing of at least some important stocks could have been foreseen as a result of new fishing technologies and practices. This lack of legal preparedness has unquestionably contributed to today's ocean fisheries crisis.' (Jacobson, 1975: 53)

3   'There can be no doubt that ocean fishing has, in general, become more efficient in recent years and there can be little doubt that fishing will, given a non-restrictive legal climate, continue to become more efficient. ... [Yet, e]fficiency is, after all the technology-product that got us into the current fisheries management crisis.' (Jacobson, 1975: 77)

4   'In a world changing as rapidly as our world has changed..., relative rates of change are exceedingly important. Although our ability to manage fish stocks has grown rapidly..., our ability to harvest has increased even more dramatically and the gap between managerial ability and exploitive technology has widened. This problem can be capsulized as one representing a growing divergence between technological capacity and management concepts adequate to fully utilize technological developments.' (Alerson and Paulik, 1973, quoted in Jacobson, 1975: 52)

5   See note 1, above.

6   'In the development of national and international oceans policy over the past half-century, technological innovation has been a silent but driving force. It has enhanced man's capabilities to recover ocean resources and, in doing so, has raised new problems of crowding and over-exploitation. The typical political and legal response to the expansion of ocean uses has been the expansion of national claims over ocean areas and the exclusion of foreign users. While clear ownership or title should facilitate the adoption of sound management policies, proper management has been an afterthought for most nations. Exclusive national control has been the goal. The claims that have been advanced have generally anticipated the existence of resources as well as the capability to control or exploit them.' (Hollick, 1981: 372)

7   To grasp the futility of a purely vessel surveillance scheme one need only note that a rectangular-shaped EEZ generated by a coastline of only 100 miles covers an area of 20,000 square miles, while visual observation from a vessel can only be accomplished for an area of less than 80 square miles. From this simple illustration, one can readily see the impracticability of a vessel surveillance scheme for an EEZ generated by a coastline of any appreciable length (or by *any* island – which would generate an EEZ area in excess of 125,600 square miles).

8   Obviously, announced or well-known patrol patterns deter illegal activity, but again, the problem of the enormity of the EEZ limits the effectiveness of this type of scheme.

9 'As a result of the GIFAs [Governing International Fishery Agreements] the situation in the 200-mile Fishing Conservation Zone of the United States is almost devoid of armed conflict, but the combination of anecdotal information, the cost of enforcement, budget restrictions, the ever increasing mission requirements of the Coast Guard, and the huge area of the economic zone suggest that violations are, or would be, difficult to detect. The problems will be greatly compounded if technology is employed by the violators to prevent their detection and arrest.' (Craven, 1985: 1152).

10 See, for example, the comments of Craven: 'Enforcement [under UNCLOS] thus implies a technology of surveillance by aircraft or on rare occasions when the lack of cloud cover permits, by satellite... .' (Craven, 1985: 1141)

11 In fact, all phases of the modern management of fisheries can make use of various satellite technologies. A partial list of these features should illustrate the wide utility of satellites: temperature measurements, biological productivity measurements, as well as ocean surface shape and roughness measurements relevant to currents. See, for example, Knauss (1985).

12 While the term 'satellite' is correct, the term 'orbiting platform' conveys a more accurate picture since most satellites carry instrumentation for many purposes, including remote sensing, data transmission, and geolocation. The NOAA TIROS-N satellites, for example, provide climate and weather monitoring, data collection and transmission, and remote geolocation (Rao *et al*, 1990).

13 'Geostationary satellites hover above a fixed point on the earth. They produce continuous pictures showing the earth below them. They relay these pictures over a low-data-rate broadcast called WEFAX.' (Systems West, 1993)

14 This area is large, though, covering from 60°N to 60°S and the same distance east to west.

15 The polar orbit remains the same, while the Earth's rotation brings different areas of the planet's surface beneath the satellite's path. Thus, the satellite will eventually fly above every spot on Earth.

16 A possible disadvantage of such a reporting system may arise from the distrust of observers and observing programs by fishermen. Replacing written reports which the fisherman can inspect with a small blackbox satellite transmitter could increase the animosity that fishers display toward observers. This could create problems for international observing efforts like those of the Inter-American Tropical Tuna Commission in areas where the fishing vessels have no obligation to allow the observers onboard. Interview by Laurel A. Muehlhausen with Dave Braatten and

Michael Scott, Dolphin Observer Program, Inter-American Tropical Tuna Commission, in La Jolla, California, USA (March 1991).

17   Although such precision is not required to enforce fisheries zones, with the addition of sophisticated equipment GPS can determine locations to within a few millimetres. Interview by James E. Bailey with Judith Collier, Strategy Implementation Manager, Positioning Resources, Ltd in Durham, England, UK (April 1994).

18   While Argos transmitters have actual distress call buttons and the units themselves are easily detachable for carrying onto a life raft, otherwise inexplicable loss of location signals should still be treated as a possible indication that a vessel was in distress.

19   See, for example, Simpson (1992).

20   'This program used a combination of AVHRR, Coastal Zone Color Scanner (CZCS), and wind field data to help locate commercial catches of tuna, swordfish, and salmon.' (Simpson, 1992: 9).

21   Xinhua General Overseas News Service, 4 January 1993, available in Lexis, Nexis, CURNWS file.

22   Science and Technology Week, Cable News Network, 5 February 1994.

23   The possibility for further reduction of the need for direct human participation in patrolling ocean areas is demonstrated by the surveillance potential of a device currently being developed by the Australian Bureau of Meteorology.
The device is called an 'aerosonde' and is essentially a solar-powered model aeroplane designed to carry weather instruments and operate largely independent of human control for several days. The aerosonde uses GPS antennae on wingtips, tail and nose to measure attitude and velocity, by keeping track of its position to within several metres.
Replacing the meteorological equipment with transmitting cameras may provide a practical alternative for those nations lacking the resources to acquire and maintain human-operated patrol aircraft.
Aerosonde information obtained from personal communication from Pete Evans, Research Assistant, Department of Applied Mathematics, University of Adelaide, South Australia, 17 April 1994.

24   'The 1982 Law of the Sea Convention is silent on marine scientific research from satellites. In fact, the subject was never formally raised during the negotiations.' (Knauss, 1985: 1210)

Bibliography

Alerson and Paulik, (1973) 'The Objectives and Problems of Managing Aquatic Living Resources', 19, FAO Technical Conference on Fishery Management and Development, Vancouver, BC, February.

Chien, P. (1988) 'You are here', *Popular Mechanics* 170: 50.

Convention on the High Seas, (1958) Article 23(1), 29 April 1958, 13 UST 2512 TIAS No. 5200.

Craven, J.P. (1985) 'Technology and the Law of the Sea: the effect of prediction and misprediction', *Louisiana Law Review* 45: 1143, 1151.

Federal Register (1994) 59, 31 March: 15180.

Guardian, The (1994) 'Plundered oceans: catastrophe threatens world's fisheries as stocks fall', *The Guardian*, 12 March, available on Lexis, Nexis, CURNEWS files.

Gulland, J.A. (1983) 'Managing fisheries in an imperfect world', in B.J. Rothschild (ed.) *Global Fisheries: Perspectives for the 1980s*: 189–90.

Hollick, A.L. (1981) *U.S. Foreign Policy and the Law of the Sea*: 372.

Independent, The (1993) 'Satellites that go fishing', 1 March, available on Lexis, Nexis, CURNWS file.

Jacobson, J. (1975) 'Future fisheries technology and the Third Law of the Sea Conference', in H.G. Knight, (ed.) *The Future of International Fisheries Management*: 52–3.

Jouventin P. and Weimerskirch, H. (1990) 'Satellite tracking of wandering albatrosses', *Nature* 343: 746.

Knauss, J.A. (1985) 'The effects of the Law of the Sea on future marine scientific research and of marine scientific research on the future Law of the Sea', *Louisiana Law Review* 45: 1201, 1210.

Muehlhausen L.A. and Vassal, C. (1992) *Contribution of Argos to World Climate Change Studies, Sixth Conference on Satellite Meteorology and Oceanography,* preprint volume: 363.

Rao, Holmes, Anderson, Winston, and Lehr (eds) (1990) *Weather Satellites: Systems, Data, and Environmental Applications* Boston: American Meteorological Society: 53–4.

Simpson, J.J. (1992) 'Remote sensing and geographic information systems: implications for global marine fisheries', Report No. T–CSGCP–025, La Jolla: University of California.

Springer, S. (1993) 'Monitoring the locations of fishing vessels by satellite', *CLS/Argos Mobile Monitoring Newsletter* 3, January.

Systems West Inc, (1993) *Weather Satellite Information Systems 2.*

UNCLOS (1982) United Nations Convention on the Law of the Sea, Article 111(1), opened for signature 10 December 1982 UN Doc. A/Conf. 62/122, reprinted in 21 ILM 1245 (1982).

29

Fisheries Violations of an Arbitrated Maritime Boundary: The Gulf of Maine Case

Douglas Day
Glen Herbert

Introduction

The extension of coastal state jurisdiction since the 1970s has increased enormously the length of maritime boundaries between opposite and adjacent coastal states. Determination of these boundaries has followed different paths. Some have been agreed or negotiated quickly, as in the case of Norway and the European Community; others have been strongly disputed, eventually being resolved by one or another kind of arbitration, as in the case of Canada and France with respect to St Pierre and Miquelon and Canada and the United States in the Gulf of Maine. The manner in which maritime boundaries are settled, together with the length of time involved in determining the boundary, may have a profound effect on the way in which transboundary resources are managed once the boundary is determined. If a boundary is settled by arbitration, it is probable that the countries involved have moved far apart in their positions in the pre-arbitration stage, a circumstance that may present serious obstacles to co-operative management of transboundary fish resources in the years following the boundary settlement and that may focus attention on the surveillance and enforcement aspects of fisheries management in order to ensure that the newly-created boundary is respected by the fishers from each country. In addition to the history of negotiations over a boundary, a key determinant of the degree to which co-ordinated management of transboundary fish resources occurs in the post-boundary settlement era is the importance of historic fishing patterns (Day, 1992: 253–64; Day, 1994: 103–26).

The delimitation of maritime boundaries between adjacent and opposite states may interfere with historic fishing patterns. Where the boundary is agreed upon or negotiated quickly, the countries involved will probably be more willing to consider reciprocal access agreements in order to preserve historic fishing patterns than where maritime boundaries are determined by arbitration. The extreme positions and strained relations that tend to develop in the pre-arbitration period and during the arbitration proceedings themselves often preclude reciprocal access agreements to transboundary fish resources in the post-arbitration era.[1] As an arbitrated boundary is likely to be an unacceptable outcome to a jurisdictional dispute for at least some fishers, fisheries violations of this boundary are likely to occur. Hence the way in which a boundary solution is developed, together with the nature of the boundary agreement (Gulland, 1980), becomes of critical importance in determining where the emphasis and problems lie in terms of transboundary fisheries management policy in the post-settlement era. In the case of a negotiated boundary, transboundary stock management may involve bilateral co-operation in setting and apportioning allowable catches, and determining the conditions of reciprocal access to each country's exclusive zone. In terms of surveillance and enforcement, the focus of attention is not the boundary itself, but rather in making sure that vessels taking advantage of the reciprocal access provisions abide by the national regulations when in the other country's exclusive zone. The European Community–Norway case illustrates this kind of situation (Day, 1992). In the case of an arbitrated boundary, the boundary itself is likely to be of much greater concern in fisheries surveillance and enforcement activities, as one or both countries strive to prevent violations of the boundary line. This has been the case in the Gulf of Maine where, since 1984, numerous violations of the international maritime boundary have occurred by American fishers.[2] Analysis of these American fishing violations and their relationship to surveillance and enforcement procedures forms the focus of this paper.

The Gulf of Maine Boundary: Background Considerations

The jurisdictional dispute in the Gulf of Maine began in the mid-1960s over the continental shelf (Day, 1988) and, with the enactment of 200 nautical mile exclusive fishing zones (EFZs) by both the United States and Canada in 1977, it took on the additional dimension of a dispute over the water column and the living resources of the sea. The major area in dispute, as delimited by the final Canadian and United States' claim lines, was the eastern part of the Georges Bank (Figure 29.1). The declaration of EFZs was followed later in the same year by the short-lived Interim Reciprocal Fisheries Agreement, which gave flag state enforcement rights in the disputed areas of the Gulf of Maine (De Vorsey, 1990). Continuing negotiations over the boundary dispute and fisheries management in the disputed zone eventually led to two linked agreements in 1979: a fisheries treaty embracing detailed measures for the conservation and management of the Gulf of Maine shared resources and an agreement to send the boundary dispute to binding arbitration. The fisheries treaty met considerable opposition in the New

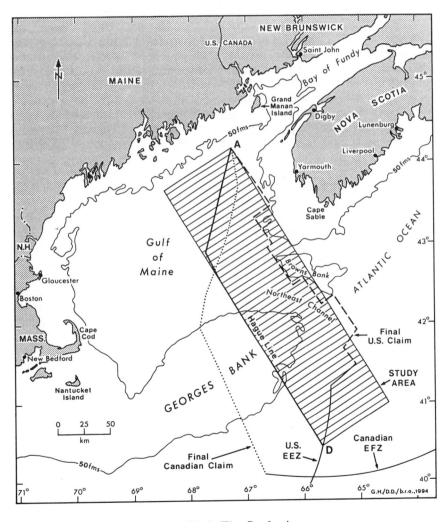

Figure 29.1 The Study Area

England and Middle Atlantic states and was not ratified by United States' Congress. Subsequently, both parties agreed to submit the boundary dispute to binding arbitration of a Chamber of the International Court of Justice (ICJ) with the condition that the Court should draw a single maritime boundary between Points A and D (Figure 29.1). The full boundary dispute in the Gulf was not submitted to arbitration, so that landward of Point A and seawards of Point D are sea areas that are still subject to jurisdictional dispute.

In its decision, the ICJ made little mention of the effect of its judgement on the management of the transboundary resources. As Figures 29.2 and 29.3 show, this area is important for both sedentary resources that straddle the boundary and fish stocks that migrate between the Canadian and American zones (Backus, 1987; Bubier and Rieser, 1986). The ICJ believed that Canada and the United States could reach agreement on fisheries management of these transboundary resources in their 'tradition of friendly and fruitful co-operation in maritime matters' (ICJ, 1984: 344, para. 240). Unfortunately, the Court's confidence was misplaced. In the years before the boundary decision, Canadian and American management philosophies and practices began to diverge significantly (Bubier and Rieser, 1986); in the years since the boundary was announced, there has been a complete exclusion of the adjacent state's fishers from each state's exclusive zone[3] and the imposition of quite different management philosophies on either side of the boundary (Day, 1992).

The boundary between A and D, referred to as the 'Hague Line' by local fishers, is located between the original claims of Canada and the United States. As Figure 29.1 shows, the United States had laid claim to the whole of the Georges Bank. which is not only important for groundfish but also contains extensive and highly valued scallop resources. During the 1970s both the Canadian and American scallop industries were expanding, and scallop fishers from both countries exploited the resources on either side of where the Hague Line was to be drawn. The ICJ's judgement gave a significant part of these scallop resources to Canada, a decision which many American fishers and other parts of its fishing industry did not agree with. This has provoked American demands for a renegotiation of the boundary under the North American Free Trade Agreement, suggestions that there should be a buffer zone which would allow American fishers to exploit waters on the Canadian side of the boundary line, and illegal entries into the Canadian zone. In Canada, detection and recording of these violations is primarily the responsibility of the Department of Fisheries and Oceans (DFO). Analysis of their reports for the study area shown in Figure 29.1 in the five-year period 1988–92 provides the basis for a study of the pattern of violations (Herbert, 1993).[4]

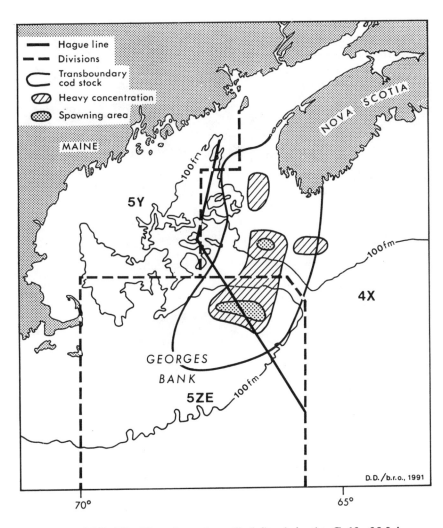

Figure 29.2 The Transboundary Cod Stock in the Gulf of Maine

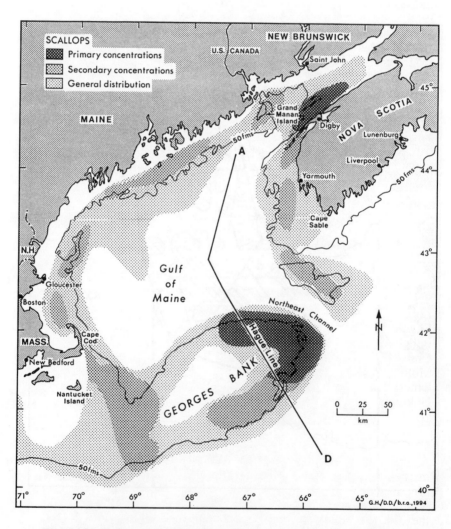

Figure 29.3 Location of Scallop Resources in the Gulf of Maine

Transboundary Violations

NUMBER, TYPE, AND TIMING OF VIOLATIONS

There were 181 known violations recorded by Canadian authorities between 1988 and 1992.[5] Table 29.1 shows that the number of known violations doubled from 1988 to 1989 (the peak year) and fell thereafter. It also reveals that more than three-quarters of the detected violations involved illegal fishing of scallop and groundfish (ie, cod and haddock) resources. Although known scallop violations peaked in 1989, there were many fewer by the end of the study period. Known groundfish violations decreased steadily to a nominal level in 1992. This decline doubtless results from the poor condition of the groundfish stocks on both sides of the boundary, the relatively low value of this fish compared with scallops, and the fact that the amount and value of potential illegal catches, together with the increased uncertainty of such catches for migratory fish compared with those for the sedentary scallops, has made the risk of detection, arrest, and penalties too great in relation to the potential returns. Although other fish stocks also form part of the transboundary resources of the region, to date they have proven relatively less important in terms of boundary violations.

Table 29.1 Known violations by fishery type

	1988	1989	1990	1991	1992	Total	%
Scallop	6	48	21	24	7	106	59
Groundfish	17	5	6	2	1	31	17
Swordfish	2	0	3	3	3	11	6
Lobster	4	5	1	3	1	14	8
Flounder	1	0	0	0	0	1	0.5
Pollock	0	0	1	0	0	1	0.5
Crab	0	0	0	1	0	1	0.5
Mollusk	1	0	0	0	0	1	0.5
Other	0	0	1	0	0	1	0.5
Unknown	3	11	0	0	0	14	8
TOTAL	34	69	33	33	12	181	100

Analysis of temporal patterns for all known violations reveals both a marked seasonality and a diurnal peaking (Figures 29.4 and 29.5). A preponderance in the second half of the year coincides with fairer weather conditions and a generally higher level of fishing activity in the Georges Bank region. It appears that the overall pattern of seasonality is conditioned by the number of illegal scallop entries in

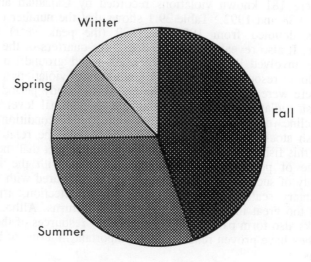

Figure 29.4 Percentage of All Violations by Seasons, 1988–92

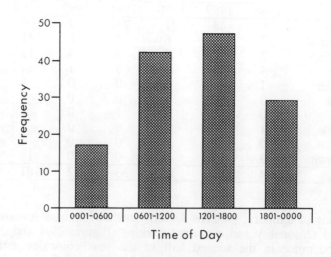

G.H./D.D./b.r.o.,1994

Figure 29.5 All Violations by Time of Day, 1988–92

summer and fall: in contrast, groundfish violations show relatively little seasonal variation and observed lobster violations show a peak in winter corresponding with the official lobster season and with rising prices in anticipation of the Christmas market. There is also a marked variation in the number of violations by time of day, the greatest number occurring during the morning and afternoon.

LOCATIONAL PATTERN OF KNOWN VIOLATIONS

The degree of spatial concentration and the locational pattern of the violations is shown by calculating the location quotients for a 30km by 30km grid covering the study area (Figure 29.6a).[6] When all violations are treated together, the location quotients are very high in squares A-5 and A-7. A-4 also shows a high concentration of violation activity. All three grid squares lie on the Georges Bank and adjacent to the Hague Line, in areas where highly valuable straddling scallop stocks are found (Figure 29.3). Beyond 30km from the boundary, the location quotients are everywhere very low or low.

Regression analysis of the total number of violations by 1km distance bands shows a distance-decay curve with a strong, negative relationship between the frequency of violations and distance from the Hague Line (Figure 29.7a). This relationship suggests a strong preference by American fishers not to risk lengthy trips across the Hague Line, and is probably based on the assumption that the risk of being detected and penalised is directly proportional to the length of time spent in Canadian waters.

SCALLOP VIOLATIONS

Given the preponderance of the scallop violations in the total number of violations, it is not surprising that the aggregate pattern of violations revealed by the location quotients is determined by the location quotient pattern for scallops (Figures 29.6a and 29.6b). However, Figure 29.6b shows that within the study area scallop violations are highly localised, and reflect the fact that scallop resources are primarily found on the Georges Bank. This map does show that two areas (B9 and C6) located beyond 30km from the boundary have medium location quotients. This, in turn, helps to account for the slightly weaker non-linear relationship shown by the distance-decay curve for scallops than for both aggregate violations and non-scallop violations (Figure 29.7b).

Detailed mapping of the 59 scallop violations for the 1988–92 period, highlights the importance of the Georges Bank and reveals that the vast majority occur within 5–10km of the Hague Line (Figure 29.8a). In particular, two specific areas on the Canadian side of the Hague Line are targeted by American vessels: the Northern

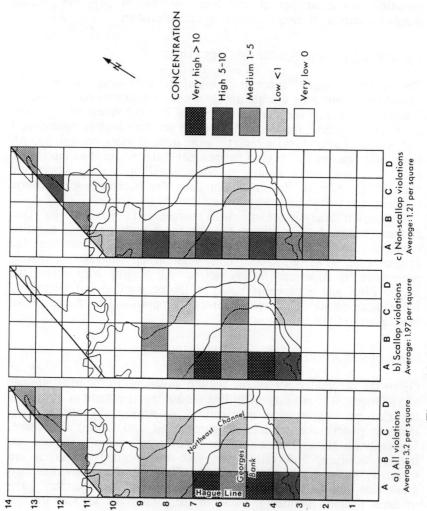

Figure 29.6 Location Quotients for Known Violations

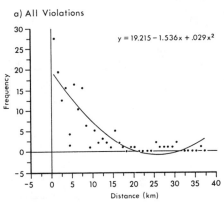

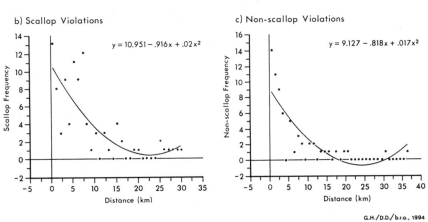

a) All Violations

$y = 19.215 - 1.536x + .029x^2$

b) Scallop Violations

$y = 10.951 - .916x + .02x^2$

c) Non-scallop Violations

$y = 9.127 - .818x + .017x^2$

G.H./D.D./b.r.o., 1994

Figure 29.7 Distance Decay Curve

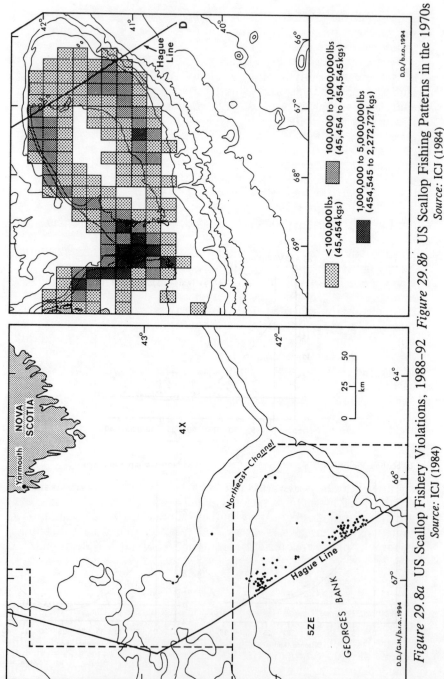

Figure 29.8a US Scallop Fishery Violations, 1988–92
Source: ICJ (1984)

Figure 29.8b US Scallop Fishing Patterns in the 1970s
Source: ICJ (1984)

Edge and the Yellowtail Hole. When violations are analysed by individual years, these twin foci are seen to be a robust feature in the locational pattern (Herbert, 1993).

This pattern can be explained by three factors: the spatial structure of surveillance activity, the proximity of valuable resources to the Hague Line, and historic fishing patterns. DFO surveillance of the study area is concentrated along the boundary, as Figure 29.9 shows. It could be argued that the higher level of surveillance effort near the Hague Line leads to a higher detection rate in that area compared with elsewhere and that this, in turn, skews the locational pattern depicted in Figure 29.6b. However, it is probable that administrative decisions by DFO as to where to concentrate patrols are conditioned by the geographical characteristics of past violations. It is known that American violators appear more willing to make a quick incursion over the Line than a more prolonged, deeper penetration of Canadian waters that carries a higher risk of detection and arrest.[7] Moreover, deeper penetrations of the Canadian zone than the Northern Edge and the Yellowtail Hole would be monitored, detected, and reported by Canadian fishers who provide a surveillance net in areas patrolled less intensively by Canadian authorities. The pattern of violations can also be explained by regarding the Northern Edge and Yellowtail Hole as intervening opportunities which provide a good abundance of high quality scallops close to the Hague Line that obviates the need for deeper penetration, even though Figure 29.3 suggests that other primary concentrations of scallops could be found closer to the Northeast Channel.[8]

The historic pattern of scallop fishing by American fishers must also be taken into account. Both the Northern Edge and the Yellowtail Hole were favoured fishing haunts of American scallop draggers originating mainly from New Bedford (Massachusetts) in the pre-boundary determination era. Figure 29.8b shows the pattern of American scallop fishing in the 1970s. It is clear that all the scallop areas showing significant location quotients were being visited before the ICJ decided on the path of the international boundary across the Georges Bank area. Geographic inertia may be contributing to the concentration of violations in these two areas, in spite of the changed political geography of the area resulting from the 1984 boundary decision.

NON-SCALLOP VIOLATIONS

A wide range of other fishing violations occurred in the period besides those involving scallops (Table 29.1). As Figure 29.7c shows, these are not so geographically concentrated but are dispersed along the full length of, but very close to, the Hague Line. The location quotient map confirms a lack of very high location quotients compared with scallops (Figure 29.6c). The pattern is controlled by American groundfish vessels making short sorties across the Hague Line and by lobster violators who prefer to have their gear very close to the Hague Line, allowing them to claim that the gear drifted across it if they are detected. This excuse is often offered when the captains of lobster boats are confronted by enforcement officers about violations. Swordfish violations are widely distributed, owing to the highly migratory nature of the species (Figure 29.7c). Fishers tend to follow the migration route of this resource and, while doing so, transgress the boundary.

Discussion

The scale, structure, and pattern of the violations described raises major questions pertaining to the peaceful management of transboundary resources in the Gulf of Maine: Why do the violations occur? How effective have surveillance and enforcement efforts been in detecting, preventing, and deterring violations? Under what conditions would the number of violations be reduced to zero or a nominal level?

THE REASONS FOR THE VIOLATIONS

Two major reasons are advanced to explain the violations. It has already been noted that, in the pre-1984 period, American fishers frequented waters that are now defined as Canadian. Given that many American fishers have a strong tradition of fishing in these waters, that many of them believe that the ICJ erred in not giving all the Georges Bank to the United States, and that there is no reciprocal access agreement to reduce the impact of the boundary, they have chosen to violate it. This is not, however, a sufficient explanation. A second major factor is the relative condition of the fish resources in the Canadian and American zones. Since 1984, there has been no co-operation between American and Canadian authorities in the management of straddling and transboundary fish resources in the Gulf of Maine, except for an agreement on co-ordinated surveillance of the boundary and enforcement procedures against violators which took effect in late 1991. Their philosophies with regard to fish stock management are very different (Bubier and Rieser, 1986; Day, 1992), with the United States managing the resources based upon the size of the reproductive stock, restricting the minimum size of fish that can be landed, and allowing unlimited entry to the fishery. It has managed its part of the Gulf of Maine resource without the use of total allowable catches (TACs), quotas and vessel licensing, while promoting a multi-species approach to harvesting. On the other hand, Canada's policy is based on controlling effort by entry limitation, vessel licensing, and the use of total allowable catches and quotas on a species and area basis. For migratory transboundary stocks, this lack of co-ordination of management philosophies and practices has led to overexploitation of the resources: for sedentary straddling stocks it has created a sharp difference in the size and quality of the scallop resource between the two sides of the Hague Line. While the American part of the scallop resource is greatly overexploited, Canada's part still yields valuable catches.

This difference encourages American fishers to cross the boundary to fish. Apparently American scallop boats are barely able to make a living by fishing only on their side of the boundary. It is estimated that a boat that crosses the Hague Line can catch up to US$100,000 of scallops per trip compared with an average of US$30,000 for fishing legally on the American side. There is evidence that many captains are unable to get crews unless they are prepared to fish illegally. Crew members can receive up to ten times as much for illegal fishing without bearing any risk of penalty for doing so, as only the captains and vessel owners can be charged if caught fishing illegally in Canadian waters.

EFFECTIVENESS OF SURVEILLANCE AND ENFORCEMENT

Surveillance and enforcement has changed significantly in the period since the boundary was announced in 1984 and this helps to explain the pattern of variation noted earlier in the annual number of known violations (Table 29.1). From 1984 to 1988, surveillance was sporadic and the manual records that were kept were incomplete. There is little doubt that the number of violations was much greater than the number officially recorded during this period. In 1989, a new system of reporting observed violations was adopted by DFO and methods of surveillance were improved. The considerable increase in the number of violations detected in 1989 stemmed from these improvements. Together with a general increase in enforcement activity, including armed boardings, they also deterred violations in 1990.

An even more fundamental change occurred in 1991. Until then co-operation between Canadian and American surveillance and enforcement authorities was almost non-existent. American violators detected in the Canadian zone would have to be arrested by Canadian patrol vessels for charges to be laid, even if hot pursuit across the boundary to make the arrest in American waters beyond their territorial sea was needed. Even if there were an arrest by American officials, the captain/owners of the vessel faced a maximum fine of US$10,000 under the Lacey Act for the importation of illegally-obtained goods whereas, if brought to trial in Canada, the maximum penalties involved a Can$100,000 fine, confiscation of catch, impoundment of the vessel, and a possible jail sentence. This differential in penalties alone made it worthwhile for violators to try and reach the American side of the boundary upon detection by Canadian authorities. In 1990, Canada and the United States reached an agreement whereby the two governments would co-operate in the arrest of violators and the United States would raise its maximum penalties for a proven violation to the level that existed in Canada prior to the agreement.[9] To accommodate these changes, violators arrested in American waters would no longer be charged under the Lacey Act but under an amended version of the Magnuson Fisheries Conservation and Management Act. In Canada, the Fisheries Act was also amended to reflect the agreement. The Agreement entered into force in late 1991 and led to a pronounced decline in the number of known violations in 1992 (Table 29.1). The improved co-ordination of surveillance and detection efforts by Canadian and American authorities (including some patrols by American authorities along the Hague Line to help prevent violations of the Canadian zone by their fishers) and the standardisation of the maximum penalties on both sides of the boundary have not only seemed to deter violators but also appear to have been successful in undermining the efforts of violators to resist arrest and retreat quickly to the American zone if detected by Canadian authorities.

Caution needs to be exercised in interpreting the decrease in known violations as an accurate reflection of the trend in actual violations. The nature of Canada's surveillance activities raises questions over the proportion of actual violations that are detected and reported. The first concern relates to the intensity of surveillance coverage in the study area (Figure 29.1) and requires an understanding of the surveillance effort. For fisheries management purposes, DFO divides eastern Canadian waters into a number of regions. The Scotia-Fundy region covers some 414,400km², and includes the Bay of Fundy, Canada's part of the Gulf of Maine, and the Scotian Shelf area to the outer limits of the EFZ and the boundary with Newfoundland. The study area is a small part of this region, covering approximately 4,320km². DFO surveillance efforts in the area are of two kinds: vessel patrols and aircraft patrols.[10] Vessel patrols in the Scotia-Fundy region are carried out by two offshore boats. Work plans for these vessels are based upon a 200 sea-day (24 hours per day) availability, but must include patrols of a variety of fisheries problem areas which are accorded priorities by DFO. Although the Hague Line has received high priority for patrols, continuous and intense surveillance in the area has not been possible. Air surveillance involves both fixed wing and rotary wing aircraft and is usually undertaken by private contractors and chartered operators, although the Department of National Defense and the Canadian Coastguard (Department of Transport) are occasionally utilised for fisheries enforcement. Work plans are developed at the beginning of the year and administered on a weekly basis in accordance with the number of air-hours assigned by the DFO to each Northwest Atlantic

Fisheries Organisation (NAFO) division per month. The Department lets the chartered operators know the routes to be checked and the days on which they are to be checked each week. Hence, the study area is not included in surveillance activities every day. A typical flight path for a fixed wing aircraft based in Halifax is shown in Figure 29.9. It suggests that not all of the study area is surveilled in detail or on a continuous basis. The spatial extent of such an air patrol is more effectively limited during poor weather conditions. The geographic coverage of the study area by a helicopter patrol, which operates from Yarmouth in south-western Nova Scotia, is much more limited than for fixed wing aircraft as the Hague Line is at the limit of its geographic range for patrol purposes.

A second area of concern involves the temporal structure of surveillance coverage. Two characteristics revealed by the analysis of known violations are the peaks during the daytime and in summer/fall. Both may be related to the surveillance schedule and effectiveness of surveillance methods rather than to the actual temporal distribution of all violations. Patrol flights occur in the daytime: at present DFO has no effective night-time surveillance capability. Continuous coverage around the clock and on each day of the year is not possible using the present system of surveillance and given present budgetary constraints. However, fishing continues throughout the day and night so that it is possible that many American boats deliberately fish in Canadian waters at night to minimise the risk of detection, making it likely that many violations go undetected because of the surveillance schedule. It is perhaps significant that when Canadian authorities used a submarine in the spring of 1993 to supplement normal surveillance efforts, the submarine spotted a dozen American vessels fishing in the Canadian zone in the early hours of the day.

The pattern of surveillance may not only help to explain the observed incidence of violations in a daily context, but also the yearly pattern of known violations. Surveillance coverage varies in its intensity, continuity, and effectiveness throughout the year being less in the winter/spring and more in summer/fall. To some extent the changing level of surveillance reflects the seasonal rhythm in the intensity of fishing effort on Georges Bank, but it is also pertinent to observe that better environmental conditions in the summer and fall are accompanied by improved visibility and calmer weather conditions, which not only provide better flying conditions but also enhance the probability of detection and aid the more accurate reporting of violations. The corollary of this is that in winter/spring there is not only less surveillance, but conditions for surveillance are poorer and so there is a greater likelihood that fishing violations go undetected.

A thorough analysis of the environmental conditions associated with the violations has not yet been attempted. However, preliminary analysis of official reports suggests that almost all known violations occur in sea conditions of 1 or 2m, and visibility conditions of at least

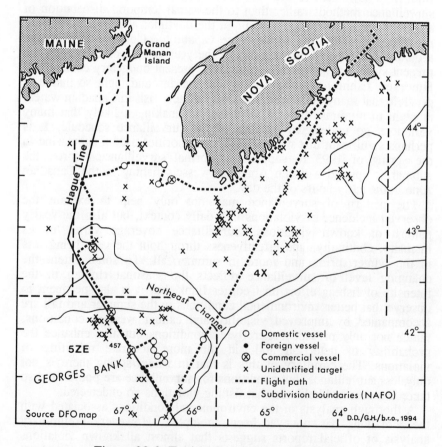

Figure 29.9 Typical Surveillance Flightpath

two, and usually at least six, nautical miles. Visibility is a key environmental factor affecting the outcome of current surveillance efforts. Records show that there are many days of poor visibility, together with stormy conditions, in the Gulf of Maine which could be accompanied by a large number of undetected violations. It is clear that for a considerable part of each day and for much of the year, illegal access to the study area by American vessels would not be deterred by surveillance craft. In spite of the advanced technology used aboard fixed wing aircraft patrols and the assistance now being given by American surveillance authorities, the possibility for non-detection of violations remains significant and so it is reasonable to conclude that many violations go undetected because of temporal and spatial holes in the surveillance net and poor environmental conditions in which to spot offenders.

A third area of concern highlights shortcomings of the surveillance/enforcement programme in terms of the detection and apprehension of violators. It is significant that Table 29.1 lists 8% of all violations as involving 'unknown' species. It is difficult for aircraft platforms to obtain a positive identification of the kind of violation resulting from American fishing vessels that have the capability to fish for a variety of species. The limitation of aircraft in this respect is an important factor to be taken into account in structuring the mix of surveillance platforms used in the enforcement process. Secondly, the number of violation occurrences that were observed over the study period far outnumbered the number of arrests and prosecutions, partly because an aircraft could detect and record a violation but was unable to make an arrest. Surface support capability is needed for this. However, the implementation of the Canada–United States Fisheries Enforcement Agreement and the inclusion of global positioning system (GPS) locations on aerial photographs of violators has raised the percentage of arrests in relation to observed violations since 1991. Prior to the Agreement coming into force, the number of prosecutions in relation to the number of known violations was small. These were mainly effected through the legal system, with consequent lengthy delays. Since 1991, not only has the number of violators receiving fines been increased but the speed with which penalties have been imposed has improved. This change results partly from the use in the United States of an administrative system of levying fines and penalties rather than making recourse to the court system. However, use of this system has also led to bargaining for fines and penalties at less than the maximum level, so that many violators have possibly been treated more leniently by this United States' system than if they had been taken to court in Canada.

CONDITIONS FOR REDUCING THE NUMBER OF VIOLATIONS

Unofficial estimates suggest that over a million dollars worth of scallops alone are lost to American boats each month through violations of the Hague Line. This raises the question of how the actual number of fishing violations could be reduced to zero or a nominal level under a regime of peaceful management of straddling and transboundary resources in the Gulf of Maine. One course of action would be to reduce the shortcomings of the present surveillance and enforcement system through increased geographic and temporal coverage of the area (possibly through the use of satellite tracking in conjunction with GPS transmitters and aircraft/vessel enforcement), continue efforts to improve co-ordination of surveillance efforts between the DFO and the American surveillance authorities, and strengthen the imposition of penalties on arrested violators. There can be little doubt that, if enforcement of the boundary is to lead to a long-term decline in the number of violations, then improved efforts of surveillance must be mirrored by quick and strict enforcement measures against violators.

However, it is suggested that the best chance for a successful enforcement of the Hague Line in the longer term lies in removing the need to violate. A major underlying cause of the violations stems from the difference in management practices between the two zones. A total lack of co-operation in management of the transboundary resources since 1984 has led to a gross overutilisation of the scallop resource in the American sector of the Georges Bank compared with that in the Canadian zone.

Conclusions

The preceding analysis has shown that the same locational pattern of violations is isolated repeatedly on an annual and longer-term basis but that there is a possibility that the temporal structure of the violations has changed. This change may have been affected by improvements in surveillance efforts, including more surface co-ordination between the Canadian and American governments and the use of a wide variety of surveillance platforms. However, there is still reason to doubt that the number of known violations is a true reflection of the number of actual violations. Many violations probably fall through the surveillance net as a result of variations in its spatial and temporal structure.

In a region where fishers from adjacent coastal states have traditionally pursued overlapping spatial patterns of exploitation, the imposition of an arbitrated boundary may lead to two kinds of fishing violations. First, there are incursions of one state's exclusive zone to tap sedentary resources that straddle the new boundary. These violations will tend to occur in areas visited historically for a resource that is no longer available to the violators. This type of violation will be encouraged if the species is highly valued and the resource is either not found on the violators' side of the new boundary or what is there has been depleted, as is the case of the American scallop resource on the Georges Bank. Secondly, there are violations that occur in terms of illegal entries to fish resources that migrate across the boundary, as in the case of groundfish in the Gulf of Maine area. Each species has different biogeographical characteristics, so that violations are more dispersed than with a sedentary resource. This study suggests that these violations occur with very short incursions into the opposite zone, probably because the resource will eventually migrate across the boundary and the low value of the resource makes the violation less worthwhile in terms of the potential gains offset against the penalties of being caught. With migratory transboundary resources, the decline of the violations in the period under study suggests that the greater the resource depletion the fewer the violations.

Surveillance and enforcement are no substitutes for successful co-operative management of the stocks on both sides of the boundary. Although adequate surveillance and enforcement may help to deter violations on straddling stocks, it is unlikely to lead to a complete cessation of violations unless there is also improving management on both sides of the boundary. So long as a sharp difference in the size and quality of the resource exists between two sides of a boundary and so long as there is a difference in legal enforcement against arrested violators, it will always be worthwhile to take the risk of crossing a boundary. In the absence of harmonious and proper management of these transboundary resources and in the absence of reciprocal access agreements, it is likely that Canadian fisheries management will have to focus indefinitely on strict enforcement of the boundary.

Notes

1   A recent example involves the Canada–France case centred on St Pierre and Miquelon. Reciprocal access by St Pierre and Newfoundand fishers to each others' waters has been a feature of treaty rights, as expressed in the 1972 Agreement between Canada and France on their Mutual Fishing Relations (Ottawa: 27 March 1972). Even though the 1992 arbitrated boundary delimitation around the islands did not set aside French treaty rights in Canadian waters, both parties have moved to limit the traditional reciprocal access rights during the post-arbitration period.
2   In the Gulf of Maine, there have been few if any violations of the international maritime boundary by Canadian fishers. However, on the west coast of North America in the Juan de Fuca Strait area, Canadian fishers have been the principal culprits in violating the Canada–United States maritime boundary. This reversal of

positions between the east and west coasts provided the framework for the 1990 Canada–United States Fisheries Enforcement Agreement, under which Canada agreed to try to prevent violations of the west coast boundary by Canadian fishers in exchange for United States' help in enforcement of the Gulf of Maine boundary.

3   Canada's fisheries policy refuses to allow access to the fish resources of its EFZ by the fishing vessels of any state that is not a member of the Northwest Atlantic Fisheries Organisation (NAFO). This policy, designed to exclude European fishing fleets from access to Canadian waters under the provisions of the UNCLOS III agreement, has been applied to the USA, as it has refused to join NAFO.

4   Violations of the boundary began in 1984, but Canadian records are less complete for the period 1984–7 so that analysis has been focused on the five-year period 1988–92. Two types of records are kept by the Department of Fisheries and Oceans: *occurrence* reports show detection of determined and suspected violations, whereas *violation* reports involve the arrest of the vessel and laying of charges, so that violation reports are a subset of occurrence reports. All violations are listed as an illegal entry into Canadian waters, but differ by type of fish involved. Claimed violations in the remaining disputed waters in the Gulf of Maine are excluded from the analysis.

5   Seventeen of these violations are not shown on the maps and diagrams that show locational analysis of the patterns as the reports do not contain precise latitude/longitude data for the violations.

6   In calculating the location quotients, the areas of squares A-11, B-12, C-13, and D-14 were pro-rated to obtain the relevant area on the Canadian side of the Hague Line.

7   The nature of the American violations is called 'dine and dash' by local authorities.

8   The distance decay curve of fishing violations may change if the quality and/or abundance of the resource at the Northern Edge and Yellowtail Hole decline or if current and projected cutbacks in the DFO budget and the requirements for new surveillance efforts around St Pierre and Miquelon and in the high seas area of the Grand Banks lead to a lower intensity of surveillance efforts along the Hague Line.

9   Agreement between the Government of Canada and the Government of the United States of America on Fisheries Enforcement, Ottawa, 26 September 1990.

10   DFO also operates an Observer Programme that involves at least 60 people and is a potential source of surveillance in the study area. These observers are primarily used on foreign vessels and

larger Canadian vessels operating legally in the Canadian EFZ. However, these observers have no real enforcement powers and they are, therefore, of little significance to this study.

Bibliography

Backus, R.H. (1987) *Georges Bank*, Cambridge, Massachusetts: The MIT Press.

Bubier, J.L. and Rieser, A. (1986) 'US and Canadian groundfish management in the Gulf of Maine–Georges Bank region', *Ocean Management* 10: 83–124.

Canadian Counter Memorial (1983) *The International Court of Justice Delimitation of the Maritime Boundary in the Gulf of Maine Area*, Canadian Counter Memorial, 28 June.

Day, D. (1988) 'Maritime boundaries, jurisdictional disputes, and offshore hydrocarbon exploration in eastern Canada', *Journal of Canadian Studies* 23(3): 60–89.

—— (1992) 'North Atlantic experience in transboundary stock management', in J.L. Suarez de Vivero (ed.) *The Ocean Change: Management Patterns and the Environment*, Seville, Spain: Department of Human Geography, University of Seville and the International Geographical Union.

—— (1994) 'Managing transboundary fish stocks: lessons from the North Atlantic', in G. Blake (ed.) *Maritime Boundaries*, World Boundaries Volume 5, London: Routledge.

De Vorsey, L. (1990) 'The Canada–United States boundary in the Gulf of Maine and over Georges Bank', *Boundary Briefing* 2, International Boundaries Research Unit, University of Durham.

Gulland, J. (1980) 'Some problems of the management of shared stocks', *FAO Fisheries Technical Paper* 206.

Herbert, G. (1993) *Fisheries Violations Across an Arbitrated Maritime Boundary: The Gulf of Maine Boundary Case,* Halifax, Nova Scotia: Department of Geography, Saint Mary's University.

ICJ (1984) 'Case concerning delimitation of the maritime boundary in the Gulf of Maine area', *International Court of Justice,* The Hague, 12 October.

30

Chile–Peru Relations:
The Special Maritime Border Zone

Hernan Santis Arenas
Monica Gangas Geisse

Introduction

According to the statistics of the Food and Agriculture Organization (FAO), in the 1980s Zone 87's production volume increased from 6 million tons at the beginning of the period, to 14 million tons at the end of the decade.

The major sources of fish production in Zone 87 are the exclusive economic zones (EEZs) of Chile and Peru. Statistically, Peru contributes 48% and Chile 46%; the remaining 6% is produced by the fishing economies of Ecuador and Colombia.

In a global context, the fishing economies of Ecuador and Peru in the period 1951–81 were strongly affected by the arrival of fishing ships from another nations, who covertly fished the EEZs of both parties without licences. In former periods, Peru and Chile's governments had complained of mutual infringements of fishing ships by both countries.

On 23 June 1947 the administration of President Gabriel González Videla, taking into account the reaction of the governments of the USA, Mexico and Argentina with respect to statements of sovereignty over the continental shelf adjacent to their coasts, together with consideration of the conservation, handling and exploitation of natural resources in these waters, decided to emphasise Chilean sovereignty over all the continental shelf adjacent to continental and insular Chilean territory. A demarcation line for a protected fishing area was established at 200 nautical miles from the continental and insular state territory.

A few weeks later, on 1 August 1947, the Peruvian government established a 200 nautical mile protected fishing area by presidential decision. It is clear that both governments were interested in securing their resources and maritime wealth against exploitation by foreign ships. The Chilean statement not only provoked reaction from America, but also decisively influenced international relations between Peru, Ecuador and Chile.

The principal purpose of this paper is to explore the Chile–Peru relationship regarding fishing activities located in the south of the Peruvian EEZ and the north of the Chilean EEZ.

As a result of co-operation between Chile, Peru and Ecuador, advances were made in the configuration of their maritime area, including the establishment of delimitation criteria. Later, Chile and Peru agreed to generate a 'Special Maritime Border Zone', and in the 1960s they tried to establish a visible marker to verify the position of the landmark that signals the western limit of the Chilean–Peruvian maritime border.

This analysis includes the events leading to Peru and Chile configuring the Special Border Zone; then some aspects of Chile and Peru's diplomatic relations in the 1990s will be examined, specifically those aspects that led to the Convention of Lima in 1993. We review the ideas of some Peruvian scholars attempting to stir up controversy in relation to the location and development of the maritime border between the territories. Each topic constitutes the result of research and reflection upon the potential for peaceful management of transboundary resources in the area.

The Special Maritime Border Zone

When the Chilean Government published its Presidential Statement of 23 June 1947, foreign offices of countries all over the world learned about the Chilean initiative: the proposal for a 200 nautical mile maritime zone. With this statement, Chile emphasised to the international community its right as a coastal State to protect, conserve and make use of all the natural resources contained in the vast extension of sea adjacent to its coast, within a breadth of 200 nautical miles.

This led to the concept of a new maritime regime, first proclaimed by Chile, then by other American states, and subsequently, after a long diplomatic juridical process, accepted by the international community, as the EEZ.

Chile proclaimed this revolutionary zone in an attempt to control competition for whales between Chilean and foreign ships fishing in the waters adjacent to Chile's coast. At the same time, when the Foreign Affairs Ministry had completed the study, and taken steps to materialise proposals, the initiative was divulged to Peruvian and Ecuadorian entrepreneurs. This made the road to diplomatic and political negotiations easier, and consequently led to an agreement.

Chile took this step, despite scarce knowledge in the 1940s. The idea was that the greater part of Chile's fishing economy came from activity in the so-called 'high seas', outside the three nautical miles contained by the 'territorial sea'.

In conclusion, Chilean authorities were interested in securing maritime resources and wealth against exploitation and degradation by foreign ships. It is also clear that in the early years Chile became isolated in its view. Chile broke from this isolation with the Statement of Santiago over the Maritime Zone, signed in 1952 with Peru and Ecuador.

THE MARITIME ZONE, 1952

Chilean authorities were aware that the statement of 1947 regarding the 200 nautical mile zone, when applied materially, generated difficulties between conterminous countries or countries with an ordinary maritime border. Because of this, in the beginning Chile oriented its international politics towards conterminous countries, with the purpose of setting up multilateral instruments to secure peaceful conflict resolution.

Whale capture along the coast of the South Pacific (the maritime zone of both countries and zone of Antarctic Seas, in the coastal waters of Chile and Peru) peaked in 1952, reaching some 20,000 specimens and generating 569,200 tons of whale oil. With an industry of this size it seemed appropriate to invite Peru and Ecuador to be involved in considerations.

The Statement concerning the Maritime Zone made at the first Conference on Conservation and Exploitation of the Maritime Resources of the South Pacific of 18 August 1952, had an economic basis, and justified sovereignty and exclusive jurisdiction in the 200 nautical mile zone in relation to other states. At the same time the governments of Chile, Ecuador and Peru searched for a definition of sovereignty and exclusive jurisdiction to which all of them could agree. For example, when considering an offshore island or group of offshore islands pertaining to one of the declaring countries, it was decided that the parallel of the point in which the terrestrial boundary of the respective states goes into the sea would be used in delimiting the maritime zone. This delimiting instrument must be used between the maritime zones of Ecuador–Peru and Peru–Chile.

The three governments were convinced of the high economic and social value of the resources located in the 200 nautical mile zone adjacent to their coasts, both geological and biological, coincident with the Humboldt Current. It seemed logical to sort out the countries' territorial relations and the relationship with other states. In this way, the 200 nautical mile maritime zone emerged as a formula for resource management.

THE SPECIAL MARITIME BORDER, 1954

The second Conference on Conservation and Exploitation of the Maritime Resources of the South Pacific, held in Lima, Peru, in December 1954, approved three special agreements in relation to the matter: the 'Complementary Agreement to the Sovereignty Statement over the Maritime Zone of 200 miles', the 'Agreement on the Special Maritime Border' and the 'Agreement on Vigilance Measures and Control of the Maritime Zones of the Signatory Countries'.

The first document gives the testimony of Chile, Ecuador and Peru who agreed to proceed jointly in the juridical defence of the principle of sovereignty over the Maritime Zone to a minimum distance of 200 nautical miles, including soil and respective subsoils. The third document says each signatory should effect the protection and control of exploitation of the wealth of its maritime zone by setting up suitable organisations.

The Special Maritime Border Agreement is the most interesting of these documents in relation to this paper. In the legal reasoning, the three governments described the difficulties of vessels of reduced size, manned by sailors with scarce knowledge of seamanship, or people without the necessary instruments to determine exactly their position on the open sea. These factors lead to innocent violations of the maritime border between neighbouring states. The governments also took into consideration the resentment originating from the application of sanctions in such cases and the possible negative effects on the spirit of collaboration and unity. In any case, the aim was to avoid the possibility of accidental infringements of the maritime zone.

Because of this, the three governments co-operated in establishing a special zone, extending to 12 nautical miles, 10 nautical miles wide, on each side of the parallel forming the maritime border between the countries. The accidental presence in that zone of vessels from any of the border countries, would not be considered a violation of the waters of the maritime zone. This does not mean that there is recognition of any right to purposeful, preconceived fishing in the Special Zone. Fishing or capture in the 12 nautical mile zone is reserved exclusively to the nationals of each country.

MARKING THE MARITIME BOUNDARY, 1969

Representatives of Chile and Peru , after years of negotiations, agreed to utilise a simple optical mechanism to help crews of fishing schooners locate the maritime border. For this purpose, they carried out a primitive geographical location of landmark No.1 of the common terrestrial border and other tasks necessary to fix demarcation points, agreed by both countries, to signal the parallel crossing the landmark No.1, placed on the coast.

When the location of the landmark was technically established, they selected two points where they put a tower in front of the landmark and behind it. These towers were provided with electrical lamps for nocturnal signalling and colour panels for day use. Thus an easy mechanism for establishing optically the line separating Peruvian and Chilean maritime jurisdiction was offered to the fishermen of Chile and Peru.

THE MAIN OBJECTIVE OF THIS SPECIAL MARITIME BORDER ZONE

It is clear that the Chilean initiative to protect, conserve and make use of all the natural resources in the 200 nautical mile zone, according to the reply of 1947, intended to address economic and biological aspects and implied, in relation to the jurisdiction of a state, the reinstatement of relations with conterminous territorial entities.

The first two Conferences on Conservation and Exploitation of Maritime Resources of the South Pacific searched for a diplomatic and peaceful solution and sought standardised sovereignty and exclusive jurisdiction for the three states. In 1952 they introduced the basic criterion for delimiting their individual zones, the parallel from the point at which the terrestrial border goes into the sea. In 1954, in an agreement over the Maritime Special Border Zone, they established an area of 10 nautical miles wide on each side of the parallel, and marked the maritime border between the two countries, 12 nautical miles from the coast.

The technical system of demarcation of 1969 specially designed for the crews of fishing vessels, completed the original plan. The coastal state had extended its economic jurisdiction and made this expansion without generating unnecessary controversy within the vicinity, and created a mechanism for the peaceful exploitation of resources from the sea.

From this point of view, the Chile–Peru Special Maritime Border is a buffer area located on the initial maritime border that was agreed in 1952.

The Peru–Chile Relationship During the 1990s

After 64 years the governments of Chile and Peru introduced a mechanism to fulfil the obligations established in the fifth article of the 1929 Treaty, and in the second article of the Complementary Protocol on the juridical regime. This involved the completion of Chile's obligations, in this case:

for the service of Peru, the government of Chile will build, supporting the costs, within the 1,570m of the Arica's bay, a docking sea wall for draft steamboats, a building for the Peruvian customs agency and a terminal station for the railway to Tacna, establishments and zones where Peru's commerce will have the independence proper of the ampler free port.

By 1986, Chile had completed the construction of the public works cited above. During 1985 negotiations about a juridical regime were opened. On 11 May 1993, representatives of both states agreed on criteria and signed the Convention of Lima, a convention on the free transit of goods, exchanging five notes on connected matters. It juridically established a territorial concession on the side of Chile for the use of port installations, and made Peru a private owner of a large area of urban land in the city of Arica. Peru also agreed to convert property into a park for the service of the people.

After some weeks, both governments sent the agreements to their respective parliaments, awaiting legislative confirmation. The Chilean Senate passed the agreement, but confirmation of the project remained obstructed in the Chamber of the Deputies. In Peru in August 1993, the Democratic Constituent Congress, the Peruvian legislative institution, began ratification, but decided to suspend any decision until a complete and detailed investigation had been undertaken.

A review of the Peruvian and Chilean press, between August 1993 and March 1994, clearly shows that a group of Peruvian legislators were attempting to generate a territorial position over the dock, the customs agency building and the railway station, hoping to enlarge jurisdiction over the esplanade between the dock and the railway station. Many less demanding members of parliament thought that the agreements should be renegotiated.

In short, the process of confirmation of the agreements was interrupted by the appearance of forms of nationalistic political thought, which shocked the government of President Fujimori.

The Aylwin administration, in the last months of its term, was disposed to complement the negotiations with other agreements, but wanted juridical conditions different to those agreed in the Treaty of 1929 and in the Convention of 1993.

As researchers of political relations between states, from a geographical perspective, we question the future of such spatial relations in the Special Maritime Border Zone of 1954, and the border in the Maritime Zone of 1952. This results from the increasingly inflexible attitude of the members of the Committee of Foreign Affairs of the Peruvian Constituent Congress, an institution that has deliberately avoided the ratification of the text of the Convention of Lima (January 1994).

In the first days of March of this year (1994), President Fujimori attempted to negotiate a complementary agreement to make aspects of the Convention of Lima clearer, but the negotiation was deferred by a change of government in Chile. However, the President hopes for intensification of economic relations and integration with Chile with the new Frei administration.

In this context how can Chile suggest to Peru any joint action in respect of increased revenues from fishing in the fisheries of both Exclusive Economic Zones? Our hypothesis is that in the immediate future nationalistic political thought will interfere, whilst on the horizon economic integration may emerge along with peaceful management of natural resources in the borderland areas.

Some Geopolitical Ideas in Peru

As an example of Peruvian geopolitical thought, we have selected the work of Morote (1986), examining in it aspects influencing the regime of the maritime border in 1952 and the Special Maritime Border Zone. The first problem which the author presents as fundamental refers to the establishment of the maritime borders with Ecuador and Chile (Morote, 1986: 53).

Morote suggests the maritime borders of Ecuador and Chile should be traced as the bisector of the angles conforming to its coastal limits, suggested to be an equitable one, rather than the parallels, because in the latter arrangement Peru yields space that affects development and security.

Figure 30.1 gives a better representation of the ideas of the geopolitical author, who affirms that the maritime limits between Ecuador and Chile:

> ... had not been established. There are fishing agreements that somebody without consulting, have convened in the parallels... In the chart of the Peruvian Sea, the sea and its borders are clearly presented. In front of Chile, must be formed the centre line of the overlapped area of the territorial sea corresponding to both countries. Zone A will be Peruvian. Zone B, without any discussion, corresponds to Peru (*sic*) (Morote, 1986: 57).

Morote concludes by saying that the situation with Chile, with regard to the spatial relationship of the two states, constitutes one of the areas of geopolitical tension affecting Peru. Morote is clearly trying to describe Peru as a victim of its neighbours.

We strongly question the influence of these thoughts, could they lead to an explosion of expressions of territorialist nationalism and opposition to debate? We try to imagine peaceful solutions to the difficulties and to contribute to the economic co-operation between the states, towards advancing effectively the physical integration of the territories.

We ask how we can reach the bilateral understanding necessary to conclude a joint political solution in respect of the prices of products

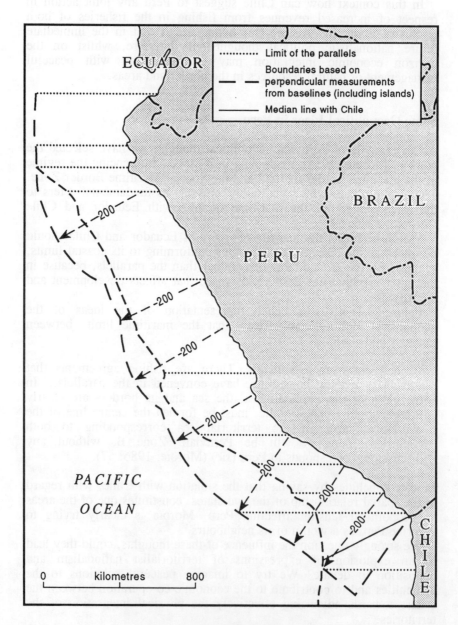

Figure 30.1 Peruvian Maritime Boundaries
Source: Marote (1986)

from this area's EEZs. These are mainly fish meal and fish oil. These products are basic in both economies. In the Chilean economy, export of marine products comes below minerals, wood and fruits. In the Peruvian case, during 1993, fishing products represented 21.9% of the volume of exports. We think for the materialisation of projects of economic co-operation and physical integration, a setting of bilateral relations free of prejudices and extreme political thought is necessary.

Summary

In IBRU's invitation to this conference, under the theme of 'Fisheries', our hosts hoped we would refer to matters of stock management in transboundary zones, located in the EEZ. It is not easy to address this topic if we do not first locate and identify the type of problems in relation to the territorial expectation of the states, including both terrestrial expectations and maritime ones.

In this example Chilean–Peruvian relations are being conditioned by former events and by forms of nationalistic political thought. During the decades of Cold War between the USA and the USSR, these forms of political thought remained buried by political difficulties between Chile and Peru. Today they are re-emerging, as in many European, Asiatic, and African areas as well as on other continents. Such re-emergence alters conditions, exacerbates bilateral relationships and changes the context of international relations – especially between territorial neighbours. This analysis of the Chile–Peru experience, without reference to other aspects of relations in new maritime territories, permits us a brief conclusion. If we wish to promote peaceful management of transboundary resources between states, we need to explore profoundly the difficulties that the past brings with it, to make them significant, and to look for rapid practical solutions. Economic co-operation, at least according to our observations in many American cases, necessitate the urgent solution of limiting past controversies. When we wish to accelerate and enlarge interstate relations in respect of fisheries, it is necessary to identify and solve problems concerning the respective maritime areas and agree on mechanisms for peaceful solutions.

Note

This paper stems in part from projects Fondecyt No. 1215/86, DIUC No. 015/90 and DTI C3020/9013, C3020/9223 and C3020/9333.

Bibliography

Ferrero, E. (1988) *Los intereses marítimos del Perú y los países del Pacífico Sur,* Lima: CEPI–UMA.

García, E. (1974) 'La doctrina de las 200 millas y el derecho del mar', in *Revista de Derecho de la Pontificia Universidad Católica del Perú* 32: 23–4.

Lagos Carmona, G. (1981) *Historia de las Fronteras de Chile. Los tratados de límites con Perú,* 2nd edn, Santiago: Editorial Andrés Bello.

Morote Solari, F. (1986) *Geopolítica del Perú,* 2nd edn, Lima: Librería Studium Ediciones.

MRE (1977) *Tratados, Convenciones y Arreglos Internacionales de Chile, 1810–1976. Tratados bilaterales Chile–Bolivia, Santiago,* Tomo II, Chile: Ministerio de Relaciones Exteriores.

31

Fisheries in the Sea of Okhotsk High Seas Enclave: Towards a Special Legal Regime?

Alex G. Oude Elferink

Since 1991 unregulated fishing activities in the central part of the Sea of Okhotsk, situated beyond the outer limit of the 200-nautical mile exclusive economic zone (EEZ) of the Russian Federation have led to notable pressures on fishing stocks in both in the high-seas enclave[1] and in the surrounding Russian EEZ.[2] The high-seas enclave in the central part of the Sea of Okhotsk makes up some 3% of the total area of the Sea of Okhotsk and measures some 300 nautical miles from north to south and some 30 nautical miles from east to west (Figure 31.1). Despite its limited size in relation to the whole of the Sea of Okhotsk, the high-seas enclave, which is also referred to as the 'peanut hole', is important for the management of fisheries stocks in the surrounding 200-nautical mile zone of the Russian Federation. It has been asserted that between 1991 and 1993, 1.5 million tons of fish were caught in the peanut hole (Zilanov, 1993).[3]

Jurisdiction over fish stocks which straddle the EEZ and adjacent areas of high seas,[4] as in the Sea of Okhotsk, is at present widely debated in the international community. International law provides that this issue has to be addressed by co-operation between the coastal state and states engaged in fisheries in the area adjacent to the coastal state's EEZ. As this solution has not led to efficient management, coastal states press for an extension of their jurisdiction over straddling stocks.

The Sea of Okhotsk provides an example of the debate over straddling stocks. The Russian Federation has advanced proposals which would give it primary responsibility for the management of the fisheries resources in the whole Sea of Okhotsk. The Russian Federation has been careful to point out that the factual situation in the Sea of Okhotsk and other enclosed and semi-enclosed seas with high-seas enclaves differs from the situation where stocks straddle between the EEZ and the high seas in other sea areas. This implies that the legal regime proposed for fisheries in enclosed and semi-enclosed seas with high-seas enclaves also has to be differentiated from that applying in other situations in which straddling stocks occur. The states engaged in fisheries in the peanut hole, such as Poland, do not reject a limitation of catches in the area, but consider that under international

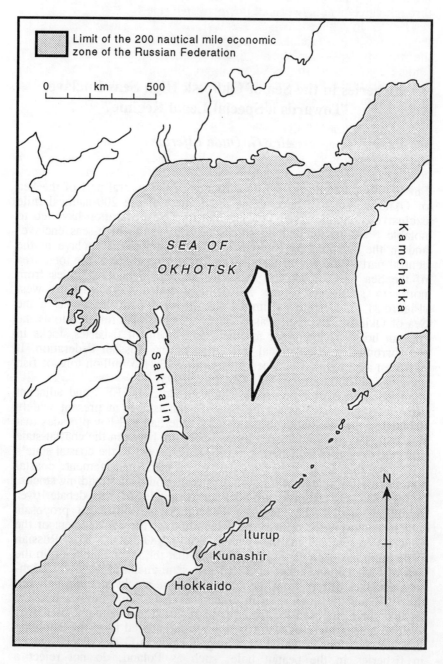

Figure 31.1 The High-Seas Enclave in the Sea of Okhotsk

law the regulation of catches in this area has to be accomplished through agreement between all the interested states.

The Sea of Okhotsk, which is situated on the north-western rim of the Pacific Ocean is almost completely surrounded by the territory of the Russian Federation. Japan, the only other coastal state, has a very limited coastal front in the southern part of the Sea of Okhotsk and its 200 nautical mile fishery zone does not extend to the high-seas enclave at the centre of the Sea of Okhotsk.[5] Although exact information on the Japanese position is lacking, it seems that Japan maintains a low profile on the regulation of fisheries in the Sea of Okhotsk. The Japanese position can be explained by the fact that generally Japan is mainly interested in preserving its existing rights in high seas fisheries, which contradicts support for extended coastal state jurisdiction in the Sea of Okhotsk.

Steps taken by the Russian Federation seem to suggest that it considers that it is the only coastal state which has a primary responsibility in regulating fisheries in the peanut hole. The Russian Federation has taken the initiative to start negotiations over fisheries in the Sea of Okhotsk, and apparently has not co-ordinated its position with Japan.[6] Legislative measures covering the high-seas enclave have been taken unilaterally by the Russian Federation, without reference to the interests of Japan as a coastal state. Russian authors have argued that the Sea of Okhotsk does not fall under the regime for enclosed and semi-enclosed seas contained in Articles 122 and 123 of Part IX of the 1982 United Nations Convention on the Law of the Sea (LOS Convention), which addresses co-operation between coastal states in such seas, because of the limited extent of the Japanese coast and maritime zones in the Sea (Molodtsov, 1993: 49). According to these authors this does not imply that the Russian Federation can be considered to have more limited rights in the Sea of Okhotsk than two or more coastal states have under Articles 122 and 123 of the LOS Convention (Molodtsov, 1993: 49–50).

Rejection of Japan's interest in fisheries management in the peanut hole as a coastal state may be subject to some doubt. Instead of an outright rejection of applying the regime contained in Part IX of the LOS Convention to the Sea of Okhotsk on purely geographical criteria, it would seem to be more appropriate to establish for specific issues whether regional co-operation is required. Such an approach would seem to follow from the object and purpose of Article 123 of the LOS Convention, which is to promote co-operation between coastal states for issues which are better resolved at a regional level than unilaterally. In the case of fisheries, if the activities of third states in the high-seas enclave have an adverse effect on fisheries resources in Japanese maritime zones, regional co-operation to address such fisheries would suggest itself.

The most important stock in the Sea of Okhotsk is Alaska pollack. There are also a number of commercial species associated with the

Alaska pollack: herring, halibut and certain marine mammals. According to the Russian Federation, the high-seas enclave in the Sea of Okhotsk is of particular importance for regulating the fishing of Alaska pollack in the Sea of Okhotsk, because in this area the various subpopulations of Alaska pollack which reproduce in other parts of the Sea intermingle. Because of this intermingling of subpopulations a permanent ban on fishing was introduced in the high-seas enclave, which was observed by states traditionally fishing in the Sea of Okhotsk. Difficulties have arisen since 1991 when fishing vessels mostly from China, South Korea, Poland and Panama started conducting fishing activities in the high-seas enclave. These fishing practices are said to have destroyed the entire system of measures for the conservation and management of Alaska pollack stocks taken by the Russian Federation. Because of over-fishing, the total allowable catch (TAC) in the Russian EEZ for the years 1992 and 1993 had to be adjusted downward in order to prevent spawning stocks from being totally eliminated (UN 164/L.21: 2).[7] Fishing for Alaska pollack in the peanut hole could also have detrimental effects for stocks of other commercial species such as herring, halibut, salmon, and certain marine mammals (UN 164/L.21: 3).

Since the commencement of large scale fisheries in the peanut hole in 1991 the Russian Federation has taken a number of unilateral steps and initiated negotiations to address this issue. One of the first reports on alleged over-fishing in the Sea of Okhotsk, which appeared in *Izvestiia* of 23 November 1991, already suggested that under international law the Russian Federation could establish a temporary moratorium on fisheries in the Sea of Okhotsk (*Izvestiia,* 1991a: 2). Russian fisheries organisations proposed in December 1991 to close the central part of the Sea of Okhotsk temporarily to hold military manoeuvres, which was rejected by the Russian Ministry of Foreign Affairs at the time (*Izvestiia,* 1991b: 7). It seems that the Russian Federation planned to conduct military manoeuvres in the high seas in the Sea of Okhotsk for a two-week period in August 1993. However, these plans in the end did not materialise.

On 16 April 1993 the Supreme Soviet of the Russian Federation adopted a resolution which provided that the Russian Federation took upon itself the responsibility for the conservation of the living resources in the high-seas enclave in the Sea of Okhotsk (Russian Federation Supreme Soviet, 1993). The resolution established a temporary moratorium on fishing in the high-seas enclave for Russian and foreign fishing vessels from 15 June 1993 until an international agreement on this issue was reached. According to the preamble of the resolution, fisheries in the high-seas enclave in the Sea of Okhotsk was addressed in this manner because international law did not explicitly provide for a regulation of this issue. Shortly after the adoption of this resolution a spokesperson of the Russian Federation Ministry of Foreign Affairs indicated that any measures taken to enforce the moratorium would not contradict international law (Diplomaticheskii Vestnik, 1993: 70).

From 31 May to 1 June 1993 the first international conference on the living resources of the Sea of Okhotsk, in which the Russian Federation, Japan, Poland, South Korea and China participated, took place in Moscow on the initiative of the Russian Federation. The Russian Federation, considering the uncontrolled fishing activities in the peanut hole harmful to the fishing resources in the Sea of Okhotsk, proposed a three-year moratorium on fisheries in the peanut hole to the Conference (Diplomaticheskii Vestnik, 1993: 69). Japan agreed to abide by this measure on a voluntary basis, as it was already doing at the time. Poland, South Korea and China declared that they were prepared to temporarily diminish their catches by 25% in the high-seas enclave in comparison with the same period in 1992 (UN 164/INF/6: 1). The Russian Federation indicated the total insufficiency of measures aimed at the partial reduction of fishing and declared its intention to take all necessary measures on the basis of the relevant provisions of international law to promote the conservation of Alaska pollack in the Sea of Okhotsk (UN 164/INF/6: 1–2). At the conference it was agreed to establish a special scientific committee to prepare a report on the condition of the Alaskan pollack in the peanut hole for the second session of the conference (UN 164/INF/6: 1).

In October 1993 the Russian government adopted a decision containing further measures to preserve the living resources and protect the Russian Federation's fishing interests in the Sea of Okhotsk. The Ministry of Foreign Affairs was charged with examining the expediency of reconsidering or denouncing bilateral fisheries and trade agreements with states whose fishing vessels were engaged in fishing in the peanut hole, and also to look into the possibility of other trade and economic measures in case of rejection by such states to support the efforts of the Russian Federation to conserve the living resources in the peanut hole. The Decision prohibits the allotment of catch quota in the Russian Federation EEZ to foreign legal or natural persons, conducting or having conducted fisheries in the peanut hole. Furthermore, the servicing in Russian ports of fishing vessels, conducting or having conducted fisheries in this area was prohibited (Russian Federation Council of Ministers, 1993: paras. 2 and 5).[8]

The Russian Federation has also taken bilateral steps in connection with the fisheries in the peanut hole. For instance, the Russian Federation has approached China to conduct scientific studies in fisheries management in the Sea of Okhotsk and to refrain from fishing the peanut hole (SWB SUW/0304). A further step taken by the Russian Federation has been to deny China, which in earlier years was authorised to fish in the Russian Federation EEZ, a catch quota in its EEZ for 1994, because of the numerous violations of the moratorium on catches of Alaska pollack in the high-seas enclave in the Sea of Okhotsk by Chinese fishermen (SWB SUW/0316). Japan and South

Korea, which also have an interest in fisheries in the peanut hole, have been accorded catch quotas of some 200,000 tons in the Russian Federation EEZ for 1994 (SWB SUW/0316).

The Russian position on the legal regime for fisheries in the high-seas enclave in the Sea of Okhotsk is based on the premise that high-seas enclaves occupying small areas within enclosed and semi-enclosed seas[9] require a specific fisheries regime.[10] The Russian Federation submits that in view of the fact that high-seas enclaves occupying small areas within enclosed and semi-enclosed seas lie across the migration routes of certain fish species exclusive to the coastal state, the basic provisions of the regime for the conservation and rational utilisation of such fish stocks should be based not only on Articles 63 and 123, but also on Articles 61 and 62 of the LOS Convention (UN 164/L.25 Annex: 4).[11] The Russian approach in practice would imply that the legal regime concerning fisheries applicable to the EEZ becomes applicable in its entirety to the straddling stocks in high-seas enclaves in enclosed and semi-enclosed seas, giving the coastal state control over fisheries in these enclaves. According to the Russian view, the coastal states of enclosed or semi-enclosed seas should independently determine the TAC for all fish stocks in these seas and should establish annual catch quotas for each species (UN 164/L.25, Annex: 4).[12] Only in cases where the TAC for the commercial stocks of enclosed or semi-enclosed seas is not fully utilised by the coastal states, shall other states be given access to the surplus of the TAC of these stocks on the basis of bilateral agreements between the coastal states and the other interested states. In the allocation of quota, priority shall be given to developing countries and states of a region whose fishermen have traditionally fished in the area concerned (UN 164/L.25: 4).[13] The Russian proposal provides that these bilateral agreements shall include, *inter alia* the following provisions:

1 The duty of the parties to ensure that fishing activities in the high-seas enclave are not detrimental to the resources of the economic zones surrounding this enclave, or to the ecosystem and environment;
2 Quotas and other restrictions on fishing activities;
3 Means of identifying vessels and fishing gear;
4 The standardisation of vessel and fishing-gear markings;
5 A system for the monitoring, inspection and surveillance of fishing vessels;
6 Measures to enforce compliance with agreements, including measures established by international law in respect of illegally flagged vessels, vessels which conceal their nationality or vessels reflagging at sea (UN 164/L.25: 4–5).

A review of the regime proposed by the Russian Federation for enclosed and semi-enclosed seas shows that it is not as much these measures related to fishing activities which differ substantially from measures proposed in connection with fisheries of straddling stocks in general, but that the major difference is whether it will be the coastal state alone which will be able to establish the TACs for straddling stocks beyond its EEZ or whether this is a matter to be agreed upon between the coastal state and interested third states.

For the Russian Federation the differentiation between enclosed and semi-enclosed seas and other sea areas is explained by its interests as a coastal state to a number of semi-enclosed seas with high-seas enclaves, while at the same time being a distant water fishing nation.[14] The attraction of a special regime for high-seas enclaves of enclosed and semi-enclosed seas is that such enclaves are relatively few in number. Apart from the Sea of Okhotsk, the Russian Federation is a coastal state in two other seas with high-seas enclaves, one being the Barents Sea, the other the Bering Sea. In these two cases the Russian Federation is one of two coastal states whose 200-mile zones are adjacent to the high-seas enclave. In the Barents Sea the other coastal state is Norway, while in the Bering Sea it is the United States. Fisheries in the Bering Sea have been the subject of extensive negotiations between the Russian Federation, the United States and the states interested in the fisheries in the high-seas enclave. In August 1992 the interested states agreed on a moratorium on the fishing of the Aleutian Basin pollack in the high seas area in the Bering Sea on a voluntary basis for the period from the beginning of 1993 until the end of 1994.[15] Under a Draft Convention on fisheries in the Bering Sea, which was adopted in February 1994, an annual Conference of the Parties will decide allowable harvest levels and establish catch quota for parties fishing in the enclave. Fishing is not allowed unless the Aleutian Basin pollack biomass is determined to exceed 1.67 million metric tons. If possible this determination is to be made by consensus of the parties, otherwise by the United States and the Russian Federation jointly, and, as a last resort, unilaterally by the United States. In the Record of Discussion accompanying the Draft Convention, the Russian Federation and the United States indicated that they intend to suspend fishing within their respective EEZs if the Aleutian Basin pollack biomass does not exceed 1.67 million metric tons and to take into account the level of fishing in the enclave in establishing annual catch quotas in their EEZs. These statements can be seen as a check on the decision making power with respect to fisheries in the enclave which the Draft Convention ultimately accords to the coastal states. The experience with regime building for the fisheries in the high-seas enclave in the Bering Sea, which has been on the political agenda for a longer time than the Sea of Okhotsk, can be expected to exercise an influence over the course of events in this latter case.[16]

Present day international law does not seem to provide a basis for the proposals of the Russian Federation for a special legal regime for straddling stocks in enclosed and semi-enclosed seas. The Articles of the LOS Convention[17] addressing stocks that straddle between the EEZ and the adjacent high seas[18] do not provide in any way for a differentiation between enclosed and semi-enclosed seas and other sea areas. As far as the application of Articles 61 and 62 of the LOS Convention to high-seas enclaves in enclosed and semi-enclosed seas are concerned, the Russian proposal that these Articles *should* apply in this case recognises that the provisions of these Articles at present do not form part of the applicable law for high-seas enclaves.[19] Existing bilateral fisheries agreements addressing the issue of straddling stocks do not seem to differentiate between high-seas enclaves in enclosed and semi-enclosed seas and other high seas areas adjacent to EEZs with straddling stocks, and are based on the regime contained in the LOS Convention which requires co-ordination of policies of the coastal state and third states engaged in high seas fisheries with straddling stocks.

Article 123 of the LOS Convention on co-operation between states bordering enclosed or semi-enclosed seas has been invoked by the Russian Federation as supporting a differentiation between enclosed and semi-enclosed seas and other sea areas. In view of the fact that Article 123(a) only provides that states bordering such seas shall endeavour to co-ordinate the management, conservation, exploration and exploitation of the living resources of the sea, this Article does not create an independent basis for coastal state rights but only provides that in enclosed and semi-enclosed seas states should co-operate. The legal basis for specific measures to be taken by coastal states is to be found in the other Articles of the LOS Convention, which as already noted, do not make a differentiation between coastal states' rights over straddling stocks in enclosed and semi-enclosed seas, and other sea areas.[20] The claim made in Russian legislation that the issue of straddling stocks in enclosed and semi-enclosed seas is not explicitly regulated under international law, justifying unilateral actions by the coastal state, is only correct to the extent that international law does not provide for a mechanism to settle disputes between coastal states and other interested states in respect of straddling stocks in general.

Moreover, it can be questioned whether it is possible to make the factual differentiation between enclosed and semi-enclosed seas and other seas, which forms the premise of the Russian proposals for a special regime in the former case. According to the Russian Federation, high-seas enclaves occupying small areas within enclosed and semi-enclosed seas lie across the migration routes of certain fish species exclusive to the coastal state. This assertion may be very hard to document by scientific evidence and it has to be asked what criteria have to be met to determine that a certain fish species uses the high seas area mainly to migrate between parts of the EEZ of the coastal states. As a result of such difficulties, a special regime for enclosed and semi-enclosed seas would seem to create a precedent for extending coastal state jurisdiction in general. It can be expected that coastal states which are faced with stocks which straddle between their EEZ and the open seas will draw an analogy with enclosed and semi-enclosed seas once a special regime for these latter seas is accepted. It may prove difficult to refute such claims with unequivocal scientific evidence.

Notwithstanding the lack of a legal basis to establish a special fisheries regime for high-seas enclaves in enclosed and semi-enclosed seas under current international law, it cannot be said that such a regime will not eventually come about in a number of cases. In the case of the Sea of Okhotsk, it can be noted that the Russian Federation is a major maritime power, which has considerable resources at its disposal to influence the outcome of negotiations of a regime for fisheries in the area. In the field of fisheries itself this can involve the access of third states to fisheries within the EEZ of the Russian Federation, denial of servicing in Russian ports of fishing vessels engaged in fisheries in the high-seas enclave in the Sea of Okhotsk, and harassment of fishing vessels of third states actually engaged in fishing activities in the Sea of Okhotsk. Third states engaged in fishing in the high-seas enclave the Sea of Okhotsk will have to weigh the short-term gains of co-operation with the Russian Federation on the Russian Federation's terms (with the consequential risk of losing all control over the terms under which fisheries are conducted to the Russian Federation) against the gains of fishing in the high-seas enclave with the opposition of the Russian Federation.

In general terms, two outcomes of the negotiations over fisheries in the Sea of Okhotsk are possible. One possible outcome is that priority will be accorded to coastal state rights and interests in derogation of the regime generally applicable to straddling stocks, which in the longer term could lead to a factual assimilation of the high-seas enclave to the surrounding EEZ for fisheries management purposes.[21] Another possibility is that the solution for the Sea of Okhotsk will follow the rules applicable to straddling stocks in general. Which of these approaches will be actually pursued by the Russian Federation is difficult to predict. Its present moves clearly show that it has a preference for the first option. The fact that until now the Russian Federation has avoided any steps that openly contradict international law[22] (although it has claimed rights to regulate fisheries in the high-seas enclave in the Sea of Okhotsk going beyond what is presently permitted under international law to the coastal state) indicates that it is not willing to achieve its preferred outcome at too high a cost. Whether the Russian Federation will continue to advocate a special regime in the longer term can be expected to depend to a large extent on the outcome of the United Nations Conference on Straddling Stocks and Highly Migratory Fish Stocks. In case the Russian Federation is satisfied that the results of this Conference can protect its interests as a coastal state, it may consider it more advisable to adopt this approach in the Sea of Okhotsk, than to opt for a special regime in this sea which might threaten to erode the compromise reached over straddling stocks at the Conference, which would be to the detriment of the interests of the Russian Federation as a long distant fishing nation.[23] Another circumstance which will influence the course of events in the Sea of Okhotsk will be the outcome of negotiations in the Bering Sea. The compromise reached in this sea, which to a large extent concerns the same interested states, could present itself as a model for the Sea of Okhotsk.[24] Both the UN Conference and the case of the Bering Sea seem to suggest that a final solution of the straddling stocks issue may be to accord preferential rights to the coastal state, while at the same time providing for some checks to avoid abuse of such rights.

Notes

1   Although regularly referred to in state practice and literature 'high-seas enclaves' are not a legal concept. Sea areas which are referred to as high-seas enclaves consist of a sea area completely surrounded by 200-nautical mile zones of coastal states, being of limited size in comparison to the surrounding zones.

2   Another problem facing the Russian Federation in the seas off its Far Eastern coasts seems to be illegal fishing in its 200 mile zone and the difficulties Russian Border Troops have in enforcing fishery regulations (SWB SUW/0303). See also Canfield (1993: 278).

3   Another figure that has been mentioned is 1 million tons for the year 1993 (SWB SUW/0302).

4   The term 'straddling stocks' will be used in this paper to refer to stocks that occur between both within the EEZ and in an area beyond and adjacent to the EEZ, and does not include stocks that occur within the EEZs of two or more coastal states. This paper will not address fish stocks in the Sea of Okhotsk which are not straddling stocks, for which stocks no management problems similar to those of the straddling stocks exist.

5   Due to a dispute between Japan and the Russian Federation over the sovereignty over two islands of the Kuriles, Iturup and Kunashir, the Habomai Islands and Shikotan, the precise extent of the maritime zones of Japan and the Russian Federation in the Sea of Okhotsk is uncertain. However, even when these disputed islands would fall under Japanese sovereignty, the coastal front of Japan remains very limited in comparison to that of the Russian Federation, and Japanese maritime zone would not extend to the high-seas enclave in the Sea of Okhotsk.

6   See also Russian Federation Council of Ministers (1993). The Decision charges the Russian Federation Ministry of Foreign

Affairs to conduct negotiations with states, whose fishing vessels are engaged in fishing in the central part of the Sea of Okhotsk. No reference is made to negotiations or consultations with Japan as a coastal state of the Sea of Okhotsk in this connection (*ibid*, paragraph 1).

7   According to one report, in the absence of immediate measures, catches of Russian fishermen in the Sea of Okhotsk would diminish by some 2 million tons within two years (*Izvestiia*, 1991a: 2).

8   For a report in English on the Decision see SWB SUW/304 and SWB SUW/0316.

9   Article 122 of the LOS Convention defines 'enclosed or semi-enclosed seas' as:

> a gulf, basin or sea surrounded by two or more States and connected to another sea or the ocean by a narrow outlet or consisting entirely or primarily of the territorial seas and exclusive economic zones of two or more coastal states.

10   The following account of the Russian position is based mainly on the Annex to the 'Letter Dated 26 July 1993 from the Alternate Chairman of the Delegation of the Russian Federation Addressed to the Chairman of the Conference' (UN 164/L.25) which was circulated at the second session of the United Nations Conference on Straddling Fish Stocks and Highly Migratory Species, 12–30 July 1993.

11   Article 63 of the LOS Convention is applicable to stocks occurring in the EEZ of two or more coastal states or both within the EEZ and in an area beyond and adjacent to the EEZ. Article 123(a) of the LOS Convention provides that coastal states of enclosed and semi-enclosed seas shall endeavour to co-ordinate the management, conservation exploration and exploitation of the living resources of the sea. Article 61 and 62 address the management of living resources by the coastal state in its EEZ.

12   Article 61(1) of the LOS Convention gives the coastal state the right to establish the TAC in its EEZ. In cases in which there is more than one coastal state in an enclosed or semi-enclosed sea, the regime applicable for the establishment of the TAC proposed by the Russian Federation would have to be elaborated, to provide for a mechanism to resolve disputes between the states concerned.

13   These provisions correspond with Article 62(2) of the LOS Convention which is applicable to the EEZ.

14   This point is very well illustrated by the Russian proposals contained in UN 164/L.25, which apart from the proposal for a legal regime for high-seas enclaves in enclosed and semi-enclosed seas gives the Russian views on the regime which should be generally applicable to straddling stocks. In this case the Russian Federation adheres to the approach, which is also contained in

Article 63(2) of the LOS Convention, that the TACs and annual catch quotas for each species of straddling stocks shall be established jointly by the coastal state and other interested states (*ibid:* 3).

15   Joint Resolution of the Fifth Conference on the Conservation and Management of the Living Marine Resources of the Central Bering Sea (August 1992). On fisheries in the Bering Sea high-seas enclave see further Miles and Burke (1989: 343–57); Canfield (1993).

16   See also Canfield (1993: 278).

17   It is assumed here that the LOS Convention reflects customary international law.

18   Apart from Part V of the LOS Convention on the regime for the EEZ, especially Article 63(2), this concerns Section II of Part VII of the Convention on the conservation and management of the living resources of the high seas, especially Article 116.

19   See UN 164/L.25, Annex: 4. On the other hand the Russian Federation seems to consider that Article 123 of the LOS Convention does already entail a differentiation in the coastal state jurisdiction over straddling stocks as regards enclosed and semi-enclosed seas and other sea areas (see below).

20   See however Molodtsov *et al* (1993: 48) where it is argued that the coastal states can take management measures concerning living resources in a high-seas enclave in an enclosed or semi-enclosed sea, which are binding on all states.

21   Taking into consideration that the central part of the Sea of Okhotsk in legal terms forms part of the continental shelf of the Russian Federation, the Russian Federation in this case to a large extent would enjoy the same rights in the high-seas enclave as it does in the surrounding EEZ.

22   Some doubt in this respect is possible as concerns the ban on servicing in Russian ports of fishing vessels engaged in fishing in the peanut hole, especially if there is a bilateral agreement between the Russian Federation and the flag state over entry into ports. In this case relevant questions would seem to be whether fishing activities in the Sea of Okhotsk concern a violation of international law justifying a reprisal by the Russian Federation and whether the Russian Federation response is in accordance with the provisions of the bilateral agreement.

23   As is noted by Canfield (1993: 279):

A successful conservation regime for the Bering Sea might inadvertently set off the same cycle of overexploitation in some other region of the world's oceans. This possibility suggests there is value in addressing these resource conservation and management issues simultaneously in regionally specific international fora.

As a matter of fact fisheries in the high-seas enclave in the Sea of Okhotsk started after long distant fishing states encountered opposition to their fishing activities in the central part of the Bering Sea.

24 See also Canfield (1993: 278).

Bibliography

Canfield, J.L. (1993) 'Recent developments in Bering Sea fisheries conservation and management', Ocean Development and International Law 24: 257–89.

Diplomaticheskii Vestnik (1993) No. 13–4: 70.

Izvestiia (1991a) 'Dostanetsia li Nam "Dyrka ot Bublika"?', 23 November: 2).

Izvestiia (1991b) 'Pora Zakryvat' Okhotskoe More', 5 December: 7.

Segodnia (1993) 'MID Nastaivaet na Moratorii na Promysel Mintaia', in *Segodnia* 15, 12 May.

Miles, E.L. and Burke, W.T. (1989) 'Pressures on the United Nations Convention on the Law of the Sea of 1982 arising from new fisheries conflicts: the problem of straddling stocks', *Ocean Development and International Law* 20: 343–57.

Molodtsov, S.V., Zilanov, V.K. and Vylegzhanin, A.N. (1993) 'Anklavy Otkrytogo Moria i Mezhdunarodnoe Pravo', *Moskovskii Zhurnal Mezhdunarodnogo Prava* 2: 39-53.

Russian Federation Council of Ministers (1993) 'On Additional Measures for the Conservation of Living Resources and the Protection of Fisheries Interests of the Russian Federation in the Sea of Okhotsk', decision of the Council of Ministers, Government of the Russian Federation, No. 962 of 22 September, in *Sobranie Aktov Prezidenta i Pravitel'stva Rossiiskoi Federatsii* 40: Item 3857 (in Russian).

Russian Federation Supreme Soviet (1993) 'On measures to protect the biological resources of the Sea of Okhotsk' resolution of the Supreme Soviet of the Russian Federation of 16 April, in *Vedomosti Soveta Narodnykh Deputatov Rossiiskoi Federatsii i Verkhovnogo Soveta Rossiiskoi Federatsii* 18: Item 638 (in Russian).

SWB SUW/0302 *Summary of World Broadcasts Weekly Economic Report Part I Former USSR* SUW/0302 WC/4 [16].

SWB SUW/0303 *Summary of World Broadcasts Weekly Economic Report Part I Former USSR* SUW/0303 WC/3 [16].

SWB SUW/0304 *Summary of World Broadcasts Weekly Economic Report Part I Former USSR* SUW/0304 WC/4 [23].

SWB SUW/0316 *Summary of World Broadcasts Weekly Economic Report Part I Former USSR* SUW/0316 WC/4 [19].

SWB SUW/304 *Summary of World Broadcasts Weekly Economic Report Part I Former USSR* SUW/304 WA/1 [3].

UN 164/INF/6 *United Nations* Doc A/CONF.164/INF/6.

UN 164/L.21 *United Nations* Doc A/CONF.164/L. 21.

UN 164/L.25 'Letter Dated 26 July 1993 from the Alternate Chairman of the Delegation of the Russian Federation Addressed to the Chairman of the Conference' *United Nations* Doc A/CONF.164/L.25 circulated at the second session of the United Nations Conference on Straddling Fish Stocks and Highly Migratory Species, 12–30 July 1993.

Zilanov (1993) *Rossiiskie Vesti,* 20 August: 7.

32

The Management of Tropical Tuna Resources
in the Western Pacific:
Trans-Regional Co-operation and Second Tier Diplomacy

Gordon R. Munro

Introduction

One of the more difficult resource management issues to have arisen as
a consequence of the implementation of Extended Fisheries Jurisdiction
(EFJ) is that of managing transboundary fishery resources. Such
resources are now commonly divided into two non-mutually exclusive
classes; fishery resources which are 'shared' by two or more coastal
states, and fishery resources which cross the boundary of the coastal
state Exclusive Economic Zone (EEZ) into the adjacent high seas,
where they are subject to exploitation by fleets of distant water fishing
nations.

No class of fishery resources more closely fits this definition of
transboundary fishery resources than the highly migratory species, of
which, in turn, the tuna species are of overwhelming importance in
economic terms. Tuna are shared widely among groups of coastal
states and are to be found extensively in the high seas adjacent to
EEZs.

Tuna resources are to be found in both temperate and tropical zone
waters. In economic terms, however, the tropical tuna fisheries are
clearly dominant, accounting for approximately 80% of the landed
value of all tuna harvests (FAO, 1993a).[1] This paper is concerned with
the single most important set of tropical tuna resources in the world,
namely those tuna resources of the western and central Pacific. It will
be argued that effective economic management of these transboundary
resources will require, not merely co-operation among regional groups
of coastal states, but also co-operation across neighbouring regions. It
will also be suggested that, while there is little evidence of biological
links between tuna stocks in the western Pacific and those in the
eastern Pacific, there are, nonetheless, opportunities for trans-Pacific
co-operation as well.

Finally, we shall argue that the extent to which trans-regional co-
operation in the western Pacific has emerged is because of the exercise
of what we have chosen to term as 'second-tier' diplomacy. First-tier

diplomacy can be thought of as formal diplomacy conducted on a strict government to government basis by professional diplomats. Second-tier diplomacy is thus informal diplomacy, which does not rely solely upon the services of professional diplomats.

Prior to discussing tropical tuna in the western Pacific and co-operative management, we digress briefly to review the economics of the management of transboundary fishery resources, and thus remind ourselves of the circumstances under which co-operation in management of such resources does, and does not, matter.

The Economics of the Management of Transboundary Fishery Resources Reviewed

The economics of the management of transboundary fishery resources is, for certain historical reasons, focused almost entirely on the management of such resources 'shared' by two or more coastal states. Economists have only recently turned their attention to the management of fishery resources to be found both within the EEZ and in the adjacent high seas (Kaitala and Munro, 1993).

If two or more coastal states 'share' a fishery resource, it is assumed that each of the coastal states will attempt to obtain the maximum economic returns from the resource over time. The first question to be asked is whether co-operation between (among) coastal states in the management of the resource is really required. It is not obvious that co-operation is, in fact, required. If each coastal state, as joint owner of the resource, sets out to manage effectively its portion of the resource, the outcome, while perhaps not ideal, may well be adequate.

Economists bring to bear on this question the theory of competitive games. In passing, the theory of games in general can be thought as a set of analytical tools for the examination of situations in which the actions of one participant will have a perceptible impact on one or more other participants.

The analysis reveals, quite unequivocally, that, if the fishery resource is genuinely shared in the sense that the exploitation of the resource by one coastal state will affect the harvesting opportunities of the other, then co-operation does indeed matter. In the absence of co-operation, both (all) joint owners of the shared resource will be driven to adopting strategies which will lead to mutually unsatisfactory outcomes, quite possibly involving serious overexploitation of the resource (see, for example, Levhari and Mirman, 1980). This is a manifestation of the famous competitive game, 'The Prisoner's Dilemma'.

The analysis has strong predictive powers. There are numerous examples in the real world of non-co-operative management of 'shared' fishery resources leading to the outbreak of 'fish wars' and serious over exploitation of the shared resource.

In analysing co-operative resource management, economists apply, not surprisingly, the theory of co-operative games. The analysis suggests that co-operation in resource management is feasible, even if the management goals of the 'joint owners' do not coincide (Munro, 1987).

The well known British marine biologist, John Gulland, usefully outlined in a study for the FAO (Gulland, 1980), the stages of co-operation in the management of shared fishery resources. The primary stage, according to Gulland, involves co-operation in fishery research. Since all joint owners have the same goal, ie, achieving increased knowledge of the resource, and since all stand to benefit, co-operation should be relatively easy to attain. Moreover, it is difficult to design an effective co-operative resource management regime until the nature of the sharing of the resource is properly understood.

The secondary stage of co-operation involves true resource management co-operation in which the joint owners will:

1 determine the optimal global harvest path through time, and by implication, the optimal biomass level;
2 settle upon the allocation of harvest shares among the joint owners;
3 determine means of implementing and enforcing the management agreements (Gulland, 1980).

The resolution of (2) may, of course, require hard bargaining. This will, however, likely prove easier than (1), if there are different views among the resource owners with respect to appropriate management goals. There is no necessary reason why the goals should coincide.

The economic analysis of this issue, drawing once again upon the theory of co-operative games, suggests that bargaining over resource management policy will prove to be more tractable if so-called side payments between and among the joint resource owners proves to be feasible. The consequence of introducing side payments into the bargaining is that the economic return from the resource in question to a given coastal state is not solely dependent upon the harvest taken in the coastal state zone. One of the more famous examples of side payments in the real world involves the now defunct North Pacific Fur Seal Agreement in which two of the four nations involved in the agreement received certain percentage shares of the harvests, even though their fleets captured none of the seals in question.[2]

Where differences in management goals exist, the differences invariably reflect the fact that, for any number of reasons, one joint owner places a higher value on the resource than does the other(s). Ideally, the management policy of that joint owner placing the highest value on the resource should prevail, with the joint owner then compensating the others through the use of side payments (Munro, 1987).

In passing, the economics of the management of transboundary fishery resources to be found within the EEZ and the adjacent high seas, to the extent that such economics has been developed, reveals the following. The economic consequences of non-co-operation between the coastal state and those distant water fishing nations exploiting the resources are at least as severe as non-co-operation among coastal states exploiting a 'shared' fishery resource. Overexploitation is all but guaranteed. Once again, the real world presents us with several examples which validate the analysis (Kaitala and Munro, 1993).

With this brief review of the economics of the management of transboundary fishery resources, we turn to an overview of the tuna fisheries of the western tropical Pacific.

A Profile of the Tuna Fisheries of Western Tropical Pacific

The fact has already been noted that approximately 80% of the world tuna harvests in value terms are accounted for by tropical tuna fisheries. The tropical tuna fisheries are, in turn, dominated by the Pacific. The Pacific accounts for 65% of the world total of tropical tuna harvests (FAO, 1993a).[3] The Pacific tropical tuna fisheries are found in three sub-regions: the Pacific Island Nations Region, South-east Asia, and the eastern Pacific, from the southern tip of California to the northern tip of Chile (Munro, 1990).

Of the three sub-regions, the Pacific Islands Region is by far the most important, accounting for approximately 50% of the total harvest. South-east Asia accounts for 20-5% of the total, with the remainder being accounted for by the eastern Pacific (Munro, 1990). Within South-east Asia, not less than 80% of that sub-region's harvest is taken in Indonesian and Philippine waters (Munro, 1990; FFA, 1992).

Thus, the western tropical tuna fisheries of the western Pacific—the Pacific Island Nations Region plus Indonesia[4] and the Philippines—constitute the most important set of tuna fisheries in the world. These fisheries yield harvests in the order of 1.4 million tonnes per annum, having a landed value well in excess of US$1billion (FFA, 1992).

South-east Asia as a major tuna producer is a relative newcomer, dating back only to the early 1980s (Munro, 1990). The Pacific Island Nations Region, on the other hand, had been a major producer of tuna decades before the onset of the UN Third Conference on the Law of the Sea in 1973.

Prior to the aforementioned Conference, the tuna fisheries of the Pacific Island Nations Region were dominated by fleets of developed distant water nations, and indeed by the fleets of one such nation, Japan. The fisheries were, and are, largely offshore and capital intensive. The resources themselves were international common property, open to all. Since the Pacific Islands were at relatively low levels of development and lacked the financial capital to acquire significant deep sea fleets, they could not effectively avail themselves of the tuna resources off their shores.

All of this was to change with the UN Third Conference on the Law of the Sea. With the consequent advent of Extended Fisheries Jurisdiction and the implementation of the EEZ regime, most of the tuna resources in the Pacific Island Nations Region came under Pacific Islands jurisdiction.

These rich tuna resources were to prove to be of prime economic importance for the Pacific Islands. However, while EFJ bestowed great benefits on the Pacific Islands, it presented them with immense management problems as well.

The Pacific Islands are widely scattered. Their EEZs collectively have an area equal to the continent of Africa (Munro, 1990). The bulk of the tuna harvests continued to be taken by distant water fleets, now ostensibly operating under licence and paying fees to the coastal states. The Islands were thus presented with an immense surveillance and enforcement problem, with which they seemed ill equipped to deal, given their low levels of development.

With the coming of the EFJ, it seemed obvious to the Pacific Islands that they had to co-operate in the management of their immense shared fishery resources, if they were to enjoy any long-term economic benefits from them. Without co-operation, the distant water fishing nations seeking access to the Pacific Islands EEZs would have had every incentive to play one Island state off against the other. Moreover, ineffective co-operation, leading to ineffective surveillance and enforcement, would have provided the distant water fishing nations with a further incentive to fish heavily and to under report (Munro, 1990).

The Pacific Islands were fortunate, as they moved towards implementing Extended Fishing Jurisdiction in the late 1970s, that they had two regional organisations in place. The older of the two was the South Pacific Commission (SPC), which includes all of the Pacific Islands, sovereign and non-sovereign. The SPC is responsible for biological research in fisheries, and thus helps to achieve the first stage of co-operative management of the tuna resources within the Pacific Island Region.

The second organisation was the South Pacific Forum which includes in its membership all of the independent Pacific Islands (plus Australia and New Zealand). In 1979, the Forum established an agency devoted exclusively to fisheries, the South Pacific Forum Fisheries Agency (FFA). The Agency would, with respect to tuna, address the legal and economic aspects of management, thus dealing with the secondary aspect of fisheries management. The FFA would, in particular, co-ordinate the Pacific Islands in their negotiations of access terms and conditions with distant water fishing nations.

At its founding, the FFA had 14 Pacific Island members. With this number of members, the FFA appeared to be too unwieldy to be effective. There was a fear that there would be no solution to the co-operative game, and that the game would degenerate into a destructive competitive one (Munro, 1990).

The tuna resources of the Pacific Islands Region are not spread evenly. The tuna resources are densest along the Equator and become thinner as one moves north and south of the Equator. Of the 14 Island members of the FFA, seven, which could be considered 'have' states, formed a sub-coalition which, because of their first meeting on the island of Nauru, became known as the Nauru Group.[5] The threat of the Nauru Group to go it alone if necessary caused the 'have nots' – the other seven – to negotiate and to make the FFA an effective organisation. The co-operative game did, in the end, have a solution.

The Nauru Group, valuing the resource more highly (by definition) than the 'have nots', dominates the co-operative management policy arrived at through the FFA. There is, moreover, evidence of the 'haves' having made ongoing side payments to the 'have nots' (Munro, 1990).

The Pacific Islands, through the mechanism of the FFA, have proven to be very effective negotiators with major distant water fishing nations, first with Japan and secondly with the United States, as American tuna fleets moved westwards during the first half of the 1980s. Through the FFA, the Pacific Islands have, in particular, succeeded in agreeing upon a common set of minimum terms and conditions of access to the EEZs, which discourages distant water fishing nations from playing one Island off against the other.

In turning now to South-east Asia, it will be recalled that, at the dawn of the UN Third Conference on the Law of the Sea in 1973, South-east Asia collectively was a minor tuna producer. Substantial potential existed, however, particularly in the waters of Indonesia and the Philippines. Efforts were made to realise this potential, first in the Philippines and subsequently in Indonesia. Total tuna harvests in the Pacific (of the primary market species) accounted for by Indonesia plus the Philippines amount to roughly 225,000 tonnes in the mid-1980s and 340,00 tonnes by the early 1990s (FFA, 1992; Munro, 1990). Further growth in the fisheries is anticipated.

While there is distant water fleet activity in the Indonesian and Philippine tuna fisheries, significantly more of the harvest is taken by domestic fleets than is the case in the Pacific Islands. This may be a factor explaining why the expansion of tuna harvests in Indonesian and Philippine waters has been accompanied by an expansion of domestic processing capacity not seen in the Pacific Islands.

One further comment is in order. Co-operation in fisheries matters is much weaker among the South-east Asian coastal states than it is among the Pacific Islands. There is, for example, little or no co-operation between Indonesia and the Philippines with respect to tuna, even though they are both major producers.

The rapid growth of the South-east Asian tuna fisheries raised an obvious question, namely, the links, if any, between the South-east Asian tuna resources and those in the Pacific Islands Region. If the regional stocks were discrete, then co-operation would be of little concern. The suspicion was, however, that quite the opposite was the case. If the suspicion was justified, then one had to be concerned, not simply with transboundary resource management co-operation in the usual sense, ie, co-operation between neighbouring coastal states, but rather with *trans-regional* resource management co-operation. The difficulty lay in the fact that fishery relations (or any other relations, for that matter) between the Pacific Islands Region and South-east Asia were, at the time, negligible. Hence, in light of the consequences of non-co-operation in the management of shared fishery resources, and in light of the magnitude and economic importance of the fishery resources involved, a potentially very dangerous situation existed.

The fishery relations between the two regions were, however, to be fundamentally altered in the late 1980s. This fundamental alteration was to come about through the application of informal, or second-tier, diplomacy under the aegis of a body known as the Pacific Economic Co-operation Council.

The PECC and Pacific Fisheries

The Pacific Economic Co-operation Council (PECC) is an informal, tri-partite body – government, private sector, academia – which has, as the name suggests, the objective of fostering economic co-operation throughout the Pacific. The PECC was established in 1980 and, at the time of writing, has 21 members.[6]

Much of the day to day work of the PECC is done through task forces or fora, which seek to identify and develop specific opportunities for co-operation in the region. One of the PECC task forces is the Task Force on Fisheries Development and Co-operation, referred to hereafter as the Fisheries Task Force, which was established in 1983. The rationale for the work of the Task Force, since the Task Force's inception, has been the impact of the New International Law of the Sea upon the Pacific. The Pacific is the single most important region in the world for fisheries, accounting for 50% of the world harvest of fish (FAO, 1993b).

The Task Force, which has Canada as its senior sponsor, did, initially at least, focus upon the developing coastal states, on the grounds that these states appeared to offer particularly good opportunities for fostering co-operation. This focus, in turn, was to result in much of the Task Force's activities being funded by the Canadian International Development Agency (CIDA). Currently, the Task Force is supported by CIDA through the Agency's Asia Branch, under a project having the title: 'Asia Pacific Ocean Co-operation'.

Over time, three sub-regional groups of Pacific developing coastal states came within the purview of the Task Force. These were and are: the Pacific Island Nations, South-east Asia – the ASEAN in particular – and Pacific Latin America. At the first meeting of the Task Force, held in the last quarter of 1984, it was agreed that more emphasis should be given to developing coastal states assisting one another: South-South co-operation. It was noted in particular that nothing had been done to advance South-South inter-regional fisheries co-operation in the Pacific.

One participant in the Task Force was an official of the South Pacific Forum Fisheries Agency (FFA). The FFA had, for some time, been contemplating the desirability of its members establishing contact with, and gaining knowledge of, the burgeoning tuna industries in the ASEAN. Such knowledge would assist the FFA members in planning the development of their own tuna industries. With this in mind, the FFA now called upon the Task Force to assist in organising a study tour, which would enable a group of senior Pacific Island officials to examine the tuna industries of Indonesia, the Philippines and Thailand. This was done, and the tour, funded by the Management for Change Program of CIDA, took place in early 1986.

The FFA, acting upon the suspicion that the Pacific Islands shared tuna resources with Indonesia and the Philippines, encouraged the study tour group to do more than examine the tuna industries *en route*. The FFA urged the group to explore with their Indonesian and Philippine hosts the possibility of establishing an informal tuna joint management committee (Munro, 1993).

The group did as it was asked and found that its proposal was received with particular warmth in the Philippines. The group's Philippine hosts suggested that the idea should be expanded upon in that inter-regional fisheries co-operation should not be confined to tuna, and that membership on the ASEAN side, rather than being confined to Indonesia and the Philippines, should be open to all interested ASEAN members. The Filipinos recommended further that a body be established to effect fisheries co-operation between the two regions, a body which they suggested might be given the title of the Western Pacific Fisheries Forum.

The study tour was completed and was deemed to have been a success. The PECC Fisheries Task Force responded to the results of the study by planning for a workshop for fisheries specialists from the two regions to determine whether the opportunities for inter-regional co-operation were more than just talk. If the workshop participants decided serious practical opportunities for co-operation did in fact exist, they would then have to go on and consider mechanisms for making the opportunities a reality.

The workshop was, after months of planning, convened in Manila in October 1987, as the ASEAN–Pacific Island Nations International Fisheries Conference. It became clear that the Conference would never have been held if it had been other than informal. Since the study tour, the first blush of enthusiasm had faded, and many in both regions began having second and third thoughts. Concerns were expressed, particularly within the Pacific Islands, about possible unwelcome entanglements. Only a conference, in which the highly experimental nature of the undertaking was recognised and in which no government would be seen to be embarrassed if the experiment proved to be unsuccessful, was feasible (Munro, 1993).

The Manila Conference, as it came to be known, was a success. From the ASEAN side, Malaysia and Thailand, as well as Indonesia and the Philippines, participated. From the Pacific Islands, both regional organisations participated, as did several national governments. Furthermore, there were at the conference/workshop observers from several Pacific Latin American countries.

In the conference, the participants agreed that there were several opportunities for practical co-operation in fisheries between the two regions. The shared tuna fisheries were, in particular, seen to provide important opportunities. Indeed, the tuna fisheries provided a critical focus for the conference (Munro, 1993).

The participants then addressed the question of a mechanism to co-ordinate and facilitate co-operation between the two regions. The Philippine proposal to establish a forum was rejected on the grounds that such a body would be excessively formal and structured. A consultative committee, on the other hand, was seen to be acceptable. Hence, it was agreed at the Conference to consider establishing the Western Pacific Fisheries Consultative Committee (WPFCC).

After many months of consultation within the two regions following the Conference, the WPFCC was formally established in late 1988. The WPFCC was to be a strictly informal body in which membership would be voluntary. A country or organisation, upon joining the WPFCC, could subsequently withdraw without penalty. A secretariat was established in Manila. A Director was appointed, who remains in office to the present day. The Director is the very able Ms. Elvira A. Baluyut, who comes from the private sector, where she serves as well as the president of a Philippine consulting company specialising in fisheries and agricultural affairs. Financial support for the WPFCC now comes largely from CIDA, through the aforementioned project, 'Asia Pacific Ocean Co-operation'.

At the WPFCC's inauguration, it was agreed that Pacific Latin American countries should be accorded special observer status. This was a reflection of a development which had occurred in the interim between the Manila Conference and the WPFCC's inauguration. The development concerned the holding of a conference modelled on the Manila Conference and held in Lima, Peru. This was the Pacific Latin America - Pacific Island Nations Conference, which was designed to explore opportunities for fisheries co-operation between the Pacific Islands and Pacific Latin American. The four ASEAN member countries which had participated in the Manila Conference had observer status. The Lima Conference, as it came to be known, led in due course to the establishment of a counterpart to the WPFCC, the Trans-Pacific Fisheries Consultative Committee (TPFCC), to facilitate co-operation between Pacific Latin America and the Pacific Islands.[7] The WPFCC and TPFCC have come to collaborate closely with one another.[8]

The WPFCC, upon its inauguration, was to be presented with its first major opportunity to co-ordinate fisheries co-operation between the Pacific Islands and the ASEAN. The opportunity was concerned with tuna research.

The WPFCC and Co-operation in Research on Shared Tuna Resources

At the time of the inauguration of the WPFCC in late 1988, the South Pacific Commission was looking forward to a major three year, multi-million dollar tuna research programme in the form of a tuna tagging project. The project would focus primarily on yellowfin tuna, but would also include skipjack and bigeye. Tagging is a powerful research tool which enables scientists, not only to trace the movement of the fish, but to also estimate key parameters pertaining to fishery population dynamics.[9]

The aforementioned suspicion that the Pacific Islands shared tuna resources with Indonesia and the Philippines had become the SPC's working hypothesis (SPC, 1993). Lacking any effective contact with their counterparts in the two ASEAN countries, the SPC scientists had no means of testing the hypothesis. In previous tuna tagging exercises, the SPC had attempted to establish links with the two ASEAN countries and to gain access for the SPC research vessel into Indonesian and Philippine waters. These exercises, in what one could term first-tier diplomacy, proved to be utterly fruitless. While we had argued earlier that establishing transboundary co-operation in fisheries research should be relatively easy, establishing trans-regional co-operation in such research proved to be very difficult indeed.

The SPC requested that the WPFCC assist the SPC in establishing the desired contacts and linkages with the ASEAN, as the SPC began its tuna research programme. If success were to be achieved, then the two regions could be seen as having moved towards achieving the primary stage of co-operative management of their presumably shared tuna resources.

The WPFCC responded to the request and did so in a deliberate step by step manner, and in a manner which exploited the WPFCC's informal nature. While this author hesitates to use the overworked expression, 'confidence building', this is essentially what the WPFCC was about.

The WPFCC commenced in 1989 with a technical workshop for tuna research scientists from the Pacific Islands, Indonesia, the Philippines, and Malaysia. As the workshop progressed, the need for a common bi-regional tuna research programme became obvious to all participants. With that need acknowledged, the WPFCC, subsequent to the workshop, arranged for exchanges of tuna research scientists between the two regions, enabling scientists from one region to attend technical scientific meetings in the other and enabling the scientists to examine the other region's tuna research techniques.

The three year SPC Regional Tuna Tagging Project (RTTP) commenced in late 1989. The WPFCC now undertook, at the SPC's request, the difficult task of gaining access for the SPC research vessel into Philippine waters. The WPFCC Director worked diligently and effectively, drawing upon her many contacts in key Philippine government departments (eg, Agriculture and Foreign Affairs). She was aided by the fact that Philippine government tuna research scientists and administrators now knew on a personal and professional basis their counterparts in the Pacific Islands. In other words, the WPFCC's step by step efforts at 'confidence building' were bearing fruit.

The WPFCC's attempt to gain access for the SPC research vessel into Philippine waters eventually met with success. In July 1990, in an historical first, the SPC research vessel entered Philippine waters and made port at the city of Cebu. The vessel then undertook several weeks of tagging in Philippine waters, with Philippine scientists on board. The Philippine Secretary of Agriculture (whose department is responsible for fisheries) publicly hailed the arrival of the vessel as 'having opened a new field of co-operation among the ASEAN and the Pacific Island Nations' (cited in PECC Fisheries Task Force, 1990).

With its success in gaining access for the SPC research vessel into Philippine waters, the WPFCC now turned to the task of gaining access for the vessel into Indonesian waters. Once again, the WPFCC's earlier efforts at 'confidence building', this time between Indonesia and Pacific Islands tuna research scientists and administrators, were to prove to be invaluable. The WPFCC achieved success a second time. The SPC research vessel was welcomed into Indonesia in March 1991 and spent several weeks tagging in Indonesian waters with Indonesian scientists on board. Once again, the vessel's arrival marked a historical first. The research vessel, upon completing its Indonesian tour, went on to make a second voyage to the Philippines.

In a sense, the inter-regional tuna research co-operation was to become self-sustaining. It has become clear to all in the western Pacific that the South Pacific Commission is the leading body for tuna research. In late 1991, the Philippine government undertook an extensive research project on Philippine tuna resources as a part of a general fisheries sector programme funded by the Asian Development

Bank. The Philippine government turned to the SPC to oversee the tuna research project and to train Philippine scientists in the collection and analysis of tuna data. The WPFCC served to broker the arrangement between the Philippine government and the SPC.

The Philippine government–SPC arrangement originally had a two-year term. The arrangement has recently been extended for a further two-year term. The advantage of the arrangement to the SPC, outside of prestige, is that it extends the Commission's knowledge of tuna behaviour in the western Pacific (SPC, 1993).

In 1993, the SPC provided assistance to the Indonesian government to deal with a serious problem affecting the Indonesian pole and line tuna fishery. The WPFCC was again called upon to broker the arrangement.

Results from the co-operative inter-regional tagging programme are now becoming available. While the scientists show the usual caution, the SPC scientists have been prepared to come to the following conclusions (SPC, 1993). First, and rather surprisingly, the movement of tuna from the Philippine EEZ into the Indonesian EEZ and into the Pacific Islands Region is very limited. On the other hand, the movement of tuna between the waters of eastern Indonesia and the Pacific Islands Region is massive and unrestricted. The tuna stocks of eastern Indonesia, and those of the Pacific Islands Region, are, to all intents and purposes, a single resource (SPC, 1993).

The consequence of the inter-regional co-operative tuna research to date have been twofold. First, there now exists a far better understanding of the nature of the sharing of tuna resources between the ASEAN and the Pacific Islands Region. As the two regions look forward to what John Gulland (1980) termed the secondary stage of co-operative resource management, it is clear that there may be little need for the Philippines and the Pacific Islands to engage in broader co-operative management with respect to conservation of the resource. On the other hand, for Indonesia and the Pacific Islands not to engage in such co-operative resource management could prove to be foolhardy in the extreme.

Secondly, the development of the inter-regional co-operative tuna research, seen as a 'confidence building' exercise, has laid the foundation for inter-regional fisheries relations, which simply had not existed before. The establishment of such relations is a fundamental pre-requisite which must be met if the secondary stage of co-operative resource management is to come to fruition.

Further Developments in Trans-Regional Co-operative Tuna Management

The Pacific Islands and the ASEAN are at a very preliminary stage with respect to the secondary stage of co-operative management of their shared tuna resources. Nonetheless, there have been some developments, in which the WPFCC has played a central role. The developments do, moreover, involve co-operation with the third regional group of Pacific tropical tuna producers in the eastern Pacific.

In late 1992, the WPFCC, in collaboration with its sister consultative committee, the Trans-Pacific Fisheries Consultative Committee, mounted a conference on the economic and legal aspects of tuna management (International Conference on the Economic and Legal Aspects of Tuna Management, 1992), which was held in Manila. The conference was tri-regional with participants from the ASEAN, the Pacific Islands Region and Pacific Latin America attending. In managing their tuna resources, the three sub-regions have an incentive to co-operate with one another in negotiating with distant water fishing nations. These fishing nations have proven quite capable of playing one region, as well as one country, off against the other.

The participants from the three sub-regions agreed on the need for their countries to work towards harmonising their relations with distant water fishing nations. It is possible that in time they will develop a common, Pacific-wide, set of minimum terms and conditions of access to the EEZ.

Of more immediate importance was, and is, the issue of high seas fisheries management. It will be recalled that tuna constitute a prime example of the second form of transboundary fishery resource that is to be found both within the EEZ and the adjacent high seas. The issue of high seas fisheries management is, at the time of writing, being addressed by a UN conference, the UN Conference on Straddling Fish Stocks and Highly Migratory Fish Stocks.

At the aforementioned 1992 conference in Manila, the three groups of Pacific tropical tuna producers discussed the high seas issue in detail. They agreed on the desirability of working towards a common position on the issue as they looked forward to the aforementioned UN conference. Some initial measures have been taken in this direction.[10]

It must be re-emphasised that these steps represent only the beginning of the development of secondary co-operative management. A great deal more remains to be done, and hopefully will be done, with the assistance of the WPFCC. A further step is in fact being planned. The WPFCC owes its origin to a study tour of the ASEAN by senior Pacific Islands fisheries officials. A reverse study tour is now being planned by the WPFCC, which consists of a tour of key Pacific Islands institutions for senior ASEAN fisheries officials. The officials would be given the opportunity to examine at first hand the highly organised and effective system of co-operative intra-regional transboundary fishery management which prevails in the Pacific Islands Region.

Conclusions

Tuna constitute the ultimate transboundary fishery resource. This paper has been concerned with the most important set of tuna stocks in the world, namely those of the western tropical Pacific. It is argued that effective economic management of the resources call, not just for transboundary co-operative resource management in the usual sense, ie, between neighbouring coastal states, but for trans-regional co-operative resource management as well.

Progress has recently been made in the first stage of co-operative resource management, in the form of fisheries research between the two relevant sub-regions, the Pacific Islands Region and South-east Asia. The co-operative management has come about through informal, or 'second-tier', diplomacy operating under the aegis of the PECC, and made possible by the generous financial support of the Canadian International Development Agency through its project: 'Asia Pacific Ocean Co-operation'.

The two regions are now approaching the difficult, but essential, secondary stage of co-operative resource management. Undoubtedly, the same second-tier diplomacy will be called upon to bring this second stage to fruition.

Notes

1   According to biologists, there are many tuna sub-species. Of these, however, only six can be deemed to be primary market species, these being albacore, bigeye, northern bluefin, skipjack, southern bluefin, and yellowfin. The percentages quoted are based upon landings of the primary market species. The two bluefin species are temperate zone species; the remainder are tropical.
2   The four were Canada, Japan, Soviet Union/Russia, and the United States. Under the Agreement, Canadian and Japanese fleets harvested zero seals. Nonetheless, Canada and Japan each received a fixed percentage of the harvest of every season.
3   These percentages are based on the harvests of primary market tropical species: albacore, bigeye, skipjack, and yellowfin.
4   Strictly speaking, eastern Indonesia.
5   The seven were: the Federated States of Micronesia, the Republic of Kiribati, the Republic of the Marshall Islands, Narau, Palau, Papua New Guinea and Solomon Islands. Among the 'have nots', Fiji served as the leader.
6   The 21 being: Australia, New Zealand, Pacific Island Nations (collectively), Brunei, Indonesia, Malaysia, Philippines, Singapore, Thailand, South Korea, Hong Kong, China, Chinese

Taipei (Taiwan), Japan, Russia, Canada, United States, Mexico, Colombia, Peru, and Chile.

7   The Latin American members of the TPFCC are: Chile, Colombia, Costa Rica, Ecuador, Mexico, and Peru. In addition, two Latin American regional organisations participate, these being the Comision Permanente del Pacifico Sur (Permanent South Pacific Commission – CPPS) and the Latin American Fisheries Development Organization (Spanish acronym – OLDEPESCA).

8   The TPFCC, and its activities, are also supported by CIDA through the project 'Asia Pacific Ocean Cooperation'.
It should be also be noted that there is reciprocity between the TPFCC and WPFCC, and that ASEAN members are accorded special observer status in the TPFCC.

9   Tuna are captured, have coded tags inserted into them and are then released. Fishermen and companies are encouraged to return the tags upon capture of the fish. A 10% return is deemed to be acceptable. Over the course of the project, approximately 120,000 tuna were to be tagged (South Pacific Commission, 1993).

10   The participants brought forth a set of principles at the Conference, the Manila Principles, which addressed the high seas issue and emphasised the need for the Pacific groups of developing tropical tuna producers to work towards a common position in light of the UN Conference (WPFCC, 1992: Attachment G).

Bibliography

FAO (1993a) 'World review of high seas and highly migratory fish species and straddling stocks', *FAO Fisheries Circular* 858, Rome: Food and Agriculture Organisation of the UN.
—— (1993b) *Fisheries Statistics 1992* 72, Rome Food and Agriculture Organisation of the UN.
FFA (1992) 'Options for tropical tuna management: considerations for the South Pacific', in Western Pacific Fisheries Consultative Committee *International Conference on the Economic and Legal Aspects of Tuna Management: Summary Report and Papers Presented at the Conference*, Manila: South Pacific Forum Fisheries Agency: 45-58.
Gulland, J. (1980) 'Some problems of the management of shared stocks', *FAO Fisheries Technical Papers No. 26*, Rome: FAO of the UN.
Kaitala, Veijo, and Munro G.R. (1993) 'The Management of High Seas Fisheries', *Marine Resource Economics* 8: 313-29.

Levhari, D. and Mirman, L.J. (1980) 'The great fish war: an example using a dynamic Cournot-Nash solution', *Bell Journal of Economics* 11: 649–61.

Munro, G.R. (1987) 'The management of shared fishery resources under extended jurisdiction', *Marine Resource Economics* 3: 271–96.

—— (1990) 'Extended jurisdiction and the management of Pacific highly migratory species', *Ocean Development and International Law* 21: 289–307.

—— (1993) 'Environmental co-operation among Pacific developing coastal states: a fisheries case study', *University of British Columbia Law Review* 27: 201–12.

PECC Fisheries Task Force (1990) 'Report of the Task Force', unpublished, Vancouver: Pacific Economic Co-operation Council Task Force on Fisheries Development and Co-operation.

SPC (1993) 'Interactions amongst tuna fisheries of Philippines, Indonesia, and adjacent western Pacific areas, based on tagging experiments', information paper prepared for the Seventh Workshop of the PECC Fisheries Task Force, Noumea: South Pacific Commission.

WPFCC (1992) *International Conference on the Economic and Legal Aspects of Tuna Management: Summary Report and Papers Presented at the Conference*, Manila: Western Pacific Fisheries Consultative Committee.

33

The Peaceful Management of Transboundary Resources in the South Pacific

Joeli Veitayaki

Introduction

The peaceful management of transboundary marine resources requires co-operation at various local and international levels and as such necessitates a basic minimum level of common understanding. Ideally, throughout the world there would be consistent stewardship policies in which the uses of ocean resources clearly reflect their diverse and delicate interrelationships. This, unfortunately, is far from the reality. Nations are rich or poor, industrially advanced or backward, and are scrambling for the resources of the oceans. Contradictions and conflicts are common, resulting ultimately in the degradation and overexploitation of resources. Describing the outcome of this situation on the fisheries sector, the UN Secretary General reported that the world's marine fisheries are now characterised by qualitative decreases in catches of the most valuable species, lesser quality as catches transfer to less valuable species, excessive costs from over-investment in boats and gear, low income for fishers, conflict among small-scale and large-scale fisheries, and change in the geography of fisheries (United Nations, 1991a and b).

The South Pacific region spans some 28 million km² of ocean, approximately 12% of the earth's surface, and includes some 27 island states or territories. The region is highly diverse; country populations vary from 2,000 to over 3.5 million. The total population is approximately 4.5 million. Under the provision of the United Nations Law of the Sea III (UNCLOS III), these small states have jurisdiction over a vast tract of the Pacific Ocean and are responsible for the proper management of all its resources. This paper will deal with the initiatives that have been taken by the island nations of the Pacific to manage peacefully the transboundary resources of the Pacific Ocean.

To date, the peoples of these small nations who are wedded to the sea by tradition, by history, and by geography, have done exceptionally well in the management of their marine resources. Not only are they earning significant revenue from the sale of fishing rights in their waters, they are also beginning to undertake environmentally sound development. These nations have illustrated to the world that UNCLOS III can work to protect and preserve their marine resources and help overcome their handicapped positions.

Part XII of the Law of the Sea Convention consisting of Articles 192–237 is on the protection of the marine environment. While nations have the sovereign right to exploit their natural resources, they are to take all measures, individually or collectively, to prevent, reduce and control pollution of the marine environment. Owing to the nature of marine environments, nations are encouraged to co-operate on a regional and global basis to formulate international rules and standards and recommended practices for protection and preservation. In the Pacific, the Regional Register is an example of an innovative tool that is proving effective in the peaceful management of transboundary resources. The initial opposition from distant water fishing nations (DWFNs) has disappeared as the nations of the region have demonstrated that the fishing of their transboundary resources by outsiders is possible only if outsiders comply with the conditions of the Regional Register.

The South Pacific nations are co-operating in their effort to adopt a consistent, intricate, system of ocean resource use. Given their small, isolated and economically vulnerable positions, these nations have realised that only effective regional effort will best represent and address their interests. Through regional organisations, Pacific nations share financial costs, expertise and experience. Furthermore, they attract more attention to their situation because the positions of regional organisations are often more prominent, providing the necessary leverage that is at times required to influence global negotiations and decision making.

The South Pacific Region - An Overview

The South Pacific, bordered by Papua New Guinea to the west, the Marianas and Guam to the north-west, the Marshall islands to the north, French Polynesia to the south-east and New Caledonia and Tonga to the south, is a unique and diverse region (Figure 33.1). The region is home to less than 0.1% of the world's population. The South Pacific nations have in common their traditional history, their smallness, and their setting within the vast stretches of Pacific ocean. They differ, however, in size, physical nature, resource endowment, and social and cultural features. The western Pacific nations such as Papua New Guinea (PNG) and the other island states of Melanesia are older, larger and richer in agricultural lands and mineral resources. The islands of Micronesia to the north and Polynesia to the east, are smaller, lower islands and atoll chains. Resources are few. In most of the islands, a lack of water limits life. For some, such as Tuvalu,

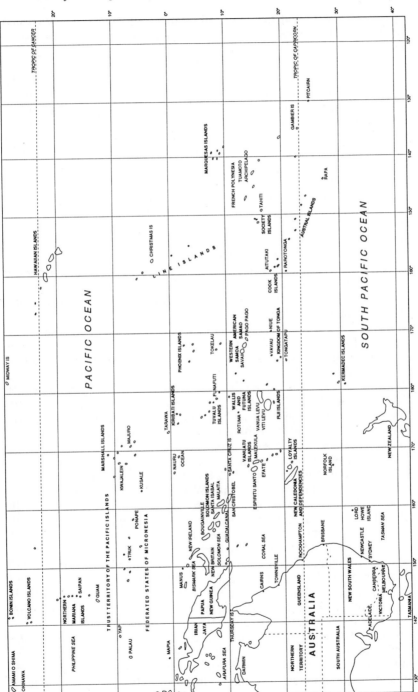

Figure 33.1 The Area of the South Pacific

Kiribati, Tokelau and the Marshall Islands, the land is so small and low that any rise in sea level is expected to cause extensive inundation and land loss.

The previously self-sufficient and independent communities of the Pacific were first integrated as part of the global system with the arrival of European explorers after 1521. Socio-economic changes including village sites, food intake, diseases, plantations, urban settlements, education and the use of money took place through time. Colonisation resulted in the subdivision of the region by Great Britain, Germany, the Netherlands, France, Japan and later Australia, New Zealand and the United States. Like other colonies, the Pacific countries provided sources of raw materials for industry and markets for goods processed by their colonial masters.

The export of *bêche-de-mer,* timber, plantation products, minerals and the alteration of the physical surroundings have caused serious environmental problems that are now the foundation for the need to implement sustainable development. There is evidence in the Pacific to show the serious environmental consequences of inappropriate development which have made Pacific Island communities and their leaders more aware of the inextricable link between environmental management and economic development.

The nations of the South Pacific are remote in their location within the world's economic system. They are on the periphery; isolated from the major core nations of Japan, Europe and North America which are the main markets for exported goods and the main suppliers of imported products. PNG is 14,469km away from Britain while Guam is 16,000km away from USA, Suva (Fiji) is 7,231km away from Japan, and Vanuatu is 16,739km away from France. The Pacific Islands are thus remote in the remotest part of the world. Within the Pacific, the countries are far from each other and are separated by vast stretches of ocean. Fiji is 2,244km away from Kiribati and 3,505km from PNG which is 4,224km from Tonga. The Cook Islands are 3,657km from Vanuatu while Western Samoa is 3,320km from New Zealand. The extreme case of remoteness is experienced within Kiribati where travel visas are required by people travelling from Tarawa to Christmas Island because they need to go through Fiji or the Marshall Islands to Honolulu and then to the Line Islands.

A small country has a small economy, a common situation in the Pacific region. The biggest countries - PNG, Solomon Islands, New Caledonia and Fiji have areas of 462,243km^2; 27,556km^2; 19,103km^2; and 18,272km^2 respectively, while the smallest ones include Pitcairn (5km^2), Tokelau (10km^2), Nauru (21km^2) and Tuvalu (26km^2). The situation is worse because of the percentage of the population who are not part of the formal sector because they are too young or too old, still residing in traditional semi-subsistence settlements or illiterate, or simply unskilled. These people cannot be part of the labour market.

The dependence by Pacific states on few commodities for export was predetermined by their colonial history. The situation is now enforced by the protectionist laws of trade practised by the nations of the world and trading blocks. To sell a product in a new market, a nation has to displace other producers in the world market arena and has to do so despite the possible existence of preferential and protectionist policies of the other producers (UNCTAD, 1985). This is a major difficulty in the Pacific because the countries export the same commodities of sugar, root crops, copra, frozen fish, timber, logs, gold and palm oil and compete at the world markets. Furthermore, as small producers, they can not influence world market trends but are sensitive to fluctuations of the world economy (Benedict, 1967).

The significance of ocean resources to Pacific islands and their attempts to manage their transboundary resources should be considered within this context. It is within the oceans that the hope of many Pacific states lie. Pacific Islanders have realised this and have undertaken to properly manage their ocean resources to allow maximum sustainable benefit to accrue to themselves.

Resource Potential

Apart from ocean mining and fishing, other resources of the sea include the harnessing of energy and the generation of power from waves and thermal sources, the development of suitable shipping and port services, and the exploitation and promotion of marine resources for tourism purposes. Ocean mineral resources are considered of the greatest economic importance. For the time being, the most commonly used marine-based minerals are sand and gravel for construction and phosphorite for fertilisers. These are found in near-shore areas and may be used without processing. Phosphate prospects are best in the Lau group in eastern Fiji. Placer minerals whose potential has yet to be fully evaluated, are important on islands with large hinterlands and where heavy minerals have been disseminated through the rocks which, because of erosion over time, free the heavy metals for concentration by wave and current energy.

Corrallium and black coral are found in the south-west Pacific and offer a possible source of income. Garnets and shells and reef detritus are present in Malaita, and the Solomon Islands and may be developed in the future.

Offshore manganese nodules are richest between the Hawaiian Islands and Baja California within the Clarion-Clipperton fracture zone (Johnson and Clark, 1988). This area, covering 4 million km^2 contains extensive nodule deposits and is where pioneering activities will take place when submarine mineral exploitation begins. Rich deposits are also found in the Cook Islands and Kiribati. Since 1980, crusts and sulphides instead of nodules have become the mineral resources of scientific and commercial significance. The highest grade crust is anticipated to occur between 15°S and 20°N in the Pacific Basin with the best deposits in the exclusive economic zones (EEZ) of one or more Pacific States. This includes the richest deposits discovered so far, south of Johnson Island. Sulphide deposits found near ocean floor spreading centres, volcanic seamount and back arc basins are still being explored. An estimated 4.5 million tons of chromite is found south of Lae in PNG. Magnetites are found in south-eastern PNG and Fiji, and may become exploitable if resources elsewhere are exhausted. Polymetallic sulphides with major components of iron, copper and zinc are abundant in the Lau Basin, the North Fiji Basin, Woodlark Basin in the Solomon Islands and PNG and the Manus Basin in PNG. Gold is found off northern Guadalcanal in the Solomon Islands and in the Kermadec Trench. Further exploration is being done on the gold enriched basin from Fiji through Vanuatu and PNG into Japan and China (FFA *et al,* 1983).

The Pacific is the most productive of all the world's oceans providing 72% of world tuna production worth about US$1.46 billion at the wharf in 1993. Inshore and near-shore fisheries of the Pacific are important in providing protein food for local communities, contributing to some of them an annual consumption per capita of up to 50kg of fish.

Unlike most of the fisheries in the northern Pacific that are now overexploited, the tuna species of the tropical central and western Pacific are under-utilised. Upwelling in the western equitorial Pacific is resposible for important tuna fisheries in the EEZs of PNG, the Solomon Islands, Kiribati, and Nauru. The present stock of skipjack is around 3 million tons compared with an annual catch of 250,000 tonnes. Yellowfin stock is presently around 600,000 tonnes with an annual catch of between 60,000 and 90,000 tonnes. Albacore and big-eye are also under-utilised. The future of tuna fishing is bright in this region, provided reasonable management procedures are adopted (Kearney, 1985). Careful research-based management is vital to ensure the continued existence of presently over-exploited species and a depleting fish stock.

The harnessing of ocean energy is expected in future because of the great potential in the Pacific and the development of appropriate technology. Thermal energy from volcanic-related activities is a notable potential source of power if the technology is developed. Shipping concerns are paramount and need to be addressed. Shipping is a primary challenge because even though the Pacific is predominantly a region of small nations for which shipping is very important, the region is geographically ideally located in the centre between the trade centres of Asia, North America, Europe, and Australia, New Zealand and the rest of the countries in the southern hemisphere. In a region characterised by vast stretches of oceans, properly planned shipping can be a major economic activity. Escalating costs of operations, handling terminal and capital port equipment are some of the main challenges that need to be addressed. Pacific nations can also take advantage of their islands' exquisite coastal areas to promote tourism and cruise tours. Such development can stimulate the development of port and shipping facilities and boost the growth of tourism without excessively pressurising the coastal states involved to provide the necessary tourist infrastructure.

Regional Co-operation

Regional co-operation contributes significantly to national ocean development through the sharing of expertise, experience, facilities and infrastructure, and the pooling of resources and markets. Regional co-operation is also effective in addressing the transboundary nature of marine environmental issues, data and information collection, marine scientific and technological advancement, and human resource development. It also facilitates conservation and management of living resources, assessment of non-living resources and efficient conduct of maritime transport (United Nations 1991a). Regional initiatives have resulted in greater success in gaining access to international assistance as it enhances the cost-effectiveness of donor assistance.

Regional co-operation in the South Pacific is advanced because the small island nations were quick to realise that their interests under UNCLOS III could best be protected through co-operative and collective effort. The oldest of the regional organisations, the South Pacific Commission (SPC) was established in 1947 by the colonial powers in the region. The SPC meets annually to discuss issues, problems, needs and ideas common to the Pacific. In 1970, the University of the South Pacific was established to provide trained expertise, research, and consultancy services geared to the needs of the region. In 1971, the South Pacific Forum was set up to provide an opportunity for the heads of governments to discuss common issues and problems. A year later in 1972, the South Pacific Bureau for Economic Co-operation (SPEC and later the Forum Secretariat) was set up to promote and encourage regional co-operation and consultation on trade, economic development, transport, tourism and other related matters. In 1977 after some lengthy and important negotiations that discussed issues of sovereignty, national obligations and effective regional approaches, the South Pacific Forum Fisheries Agency (FFA) was established to co-ordinate co-operation and mutual assistance amongst member nations regarding fishery policies, fishing limits and the maximisation of benefit from the exploitation of marine fisheries resources. In the same year the Pacific Forum Line, a joint venture, was formed to provide shipping services in the region and address common transport problems. 1980 saw the establishment of the South Pacific Regional Environment Programme (SPREP) to develop regional co-operation and technical support on all aspects of the environment while in 1984, the South Pacific Applied Geoscience Commission (SOPAC) was set up to conduct mineral exploratory work in the near-shore and offshore areas. Regional co-operation is working in the Pacific and should be encouraged to continue.

Peaceful Management of Transboundary Fisheries Resources

The many conventions and treaties that the South Pacific member countries have signed testify to the good work that they are currently doing to manage their marine resources properly. None of the regional organisations has done better in this respect than the South Pacific Forum Fisheries Agency (FFA). The scope of this paper will not allow discussion of all the treaties and conventions that have been finalised through the FFA, but some brief discussion on what has been done should illustrate the achievements of South Pacific member countries in their management of transboundary resources (Table 1).

The FFA Convention which established the FFA has been signed and ratified by all 16 of the member countries. Together, the South Pacific countries are taking an active role in the management of the tuna stock within their EEZs and the South Pacific in general. Although only Fiji, the Marshall Islands and the Federated States of Micronesia have ratified or acceded to the Convention all of the nations in the region have claimed maritime zones and are benefiting from their provisions (Figure 2). There is hope that the remaining Pacific Island states will ratify the Convention soon.

THE REGIONAL REGISTER

In May 1983, working through the FFA, the countries of the South Pacific established a Regional Register for Fishing Vessels which is a co-operative form of exercising control over fishing operations. Fully aware of the importance of controlling distant water fishing nations (DWFNs) in their EEZs and the financial burden regular surface and air surveillance can cost, the member nations agreed to an innovative control and enforcement alternative. The Regional Register for Fishing Vessels is cheap, provides effective control of DWFNs, and transfers more of the responsibility for the proper management of fisheries resources on to the users, who are provided with incentives for voluntary compliance with national laws and fisheries access agreements. Under the Regional Register the South Pacific countries

Table 33.1 Treaties in the South Pacific

	FFA Convention		US Treaty (and amendments)			Wellington Convention		Niue Treaty		Nauru Agreement		Palau Arrangement	
	Signature	Ratification	Signature	Ratification	Approval	Signature	Ratification	Signature	Ratification	Signature	Ratification	Signature	Ratification
Australia	X	X	X	X		X	X	X					
Cook Islands	X	X	X	X	X	X	X	X	X				
Federated States of Micronesia	X	X	X	X		X	X	X		X	X	X	
Fiji	X	X	X	X			X			X	X	X	
Kiribati	X	X	X	X		X	X			X	X	X	
Marshall Islands	X	X	X	X		X		X		X	X	X	
Nauru	X	X	X	X		X	X	X	X	X	X	X	
New Zealand	X	X	X	X		X	X	X	X				
Niue	X	X	X	X		X		X		X	X	X	
Palau	X	X	X	X		X		X		X	X	X	
Papua New Guinea	X	X	X	X	X								
Solomon Islands	X	X	X	X		X		X		X	X	X	
Tonga	X	X	X	X	X			X					
Tuvalu	X	X	X	X	X	X		X			Acceded	X	
Vauatu	X	X	X	X		X		X					
Western Samoa	X	X	X	X	X			X					

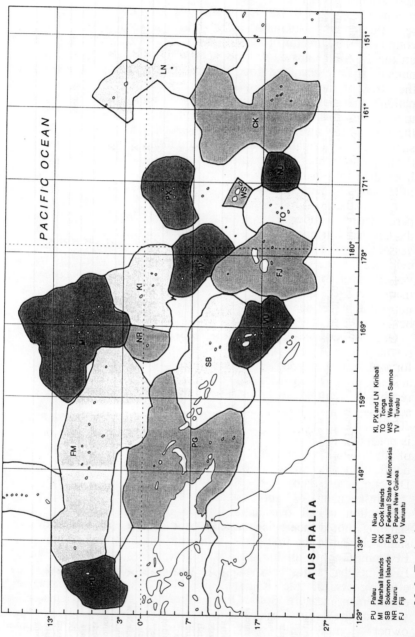

Figure 33.2 Exclusive Economic Zones (EEZ) of the Forum Fisheries Agency (FFA) Island Member Countries
Source: Forum Fisheries Agency (1989)

will not license foreign fishing vessels for tuna unless the vessel is in good standing on the Register. All fishing boats in the region are required to register. Properly completed application forms for registration can be submitted by the boat operators or by the member country to the Director of the FFA who enters the details of the vessel on the FFA's database. All the vessels in the Register are given a number and are accorded good standing which allows them to fish in the EEZ of any member country provided they comply with the national fisheries laws and access agreements. Each participating state must nominate a national correspondent with whom the Director of the FFA is to liaise. In the absence of such nomination the Director shall use his normal channel of communication with the countries. Participating states are to provide the FFA with registration and licensing information while the FFA is to circulate register information to member states.

The withdrawal of good standing may be instigated by any participating member country after it has made full investigations into the alleged infringement and has obtained an explanation from the vessel operator concerned. Supporting documentation including evidence of the alleged offence, response to the evidence by the vessel's operator, and a record by the member country concerned are made available through the FFA. The Director of the FFA must notify the vessel operator when a withdrawal request for his vessel is being considered.

Once a vessel's good standing has been withdrawn, the vessel retains that status even if it is sold, renamed or re-flagged. Approval for withdrawal of good standing requires a favourable response from at least 10 of the participating member nations with no dissenting responses. The Director of the FFA must notify all participating states accordingly and indicate when the withdrawal date is to become effective. This is an important part of the Register because no country is permitted to license a vessel unless it is in good standing. The date of the withdrawal must be no earlier than 14 days after the notification date and stands unless an objection is received by the Director before then.

Reinstatement of good standing becomes effective upon the satisfaction of all outstanding requests. The restoration of good standing should then be requested by the country that applied for the status change in the first place. When this occurs, the Director of the FFA must notify all the other members. Good standing within the FFA member states has been withdrawn only twice, indicating the effectiveness of the Regional Register as a management and enforcement measure. So far, the prospect of a change in status of the vessel on the Register has been sufficient to make vessel operators and owners comply with court orders or to enter into settlement negotiations regarding the payment of compensation for infringements.

In early 1984, a member country requested the withdrawal of the good standing of a US purse-seiner for allegedly fishing illegally, and the refusal of the ship's captain to submit to the legal process in the country where the incident took place. The fishing boat was taken to Hawaii where it was repainted and renamed in an attempt to circumvent the removal of the vessel's good standing on the Register. The FFA continued to process the withdrawal of the vessel's good standing. Realising what was happening, the owners of the vessel decided to comply with the demands of the Register. They went back to the country where the infringement took place and agreed to go to court to pay compensation for the vessel's illegal activities. A fine totaling of more than US$1 million was paid by the vessel owners so that the vessel's good standing remained (Doulman and Terawasi, 1990). In 1991, an unlicensed Taiwanese purse-seiner was photographed by an Australian surveillance plane inside Tuvalu's EEZ. The owners of the vessel paid US$75,000 to avoid the threat of blacklisting on the Register.

In 1990, a requirement for an annual renewal of registration was introduced to ensure that the Register included only the vessels fishing in the South Pacific region. In 1989 before the introduction of this procedure, 2,260 vessels were in the Register and included some vessels that had long since left the trade. To date the Register holds 1,000 foreign fishing vessels which the FFA believes is a more realistic representation of the number of fishing boats in the region for the 1992/1993 period. This feature of the register should improve as more information becomes available to the FFA and as the system becomes more streamlined. The arrangement at present is adequately meeting the increasing demand to license new vessels with improved compliance by vessel operators. Regular communications have been enhanced by the use of the new PEACESAT and the Maritime Surveillance Communications Network (MSCN).

THE MULTILATERAL TREATY WITH THE USA

In 1987, the nations of the Pacific made history when they signed the multilateral treaty with the USA which is perhaps the most comprehensive fisheries access agreement in the world considering the USA's present negative stand on UNCLOS III. The USA, eager to remain friendly with the South Pacific states given the increased activities of the Soviets in PNG, Solomon Islands, Vanuatu and Kiribati at that time, and aware of the depletion of their own tuna resources in the north-eastern Pacific, signed the treaty with the FFA member countries. Under the treaty, the USA recognises the coastal states' sovereign rights over fisheries resources in their EEZ and pays for licences. The South Pacific nations on the other hand, have the right to enforce the treaty under their legislation without fear of facing a penalty under the Fishermen's Protective Act (FPA) or a ban under the Magnuson Act. These two USA domestic laws were central to international controversies in 1982 when PNG confiscated the USA purse-seiner *Danica* and in 1984 when the Solomon Islands seized the *Jeannette Diana* for illegal fishing. After such bitter tuna-related disputes, a multilateral fisheries treaty with the USA Government was a major achievement for the South Pacific countries.

The treaty marks the first time ever that the USA has agreed not only to recognise the right of coastal states over highly migratory species but also the commitment to pay for the right to fish for them. Provisions of the Multilateral Treaty include access to the EEZs of South Pacific nations which allows US fishing vessels to fish in the EEZs of South Pacific nations subject to certain regulatory conditions and control. For instance, the US fishing vessels do not have access to the entire EEZs of the Pacific nations, but only to the Limited Area which excludes internal waters, territorial seas and archipelagic waters. The conditions of access include: procurement of a fishing license; permission to catch only tuna; use of only licensed purse-seiners and the observation of the requirements of the Regional Register of Fishing Vessels. Like all other fishing boats in the region US tuna vessels must have good standing on the Register, from which they can be withdrawn, resulting in the loss of their licence.

The application fee and licence are paid for by the USA government. The Multilateral Treaty imposes clear obligations on the USA to ensure that fishing vessels flying its flag comply with the terms of the Treaty. This measure is seen as an assurance to member nations that they will not be undermined in any way and that their management effort is supported by the US government. On the other hand the Pacific Island member states are given the authority to enforce their own fisheries laws and regulations against any US fishing vessels that violate the terms of the Treaty. This condition is interesting because by making the commitment of the non-imposition of embargo, the USA has nullified its domestic FPA and Magnuson Acts in its relation with the Pacific Island states (Sutherland and Tsamenyi, 1992).

In the five years since 1988, the US paid US$60 million for 60 purse-seiners to fish for tuna in the limited area as determined by the FFA. The access agreement has now been extended for a further 10 years with a review prior to the end of the first five years. With the extension, the US will pay FFA member countries US$18 million annually for 55 purse-seiner licences, five of which must be reserved for joint venture arrangements. As in the previous agreement member governments share 15% on an equal basis, while the remaining 85% is shared according to the catch from the EEZs of the nations.

The control that has been sought by the FFA member countries seems to be attainable given the current good relations that now exist in the South Pacific. Only last year (1993) FFA member countries decided to levy an annual administration fee of US$100. To date all fleets have complied. There are indications that multilateral arrangements will be adopted by other DWFNs. This has been a long struggle and member nations are beginning to see positive signs of change. Japan and Taiwan are now engaged in negotiations with the member nations on treaties similar to the one with the USA. There is now co-operation with the member countries on matters relating to licensing and monitoring. Research continues in Japan, Australia, New Zealand, USA and the FFA for an appropriate transponder system that can provide accurate position information for fishing vessels on a 'real time' basis. Unlike the above-named DWFNs, South Korea has not been forthcoming and continues with its single-year access agreement. This position has isolated South Korea and has threatened long-term security access to the region.

THE WELLINGTON CONVENTION

The Wellington Convention had its beginning in the Tarawa Declaration of July 1989. This Convention bans driftnet fishing within the Pacific and is the basis of the present United Nations moratorium on driftnet fishing in the high seas. Concerned about the vast increase in the number of Japanese, Taiwanese and Korean gillnet fishers in the Pacific in the late 1980s, the FFA states signed the Tarawa Declaration banning driftnet fishing from the Pacific's EEZ and pockets of high seas surrounded by the EEZ of Pacific nations. The gillnet fishers, despite great resistance initially, are observing the ban.

THE NIUE TREATY

The Niue Treaty formalises the arrangement whereby the countries of the region can rely on each other for the control and enforcement of their regulations relating to fisheries use. Under the Treaty, France, Australia and New Zealand, which have assisted in the development of surveillance capacity within the region, lead the other member nations in their attempt to control fishing in their areas. French, Australian and New Zealand surveillance patrol flights continue in the Pacific. Effort is now being made to involve commercial airlines, and ships to assist in the enforcement of the region's management and conservation decisions.

The capacity of the South Pacific states to enforce their laws within their EEZs continues to be greatly enhanced by the provision by Australia of Pacific Patrol Boats and their development of a computer-based mapping system which will be distributed to all national fisheries offices. In the near future, the system will provide for real-time display of locations and vessel activity providing a mechanism to monitor individual vessel and fleet operation within their areas. The capacity of the member states is expected to improve with the use of modern telecommunication facilities. The regional MSCN has been implemented in the region in the last two years and should improve the member countries' control and enforcement capability. Intra-regional co-operation is best illustrated by the case between Tonga and Tuvalu where the former has agreed to use its patrol boats donated by Australia to patrol both of their EEZs.

The ban on transhipment at sea was implemented in the middle of 1993 and has been an additional source of revenue to Pacific Island states. Transhipment has contributed significant income through registration, port, transhipment fees and the provision of fuel, agency service and travel expenses. In 1993 the ban on transhipment provided approximately US$700,000 for member countries. Around US$1.5 million is expected in 1994. In-port expenses are expected to boost local economies in the FFA countries. A purse-seiner spends about US$10,000 per transhipment. In the second half of 1993 the 360 transhipment operations that took place brought in US$3.6 million. Improvement in supply and services at the local ports can easily earn US$10 million annually which will be valuable to the Pacific.

Conclusion

It is evident that collectively the small nations in the South Pacific are making a difference. These nations are achieving 'watermark' accomplishments because of their common understanding and co-operation. There are still major frontiers that need to be addressed, but with the bond these nations now have, little is impossible. Fisheries management is more critical now because of the increase in population, efficiency of fishers, depletion of fish stocks and the increasing monetisation of fisheries resources. Traditional fishing methods are being abandoned while more efficient methods have been adopted to maximise output. Fishers are venturing further away from their bases, expanding the areas of depleted fisheries in the process. Management and conservation, although necessary, is difficult to promote because it contradicts the maximisation of catch that is aspired to by all fishers. These are the reasons why we need to learn from the South Pacific example.

The countries of the South Pacific are also party to other international conventions such as the South Pacific Nuclear Free Zone Treaty, the Conservation of Nature in the South Pacific, and the South Pacific Environment Programme Action Plan. All the above conventions directly affect the proper management of the marine resources which are part of the overall environment for which the people of the region are responsible. Fisheries resources are by their nature transboundary and it is appropriate that users co-operate to ensure a sustainable peaceful co-existence. It is in this aspect that the experience of the South Pacific member states is most noteworthy.

Bibliography

Benedict, B. (1967) 'Sociological aspects of smallness', in B. Benedict (ed.) *Problems of Smaller Territories,* London: Athlone Press.

Connell, J. (1988) *Sovereignty and Survival: Island Microstates in the Third World,* Research Monograph 3, Sydney: University of Sydney.

—— (1990) 'Modernity and its discontent: migration and change in the South Pacific', in J. Connell (ed.) *Migration and Development in the South Pacific,* Pacific Research Monograph 24, Canberra: ANU.

—— (1991) 'Island microstates: the mirage of development', *The Contemporary Pacific* 3 2: 251–87.

Doulman, D.J. and Terawasi, P. (1990) 'The South Pacific regional register of foreign fishing vessels', *Marine Policy* July: 324–32.

FFA (1993) 'Director's annual report 1993/1994', unpublished, Forum Fisheries Agency.

FFA *et al* (1983) 'EEZ management course participants report', Forum Fisheries Agency, IOI and IMR.

Johnson, C.J. and Clark, A.L. (1988) 'Expanding horizon of Pacific minerals', in E.M. Borgese, N. Ginburg and J.R. Morgan (eds) *Ocean Yearbook 7,* Chicago and London: University of Chicago.

Kearney, R. (1985) 'Fishery potential in the tropical, central and western Pacific: environment and resources in the Pacific', *UNEP Regional Seas Report and Studies* 69: 75–84.

Sutherland, W. and Tsameny B.M. (1992) *Law and Politics in Regional Cooperation: A Case Study of Fisheries Cooperation in the South Pacific,* Hobart: Pacific Law Press.

UNCTAD (1985) 'Examination of the particular needs and problems of island developing countries', in E. Dommen and P. Hein (eds) *States, Microstates and Islands,* London: Croom Helm.

United Nations (1991a) 'Realisation of benefits under the United Nations Convention on the Law of the Sea: Measures taken in response to needs of states in regard to the development and management of ocean resources, and approaches for further action', *Report of the Secretary General* A/46/722, United Nations.

—— (1991b) *Report of the Secretary General - Law of the Sea* A/46/724, United Nations.

Index